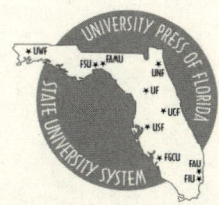

Florida A&M University, Tallahassee
Florida Atlantic University, Boca Raton
Florida Gulf Coast University, Ft. Myers
Florida International University, Miami
Florida State University, Tallahassee
University of Central Florida, Orlando
University of Florida, Gainesville
University of North Florida, Jacksonville
University of South Florida, Tampa
University of West Florida, Pensacola

The Wakefield Master's Dramatic Art

A Drama of Spiritual Understanding

Liam O. Purdon

University Press of Florida
Gainesville · Tallahassee · Tampa · Boca Raton
Pensacola · Orlando · Miami · Jacksonville · Ft. Myers

Copyright 2003 by Liam O. Purdon
Printed in the United States of America on acid-free, TCF (totally chlorine-free) paper
All rights reserved
08 07 06 05 04 03   6 5 4 3 2 1

Library of Congress Cataloging-in-Publication Data
Purdon, Liam O.
The Wakefield Master's dramatic art : a drama of spiritual understanding / Liam O. Purdon
p.   cm.
Includes bibliographical references and index.
ISBN 0-8130-2603-2 (cloth : alk. paper)
1. Towneley plays. 2. Mysteries and miracle-plays, English—England—Wakefield—History and criticism. 3. Christian drama, English (Middle)—History and criticism. 4. English drama—To 1500—History and criticism. 5. Bible plays, English—History and criticism. 6. Space and time in literature. 7. Spiritual life in literature. I. Title.
PR644.T6P87 2003
822'.05160901—dc21   200204030

The University Press of Florida is the scholarly publishing agency for the State University System of Florida, comprising Florida A&M University, Florida Atlantic University, Florida Gulf Coast University, Florida International University, Florida State University, University of Central Florida, University of Florida, University of North Florida, University of South Florida, and University of West Florida.

University Press of Florida
15 Northwest 15th Street
Gainesville, FL 32611–2079
http://www.upf.com

For my father,
Roger Anthony Purdon,
and to the memory of my mother,
Marie Tully Purdon

Contents

Preface ix

Introduction 1

1. The Abuse of Time and Space in the *Mactatio Abel* 21

2. The Abuse and Use of Time and Space in the *Processus Noe cum filiis* 46

3. *[Prima] Pagina Pastorum* and the "Inventive" Speculative Creaturely Triune Mind 67

4. *[Secunda] Pagina Pastorum* and the "Inventive" Empirical Creaturely Triune Mind 103

5. *Magnus Herodes* and the Degradation of the Rational Soul 152

6. The Repudiation of the Eschatology of Labor in Two "Passion Group" Revisions and the *Coliphizacio* 191

Conclusion 224

Notes 227

Bibliography 281

Index 300

Preface

In a study of the Wakefield Master's unique artistic contributions to the fifteenth-century Towneley play collection, as we seek to plumb both the meaning and the aesthetic complexity of each play and play revision attributed to this singular late-medieval playwright, the most fruitful approach appears to be a demonstration of spirituality's centrality to the technological mastery of nature's temporal and spatial dimensions, to the orientation of the mind itself that both speculatively and empirically engages nature and artifice in the world about it, and even to the understanding and proper use, as opposed to abuse, of any practical art or *techne*. As the Master invites Corpus Christi audiences to recognize the expression or denial of their own spirituality *in* and *through* dramatized moments of biblical history anachronistically modified by the things and kinesis of everyday late-medieval life, we and they are afforded the singular theatrical opportunity to observe—and, to a limited extent, participate in—what might be called an iconic material anthropology of spirituality. This unique dramatic experience involving the effective artistic deployment of an extensive, imaginative anachronism repeatedly asserts the primacy of spiritual cooperation between humankind and God, especially through what is done by humankind in its technological mastery of nature, and by demonstrations of the mind as it orients itself in preparation to comprehend the world as the *opus Creatoris*. In this way, the artistic achievement of the Wakefield Master's dramatizations of select moments in biblical history may be seen to be analogous to the moments of "history" that are "made" by the artist/arranger of the famous fourteenth-century Luttrell Psalter, who makes history not by the accurate or verisimilitudinous representation of the complexity of late-medieval English manorial life but rather by the imaginative shaping, as Michael Camille has recently demonstrated, of chivalric identity, the complexity of manorial life's many aspects, and even the basis of the fourteenth-century cultural distinction between what is real and what is illusory.[1] While the Luttrell Psalter calls attention to the dialogic relation between the "'sacred centers of pages' and the chaotic borders, home to fantastic marginalia,"[2] the Wakefield Master's greatest works, the two shepherds' plays and the *Magnus Herodes*, establish as their "sacred centers" the prosopopeia of either spirituality's noesis or its absence, and so create an innovative dialogic relation with the theatrical margin or "border," which in this case includes the audience, at least in part, as the metadramatically fantasticized other.

The scope of the following argument, accordingly, includes consideration of a significant portion—nearly half the lines—of the late-fifteenth-century Towneley collection of plays, a collection twice edited prior to the publication of Martin Stevens and A. C. Cawley's most recent edition,[3] and a collection preserved in the "unique incomplete MS," as Stevens and Cawley have described it, "now held by the Henry E. Huntington Library and Art Gallery at San Marino, California, under accession mark HM 1."[4] The portion of the collection treated by this study consists of a number of play revisions appearing in the latter part of the manuscript as well as six complete plays. The first two of the latter, the *Mactatio Abel* or *The Murder of Abel* and the *Processus Noe cum filiis* or *Noah*, are the manuscript's second and third plays; the next three, the *[Prima] Pagina Pastorum* or the *First Shepherds' Play*, the *[Secunda] Pagina Pastorum* or the *Second Shepherds' Play*, and the *Magnus Herodes* or *Herod*, are the manuscript's twelfth, thirteenth, and sixteenth plays, respectively; and the last, the *Coliphizacio* or *The Buffeting*, is the manuscript's twenty-first play. The play revisions, long as well as short portions of a number of works that deal primarily with the characters of Pilate and Tutivillus in the "Passion group" of plays in the manuscript's latter part, include lines and stanzas from the twentieth play, the *Conspiracio* or *The Conspiracy and Capture*, the twenty-second play, the *Flagellatio* or *The Scourging*, the twenty-fourth play, the *Processus Talentorum* or *The Play of the Dice*, the twenty-seventh play, the *Perigrini* or *The Pilgrims*, and the thirtieth play, the *Iudicium* or *The Judgment*.[5]

Setting out to recuperate the Wakefield Master's distinct dramaturgical accomplishment, this study attempts to understand the nature of the Master's artistry in relation to the principal aesthetic ideas informing dramatic performance theory and practice of the time in which the Master's well known revisions and plays were completed and included in the Towneley collection. If a collateral benefit of this approach is to place the Wakefield Master in the correct literary pantheon—that is, among the great dramatic geniuses leading up to Marlowe, Jonson, and Shakespeare—then so much the better. More important, however, is the principal consequence of this study: the demonstration of how this playwright's repeated attempts to assert a medieval worldview—that is, his repeated, concerted effort to engage the Corpus Christi audience imaginatively in the theatrical experience of the fundamental principles informing the expression of traditional medieval belief and civic conservatism—nearly always result, either intentionally or inadvertently, in intimations of modernist protocols and habits of thinking and understanding. This paradox within his art identifies the Master certainly as a transitional figure, not only in drama, but also in the history of ideas. Furthermore, it provides us with insight into the late-fifteenth-century or late-Gothic mind itself, a mind that certainly looks backward to reassert the greatness of the past in the present moment, but also a mind that anticipates the future or modernity by means of the emphasis it places upon the "discovery of the world in its infinite variety"—that is, on the "reconstruction" rather than on the "representation" of the world itself[6]—that inevitably arises as the result of the very process of cultural retrieval to which the Wakefield Master, and other artists like him, are committed in the waning years of the fifteenth century.

Incomplete is a preface of this kind without acknowledgment of the many who have provided one form of assistance or another toward completion of the study. A humble expression of gratitude is offered to Professors Michael Arthur, Claude Jones, Alexander Bell Hay Allen, Evelyn Shellard, Ira Clark, the late Arthur Kouguell, Esq., and Jackson Cope, all of whom taught me, in one field of study or another, the value of examining drama as closely and exhaustively as possible; to Professors John T. Irwin, Jane Chance, David Minter, Stanley E. Fish, Lois Roney, and T. Daniel Kelly, who helped develop in my thinking, in and through their respective fields of specialization, an understanding as well as an appreciation of semiotics, deconstruction, and medieval history and iconography; to Professors David Pike, Thomas Bisson, Karen Nicholas, the late Charles Garside, and the late Andrew Jitkoff, who reoriented my understanding of history and historiography; to Professors Julian N.

Wasserman, S. R. Olsen, Laura Hodges, and James J. Paxson, who were gracious enough, after reading chapters or the entire manuscript, to offer many insightful comments and helpful corrections; to Ann Marlowe, who carefully copyedited the manuscript, and to project editor Jacqueline Kinghorn Brown, who watched over the book from manuscript to final proof pages; and finally to my wife, Dianne, Steinman Ferguson, and little Carly, all of whom waited patiently—at the lake and elsewhere—many more months and years than they should have for this project to be completed.

Introduction

Historicist treatments of medieval culture have begun to elucidate many of the ways in which people of the later Middle Ages understood and purposefully shaped the world around them.[1] Yet medieval British drama, which expressed and even furthered this new practical and philosophical response to created reality, has received puzzlingly little critical examination in this regard. This is especially true in the case of the Towneley *regenall,* in which appear, in nearly all of the extant works included in that collection of plays, numerous instances of this new intellectual spirit regarding the relationship between the world and its Creator—instances of images as well as examples of a new appreciation for and redefinition of such concepts as nature, labor, and technology. The act of pulling as if by some kind of "gyn" in the *Processus Crucis* and the presence of the stalled heavy plow and plow team at the beginning of the *Mactatio Abel* come as readily to mind, in this regard, as do the mill wheel in the *[Prima] Pagina Pastorum,* Tutivillus's description in the *Iudicium* of the parvenu's "luddokkys" or buttocks bulging like "walkmylne cloggys," the music of David's "mynstrelsy" in the *Processus Prophetarum,* and even Centurion's empirically-based asseveration in the *Resurreccio Domini* of nature's expression of solemn sympathy in response to the Crucifixion.[2] Indeed, the range of images and types of medieval materialities and technology throughout the *regenall* is exceeded only by the frequency of their appearance.

Several explanations have been offered for this distinctive feature of the Towneley plays in general. Most persistent in the last century perhaps was the argument that such references to medieval technology or to other related aspects of contemporary medieval life were evidence of "realism" in the plays.[3] This approach to making sense of topical allusions or the presence of contemporary medieval actualities or materialities in many of the works, though now discounted by most scholars of medieval drama, was not entirely inconsistent with what V. A. Kolve, in his *The Play Called Corpus Christi*, later described as an artistic program of pervasive incorporation of direct, unselfconscious dramatic anachronism primarily for the sake of convenience in the Corpus Christi pageants.[4] Inclusion of this sort of historical verisimilitude, in other words, was a way in which medieval British playwrights—and most particularly the Towneley collection's Wakefield Master[5]—invigorated their writing through incorporation of colloquial dialogue while anglicizing costume and setting to make "foreign" stories or even familiar Old Testament ones "immediately clear and meaningful to an English audience."[6] In this regard, the function of Cain's "pudding in the pot" remark (2/388) becomes readily understandable: it provides an easily recognizable domestic metaphor of the irrevocable change in the world resulting from Abel's death. Noah's use of the lunar calendar to emphasize the duration of the Flood (3/661) could likewise be seen to offer a reassuring, though inaccurate, temporal determinacy. The brightness of Abraham's menacing steel blade brandished over Isaac (4/201)—a blade of steel reminiscent of God's previous description of Noah's "true-as-steel" loyalty (3/175)—could be viewed similarly as a reminder of the latest advances in regional weapons metallurgy and manufacture, while Caesar's expectation of homage from "castles, towers and towns" (9/14–15), an example of what James J. Paxson has identified as "futuristic retro-active anachronism,"[7] could perhaps be understood to be the expression of a longing for the former—but by no means forgotten—political system of feudal reciprocities, which had now become more and more transformed and obscured by the emerging commercialism and market economies of late-fifteenth-century England.

Another kind of anachronism identified and acknowledged by Kolve to be present in medieval drama, and especially in the Wakefield Master's contributions to the Towneley collection, is more pertinent to this study—and appears also to be of more interest to Kolve—because it involved a "conscious artistic intention," both for secular purposes and for the religious end of linking the "past with present Christian relevance."[8] For Kolve, this type of anachronism often included not only anglicization in the form of geographical dislocations and transpositions, which resulted in the creation of a metaphysical "place" of action in the plays, but also the transposition of history for the purpose of making a doctrinal point.[9] Among the most noticeable effects wrought by this kind of anachronism, Kolve notes, was that "the Jews are largely expunged from the picture in order that the guilt of Christ's death and the blessing of His sacrifice may both be felt as local."[10] It may be, as Kolve proceeds to observe, that this particular localizing explains why no surprise is felt in the *Iudicium* when the devils identify the place of Doom as being up Watling Street in Wakefield.[11] It may also be that this kind of localizing was an expression of medieval Christian, as well as civic, anti-Semitism. But more important is Kolve's point about the feeling of guilt and joy in response to Christ's sacrifice—a point that anticipated what D. W. Robertson Jr. identified as tropological verisimilitude in the drama in general, and in the Wakefield Master's contributions to the Towneley collection in particular.[12] In other words, creating a metaphysical history and place—that is, presenting the idea of a time outside of time or "time as artifact," and the idea of space beyond the spatial, ideas Kolve treats later in his chapter to complete the discussion of anachronism[13]—enabled medieval mystery play playwrights, dramatists especially like the Wakefield Master himself, to make the spiritual significance of their narrative—the perennial discovery of Christ in one's heart, or spiritual understanding—immediately available and meaningful to their audience in practical terms they could readily understand, feel, and respond to.[14]

That the practical terms chosen by the Wakefield Master[15] to facilitate the understanding and feeling of spiritual significance primarily included images and examples of medieval technology—namely, actual medieval machines, practical techniques, and even less obvious but no less actual forms, such as rudimentary cost/benefit assessments—is partially explained by the presence and availability of the many techniques or tools and technologies used by people in their various daily productive pursuits in the Yorkshire towns, villages, and countryside with which the Towneley *regenall* was initially associated. Indeed, the Wakefield Master did not have to look far for the things—the plows, the pillories, the plumb lines, the scaffolding, the laborers—that might be appropriated as matter for this type of anachronistic verisimilitude in his unique artistic creations and revisions.[16] There was in the immediate area—that is, the Yorkshire West Riding, the region where many of the Towneley plays not only were probably first performed, in the latter half of the fifteenth century,[17] but also probably came to enjoy the distinction of being included in a cycle, in the sixteenth[18]—no shortage of readily imitable examples of either medieval manufactured goods or manufacturing technologies that could easily be appropriated for artistic purposes by an inventive and innovative playwright looking for obvious and effective ways to introduce ethical and spiritual distinctions and associations through familiar images of procedures, tools, machines, and the like. In fact, when Wakefield, the West Riding town specifically identified in several of the *regenall's* plays,[19] first began to experience economic prosperity in the latter half of the fifteenth century as the result of increased trade in products of wool and cloth manufacturing,[20] one did not have to travel far in the West Riding to behold varieties of machines at work and people engaged in their daily occupations, employing different kinds of technologies.

Despite calamitous economic upheaval and political uncertainty in northern England during the first half of the fifteenth century, the impressive machines of the fulling mills on the banks of the Aire, Calder, and Colne,[21] the power technology of emerging textile manufacturing, would frequently have been in operation in the latter half of the century, preparing the fabrics that would eventually be transformed into cheap broadcloth or kerseys, for which the region had come to be known.[22] The forges located on the Wakefield Manor, as well as in the woodlands of Outwood and Hipperholme,[23] would likewise have been at work creating the various iron goods needed by local agriculture and rudimentary manufacturing. Mining on the Wakefield Manor, and on the nearby manor of Pontefract, too, would often have been seen producing not only the mineral or sea-coal that was used as fuel by the nearby forges,[24] but also the great quantities of lead needed for roof and gutter construction in large-scale building programs in Wakefield itself, such as the expansion of All Saints, the site of the tallest spire in all of Yorkshire (247 feet), and similar programs in the rest of the West Riding, especially those involving Fountains Abbey, Roche Abbey, Kirkstall Abbey, Bolton Priory, Selby Abbey, Wadworth Chapel, and Ripon Cathedral.[25] Traffic in raw materials such as quarried stone and in livestock on the "Wakefield Gate," the drove road, or on the Grand Trunk (now the A1), the great road dating back to the Roman occupation of the British Isles, would certainly have contributed to the spectacle as well.[26] And the hustle-bustle characteristic of traditional fairs in Wakefield and in the immediate area—fairs such as the famous Woodkirk or "Lee" Fair[27]—would have reminded even the casual onlooker of how much the West Riding had come to be a region synonymous with the various technologies involved with, and supporting commerce and trade in, agriculture and rudimentary manufacturing.

I

Yet a more compelling explanation for the appropriation of the matter of contemporary technology as distinctive feature of the anachronistic tropological verisimilitude in the Wakefield Master's drama can be traced to one of the principal axioms of the age, an axiom emphasizing the belief that humanity's productive pursuits were an integral part of divine "governance" in the world. This idea, found in *Notae super Johannem secundum magistrum Gilbertum,* is implicit in the distinctions made by Gilbert de la Porrée in regard to the three aspects of the great work of God—that is, the divine creative action, the operations of nature, and the things made by men:

> It is asked whether artificial things—footgear, cheese, and like products, which we say are works of man and not of God—have been made by God. —Indeed, all things have been made by God as their author; but certain things are called God's works just as they are, namely those which he makes by himself and neither after some resemblance in nature nor through the intermediary service of someone else, as he makes heaven and earth. Others are called works of nature, and these are created by God after some natural resemblance, as a seed from other seeds, a horse from other horses, and similar things from their similars. Others which he makes through the intermediary service of man are called works of men. God, therefore, is the sole author of all things; but there are different ways of making, both as to authority and as to intermediary service, such that on the one hand man is said to be the author, and on the other hand, God. In a similar manner we customarily say that some rich man has built many buildings which in fact a carpenter has built, but the one has built them only by his authority and command, the other by his service.[28]

This feature of the age's religious metaphysics—this definition of man as artisan (*homo artifex*) in relation to God's creative work (*opus Creatoris*) and the work of nature (*opus naturae*)—was drawn from the commentary of Chalcidius upon the *Timaeus* and later amplified by the masters of Chartres until it "furnished a complete vision of the world and a definition of man, and even the guidelines for man's productive activity."[29] Fundamental to this view of humanity's serving God cooperatively by serving itself in the technological mastery and practical use of nature— and a fact that must be considered in light of the Wakefield Master's incorporation of the varietal anachronism of *techne* as well as technology in his drama—were two profoundly influential perceptual changes occurring over a period of approximately 1300 years that led, eventually, to the association between spirituality and the ethical use of technology.

The first of these changes was the gradual emergence in the West of a new attitude toward nature and technology. This view was the product of two mutually exclusive but complementary forces. One was an agricultural revolution in northern Europe inaugurated by the invention and advent of the heavy plow and the rise of the agricultural cooperative to pool plow-team animals to power this new agricultural technology.[30] As the "standard of land distribution ceased to be the needs of a family and became the ability of a power engine to till the soil," White observes elsewhere, humanity "ceased to be nature's child and became her exploiter."[31] This change from subsistence to cooperative farming, while archaeologically suggested by the three-field rotational planting system, was recorded and preserved by illustrated calendars, which offer the collateral benefit of visually instructing the observer in the fundamental perceptual changes in outlook often depicted in and by them. Until about the ninth century, secular calendars revealed the "months as static personifications holding symbolic attributes."[32] While this artistic tendency continued in Byzantium well into the later Middle Ages, calendar illustrations in the West dramatically changed after the ninth century, showing active scenes such as those involving "plowing, haying, harvesting grain, wood chopping, men knocking acorns from oaks so that pigs can eat them, [and] pig slaughtering."[33]

The second force precipitating a change in attitude toward nature and technology was a revolution in spirituality resulting from the slow Christianization of the common people. This revolution involved the early Church's rejection of pagan animism and the eventual secularization of the sacred.[34] What this rejection eventually led to was nothing short of the creation of a "new abstraction of spirit from matter," which in turn "fostered a new flexibility in the human utilization of matter."[35] Accordingly, the cumulative effect of these two forces was a firmly established belief that the world had been created for humanity's benefit, and that humanity had a spiritual responsibility to master it through the utilization of all technological means at its disposal.[36]

Occurring concomitantly with the evolution of this new understanding of nature and technology was the emergence of a positive attitude toward technology and labor.[37] The origin of this view was to be found in the early Church's gradual acceptance of the Benedictine affirmation of labor, an affirmation made explicit by the famous Benedictine expression *laborare est orare*, which gave a new psychic dignity to labor as well as to the things used to facilitate work.[38] Signs of this new attitude fostered by Western voluntarist theology—a testament to the force of its impact on the previous negative outlook of classical antiquity with regard to labor[39]—made their appearance gradually between the fifth and eleventh centuries as improved methods in agriculture, warfare, and rudimentary manufacturing production were developed in the Frankish regions.[40] Too many examples exist to be cited in this introduction to document the extent of this evolution in outlook, but a sampling demonstrates just how far-reaching and profound the effect was of the new appreciation not only of technology and labor but also of the spiritual implications the ethical relation between the two had for late-medieval society.

One of the earliest known illustrations of this new tendency in thinking—an unusually sophisticated one, which features purposeful labor utilizing machine technology—can be seen in the ninth-century Utrecht Psalter in the illumination decorating Psalm 63 (64) (Utrecht Univ. Lib., Aev. med., script. eccles. 484, fol. 35v). In this particular example, the monastic illuminator, following and yet embellishing his biblical source in a singular way, emphasizes the importance of the relationship between labor and the things used to facilitate it. He conforms to the text in his presentation of the adversarial camps of the righteous and the workers of iniquity—the former, a smaller group, possessing the high ground, God's blessing, and the protection of an angel, in the upper right-hand corner of the folio; the latter, a heavily armed multitude, attacking from the lower left-hand corner. Between the two camps can possibly be seen an illustration of Hell's mouth or the snare referred to in verse 6 of the text. However, the central interest of the picture, as White has pointed out,

> lies in the sharpening of a sword in each camp (cf. verse 4), but by very different means. The iniquitous are content to employ an old-fashioned whetstone. The virtuous, in spectacular contrast, are using the first known example of the rotary grindstone, and it is being turned by the first mechanical crank to appear outside China. Since the substitution of continuous rotary motion for reciprocating motion was basic to the development of machine design, this illumination marks a great moment in the history of technology. But its psychological content is no less portentous than its purely technological import.[41]

Other signs of this new tendency in thinking were available, too; notable among these is one appearing a century after the Utrecht Psalter in an illumination in the Eadiwi Gospel Book produced at Winchester. The illumination in this case involves the subject of God innovatively transformed into the image of one whose labors are advantageously supported by technology. The monastic illuminator, possibly inspired by Wisdom 11:21, shows "the hand of God—now the master craftsman—holding scales, a carpenter's square, and a pair of compasses."[42] While it spread, this new view of God was modified, later illustrations picturing God holding only the compass. Such modification notwithstanding, the symbol of the medieval and renaissance engineer, the compass, continued to be associated with the deity. The persistent vitality of this iconographic tradition of linking the tools of *homo artifex* and the *opus Creatoris* appears in such examples as *The Holkham Bible Picture Book*, the *Bible Moralisée* in the Bodleian, a Bible in the British Museum (Royal, 19 D iii, vol. 1, fol. 3v.), a Bible at Chantilly (MS fr. 1045, vol. 1, fol. 1), and Boccaccio's *Des cas des Nobles Hommes et Femmes*.[43]

A more elaborate—in fact, a somewhat analytical—example of this new attitude toward the association between technology and labor, signaling yet another mutation in the evolution of its expression, can be found in the twelfth-century *De diversis artibus*, a "religiously motivated codification of all the skills available for the embellishment of a church," produced by the theologically sophisticated and technologically learned German Benedictine Theophilus.[44] The identification of ethics and spirituality with the mastery of technological skills is emphasized in each of the three prefaces to this major document in the history of technology. The third preface is the most pertinent to the present study because in it Theophilus assures the reader, the anticipated apprentice monk, that if he has employed his technical skill righteously and has wisely labored, by following the wisdom of David, to embellish the house of God, the place of prayer, then he cannot "but believe with a full faith" that his "heart has been filled with the spirit of God."[45] With these words Theophilus indicates that the ethical exercise of masterful technological skill for the purpose of furthering monastic church decoration is, ipso facto, evidence of spirituality. What is more, if such an association is gainsaid, Theophilus adds that whatever is learned, understood, or devised cannot be doubted since it is "ministered" to one "by the grace of the sevenfold spirit," the "proof" of which immediately follows. Through the spirit of wisdom, Theophilus argues, the skilled artisan knows "that all created things proceed from God, and without Him nothing is." Through the spirit of understanding, he adds, one receives "the capacity for skill—the order, variety and measure with which to pursue . . . varied work." Through the spirit of counsel, one openly works and teaches in all humility, displaying one's talent "faithfully to those wishing to understand." Through the spirit of fortitude, one drives "away all the torpor of sloth" and sees through whatever is essayed "with energy . . . [and] full vigour to completion." Through the spirit of knowledge that has been accorded the skilled artisan, the artisan is the "master of . . . [his] skill, and with the confidence of a full mind, [employs] that abundance for the public good." Through the spirit of godliness, one regulates "with pious care the nature, the purpose, the time, measure and method of the work and the amount of the reward lest the vice of avarice or cupidity steal in." And finally, through the spirit of the fear of the Lord, one remembers that one can do nothing of oneself—that one can have or intend nothing, unless accorded by God.[46]

This equating of spirituality with the ethics of labor and advanced technology in a monastic setting was hardly an anomaly, as is revealed by other contemporary voices from the cloisters. One of these, Abbot Arnold of Bonneval, the author of the life of Saint Bernard, describes the rebuilding of Clairvaux in 1136 in terms emphasizing the innovative quality of the abbey's water-powered machines for milling, fulling, tanning, blacksmithing, and other industries.[47] Similar interests are obvious in another contemporary account of the same rebuilding program. The anonymous author in this instance "is particularly taken by an automatic flour sifter attached to the [monastery's] flour mill . . . makes a little monkish joke, saying that the stamps of the fulling mill have remitted the penalty for the sins of the fullers . . . thanks God that such machines can alleviate the oppressive labors of both man and beast . . . [and finally] offers a picture of the abstract power of water flowing through the abbey seeking every task."[48]

II

This new outlook involving labor, nature, and technology, which over time had gradually become part of the social ideal, was given new impetus in the twelfth and thirteenth centuries by two remarkably influential forces that changed the intellectual landscape of late-medieval Europe. The first force was Hugh and Richard of Saint Victor, who effected the transition of the dignity of manual labor into the world beyond the cloister.[49] To achieve this end, Hugh of Saint Victor, first in the *Didascalicon* and next in the *Epitome* and *De grammatica* (Richard of Saint Victor furthering the cause in the *Liber exceptionem*), gave "an unprecedented psychic dignity and speculative interest to the mechanic arts."[50] These arts were likened to the traditional liberal arts in the Victorine scheme as a practical way of furthering the unity of philosophy, the conception and institution of which was to help overcome human defect.[51] The reasoning behind this new combination was that the mechanical arts could compensate for human weakness in ways the liberal arts could not. Hugh argued that while speculation provides truth and so eliminates ignorance, and while ethics aids virtue and so eliminates vice, the mechanical arts support the bodily needs of the race and so compensate for the physical defect of inherent human frailty. What is more, this kind of support was not conceived of as something external alone, but as having an internal dimension. Thus, when enumerated, the mechanical arts possessed, like their liberal sisters, their own *trivium* and *quadrivium*. The arts that gave support externally and comprised this new *trivium* were, according to Hugh, fabric making, armament, and commerce. The first of these protectively clothed the body, and the second the warrior. The third protectively clothed the merchant, not by means of a particular kind of garment, but rather by a kind of rhetorical eloquence that enabled the "trade of mankind" to be conducted in "secret places of the world," on "shores unseen," in "fearful wildernesses," and in "tongues unknown."[52]

The arts that gave support internally by feeding or nourishing, the new *quadrivium*, consisted of agriculture, hunting, medicine, and theatrics. The first two provided nourishment through alimentation, and the third, using different kinds of nourishment, helped to preserve or restore health. The fourth nourished in the sense that dramatic performance provided an "enjoyment that refreshed the mind." A collateral benefit also accrued. The mind's being refreshed or at least distracted by theatrical events forestalled the tendency to desire to go to public houses, where might be committed "lewd or criminal acts."[53]

While the view proposed by Hugh and repeated by Richard met with opposition in the form of a continued upper-caste prejudice against manual labor—a prejudice gradually strengthened as twelfth-century translation projects involving the cultural retrieval of classical Greece and Rome led to a revival of ancient attitudes[54]—the rise of Scholasticism and the universities, later coupled with the new natural theology of the Franciscans,[55] assured the continuation and refinement of this outlook.[56] The furthering of the fundamental change in attitude toward nature—and, implicitly, toward technology—was given monumental expression at this time in the emergence of the artistic style known as the Gothic, which placed value on the objects of creation as things important and interesting in and of themselves. Calling attention to this empirical interest in nature, Lynn Thorndike suggests it is implicit practically everywhere in the artifacts of the age:

> One has only to examine the sculpture of the great thirteenth century cathedrals to see that the craftsmen of the towns were close observers of the world of nature and that every artist was a naturalist too. In the foliage that twines about the capitals of the columns in French Gothic cathedrals it is easy to recognize . . . a large number of plants. . . . But it is not merely love of nature but scientific interest and accuracy that we see revealed in the sculptures of the cathedrals and in the note-book of the thirteenth century architect, Villard de Honnecourt, with its sketches of insect as well as animal life, of a lobster, two parroquets on a perch, the spirals of a snail's shell, a fly, a dragonfly, and a grasshopper, as well as a bear and a lion from life, and more familiar animals such as the cat and swan. The sculptors of

gargoyles and chimeras were not content to reproduce existing animals but showed their command of animal anatomy by creating strange compound and hybrid monsters—one might almost say, evolving new species—which nevertheless have all the verisimilitude of copies from living forms. It was these breeders in stone, these Burbanks of the pencil, these Darwins with the chisel, who knew nature and had studied botany and zoology in a superior way to the scholar who simply pored over the works of Aristotle and Pliny.[57]

Further refinement of the attitude toward labor could be seen in new contemporary views of spirituality and theology arising in response to the emerging diversification and division of labor. This could be seen in the gradual supplanting of penitential labor by the idea of labor as a positive means to salvation, by the rise in importance, after the beginning of the thirteenth century, of the saintly worker as opposed to the working saint, and by the rehabilitation of Martha and the idea of the active spiritual life.[58] It also resulted from reconsideration of the relationship between Adam's prelapsarian vocational labor and the Creator's work, which later, in mendicant confessor manuals, was often presented thematically in one of three principal ways—that every Christian is essentially defined in relation to his profession, that all labor deserves compensation, and that every profession based on labor is justified.[59] Indeed, to realize just how far-reaching and influential the idea of work as preliminary means to salvation had become in the later Middle Ages, one need only listen to part of a sermon on the Last Judgment prepared for the first Sunday in Advent emphasizing the importance of ordering one's life by getting "wyth swynke":

> Wherfor he þat wyll scape þe dome þat he wyll come to at þe second comyng, he most lay downe all maner of pride and heynes of hert, and know hymselfe þat he ys not but a wryche and slyme of erth, and soo hold mekenes yn his hert. He most trauayl his body yn good werkes, and gete his lyfe wyth swynke, and put away all ydylnes and slewth. For he þat wyll not trauayle here wyth men, as Seynt Barnard sayth, he schall trauayle ay wyth þe fendes of hell.[60]

III

The integral relation between this renewed interest in nature, labor, and technology and the religious metaphysics of the age, which defined man as artisan in relation to God's creation and the work of nature, would understandably have encouraged a playwright like the Wakefield Master to appropriate the anachronistic matter of contemporary medieval technology in his drama for the instructive and even hortatory purpose of engaging the Corpus Christi audience's thinking in terms of the idea of *use*—that is, in terms of their understanding of the difference between use and enjoyment, the conceptual distinction fundamental to the medieval philosophical doctrine of beauty.[61] The effect of this anticipated kind of involvement in response to anachronism, a final explanation for a varietal anachronism's inclusion in the Wakefield Master's artistic strategy, would have manifested itself immediately, as Robertson contends, in the audience's feeling and subsequent realization of something of the play's characters either in themselves or in their fellow townspeople,[62] a feeling not only reassuring but even gratifying if the experience of this perception—this moment of tropological insight—was characterized by the expression of charity, and correspondingly disconcerting if this perceptual moment was characterized by the expression of charity's opposite.

But the effect of the audience's understanding the relevance between important events in biblical history and present Christian ethical conduct, through anachronistic images and examples of technology functioning instructively either as means to the greater end of loving God or as ends in themselves, would have challenged the audience to come into knowledge of an unknown thing through the agency of their own reason. This anticipated intellectual response to the drama, primarily the result of the narrative particulars of the plays' predictable dramatic mimesis, is what the later Middle Ages would have understood to be the act of invention,[63] the act of mind about which White no doubt is thinking in his word choice when he describes late-medieval men and women, many of whom would very often have been Corpus Christi drama audience members, as "active" seekers of understanding divine nature as it is reflected in the pattern of creation.[64] But a clarification needs to be made here. This idea of invention is not to be confused with the *inventio* or *heuresis* of classical antiquity—with the act of "coming upon," a "discovery of that which is there, or already is there, to be discovered."[65] Rather, it was the elicited engagement of the intellect in the response-form of the *modus interpretandi* or the engaged cognitive ability to make meaning out of a challenging interpretive circumstance.[66] This idea had been set forth and elaborated by Saint Augustine in his discussion of sacred rhetoric in the first three books of *De doctrina christiana,* where responsibility for making meaning is effectively transferred from the writer to the reader, whose interpretive task is to make, not *res,* but *signa* meaningful.[67] This understanding of the treatment of meaning's ambiguities from the perspective of the reader, as might be expected, did not long remain a textual concern alone. By the latter part of the fifteenth century when the Wakefield Master began writing and revising the Towneley plays for which he is known, evidence of this perceptual tendency could be found in examples that emphasize a rational approach to understanding natural phenomena through the adoption of an experimental method involving actual observation while calling often for advancements in technology to insure precision—instances such as those having to do with astronomical calculation or the *computus.*[68] So appearance in the Corpus Christi play performance setting of this same transference of intellectual responsibility—now from playwright to audience—would not have been a surprising feature of the feast-day theatrical event. But startling are the aesthetic implications such transference of responsibility had on the Wakefield Master's exploration of the relation between invention and dramatic mimesis. In his dramatic work, where aesthetic distancing is not neutral but, to a degree, inhibitory, the intellectual ability to comprehend the difference between use and enjoyment and, further, to recognize that distinction in its various deployed forms in the drama (a response principally evoked by the dramatic mimesis of the plays and play revisions themselves) was also challenged, at decisive moments in the plays, by introduction of the opportunity to participate in the affective experience of *caritas* or *cupiditas* through inclusion of dramatic methexis, one of two ideas considered by Aristotle in his theory of tragedy, the mode of artistic action providing a rhythmic or participatory dimension of performance as opposed to the mimetic or ritual dimension.[69] Its inclusion, as in any other art form, destabilized the privileged position—the aesthetic distance—of the audience member or spectator and, as a result, compelled that same individual, now through a perceptual contrast, to assume responsibility, even if only momentarily, for making meaning or for responding inventively to an immediate interpretive circumstance presented by the particulars of the play narrative or action. This distinctive feature of the dramatic presentation would certainly have drawn the Corpus Christi audience "closer" to the events and characters presented on stage. But more important than this impressionistic effect was the fact that the perceptual contrast caused by the introduction of dramatic methexis also afforded each viewer the possibility of the tropological cognitive experience fundamental to the religious metaphysics of the age—the tropological cognitive experience, in other words, implicit in allegoresis or the interpretive ability to supply "inventively" an ulterior structure of ethical and spiritual meaning to the action of the play being performed on the pageant wagons before the audience.[70]

IV

The opportunity to consider and even experience such "inventiveness," as well as the new understanding of nature and labor, from the viewpoint of this distinctive apostolic consciousness occupies, in varying degrees of elaboration, the attention of each of the three groups of plays or play revisions attributed to the Wakefield Master—the first group being the *Mactatio Abel* and the *Processus Noe cum filiis*, the second the *[Prima] Pagina Pastorum*, the *[Secunda] Pagina Pastorum*, and the *Magnus Herodes*, and the third the *Coliphizacio* and two "Passion group" revisions. The most extensive treatment of this particular consciousness, and one that introduces several structures of reference that are presented as "anterior to the texts and from which those texts are seen to emerge as if organically,"[71] is to be found in the second group, the plays set in the sixth age or the time of renewal.[72] The first of these works, the *[Prima] Pagina Pastorum*, introduces through action involving a variety of deployments of tropological anachronisms of technology, the most obvious of which is the *techne* of medieval British shepherding, numerous narrative particulars that invite the perception of the inherent structure or condition of the "inventive" speculative creaturely triune mind—that is, the noesis characteristic of the mind cognitively disposed to serving God cooperatively by serving itself through technological mastery and practical use of nature. The play suggests, principally through its dramatic mimesis but also through carefully staged moments of dramatic methexis, that the qualitative metaphysical condition of the pastoral mind—that is, the condition of mind of the local everyman figure—must first encompass, if it is to appreciate fully the experience of God in the Nativity by being cognitively "priestlike" in its response,[73] such a noetic disposition, in its acts of "invention" or meaning-making, as to enable it to accept proof both by reason and by authority. This is what becomes noticeable as Gyb, Iohn Horne, and Slawpase are awakened by Angelus and begin "inventively" and analytically to reconstruct, as well as act upon, the message that has been sung to them—a far cry from what they do in the play's first half as they perceive and respond to the world about them by means of the *phantasmata* of "imaginacioun." In a way, then, the *[Prima] Pagina Pastorum* offers the audience a dramatized *allegoria* of what Peter Lombard means by the quality of mind he identifies as *sapientia* in his *Sententiae* (2.24.6–11).[74] Thus, the first of the shepherds' plays turns the audience's attention to "the true understanding of things."

The second play of this group—and perhaps the most famous of all the plays in the Towneley collection, as well as in all of medieval British drama—the *[Secunda] Pagina Pastorum*, innovatively modifies the dramatized *allegoria* of mind presented in the *[Prima] Pagina Pastorum* by introducing narrative particulars that invite the perception of the complementary empirical condition of the "inventive" creaturely triune mind. Again, this view of mind is evoked by action involving a variety of deployments of tropological anachronisms of *techne* or technology associated with the medieval pasture and manorial farm. As a result, the play suggests, principally through its dramatic mimesis, and through select instances of dramatic methexis as well, that the adoring shepherd's mind must be able not only to accept proof by reason and authority but also to combine that noetic disposition of mind with a will properly ordered by *caritas* to ascertain truth through experience or experiment involving the senses. This is what is dramatized, for example, as Daw, shortly after returning to Mak and Gyll's to offer "That lytyl day-starne" a sixpence, engages in a process of inspection that eventually leads the other shepherds and himself to the realization, despite the many obstructions to interpretation put in their way by the ever-inventive Mak and Gyll, that the newborn is actually their missing sheep. In this regard, then, the *[Secunda] Pagina Pastorum* offers the audience a dramatization of what Peter Lombard means by the quality of mind he identifies as *scientia*. In other words, the play turns the audience's attention to "how to perceive and express what is known." The argument for this play's being the better or more sophisticated of the two shepherds' plays, a viewpoint based partly on the notion of the *[Prima] Pagina Pastorum*'s having been modified and transformed into the more refined *[Secunda] Pagina Pastorum*,[75] is thus not supported by the internal evidence of the plays themselves. In fact, both works, as will be demonstrated shortly, have to be presented—one perhaps at the end of the first performance day and the other at the beginning of the second, a conjecture first made by Elizabeth Jergens-Forsythe, and more recently by Lois Roney[76]—as they offer, together, an instructive dramatized *allegoria* of the totality of mind— that is, of the proper union and working in concert of *sapientia* and *scientia*, the reward for which consists of both spiritual profit and delight.

The final play in this second group of the Wakefield Master's works, the *Magnus Herodes*, introduces, after a separation consisting of the *Oblacio Magorum* and the *Fugacio Iosep et marie in egiptum*, a stark contrast to the two shepherds' plays through one of the most vigorous and memorable dramatic disavowals of the tropological cognitive experience fundamental to the apostolic consciousness identified with the religious metaphysics of the age. This disavowal—more than just parody, though certainly utilizing it[77]—is presented by means of dramatized *allegoria*, in response to which the audience is invited to perceive the repudiation of the "inventive" speculative creaturely triune mind. Like the shepherds' plays before it, the *Magnus Herodes* introduces this disavowal by means of action that, including the deployment of tropological anachronisms of technology, involves dramatic mimesis. But different here is the greater frequency of deployments of dramatic methexis.[78] Consequently, the audience is repeatedly given the opportunity to understand and even feel the perilous tropological condition of the cognitive experience leading to the degradation of the human soul—that is, the utter corruption of the divine reason, divine will, and divine memory— or of the Image of God within the creaturely triune mind itself. This is most obviously demonstrated in the play's first scene by examples of the disordered or erratic will, a volitional errancy repeatedly expressed by Herod. This corruption is also evidenced in the degradation of the memory, a degradation that takes the form of homologous Herodian *phantasmata*. And this metaphysical destruction is completed through multiple instances of the degradation of the reason, a degradation evinced by repeated homologies of the defective *disputatio*, the very habit of mind or process of logical argumentation associated with late-medieval

Scholasticism. The cause of this perilous condition, to complete the dramatized *allegoria* of noetic dysfunction here, is revealed to be the destruction of innocence, a destruction explored later in "The Slaughter of the Innocents," the play's second scene. And the play concludes with a demonstration of the chilling consequence of this destruction or degradation: the perceptual experience of living life in a state irrevocably bereft of grace, in which no light of truth, or of the Truth, illuminates anything.

Along with the dramatization of the process of the mind that either accepts or does not accept the responsibility for making meaning, the Wakefield Master's works, again by an innovative combination of allegorized dramatic mimesis and methexis, also provide the audience with the opportunity for making meaning themselves through consideration of late-medieval attitudes toward nature. This opportunity is offered by the Master's first group of plays in the Towneley collection. Both of the plays here call attention to the idea of human utilization of matter. But each presents a different emphasis. The first, the *Mactatio Abel*, calls attention to the technological mastery and practical use of nature, not as a way of serving God cooperatively, but rather as an end in itself. Neither time nor space is properly *used* here, so nature remains underutilized or even unutilized—an irony, given Cain's conspicuous exploitive attitude and distinct possessiveness. What is more, as materiality or created reality is abused as an end in itself to be enjoyed, there is not even a proper serving of the self.

The *Processus Noe cum filiis*, the second play in this group, introduces an instructive contrast to the *Mactatio Abel*, the effect of which is heightened by a modification of historical continuity wrought by the play's placement in the *regenall* directly following the *Mactatio Abel*. In this work, Noah and his family, the rest of the remnant, learn after—and as the direct result of—the Flood how to recreate the spirit of cooperation with God through proper technological use of time and space. They come to this knowledge by formulating several practical arts, whose nautical and post-cataclysm application gives rise to new social structures to serve God cooperatively through a conspicuously practical and technological serving of self. While the *Mactatio Abel*, in other words, enables the audience to realize intellectually as well as affectively the limitations of false *enjoyment*, the *Processus Noe cum filiis* reacquaints the audience, in much the same mimetic way, with the idea of proper *use* through the demonstration of a preferred spiritual responsibility, whose concomitant mastery of nature involves the utilization of all technological means at its disposal. The dramatized *allegoria* of these plays does not operate as noticeably "as a deep re-causing of the text as if from within the text"[79] as it does in the second group, not because the two plays here are less aesthetically sophisticated than the shepherds' plays and the Herod play, but rather because the historical period of erring in which they are set—that is, the first and second ages in the Augustinian schema—focuses attention more on the material cause of, rather than on the "inventive" or interpretive response to, aberration.

A final opportunity for audience members to experience fully the responsibility of "inventive" meaning-making—that is, of responding interpretively to the dramatized *allegoria*—is offered by the Wakefield Master in the last group of his works, which consists of the complete play titled the *Coliphizacio* and revisions appearing in portions of several other plays, nearly all of them in the "Passion group." This heterogeneous collection of works collectively invites the perception of the tragic refusal to serve God cooperatively, in the time of reconciliation, manifested in the repudiation of the eschatology of labor or the understanding of work as a constructive or practical preliminary means to salvation. In the first of the two revisions identified as the focus of the Master's redactive art in this study, for example, Pilate is presented as the arch abuser of the kind of mastery of *techne* that should effect such cooperation. As Pilate is a Roman procurator, his disavowal of labor's eschatological value is introduced by the Wakefield Master through two kinds of legal abuse. One involves improper conceptualization of rule or the abuse of the *techne* of "sovereigntée." The other involves the improper action of rule or the abuse of the legal *techne* of "mastry." In the second revision, Tutivillus, the famous recording demon, reintroduces the repudiation of the eschatology of labor, initially by demonstrating himself the very abuses he is designed to record, and then by calling attention to the psychology of sloth as the principal motivation for denunciation of any relation between labor and salvation.

The final work in this group, the *Coliphizacio,* offers another view of the repudiation of labor's salvific effect within the broader context of the corruption of institutional thinking and action. This corruption is evidenced in a number of ways in the play. The torturers, for example, do not actually torture because they lack the intelligence that would enable them to engage in this particular art or *techne*. The high priests, Caiaphas and Annas, find themselves in a position where they have to do what the torturers have failed to accomplish. While they prove more adept at the art of torture than the nominal torturers, their failure to extract confession creates more problems for themselves as well for the pharisaical outlook they espouse. Finally, the Buffeting proper, presented as a variant form of the late-medieval British judicial process known as *peine forte et dure*, reveals how ineffectual and, ultimately, how intellectually impoverished are even the most complicated and sophisticated human institutions when they lack the firm buttressing of spiritual understanding.

V

Just how the Wakefield Master reshapes and gives new life and meaning to the commonplace tools, machines, practical arts, and techniques of his day as part of an imaginative dramatic recasting of anachronized biblical history to enable Corpus Christi audiences to realize the spiritual implications of a life lived ethically by means of technology, in an age whose empirical temper is evidenced as much by the blacksmith shop as by its sacramentalism,[80] is the subject of this study. The discussion here of how the Wakefield Master's unique dramatic art invites his audience to renew understanding of itself as community—that is, as a collective of individuals living in a constructive and practical relation to the materiality of created reality and its Creator by scrutinizing everything they may have previously taken for granted about themselves as well as the world around them and its inherent order—should foster new interest, not only in this singular fifteenth-century British dramatist about whom little, lamentably, is known, but also about the various forms of technology and practical arts and techniques he so readily and effectively incorporated in his drama.[81] Ambitious as this aim may be, it is further hoped *The Wakefield Master's Dramatic Art* will rekindle interest in the six plays themselves and the various play revisions attributed to this dramatic genius, for his works—the fragments as well as the complete plays—never cease to delight and instruct in ways that even now will certainly move the interested audience member or reader to a greater comprehension of the fifteenth-century mind, and the importance that mind placed on spiritual understanding.

1

The Abuse of Time and Space
in the *Mactatio Abel*

The first play in the Towneley collection attributed to the Wakefield Master, the *Mactatio Abel,* wastes little time before challenging the audience, by means of the innovative artistic strategy involving the anachronistic verisimilitude of technology, to assume the responsibility of making meaning out of the decisive historical moment of the first act of manslaughter. Despite evidence of an extra-play or collectionwide thematic function, an unusual comic element, extensive editing, and a distinctive metrical complexity involving the widest variety of stanza forms and kinds of versification found in Huntington MS 1,[1] the *Mactatio Abel*'s use of the artistic strategy of linking the past with present Christian relevance through images and examples of contemporary medieval technologies effectively turns the audience's attention to the thematic concern of the improper *use* or abuse of nature. Revelation of this concern illuminates the motivation behind the more noticeable feature in the play of Cain's well-known obdurate impenitence, a theme that would have been anticipated by the Master's initial audiences,[2] and one that is developed by much of the play's action, such as the instances of foul wrath,[3] improper familial relations, improper stewardship, lack of feudal reciprocity, and even poor plowmanship.[4] But the serving of the self through the technological mastery and practical use of nature as, simply, an end in itself—that is, as a form of incorrect enjoyment—is of more interest to the Wakefield Master for the compelling reason that it offers his audience a dramatization of irresponsibility contrary to the prevailing medieval ethical attitude toward space, time, and the relation between the two. Four instructive instances of this irresponsibility and their particular consequences with regard to the abuse of nature are presented for the audience's consideration in the *Mactatio Abel* through the innovative elaboration of the anachronistic verisimilitude of technology in the play's four scenes and induction.[5]

I

The Wakefield Master's first treatment of incorrect *use* of nature, occupying the audience's attention in the induction (2/1–24) and "The Fraternal Encounter and Interview" (2/25–171), the play's opening scene, begins with a dramatic abuse of space. Evidence of this abuse arises in Garcio's induction proclamation. Aside from establishing the play's beginning, this proclamation demonstrates incorrect use in two ways, though both demonstrations have a practical as well as a salutary dramatic result. The first, the consequence of incorporation of direct discourse, destabilizes the expectation of the privileged view or "alienation" of the spectator in response to mimetic art, dramatic or otherwise. In other words, the "space" of the drama is initially disrupted by introduction of the participatory element of methexis, which has the effect of drawing the audience "in" or "closer" to the action on and before the pageant wagon.[6] The second abuse of space involves the proclamation itself, the purpose of which is to extend Cain's voice, the voice of Garcio's master, *in* and *over* the world. The extension of voice through an act of broadcast communication like this one, Lynn White Jr. has indicated in a study devoted to a different but related subject, is one of two principal means by which the conquest of matter—and, by implication, the conquest of space—is achieved.[7] While the proclamation's first words consist of a formulaic language of sorts—"All hayll, all hayll, both blithe and glad" (2/1)—and so suggestively remind the audience of heraldic proclamative language and its effect,[8] the nearly immediate degeneration of Garcio's expostulations into a harangue or rant, including curses interspersed with vulgar threats to get the imagined or even actual audience members to come to order—

Be peasse youre dyn, my master bad,
Or els the dwill you spede (2/3–4)

and

Bot who that ianglis any more,
He must blaw my blak hoill bore,

Both behynd and before,
Till his tethe blede (2/6–9)

—demonstrates how ineffectual *in* and *over* the world or space are both Garcio and, by implication, Cain, his master. As if this were not enough, the Wakefield Master also has Garcio repeatedly underscore this ineffectuality with regard to space, by stating this is not the first time he has come forward to proclaim on behalf his master—"Wote ye not I com before?" (2/5), then by forbidding the "Felows" to make noise or to cry out (2/10–11), then by enjoining the same to welcome Cain should he choose to appear (2/23), then by engaging in name-calling, identifying certain members of the audience as "Harlottys" (2/22), and finally by calling for the same to control their hostility and anger by covering their teeth with their lips (2/21).[9]

The combination of the plow team and plow Cain drives onstage at the beginning of "The Fraternal Encounter and Interview" images this same kind of incorrect or improper use of space. Mismatched as it may be, the team's size of two, four, or even eight or nine animals[10] combined with the heavy plow—the kind perhaps having wheels, coulter, flat plowshare (set at right angles to the coulter), and a moldboard slicing the turf to the left or right—suggests not only an ambitiously large area or space to be tilled and put into agricultural production,[11] but also the concomitant spirit fundamental to the medieval agricultural cooperative.[12] However, while the animals and this revolutionary farming device imply the possibility of a cooperative agricultural community, such is not the obvious outcome. Neither does the device plow, nor is a unanimity of purpose, agricultural or otherwise, expressed by either Cain or Garcio.[13] In fact, the correlative image presented here of the improper master-servant relationship[14] further suggests the impossibility of cooperation, first as Cain strikes Garcio and then as Garcio returns blow for blow, defiantly threatening his master with

Yai, with the same mesure and weght
That I boro will I qwite. (2/53–54)[15]

The dramatized elaboration of the mind that does not willingly serve God cooperatively in its technological mastery and practical use of nature at this point in the play also involves the demonstration of the improper use of time as an end in itself. Such a demonstration begins as soon as

Cain drives the plow team and plow, the great laborsaving device of medieval agriculture, out in full view of the audience. Cain's initial action gives the impression of saving and even mastering time, since one can literally *make* time by utilizing this particular farming technology, and since it is through laborsaving devices such as this machine that time is mastered and controlled.[16] However, the opposite occurs as soon as the entrance is completed. As the plow comes to a dead stop, the futility of controlling or even simply using time is dramatically evidenced. The point is repeated shortly afterward as Cain's ignorance of productive plowing procedure is demonstrated in several ways. First, while suggesting he knows that in order to plow he needs to be working with at least one other person—

> What, boy, shal I both hold and drife?
> Heris thou not how I cry? (2/39–40)

—Cain, nevertheless, is initially alone,[17] the opposite of proper or practical procedure suggested, for example, by the British Museum illustration of the four-ox plow in action.[18] Further, while he maneuvers the plow team and plow on or near the stage so that he might enlist the support of Garcio, Cain does not identify and call only the lead animal by name, the customary way to get a team of four or even an inconceivably large team of eight or nine animals to work productively.[19] Instead, he summons each animal as if it were the lead, cursing one at one moment, judging another the next—creating, in short, a general confusion:[20]

> Io furth, Greynhorne! and war oute, Gryme!
> Drawes on, God gif you ill to tyme!
> Ye stand as ye were fallen in swyme.
> What, will ye no forther, mare?
> War! let me se how Down will draw;
> Yit, shrew, yit, pull on a thraw!
> What, it semys for me ye stand none aw—
> I say, Donnying, go fare!
> Aha, God gif the soro and care!
> Lo, now hard she what I saide;
> Now yit art thou the warst mare
> In plogh that euer I haide. (2/25–36)

Cain's ignorance of the right kind of plow team for the job at hand further points to ineffective and unproductive plowing methods and the consequent loss and lack of mastery of time. While evidence might exist in medieval England for such mixed teams as Cain's,[21] they would not have made much sense in the field, since the horse, exerting roughly the same pull as the ox, would produce fifty percent more foot-pounds per second and would have more endurance—at least two hours more per day—than the slower beast of burden.[22] Practical considerations aside, too, such a combination of animals, an unusually weak team despite its numbers (whatever those numbers may be),[23] would have demonstrated a disregard for the figurative biblical injunction against uneven yoking and so offered to the actual working community a conspicuously instructive image of spiritual as well as agricultural confusion.[24]

Cain's ignorance of the proper maintenance of the plow and plow team completes the picture of agricultural inefficiency resulting from faulty procedure based in improper *use*. Walter of Henley's *Husbandry* indicates that it was advantageous in the manorial setting to tend carefully to the animals on the farm, whether in the pasture, folds, or stables.[25] The reason given for this attitude—nothing more, really, than medieval predial common sense—was that the better the health and physical condition of the animal, the more productive it would be. Such, however, is not heard or even suggested when the dialogue between Cain and Garcio commences. The audience immediately learns that the animals have not been fed, a fact over which Cain himself expresses concern—

Gog gif the sorow, boy!
Want of mete it gars. (2/44–45)

—and that the team has been improperly harnessed to the plow, tied by the neck in a primitive kind of choke harness that minimizes the animal's pulling power since the makeshift device, as Garcio himself declares, is weighted down with stones:

Thare prouand, syr, forthi,
I lay behynd thare ars,

And tyes them fast bi the nekys,
With many stanys in thare hekys. (2/46–49)

In fact, it is a wonder that the plow team and plow can even be driven onstage, given the suggested physical condition of the animals and the description of the rig's setup. That Garcio, when ordered to plow, starts but then abruptly stops is explained, then, no more by his obvious combative contrariness than by the odd way things are being done down on Cain's farm. The stalled plow, which must remain in view (even if off to the side) during the entire performance, "gives perspective to the action at hand," as Edmund Reiss observes,[26] but perhaps for a reason other than the one he suggests; it does so, in other words, by reminding the audience of the lack of proper *use* of nature through the failure to master either time or space, the result of the refusal to serve the self as a principal way of serving God cooperatively.

II

Further elaboration of the abuse of nature arises at the end of the play in the fourth scene or "The Cover-Up" as the Wakefield Master shifts attention, again, to the improper practical *use* and mastery of space and time as ends in themselves, in the demonstration of malice-induced faulty volition as source of motivation. The explicit manipulation and self-serving *use* of the *techne* or practical art of legal process, the initial example of this new emphasis involving the abusive control of space, occurs as Cain unsuccessfully attempts to enlist Garcio's support and participation in history's first cover-up.[27] First, Cain attempts to gain control of the world or space by creating a situation in which the response of the "bayles" is inevitable. To Garcio he admits killing Abel, and invites the boy "To ryn away with the bayn" (2/399)—to become an accomplice. Put in this position of potential legal jeopardy, Garcio does not raise the hue and cry, since he has no sense of civic duty to begin with, but he does demonstrate immediately an understanding of the implication of his being made accessory after the fact, an understanding he conveys to Cain when he exclaims: "We! out apon the, thefe!" (2/400).[28] Even though the admission is quickly dismissed by Cain as merely a "skaunce" (2/403) or jest, the degree to which Cain is ready to scheme to evade criminal liability is now fully apparent.

The second part of Cain's explicit maneuver, a consequence of the first, consists of offering Garcio a pardon:

A, syr, I cry you mercy! Seasse,
And I shall make you a releasse. (2/408–9)

The "releasse" is ostensibly meant to help Garcio, but in fact has the effect of inculpating the boy by identifying him as the guilty party, the one in need of exoneration.[29] What is more, as a diversionary disinformation technique of sorts, the release turns attention away from Cain, the actual fratricide.[30]

To insure against the undoing of this fabrication, Cain executes the final part of the explicit maneuver by making the deception convincing. First, he nullifies the substance of Garcio's responses to the implied inculpation. In his questioning of Cain's admission to the killing, for example, Garcio asks Cain whether he has slain his own brother, attempting to call attention to the actual guilty party as well as to the act itself. Cain, as has been noted, dismisses the admission as a "skaunce." Similarly, when Garcio suggests pronominally that guilt through association affecting him may actually have a deleterious effect upon its author, Cain—

We mon haue a mekill myschaunce
And the bayles vs take (2/406–7)

—Cain treats the notion dismissively and offers the "releasse." Secondly, Cain gets not only Garcio but, implicitly, the rest of humanity—"both man and wife" (2/415)—to abet him in the deception. This is done by trying to get Garcio to proclaim, "Oyes, oyes, oy!" (2/419), a series of expletives shouted to give authority to the disinformation while appropriating Garcio's voice, and then by offering a "payoff"—that is, by promising good fortune to all who conform to the script of the cover-up:

And whoso will do after me,
Ful slape of thrift then shal he be. (2/416–17)

Another example of malice prepense in the abuse of the legal practical arts to master space, as well now as time, arises as the full text of the proclamation of the King's Peace is introduced. As the well-known twenty-line stichomythic exchange between Garcio and Cain begins (2/420–39), the performance-selective reality of the dialogue provides the opportunity for creating the illusion, not that the King's Peace is necessary, but that the peace has already been broken. The first indication that this is so comes with the emphases in the "wrytys" itself. That no one is to find fault with Garcio and, by implication, Cain, and, further, that all should believe these two are true, beyond reproach, and even worthy of "devout love," suggests the two have previously been faulted or at least perceived to be untrue and unworthy. Another indication that the peace has already been broken, another justification for the imposition of a penalty, occurs toward the end of this comic exchange between Garcio and Cain as the latter, hoping Garcio has been silenced once and for all, attempts to mulct those physically near to him, and perhaps the audience as well, as the incorporation of the methexis of direct discourse again suggests is occurring:

> Long or thou get thi hoyse and thou go thus aboute!
>
> Byd euery man theym pleasse to pay. (2/439–40)

But for Garcio's humorous sustentative and substantive replies to each of Cain's pronouncements in the stichomythic exchange, Cain's proclamative disinformation would, no doubt, have the authority of truth and so shape perception of Cain and Garcio. Revealing as the stichomythic undoing of this sham may be,[31] however, more important is the anger this response engenders in Cain, for the revelation of that emotion, most noticeable as Cain thinks of Garcio in terms of Abel—

> We! com downe in twenty dwill way!
> The dwill I þe betake;
> For bot it were Abell, my brothere,
> Yit knew I neuer thi make (2/442–45)

—discloses the prepensive nature of the malice motivating Cain's actions, since Cain is now making a comparison, and calling attention to that comparison, *prior* to acting.

This quality of malice is also shown in the final lines of the play to be a principal part of Cain's abuse of technology to master time as an end in itself. Once again this abuse returns attention to the plow, which during the entire play has remained idle. After telling Garcio to go to the device and walk before it—the proper way, ironically, of using this agricultural technology—Cain threatens Garcio, warning him never again to annoy him as Garcio has done through the stichomythic disclosures Garcio has just made about his relation to his master, as well as about his master's guilt in the matter of the first-ever fratricide. If Garcio does not heed this warning, Cain indicates that the plow, the great laborsaving device enabling people to *make* and thereby *master* or properly *use* time, will be transformed into the gallows,[32] another medieval technology,[33] the purpose of which is to end time. The suggestion that Garcio will suffer a fate similar to Abel's if he does not conform to Cain's wishes by assimilating the principles of the other "lore" Cain says he will teach Garcio restates, in a final, chilling way, the prepensive desire to do another harm while possibly also introducing an imaged corruption of "streeking the plow," the immediate effect of which is the suggestion of the field's being turned into a graveyard.[34]

III

Refusal to serve God cooperatively, by improperly serving the self in the technological mastery and practical use of nature, is elaborated in the *Mactatio Abel's* middle section, or second and third scenes, through the abuse of invention and innovation. This is, understandably, the most extensive treatment of the idea of abuse in the play, for obvious dramatic and thematic reasons. The account in the play's third scene, "The Killing of Abell," of the first fratricide introduces the misuse of invention—the abuse, in other words, of the discovery and material application of what is latent in nature for the purpose of technologically fulfilling the divine will in the world.[35] This abuse, of course, occurs as the jawbone is picked up by Cain and turned into a weapon. With this new technology, one unique to the English tradition of the Cain and Abel story,[36] Cain "chastises" Abel suddenly by "twaining" him from life with one quick thrust:

> With cheke-bon, or that I blyn,
> Shal I the and thi life twyn.
> So, lig down ther and take thi rest;
> Thus shall shrewes be chastysed best. (2/326–29)

As a weapon per se, this invention fulfills its purpose of "twaining" or killing much as the jawbone, as part of the skeletal structure, fulfills its purpose of enabling the teeth it supports to "twain" things in the act of chewing. However, while this weapon allows Cain, in a sense, to serve himself in a technological mastery of nature, this mastery turns out to be an abuse, since the purpose of the material application is not service in cooperation with God but rather the thwarting of God's purpose through the silencing of Abel, the voice of the divine will in the world. The immediate consequence of Cain's estrangement from God and society through this abuse of invention implicit in the act of killing is suggested, on the one hand, by Cain's desire to find sanctuary in "som hole" for forty days (2/342), a telling legal anachronism in the play,[37] and, on the other, by the illusion of distance created twice as God calls out to Cain to consider what he has done:

   Caym, Caym! (2/343)

and

   Caym, where is thi brother Abell? (2/346)

Equally important, however, is the estrangement or disorder Cain also suffers within himself as a result of the abuse and killing. As if to compensate for the greater alienation he now feels as a fratricide, Cain broadens the focus of his anger, which originally was directed only at God and Abel, to include the entire imagined and perhaps even actual audience, yet again through the methexis of direct discourse:

   Yei, ly ther, old shrew! ly ther, ly!

   And if any of *you* thynk I did amys,
   I shal it amend wars then it is,
   That all men may it se:
   Well wars then it is,
   Right so shall it be. (2/332–37; italics mine)

Stevens and Cawley suggest the use of "amend" here is ironic in that Cain is promising to make the amends for the crime worse than the crime itself.[38] This irony, however, becomes even more trenchant in light of the morality of technology if the medieval meaning of "to improve on" for "amend" is considered in this context.[39] To improve an invention or, in other words, to create an innovation whose purpose has already been proved to be contrary to the divine will in the world is to be even more committed, it would seem, to the condition of erring by furthering and making irrevocable the disconnect between morality and technology.

   Two other kinds of abuse of invention betraying like impetuous force and involving material application occur just before and after the killing; as they frame the first fratricide, they deserve consideration here. In each of these, inventive lingual or lingual-physical acts are performed by Cain to separate the space and time he inhabits from that created by God. One inventive lingual-physical act occurs just prior to the killing as Cain attempts to encourage Abel to flee with him, in a way reminiscent of Jonah's thinking in the late-fourteenth-century poem *Patience*,[40] when Cain suggests they flee to where God will not be able to see them:

> No, bot go we hens sone;
> And if I may, I shall be
> Ther as God shall not me see. (2/307–9)

An inventive lingual-physical act precedes this argument in support of flight, too. In this instance Cain, through the act of linguistic identification or naming, attempts to reduce God's significance by identifying God as a "hob" or sprite, and by locating God in a space different from the one he occupies:

> Whi, who is that hob ouer the wall?
> We! who was that piped so small? (2/299–300)

This identification, including the concomitant denunciation of God as "out of hys wit!" (2/302), is made not only for the purpose of extending the "claim of madness to God Himself"[41] but also for the purpose of furthering the differentiation of space, which has the correlative benefit of enabling Cain to ignore God's previous injunction to tithe correctly and, equally important, to deny the previous judgment of his own rebelliousness (2/293–94).

A similar abusive preemptive move involving an abuse of linguistic invention alone is made by Cain just after he has killed his brother and Abel's blood has cried out for vengeance. In response to Abel, God calls out for Cain to tell Him where Abel can now be found. Rather than comply, Cain equivocates by answering God's question with a question of his own:

> *Deus.* Caym, where is thi brother Abell?
> *Caym.* What askys thou me? (2/346–47)

Questioning God's questioning in this manner is an attempt to preclude the possibility—or, dramatically, to limit the extent—of God's perception by suggesting it is, in fact, a misperception, a suggestion for which Cain has already prepared the audience by questioning, first, who it is calling to him and then the very limit of God's visual field:

> Deus.   Caym, Caym!
> Caym.   Who is that that callis me?
>   I am yonder, may thou not se? (2/344–45)

The most remarkable act of inventive linguistic abuse through preemption that Cain performs with impetuous force and even vehemence, however, follows shortly afterward as God readies Himself to offer his "malison." Rather than wait for the judgment, Cain instead gives himself his own curse, which curiously includes an appended condition.[42] What he says as he bereaves God of voice to offer the sole judgment on himself is that any who might meet him must kill him "hardely":

> Yei, dele aboute the, for I will none,
> Or take it the when I am gone.
> Syn I haue done so mekill syn
> That I may not thi mercy wyn,
> And thou thus dos me from thi grace,
> I shall hyde me fro thi face.
> And whereso any man may fynd me,
> Let hym slo me hardely. (2/358–65)

Furthermore, the condition appended here is that if one does comply, then one must also bury Cain as "hardely" as one has slain him, in "Gudeboure at the quarell hede" (2/368–69). In other words, the judgment he passes on himself turns also into a financial threat of sorts that he believes no one will challenge,[43] as the contempt expressed in his final words implies:

> For, may I pas this place in quarte,
> Bi all men set I not a fart. (2/370–71)

Ironically, however, this forceful preemption is itself preempted by God, as God turns the curse into a protective sign[44] and increases the penal consequences of killing Cain to be a deterrent against any kind of future manslaughter:

> Nay, Caym, it bese not so;
> I will that no man other slo,
> For he that sloys [the], yong or old.
> It shall be punyshid sevenfold. (2/372–75)

The linguistic separation of God from the space and time Cain inhabits is thus effectively reversed in a single instant by God's revalorization of the meaning of the first act of killing. All of Cain's abusive linguistic inventions have, thus, been in vain.

IV

The second way God is not served cooperatively by the technological mastery and practical use of nature in the second scene or "The Tithing" involves explicit abuse by means of the adoption of innovative accounting strategies to avoid God—that is, the adoption of two sets of innovative acts of mind (the creation of artificial intelligence, in a sense) to postpone or, if possible, to put off indefinitely the acknowledging of God. The first set of such abuses begins as soon as Abel has acquainted his brother with his "sawe" concerning tithing and the need to be cleansed "from the feynd" in preparation to perform the ritual sacrifice. It is then that Cain presents practical and ethical technology assessments—that is, rudimentary cost-benefit analyses of sorts, of the pre-Cartesian measurable *res extensa* and of the incommensurable *res cogitans*—as arguments for not accompanying Abel to participate in the giving.[45]

Technology assessment, the perceived and estimated value of the relationship between technology and society, as well as between technology and nature, was as much a feature of medieval thinking as it is of our own today. While no medieval person used the term "technology assessment," a phrase of fairly recent coinage,[46] examples of medieval people engaged in this type of estimating and appraisal are readily available. One of these arising during the latter part of Edward III's reign serves as an instructive illustration of this tendency that is true in any age.[47] Perceiving a decline in English archery in 1365, Edward, one of the great militant kings of medieval British history, banned a variety of sports, including bowling, quoits, handball, football, club ball, hockey, and cockfighting—by 1388, tennis and dice had been added to the list—so that time usually spent participating in these activities could be devoted to practicing with bows and arrows, the principal weaponry of the age. Edward's understanding of the importance of the longbow in relation to society and his future political ambitions led him to take the stringent measures he did.

While his lack of understanding of the complexity of popular life and leisure in the latter part of the century eventually undermined the measures imposed and did not halt the decline of the bow as the weapon of choice—a decline that continued until the sixteenth century when the bow was officially replaced by the technologically inferior musket—Edward's assessment of the problem and identification of the remedy, flawed as it turned out to be, nevertheless demonstrated an attempt at understanding the ethical and practical implications of the relationship between a particular weapons technology and society, on the one hand, and between that same technology and human nature, on the other.

As Cain engages in a like appraisal in the tithing scene, however, the Wakefield Master makes it clear that the practical art of technology assessment in this case is not being utilized to remedy a problem but rather to create one—that is, to provide the mind with a subtle means of avoiding cooperative service with God as it serves itself in the technological mastery and practical use of nature. The practical analyses offered by Cain in the first part of the assessment are presented one after the other. First, he raises the issue of the cost of interrupting production by pointing out the impracticality of leaving the plow when it is in operation, even though, ironically, the great plow Cain has driven into view at the beginning of the play is standing idle in full view on or off to one side of the stage:

> Shuld I leife my plogh and all thyng,
> And go with the to make offeryng?
> Nay, thou fyndys me not so mad!
> Go to the dwill, and say I bad! (2/93–96)

The second rudimentary cost-benefit argument follows nearly immediately, in response to Abel's characterization of Cain's expressed reluctance to tithe as "vayn carpyng" (2/99). In this attempt to forestall Abel, Cain argues against giving on the grounds that such an investment would not be profitable since his current "wynnyngys," the source of his investment, have, as the result of poor recent production, turned out to be "meyn" (2/113). Cain's position here is buttressed by the apparent fact, to which Cain alludes, that the present moment is a time of recession in the actual economy of the area. Not only is Cain unable to receive credit from God—"I traw that he will leyn me noght" (2/117)—but his previous contribution in the form of a farthing to increase the economy of spirituality has not yet resulted even in a modest return since the coin, as far as Cain can see or judge, is still in the priest's hand (2/106–7).[48] Were everyone to invest during a recession, an economic turnaround might occur. For Cain to do it himself, or even with Abel, however, does not make good production/investment sense to him.

The first ethical production-cost-benefit analysis presented for not tithing—that is, the cost-benefit analysis of the *res cogitans*—calls attention a second time in the play to the late-medieval agricultural cooperative. The new plow, like the one Cain has driven onstage, revolutionized not only plowing but also the social experience of the manorial peasant group. The plow's size, requiring perhaps as many as four yokes or harnesses, created the need for pooled plow teams and field labor, not to mention the reorganization of the fields under cultivation.[49] As Abel responds to Cain's acknowledgment of a lack of creditworthiness with God in the previous argument for not tithing, Cain quickly rejoins by pointing out that the social experience of the cooperative has also not been characterized by sharing.

First, he indicates that God has lent him nothing, the result of God's being his "fo," not his friend. Second, he points out that, these differences aside, God has not even cooperated by offering seed at a crucial time when the need was great:

> When I should saw and wantyd seyde,
> Then was myne not worth a neld.
> When I should saw, and wantyd seyde,
> And of corn had full grete neyde,
> Then gaf he me none of his. (2/124–28)

In other words, God's unwillingness to make resources available when circumstances required such an action for the benefit of the group demonstrated an attitude contrary to the ethos of the cooperative. It is for this reason Cain, with an air of self-satisfaction, concludes by saying

> Hardely hold me to blame
> Bot if I serue hym of the same. (2/130–31)

It would be wrong or unethical of Cain, according to the limited logic of his own analysis, to serve God in any way other than that in which God, as member of the medieval agricultural cooperative, has apparently served him.

The second set of practical and ethical cost-benefit analyses Cain musters to further his strategy of avoidance has to do with "prow" or "good." In this set, the ethical analysis—that is, the cost-benefit analysis of the *res cogitans*—is presented first. In response to his brother's continued requests to tithe, Cain maintains that giving away his "good" or profit would have a negative socioeconomic impact.[50] In other words, tithing would impoverish him and reduce him to economic dependency:

> For had I giffen away my goode,
> Then myght I go with a ryffen hood,
> And it is better hold that I haue
> Then go from doore to doore and craue. (2/142–45)

The short- and long-term consequences of this condition were well known to many in England at this time. In his discussion with Hunger in passus VI of *Piers Plowman*, for example, Piers points out that the problem with beggary is not that the destitute need to be fed; instead, they need to be mastered or taught to work since, when the goad of hunger is not present, "they will work badly."[51] Cain's analysis argument thus may reveal an inveterate possessiveness, but it also introduces a socioeconomic issue affecting the lower end of the very caste structure of medieval British society.

The practical "prow" cost-benefit analysis follows Abel's expressed fear that they have delayed the tithe too long; this attempt to continue to put off giving turns attention to the *res extensa*. Cain tells his brother that it makes no sense to tithe since were he to give away part of his "warldys," then he would not be able to enjoy fully what he has worked so hard to obtain and now possess.[52] Wearing shoes with ripped hose, he points out aphoristically, defeats the purpose of working for the shoes in the first place (2/154–55). Cain does agree to Abel's request afterward, but his concession reiterates the practical profit incentive he has just finished articulating. The point he is making, though conspicuously off the mark,[53] is that he would be more amenable to the request to tithe if some "prow" were to result.

V

The final way the deliberate refusal to serve God cooperatively through the technological mastery and practical use of nature is brought to the fore again in the third scene or "The Tithing" as Cain, having finally accompanied Abel to the tithing place, explicitly distorts the tallying procedure by an innovation that works to his own benefit. Even though his improper *use* of production or "prow" cost-benefit analyses to keep from having to give a portion of his wealth proves, in the final analysis, to be ineffectual, Cain shows he is not without means of continuing to forestall the act of sacrifice and giving. This particular abusive ingenuity furthering Cain's recalcitrance and impenitence is manifested as soon as he begins counting out the sheaves of "corn" or grain in his tithe offering. His unique arithmetic method here, one of the more humorous moments in the play, has been called a number of things, including a model of disorder, sleight of hand, bad ring-giving, and subterfuge.[54] While certainly an evasion, this comical arithmetic event into which the tithing turns is fundamentally an abuse of innovation since its objective is the distortion of offering and distinction, which is effected by means of manipulating the practical art of counting to one's own advantage.

The distorted innovation that undermines collaboration with God in this case is introduced, first, in terms of its opposite. Evidencing the influence of the second controlling principle of Scholasticism, *concordantia*,[55] the Wakefield Master begins, for purposes of clarity, by introducing the proper method of making the tithing prayer in the form of a procedural model that is empirically demonstrated to Cain by Abel, as Abel himself first tithes before God:

> God that shope both erth and heuen,
> I pray to the thou here my steven
> And take in thank, if thi will be,
> The tend that I offre here to the,
> For I gif it in good entent
> To the, my Lord, that all has sent.
> I bren it now with stedfast thoght.
> In worship of hym that all has wroght. (2/176–83)

Like the medieval *computus* in its objective, the design to be followed through the act of giving properly, as articulated in the prayer, allows for what Boethius called *commercium* (V. Prose III)[56]—the experience of the nexus between the macrocosm and the microcosm, between the heavens *beyond* space and time and the individual *in* space and time.[57] This nexus or unity results from the simultaneous perception in the prayer of two things: the ordered relation of the self to God—that is, the proper condition, in the Pauline sense, of the "exterior" man—and its prerequisite inner condition, the proper order within the self, or the proper condition of the "interior" man.

The former is established two ways at the beginning and end—in the frame, as it were—of the prayer. First, God is identified as the shape-maker or architect of the earth and heavens, of time and space. In short, God is properly recognized as "hym that all has wroght." Secondly, the reverence due God as architect of the cosmos is given by Abel, at the outset as he kneels to show respect and identifies God as his lord, and then in closing as he identifies God as the deity whom he worships. Similarly, proper order within the self or of the "interior" man is acknowledged in the middle of the prayer in two ways as well. The first employs volition to reveal the "inner" quality of the self. In this case, the proper attitude of will is identified as "good entent" (2/180). The "exterior" quality of the properly ordered self—the demonstration or expression of "good entent"—follows in the identification of the rational ceremony of sacrifice as the act of burning the tithe "with stedfast thoght" (2/182). What Abel wills with regard to God, as the model thus demonstrates, Abel does in response to God.[58]

The abuse of the tithing prayer results from Cain's innovative approach to the "inner" and "outer" parts of the prayer model concerned with the proper ordering of self in preparation for sacrifice and giving. This approach changes the experience and expression of the ordered self, shifting the object of the prayer from nexus or unity, as in the *computus* or the *commercium* of *The Consolation of Philosophy*, to something more like a balance revealing a relative bargaining strength, as in the medieval manorial *compotus* or annual audit.[59] The first indication of this involves Cain's modification of Abel's "good entent." What is wilful obedience in the model becomes, for Cain, obdurate wilfulness. This is not a new revelation about Cain: he is, historically as well as dramatically from the moment he appears onstage, a convincing personification of *duritia cordis*. However, unique about this modification of proper submission is its purpose. Until this moment in the play, nearly everything said or done by Cain has either revealed or contributed to his recalcitrance. Now an explanation is given in passing for this attitude, which is unmistakably heard at the beginning of the tithing scene as Cain emphatically states:

> It is full sore myne vnthankys,
> The teynd that I here gif to the
> Of corn or thyng that newys me. (2/189–91)

What makes Cain the way he is, as the end of his version of the tithing prayer suggests, is, in other words, lack of conscience.[60] As he tries to persuade Abel to "chaunge [his] conscience" (2/265) to be like him, Cain also demonstrates that his inability to judge between right and wrong has altered the fundamental attitude of his will so that all he does or says results from, as well as betrays, a "bad entent."

Abusive innovation distorting the expression or demonstration—that is, the "outer" quality—of "good entent" in Cain's version of Abel's prayer includes direct and indirect modification of the act of obedience and steadfast thought in the relationship either between Cain and Abel, between Cain and God, or both. As soon as Abel has finished tithing and been ordered by Cain to rise to make way for the next act of sacrifice, indirect modification of obedience begins. Cain's purpose in regard to his brother is not to challenge God directly but rather to enlist the support of another in repudiating the need to collaborate with God. It is perhaps for this reason Cain has been viewed by some as satanic.[61] Whether this association is justified, it is certain Cain wants company in his misery and so tries to persuade Abel to "chaunge [his] conscience." What is more, the strategies he employs to effect this conversion are themselves acts of artful but deceptive indirection. First, for example, he tries to inveigle by introducing a tithing hypothetical. Though against giving his "good away," he entertains momentarily the thought of giving, and of what Abel's response would be:

> Bot had I gyffen hym this to teynd,
> Then wold thou say he were my freynd. (2/216–17)

Next, by asking Abel to help in the sheaf selection process while he closes his own eyes, Cain attempts to make Abel an accomplice in the wrongful act of mis-tithing:

> We! com nar, and hide myne een;
> In the wenyand, wist ye now at last!
> Or els will thou that I wynk?
> Then shall I doy no wrong, me thynk. (2/227–30)

Finally, after being chastened for not dreading God, Cain tries to elicit Abel's sympathy by explaining that his reluctance to tithe results directly from the hardships suffered at the time of the harvest:

> For that, and this that lyys here,
> Haue cost me full dere:
> Or it was shorne, and broght in stak,
> Had I many a wery bak. (2/241–44)

It is no wonder that, when none of these attempts to gain support works, Cain becomes irate and resorts to threatening Abel:

> For if thou to my teynd tent take,
> It bese the wars for thi sake (2/251–52)

and

> Yei, kys the dwills ars behynde;
> The dwill hang the bi the nek!
> How that I teynd, neuer thou rek.
> Will thou not yit hold thi peasse? (2/268–71)

So much effort to reap so little a return or "prow" is certainly frustrating for a temperament like Cain's, governed as it is by materiality and acquisitiveness, and bereft of spirituality.

A similar belligerence characterizes the direct innovative modification of obedience in the relationship between Cain and God. From the moment he readies himself to tithe, Cain demonstrates an obvious defiance toward God in what he does and says. To begin, he refuses to perform the obligatory deferential genuflection, the attitude of submission assumed by Abel during his act of sacrifice. When reluctantly giving God two sheaves of corn—first, one that "we [may] best mys" (2/221), and then another that is distinguished from the good ones as "Nawder of thise ii" (2/254–55)—Cain offers the worst of each part of the harvest. His preemption of God's judgment regarding his first act of giving by means of his own favorable procedural assessment—

> Let me se now how it is—
> Lo, yit I hold me paide;
> I teyndyd wonder well bi ges,
> And so euen I laide (2/231–34)

—likewise nullifies not only God's authority but also the authority of the tithing model itself since, by his own admission, he has given not by design but merely "bi ges."

Cain's final characterization of this enacted or direct defiance—he calls it "skill"[62]—might also be considered another way of preempting God's judgment. Within the context of the innovation of the prayer, however, inclusion of this term serves to remind the audience of the modification of the "stedfast thoght" with which Abel has just made his sacrifice. Cain recasts his brother's rational buttressing of faith, for himself, through an abusive, innovative combination of tallying and anecdotal/analytical response. The first part of this strategy involves creating the impression of steadfastness through the illusion of numerical consistency. To do this, counting and counting-repetitions are employed by Cain as he reviews the sheaves, one by one, to be tithed.[63] Conventional scholarly wisdom has been that Cain identifies ten sheaves in the first tithing exercise, enunciating the simple arithmetic progression of the decimal counting system.[64] Such a medieval theatrical activity alone, of course, suggests a kind of steadfastness, not only numerically, but also in terms of purpose. However, an even more convincing illusion of consistency is created if Cain's counting out of the sheaves is considered to be not a decimal but rather a vigesimal arithmetic progression, in which the counting out of two piles of sheaves is conducted as in the medieval tally or *compotus*.[65] When Cain begins with "One shefe, oone," in other words, he is not pointing to one sheaf alone and then emphasizing it, but rather putting down one sheaf on either side of the tally stick as was customarily done in the medieval tally. Likewise, "and this makys two" is not a simple sum, but rather the placing of the second sheaf on each measuring pile, increasing the total number of sheaves, after this second count, to four, then to six after the third, to eight after the fourth, and so on down to twenty after the tenth. Cain's use of the word "thrafe" (2/199), a medieval measure of "corn" or grain consisting of two stacks,[66] suggests that such a kind of tallying is, in fact, occurring, a suggestion echoed by the balanced metrical structure of each line. What is more,

Cain's role as steward, initially marred though it is by his inability to control space and time through an inept handling of the plow and plow team, also increases the likelihood of there being not one but two piles of sheaves tallying with each other on the stage as the twenty-first or the odd-sheaf-out is reluctantly given as a tithe, since the steward or reeve was usually the manorial overseer and representative who engaged in the tally at the time of the annual audit. The dramatic visual effect of these measured piles of grain, moreover, provides an objective correlative of the illusion of steadfastness and balance, which, for the successful medieval manorial *compotus,* was an indispensable feature of the annual audit performance response.

Cain's innovative recasting of the kind of thinking Abel maintained steadfastly in tithing is perhaps not as dramatically effective as the transformation of steadfastness in the demonstration of tallying numerical constancy, but, as the second part of the strategy recasting Abel's rational buttressing of faith, it is no less important. In the first tithing exercise, for example, it is as thoroughly developed as the sheaf counting. Once he has counted out the first set of corn stacks, Cain removes the sheaves from tithing consideration with a simple dismissive statement of fact: "Bot nawder of thise may I forgo" (2/195). Next, having added another sheaf to each stack, Cain again withdraws the grain from consideration. But this time the reason is offered in the form of a value judgment:

> Yei, this also shall leif with me,
> For I will chose and best haue—
> This hold I thrift—of all this thrafe. (2/197–99)

After a fourth sheaf is distributed to each side of the tally, the thinking enunciated at the withdrawal of the latest produce from the tithe takes the form of a lengthy anecdotal analysis of the harvest—one reminiscent of earlier production cost-benefit analyses or technological assessments used to put off tithing and so preclude collaboration with God:

> Wemo, wemo! foure, lo, here!
> Better greved me no this yere.
> At yere tyme I sew fayre corn,
> Yit was it sech when it was shorne:
> Thystyls and brerys—yei, grete plenté—
> And all kyn wedys that myght be. (2/200–205)

Reasoning for not giving the fifth sheaf, too, advances the transformation of thought yet another step. In this case Cain, now halfway through the count, questions his present activity aphoristically: "Deyll I fast thus, long or I thrife!" (2/207). Finally, after the seventh sheaf is dealt, Cain completes the evolution of his thinking by offering the conclusion that God will not get, nor even see, any of the grain under consideration in this portion of the tithing. Three more sets of sheaves are put down to complete the tally, but the conclusion does not change except for the inclusion of the tithing hypothetical, which only further emphasizes the conclusion, and the inclusion of the word "goode" for the corn that has been deemed too good to be given as a sacrificial offering. The consideration of the withheld sheaves as "goods" or "wealth" may suggest Cain's acquisitiveness. He is, after all, viewed as "possessor" in medieval exegesis.[67] But it also introduces a far more complicated way of thinking than the bald statement given as the reason for not giving up the first sheaves at the beginning of the exercise. To conclude Cain is now viewing the grain before him as a fungible may be going too far. But it would not be an exaggeration to say that, by the time he finally does part with a sheaf of corn—the one he may "best mys"—he has demonstrated a remarkable cognitive agility or "skill," one like that of the successful manorial reeve or steward, such as Chaucer's Reeve Oswold, who has never been caught in arrears at the time of the annual audit.[68] The problem with this, however, is that the context in which Cain exercises his singular skill is a tithing, not the *compotus*, and so the ability demonstrated, in the final analysis, is a demonstration of false, not true, husbandry.[69]

The abusive innovation of the tithing prayer, though remarkably forceful dramatically, proves ultimately to be faulty because it is explicitly self-serving and so does not last as the final part of the tithing exercise begins. The illusion of steadfastness through numerical constancy, for example, degenerates into the calling out of random numbers as Cain, counting out more and more sheaves, apparently now in groups, puts down twelve, then fifteen and sixteen, until he is interrupted. The recklessness of this change in counting procedure is noticed by Abel, who, long an advocate of Cain's tithing reform, identifies Cain's latest treatment of the sacrifice as being "of the warst" (2/226). In addition, the illusion of thinking by means of cognitive agility is also quickly debased as Cain abandons his "skill" or practical art by introducing into the argument, for the purpose of refraining from further giving, such emotive and volitional elements as the superstition of the "wenyand" (2/227–30), the delusionally favorable assessment of his own previous tithing generosity (2/231–34), *podex* and defecation obscenities (2/236–40), an appeal for sympathy (2/241–46), threats (2/251–52 and 268–69), and the expression of exasperation (2/270–71). Accordingly, bereft through the tithing-prayer alternative he has innovatively fashioned in an effort to continue to avoid collaboration with God, Cain finds himself at the moment of sacrifice and giving, to continue the *compotus* metaphor, caught in arrears—that is, he finds himself vulnerable in a way he has not hitherto been, his lack of conscience or "bad entent" paradoxically put in relief as his tithe-burning suddenly belches forth a billow of choking smoke. This nearly asphyxial pyrotechnical cloud,[70] the only one of its kind in all of the mystery plays,[71] introduces the potential for ecological crisis when technology is abused as an end in itself and not employed as a means to the greater end of using and enjoying nature properly in a cooperative mastery with God.[72] What is more, it signals the condition of a crisis of "spiritual ecology" within Cain himself,[73] the cause of which is Cain's perverse wilfulness to abuse technology for the purpose of maintaining the condition of *duritia cordis*.

The killing of Abel, then, in the Wakefield Master's *Mactatio Abel*, as most criticism of the play agrees, involves, as much as the actual wielding of the lethal jawbone, the consequence of Cain's insistence upon remaining distant and alienated from God. What is more, of these two kinds of "killing," the latter is presented as the more serious because it is in this way—that is, by repeating or reasserting in one's own heart the wilful attitude informing the recalcitrance behind and eventually leading to physical violence—that one becomes, to quote Garcio, one of "Cain's men," one who must endure the perennial tropological condition consisting of the fate suffered by Cain himself.[74] The Wakefield Master, like other Towneley playwrights whose purpose it is to effect moral—and, by extension, civic—reform through their dramatic art, wants the audience to understand this fact and thereby avoid this "inner" condition of disorientation and disorder by recognizing its "outer" signs. To facilitate such recognition, obvious as well as subtle "signs" are integrated within the dramatic texture of the play. Of the former are such elements as Cain's repeated anachronistic belligerence or rejection of the proper master-servant relationship, or of its politicomilitary equivalent involving the proper vassalic relationship informing feudal custom and practice. Of the latter are the various instances of the mind's refusal to serve God cooperatively through the anachronistic abuse of technology to serve itself in an improper mastery of time and space. Of these two types of "signs," the subtle offer a greater interpretive challenge because they not only reveal how complex is the "interior" condition of disorientation and disorder of the perennial Cain, they also explain how the seemingly disparate "exterior" or obvious "signs" in the play are actually related.

2

The Abuse and Use of Time and Space in the *Processus Noe cum filiis*

The *Processus Noe cum filiis*, the second Towneley play attributed to the Wakefield Master and the first to be written entirely in his thirteen-line signature stanza,[1] begins with the unfolding moment of nexus between created and uncreated reality at the outset of the second age in the time of erring, just before God and Noah, their monologues done, enter into a dialogue. This is the same type of nexus Abel momentarily achieves through his tithing prayer in the previous play in the collection, the *Mactatio Abel*, and the same nexus that is undone just as quickly by Cain through his subsequent disastrous mis-tithing. While a like kind of nexus can be found in the Bible and in the two York Noah plays—the Towneley play's three principal sources[2]—the Towneley *Processus Noe* is distinctive in that it presents Noah as the initiator of this unique experience of union.[3] Noah's role here, one that is put in relief dramatically by his expressed desire to be distinguished from the rest of creation, sets him apart as being alert, receptive, and responsive at a time in the history of the world when the rest of creation is obviously not. Not unexpected as the result of this innovative modification of principal source material is the fact that Noah is chosen by the Wakefield Master to be, in created reality as well as in the design of history conceived of in the Towneley collection, the initial exemplar of the mind that serves God cooperatively by serving itself in the technological mastery and practical use of nature.[4] Not unexpected, too, is the fact that explicit mastery and practical use of nature here is conceived in terms of a proper attitude toward—as well as *use* of—time and space. Unusual from the point of view of conventional medieval Noah plays, however, are the artistic ways in which the Wakefield Master elaborates, without compromising dramatic unity or coherence, Noah's exemplarism by means of the tropological anachronistic verisimilitude of medieval technology, the dramatic effect of which again challenges the audience to assume responsibility for making meaning in response to the play.

I

The first of these ways, occurring in what might be considered the play's first scene or "The Problem,"[5] consists of the summoning of the archetype or the anachronistic exemplary model[6]—a summoning, that is, introducing a set of medieval presuppositions about technology involving the ideas of cooperation with God, the serving of the self through the technological mastery and practical use of nature, and the integral relationship between the two. Most noticeable about the innovative presentation of the anachronistic medieval notion of cooperation, especially in the third or "Dialogue" episode between God and Noah (3/235–62), as well as in Noah's and God's monologues before it, is the emphasis the Wakefield Master places on the expression of collaboration in the mouths of both Noah and God. The latter, for example, articulates a willingness to work closely with Noah owing to Noah's singular and distinctive work ethic and previous "true-as-steel" obedience:

> Thou was alway well-wirkand,
> To me trew as stele,
> To me bydyng obediand. (3/174–76)

For this reason God, making the same distinction found in John 15:13, refers to Noah as "my freend" (3/170) and identifies Noah's future reward as the "Frendship" they now—and will afterward continue to—enjoy:

> Frendship shall thou fele
> To mede. (3/177–78)[7]

A similar sentiment can be heard repeatedly in Noah's replies to God toward the end of the same episode. This is apparent in Noah's initial expression of civility and curiosity. Noah's use of the anachronistic Franciscan *Benedicité* (3/235) and his inquiring after God's name, the first two things Noah says after hearing God speak of the marvel about to occur, imply an appreciation for all of creation as well as a respect for—

and an immediate friendly or loving interest in—the divine visitor.[8] A reassertion of this collaborative spirit and its importance is underscored at the end of the exchange in Noah's acknowledgment of the need for God's blessing as the only means of empowerment:

> Blis vs, Lord, here
> For charité I hit crafe;
> The better may we stere
> The ship that we shall hafe,
> Certayn. (3/252–56)

Noah's inclusion here of the anachronistic "charité" also reasserts the collaborative spirit already expressed by both God and Noah, since the relationship implied by this word is based upon a reciprocity and friendship whose immediate and long-term benefits both parties understand and appreciate—the result, of course, of a millennium of Christianity's influence upon thinking and action in the West.[9]

A like sentiment of cooperation is articulated in the two preceding monologues as well. It is there, for example, in Noah's initial plea to God when Noah—wanting to distinguish himself from the rest of creation that

> Most party day and nyght,
> Syn in word and ded
> Full bold (3/72–74)

—calls out to God, not only to identify himself as God's "seruant" but also to invite God, as "Comly kyng" or master, to keep him, Noah, from sinning "This warld within" and to preserve his "fry" and himself eventually in God's "hall / In heuen" (3/96–104).[10] That Noah ends this plea by importuning God to hear his voice or "stevyn" (3/104) is accordingly not just an emphatic, though such an effect is established by the usage; rather, it serves again to remind the audience of the spirit of cooperation, anachronistic as it may be, since it is through voice or communication that, as the scene's later dialogue demonstrates and may even be seen to emblematize, the reciprocity of collaboration is established. As might be expected, the same spirit of cooperation characterizes the end of God's subsequent monologue as God identifies Noah as his servant, hastens to the human to warn him of the impending cataclysm, singles out Noah as one who shall receive great profit owing to his consistent cooperative spirit, which is untainted by the contrariness of "stryfe" (3/154–60), and finally identifies Noah as his "freend" (3/170).

The serving of self in the technological mastery of nature or, more specifically, in the explicit mastery and proper use of time and space in the first scene is also informed, in its introductory elaboration, by such a spirit of cooperation. In the "Dialogue" episode, for example, this mastery of nature—that is, this medieval Christian ethical imperative—figures prominently in the directions God cooperatively gives Noah to preserve the remnant. The first thing to which God calls attention is how time will be saved in terms of space. If the remnant is to survive, as God enjoins Noah it must, then the layout of the Ark, the means of the remnant's rescue—and, ultimately, of time's preservation as well—must be clearly and carefully delineated. The dimensions of the hull, its length and breadth and depth, accordingly are given first, followed by anachronistic conventional medieval maritime advice on ark hull waterproofing, both inside and out, with pitch and tar:

> Of lennthe thi ship be
> Thre hundreth cubettys, warn I the;
> Of heght euen thirirté,
> Of fyfty als in brede.
> Anoynt thi ship with pik and tar
> Without and als within,
> The water out to spar:
> This is a noble gyn. (3/179–86).[11]

Then the spatial organization of the interior is elaborated, including identification of "Parloures," "houses of offyce," and "chambres," measurements for the "wyndo," and a hull modification to permit "On the syde a doore" (3/188–98).[12] Interspersed among these anachronistic spatial directions to save time, interestingly enough, are several temporal admonitions made by God to save space—that is, to insure the construction of the Ark by insuring that the cooperative spirit is maintained. In the first of these God interrupts Himself to warn Noah that he should let no man "mar" (3/187) his endeavor—that is, turn his attention away from the enterprise upon which he has embarked at God's behest. Not long afterward God, again interruptively, warns that no one shall distract Noah, either by fighting with him or by doing him any kind of harm (3/200–201). In the next stanza God prescribes the Ark's seven-day construction deadline as well as the forty-day duration of the vessel's seaworthiness (3/215–17). And a final temporal admonition completes God's opening of the "Dialogue" episode when the importance of careful provisioning is introduced. While the three previous temporal admonitions aim to assure the establishment and maintenance of the Ark's or the container's spatial integrity, this final one has as its object the analogous maintenance, through life-sustaining alimentation, of the Ark's cargo or the contained sentient life housed within the spatial dimensions of the vessel.

II

Cooperation in terms of mastery of nature or the explicit proper *use* of time and space is also brought to the audience's attention by means of the Gothic stylistic feature of *concordantia*,[13] in which cooperation's obverse and the consequence thereof are elaborated for the purpose of rationally considering the implications of cooperation's absence. This instructive contrast's rhetorical as well as dramatic effect, the second of the ways in which Noah's exemplarism is elaborated, is included by the Wakefield Master earlier in the first scene's opening monologues. For example, while repeating the story of humanity's creation to reestablish the historical focus of the entire play collection,[14] Noah's monologic prayer reveals, by means of the anachronism of history, that the result of temporal order's disruption is punishment in the form of suffering of indeterminate duration, the very kind of punishment whose imminent threat eventually leads Noah himself, in fear, to seek God's mercy by asserting a collaborative relationship.

The first indication of this consequence arises in the indeterminate space of "in heuen" (3/16), according to Noah's account of history, as Lucifer undermines the "Full mervelus," newly established angelic hierarchy. This act, characterized here as an unkindness, or unnaturalness, is the result of pride and is associated by the Wakefield Master with chance or accident through the metaphor of the throw of the dice—an act, in other words, occurring in time:

> Yit was ther vnkyndnes
> More bi foldys seuen
> Then I can well expres,

Forwhi
Of all angels in brightnes
God gaf Lucifer most lightnes,
Yit prowdly he flyt his des,
And set hym euen hym by. (3/19–26)

The consequent punishment of open-ended suffering comes in two parts. The first brings degradation to Lucifer and his cohort, and brings it more suddenly than sudden—that is, "in a brade" (3/32). The other part, the beginning of eternal punishment, follows immediately, Lucifer and "all his menye" made, according to Noah, "vnglad" forever (3/33–35), their fate to "burn in bayle for ay" (3/38) or to suffer forever in the paradoxical determinate indeterminacy of undying death.[15]

The second temporal disruption to be acknowledged in the monologic prayer occurs in the more determinate space and time of "Paradise," after the creation of Adam and Eve. Because "man" is tempted by the "feynd" and succumbs to sin, and because Paradise is defined as a space where "myght no syn abide" (3/56), man is hastily put out of "That place [where original order is] to be restord" (3/42). That man is removed "full hastely . . . in þat tyde" (3/57–58) is to be expected by the order of temporal disruption leading to punishment already established in the monologic prayer. That man must face yet another punishment involving temporal indeterminacy comes as no surprise either, for the same reason. What differs is the paradoxical nature of the punishment's indeterminacy in this new instance. Man's punishment consists of a limitless and severe misery, whose indeterminacy is now a function of man's own consciousness or what is known by man:

And therfor man . . .
Was put out . . .
In wo and wandreth for to be,
In paynes full vnrid
To knowe:
Fyrst in erth, and sythen in hell
With feyndys for to dwell. (3/57–63)[16]

The final temporal disruption included in the monologic prayer is identified by Noah as happening in the present moment, in the even more determinate space of "erth" or created reality where diurnal distinction is now an observable fact. In the spatiotemporal experience of "erth," says Noah, the disruption is to come since

> Euery liffyng leyde,
> Most party day and nyght,
> Syn in word and dede
> Full bold:
> Som in pride, ire, and enuy,
> Som in couetous and glotyny,
> Som in sloth and lechery,
> And other wise manyfold. (3/71–78)[17]

While this disruption's consequence is pending and acknowledged here only implicitly in Noah's reference to God's inevitable vengeance (3/80), the two-part plea Noah makes to be recognized as unique in his collaborative obedience, and to be saved, along with his "fry," in God's "hall / In heuen" (3/99–100) as God's servant, is intended to forestall suffering of an indeterminate temporal duration by inviting an immediate response or acknowledgment from God.

The need to have proper mastery over time and space is demonstrated implicitly in God's subsequent monologue, too, as the consequence of the disruption of spatial order is revealed to be the destruction of space itself. The disruption of spatial order that God feels justifies this outcome is implied by God in His monologue's first stanza when He acknowledges that all of the order He has given to creation—that is, the anachronistic social distinction between "Duke, emperour, and kyng" (3.107) as well as the emotional distinction between pleasure on land and at sea (3/109–10)—has not reaped the expected bountiful harvest of love and obedience for the creator by the created. Implication quickly becomes declaration in the next stanza, as God argues that man, fashioned "to be / All angels abuf" and "Like to the Trynyté" (3/119–21), lies full low in space, glutting himself almost in a porcine way on all manner of sin. The part of creation, in other words, that should have transcended the spatiotemporal, God declares, is now so low or "in erth" (3/124)—that is, *of* the spatial—as to be degraded to the point that warrants destruction of "medillerd" (3/145) or of the spatial in its entirety:

> And now in grete reprufe
> Full low ligys he,

In erth hymself to stuf
With syn that displeasses me
Most of all.
Veniance will I take
In erth for syn sake;
My grame thus will I wake
Both of grete and small. (3/122–30)

The obverse of a proper collaborative spirit, as well as the effect it has on the serving of the self through the mastery of time and space, is reintroduced by the Wakefield Master in what might be considered the play's interludes, the first of which begins the play's next scene, "The Solution," the dramatic moment when Noah finally sets himself to the task of saving time by collaboratively reconstructing space according to God's specifications, and saving space by collaboratively completing the task forthrightly according to God's admonitions. Some critics of the play have argued that the principal function of these interludes or "fabliaux," as they have been identified, is to provide the opportunity to test the resiliency of the very fabric of drama by including a farcical element.[18] While both of these portions of the play certainly present unusual actions as Noah and Uxor Gill exchange insults and, eventually, engage in fisticuffs, the purpose of the inclusion of the farcical or fabliau may not be solely to examine the dramaturgical implications of comedy or even to provide the kind of comic relief that is afforded by what, in contemporary theater, would be considered slapstick. Rather, the purpose of the inclusion, it would seem, is also instruction[19]—that is, providing the challenging interpretive opportunity to arrive at an understanding of how, within a recognizable, plausible domestic context, the abuse of the collaborative spirit between humankind and God inevitably leads to the loss of mastery of time and space, a loss whose result may have dire consequences, as the Wakefield Master has already implicitly shown in the play's first scene.

In the first interlude (3/263–355), for example, lack of a cooperative spirit is clearly evidenced, first, as Uxor Gill insults Noah by demeaning him as one who wears "Stafford blew" (3/290), an anachronistic textile expression of contempt whose meaning would not have been lost on the Wakefield Master's initial audiences.[20] Next it is reasserted in Noah's obscene reply to Uxor Gill as he calls her by the predial commonplace "ram-skyt" (3/313).[21] Eventually it is made even more obvious dramatically as the husband and wife exchange blow for blow (3/318–32). More important, however, is the way the interlude reveals how such lack of collaborative spirit results in a loss of mastery and practical use of nature. It does this, first, by demonstrating how the abuse of time leads to the lack of control—or the waste—of space. This consequence is brought to light as soon as God withdraws. In Genesis 6:22, Noah obeys God directly: he does "all things which God commanded him." Here, however, Noah, having forgotten God's initial admonition concerning interference and delay, mars his own present efforts and invites like response to future efforts by abandoning the project to inform Uxor Gill of the divine interview that he acknowledges fatalistically beforehand she will not, in her peevishness, be interested in hearing anything about:

> My [wife] will I frast
> What she will say,
> And I am agast
> That we get som fray
> Betwixt vs both,
> For she is full tethee,
> For litill oft angré;
> If any thyng wrang be,
> Soyne is she wroth. (3/265–73)[22]

By not utilizing time properly, in other words, space or the Ark remains only an unrealized or unactualized potentiality. Similarly, the interlude reveals how the loss of collaborative effort results in a loss of mastery and practical use of nature by demonstrating how the abuse of space leads to the lack of mastery—or the waste—of time. Evidencing this are the two innovative asides made by Uxor Gill and Noah here, asides that are reminiscent of Garcio's address to the audience at the beginning of the *Mactatio Abel*, and of his candid responses to Cain in the stichomythic exchange near the end of the same play. In Uxor Gill's, the more extensive of the two, the stage or the spatial is misused for the purpose of delivering a digressive condemnation of "ill husbandys" in general, and of Noah in particular:[23]

> We women may wary
> All ill husbandys;

I haue oone, bi Mary,
That lowsyd me of my bandys!
If he teyn, I must tary,
Howsoeuer it standys,
With seymland full sory,
Wryngand both my handys
For drede;
Bot yit otherwhile,
What with gam and with gyle,
I shall smyte and smyle,
And qwite hym his mede. (3/300–312)

In Noah's, which is delivered in the middle of their first fight, the stage or the spatial is "misused" in the same way to comment on Uxor Gill's contrariness, as well as on her tendency to exaggerate:

For all if she stryke,
Yit fast will she skryke;
In fayth, I hold none slyke
In all medill-erd. (3/335–38)[24]

The result of this dramatic maneuver in both instances, even if the asides involve turning only to imagined portions of the audience rather than the actual Wakefield citizenry in attendance, not only reveals a stalemate,[25] it also momentarily transforms the dramatic mimesis into a dramatic methexis,[26] the purpose of which is to create a set of aesthetic, tropological moments during which the audience is enabled to understand fully the experience and implications of lack of cooperation through the pertinent anachronism of topical domestic abuse and marital disharmony. Ironically, while the privileged point of view of the spectator is destabilized here by this innovative dramatic technique involving the "space" of the performance reality to provide a moment of ethical insight—while, in other words, "space" is properly *used* to effect understanding at this point in the play—the fact that a topical rather than a biblical historical matter occupies the audience's attention, if only briefly, suggests a willingness to allow impairment of the mastery and practical use of time. Robbing Peter to pay Paul, however, appears to be an acceptable sacrifice for the Wakefield Master if the end of comprehending the importance of cooperation is shown to justify the means of attaining such knowledge.

The second interlude, occurring between the construction of the Ark and the beginning of the cataclysm (3/417–598), functions much the same way as the first, demonstrating again how the lack of collaborative spirit results in the loss of mastery and practical use of nature. What differs here is the degree and complexity of the demonstration. The Wakefield Master again reveals how the abuse of space leads to the loss of temporal mastery by means of another set of innovative asides. In this case Uxor Gill uses the stage or abuses the play's performance reality "space" to denounce "ill husbandys," this time in a way much more virulent in its wish for the demise of husbands like her own:

> Lord, I were at ese
> And hertely full hoylle,
> Might I onys haue a measse
> Of wedows coyll.
> For thi saull, without lese,
> Shuld I dele penny doyll;
> So wold mo, no frese,
> That I se on this sole
> Of wifys that ar here,
> For the life that thay leyd,
> Wold thare husbandys were dede;
> For, as euer ete I brede,
> So wold I oure syre were! (3/560–72)

Noah, likewise, abuses the play's performance reality "space" to articulate a predictable misogamist and misogynous view, this time one nearly as militant as Uxor Gill's preceding condemnation:

> Yee men that has wifys,
> Whyls thay ar yong,
> If ye luf youre lifys,
> Chastice thare tong.
> Me thynk my hert ryfys,
> Both levyr and long,
> To se sich stryfys,
> Wedmen emong.

> Bot I,
> As haue I blys,
> Shall chastyse this. (3/573–83)

Both these departures from the events of the drama, again, momentarily rupture dramatic time in the way the first set does in the first interlude. As might be expected, this rupture of temporal flow also contributes to the Wakefield Master's demonstration of how the abuse of time—in this instance, the obvious delay in getting aboard the Ark—leads to the loss of mastery, or the waste, of the spatial. The Ark, the purpose of which is to preserve time as well as space through the proper use of space over a defined period of time, is obviously underutilized owing to this ostensible and deliberate abuse of time. But what is novel here—what extends and makes more intricate the elaboration of this demonstration of mastery's loss—is the Wakefield Master's inclusion of yet another abuse, one involving the misuse of both time and space simultaneously.

The interpolated abuse in question is a faulty rudimentary technology assessment, not the kind of faulty technology assessment deliberately made by Cain in the *Mactatio Abel* and discussed in the previous chapter,[27] but rather the sort left incomplete through inadvertent omission of pertinent matter. This type of accidental abuse is introduced three times, with spatial resonances, in this part of the interlude—once *before* the ship, once *from* the ship, and once *on* the ship—and as the events that comprise it unfold each time, an intergenerational response is included, the first made by the sons, the next by the daughters-in-law, and the final one by the sons again, to correct the omission.

The first time this happens, Noah is in the process of telling Uxor Gill that the world will be destroyed by the flood God has ordained, and that the ship before them is their only hope of survival—that is, if they hurry to board it. The note of urgency informing this account is sounded again by Noah shortly afterward in his expression "Without more dere" (3/459), and immediately each of his sons acknowledges the need to make haste and do what must be done to be ready for embarkation. The technological solution to the catastrophic meteorological event about to occur is identified exactly by Noah as the anachronistic "ship" God has had him build to save Uxor Gill, himself, and their "barnes that ar bayn, / And thare wifys thre" (3/444–45). Missing from the response, however, is what Uxor Gill asked for initially when Noah first introduced the problem of the impending cataclysm indirectly and metaphorically by means of the figurative expression

> Ther is garn on the reyll
> Other, my dame. (3/430–31)

While Noah speaks of yarn, Uxor Gill wants an exact explanation of everything:

> Tell me that ich a deyll,
> Els get ye blame. (3/432–33)

In other words, she wants an appraisal of the device's practicality and worth. In fairness to Noah, his pronouncement includes the scope of the impending destruction as well as acknowledgment of the ship or the means of surviving the destruction. But omitted here is any expert judgment or even explanation of how the practical art or *techne* of shipbuilding or the device of the vessel will enable all to survive divine wrath and will return everyone to safety. Accordingly, Uxor Gill expresses fear (3/453–55) and then anger (3/467–68) at what is happening about her. And for this reason, finally, she refuses to approach the Ark, saying,

> I was neuer bard ere,
> As euer myght I the,
> In sich an oostré as this!
> In fath, I can not fynd
> Which is before, which is behynd.
> Bot shall we here be pynd,
> Noe, as haue thou blis? (3/475–81)

The nature of the Ark, as well as its function, the combination of which would lead to a judgment of value, has not, in other words, been made understandable to her (she calls the Ark an inn or possibly even an oyster[28]), which needs to be done to help her recognize the value and applicability of the innovative vessel technology in this particular threatening situation. As a result, Uxor Gill returns to her "rok" and to the anachronistic technology of spinning,[29] a technology with which she is familiar, and so the proper utilization of the Ark or the technological mastery of space is yet again postponed.

The second faulty technology assessment follows immediately and presents virtually the same problem. In this instance, Noah calls out from the Ark for Uxor Gill to board the vessel. While he does not repeat this time that it is God who is the author of the impending cataclysm, he increases the urgency of his plea by describing the threatening storm clouds and the planetary sign that traditionally bodes meteorological ill.[30] While two of the three daughters-in-law follow Noah's lead and repeat the chilling weather forecast as a way of trying to persuade Uxor Gill to join the remnant and embrace the technological invention of the ship, the third picks up on Uxor Gill's reference to her "spyndill" and attempts to convince her mother-in-law, logically, that she can spin as easily *in* the Ark as she has been doing *before* it. But, again, none of these words, words either of encouragement or, later, of hostility from Noah, from the beginning to the end of this sequence, explains *how* the Ark works and *how* it will insure safety and rescue. The way the technology provides a solution, in other words, still remains unexplained.[31]

In the end, of course, it is not the technology assessment that makes Gill change her mind. Rather, it is the actual physical experience of the rising waters that impels her to join the family and remnant on board the vessel; as the water "nyghys so nere," Uxor Gill springs into action and clambers aboard the Ark.[32] Once there, however, she encounters yet another faulty technology assessment of sorts, one that unfolds as soon as Noah addresses her. Noah identifies Uxor Gill as the party responsible for the price that must be paid for delaying the embarkation, and for continuing the delay, implicitly, through lack of cooperation. Again, what is missing is an explanation of the technological solution, which is the vessel, to the problem facing the remnant. Without this clarification Uxor Gill, even now aboard, remains steadfastly unwilling to participate, saying,

I will not, for thi bydyng,
Go from doore to mydyng. (3/543–44)

Without the situation being made understandable, again,[33] proper order is postponed one more time, and in fact, as the consequence of this final postponement, physical violence—another way of losing mastery of time, as was noted in the discussion of the previous interlude—breaks out after both Noah and Uxor Gill misuse space and rupture dramatic time, a second time, for the purpose of delivering their lengthy militant asides condemning the other and his or her gender. It is only with the final intergenerational response from the sons that order is reasserted, though by this point a peaceful settlement is probably desired, since both Noah and Gill are noticeably, and admittedly, exhausted by their hostilities.[34]

III

A third way the Wakefield Master presents the idea of the mind that serves God cooperatively by serving itself in the technological mastery and practical use of nature arises in the lines devoted to the anachronistic construction of the Ark,[35] the middle part of the play's second scene, a part carefully interpolated between the two interludes to put the actual shipbuilding and its import dramatically in relief, much as a Gothic bas-relief works visually by means of contrast. Here, as Noah works assiduously, with or without an actual ax,[36] time is used properly to affect space, and as the invention that is the Ark comes into existence,[37] space is used—or, more precisely, fashioned—properly to affect time. What distinguishes this act is that cooperation no longer consists of a one-to-one engagement as in the first scene's third or "Dialogue" episode. Rather, the collaborative spirit, though divinely inspired, is now solely expressed by Noah in response to the guidelines God has left behind.[38] While this experience of cooperation is at one remove from the actual experience of God, expression of this spirit is no less intense as it is developed in three distinct, unilateral ways, each of which reasserts the collaborative spirit Noah and God enjoyed initially.

First, it is made evident in the recognition and remembrance of God, which Noah articulates at important moments in the construction process. Before setting out on the ambitious adventure of "wrightry," for example, Noah, in a way reminiscent of Theophilus's advice to the apprentice monk in the third preface to *De diversis artibus*,[39] anachronistically invokes the Trinity as a way of reminding himself that his skill as shipwright is inextricably linked to the triune God:

> Now assay will I
> How I can of wrightry,
> *In nomine patris, et filij,*
> *Et spiritus sancti. Amen.* (3/361–64)

Next, as he is busily working, Noah does not forget to identify and take cognizance of his inspiration and guide. This occurs first as Noah says the

Trinity will send help (3/367–68), shortly afterward as he praises God for having sent a remedy—"Now blissid be he / That this can amend" (3/371–72)—and thirdly as the Ark's window and door are completed "Euen as [God] saide" (3/405). Finally, when all work on the Ark is finished, Noah reintroduces the guiding effect of the collaborative spirit when admitting the ship is "better wroght" than he "could haif thoght," a fact for which he is thankful and which he attributes to "Hym that maide all of noght" (3/413–16).

The same collaborative spirit is rearticulated here in that it is identified as the source of a series of nearly miraculous project completions. The first of these is the construction of the hull, which, when finished, conforms exactly to the specifications given by God, a fact ascertained through measurements made by Noah himself after—*not* before—the construction.[40] The next is the making of the mast. That this construction is also miraculous is attested by the fact that the job is completed despite the acknowledged advanced age of the worker himself. The third of these miraculous project completions is the building of the superstructure and the fitting out of the vessel. Everything is done with such perfection that the contrivance itself, Noah concludes, "may neuer fayll" (3/294), again a testimonial to the value of the collaborative spirit that has equipped Noah with the actual design to follow.

The final unilateral assertion of the divinely inspired collaborative spirit can be found in the Wakefield Master's adroit imaging of dedication to purpose that Noah displays approximately halfway through the construction process. While he is old and physically unsuited for the job—his bones, he claims, are so "stark" that they "wark" (3/388–89)—Noah nevertheless gives his all, and more, to complete the project expeditiously as he has been enjoined by God. Though he complains that he has thrown out his back (3/382), that his performance in the task at hand is "a sory note" (3/383), and that he must have been a fool to undertake such a work at such an advanced age (3/385–87), his tenacious commitment to completing the divinely laid-out project exemplifies what is fundamental to the collaborative spirit. This is the spirit of a servant ready to do his master's bidding. It is also that of a friend ready to help another friend. But even more so, it is the attitude of a worker who makes the work before him not just a work to be completed but rather *his own* work or labor, to be seen through to the end, to be completed to the best of his ability.[41] The image capturing this (obviously preferred) kind of dedication essential to cooperation literally unfolds before the audience's eyes as Noah, casting his "gowne" aside, readies himself to "wyrk" in his "cote" (3/378–79). It goes without saying that this image of labor as dramatic expression of the collaborative spirit is an anachronistic displacement of the Benedictine idea *Laborare est orare*.

IV

The final way the Wakefield Master anachronistically elaborates Noah's exemplarism as expression of the mind serving God cooperatively by serving itself in the technological mastery and practical use of nature is set in yet another historical context in the play's final scene. Unique about this treatment is that, within this new set of circumstances, neither God nor even a divinely wrought, explicit design or guideline to follow is present. In the face of this troubling absence, all the remnant has to go on is the principle inferred directly and indirectly in the previous scenes and interludes concerning the collaborative spirit's transformative effect—an effect implicit in the change between God's view of Noah as "seruant" and as "freend" in the first scene, and explicit in the completion and maiden voyage of the Ark itself, with the remnant in its entirety finally aboard, in the second. This perceptual, inferential knowledge may not seem to be enough to save the remnant, especially as the cataclysmic waves begin breaking against the Ark's hull. But it is indispensable to the salvation of Noah and his family because it enables them to understand how proper *use* of space and time affects time and space, respectively, and how this cumulative spatiotemporal effect, in turn, allows all to reexperience collectively, as well as understand, what it is to be *in*, even in the absence of God and the divine guideline, the very collaborative spirit or friendship expressed and enjoyed by Noah—both indirectly and individually, when building the Ark according to the guidelines left by God, and directly and jointly, earlier on when engaged in the initial dialogue with God.[42]

The most obvious indication that this practical understanding has been fully assimilated by the remnant and now informs their outlook and behavior arises in the last scene's first episode, "The Mensuration," as Noah, Uxor, and their children, having taken their stations in the Ark to weather the storm, begin to cooperate,[43] evidencing a friendship, in the form of the construction of the new social order of the family, an order resounding the exemplaristic spirit of collaboration itself.[44] This noticeable ethical change is first directed at the sons, those who embody and articulate the norm of the marital state,[45] as Noah says he will comply with their wishes by no longer being angry (3/605–7). It is next demonstrated by Noah and now-Dame Uxor themselves, each toward the other, as Noah cautions Dame Uxor to "take hede" of the flood waters, and as she observes, now more active and engaged than her York and Chester counterparts,[46] that the remnant or family is "in grete drede" (3/615). It is completed, finally, as both Noah and Dame Uxor pray to God in this time of peril and need, an act asserting the nexus between the microcosm and macrocosm:

> Noe.   Help, God, in this nede!
> As thou art stereman good,
> And best, as I rede,
> Of all,
> Thou rewle vs in this rase,
> As thou me behete hase.
> Vxor.   This is a parlous case;
> Help, God, when we call! (3/617–24)

Further demonstrations of the assimilation of this practical understanding are elaborated in each of the scene's three episodes. This is first evident in the temporal transformation of space through mensuration and is brought to the audience's attention as soon as Noah, in the midst of the cataclysm, lowers the anachronistic plummet. This activity is performed three times in the first part—at varying intervals that are inversely proportional to the depth of water being recorded. In the first instance Noah determines the flood to have crested at "Cubettys xv" above "all hillys bedeyn" (3/638–40). This determination of great depth is associated with the relatively short forty-day duration of the rains. After the second lowering, Noah is amazed by how much the water level has dropped; the time now associated with the lowering of the plummet is the much longer duration of three hundred fifty days, or an entire lunar year, after the cataclysm's beginning.[47] At the time of the final measurement, Noah prepares again to lower the plummet but innovatively puts his finger into the water instead to demonstrate that the flood has completely receded. Time now, at least as presented in the Towneley collection, is without durational limit as the time of the second age has ended and the new temporal period, the third age, has begun. The increasing enthusiasm and joy evidenced by Dame Uxor from the moment of the second instance of measurement—she now calls Noah "husband" (3/672) in response to his latest polite form of address, "Dame"—leads her here to inquire what their location may be. The identification of the place as the "hyllys of Armonye" (3/674) offers a locational description whose homonymic implication "hills of harmony" reminds the audience of the transformative effect of the collaborative spirit now informing activity on board the Ark.[48] As this scene comes to an end, the "mery chere" (3/671) of deliverance from antediluvian hills of disharmony and the chaos of the cataclysm is thus shown to be the result of technological mastery and practical use of nature in the form of mensuration—that is, the temporal organization of space.

Another demonstration of the assimilation of practical understanding occurs in the spatial transformation of time that occupies the attention of the final scene's second part, as the "wedir" brightens and Noah and Dame Uxor begin to structure the cosmos by means of a rudimentary planimetry. This organizing of the universe—initiated here by Dame Uxor's interpretation of the "hyllys" seen by Noah and herself as "Tokyns full right" of mercy, an interpretation based upon the east-west axial orientation made earlier by Dame Uxor in the cataclysm observation concerning the sun's shining in the "eest" (3/655)—is now modified by the inclusion of a different directional axiality, one added by Noah as he lets a "fowll" further discover

> Of mercy som tokynyng,
> Ayther bi north or southe. (3/688–89)[49]

The dispatching of the raven and the dove for this purpose, in other words, is not only to verify the initial tokening but also to insure that a "tokynyng" is found. Though Dame Uxor's choice of the raven is offered in good faith,[50] the raven's nature leads Noah, who later reveals a knowledge of the creature's habits (3/723–28), to include an alternative avian search modality. (Mastery and practical use of nature imply, after all, the elimination of abuse as well as the minimization of error.[51]) Accordingly, when this second part or episode concludes after the dove's return, the more ambitious project of organizing the temporal dimension of the cosmos by means of a spatial, linear extension from *and* through a point of origin, which is completed by inclusion of a similar transverse linear extension to form a directional biaxiality or cosmological centrosymmetry, leads Dame Uxor to conclude that deliverance is more than just the experience of joy; it is now also a "trew tokyn" (3/748)—that is, something to be carefully interpreted—of the remnant's salvation, whose full understanding leads to an assured futurity, as is implied by Dame Uxor's change of tense in the next line, "We shall be sauyd all" (3/749).

As the veracity of this tokening is confirmed, first by Dame Uxor, who empirically observes a coincidental, definite drop in the water level of one fathom and more (3/753),[52] next by the sons pointing out in sequence that the flood is gone and the Ark has gone aground (3/755–60), and last by Noah, who orders the disembarkation "Apon land here anone" (3/761), a final demonstration of the full assimilation of this practical knowledge that leads to the collective experience of the collaborative spirit, through the act of interpretation that, in turn, leads to the expression of sympathy, completes the play by shifting attention now to the spatial transformation of time and a temporal transformation of space through the combination of anachronistic communication acts and rudimentary social engineering principles. The way this combination effects the former of these transformations is evidenced as Noah and Dame Uxor, practicing a conjugal conformity whose propriety is suggested by dialogue that now leads to complete explanation, remark how space in its new, postcataclysm condition leads to the concept of "grace" (3/797). While those who have perished in the waters of the Flood must now, according to Noah, suffer "payn" (3/791), escape from that punishment is possible, but only through the unconditional love of "he that myght hase" (3/795). The same proper conjugal conformity and communication between Noah and Dame Uxor also effects the temporal transformation of space and thereby completes the play. The new time of grace that has resulted from the Destruction changes the idea of space into "place." This "place," however, is no ordinary location, but rather a space like the Ark. It is a vehicle, in other words, because it is Noah's hope that, in it, he and the rest of the remnant may come to God's "light"

With his santys in sight,
And his angels bright. (3/803–4)

The implication of this new view of the spatiotemporal with which the audience is left, then, is that the space/place they now inhabit is not something to be taken for granted, but rather, like the time granted all in life, something to be *used* properly, so that, ultimately, they may experience the greatest enjoyment possible—the same cooperative relationship with God that Noah, first, enjoyed as means of renewing life and the cosmos. Understanding of this implication, to put the matter another way, leads to the realization that the technological mastery and practical use of nature, the very means of serving the self in the cooperative serving of God, consists of the attainment of an ethical perspective that sees the value of all things *in* and *of* creation as they pertain to the meaning and love of God.

3

[Prima] Pagina Pastorum and the "Inventive" Speculative Creaturely Triune Mind

While confirmation of the radical change in her own character from Uxor to Dame, "Dame" Uxor's incisive interpretation of the "trew tokyn" of the dove's return to the ark at the end of the *Processus Noe cum filiis* also raises the question of what actually constitutes the kind of mind that readily serves God cooperatively by serving itself through the technological mastery and practical use of nature. The phenomenological question of the constituent features of such a mind—that is, the separate intrinsic features of which it might consist as well as the combination or action of those features that readily disposes it to receive God's message in this new age of empirical and subjective religious experience—and the practical correlative question, also, of how that mind actually serves itself with regard to nature, are not explored and answered, however, until the Wakefield Master revises the two shepherds' plays and the Herod play, plays of the second group of works attributed to the Master and set in the time of renewal or the sixth age.[1]

The first of these in the order of their appearance in the collection to receive the impress of the Master's pen, the *[Prima] Pagina Pastorum*,[2] whose original source is Luke 2:8–20,[3] offers the first view of—and sets the stage for—this subject. It does this by identifying as its focus the elaboration of the intricate relationship between the Trinitarian soul, as originally conceived of by Saint Augustine, with its emphasis on will, memory, and intellect, and the fundamental speculative processes or "motions"—that is, actions—of the soul[4] that distinguish between the Christian as active seeker of an understanding of the divine nature as it is reflected in the pattern of creation and the Christian as passive recipient of spiritual messages through natural phenomena.[5] This relationship was not new, nor was expression of it restricted to theological writings. Its origin, of course, could then, as now, be easily traced to a number of ideas articulated first by Saint Augustine. One of these, the correspondences between the Father, Son, and Holy Ghost and the creaturely trinity of the divine mind or memory, the divine intellect, and the divine will or love, is considered at length in *De Trinitate*. Another of these ideas can be found in *De Musica* where the difference between the "blessed state" and the condition of the diminished soul is delineated. Yet another is in the "Letter to Nebridius," a letter roughly contemporary with *De Musica*, in which are identified the three principal origins of fantasy: the senses, the imagination, and the reason. And of course there was *De doctrina christiana*, in which the active seeker is conceived of as one who has mastery of the speculative ability to interpret and convey intelligibly both literal and figurative meaning—that is, one who has willingly assumed the responsibility of making meaning through mastery of the *modus interpretandi* and disseminating meaning through mastery of the *modus proferandi*.[6]

Like so many other important concepts concerning the nature of piety itself in the Middle Ages, the relationship between the Trinitarian soul and the speculative process implicit in practical Christian allegoresis, as well as interpretive response to it, was also affected by—indeed, swept along in—the allegorical current of the age, which, "far from shrinking, flowed on and on in an ever widening channel." It is not necessary here to rehearse the elaborate argument that has been eloquently made and convincingly repeated treating the ways in which figural and personification allegory, as well as the allegorical method itself, had become, by the twelfth century and afterward, the universal artistic vehicle of nearly all pious expression.[7] What needs to be considered, rather, is how this distinctive mode of expression was artistically appropriated and innovatively transformed by the Wakefield Master, in three plays set in the time of the sixth age's beginning, to provide the audience with elucidated examples of the unseen conflicts of the soul by means of a consistently sustained figural allegory through a process of dramatization incorporating the anachronistic verisimilitude of various medieval technologies, the most obvious of which is the practical art of shepherding.

The artistic decision to dramatize in the *[Prima] Pagina Pastorum* the relationship between the Trinitarian soul and the propensity to seek an understanding of the divine nature as it is reflected in the pattern of creation, however, while calling attention again to the conspicuous empirical temper of the age,[8] established for the first time in the history of medieval British drama the need for a distinctive dramaturgic inventiveness[9] ready to meet the challenge of conveying the complexity of qualities and states of mind, including the rhythm of the soul itself, in easily recognizable terms of character and anachronism, including the popular Nativity tradition, without either deviating from fundamental aesthetic principles of late-medieval Gothic art or compromising the integrity of biblical history. As this chapter and the next two will demonstrate, that challenge is amply met; what results, in fact, far exceeds in artistic genius anything else written by contemporary medieval playwrights, those working alongside the Wakefield Master in the Towneley collection as well as those contributing to the other play collections or cycles.

I

While definition, elaboration, and dramatization of the intrinsic speculative mind of the active seeker for an understanding of the divine nature in created reality—that is, the dramatic mimesis, as well as methexis, of the "inventive" speculative creaturely triune mind—is the object of the revision of the collection's first shepherds' play, adherence to the Gothic stylistic principle of *concordantia*, as is briefly the case in the *Mactatio Abel* and more so in the *Processus Noe*,[10] again leads the Wakefield Master first to investigate thematically the opposite mental condition of being bereft of the ability to engage in either the *modus interpretandi* or the *modus proferandi*. In other words, the *[Prima] Pagina Pastorum*, which consists of four distinct scenes,[11] is so arranged that the audience is initially introduced to the opposite, or what will be called, for purposes of simplification and clarity in this and the next chapter, the "uninventive" mind, speculative or otherwise.[12] This concept may seem to be a contradiction in terms, especially to the contemporary sensibility, since the play's conclusion involves a visit to Bethlehem for the purpose of adoring and giving presents to the Christ Child, and also since some of the most inventive and imaginative goings-on in all of medieval British drama occur in this play's first two scenes, which comprise more than half the lines of the entire work. But compromised as symmetry may be by this arrangement, such an emphasis would not have been jarring at all to the play's initial late-medieval West Riding and Wakefield audiences, since discerning the ethical implications of the difference between the noesis of the "inventive" speculative mind and that of the "uninventive" speculative mind was more important than merely enjoying "imaginacioun's" inventive deceptiveness.[13]

The "uninventive" speculative mind, as conceived of artistically and presented dramatically through anachronistic character and action in the play's first scene by the Wakefield Master, is thus the mind of a diminished spirit and soul. This mind is still possessed of memory, intellect, and will (hence the modifier "speculative"), but since the spirit has turned away from God-its-Master to follow its servant the body[14]—that is, since the spirit has entered into a state of suffering, not from the body, but from itself as it has adjusted itself to the body[15]—each aspect of this mind's triune nature is lessened and enfeebled, though not extinguished. Such a mind is not well suited to the intellectual and volitional rigors of either the *modus interpretandi* or the *modus proferandi*. In fact, such a mind, in light of the contaminated condition of the spirit, is incapable of mastering any sort of *techne*, let alone the more complicated intellectual arts involving reason or analysis, and so is aptly characterized as being passive. While the action of the diminished spirit, like that of its opposite the living spirit, continues to adjust the body to the stimuli it receives for the purpose of producing sensations and forming *phantasiae*—that is, images of things actually experienced—what this passive "uninventive" speculative mind ends up being most prone to producing is little more than the *phantasmata* of things not actually perceived—that is, strange and unanticipated combinations of *phantasiae* stored in memory, or, as Saint Augustine puts it in the "Letter to Nebridius," the creation of deceptive classes of *phantasiae* originating with the imagination and reason, such as imaginary objects and fictions and imaginary abstractions.[16]

Evidence of the "uninventive" speculative mind in the play's first two scenes, as the preceding definition might lead one to anticipate, involves the dramatized *allegoria* of at least three things. The first of these, the most immediately obvious to the audience in the staging of the first scene's action, is the consistent passivity or indolence of the characters themselves. This is made apparent in the general languor or dullness with which Primus Pastor (Gyb) and, next, Secundus Pastor John Horn (Iohn Horne) first appear onstage in the anachronistic West Riding sheep run of ancient Judea. Gyb enters and makes his complaint to God for sixty-five lines. Then, unbeknownst to him, John enters to do the same thing. Unbeknownst to John, likewise, is Gyb's presence, something he discovers only after completing his nearly-as-long prayer of fifty-two lines. Neither shepherd, demonstrates the perspicacity expected in a person whose job it is to keep watch over a flock of sheep. What is more, their nearly sedentary condition at this moment is the opposite of the active life normally associated with late-medieval British shepherding.[17]

A like passivity is heard in much of the first scene's language: implicitly in the many clichés, for example, exchanged by Gyb and John as they accost each other,[18] and again in Gyb's very first despairing words as he observes that the dead are luckier than the living because they do not have to feel, as now he must, the condition of being downcast:

> Lord, what thay ar weyll
> That hens ar past!
> For thay noght feyll
> Theym to downe cast. (12/1–4)

Passivity's explicit articulation afterward, as Gyb and then John pray to God and Christ, respectively, to save themselves in some form or fashion, is also noticeable. Gyb, who has lost his flock as well as the means to purchase new sheep, begs God, when he is ready to gamble for the purpose of turning his fortune around, to be prepared, as it were, to hedge his bet by sending "grace" (12/61) should matters worsen and what little luck he has give out. John, employing the conspicuously anachronistic Franciscan "Bensté, Bensté," prays to Christ to be saved from all manner of men, including "robers and thefys" and "bosters and bragers" and especially the ever-present parvenu who

> will make it as prowde
> A lord as he were,
> With a hede lyke a clowde,
> Felterd his here. (12/92–95)

Neither Gyb nor John, in other words, wants to act or to assert himself to change his lot; rather, both want some sort of intervention, preferably divine, to aid them and protect them from situations or other individuals whose presence or effect they do not want to endure.

Added to these examples is the pervasive lethargy of the scene. Even after the arrival of Tercius Pastor (Slawpase) and Jak Garcio—both of whom stir things up to a noticeable degree, Slawpase in his denunciation of his elder pastoral brethren, and Jak in his denunciation of all three shepherds as bellwether fools—virtually no action occurs, except for the emptying of a sack of milled meal, the participation in an imaginary feast, and the circulating of an actual ale cup, from which many sips are taken,[19] before the second scene comes to an end with everyone going off to sleep. In fact, as he advises everyone to go take his rest since night is fast approaching, John Horn acknowledges that he is ahead of everyone as he is "euen redy dyght" (12/415). He may not be asleep yet, but he might as well be.

II

The second thing presentation of the "uninventive" speculative mind leads the audience to expect in what little there may be of the first two scenes' action is the demonstration of the workings of memory, since it is from this faculty of the diminished spirit's creaturely triune mind that many *phantasiae* are recollected to be combined with each other to form *phantasmata*. In the litany of woe presented by Gyb in the opening of the first scene, simple examples of memory are brought to the audience's attention almost immediately in two ways. One involves the linking of the past with the present through repetition of adverbial expressions to emphasize the uncertainty of life. As he begins, Gyb points out in an act of remembrance that much unhappiness or ill has long endured in the world—unhappiness or ill that is the direct result of things being good one moment and bad the next:

> Here is mekyll vnceyll,
> And long has it last:
> Now in hart, now in heyll,
> Now in weytt, now in blast;
> Now in care,
> Now in comforth agane;
> Now is fayre, now is rane;
> Now in hart full fane,
> And after full sare. (12/5–13)

The act of memory is also emphasized by Gyb in his use of the exemplum of the horseman Jack Copé to illustrate anew the vicissitudes of life. Fundamental to Gyb's use of this figure is a presumption that the audience remembers who "Jack Plenty" represents in terms of acquisition and the degree of limited upward social mobility possible in fifteenth-century English and Yorkshire society.[20]

A more elaborated view of the action of memory, this time by means of analogy, is introduced at the end of the first scene as Tercius Pastor or Slawpase, having entered the sheep run, denigrates the mental acuity of his elder pastoral brethren. While beginning to instruct them in his "lawe" after having witnessed the well-known pastoral quarrel over the imaginary sheep (12/234), Slawpase employs the ground-meal-sack exemplum (12/238–53) to enable Gyb and John to see how that portion of the divine triune mind in them just does not work—that is, actually to see or witness how sensations or *phantasiae* apparently do not stick in either of their memories. Whether the exemplum achieves what Slawpase intends is certainly debatable, since the emptying of the sack's contents on the ground puts Slawpase's own intellect in a questionable light.[21] Be that as it may, Slawpase concludes, using the mess he has created as a visual reminder of Gyb's and John's lack of mental capacity to remember, that

>   youre wyttys [are] thyn,
> And ye look well abowte,
> Nawther more nor myn;
> So gose youre wyttys owte,
> Evyn as it com in.
> Geder vp
> And seke it agane! (12/247–53)

That John Horn's reply to this demonstration, on the one hand, superficially praises—as John's rhetorical question to Gyb, "May we not be fane?" (12/254), suggests—and on the other hand implicitly condemns, by identifying the now-contaminated meal on the ground ironically as the source of "Wysdom to sup" (12/256), may not disprove Slawpase's conclusion. But it does show that, diminished as his spirit may be, John and, by implication, Gyb are not completely bereft of "wyttys" as Slawpase believes them to be.[22]

Other instances of the working of memory are also brought to the audience's attention as events unfold in the second scene. One of these, the menu for the "Grotesque Feast"[23] that is elaborated by each of the shepherds in the scene's first episode, reveals, by means of gastronomic anachronism, how memory serves to establish social distinction through social convention. Gyb and John, whose desire it is only to sit down and drink (12/276), reluctantly accommodate Slawpase, who insists, almost vehemently, upon turning the activity into a feast:

> Yey, torde!
> I am leuer ete;
> What is drynk withoute mete?
> Gett mete, gett,
> And sett vs a borde;
>
> Then may we go dyne,
> Oure bellys to fyll. (12/278–84)

What they offer to this imaginary pastoral repast[24] has been characterized as plebeian fare.[25] Gyb, for example, is ready to give, along with a great deal of mustard, a well-sauced "foote of a cowe," as well as a powdered "pestell of a sowe," "two blodyngys," a "leueryng," some "befe," and "moton" from "an ewe that was roton" (12/309–19). In addition to the "browne of a bore" (12/306), John is ready to add to this gallimaufry an "ox- tayll / That wold not be lost," a "good py," "two swyne-gronys," and everything of a hare but its "lonys" (12/322–34), or, in other words, everything but its tender flesh. What Slawpase is ready to bring to "borde," on the other hand, is the sort of dishes, with some puzzling exceptions, one would expect to find on a medieval aristocrat's table, including

> The leg of a goys,
> With chekyns endorde,
> Pork, partryk to roys,
> A tart for a lorde (12/336–39)

and

> A calf-lyuer skorde
> With the veryose. (12/341–42)[26]

That Slawpase introduces this menu as something "to recorde" indicates it may be a list of things heard or read rather than actually experienced, as many of the items are reminiscent of descriptions of feast items in the Harley text of John Russell's *Booke of Nurture*.[27] This fact notwithstanding, the recital of these particular dishes, while whetting the appetite like the smell of a "Good sawse," appears to have as its principal purpose the demonstration of social distinction, a distinction not lost on Gyb, who immediately denounces the foregoing as something one might expect to hear from a member of the clergy.

One last event in the second scene that reminds the audience of the "uninventive" speculative mind's action in terms of memory arises at the end of the drinking bout as the two older shepherds demonstrate how memory, even in a diminished and weakened condition, can provide a satisfactory means of requital. They do this in two ways. First they deprive Slawpase of his share of the good ale of Healy by outwitting him through the feigned act of forgetting that he is part of the drinking activity and contest. This happens in stages. The older shepherds start by maneuvering Slawpase into a position where he only just gets to wet his lips with the "holsom ayll" of Healy.[28] Gyb wishes out loud that Slawpase's "gramery" might actually have some practical benefit by providing the company with some "drynk." John answers his pastoral colleague, and the ale cup he offers is passed from one shepherd to the next, Gyb taking the first swallow and exclaiming the contents to be nothing less than the "boyte of oure bayll" (12/357), an exclamation with obvious parodic Eucharistic implications.[29] Slawpase is next in line, but before he has taken more than a sip, the cup is snatched away from him by John, who claims, by means of *phantasma*, that Slawpase has taken more than his fair share. Gyb, here playing good shepherd to John's bad shepherd, attempts to defend Slawpase, but John will have none of it, downing the remaining contents of the cup after reciting a tavern drinking-prayer of sorts:

Be thou wyne, be thou ayll,
Bot if my brethe fayll,
I shall sett the on sayll;
God send the good gayte! (12/370–73)[30]

As the second stage of the maneuver to exclude Slawpase begins, Gyb and John, utilizing a strategy similar to the vaudeville routine of the "inside joke" perfected by Bob Hope and Bing Crosby in all of their *Road* movies as a way of extricating themselves from threatening situations, produce a second bottle of the same good ale.[31] As John brings the new bottle forward, Slawpase, in an interruptive way, attempts to use the discovery to reingratiate himself in the pastoral group. However, John not only ignores Slawpase here but also reasserts the exclusion by quickly changing the subject to introduce the drink-for-a-song contest:

> *2 Pastor.* Yit a botell here is—
> *3 Pastor.* That is well spoken;
> By my thryft, we must kys!—
> *2 Pastor.* That had I forgoten.
> Bot hark!
> Whoso can best syng
> Shall haue the begynnyng. (12/378–84)

Since the contest is fixed from the start, both Gyb and John sing, leaving Slawpase out of the activity. As a reward for their performance, the two older shepherds help themselves to the bottle, Gyb congratulating John and himself on a job well done. When Slawpase finally exclaims they have taken more than their fair share, using the metonymic expression "dronken a quart" (12/393), Gyb in feigned high dudgeon claims "Ther is drynk enogh" (12/397). Of course, there is not, as Slawpase quickly discovers, and he accuses Gyb and John of being "knafys," an accusation Gyb admits the truth of in his subsequent "Nay, we knaues all" (12/400) retort.

The second part of the requital is put into play as soon as Slawpase is calmed down by Gyb and John, who declaim against brawling and introduce the idea of almsgiving, another idea used to change the subject and promote forgetting. Slawpase, again looking to be admitted to the pastoral brotherhood, agrees to this act of charity, declaring it will have a beneficial effect on all their souls. Introducing this self-serving observation, however, he does not remark the words Gyb employs ironically to encourage him to prepare the alms—"Geder vp," the very words he himself used earlier in the lesson when attempting to instruct by humiliating Gyb and John with the empty-sack exemplum (12/253):

> *3 Pastor.* Syrs, herys!
> For oure saules lett vs do
> Poore men gyf it to.
> *1 Pastor.* Geder vp, lo, lo,
> Ye hungré begers frerys! (12/408–12)

III

The last—and perhaps most important—thing anticipated in the presentation of the "uninventive" speculative mind is the presence of *phantasiae* and *phantasmata*, and of action based upon or involving such images and imaginings. Several fictitious creations arising from memory unfold as each shepherd is introduced in the play's first scene, and while some of these products of the "imaginacioun" appear to be only incidental or ornamental, all of them are integral to the play's thematic development, functioning much the same way gargoyles and other strange and imaginary homologous figures decorating the Gothic cathedral façade instruct and elicit a response in the onlooker.[32]

In the second scene or "The Pastoral Celebration," for instance, the first of two examples demonstrating the capacity for creative fantasy of the diminished spirit's memory is brought to the audience's attention by the substance of the "Grotesque Feast." While the order of the dishes in this meal may suggest the customary progression in a feast from first course to second to third and so on,[33] the many odd combinations of aristocratic and plebeian menu items—even where some of these foods may be theologically or typologically meaningful[34]—along with the feast's imaginary nature, offer a series of gastronomic *phantasmata*, which reveal an energetic but circumscribed working of memory, as has already been noted, as the diminished spirit adjusts the body—in this case a malnourished body—to the stimuli it receives or can only remember having received.[35]

Not as extensive in scope, but certainly as odd in terms of its construction, which consists of apparently garbled images or the *phantasiae* of liturgical Latin,[36] is the bedtime prayer delivered by Slawpase as the shepherds retire at the end of the celebration, the second example in this scene of the capacity for creative fantasy of the creaturely triune mind's enfeebled memory:

> For ferde we be fryght,
> A crosse lett vs kest—
> Cryst-crosse, benedyght
> Eest and west—
> For drede.
> *Iesus onazorus*
> *Crucyefixus,*

Morcus, Andreus,
God be our spede! (12/417–25)

Stevens and Cawley point out that this hodgepodge of a night spell "amounts to a conflation of the following prayers recorded in a York *Horae* of 1555:

> In nomine Patris et Filii et Spiritus sancti.
> Marcus, Mattheus, Lucas, Joannes. Amen.
> Jesus nazarenus crucifixus, Rex Judeorum, Fili Dei,
> miserere me. Amen.[37]

An earlier—and quite complex—example of this peculiar capacity of memory is brought to the fore in the first scene or "The Shepherds' Convocation" as the quarrel between Gyb and John begins to heat up. After they bemoan their plight as shepherds, Gyb informs John that he is on his way to the fair to purchase more sheep. John, interestingly, questions the condition of Gyb's mind by asking "dreme ye or slepe?" (12/147) and pointing out there is no place to pasture a flock in the immediate area, an ironic thing to say, given the size of the vast Pennine sheep runs owned by the landed gentry and by the various monastic houses in the region surrounding Wakefield.[38] Undismayed, Gyb replies he will work his sheep

> Wheresoeuer lykys me;
> Here shall thou theym see. (12/154–55)

This attitude only disturbs John the more, and he next insists Gyb cannot introduce even one sheep to the place where they are now standing. The performance-selective reality of the exchange, by this point in the unfolding quarrel between the shepherds, no doubt reminded the initial West Riding and Wakefield audiences of like pasturage-rights disputes that must have been frequent in their day.[39] But what the quarrel leads to next is unanticipated—more startling, in fact, than even this momentary methexical destabilization of the spectator's privileged mimetic viewpoint by the introduction of this commonplace topical irony.

As John, now nearly in a state of exasperation over Gyb's continued stubbornness, questions whether Gyb is drunk to think he can move about freely, with or without a flock of one hundred sheep, Gyb introduces the ovine *phantasma*⁴⁰ by first urging forward the bellwether of an imaginary flock with an expression that would likely be heard on any given day in the vast Pennine sheep runs of the Yorkshire West Riding:

> 2 *Pastor.* What, art thou in ayll?
> Longys thou oght-whedir?
> 1 *Pastor.* They shall go, saunce fayll.
> Go now, bell-weder! (12/161–64)

Gyb's command forces John's hand, as it were, and he has no choice but to engage in the fantasy, which he does as wholeheartedly as Gyb. This can be heard in John's immediate use of a call commonly employed by shepherds driving a flock from one pasture to another: as Gyb urges his imaginary lead sheep on, John halts the ovine progress abruptly by exclaiming, "I say, tyr!" (12/165).

What follows next, in an astounding moment of medieval dramatic innovation in which the resiliency of dramatic illusion itself is tested in a way different from that in the interludial asides in the *Processus Noe*,⁴¹ is a series of shepherding calls, each one answering the preceding, that further establishes the dramatic presence and seeming reality of the ovine *phantasma*. First Gyb answers John's "tyr!" with

> I say, tyr, now agane!
> I say skyp ouer the plane. (12/166–67)

What this reply means in terms of staging, of course, is that the imaginary animal that has been first urged forward, and next urged to turn back, is now urged to move forward again, an action that would be counterproductive for any shepherd driving a flock in any direction.⁴² To turn another circle, John now introduces a new shepherding command, with the same animation and vigor, to redirect the imaginary lead sheep when he exclaims

> Wold thou neuer so fane,
> Tup, I say, whyr! (12/168–69)

Not to be outshepherded, Gyb answers with yet another, more forceful herding exclamation following an interrogative motivated at least in part by exasperation—

> What, wyll thou not yit,
> I say, let the shepe go?
> Whop! (12/170–72)

—and so begins the imaginary animal's third turn.

While the completion of this circle is not achieved by countermand in this instance, the turn is nevertheless halted by John, whose subsequent "Abyde yit," as well as the action it implies, nearly precipitates a violent outburst from Gyb. The threat Gyb makes against John here—

> Will thou bot so?
> Knafe, hens I byd flytt.
> As good that thou do,
> Or I shall the hytt
> On thi pate—lo,
> Shall thou reyll! (12/173–78)

—may be as real as the felt or sensed dimensionality given to the imaginary sheep through the accumulated force of the pastoral directional commands. But even more important is the fact that the ovine *phantasma*, by this point, has taken on a life of its own, one that now exerts a control over Gyb much the way excessive thought of the beloved in Guillaume de Lorris's earlier part of the *Roman de la Rose* controls the lover.[43]

The extent to which things have gone from bad to worse here, in terms of "imaginacioun," is suggested by Gyb's absurd demand that John back off to give his imaginary animals "space" (12/179). It is reaffirmed, however, quite startlingly and cleverly, from a dramatic point of view, by the introduction of Slawpase into the scene. Slawpase, who has observed but not heard the specifics of the squabble between the two older shepherds in his approach from the mill, is told by Gyb that John has interfered with his shepherding and has not allowed his flock to pass:

> Hark what I meyn
> You to say:
> I was bowne to by store,
> Drofe my shepe me before.
> He says not oone hore
> Shall pas by this way;

Bot, and he were wood,
This way shall thay go. (12/186–93)

The complaint seems legitimate, but when Slawpase asks where the sheep in question are now—since he has not, from the moment of his arrival, seen any animals in the immediate area[44]—John's reply that no such animals ever existed leads him to conclude, "Ye fysh before the net," which is to say, the foolishness of both Gyb and John is unparalleled. Limited as it may be, the intellectual perspective that Slawpase's presence and immediate conclusion introduce into the scene thus puts in relief the full extent to which actuality is obscured and distorted by the illusory reality of the ovine *phantasma*.[45] That this presence and conclusion also explode Gyb's imaginary fictions as suddenly as the dreamer/narrator is startled back into consciousness at the end of the *Book of the Duchess* by the knight in black's "She ys ded!" also follows logically since *phantasmata*, having by definition no basis in fact or actuality, cannot stand up to scrutiny exerted by even a diminished degree of rational comprehension.

Also revelatory of the extent to which this *phantasma* has turned actuality upside down are Slawpase's subsequent use of the Moll allusion and the commentary he delivers in yet another aside like those made by Uxor Gill and Noe in the *Processus Noe*. With regard to the latter, Slawpase, whose intellect is seriously compromised—as has been noted in his use of the emptied-sack exemplum—has enough intelligence at this point to diagnose the problem of his pastoral colleagues as resulting from the tendency of memory, in its capacity as storehouse of *phantasiae*, to create distortive imaginative fiction. He makes this point when opining aphoristically, with unanticipated common sense and short-lived perspicacity, that the shepherds, fighting over nothing actual, possess the sort of "wytt" that would "Make a shyp be drownde":

It is wonder to wyt
Where wytt shuld be fownde.
Here ar old knafys yit
Standys on this grownde:
These wold by thare wytt
Make a shyp be drownde;
He were well qwytt

> Had sold for a pownde
> Sich two.
> Thay fight and thay flyte
> For that at comys not tyte;
> It is far to byd 'hyte'
> To an eg or it go. (12/205–17)[46]

While Slawpase's introduction of the Moll story,[47] an allusion directed at the shepherds themselves this time, serves also as reminder of actuality's topsy-turviness as the result of Gyb and John's elaborated ovine *phantasma*, its purpose is initially corrective, pointing to the dangers inherent in such distortions of actuality:[48]

> Ye brayde of Mowll
> That went by the way—
> Many shepe can she poll,
> Bot oone had she ay.
> Bot she happynyd full fowll:
> Hyr pycher, I say,
> Was broken.
> 'Ho, God!' she sayde.
> Bot oone shepe yit she hade;
> The mylk-pycher was layde,
> The skarthis was the tokyn. (12/220–30)

In addition, the rebuke or lesson[49] of which Slawpase suggests the shepherds ponder the meaning in regard to the effect of herding a flock of imaginary sheep—that is, the tropological danger of daydreaming or considering a *phantasma* that leads eventually to the loss of the milk pitcher and its contents, an inferrable fact from the "skarthis" on the ground—implicitly introduces the idea of skepticism, the need to know things empirically, a means of knowing that will be developed in much greater detail in the Towneley collection's next play, the *[Secunda] Pagina Pastorum*.

In this way, Slawpase's anecdotal inclusion anticipates the function of Jak Garcio's arrival at the end of "The Shepherds' Convocation." The source of a considerable degree of scholarly puzzlement,[50] Jak, impish like a gargoyle though he may be, is introduced for the instructive purpose of denouncing all manner of *phantasmata*, as defined by Saint Augustine—that is, those *phantasiae* originating with the senses and imagination, as in the case of the two older shepherds, as well as those originating with the reason, as in the case of Slawpase.[51] No illusory reality as the result of the action of the diminished spirit upon the body, in Jak's view, has any value, and so he describes all three shepherds as the bellwethers of all the fools in creation, more foolish in fact than even the "fools of Gotham," those who would teach others about wisdom when they themselves lack it,[52] or, in other words, those who have no self-knowledge or perspective. Gyb's continuation of the ovine *phantasma* at this point, by asking Jak how the sheep are doing in the pasture, does not elicit an angry response from Jak as might be expected, but rather a hyperbolic imaginative fiction[53]—not the acknowledgment of a miracle[54]—that the animals, despite the winter chill, are in summer fields, in grass so abundant it comes to the sheeps' knees. Those whose creaturely triune mind is contaminated by the effect of the diminished spirit's action in response to the body as it adjusts the body to the stimuli it receives are not the sort of individuals to be chastised but rather souls that should be reasoned with gently, to be led to the point of understanding. This is why Jak's denunciation concludes enigmatically. On the one hand, he wishes simply to distance himself from those who have eyes but do not see; on the other, he lets the shepherds know that, should they wish to, they may reverse their lot and actually begin to see or understand that the beasts they have imagined into existence do not actually live and breathe, but only after they themselves have taken the initiative to engage their wills to do so:

> Amen.
> If *ye will ye may se;*
> Your bestes ye ken. (12/273–75; emphasis mine)

IV

The intrinsic "inventive" speculative creaturely triune mind as conceived of allegorically and configured dramatically by the Wakefield Master, on the other hand, is the preferred mind, the mind of the robust or fully living spirit. While this mind is possessed of memory, intellect, and will, the quality of these faculties is the opposite of that in the "uninventive" creaturely triune mind. They are, in other words, "divine," as Saint Augustine describes them in *De Trinitate* (10.4.19).[55] What is more, since no *phantasmata* are produced from the memory in this mind,[56] the result of only reasonable images or *phantasiae* being produced by the robust spirit's action on the body as it adjusts the body to the stimuli the body receives, the "inventive" speculative mind or the "blessed state of mind," as Saint Augustine also calls it, is ready to engage in the intellectual and volitional rigors of the *modus interpretandi* as well as the *modus proferandi*. In fact, because it is so strong and active, and because it is, in this invigorated condition, a creaturely trinity in which is possessed, properly speaking, the Image of God,[57] this mind employs the *techne* of meaning-making *inventio* to arrive at that which is "trew" by means of deploying two distinct analytical actions. These actions, known to the Middle Ages in various forms but described most helpfully by Hugh of St. Victor in the *Didascalicon*, involve what Hugh calls, in his discussion of the method of expounding a text, analysis through separation into parts and analysis through examination:

> We analyze through separation into parts when we distinguish from one another things which are mingled together. We analyze by examination when we open up things which are hidden.[58]

What is clear about this late-medieval conception of mind, as opposed to that of the diminished spirit, is that "imaginacioun," for it, is neither source of beauty nor source of anything else but trouble.

Evidence of the "inventive" speculative creaturely triune mind in the play's third scene, "The Annunciation," as the preceding definition should lead one to anticipate, results from the dramatized *allegoria* of the condition as well as praxis of the "divinity" of the creaturely triune mind. This creaturely noetic "divinity," as the Wakefield Master presents it, is characterized by three things, which are introduced, one after the other, as soon as the angelic prophecy and song are completed and the shepherds have awakened. The first of these is the interaction of memory and intellect that is normally associated with the living or robust spirit. This interaction is presented sequentially in the first part and in the first section of the second part of the third scene's second episode, and consists of approximately half of the scene's lines. Of even greater interest—though not unexpected, since this episode marks the beginning of the pastoral intellectual response to the Annunciation—is how much this, as well as the subsequent noetic interaction presented in the remainder of this episode, conforms to Saint Augustine's description of "the way of discovering those things which are to be understood" in the second and third books of *De doctrina christiana*.

The first instance of the mnemonic/intellectual response, introduced in the first section of the second episode's first part (12/439–77), addresses the issue of the "unknown literal"[59] by means of a rudimentary *disputatio* methodology,[60] now delivered in complete stanzas,[61] each of which emphasizes the effect of the intellect upon the memory. Gyb, in other words, presents a supposition, which is then followed by a two-part corrective refutation or "consequent" consisting of John's and Slawpase's responses. Gyb's supposition or *videtur quod*, the initial pastoral response to the angelic prophecy and song—the nucleus, as it were, of the play[62]—is that the sound he remembers he heard was that of a nubilous voice of some sort, possibly the type of voice, Stevens and Cawley point out, heard from a cloud as in Exodus 24:16 and Luke 9:35.[63] Though he begins his response by acknowledging that the sound was a "wonder curiose" song that had structure since it appeared to consist of "small noytys," the remembered acoustical effect of the experience is of a shrill noise apparently made by one who "scremyd on lowde" (12/448). As a result, Gyb is fearful enough to pray to God to save his brethren as well as himself (12/443). This evoked emotional response of trepidation to tone, combined with the unusualness of the event itself, limits Gyb's understanding of the experience and its source to simplistic response or generalization.

John's *sed contra* in reply to Gyb's initial *videtur quod*, the first part of the corrective refutation to be introduced, begins its rebuttal with a clearly stated denial—

Nay, that may not be,
I say you certan (12/452–53)

—and then offers as a *respondeo dicendum* an identification of the voice. John declares that the voice heard not only spoke to all three shepherds but also was the voice of a man, though the speaker was an angel. That John was frightened by this supernatural experience is something he readily admits, but the fear in his case does not lead to confusion of emotional response as with Gyb, but rather to an attentiveness—that is, a presence of mind or intellectual response—enabling John subsequently to clarify the angelic message's import. Part of this clarification is a delineation of the angel's subject. John declares that the celestial visitor spoke of a "barne" (12/461). Another part is a delineation of the subject's implication. With the subject clarified, John concludes to his fellow shepherds that they must seek the child, and that the star they see "That standys yonder owte" stands for or "betokyns" the object of their quest (12/462–64). John has, in other words, intellectually revealed or explained the *unknown* signs, both the natural and the conventional—that is, those appearing in nature and those incorporated in the angelic voice.[64]

The second part of the *respondeo dicendum* in reply to Gyb's initial *videtur quod* follows as Slawpase, carefully remembering what he has just heard and previously seen, completes the first section of the second episode's first part. Slawpase offers two things. One is a synthesis, the object of the intellectual endeavor, of elements of the two previous pastoral responses to the angelic annunciation. The synthesis first confirms John's identification of the angelic voice. This Slawpase does by saying that, while he might have considered the whole thing nothing more than a "thoner-flone" or lightning bolt, he did behold the marvel himself with his own eyes (12/465–70). The synthesis then confirms Gyb's response to the unusual acoustical dimension of the experience by saying that he, Slawpase, also heard a "mery gle" that was delivered, if he did not dream all of this, in a speaking voice that tonally was like a "skreme" (12/471–75). The second thing offered by Slawpase, directly following the synthesis, is an elaboration of John's explanation. This elaboration introduces the name of the city of "Bedleme" or Bethlehem, to which the shepherds need now to travel, and the purpose of that travel. As they go to "Bedleme," which reminds the audience of the latter part of the angelic song, they will journey, as Slawpase indicates, "To wyrship that lorde" (12/477), which also reminds the audience that Slawpase has remembered the initial and most important part of the angelic song sung to the shepherds, the verses that inform them they shall "give praise to the Lord Perpetual," who has been born for their sake this very day:

Herkyn, hyrdes! Awake!
Gyf louyng ye shall;
He is borne for youre sake,
Lorde perpetuall. (12/426–29)

The second instance of the mnemonic/intellectual response, introduced in the second section of the second episode's first part (12/478–

503), addresses the issue of the "unknown figurative" or unknown sign[65] using the same methodology as before, but now in a more sophisticated way, one characterized by memory's influence upon intellect. The shepherds speak in the same order, with Gyb again offering the section's supposition or *videtur quod*. Gyb's assumption about the child of whom the angel has sung is that this newborn must be literally the very same infant

> That prophetys of told,
> Shuld make them fre
> That Adam had sold. (12/479–81)

Gyb's literal-minded introduction here of the prophets, the voices of traditional authority from the past, signals the beginning of a new, more complicated emphasis upon memory in the form of a "repetitive aesthetic pattern" involving a "modified" *Processus Prophetarum*, as E. C. Dunn has argued, linking this play with the liturgical drama before it.[66]

The corrective refutation that follows is again led by John, who this time introduces the *sed contra* to Gyb's *videtur quod* by declaring the necessity to take "tent" or heed (12/482). Unlike in the first section, John does not deny or reply in the negative to what Gyb has said, since Gyb has spoken accurately if only literally. Rather, he refines Gyb's generalization through elaboration and clarification to explain the unknown sign's meaning.[67] To give his explanation authorial ballast, John turns to the "wordys of Isae." Now engaged in a conventional act of remembrance by using textual authority—that is, by relying upon words that are "inrold" (12/483)—John identifies the child as the one prophesied in the Old Testament book to be—

> kyng with crowne
> Sett on Dauid trone. (12/487–88)

The child, in other words, is to be the fulfillment in the present of what was anticipated in the past. This revelation of the unknown sign's meaning or typological forecast, John concludes, is new and unique, since no one else has ever seen with his or her eyes what the shepherds themselves now have experienced and beheld.

The second part of the corrective refutation to the "unknown figurative," Slawpase's contribution here to the *sed contra* in response to Gyb's *videtur quod*, does not offer a synthesis as in the previous section, but rather a further clarification of the typological relation between David's throne and the new child who is to wear the "crowne" and, in fulfillment of the figure, sit on that throne. How Slawpase does this is by introducing, also from Isaiah, the genealogy and function of the Virgin, on the one hand, and the meaning of the Virgin's function, on the other. The Virgin, according to the genealogy—that is, according to the historical record of memory—is descended from Jesse, and her function is to

> Bryng furth, by grace,
> A floure so bold. (12/495–96)

The inference that she has done this leads Slawpase to the beginning of the *respondeo dicendum* or the elucidation of her function's meaning, which is not only to "vphold" or confirm the validity of the words that prophesied the advent of the child, but also to engender in the shepherds, as well as in any audience member interested in considering the tropological moment of the event's significance, trust in the event's veracity. While Slawpase's final words here—

> Exiet virga
> *De radice Iesse* (12/502–3)

—may not be from Isaiah itself but from an intermediate source, such as a *Prophetae* play like that of Limoges,[68] they nevertheless capture the gist of the biblical passage and, in demonstrating a dramatic improvement over the garbled grammar and syntax of the night spell concluding the play's first scene, reveal a dramatic change in this the most intellectual, if also the most pedantic, pastoral voice of the play's first half.

The final instance of the mnemonic/intellectual response, presented in the first section of the second episode's second part (12/504–55), addresses the "ambiguous literal"[69] and is much more elaborate in its construction than the two previously demonstrated mnemonic/intellectual approaches to the "unknown literal" and the "unknown figurative." Part of the reason for this is that now both memory and intellect are shown to have a decisive influence upon the other. This can be seen immediately in the presentation of the supposition in this instance, made in response to prophetic signs found in "oure faythe alyene" (12/507), which is protracted by the introduction of a typological precedent. Completing the modified *Processus Prophetarum* through acknowledgment of the Erythraean Sibyl and Nebuchadnezzar—and thereby establishing an internal coherence by linking the episode's second part to its first—Gyb begins this section by alluding to the story of the three children of Judah as an ambiguous but comprehensible literal sign of Christ's birth since, as he observes, the fourth child in the story that

> stode before,
> Godys son lyke to bene. (12/510–11)

Gyb's surmise puts him in good intellectual company, since this is the interpretation of the sign offered in the *Sermo contra Judaeos*.[70] And John's immediate reply—that

> That fygure
> Was gyffen by reualacyon
> That God wold haue a son (12/512–14)

—confirms the accuracy of Gyb's typological interpretation. The second "ambiguous literal" presented here, the one that leads eventually—but indirectly—to the formulation of the section's supposition or *videtur quod*, offers an interpretive problem of sorts, however. While the image of "A bushe burnand, lo!" (12/520) introduces an "ambiguous figurative," the next type of sign to be dealt with by the shepherds, it is not this figurative element that proves to be the interpretive obstacle, since its typological meaning is understood by the shepherds to be a prefigurement of the Virgin Birth. Rather, what constitutes the problem in this instance, as Gyb ponders it, is the ambiguity of the literal or actual act of birth in this case. In other words, while he can understand the concept of "holy vyrgynyté," Gyb, too close in his thinking to the sheep runs and the realities of ovine animal husbandry, cannot comprehend how the Virgin can remain "vnfylyd" and yet "haue a chyld," because "Sich was neuer sene" (12/525–30). His inability to grasp the meaning of this particular "ambiguous literal" thus establishes an assumptive doubt about the role of the Virgin advanced previously in the pastoral response to the "unknown figurative," one that invites yet another mnemonic/intellectual response.

As in the previous cases, the corrective refutation or *sed contra* is begun by John, who in this instance first hushes Gyb with an expletive— "Pese, man" (12/532)—and then claims his brother shepherd's error is the result of beguilement. Continuing the *sed contra*, John rebuts Gyb's assumptive doubt by assuring his fellow shepherd that he will have empirical proof of the "Greatt meruell" of the undefiled maiden and her son as he will soon behold the two with his own eyes (12/533–37). The assurance implicit in this kind of evidence enables Gyb to overcome his doubt, the expression of which change is immediately heard, on the one hand, in his acknowledgment of the importance of faith, as he observes nothing is impossible if it is God's will, and, on the other, in his acknowledgment of the importance of belief, as he observes all

>   shal be stabyll
> That God wyll haue done. (12/541–42)

Further reassurance to buttress the correctness of this conversion follows as John, again reminding the audience of the importance of the act of remembrance, introduces testimony in support of Gyb's recognition of the value of faith and belief by including the remainder of the modified *Processus Prophetarum* presented thus far in this episode of the play's second scene:

> Abacuc and Ely
> Prophesyde so,
> Elezabeth and Zacharé,
> And many other mo;
> And Dauid as veraly
> Is witnes therto,
> Iohn Baptyste sewrly,
> And Daniel also. (12/543–50)

Slawpase's conclusion or the *respondeo dicendum*, which brings this corrective mnemonic/intellectual refutation to an end, is an expected final contribution here, since the mnemonic/intellectual and the intellectual/mnemonic response to the Annunciation has led the shepherds from a confused, emotional reaction to the supernatural, short-lived as it may be, to what now amounts to a logical proof of the nexus between uncreated and created reality.[71] Slawpase's use of the actual language of logical discourse here, as he begins with "So sayng" (12/551), is an expected feature of this final response, not because Slawpase has been associated in the play more consistently than the other shepherds with the speculative creaturely triune mind's faculty of reason, but rather because the new pastoral understanding of the "Greatt meruell" attained by the interaction of memory and intellect thus far requires a more precise mode of expression than hitherto used to comprehend the angelic song.

Slawpase's subsequent observations, accordingly, evidence this new attitude toward style and usage. In the two related brief statements that follow to complete the refutation, Slawpase affirms the fact, ethical purpose, and teleological dimension of Christ's divinity. For Slawpase, Christ is "Godys son alon" (12/552). What is more, He is the source of life for all since "Without hym shal be none" (12/553).[72] And, finally, Christ's mastery and sovereignty are eternal as

> His sete and his trone
> Shall euer be lastyng. (12/554–55)

V

The second thing the creaturely noetic "divinity" associated with the living or robust spirit is characterized by is the action of volition on the intellect, the second feature of the "inventive" speculative mind to be anticipated in this portion of the play. This interaction, which is again introduced by means of the dramatized *allegoria* of the *disputatio* methodology—though now with an emphasis on volition as the motivating factor of intellect—addresses the issue of the "ambiguous figurative"[73] in the second section of the third scene's second episode (12/556–624). Since Saint Augustine observes in *De doctrina christiana* that the ambiguities of figurative words "require no little care and industry,"[74] the Wakefield Master carefully demonstrates, again through the drama of anachronistic pastoral response, how the effect of volition on intellect leads to the utilization of the *modus interpretandi*, through both analysis by examination and analysis by separation. This engagement of interpretive ability comprises the corrective refutation, which follows an elaborated supposition, one this time consisting of remarks made by the two older shepherds, Gyb and John.

Linking the final section of the pastoral intellectual response to the previous mnemonic/intellectual response to the Annunciation, Gyb begins the configuration of this final section's supposition or *videtur quod* by introducing yet another prophetic affirmation of the "Greatt meruell." He does this, in this instance, by quoting and reversing the order of the lines of the Fourth Virgilian Messianic Eclogue to repeat the order of the presentation of Christ and the Virgin established in earlier pastoral exchanges in the episode:

> Virgill in his poetré
> Sayde in his verse,
> Euen thus be grameré,
> As I shall reherse:
> *Iam noua progenies celo demittitur alto;*
> *Iam rediet Virgo, redeunt Saturnia regna.* (12/556–59+)

The immediate rancorous and even obscene reply from John in response to Gyb's "grameré"—

> Weme! tord! what speke ye
> Here in my eeres? (12/560–61)

—a reply that completes the configuration of the supposition here, is not motivated by the artful modification of the Virgilian text, but rather by the topical association John makes between the "Laton" language and the friars. Friars, as Stevens and Cawley observe in their quotation from Owst, "generally communicated their learning in Latin 'to keep the fruits of [their] labours to [their] equals if not entirely to [their] own orders, away from the half-literate priest or the layman.'"[75] Accordingly, John's vigorous denunciation of the Latin, a condemnation of the medium by which the figurative is conveyed—not on linguistic grounds as might be expected, but rather on those involving the sociopolitical decision to use language to maintain a hegemonic ideological exclusivity—completes the supposition whose refutation requires a wilful intellectual response to demonstrate the validity of a figure, especially when it is ambiguously presented linguistically.

Such is what follows in the first part of the corrective refutation (12/567–85), which is begun this time by Gyb, who initiates the *sed contra*, on the one hand, by indirectly characterizing as foolishness the allowing of a topical issue to obscure the meaning of a messianic figure, and, on the other, by directly calling for instruction to preclude any further foolishness and to correct the pastoral response:

> Herk, syrs! ye fon.
> I shall you teche. (12/567–68)

As he continues, the action of the will on the intellect in response to the denunciation of the "Laton" leads Gyb to offer the beginning of the *respondeo dicendum* by engaging in the *modus interpretandi*, first, through analysis by examination. That feature of the *techne* or method of exposition employed by Gyb here to "open up things which are hidden" consists of two parts. The first of these involves the hermeneutic translative act of revealing, to continue to use Hugh of St. Victor's terminology,[76] the letter, sense, and deeper meaning of the first line of the eclogue in a prototypical way. The letter and sense are conveyed through the identification of the child who has been sent from heaven, and of the mother who shall conceive him "full euen" (12/569–74). The deeper meaning or *sententia*, likewise, is conveyed in this first interpretive translation through the acknowledgment of the conception's purpose, which is to introduce the New Dispensation, as well as the purpose of this: "Oure mys to amend" (12/572).

The second part of the exposition, which follows immediately, involves the hermeneutic translative act of revealing and elaborating the deeper meaning of the second line of the eclogue, introducing an emphasis here noticeably distinguishing this part of the exposition from the first. In the Virgilian text the return of Saturn's reign is presented as straightforward metaphor of the return of the Golden Age. In Gyb's exposition of the line, however, "Saturnia" is introduced, as he interpretively—some might say loosely—translates it in light of the conventional mythographic associations between the idea of the Old and the Greco-Roman figure of Saturn,[77] as metaphor of the Old Dispensation. But what is important to note about the incorporation of this more complex metaphor is that it is not introduced here to signal the return of the old but rather to herald the beginning of the new, since "Saturne," as Gyb continues the exposition,

> shall bend
> Vnto vs,
> With peasse and plenté,
> With ryches and menee,
> Good luf and charyté
> Blendyd amanges vs. (12/576–81)

In other words, the introduction of the mythographized Saturn here provides Gyb with an evolved metaphoric means of revealing how the combination of the Old Dispensation with the New, the fulfillment of messianic prophecy, leads to a new kind of Golden Age in which material and spiritual abundance exist simultaneously, an abundance Slawpase holds to be "trew" as soon as the "kyng commys new" (12/582–85).[78]

The action of the will on the intellect also leads to engagement of the *modus interpretandi* through analysis by separation. This occurs as John, now taking the lead of the pastoral group, returns attention, still in the first corrective refutation, to the angelic song that conveyed the matter of the Annunciation in the first place. This consideration begins a three-part analytical process (12/586–624) by which the song is disassembled and reassembled or reconstructed, as it were, for the purpose of understanding it. John says he wishes they

>   knew
> Of this song so fre
> Of the angell; (12/588–90)

the separation into parts is then begun. This late-medieval deconstruction, simplistic as it may be, reveals a musical rather than a rhythmic complexity that startles even John, who now, inspired by God, remarks of the elaborate style of this "mery song" that it has the unique feature of "Foure and twenty to a long" (12/598) or, as Nan C. Carpenter has observed, "twenty-four semi-minims to a long."[79] While he questions the accuracy of this ratio, Gyb does, in reply, call attention to another stylistic feature of the song, the exactness of the tonality. Of the notes, he observes

> Thay were gentyll and small,
> And well tonyd withall. (12/604–5)

The sophistication of analytical ability demonstrated by the shepherds here, an expected outcome given their sequential interpretive response to literal as well as figurative unknowns and ambiguities throughout the scene, supports JoAnna Dutka's observation that this initial musical discussion emphasizes the beauty of the performance over the rhythmic complexity of the *Gloria*.[80] The shepherds' individual and collective attainment and development of the "inventive" speculative creaturely triune mind, in response to the Annunciation, has thus rationally predisposed them to desire understanding of the proper function of the beautiful in a moral sense.

What remains for the shepherds to do, now that they have acknowledged, and enabled the audience to understand, the prominence of aesthetic matters in the experience of the tropological, is to complete the *respondeo dicendum* or analysis by separation and so bring closure to the scene's second episode. This is done in two ways by the performance reconstruction of the angelic song (12/608–24). One, the reconstruction enables the shepherds to reintroduce, as they ready themselves to give their own songful interpretation of the *Gloria*, the first of two final demonstrations in the play of the action of will upon the intellect. Most noticeable about this first demonstration of volition is the comedic—some might say almost slapstick—element. As they prepare themselves to sing, the shepherds begin to squabble over what might be considered artistic differences.[81] Gyb, for example, encourages Slawpase to break out his voice and show he can sing the high notes since Slawpase, after some previous hesitation, has told his brethren he can remember all of the angelic song's minims, crotchets, and quavers, an impressive act of memory, to say the very least:

Yee, bot I can thaym all;
Now lyst I lepe. (12/606–7)

Slawpase's reply, that he cannot sing without support, elicits a contemptuous jibe from John, who declares Slawpase lacks courage, his heart is in his stockings. The emotional turmoil of the moment is heightened by the threat that follows from Gyb, who declares that Slawpase risks a "skelp" or slap if he forgets the song. But the threat also functions to set the limits of the comedic action. Slawpase's immediate rejoinder, that Gyb is a "qwelp" on account of the "angre" he has just displayed, brings the squabble to a sudden halt by revealing that this limit has just, in fact, been overstepped. The sobering effect of this reply shows that the "inventive" speculative creaturely triune mind, while capable of comedy, prefers limitation or rational circumspection.[82] Further evidence of this tolerance and restraint is evinced immediately afterward as John and Gyb, though still somewhat emotional, tell Slawpase to begin.

The final demonstration of the action of will upon the intellect, the preferred one of the last two in the play, begins as soon as the shepherds, now in unison, perform the *Gloria*. JoAnna Dutka's observation about the uniqueness of the "intimate knowledge revealed in [the Wakefield shepherds'] plays of both musical style and musical technique as well as the use of purely musical means for a dramatic purpose"[83] suggests that this performance, not a parody as in the shepherds' songs found in the other Corpus Christi pageants and cycles,[84] offers auditory proof that the shepherds have learned the true use of natural and artificial beauty,[85] which is the reasonable enjoyment of all things of creation as principal means to the greater end of loving God. Accordingly, the attainment of this charitable outlook, the noetic object itself of the pastoral intellectual response to the Annunciation, is finally sounded, as soon as the shepherds have finished singing, in the ironic compliment John gives to Slawpase—

> Fayr fall this growne!
> Well has thou hyde. (12/623–24)

VI

To complete the presentation of the "inventive" speculative creaturely triune mind in preparation for the play's conclusion, the Wakefield Master turns the audience's attention to one other feature of "divine" creaturely noesis, one directly related to the interaction of the will and intellect just considered. As the action of the will upon the intellect has enabled the shepherds to achieve a new experience of social unity, based upon the integral relation between ethical understanding and spiritual insight, so the action of the intellect upon the will is shown now to have importance as well, for as Saint Augustine indicates in *De doctrina christiana*, one must not only learn the "way of discovering those things which are to be understood," but also practice a "way of teaching what we have learned."[86] While the Wakefield Master does not formally define what this practice must consist of—his work, after all, is a drama and not a philosophical text—two things that comprise a guideline of sorts are identified, both here and in the final scene of the play.

In the lines that follow the pastoral imitation of the angelic song, the first part of this guideline, the readying of the self for the demonstration of wisdom, is shown to be the direct result of a concerted action of the intellect upon the will. This deliberate action is evidenced in five ways in the second scene's final episode, in a sequential order of ascending importance, beginning with effects that can be categorized as actual, continuing with those that are morally practical, and concluding with one that is certainly ethical.

The first of these effects, the least significant of all, involves the engendering of a resoluteness to do or proceed. This is articulated immediately at the beginning of the scene's third and last episode (12/625–59), as John invites his fellow shepherds to run with him since he can no longer remain idle (12/625–26). The second way this action is presented, the second actual effect, arises as the shepherds, now fully under way, discover they are traveling during the new moon and so have no natural light by which to see (12/627–33). Despite the adversity of the circumstances, the shepherds not only repeat the resolve they have initially demonstrated by their agreement to hold to their purpose (12/629–31); they also display unusual ingenuity in calling on the navigational technique of following a directional bearing—that is, dead reckoning, which in this case is to travel in an eastward direction (12/632–33). Technology, when properly used, is shown to be a very reliable human-made means to an end greater than the mere enjoyment of the application and efficiency of the technology or practical art itself.

The third instance of this action, one modified this time by the engagement of all faculties of the "divine" speculative creaturely triune mind, leads to the articulation of humility (12/634–46), the first of the two practical moral effects. As Gyb wishes he and his fellow shepherds might see "This yong bab," John reminds the group that this desire is not novel but part of a tradition reaching far into the past and beginning with the prophets. The reply Slawpase offers, while elaborating this tradition through acknowledgment of the saints who were inspired by the prophets, introduces the condition of their seeing the child, when others have not, as reason for joyous expression of humbleness:

> And God so hee
> Wold shew vs that wyght
> We myght say, perdé,
> We had sene
> That many sant desyryd,
> With prophetys inspyryd. (12/639–44)

This asseveration of modesty is followed, next, by the fourth action of intellect upon the will or the second practical moral effect, which takes the form of a prayer that such a condition might be fulfilled:

> 2 *Pastor.* God graunt vs that grace!
> 3 *Pastor.* God so do.
> 1 *Pastor.* Abyde, syrs, a space. (12/647–49)

And as soon as the prayer is answered and the shepherds are guided to find their "gate" by the blazing star—that is, by the effect of grace itself[87]—the final action of intellect upon will or the ethical effect is presented. Now, at the stable housing the manger, the shepherds, exercising a new civility, decide that the eldest should lead the way on this last leg of their journey:

> 3 *Pastor.* Who shall go in before?
> 1 *Pastor.* I ne rek, by my hore.
> 2 *Pastor.* Ye ar of the old store;
> It semys you, iwys. (12/656–59)

They put in action, in other words, the commandment to honor the parent, the generation that has come before. That is, their ethical sense comes into being as they agree to participate in an historical tradition.

VII

The practical demonstration of wisdom, the second feature of the practical guideline or the actual "way of teaching what has been learned," is presented twice in "The Adoration," the play's final scene. It appears first in—and informs—the scene's entire "Gift-Giving" episode. As soon as they are demonstrably ready to share virtuously in what they have learned, and are in the proximity of the Christ Child Himself, the shepherds engage in the *modus proferandi*.[88] What is unusual about this first instance of teaching, a testament to the transformative effect of the entire pastoral intellectual response to the Annunciation, is how each shepherd's combination of wisdom and eloquence enables him now to be heard intelligently, willingly, and obediently.[89] More remarkable still is the fact that, while each shepherd employs the subdued, moderate, and grand styles to achieve these effects in the process of making his offering, each also convincingly demonstrates he has heeded Saint Augustine's important injunction to attend to and fulfill all three styles as much as can be done, even when ostensibly using only a single style.[90]

This injunction notwithstanding, all three offerings, it should be noted, evidence incorporation of the grand style in the metaphor of the triune God they cumulatively generate. In the first act of adoration Gyb's repetition of the sociopolitical language of feudatory rank in late-medieval culture—"kyng," "duke," "knyght"—introduces the suggestion of the authority figure or the Father. In the next act of adoration, John's repetition of affectionate terms—"lytyll tyn mop," "lytyll mylksop"—introduces the suggestion of the child or the Son. And in the final act of adoration, Slawpase's repetition of images of power, miraculous and otherwise—"maker of man," "so as I can," "I cowche to the than"[91]—introduces the idea of an intangible power, which suggests the Holy Spirit of God.

Each offering also employs something resembling the moderate style in its rhetorical repetitions of exclamatory salutations. In the first act of adoration, for example, Gyb offers the Christ Child seven emotional—but not ostentatious—greetings beginning with "Hayll" before calling attention to the gift he has brought. In the second act of adoration, John offers five equally emotional salutations, beginning with the same term of greeting, before turning to his gift. And in the final act of adoration, Slawpase accosts the Christ Child much the same way John has.

But it is, finally, each shepherd's use of the subdued style that shows the influence of the Augustinian rhetorical corrective the most, and reaps the benefit of becoming the most compelling manner of presentation in the play. Partly this is because the style, as Saint Augustine puts it, "does not come forth armed or adorned but, as it were, nude," so its incorporation serves as a source of great delight.[92] When Gyb begins to speak in this way—

> I pray the to take,
> If thou wold, for my sake—
> With this may thou lake—
> This lytyll spruse cofer (12/669–72)

—the genuineness of his charity and goodwill resounds as a truth both "demonstrated, defended, and placed in triumph as a source of great joy."[93] The same is true for John when, having made the offer of the ball, this second oldest shepherd apologizes that his means are scant—

> That thou wold resaue!
> Lytyll is that I haue;
> This wyll I vowchesaue,
> To play the withall. (12/682–85)

And so too for Slawpase, especially as he takes one last opportunity to demonstrate his learning:

>   Here I ordan,
> Now at oure metyng,
> This botell—
> It is an old byworde,
> 'It is a good bowrde
> For to drynk of a gowrde'—
> It holdys a mett potell. (12/692–98)

The other reason this disarmingly simple style is most persuasive is because it invites, in its unimpeded genuineness, the play of figurative expression. This can be seen in two ways. The first is implicit in the historic divergence in scholarly response that the "Gift-Giving" episode has elicited, a divergence that, at the risk of oversimplification, views the gifts as, on the one hand, a homely or humorous touch and, on the other, a means of conveying iconographic and allegorical significance.[94] The second—and more important—is implicit in the figurative "play" or meaning hitherto overlooked by scholars concerning the gifts' manufacture. All of the presents offered by the shepherds are images of anachronistic technology themselves and also are the products of the new manufacturing technologies of late-medieval society. They may or may not have domestic or iconographic significance, but as images or products of technologies, they all have one thing in common: as the shepherds introduce them, their purpose is repeatedly articulated to be the giving of pleasure. This makes the gifts, interestingly enough, like the triune nature of God Himself, the source of the wisdom of which they themselves are an end or product, and in this way they offer the audience a convincing reminder of why the "inventive" speculative creaturely triune mind, especially with its predisposition to engage in the *modus interpretandi* and the *modus proferandi*, is preferred over the "uninventive" speculative or imaginative mind, as the only kind of mind with which to serve God cooperatively in the serving of the self through the technological mastery and practical use of nature.

VIII

The final practical demonstration of wisdom or teaching completes the play as soon as Mary has given God's reward to the shepherds in "Mary's Response," or the last scene's second episode. This reward has two parts.

In return for the shepherds' attainment of the "inventive" speculative creaturely triune mind that has led to their persuasive expression of charity, they are promised, in the present moment and forever, God's

> blys full euen
> Contynuyng. (12/706–7)

Besides the certainty of this "good grace" now informing the shepherds' lives, Mary gives them the unconditional promise of assured divine support in the future, as well as "good endyng"—that is, eternal life beyond. In addition, she tells the shepherds to repeat the good works they have done through further pastoral engagement in the *modus proferandi*— that is, through the telling "furth of this case" (12/709). To put this in a way that has already been considered, the full import of Mary's reward encourages the shepherds to continue to serve God cooperatively by serving themselves in the technological mastery and proper use of the spatial through their telling "furth" or teaching, and in the technological mastery and proper use of the temporal, until their own "endyng," through their acceptance of the miraculous indwelling presence of divine inspiration, whose continuing effect will be to make their teaching ever more persuasive.

The divine gift not only is received as graciously as it is given, it also inspires the shepherds to begin again "teaching what has been learned," in an innovatively new way of combining the wisdom and eloquence they have already demonstrated. They will bolster their lesson mnemonically, they declare, by telling of what they have witnessed through their own acts of adoration, and by utilizing the practical art of music, its pedagogical advantages now known to them, to commit to mirthful and playful song the expression of the very tropological joy the experience of "this lam" has evoked in their own hearts. As they sing in the presence of the Christ child and the play comes to an end, they prepare to begin the pastoral annunciation of the miracle they have experienced and seen.

IX

Consideration of the difference between the "uninventive" speculative mind and the "inventive" speculative mind in the *[Prima] Pagina Pastorum* convincingly puts to rest any notion that the first of the Wakefield Master's two shepherds' plays in the Towneley *regenall* is something of an "inchoate" version or artistic false start.[95] This play may not possess the *[Secunda] Pagina Pastorum*'s Mak and Gyll, but the complexity of the design of mind that it develops in its deep structure through the dramatized *allegoria* of hermeneutical pastoral response, a design that appears noticeably to owe much of its inspiration as well as substance to definitions of the creaturely triune mind and its interpretive or "inventive" action as elaborated by Saint Augustine in *De doctrina christiana* and other works, suggests that, in its day, the *[Prima] Pagina Pastorum* was a play whose message was as carefully heeded as the next play in the collection is enjoyed by contemporary audiences. David L. Jeffrey's insightful observation[96] that this pair of plays represents two stages of a dramatic *débat* serves to remind us of the value and complexity of the intellectual dimension of the *[Prima] Pagina Pastorum*. What is more, because it so thoroughly elaborates the configuration of mind that embraces and conforms to authority through memory while engaging memory by intellect and volition, it also raises the question of what other kind of mind might be conceived of, since the cooperative serving of God also involves the technological mastery and proper use of nature. That question is answered, as the next chapter will demonstrate, by the *[Secunda] Pagina Pastorum*, the second of the shepherds' plays included in the Towneley collection.

4

[Secunda] Pagina Pastorum and the "Inventive" Empirical Creaturely Triune Mind

While a theological rather than literary difference between the Towneley collection's two shepherds' plays was identified by Sir E. K. Chambers in his magisterial study of medieval drama nearly a century ago,[1] it has since been demonstrated convincingly that an equally profitable way of critically approaching these dramatic works consists of considering how the two, as alternate versions of the same story,[2] complement each other philosophically. First to do this persuasively as well as instructively was Lois Roney, whose incisive examination of the Wakefield Master's incorporation of the late-medieval scholarly debate—the debate as to which is nobler among the faculties of the human soul, the intellect or the will—as the informing structural principle in these plays has provided a new practical and ethical critical context within which to understand hitherto overlooked differences and similarities between the two plays in terms of characterization, action, theme, and the like.[3]

A modification of this "context" through consideration of the *[Secunda] Pagina Pastorum* as yet another dramatized *allegoria* of the axiomatic medieval mind predisposed to serving God cooperatively by serving itself in the technological mastery and practical use of nature would now seem, however, to be in order, especially in light of several of the conclusions made in the previous chapter concerning the qualities and praxis of the "inventive" speculative creaturely triune mind. Thus, while the *[Prima] Pagina Pastorum* invites the audience to experience the qualitative metaphysical condition of the mind of the active seeker of divine revelation in terms of "inventive" speculative response or interpretive understanding, the *[Secunda] Pagina Pastorum* completes that view of mind, as this chapter will demonstrate, by modifying the "inventive" speculative creaturely triune mind through the addition of a quantitative empirical dimension. In other words, while the first of the shepherds' plays introduces as fundamental to meaningful pastoral hermeneutical performance the Augustinian combination of authority (memory) and reason (intellect and volition) in response to "unknown" and "ambiguous" literal and figurative signs, as well as other interpretive challenges, the Wakefield Master uses the second to complete this *allegoria* of noesis through the addition of the function of sentiency in successfully dealing with all *circumstantiae* of any literal or figurative interpretation, no matter what the actual context may be.[4]

I

While definition and elaboration of the intrinsic "inventive" empirical creaturely triune mind of the active seeker for an understanding of the divine nature in created reality occupies the focus of the last three scenes of the four-scene-long *[Secunda] Pagina Pastorum*,[5] a continued adherence to the Gothic stylistic principle of *concordantia*,[6] as in the case of the *[Prima] Pagina Pastorum* before it, leads the Wakefield Master again to investigate first the noetic, ethical, and spiritual implications of the "uninventive" empirical creaturely triune mind. This investigation for purposes of *claritas* through contrast leads to an expectation that slightly differs from that in the *[Prima] Pagina Pastorum*. The effect of the diminished soul upon the creaturely triune mind here is the same as in the *[Prima] Pagina Pastorum*—that is to say, the mind as it is initially presented is passive and incapable of engaging in any kind of *techne* or art whatsoever—but the emphasis is noticeably altered. While the diminished spirit in this view of mind, configured and staged again by means of the dramatized *allegoria* of pastoral response, continues to adjust the body to the stimuli it receives for the purpose of producing sensations and forming *phantasiae*, what this kind of evoked "uninventive" empirical creaturely triune mind ends up being most prone to producing in its enfeebled and passive condition, as the play's action begins, is not only the expected *phantasmata* of "imaginacioun" but also the memory of sensation itself.

What distinguishes the evocation of the "uninventive" empirical creaturely triune mind through the drama of pastoral response in the two episodes of the *[Secunda] Pagina Pastorum*'s first scene, aside from the startling economy with which it is elaborated,[7] is its regularity and predictability. As each shepherd is introduced and begins his complaint in the first episode, for example, the audience is invited to witness the experiential qualities of sensation, passivity, and "imaginacioun," as well as this particular order of exposition, with only slight modification in its final occurrence. By contemporary dramatic standards such repetitiveness might seem an artistic flaw, even when the matter of some of the qualities differs from shepherd to shepherd. But such is not the case here, since the predictable repetitions resonate each other, reminding the audience, even in the festive theatrical setting of the Corpus Christi pageant wagons and feast-day celebration, of the High Gothic stylistic principles of totality, progressive divisibility or homology, and distinctness[8] they came to expect in the structural design and decoration of the Hall church edifices, such as York Minster or even nearby Wakefield's All Saints, in which they no doubt frequently gathered to worship.

As Primus Pastor (Coll) announces his presence by beginning his complaint,[9] the paradigmatic pattern of the diminished soul's effect upon the "uninventive" empirical creaturely triune mind begins to unfold.[10] The first distinct quality to be noticed in this pattern, evidence itself of the deductive cogency of this repetition, is the memory of sensation. For Coll, this is not a pleasant recollection. To begin, he has nearly suffered the full effect of exposure, the result of his having to be out in the sheep runs at all times of day, in all kinds of inclement weather. In this first example of the dangers of hypothermia to be recorded in medieval drama, Coll acknowledges he is nearly "dold" (inert) as "these weders are [so] cold" (13/1). Some mobility is left in his extremities, but his fingers, he tells the audience, "ar chappyd" (13/6) and his legs, which now "fold" beneath him, do not have their normal strength.[11]

The next distinct quality of mind to be evoked in this sequence is passivity. This state of mind is introduced here, first, through demonstration of a conspicuous lethargy inimical to the pastoral way of life, one reminiscent of the torpor characterizing the shepherds in the first two scenes of the *[Prima] Pagina Pastorum.* Coll admits that he is not as vigilant as one might expect a shepherd to be while tending the flock. In fact, the reason he is suffering so from the cold is that he "nappyd" for a long time out in the fields (13/4) under the lowering elements. His listlessness, Coll suggests, is the consequence of his spirit's not being as robust as it should be. That it has entered into a state of suffering, not from the body, but from itself as it has adjusted itself to the body[12] is attested by Coll's admission, not only of his current loss of will, but also of an incipient despair:

> It is not as I wold,
> For I am al lappyd
> In sorow. (13/7–9)

The mental quality of passivity is also evoked here through reference to the principal contemporary socioeconomic injustice perpetrated against "sely husbandys" like Coll himself. With population declines due to disasters and consequent social upheavals beginning in the previous century with crop failures, loss of townships to the sea through erosion, the sheep murrain, cattle plagues, the Scots invasions, and the Black Death's spread throughout England,[13] and continuing into the fifteenth century as the direct consequence of the Wars of the Roses, St. Albans, and the general lawlessness of the time—a lawlessness most succinctly imaged by the notorious Halifax gibbet[14]—the region witnessed dramatic demographic changes. As more land continued to become available, there arose a new "class" of relatively wealthy landholding Yorkshire farming families that founded dynasties of yeoman and minor gentlemen.[15] Owing to the size of some of these new farms, manorial operations were often, of necessity, largely in the control of "men that ar lordfest" (13/29) rather than the lords themselves, especially in the East and West Ridings.

As a result of these administrative and demographic changes, the way of life to which "husbandys" like Coll were accustomed was irrevocably altered. These new manorial farm administrators or "gentlery-men" (13/26), as Coll identifies them, often reduced or even stopped farm production by causing the "ploghe [to] tary" (13/30). Such a strategy, born either of idleness or of the desire to raise commodity prices, frequently ignored the immediate effect that curtailing production had on the manorial labor force, the agricultural community that still looked to subsistence farming for most of its income. Without access to the fields, these "husbandys" could not even feed themselves and their families. The lengthy list of descriptive terms Coll offers to image exactly the plight he and others like him now have to suffer as the "tylthe" of their "landys / Lyys falow as the floore" (13/20–21) emphasizes resignation and inaction, nearly a complete loss of will. Coll underscores the condition of oppression through bereavement of will in his choice of specific terms emphasizing passivity when he says he and others like him have been forced to become "nerehandys / Outt of the doore" (13/16–17) and

> We ar so hamyd,
> Fortaxed and ramyd,
> We ar mayde handtamyd. (13/23–25)

Passivity also informs one final dramatic expression of the ruinous effect of this subjection. As he observes that the "gentlery-men" have brought "husbandys" like himself "In ponte to myscary / On lyfe" (13/34–35), Coll says that these administrators have held the work force down, as it were, to the point of creating great trouble for all:

> Thus hold thay vs hunder,
> Thus thay bryng vs in blonder;
> It were greatte wonder
> And euer shuld we thryfe. (13/36–39)

The final distinct quality of the "uninventive" empirical creaturely triune mind to be evoked in the first complaint is conceived of by the *phantasma* of "imagined" interaction with the very perpetrator of this oppressive condition—the new farm administrator or "gentlery-man" himself. This extensive creation of "imaginacioun," while the product of a diminished spirit acting on an enfeebled mental condition, nevertheless calls attention instructively to two alarming ways in which the manor farm workforce is currently suffering at the hands of this new class of overseers. The first of these, what would now be considered the theoretical one, consists of the mindless conformity demanded of everyone by the new supervisory authority. A far cry from the reciprocity that once informed the old feudal relation between lord and vassal, this new social compliance is both primitively coerced and absurd. The coercion, Coll points out, inheres in a very real threat of retaliation that now affects everyone working on the manor farm. The "gentlery-men," as the result of their "mantenance" by "men that ar gretter" (13/51–52), now have the power of "purveance."[16] While this entitlement to preempt and requisition is bad enough on its own, since its enactment interrupts the continuity of any agricultural operation, its widespread acceptance and continued implementation have now become insupportable as it is often made use of simply on a whim or as the result of a "boste and bragance" (13/50).

The conformity-insuring absurdity that now is also a reality on the manorial farm, Coll indicates, has arisen from the curtailment of any kind of meaningful dialogue between the "gentlery-men" and the manor farm workforce. Communication has broken down because no one can believe anything that is said by any of these new manorial supervisors, who neither know nor care to know anything of farming or of those who work the fields, and because none of these "gentlery-men" can brook even the slightest challenge or questioning of their decisions:

> Wo is hym that hym grefe
> Or onys agane-says!
> Dar noman hym reprefe,
> What mastry he mays;
> And yit may noman lefe
> Oone word that he says—
> No letter. (13/42–48)

The second way the manor farm workforce is mistreated by the "gentlery-men," what would now be called the actual one as opposed to the theoretical, is dramatized by the Wakefield Master through the *phantasma* of the abuse of purveyance in action. This fantasy involves an imagined encounter with an overseer's serving man or "swane / As prowde as a po" (13/53–54). The act of preemption or requisitioning in this instance, made worse by being delegated to an underling, is the indiscriminate borrowing of a "wane" and "ploghe" (13/55–56). Not only does Coll have to give up the farming technology he is using and so interrupt the workday on the farm but, even more annoying, he also has to feign gladness when accommodating the serving man. In other words, members of the workforce, by being unable to protest the harm done them, suffer insult added to their injury:

> Ther shall com a swane
> As prowde as a po;
> He must borow my wane,
> My ploghe also;
> Then I am full fane
> To graunt or he go.

> Thus lyf we in payne,
> Anger, and wo,
> By nyght and day. (13/53–61)

Worse, "husbandys" like Coll dare not resist or deny the unscheduled requisitioning for fear of severe retaliation:

> He must haue if he langyd,
> If I shuld forgang it;
> I were better be hangyd
> Then oones say hym nay. (13/62–65)

In a sense, then, members of the workforce are bereaved not only of the actual means of farming but also of any reasonable response to the injustice now apparently visited upon them with increasing frequency.

Elaboration of the "uninventive" empirical creaturely triune mind continues to unfold when Secundus Pastor (Gyb) enters the scene. Following the pattern established by Coll—though unaware of Coll's presence off to his side[17]—Gyb calls attention, first, to his memory of sensation. For Gyb too, this recollection is not pleasant. The cold, damp, stormy weather has not only made his eyes water but also made his shoes, at times, freeze to his feet:[18]

> Lord, thyse weders ar spytus
> And the wyndys full kene,
> And the frostys so hydus
> Thay water myn eeyne,
> No ly.
> Now in dry, now in wete,
> Now in snaw, now in slete,
> When my shone freys to my fete
> It is not all esy. (13/83–91)

What distinguishes his response to the alternating meteorological phenomena of dry weather, rain, snow, and sleet, however, is his desire to know what this unpredictable weather may mean. Though he has not fallen asleep on the job the way Coll has, and so has not suffered his pastoral colleague's alleged near frostbite, Gyb is nevertheless unable to explain "Why fares this warld thus" (13/81). What he makes up for in volition, in other words, Gyb seemingly lacks in "divine" intellect or reason.

The second quality of the "uninventive" empirical creaturely triune mind to be evoked in Gyb's complaint follows predictably as Gyb turns his attention to the plight of "sely wedmen" like himself. The oppression that leads to dismay and a subsequent loss of will here is domestic rather than socioeconomic. The passive state of mind directly caused by the marital relation is considered by Gyb in terms of three distinct types of suffering. The first of these is childbearing. This obstetrical reality, one apparently so distasteful to the Wakefield Master that he has to employ the fabulous barnyard exemplum of Sely Copyle to describe it as well as its effect, leads, Gyb suggests figuratively, to a kind of incarceration. As soon as Copyle prepares to give birth, in other words, her barnyard "cok" must suffer "wo," for Copyle's groaning or clucking signals that the barnyard feathered spouse "is in the shakyls" (13/104).[19]

Gyb now introduces a second kind of marriage-induced suffering resulting in a passive state of mind: resignation. While Gyb himself is (somewhat) immune, having learned the lesson that wedmen "Haue not all thare wyll" (13/105–6), others are not so fortunate. Learning that being bound means having to "abyde" (13/116–17), as Gyb describes it, implies two distinct forms of paradoxical compliance. One, the wedman must willingly accept being bereaved of will in responding physically to any annoyance arising in or from the marital relation:

> These men that ar wed
> Haue not all thare wyll;
> When they ar full hard sted,
> Thay sygh full styll. (13/105–8)

Second, the wedman must willingly accept being bereaved of will in responding verbally, even when hard pressed to do so:

> God wayte thay ar led
> Full hard and full yll;
> In bowere nor in bed
> Thay say noght thertyll
> This tyde. (13/109–113)

Gyb now calls attention to a third kind of suffering in marriage leading to passivity, one he says it breaks his heart to witness (13/120): the new conjugal reality, not of serial monogamy, but of polygamy, causing wonder "now late in oure lyfys."[20] This leads to a bereavement of will,

Gyb speculates, simply through the increase in suffering that will occur with quantity. In other words, if having one wife causes "wo," having several will bring even greater debilitating desperation:

> Som ar wo that has any.
> But so far can I:
> Wo is hym that has many,
> For he felys sore. (13/127–30)

The completion of the paradigmatic pastoral complaint here introduces a *phantasma* of a different sort from the one in the first complaint. For Coll, the illusory "gentlery-man" is objectified through consideration of his nature from two distinct analytical perspectives, both of which are presented in the third person; here, however, the *phantasma* involves illusory "yong men" in need of advice concerning marriage and explores yet again the relationship between stage and audience through dramatic methexis. Reminiscent of the asides in the *[Prima] Pagina Pastorum,* and in the *Processus Noe cum filiis* and the *Mactatio Abel* before it, this direct or second-person address to imagined or actual playgoers enables members of the Corpus Christi audience to experience and understand two things simultaneously.[21]

The first is what it is really like to be in a marital relationship that is not to the liking of the "sely wedman." As Gyb begins his rather strident two-stanza denunciation of marriage—admonishing the "yong men" to think twice about "wowyng" and "wedyng" and to understand that what is done in an "owre" may have an effect for a lifetime—members of the actual audience, maneuvered as they are into the experience of the marital condition's passive suffering, will likewise "sygh full styll" since "they ar full hard sted" (13/107–8). In other words, audience members are invited to be participants in a dialogue through the methexis of direct address employed by Gyb, but as soon as the dialogue begins, those same audience members, like the husband in "shakles" previously described, are bereaved not only of voice but of any meaningful response. The assumed dialogue resulting here thus has much the same effect as the monologic dialogue in the *Wife of Bath's Prologue* as Dame Alys launches into the imagined rant against "Sire olde kaynard," the composite old husband consisting of her first three elderly spouses.[22] Like Chaucer's artistic creation, too, this unusual form of dialogue leads to a revelation concerning illusion's consequence, for as Dame Alys concludes that her rant is nothing more than the product of "imaginacioun" when she admits what she "sayde" to her composite husband was all a lie or "fals,"[23] so Gyb's denunciation leads to an understanding of the dislocative and debilitating effect that "imaginacioun" can have on anyone's outlook, as well as life.

What distinguishes the Wakefield Master's artistic creation from Chaucer's is that the audience members discover at this moment the second thing to be experienced and understood here, yet another effect of the *phantasma*: that participation in the imaginative creation requires them willingly to suspend not only their disbelief as they mutely participate in the monologic dialogue but also, as a consequence and by a like act of volition, their belief in the institution and sacrament of marriage—at least until Gyb has concluded his rant with the depiction of his own bleak marital situation. Having to forgo perception of disagreement as well as perception of agreement while realizing they are powerless to change their situation, spectators are thus provided the opportunity to know what it is to be bereft momentarily of both intellect and will. Whereupon, to put this bereavement in perspective, another loss occurs. As they find themselves intellectually and volitionally immobilized by the performance reality of the monologic dialogue, audience members also find their ability to remember compromised. As they mutely participate in the monologic dialogue, in other words, they have no choice but to accept the false or fabulous that Gyb introduces as the truth about his spouse. Even though he manages to sound conventionally authoritative by beginning with an expression one might hear a priest use,[24] his hyperbolic description of his wife—likening her in sharpness of attitude to a "thystyll" and "brere," and in facial appearance and physical size to hog's bristle and whale, respectively—defies any degree of reasonableness, positing an implausibility as plausible:[25]

> For, as euer rede I pystyll,
> I haue oone to my fere
> As sharp as thystyll,
> As rugh as a brere;
> She is browyd lyke a brystyll,
> With a sowre-loten chere;
> Had she oones wett hyr whystyll,
> She couth syng full clere
> Her Paternoster.

> She is as greatt as a whall,
> She has a galon of gall;
> By hym that dyed for vs all,
> I wald I had ryn to I had lost hir! (13/144–56)

The third and final elaboration of the "uninventive" empirical creaturely triune mind in the first scene's first episode follows immediately after Coll and Gyb have encountered each other and inquired after the youngest shepherd, Tercius Pastor (Daw), who has been in a different part of the pasture minding the flock. In this instance, the order but not the substance of the exposition is modified. As Daw, recognized by his pastoral colleagues but unaware of their presence, makes his entry and begins his complaint, he first introduces the established paradigmatic quality of mind of passivity as he calls upon Christ's sacrifice and St. Nicholas to help him in this time of need:

> Crystys crosse me spede,
> And Sant Nycholas!
> Therof had I nede;
> It is wars then it was. (13/170–73)

It is not this entreaty alone that signals a lack of volition, however, though such an impetration would imply the condition exists, at least to a degree. Rather, it is the following explanation for the prayer, the introduction of a modified *contemptus mundi*,[26] that calls attention to Daw's feelings of helplessness and need for aid. For Daw, inaction and dependence upon another are apparently the direct consequence of the world's changing and unpredictable nature, "With meruels mo and mo" (13/180). The only solution in his present circumstances, if divine aid is not forthcoming, is a kind of renunciation in which one abandons everything in the hope of survival:

> Whoso couthe take hede
> And lett the warld pas,
> It is euer in drede
> And brekyll as glas,
> And slythys. (13/174–78)

Daw next calls attention to sensation, in the second part of his complaint, as he likens current meteorological conditions to those experienced by Noah at the time of the Flood.[27] The winds and rains are now so keen, he observes, that those caught out in them unprotected are virtually immobilized. What is distinctive about this kind of weather-induced paralysis, however, is that it is linked with sensation. Shepherds like Daw who are exposed to the winds and rains, in other words, find themselves either staggering or standing "In dowte":[28]

> Was neuer syn Noe floode
> Sich floodys seyn,
> Wyndys and ranys so rude,
> And stormes so keyn
> Som stamerd, som stod
> In dowte, as I weyn. (13/183–88)

The temptation to argue that "dowte" or fear, as it is used here, describes feeling rather than sensation is expected but not justified, since the experience of fear, for the medieval mind, was understood to be the act of the senses shrinking from sensible things.[29]

Daw completes his elaboration of the principal features of the "uninventive" empirical creaturely triune mind by turning attention, like Coll and Gyb before him, to the ever-elusive *phantasma* and its effect. What distinguishes this final pastoral expression of "imaginacioun" is that it reveals the potentially powerful transformative effect that strange and unanticipated combinations of *phantasiae* stored in memory can have upon perception. In this instance, the transformative effect or "sodan syght" consists of what Daw sees or thinks he sees in the dark fields and sheep runs "When othere men slepe" (13/199). As he looks in the direction of Coll and Gyb, for example, he concludes he sees "shrewys pepe" (13/203). This identification of the two older shepherds as "shrewys" and then as "wyghtys" (13/202) provides a moment of ironic humor since it is clear that Coll and Gyb are indeed rascals, who have taken advantage of their younger pastoral colleague by making him do most of the physical labor. But like the performance reality of the *phantasma* of the sheep-turn in the *[Prima] Pagina Pastorum*, it also serves to remind the audience how convincing can be an illusion or the product of "imaginacioun," especially as Daw picks up the pace of his walk and moves his actual sheep in a new direction to avoid the danger he believes lies in wait, threatening both livestock and himself:

> Yit me thynk my hart lyghtys;
> I se shrewys pepe.

> Ye ar two all-wyghtys—
> I wyll gyf my shepe
> A turne.
> Bot full yll haue I ment,
> As I walk on this bent;
> I may lyghtly repent,
> My toes if I spurne. (13/200–208)

The second episode in the first scene reintroduces all of the qualities of the "uninventive" empirical creaturely triune mind in an innovative dramatic way. The first of several dramaturgic tours de force in the play, this episode reminds the audience of the array of these qualities through a sequence consisting of two dramatizations, the complementarity of which establishes what might be considered an inchoate *rahmenerzählung* or play-within-the-play structure.[30] The first of these dramatizations or moments of self-conscious artistic expression involves a performance combination of the form and substance of the first episode's three *phantasmata*. This arises in the encounter between the two older shepherds and Daw at the beginning of the episode. As they confront the youth, who has arrived late and who is now busy turning the sheep away from them, Coll and Gyb assume the role of the "gentlery-men" about whom Coll himself initially complained. No actual preempting or requisitioning occurs here, but both older shepherds demonstrate the transformative effect and methexis of illusion through their convincing expression of the insensitivity typical of the "gentlery-man" who would, on a whim, interrupt farming operations to appropriate a wagon or a plow. Coll reveals this first in his response to Daw's request for food and drink. The irony is not lost here, for his uncharitable act of cursing the young shepherd and calling him a lazy servant (13/213–14) has the same preclusive effect Coll himself complained about in his earlier list of grievances against the administrator's underling who is unwilling to enter into any kind of dialogue with the manor farm workforce. Gyb repeats this kind of insensitivity. On the one hand, he too dismissively and preclusively labels Daw, as one who "raves" or has lost his reason (13/215). On the other, he curses the young shepherd (13/218) and then, after admitting that Coll and he have eaten, offers a specious appeal to reason justifying the rather uncharitable act of not saving any food for Daw, late though Daw may be:

> Abyde vnto syne;
> We haue mayde it,
> Yll thryft on thy pate!
> Though the shrew cam late,
> Yit is he in state
> To dyne—if he had it. (13/216–21)

The second innovative dramatized *allegoria* reminding the audience of qualities of the "uninventive" empirical creaturely triune mind complements the first by demonstrating how the product of "imaginacioun," if not checked by a properly wilful and reasonable response, perpetuates the diminished spirit's effect upon the body and eventually leads to the creation of *phantasmata*. In this instance, what results is partly anticipated and partly not. The former arises in the kinds of suffering to which Daw, like so many other members of his social caste, is subjected. Among these unpleasant experiences, the articulation of which comprises the first stanza of Daw's lengthy response to his older pastoral colleagues, are memories of painful sensations as well as of social injustice. The sensations include hunger pangs,[31] the result of not receiving meals on a regular basis, and physical distress, the result of being "oft weytt and wery" (13/222–26) working in the fields while the "master-men" are asleep. The memory of social injustice involves the loss of wages or delay in receiving remuneration for work completed:

> Bot nately
> Both oure dame and oure syre,
> When we haue ryn in the myre,
> Thay can nyp at oure hyre,
> And pay vs full lately. (13/230–34)

The unanticipated result of the unchecked "imaginacioun," likewise, arises in the articulated *phantasma* of defiance. This challenge to authority, comprising the second stanza of Daw's response and the remainder of the scene's second episode, possesses two parts, the combination of which assures the audience of the illusory nature of the challenge itself. It begins with a work and wage statement, in which Daw introduces the new "trouth" or belief concerning output in relation to the amount of food he receives. He threatens that little work will result if only meager "fayr" is provided:

> Bot here my trouth, master:
> For the fayr that ye make,
> I shall do therafter—
> Wyrk as I take.
> I shall do a lytyll, syr,
> And emang euer lake,
> For yit lay my soper
> Neuer on my stomake
> In feyldys. (13/235–43)

This threatened work slowdown is followed by yet another challenge as Daw observes he has no reason to "threpe" or haggle over the terms of his work since he can easily abandon his current servitude simply by running away (13/244–45). Daw's reminder to Coll and Gyb that they get what they pay for, the conclusion to the consequent *phantasma* of defiance, recapitulates the point of these two threats aphoristically, driving home, as it were, the lesson to be learned about the effect of exploitive servitude.

Convincing and alarming as the expression of seditious defiance presented here may be, its being nothing more than a performance reality illusion consisting of strange and unanticipated combinations of *phantasiae* retrieved from the memory—that is, its being an illusion consisting of nothing more than sound's fury symbolizing nothing—is adroitly revealed by the second part of this *phantasma* as Coll and Gyb quickly and easily put down this potential pastoral uprising by silencing Daw. Suggesting that the youngest shepherd's words are not those of sedition but rather the kind one might expect from a lover wooing, Coll effectively and nearly jokingly dismisses the *phantasma* of defiance by transforming it into a socially acceptable form that someone like himself is not in a position to consider the merits of, since he has nothing to offer in the way of a dowry:

> Thou were an yll lad
> To ryde on wowyng
> With a man that had
> Bot lytyll of spendyng. (13/248–51)

Gyb's response is less subtle than Coll's, but the result is the same. His characterization of Daw's threat as nothing more than chatter and tricks to be scorned (13/252–257) dispels the seditious pronouncement so effectively that, by the time he is done, normative order is reestablished. This is not necessarily a good thing, as Daw's subsequent admission concerning the location of the flock raises the possibility of trespass.[32] But at least the danger of treacherous defiance has been shown, in this instance, to be nothing more than the fleeting product of "imaginacioun" and not an actuality. Enfeebled though the spirit of each of them may be, the three shepherds, in other words, are not entirely bereft of will, intellect, or memory. What is more, while the harmony they achieve collectively as they start their three-part song at the end of the first scene does not even begin to approximate the complexity of harmony they achieve later in the play in their response to the *Gloria*,[33] it nevertheless demonstrates a marked improvement over the initial condition of the suffering of the soul expressed in each of their earlier complaints.

II

These initial signs of the shepherds' transformation at the end of the play's first scene ready the audience for the next sequence of events, the most famous in all of medieval British drama, a sequence that follows immediately with Mak's entrance. The arrival of this comic or farcical character[34] signals a fundamental change in the play as well as in the outlook of the shepherds, as the *[Secunda] Pagina Pastorum*'s second scene turns into a new kind of pastoral celebration or interaction. Here is no "Grotesque Feast." Rather, this drama of pastoral response, through a feast of intellectual grotesqueries, explores not only what constitutes the "inventive" empirical creaturely triune mind, but also what the hermeneutical effect and ethical value of such a mind may be, especially as that mind interpretively engages the world about it and the *signa* it encounters through that engagement.

Like that implicitly introduced in the *[Prima] Pagina Pastorum*, this dramatized *allegoria* of mind reflects the Image of God in terms of the "divinity" of its creaturely triune nature. In other words, this mind, as evoked here within the deep structure of the play, is the kind of mind that can engage in and utilize the *techne* or practical art of the *modus interpretandi* in analysis by separation and analysis by examination because it consists of "divine" intellect, volition, and memory, and also because it is acted upon by a living or robust spirit. This new conceptual configuration of mind is distinguished from the "inventive" speculative creaturely triune mind elaborately evoked in the *[Prima] Pagina Pastorum*, however, by its inclusion of sentiency. It works, then, not only through reason and authority but also through experiment or by "preve," to repeat a term the malcontent Froward will use in the *regenall* in the play titled the *Coliphizacio* (21/558), the last of the plays attributed to the Wakefield Master. That is, the conception of mind introduced by the *[Secunda] Pagina Pastorum's* second scene establishes an emotional basis for the objective investigation of nature and so shifts the focus of concern from a noesis informed by a hierarchical-qualitative *scientia*—or the noesis of tradition and authority—to that informed by an egalitarian-quantitative *scientia*—or the noesis of modernity.[35]

The second scene or "Pastoral Perscrutations" fosters this new outlook by turning attention to the features and praxis of the "inventive" empirical creaturely triune mind through sets of encounter/investigations or "perscrutations," to use the medieval term,[36] that occupy the focus of both of the scene's episodes. The first episode, "The Pretentious Impersonation," establishes the pattern by which this kind of mind is to be considered. Reminding the audience of the second and third episodes of the *[Prima] Pagina Pastorum's* "Annunciation" scene, this episode begins by examining the features and praxis of the "inventive" empirical creaturely triune mind in response to the *circumstantia* of the "unknown literal."[37] The influence of *De doctrina christiana* is again notable on conceptualization of mind, but the principles governing hermeneutical pastoral performance are not incorporated here the same way as in the previous play, owing to the emphasis on sentiency that distinguishes this kind of mind.

For example, the *circumstantia* of the "unknown literal" is clarified for the audience at this point, as soon as Mak stops singing and starts speaking, which marks the beginning of the comic subplot of the play. It is instructive that his first observations call attention to how he himself embodies the condition of the diminished or enfeebled spirit that the shepherds, through complaint or reaction, evoke in the play's first scene. Mak is, in other words, a performance-reality living personification of the condition the shepherds have temporarily suffered but do not wish to continue being subjected to. What distinguishes Mak's acknowledgment of this condition of spirit is his personification of the thoroughness of its effect on the mind. This is already noticeable in Mak's initial identification of God, and of his own relationship to the deity. As he begins to speak, Mak evidences spiritual estrangement in terms of faulty memory. He calls out not to the god found in Christian literature but rather to the god of rabbinical tradition:[38]

> Now, Lord, for thy naymes vii,
> That made both moyn and starnes
> Well mo then I can neuen,
> Thi will, Lorde, of me tharnys. (13/274–77)

Further evidencing this effect, Mak next exhibits faulty intellect or reason, suggesting that his being at odds with himself is the principal motivating force affecting mind:

> I am all vneuen;
> That moves oft my harnes. (13/278–79)

Mak then articulates a final effect of the diminished or enfeebled spirit upon the mind as he admits he is bereft of his own volition. When Coll asks him to identify himself, Mak points to this absence as a distinguishing feature of his present state:

> Wold God ye wyst how I foore!
> Lo, a man that walkys on the moore
> *And has not all his wyll.* (13/284–86; emphasis mine)

Elucidation of the features and praxis of the "inventive" empirical creaturely triune mind in response to this elaborate *circumstantia*—this first part, that is, of this feast of intellectual grotesqueries—unfolds in a sequential process consisting of sensory response preceding and, eventually, inciting mental process in such a way as to evoke engagement of the *modus interpretandi* for the purpose of dealing effectively with Mak's "mak-ness," this unexpected *circumstantia* of ethical and spiritual "unevenness." The first sense to be introduced here is hearing. Right away, a degree of error is evidenced: Mak's discordant contribution to the shepherds' rudimentary pastoral harmonizing startles the shepherds as much as it must the audience. But this particular sense does not prove strong enough to afford immediate understanding or even identification of the source of this cacophonous "unknown literal." Coll is limited to asking who it is that "pypys so poore" (13/283).

The next sense to be introduced is sight. When this occurs, error is quickly eliminated. The acuteness of visual recognition, which involves memory, is partly responsible. So are the other features of the "inventive" empirical creaturely triune mind, for as soon as the memory is called upon, the intellect and volition are aroused and the process of analysis inevitably begins. This first instance of the praxis of this conception of mind in the form of the *modus interpretandi* involves, in Hugh of St. Victor's words, distinguishing "from one another things which are mingled together."[39] This mental act of discernment and separation is articulated in Gyb's identification of Mak by name, and furthered by his request of Mak to offer news of his doings:

> Mak, where has thou gone?
> Tell vs tythyng. (13/287–88)

After this rudimentary analysis by separation, evocation of the entire mental process implicit in the *modus interpretandi* is completed as Daw joins the dialogue with a rudimentary analysis by examination. He "opens up things which are hidden,"[40] in other words, by offering a humorous but cautionary observation about Mak's nature, the gist of which is that no one's belongings are safe with Mak around:

> Is he commen? Then ylkon
> Take hede to his thyng. (13/289–90)

The stage direction *Et accipit clamidem ab ipso* that immediately follows, interestingly enough, offers a complementary enacted imaging of the opening up of things which are hidden, for when the cloak covering Mak's tunic is removed—a cloak Mak has appeared in to create the illusion of being someone he is not—the actual Mak is revealed.

The second perscrutation of the first episode's set of encounter/investigations, directly following this revelation, introduces the more challenging *circumstantia* of the "unknown figurative." Here Mak makes sudden innovative use of the literal sign of his being the king's "yoman," with its figurative meaning of a degree of social importance and distinction, articulated in hopes of precluding further inquiry into his presence and purpose. This impersonation through the self-serving manipulation of an official signifier, though lacking the visual support that the cloak-disguise was intended to provide, is momentarily convincing. Its believability is the consequence of two distinct but complementary elements—the actual roleplaying as yeoman, and a linguistic manipulation that furthers the impersonation. The former includes the expression of two aspects of the abusive attitude associated with the more active and officious underlings of the ruling caste, underlings such as the "gentlerymen" about whom Coll has complained. In the first of these behavioral stereotypes, Mak demonstrates arrogance as he stops the pastoral analysis with a rhetorical interjection to identify himself as a member of officialdom. In doing this, he reveals a pride in himself as he calls attention to his social rank and function. Not only a "yoman" to the king, he is, he adds peremptorily, a messenger to "a greatt lordyng" (13/294). Mak also evidences the disdain usually associated with such arrogance as he directs at the shepherds a contemptuous "Fy on you!" (13/296) before ordering Coll, Gyb, and Daw from his presence and reminding them of the "reuerence" due one of his social station.

The other abusive behavioral stereotype of the ruling-caste underling to be expressed here follows the shepherds' first reply to Mak's feigned superiority as Mak attempts to coerce submission through his position's inherent power. Again, to preclude further scrutiny of his presence and purpose, Mak threatens the shepherds that he has only to utter "a worde" about what they have done and the consequence will be a thrashing:

> Ich shall make complaynt,
> And make you all to thwang
> At a worde,
> And tell euyn how ye doth. (13/307–10)

The second way Mak's impersonation is made more credible is through the manipulation of language and intonation. This linguistic manipulation is apparent in Mak's incorporation of several Southernisms in his speech. The first-person-singular pronoun "ich" alerts the audience to this dialectical strategy. Several other expressions or terms foster the illusion, among them the imperative "Goyth hence" and the indicative "doth" (13/296 and 309).[41]

The combination of this prestige language, only just suggestive as it may be,[42] with the strutting and fretting pejoratively associated with the ruling-caste underling creates a *circumstantia* to challenge even the most incisive and effective hermeneutical response. Unlike in the first perscrutation, however, a sequence of sensory activity is not necessary here to incite mental response, as Mak already occupies a position in the shepherds' visual field. Nevertheless, the strategy employed by the shepherds does not forget the elusiveness of the "unknown figurative" before them. In their response, the shepherds do two things to reveal the truth momentarily obscured by the impersonation. One is to evidence a knowledge of the thing before them.[43] This is done in three ways. First, all three shepherds repeatedly identify Mak by his given name: everyone is reminded of Mak, as "Mak" is repeated five times in this sequence (13/301, 302, 310, 313, and 315). Next, Gyb reminds everyone of Mak's reputation as a thief (13/321–25) and Daw aphoristically likens Mak to the devil (13/332–33). Then shortly afterward, toward the end of the perscrutation, Coll inquires about Mak's wife, Gyll. This may seem an act of politeness; concern, in fact, is even suggested by Coll's repeated inquiry

> How farys thi wyff? By thi hoode,
> How farys she? (13/339–40)

But the actual reason for this brief display of emotional interest is that part of Mak's "mak-ness" is the presence of his spouse. The knowing of Mak, in other words, is not complete without the knowing of Gyll, who, as Mak relates it, is as much a creature of appetite as he is (13/341–64).[44]

The second thing of which the shepherds demonstrate knowledge here is language. Not only do they know the thing, they know the words associated *with* the thing. At first, they refer to the linguistic dimension of the *circumstantia* in general terms. Coll, for example, questions why Mak makes it so "qwaynt" (13/300). Gyb, likewise, says, "lyst ye saynt? / I trow that ye lang" (13/302–3). And Daw refers to Mak's ability, in his impersonation, to make specious use of words—that is, to "paynt" (13/304). In the second reply to Mak, however, the response becomes more specific. All three shepherds, as we have noted, call Mak by name. What is more, Coll identifies the dialect employed by Mak as Southern, and then follows that identification with an obscene denunciation:

> Bot, Mak, is that sothe?
> Now take outt that Sothren tothe,
> And sett in a torde! (13/310–13)

Further denunciations and even threats follow as Gyb and Daw speak, but the effect is the same. The purpose of identification and threat is to make the actual presence, as well as the linguistic dimension of the "unknown figurative," a known actual and literal. Coll's final question to Mak in this sequence, "Can ye now mene you?" (13/320), provides closure as well as an epigrammatic expression, interestingly enough, of the object of this process of interpretation and demystification.

The shepherds' sudden fatigue—they nearly collapse, one after the other, almost as if they were puppets—may seem, at least to the contemporary sensibility, an awkward transition, if not simply bad drama, but for the medieval Corpus Christi audience, it would have made sense, since the *circumstantiae* of both the "unknown literal" and the "unknown figurative" comprising "The Pretentious Impersonation" are, by this point, successfully expounded, bringing the first set of perscrutations to its anticipated conclusion while providing one more opportunity, in terms of hermeneutical pastoral response, to assert the value of knowing the thing, as Daw, the last of the shepherds to fall asleep, insists that Mak lie down with Coll and Gyb and himself. Though the mental activity that brings on sleep at the end of the "Grotesque Feast" in the *[Prima] Pagina Pastorum* is certainly qualitatively different from the mental activity demonstrated here in this intellectual feast of grotesqueries, their effects, the Wakefield Master appears ready to remind his audience, are remarkably similar. Though ethically and spiritually the opposite of imagining, thinking is similarly, if not equally, physically taxing.

III

While closure is achieved in one sense at the end of "The Pretentious Impersonation" or the first episode of the *[Secunda] Pagina Pastorum*'s second scene, especially as the shepherds and Mak prepare to sleep, in another sense it is not. Mak's prayer, though associated with this transition to sleep, signals also the introduction of the principal defining element of the next set of *circumstantiae* to be scrutinized, again by perscrutation, in the next episode. As the shepherds doze off and the transition into "The Deceptive Nativity" is completed, the audience is introduced for the first time to the "ambiguous literal."

The evocation of this challenging hermeneutical *circumstantia* is elaborated in two principal ways. The first of these involves the deployment of two preliminary instances of uncertainty in the first part of "The Parodic Nativity" or "The Set-Up"—instances that are not only memorable but also quite instructive concerning the linguistic and anthropological depth of the Wakefield Master's dramatic art. The initial uncertainty or "ambiguous literal" here arises in terms of the subtle and momentary subject-object confusion created by Mak's innovative modification of Christ's last words on the cross, the Lucan prayer *"in manus tuas commendo spiritum meum"* (23:46). Mak's version following Daw's last utterance, *"Manus tuas commendo, / Poncio Pilato"* (13/384–85) or "I commend thy hands to Pontius Pilate," as Stevens and Cawley have observed about the line, is not an instance of Mak's commending himself to the "untender mercies" of Pontius Pilate.[45] But nor is it entirely, as they contend, a blasphemous parody in which Mak elliptically commends Christ into the hands of Judea's Roman procurator.[46] In this instance, Christ is neither the direct object nor the subject of the declaration, though a Christological resonance is certainly evoked by the line's source. Rather, the antecedent of the fourth-declension feminine accusative plural *"manus tuas,"* in this instance and according to the dramatic logic of the scene, is Daw, the last of the shepherds to speak to Mak and the only one of the three possessing, it should be remembered, enough presence of mind to order Mak to sleep where he might be easily controlled. Accordingly, by suggesting that the youngest and most astute of the shepherds suffer the same fate that Christ does at the hands of Pontius Pilate, Mak's modification of the line has the effect of transforming Mak himself, if only momentarily, into one of the priests and elders in the gospel story that turn Christ over to the authorities. He identifies himself, in other words, with the Pharisaic problem rather than the Christian solution. Clearly, as the divergence in critical response to this odd initial prayer demonstrates,[47] much uncertainty is created by the incorporation of the unanticipated grammatical form, which requires nothing less than a concerted effort to construe its meaning.

Such effort is also necessary to make sense out of the next preliminary contribution to the episode's evolving complex *circumstantia* of the "ambiguous literal." This too is offered in the initial "Set-Up" by Mak, who, having now arisen and moved (presumably) to one side of the shepherds, begins preparation for casting the night spell. Not wanting his unbridled appetite to be discovered and restrained, Mak creates the illusion of having mastery of the necromantic arts to help him carry out his plan of stealing a sheep. He draws a circle around the sleeping shepherds while performing what appears to be an incantatory suffumigation in the form of a few "good wordys":

Bot abowte you a serkyll

> As rownde as a moyn,
> To I haue done that I wyll,
> Tyll that it be noyn,
> That ye lyg stone-styll
> To that I haue doyne;
> And I shall say thertyll
> Of good wordys a foyne:
> 'On hight,
> Ouer youre heydys, my hand I lyft.
> Outt go youre een! Fordo youre syght!'
> Bot yit I must make better shyft
> And it be right. (13/400–412)

The hope here is that the various parts of the rite will have the combined effect of impairing the shepherds' senses, at least until noon of the next day. None of this so-called magic is necessary, of course, since the shepherds are, by their own admission, exceptionally fatigued from being "forwakyd" and "cold and nakyd" and "forrakyd," and from having to respond interpretively in the first set of perscrutations to the *circumstantiae* of the "unknown literal" and the "unknown figurative" embodied by Mak. But even if the magic were needed, the situation is made startlingly comical, as well as decidedly ambiguous, by the fact that Mak's casting of the spell appears to be contrary to conventional necromantic wisdom and practice. Antonius de Monte Ulmi points out, for example, in his influential late-fourteenth-century treatise *De occultis et manifestis*[48] that the magic circle cast by the necromancer is made around himself, not around some other person or thing he wishes to influence. The reason for this distinction and orientation to self is that the spell is supposed to protect and empower the one who makes the invocation. Lynn Thorndike's gloss of Ulmi's discussion of the circle clarifies this distinction:

> The magic circle is made to safeguard the invoker and his associates from the attacks of spirits. The circle is so employed because it is the most perfect and capacious figure and a symbol of the prime mover. It keeps off the spirits because the names of God are written on it by the exorciser with great devotion and contrition.... The circle and those within it should be suffumigated with consecrated words and

Christian prayers.[49]

Who it is exactly that is benefitting from Mak's apparently confused exercise of the necromantic arts in this instance, thus, is left unclear. This ambiguity is something the play never addresses, though; luckily for Mak, the shepherds do not awaken until after his return from hiding the stolen sheep.

Such a coincidence works as much to the Wakefield Master's advantage as to Mak's, for the return from concealing the nabbed "fatt shepe" introduces the culmination of the second and more extensive way in which the challenging hermeneutical *circumstantia* of the "ambiguous literal " is evoked in the play. Before this portion of the evocation there is a sequence of actions that repeatedly reminds the audience of uncertainty. Mak, for example, remarks earlier in the episode how soundly the shepherds are sleeping, then makes his way to the herd to choose his "fatt shepe" and steals the animal at the end of the first part of "The Set-Up"—a fact of which the audience is fully aware, their role as witnesses to the act presumed by their play performance attendance. Yet as he makes off with his ill-gotten gains, Mak identifies the theft as "borrowing" (13/425).[50] The disappearance of the animal thus introduces an ambiguity about an actual or literal thing, and that ambiguity is made even more enigmatic by an authorial characterization, biased as it may be, of the theft's being an act to which no criminality should be attached.

The next incident in this second part of the scene's sequential evocation of the *circumstantia* of the "ambiguous literal" follows this instance of, as it were, adroit medieval public relations disinformation as Mak, with sheep in hand, reaches the door of Gyll's and his dwelling and calls out to Gyll to let him in. Mak, now a felon, does not want to be seen and held accountable for the disappearance of the sheep, or simply for being where he should not be at an hour when most are safely within their own dwellings. The "ambiguous literal" in this second part of "The Set-Up," of course, is now embodied by Mak himself, since Gyll does not know who it is knocking at the door:

Who makys sich dyn
This tyme of the nyght?
I am sett for to spyn;
I hope not I myght

> Ryse a penny to wyn,
> I shrew them on hight! (13/428–33)

This embodying of ambiguity, while possibly reminding the audience of Mak's earlier self-description of "unevenness," is quickly superseded, however, by yet another like embodiment of the "ambiguous literal" once Gyll, now fully informed of the theft, persuades Mak that he cannot eat the sheep right away but must bide his time until it is safe to do so. While Mak's desire is to appease his physical appetite immediately since he has not had such a craving for "shepe-mete" in a "twelmothe," Gyll's "bowrde" or strategy to conceal the stolen sheep makes more sense than being found out, and so Mak follows her lead. What is distinctive about this reintroduction of the "ambiguous literal" or, in Gyb's later words, this instance of "hee frawde," is the complexity of its construction as it is deployed before the audience.

The elaboration of this final "ambiguous literal" is the culmination, in a sense, of all previous instances of the "ambiguous literal" in this initial part of the scene's second episode because it consists, on the one hand, of an actual or physical dimension, such as the purloined sheep or Mak himself, and of a nonactual or abstract dimension, such as the prayer and subsequent night spell, on the other.[51] The latter dimension is the more extensively developed here, partly because of the durational nature of drama itself, but mostly because assertion of the abstract creates an expectation that orients perception of the actual.

One way the Wakefield Master thus adjusts perception in Mak and Gyll's favor in "The Set-Up's" third part is by considering the abstract or generic in terms of a well-known medieval convention, the dream-vision—here Mak's dream-vision of a "knaue-childe's" birth, the dream-vision he collusively tells Gyll he will fraudulently recount (13/486–88), and the one he claims has just "flayd" him on awakening in the presence of the shepherds:

> I thoght Gyll began to crok
> And trauell full sad,
> Wel-ner at the fyrst cok,
> Of a yong lad
> For to mend oure flok.
> Then be I neuer glad;

> I haue tow on my rok
> More then euer I had.
> A, my heede!
> A house full of yong tharmes,
> The dewill knok outt thare harnes!
> Wo is hym has many barnes,
> And therto lytyll brede. (13/556–68)

The recounting of this "sweyven," a *visio* or direct, literal prevision of the future,[52] adds credibility to the disguise and impersonation eventually used to deceive the shepherds.[53] It does this in two ways. First, it anticipatorily invests the disguised sheep with the authority implicit in medieval dream-vision convention itself. This act of revalorization creates the presumption of there being an infant in the cradle. Second and more important, it introduces, also in an anticipatory way, a circumstance that can possibly be confirmed. Such an eventuality, of course, does occur when the shepherds come looking for their missing sheep. As they confront Mak, their only suspect, the door is opened, as it were, for Mak to demonstrate the validity of the previously acknowledged *visio*, which almost—though certainly erroneously—takes the appearance of a proof:

> Well qwytt is my hyre—
> My dreme, this is itt—
> A seson.
> I haue barnes, if ye knew,
> Well mo then enewe;
> Bot we must drynk as we brew,
> And that is bot reson. (13/718–24)[54]

The second way perspective is reoriented or readjusted is by deploying the abstract "ambiguous literal" in a series of contextual emphases. Most noticeable among these in the episode is inclusion in the action of three concurrent and complementary modes of discourse. The first mode involves direct performative contributions to the impersonation and disguise. One instance of this arises in the episode's fourth part or "The Encounter" as Gyll prepares Mak for his role as father by instructing him to sing "lullay" while she makes postparturient groans. As she increases their frequency, she adds, Mak is to increase the tempo of the lullaby:[55]

> Com and make redy all,
> And syng by thyn oone;
> Syng 'lullay' thou shall,
> For I must grone,
> And cry outt by the wall
> On Mary and Iohn
> For sore.
> Syng 'lullay' on fast
> When thou heris at the last,
> And bot I play a fals cast
> Trust me no more. (13/636–46)

The purpose of this strange cacophony is to evoke the reality of postnatal parental response, a reality that, again, presupposes and thereby further establishes the presence of a newborn in the shepherds' cognition.

A second instance of direct performative contribution also implying the existence of an infant—an instance innovatively introduced by Mak himself—likewise involves postparturiency. As the shepherds enter Mak and Gyll's dwelling in "The Encounter," Mak urges the visitors to speak softly so as not to disturb a woman still ailing from the arduous experience of childbirth:

> As far as ye may,
> Good, spekys soft,
>
> Ouer a seke womans heede
> That is at maylleasse.
> I had leuer be dede
> Or she had any dyseasse. (13/697–702)

By asking the shepherds to alter their behavior by quieting down, Mak demonstrates the degree of conjugal concern and commitment that would be expected of one who has just become a father. This concern, in yet another innovative way, collaterally implies the presence of the newborn itself, the arrival of whom has caused the "maylleasse" of the mother, Gyll, and the consequent need for the paternal expression of sympathy, especially to relieve the spouse's suffering.

The effect of the second concurrent mode of discourse complementing the two direct performative contributions just mentioned is noticeable in this part of the episode, too, though the mode's orientation is less direct. This mode of discourse, one that is more *about* than a direct contribution *to* the disguise and impersonation, differs in focus, its purpose being to maintain and assure the credibility of the disguise. The first instance of the effect of this complementary mode of discourse arises later in "The Encounter" as Mak challenges the shepherds to ransack the house if they suspect Gyll and him of thievery (13/742–46). The challenge does not dissuade the shepherds, who are intent upon finding some evidence of their missing sheep. But it does not undermine the fraud, either, it being the expression of a calculated risk that subsequently works in Mak and Gyll's favor. Indeed, when no evidence of the missing sheep turns up, the fact that the challenge was made in the first place adds directly to the exoneration of Mak on the one hand, while indirectly reaffirming the credibility of Gyll's impersonation and the sheep's disguise on the other.

Another instance of this second mode of discourse's effect is noticeable here as Mak first chastizes the shepherds for intruding in his household and then chastizes Gyll for becoming distraught over that intrusion. Equally severe are the criticisms Mak levels at the visitors and at his wife, and in both cases it furthers the credibility of the deception. He shames the shepherds, not for having assumed Gyll's and his guilt, though that is the subtextual implication, but for having ignored the reality of Gyll's postparturiency:

> Wyst ye how she had farne,
> Youre hartys wold be sore.
> Ye do wrang, I you warne,
> That thus commys before
> To a woman that has farne—
> Bot I say no more. (13/766–71)

Likewise, he sternly silences Gyll not simply for having reacted as she has to the intrusion, though he acknowledges this has been decidedly annoying, but rather, in part, because she has gotten dangerously close to revealing the truth by overacting, even making a hyperbolic asseveration that mentions eating the child, and in part because he wishes to reinforce the illusion of being a caring spouse who would want to help his wife regain her equanimity—a transformation that not only quiets and soothes her emotions but also relieves his:[56]

> Peasse, woman, for Godys payn,
> And cry not so!
> Thou spyllys thy brane

And makys me full wo. (13/777–80)

The effect of a final concurrent mode of discourse complementing the direct and indirect performative contributions to the impersonation and disguise is faintly detectable here in "The Encounter" as well. This emphasis completes the deployment of the abstract "ambiguous literal" in this part of the episode by offering information that is correlated to the disguise and impersonation. Such existential contextual emphasis first arises as Mak greets the recently arrived shepherds and inquires why they appear to "ayl." The inquiry allows Mak to demonstrate sympathy while establishing a fraternal solidarity with the shepherds, something Mak is ready to do for the simple practical purpose of diverting their attention from him, as well as from the object of their search, the swaddled sheep:

Syrs, drynkys!
Had I bene thore,
Som shuld haue boght it full sore. (13/733–35)

The second instance of an existential mode of discourse arises shortly afterward and concludes "The Encounter," after the shepherds have turned up nothing that establishes either Mak and Gyll's guilt or the whereabouts of the missing sheep. While Gyb rather sheepishly apologizes for the accusation he and his two brethren have made against Mak by declaring Mak's inclusion in their friendship, Mak replies with a "thanks-but-no-thanks" valediction—

We? Now I hald for me,
For mendys gett I none.
Fare well, all thre!—
All glad were ye gone (13/818–21)

—that not only asserts his independence but also functions as another way of turning attention from him as well as from the disguised sheep and postparturiency impersonation. By cutting himself off from the shepherds, in other words, Mak hopes to benefit from the distance such separation implies.

While the abstract dimension of the "ambiguous literal" creates an expectation that orients perception of the actual, the deployment of the actual itself in terms of disguise and impersonation is also necessary to the furtherance of the *circumstantia*'s credibility. Of the two, disguise is the less elaborately developed element of the actual features of the "ambiguous literal" for obvious reasons. Impersonation is more complex in its deployment, though not as much as the generic effects of the contextual emphases' modes of discourse, the means by which the audience is repeatedly reminded of the abstract and its function in regard to orienting the perception of the actual disguise and impersonation. Gyll's contribution to this aspect of the "ambiguous literal" consists of two things and completes the deployment of the *circumstantia*.[57] The first of these is the plan to create the object of the "ambiguous literal" itself. Gyll introduces this in the second part of "The Set-Up" in two ways. The first, she informs Mak, involves the procedure by which she will disguise the sheep:

> I accorde me thertyll;
> I shall swedyll hym right
> In my credyll.
> If it were a gretter slyght,
> Yit couthe I help tyll.
> I wyll lyg downe stright.
> Com hap me. (13/622–28)

The second is the intended impersonation of the postparturient. Here, as we have seen, Gyll instructs Mak in the way in which he is to sing the lullaby while she groans. While the song is to become louder and faster, what is more important is her assurance, in her final boast, that she will play her part as convincingly as the circumstance warrants. This statement of intention galvanizes the will and sets the construction of the "hee frawde" in motion.

The second thing Gyll contributes to the actual dimension of the *circumstantia* of the "ambiguous literal" is the execution of the plan she has outlined in the second part of "The Set-Up." The execution consists of two responses by Gyll at different moments during "The Encounter" when one or all of the shepherds begin to get too close to her and the swaddled sheep. The first moment comes when the three shepherds enter Mak and Gyll's dwelling. At that decisive instant Gyll exclaims, not only to reassert Mak's appeal for quiet and sympathy, which implicitly reacknowledges the presence of the newborn, but also to limit the shepherds' field of inquiry, which cannot be allowed to include a close approach to the cradle for obvious reasons:

> Go to anothere stede!
> I may not well qweasse;
> Ich fote that ye trede
> Goys thorow my nese
> So hee. (13/703–7)

The second moment occurs approximately sixty lines later, toward the end of "The Encounter," as Coll, aphoristically reminding Mak of his larcenous tendencies, moves apparently too close to the truth, both verbally and physically. Gyll again exclaims, this time using two expletives—"I swelt!" (13/759) and, later, "A, my medyll!" (13/772)—that are more dramatic and emotionally charged than "Go to anothere stede," the first expletive in this sequence. What follows each exclamation is intended, again, to limit the pastoral field of inquiry. The circumscribing of Coll's perception, in particular, is effected each time here through the absurdity that inheres in the ironic audacity of each rejoinder made. In the first instance, Gyll's rejoinder to Coll's intimation of Mak's guilt is an impugning of the shepherds' motives. As she continues to exclaim, Gyll denounces the shepherds as thieves who have come to rob Mak and her:

> Outt, thefys, fro my wonys!
> Ye com to rob vs for the nonys. (13/760–61)

The absurdity of Gyll's audacious stance introduces a dramatic irony that cannot be ignored despite Mak's nearly concurrent "contextual" attempt to elicit a sympathetic response "To a woman that has farne" (13/770). In the second instance Gyll's rejoinder, reaffirming her innocence by exaggeratedly alleging she would eat her own newborn were she guilty of gulling the shepherds, introduces a cannibalistic absurdity that would cause anyone within earshot to hesitate:

> A, my medyll!
> I pray to God so mylde,
> If euer I you begyld,
> That I ete this chylde
> That lygys in this credyll. (13/772–76)

The cumulative effect of these actual contributions to the "hee frawde," artfully combined with the perception-orienting abstract contributions to the *circumstantia* of the "ambiguous literal" that are carefully paced and incrementally introduced, results in an interpretive challenge far exceeding in complexity that posed by "The Pretentious Impersonation."

IV

With a dramatic construction as elaborate as the one establishing this initial part of "The Deceptive Nativity," nothing less than the most astute hermeneutical pastoral response—that is, nothing less than an act of perception involving the combination of the speculative creaturely triune mind and the full engagement of sentiency buttressed by the memory of the thing as well as the language or words associated with the thing—would be expected or called for here. And such is nearly what the shepherds achieve in three distinct ways as they awaken to engage in the scene's second set of perscrutations for the purpose of discovering their missing sheep. While the shepherds demonstrate a rigor and exactitude in what they do and say in response to Mak and Gyll, a flaw in their thinking vitiates each conclusion at which they arrive in this part of the episode as they try to unravel the tangled web of the "ambiguous literal." None of this is accidental, of course. All of it, in fact, is intended, not only to provide this scene's unique comedy, but also to prepare the audience for a correction in the hermeneutical pastoral response that eventually must be made in preparation for dealing with the final *circumstantia*, the "ambiguous figurative," the introduction of which concludes the second scene.

The first encounter/investigation, thus, begins in "The Set-Up's" third part as Daw, the last of the shepherds to wake, inquires hastily and somewhat nervously after Mak's whereabouts. This is immediately explained as he begins to recount the dream he has just had concerning the theft of a sheep from the flock. The dream, a *somnium* according to medieval dream psychology, featured Mak who, disguised in a "wolfe-skyn," quietly trapped a "fatt shepe" with a "gyn" and made off with it (13/530–37).[58] Daw's readiness now to accuse this wolf-in-wolf's-clothing, a consequence of the dream experience itself, is predicated as much upon his assumption in the previous episode about Mak's ethics as it is upon the assumed credibility of dream-vision authority. The subsequent acknowledgment by Coll of Mak's presence among the shepherds, however, refutes by means of ocular proof both that authority and Daw's previous assumption, which has led, as we have seen, to the interpretive consequence—the inference of Mak's guilt. As Coll subsequently corrects Daw by suggesting, on the one hand, that his mind has been enfeebled by the dream—

> Be styll!
> Thi dreme makys the woode (13/538–39)

—and by identifying the dream, on the other, as a "fantom" (13/540)—that is, an example of the *visum* of medieval dream convention—the irony the audience is invited to enjoy and appreciate arises, not in or as the result of Daw's reliance upon dream-vision authority, which is not incorrect as it turns out, but rather in the faultiness of the ocular proof itself to which attention is called by Coll to disprove that authority. This first response, then, alerts the audience to the potential unreliability of the empirical method, especially when the interpretive *circumstantia* in question is as complex and elusive as the one prepared for the shepherds by the felons, Mak and Gyll.

The next pastoral encounter/investigation follows immediately as the shepherds, having now taken inventory of their flock and reconvened at the "crokyd thorne" to exchange news, do, in fact, discover that a "fat wedir" is missing. Again, the potential unreliability of the empirical hermeneutical method is demonstrated as the process of inference, not influenced this time by the convincing impersonation of innocence embodied by Mak, is shown to be based simply upon their assumption of his guilt. At first, there is a hesitancy about arriving at such a conclusion so quickly. As soon as the theft is discovered by Coll, Daw identifies the thieves as Mak and Gyll and confirms that identification upon an oath:

> Now trow me, if ye will—
> By Sant Thomas of Kent,
> Ayther Mak or Gyll
> Was at that assent. (13/660–63)

This snap conclusion, however, is immediately condemned by Coll, partly on the grounds that the facts do not support it. Attempting to calm his pastoral colleague, Coll reminds Daw that he saw Mak with his own eyes:

> Peasse, man, be still!
> I sagh when he went. (13/664–65)

Another reason—the more important one—for this immediate corrective response, however, is that such an identification without factual basis constitutes a slander, the commission of which should lead one to repent and seek forgiveness:

> Thou sklanders hym yll;
> Thou aght to repent
> Goode spede. (13/666–68)

One need not be reminded here, in other words, that this process is fraught with danger, not only that implicit in being illogical, but also that of doing spiritual harm to oneself by succumbing to an enfeebled and potentially reckless state of mind. However, as soon as Gyb speaks up and agrees with Daw's conclusion that Mak and Gyll are the culprits—

> Now as euer mygth I the,
> If I shuld euyn here de,
> I wold say it were he
> That dyd that same dede (13/669–72)

—all three shepherds tacitly accept the assumption-based conclusion by agreeing to go to Mak and Gyll's to determine its validity. The conception of hypothesis, in other words, is shown to have currency. That they become examples of Kolve's "rennyng" men at this point[59]—each one energetically assuring the other he will not partake of any kind of alimentation or physical ease until the truth is finally known—serves, once again, to remind the audience of the hazards faced by anyone venturing into the uncharted waters of the empirical hermeneutical response.

The third encounter/investigation occupies the entire "Encounter" or fourth part of the scene's second episode and begins as soon as the shepherds, now within earshot of the object of their scrutiny, hear the strange croaking coming from the dwelling of Mak and Gyll. Like the two previous attempts just considered, this perscrutation allows the audience to witness flawed thinking in response to the "ambiguous literal." This instance of the failure of the empirical hermeneutical response is distinguished, however, by the extent of its elaboration, for in this perscrutation the shepherds, their perceptual faculty readied by their two interpretive "warmups," confront the complex *circumstantia* ingeniously wrought by Mak and Gyll precisely in anticipation of this encounter.

While the *circumstantia* of the "ambiguous literal" presents, as we have seen, a formidable interpretive challenge, what initially undermines the shepherds' efforts is their collective desire to discover evidence to demonstrate the validity of their assumption-based conclusion about Mak and Gyll's guilt, the conclusion at which they have jointly arrived in their thinking, and not by evidence. This preoccupation with proving the assumption's correctness, while limiting the focus of their inquiry, does not lead them to act recklessly, as might be expected. From the moment they begin interacting with Mak and Gyll, they exercise a caution possessing nearly the precision of a judicious methodology. One way in which they demonstrate this care is by gradually revealing to Mak that their mood is sad because they have lost one of their sheep:

> 2 *Pastor.* Nay, nawther mendys oure mode
> Drynke nor mette.
> Mak. Why, syr, alys you oght bot goode?
> 3 *Pastor.* Yee, oure shepe þat we gett
> Ar stollyn as thay yode;
> Oure los is grette. (13/727–32)

What is more, they do not come right out and accuse Mak and Gyll of the sheep stealing. Instead, they couch the accusation in an artful indirection, suggesting they have come gradually to the conclusions made by others who have identified Mak and Gyll as the culprits:

> Mak. Syrs, drynkys!
> Had I bene thore,
> Som shuld haue boght it full sore.
> 1 *Pastor.* Mary, some men trowes that ye wore,
> And that vs forthynkys.
> 2 *Pastor.* Mak, some men trowys
> That it shuld be ye.
> 3 *Pastor.* Ayther ye or youre spouse,
> So say we. (13/733–41)

But while the shepherds are not led astray by the desire to prove Mak and Gyll's guilt, the attitude engendered in them by that desire does predispose them to accept, without hesitation, the abstract as well as actual features of the elaborately wrought *circumstantia* involving the impersonation and disguise. This predisposition, in turn, makes the shepherds vulnerable to error for obvious reasons. And unbeknownst to the shepherds, this vulnerability provides the mechanism, as it were, for one of the most ironic and humorous moments in this scene.

Regrouped after having thoroughly searched through Mak and Gyll's dwelling, Gyb concludes their sheep has been slain, Daw exclaims he has found neither fresh nor cured meat but only empty platters, and Coll admits they have made a mistake and been beguiled. In the midst of this expression of disappointment and failure, Daw adds, to emphasize his personal frustration, that the only thing of note he has encountered in the newborn is its smell—one that is more potent than that of any tame or wild living animal he has ever experienced:

Whik catell bot this,
Tame nor wylde,
None, as haue I blys,
As lowde as he smylde. (13/790–93)

The irony of this observation—that is, of Daw's looking exactly at, and even recoiling from the odor of, the very thing he has come to find, but seeing and understanding only what Mak and Gyll want him to see and understand because of his desire to validate the assumption-based slanderous conclusion he himself previously articulated and accepted as true about Mak and Gyll's guilt—is something the Wakefield Master exploits here to its fullest for obvious dramatic and philosophical reasons. This is done, first of all, by having each of the other shepherds commit the same fault. Gyb follows Daw's lead by looking at the infant and asking whether the child is a "knaue" (13/800), a word choice whose irony scholars have duly noted.[60] Coll, who does not look at the infant and does not see the sheep the way his pastoral brethren do, nevertheless evidences the same prejudicial purblindness. When Daw asks Mak who the child's godparents are, godparents who have hastily been identified and chosen, Coll suggests in an aside that Mak's response will be a lie (13/810). The immediate identification of Parkyn, Gybon Waller, and "gentill Iohn Horne," however, vitiates this latest assumption-based slanderous and prejudicial conclusion, and reminds the audience, once again, that the essential and actual contributions *to* and *about* the *circumstantia* of the "ambiguous literal" are both sophisticated and artfully wrought. Mak and Gyll, in other words, are ready for any contingency.

Whether Mak and Gyll are aware of it or not, their choice of "gossyppys" in this instance demonstrates, yet again, just how ready the Wakefield Master is to exploit a dramatic opportunity. And this is what he does as he has Mak include Gyb and John here in the list of godparents. Stevens and Cawley remark that Mak's identification of John in terms of the "garray" reminds the audience of the quarrel that precedes the "Grotesque Feast" in the *[Prima] Pagina Pastorum*. One conclusion they make based upon this coincidence is that the "allusion, if such it is, may also be evidence that the first pageant continued to be acted after the second was written."[61] Another conclusion, however, can and should also be drawn from this coincidence, especially in light of what has just been said about the prejudice that, displayed or expressed by each of the three shepherds, consistently leads to the failure of the empirical hermeneutical response. Mak's choice for godparents of the two shepherds who, in the previous play, create and participate in the most sophisticated ovine *phantasma* in all of medieval British drama realerts the audience, by means of dramatic irony, to just how real or actual the deceptive product of "imaginacioun" can be. In a sense, then, the allusion has something of the self-congratulatory about it. The *phantasma* of Mak and Gyll's "gyn," so Mak seems to be suggesting, rivals that associated with Gyb and John's imaginary sheep turning round in circles in the medieval Pennine sheep runs of ancient Judea. But because it introduces something that is not actually seen, though completely in view, the allusion, if allusion it is, also reemphasizes a disconnection between object and observer when any sort of prejudice in thinking affects perception.

This last point is important, not only because it explains the failure of each hermeneutical pastoral response to the *circumstantia* of the "ambiguous literal," but also because it prepares the way for inclusion of the "ambiguous figurative," which is introduced in "The Discovery," the scene's final part. The shepherds' failure to deal effectively with the "ambiguous literal" might lead one to conclude that the introduction of this final *circumstantia* promises nothing more than further disappointment and frustration since, as Saint Augustine says, the "ambiguous figurative" is something that requires "no little care and industry" to understand.[62] However, while they discover they must confront this new interpretive challenge, the shepherds also, in a moment of near-miraculous but certainly evangelical insight, find the means of overcoming the prejudice that has hampered their efforts, up to this point, in response to the "ambiguous literal." As they leave Mak and Gyll's dwelling, Coll asks his colleagues if anyone has thought to give the child a gift. In other words, he asks his fellow shepherds if anyone has demonstrated charity—what Saint Augustine calls the "motion of the soul toward the enjoyment of God for His own sake, and the enjoyment of one's self and of one's neighbor for the sake of God."[63] When it is apparent no one has, Daw runs back to offer a present, and the action of the scene's final part begins. On the face of it, this blossoming of charity may not seem significant. However, once this orientation of the soul is established (and the soul is thereby reinvigorated by the spirit), then the function of the creaturely triune mind, combined with the full perceptive power of sentiency, is no longer encumbered by prejudice of any sort and so is "divine" in its freedom to engage in the *modus interpretandi* or, in Hugh of St. Victor's terms, in analysis by separation as well as analysis by examination.

And this is what happens as soon as Daw approaches the swaddled infant to make it an offering of at least an anachronistic sixpence. Though Mak tries to keep the shepherd at a distance, Daw's anachronistic charitable enjoyment of the infant for the sake of God—he does, after all, want also to give "That lytyll day-starne"[64] a kiss—leads him into proximity with the newborn. And that proximity in turn enables him to discover, once the "clowtt" has been lifted up or once things have been opened up that formerly were hidden, that the child has a "long snowte" (13/842–45). This discovery has a ripple effect that leads to related but separate discoveries. Coll, for example, remarks the child's deformity. And Gyb suggests the botch of nature before them is not unexpected, given who the child's parents are. While Gyb makes this unkind statement indirectly by means of aphorism, he also gets a better look at the newborn and, before finishing speaking, points out the child actually looks like their missing sheep. The senses, like the speculative creaturely triune mind, are thus unencumbered and able to respond freely and cogently as the result of charity.

This conclusion is repeated by the other shepherds once they have also taken a "pepe" or gotten ocular proof of the sheep, and the conclusion they draw from this inference is that they have been had, that the "qwantt gawde" is a "hee frawde." While Daw's expression evidences the greatest frustration, especially as he says of Mak and Gyll such things as "Lett bren this bawde" (13/859) and "Hang at the last / So shall thou" (13/862–63), what finally is more important than this display of emotion, dramatic as it may be, is the brief analysis by examination and separation into parts he makes as he discloses the mechanism, as it were, of the disguise. He first distinguishes from one another things that are mingled, as he points out how the "foure feytt" are tied to the sheep's middle, preventing any movement. At the same time he opens up what is hidden, not only by revealing and explaining the swaddling technique, but also by suggesting a connection between the sheep and the diabolical. The obvious relationship, of course, involves the horn and the crooked snout, prominent features of the conventional medieval devil physiognomy.[65] But also implicit here is the sheep's constriction as an expression of the motion of the soul toward the enjoyment of a corporal thing for the sake of something other than God. What should be the embodiment of charity, it turns out, is the embodiment of the effect of cupidity—its opposite.

While the shepherds demonstrate they now can understand the "ambiguous literal" for what it is—that is, they can see through the disguise and the attendant impersonations—the final test of successfully responding interpretively to the "ambiguous figurative" yet awaits them. This test unfolds two ways as Mak and Gyll persist in maintaining their innocence and even victimization. The first of these ways, interestingly enough, involves an appeal to sympathy by means of the "ambiguous figurative." This appeal is presented in the sudden image configuration Gyll composes as she takes, without aid of stage direction, the swaddled sheep and places it upon her knee, saying:

A pratty child is he
As syttys on a womans kne;
A dyllydowne, perdé,
To gar a man laghe. (13/877–80)

This act, which certainly is more effective if it is carried out as part of the performance reality of the scene's action, introduces an appeal to religious sentimentality through the power of analogy by mimicking popular devotional representations of the seated Madonna with the Christ child on her knee, representations such as those found in the late-thirteenth-century B.N. MS. Lat. 17326 illustration *The Adoration of the Magi,* in *The Virgin of the Portal* at Notre Dame in Paris, or in the early-thirteenth-century *Notre-Dame de la belle verrière* in the window at Chartres.[66] This emotionally charged analogy, whose purpose it is to elicit in the observer the desire to take a literal as a figurative, a desire as counterproductive to the furtherance of charity as that of taking a figurative as a literal, has as its object, to use Saint Augustine's words, the confusion of anyone "who uses or worships a significant thing without knowing what it signifies."[67] Now fully and finally in command of the "inventive" empirical creaturely triune mind through the incorporation of charity, the shepherds, however, are no longer the kind of individuals who might potentially suffer such an intellectual "servitude." What is more, because they now have the power not only to know what a sign is but also to know what any sign might mean, Daw dismisses this first instance of the "ambiguous figurative," on the one hand, by calling attention to the meaning of the sheep's "eere-marke," which is a signifier of the shepherds' possession, and, on the other, by acknowledging the sign itself, which he concludes is a "good tokyn" (13/882).

The second way the final test to which the shepherds must respond unfolds involves the evocation of fear by means of the "ambiguous figurative."[68] This emotion is evoked in two ways, each involving popular belief in the preternatural. First, Mak, trying to make the shepherds forget the sheep's identification, informs them that he has it upon clerkly authority that the newborn has been bewitched, the reason for its broken nose:

> I tell you, syrs, hark!—
> Hys noyse was brokyn.
> Sythen told me a clerk
> That he was forspokyn. (13/883–86)

When this attempt elicits only the threat of vengeance from Coll, who calls for a weapon, Gyll, offering a new tack, claims that Mak's and her child is actually a changeling:

> He was takyn with an elfe,
> I saw it myself;
> When the clok stroke twelf
> Was he forshapyn. (13/890–93)

In other words, in both instances Mak and Gyll try once more to elicit in the observer the desire to take a literal as a figurative. However, since the shepherds know how, within the framework of the expression of charity, to distinguish signs as well as their meanings, Mak and Gyll's efforts, entertaining as they may be, are yet again in vain.

Furthermore, while the threat of punishment escalates to the point of the shepherds' calling for the most severe retribution against Mak and Gyll—with Coll, the least likely, surprisingly pronouncing the felons' death sentence since they persist in maintaining their innocence—Mak's last-minute appeal for mercy mollifies the shepherds, and the punishment finally takes the puzzling form of the canvas toss. Several have offered explanations for this unusual event in the play: one says the toss suggests cowardice, another that it is meant to humiliate the person who has staged a pseudo-nativity.[69] However, while these interpretations are intriguing, important to remember is the emphasis Daw himself places on the punishment's not being an act of quarreling or chiding, and on its being carried out expeditiously:

> Syrs, do my reede:
> For this trespas
> We will nawther ban ne flyte,
> Fyght nor chyte,
> Bot haue done as tyte. (13/901–5)

These qualifications, which together suggest a nonpunitive action that will eliminate the need for further correction of Mak and Gyll, imply, by the process of elimination, a transformation of the felons' nature into one that is compatible with the shepherds' new outlook—that is, with their newly attained, intellectually and empirically buttressed expression of charity.

How a canvas toss and the renunciation of vice may be related, however, is a difficult proposition to ponder unless these two obviously disparate things are examined within the speculative framework of medieval mathematical physics. For such a consideration, the *Calculationes* of Richard Suiseth or Swineshead, the medieval mathematician also known as Calculator, may be able to shed some light. In this celebrated work, which is yet to receive scholarly treatment in the form of a modern edition, Swineshead's fifth-chapter discussion of rarefaction and density offers a possible way of viewing the canvas toss as an actual rudimentary technological means by which the density of Mak's uniform deformity—that is, the source of the "unevenness," to use his own word, of a life that is both ungoverned by reason and given over to sensation and appetite—is rarefied and thereby transformed.[70] The toss, consisting of a levitation of decreasing velocity and possessing a point that remains "quiet"—that is, the apex of the toss's arc—while others are in movement, dramatically images the rarefaction of Mak in terms of the ratio of his mass to his volume. In other words, as his volume is seen visually to increase in extent or vertically by the force of the toss, the extent of his mass is correspondingly diminished. As a result, the troublesome deformity, the density that has led to his "unevenness" in the first place with all its consequences, is made to evanesce suddenly right before the onlooking audience.

V

This brief foray into medieval mathematical physics, a highly complicated practical art, may seem out of keeping with the tenor or normative expectations of a nativity play, no matter how innovative the playwright may be in his treatment of subject matter. However, such an abstract/actual or "inventive" empirical way of understanding this particular difficult feature of the play's action should not come as a surprise, given the emphasis the previous scene's perscrutations place upon the combination of mind and senses, or of the abstract with the physical, for the purpose of successfully interpreting any phenomena *in* or *of* created reality. What is more, this outlook is even anticipated in that the shepherds receive, after the next scene has begun and the angelic *Gloria* has been sung, the charge of comprehending the full implications of the promise of God's being made their "freynd"—that is, of the uncreated's or the abstract's taking form in the created or physical.

To begin to comprehend the full import of this promise, the third scene of the play, "The Annunciation," provides the dramatic opportunity for the new "inventive" empirical creaturely triune mind to be exercised in such a way as to demonstrate its complete effect on the duality of the human condition, or, to be more specific by using the Pauline distinction, on the "interior" and "exterior" man. The latter receives initial treatment here. As soon as the shepherds have awakened, attention is directed to the "qwant stevyn" they have just heard. While all three have something to say—which they say in the order of their appearance in the play, an order of presentation they repeat throughout the scene—their particular emphases assert the four principal qualities of the "inventive" empirical creaturely triune mind. In the first go-round, for example, as all three comment on the angel's appearance and song,[71] the importance of memory is emphasized by what is recollected about the extrinsic event (13/933–43). While Coll remarks the marvel, what Gyb and Daw remember as most important about the experience is that the angel spoke of "Godys son" (13/937). This emphasis, in turn, leads to the assertion of the next quality of the creaturely triune mind, the intellect or reason, as Coll interprets the function of the star over Bethlehem. Following this, the will, as well as sentiency, is introduced as Coll concludes they must decamp to travel toward the star and find the place where

> lygs that fre
> In a cryb full poorely,
> Betwyx two bestys. (13/930–32)

As attention is next turned to the vehicle of the "qwant stevyn," the same qualities of the "inventive" empirical creaturely triune mind are again evoked in the same order—memory, intellect, will—though the center of gravity of the emphases shifts now more toward the will (13/944–58). The emphasis upon memory is introduced only briefly as Gyb asks the others if they remember the angelic song itself. The intellect is subsequently asserted in terms of distinction, as Gyb asks whether the musical line of the song that was "crakyd" consisted of "Thre brefes to a long" (13/948), and the others agree.[72] When Daw concludes by observing nothing was amiss, Coll's claim that he can repeat the song as part of a joint musical effort calls attention on the one hand to the will, which is expressed shortly afterward by several pastoral exclamations in a row (13/955–57), and on the other to sentiency, which is heard as all three shepherds, in unison, re-sing the angelic song.

How long this volitional performance turns out to be is not indicated by the text of the Towneley collection, but it is certain that when the shepherds are done singing, attention turns to the intrinsic matter of what the message of the "qwant stevyn" means for the shepherds in terms of action. This new consideration of the effect of the angelic Annunciation on the "interior" man shifts the emphases this time to the intellect or reason (13/959–71). To be sure, this sequence begins with the predictable assertion of memory, as Gyb reminds his brethren that the angel bade them go quickly to Bethlehem, and concludes with an assertion of will followed by sentiency, as Coll urges everyone forward, regardless of his present physical condition, to behold "that chyld and that lady" (13/970). But what is singled out as important here is the intellectual understanding of what the promise means to each shepherd in terms of feeling. For each, this involves two sets of distinctions. The experience of "myrth" (13/964), which results from being "mery" (light or incomplete) rather than "sad" (heavy, complete or serious),[73] is now to characterize everyone's expression or "exterior" self. And to characterize the "interior" self at the same time, as a way of compensating the deficiency of the outer man, is now the reward-experience of "Euerlasting glad" (13/965), the expression of which is not raucous but rather "withoutt noyse" (13/967).

The point to be understood about this intrinsic matter of the new kind of joy that is the shepherds' to experience is that it shifts the center of gravity of the pastoral emphases in the final part of "The Annunciation" to the assertion of the new quality of mind involving sentiency, since the new feeling will gladden even if one be "wete and wery" (13/969). This final go-round is the longest of the four in this scene, but the structure with its predictable order can easily accommodate such an elaboration. The quality of mind introduced first is memory, as Gyb, now offering an abbreviated *Processus Prophetarum,* calls attention to the miraculous birth as typological fulfillment of prophecy (13/972–84). The intellect or reason is expressed next (13/985–97) as Daw deduces that the others, and he himself, may now experience the "Euerlasting glad," and speculates on the beneficial effect that would certainly result from his interview with the "chylde":

> Lord, well were me
> For ones and for ay,
> Myght I knele on my kne,
> Som word for to say
> To that chylde. (13/989–93)

The qualities of mind, will, and sentiency are next expressed by Coll, who is obviously less opportunistic than his colleague Daw. Turning first to the will, he indicates that the pastoral group now has the opportunity to experience the same desire that informed the vision of "Patryarkes" and "prophetys beforne" (13/998–1001). What is more, he adds that the same group, because of its place in history and because it has been singled out by God's "messyngere," can now, poor as the shepherds may be, fulfill that very desire. The benefit accruing from such a volitional action, the final elucidation of the "tokyn," he concludes necessitates the engagement of the final quality of mind, sentiency, for it is only after he has beheld and felt the child that the "true as steyll" confirmation of the truth of the prophets' words concerning the shepherds' role in the matter of the New Dispensation can be accepted:

> *When I se hym and fele,*
> *Then wote I full weyll*
> It is true as steyll
> That prophetys haue spokyn:
>
> To so poore as we ar
> That he wold appere,
> Fyrst fynd, and declare
> By his messyngere. (13/1007–14; emphasis mine)

Coll's emphasis upon sentiency and proof by "fele," which here completes the dramatic redeployment of the totality of qualities of mind of the "divine" "inventive" empirical creaturely triune mind, demonstrates the readiness of the shepherds to incorporate in their mental outlook and cognition the final feature of charity that has been shown to be, embodied previously as it is in Daw's desire to offer the disguised sheep a sixpence, the keystone of this new dramatized *allegoria* of the conceptualization of mind. Accordingly, as the shepherds approach the place where the child is to be found, and enter together to behold "that bright," they express the enjoyment both "of themselves and of their neighbors for the sake of God" by praying to God to grant them something of joy or mirth with which to comfort His child:

> Lord, if thi wylles be—
> We ar lewde all thre—
> Thou grauntt vs som kyns gle
> To comforth thi wight. (13/1020–23)

VI

The granting of the shepherds' prayer, which introduces the play's final scene or "The Adoration," provides the Wakefield Master with the opportunity to do two things before ending the play. The first of these, a preventive of sorts so that the audience will not forget what it has just beheld in the two sets of perscrutations in the second scene, is to dramatize the defining expression—that is, the essence or quiddity—of this new conceptualization of mind. As this mind has been revealed to apprehend by means of the vital and vitalizing nexus between the uncreated or abstract and the created or actual, what is shown to constitute this defining expression, in the final analysis, is understanding articulated by means of analogy. Each charitable act of giving that occurs in the first half of "The Adoration" thus unfolds according to this informing principle.[74] What is distinctive about each instance is that the analogy arising as the result of the dramatic pastoral response involves a perception of the incarnation of divinity to which a particular gift and its implicit source are eventually equated.

In the first act of giving, by Coll (13/1024–36), the perception is that divinity's incarnation consists of the young child on the one hand and of the maker and protector on the other. In other words, it involves attributes of something both old and young at the same time. The choice of the gift of the "bob of cherys"[75] as an analogy of this paradoxical condition is explained when the plant's own nature, its rejuvenescent vegetable organics of the new fruit's relationship to the old stem and branch, is considered within the context of the implicit comparison.

In the next act of giving, by Gyb (13/1037–49), the perception is that divinity's incarnation consists of the young child or the "lytyll tyne mop"[76] on the one hand and, on the other, of the maker and the "sufferan sauyoure." In other words, it involves attributes of something both old and young, and powerful. The choice of the gift of the "byrd" as an analogy of this new paradoxical condition is revealed when the creature's own nature, its rejuvenescent sentient animal organics, is taken into consideration within the context of the implicit comparison. The animal organics provides a way of understanding the paradox of the old and new, as does the vegetable organics in the instance of the previous gift; the powerful is implied by the creature's quality of sentiency.[77]

In the final act of giving, by Daw (13/1050–62), the perception is that divinity's incarnation consists, on the one hand, of the essence of God or Godhead and, on the other, of the attractiveness of God or God as "derlyng dere." In other words, it involves both the uncreated and created natures of God. The choice of the gift of the "ball" for "tenys" as an analogy of this paradoxical condition is explained when the ball's own nature, its being a product of technology, is considered within the context of the implicit comparison.[78] Because of its linen core, the ball, on the one hand, can be seen as the product of the interplay between sentient animal organics and vegetable organics. In other words, the ball is the technological achievement of the transformation of the linen that is made from flax into something uniquely different from the cloth that initially results from the actual spinning process. The ball as analogy of Godhead, on the other hand, can be seen in the rejuvenescent function of the device itself. As one goes "to the tenys" and plays with the ball, despite Edward III's prohibitions against the game, one finds a means of creating oneself anew or recreating oneself, the analogous act the uncreated performs when giving definition to the uncreated—that is, when engaging in the act of creation itself.

The second thing the granting of the shepherds' prayer enables the Wakefield Master to do is to conclude the play, as the *[Prima] Pagina Pastorum* ends, with the introduction of the *modus proferandi*. As soon as Mary assures the shepherds they shall be kept from "wo," they are enjoined to "Tell furth" as they "go" (13/1074). This request to engage in the *artes predicandi* and the *modus proferandi* is immediately answered by the shepherds, who, in departing, repeat the miracle of the nexus between the uncreated or abstract and the created or actual. They do this by joining once again in song, the vitality of which is suggested by Daw's final pronouncement:

To syng ar we bun—
Let take on loft! (13/1087–88)

The ease with which the shepherds (presumably) harmonize now is the result of their having once again apprehended the vital and vitalizing link between the uncreated and the created, this time the former acknowledged in terms of the grace that has been discovered and is now to be enjoyed, and the latter in terms of the embodiment of grace in the "lady, / So fare to beholde, / With thy childe on thi kne" (13/1076–78), a far cry from what the shepherds experienced in beholding Gyll earlier in the play.

Like the *[Prima] Pagina Pastorum* before it, the deep structure of the *[Secunda] Pagina Pastorum* thus offers the audience a thoroughly developed view of mind by means of the drama of pastoral response. The distinguishing feature of this view, of course, is the emphasis it places upon sentiency and upon sentiency's role in terms of cognition and understanding. This noetic conceptualization is not presented as an alternative to the noetic configuration presented in the previous play. Rather, it is a view of mind that is advanced for the purpose of complementing the view of mind advanced by the previous play, for together the "inventive" speculative/empirical creaturely triune mind is that of the active seeker, in all senses of the term, of divine nature in created reality. The view of mind that can be perceived from the combined dramatized *allegoriae* presented by and consisting of the two shepherds' plays in the Towneley *regenall* is, thus, the mind of the new age of religious subjectivism—the mind, in other words, in which the combination of *sapientia* and *scientia*, informed by reason, evidences the "divinity" of the rational soul.

5

Magnus Herodes and the Degradation of the Rational Soul

While the Towneley collection's two shepherds' plays, as the two preceding chapters have suggested, may be seen to form an extended dramatized *allegoria* of the bilateral constituent features of the rational soul or of the "inventive" speculative/empirical creaturely triune mind of the active seeker for an understanding of divine nature as it is reflected in the pattern of creation—an interpretive outcome expected of plays preparing the audience for the subjective religious experience of Christ's Nativity—the Wakefield Master's *Magnus Herodes,* the third of his plays also set in the time of renewal, introduces a thematic contrast that, for the audience, is as chillingly provocative as it is instructive. The second Towneley play to present Herod Ascalonita—the first of the two or even three Herods often dramatized elsewhere in medieval pageants[1]—the *Magnus Herodes* establishes this contrast by means of a dramatic allegorizing of the condition of mind resulting when, through wilful and impious perversity, the spirit suffers so grievously from itself that the soul is said to be "dead" or abandoned by God. Jeffrey Helterman and John Gardner have identified this mental and spiritual condition as that of the Antichrist or of a figure or type of the Antichrist,[2] a conclusion supported, as they argue, by the play's noticeable use of traditional allegory.[3] While this identification is buttressed by Herod's many startling expostulations and actions, as well by the conventional typological association between Herod and the forces of Lucifer,[4] the condition of mind predisposing Herod to act and think *like* the Antichrist, and thereby anticipate the Antichrist,[5] appears to have been of equal interest to the Wakefield Master. This is perhaps so because such a dramatization would offer an instructive contrast to the *allegoria* of mind dramatically evoked by the combination of the two revised shepherds' plays earlier in the collection. What is more, such a dramatization would present the aesthetic challenge—and reap the eventual hortatory benefit—of eliciting from Corpus Christi audiences the appropriate ethical reaction of reproof in response to wilful impiety—that is, to the tropological cognitive experience most obviously antithetical to the apostolic consciousness fundamental to the religious metaphysics of the age.

Indeed, many late-medieval spectators at the Corpus Christi celebration would have been eager to witness the dramatized condition of this *mentalité* on the stage because of what generally was understood to be the paradoxical nature of a rational soul that is bereft of the life it derives from God even when the body is still living. Since it is immortal, the soul, though "dead" as the result of its abandonment by God, never ceases to exist and to feel, even if only in the slightest degree.[6] In this paradoxical immortal living-death-like state—in this condition of "presumption," the first of two aspects of the sin against the Holy Spirit[7]—the spirit, in adjusting the body to the stimuli it receives, would continue to produce sensations. But because of the spirit's concomitant degradation, the sensations experienced, as well as the *phantasiae* or images formed or combined as the result of this activity, would be grossly deceptive to the victim, while horrifying to the onlooker. Cognition would also be affected. Each part of the speculative creaturely triune mind, in other words, would evidence the effect of being wrongly directed by a spirit that is ruled by the body, its inferior.[8] The perversion of reason, memory, and will would result in the evil of the condition of confusion and disorder.[9]

I

To dramatize this debasement of the properly ordered or rational soul—that is, of the Image of God within the speculative creaturely triune mind—the Wakefield Master does two things. First, to provide the audience properly with a vantage point from which to respond analytically to what is to come, he deploys the theatrical innovation of a preliminary dramatic irony by altering the conventional performance order of the plays. This is done both to achieve the practical hortatory effect of precluding empathetic identification with Herod and to establish a contextual contrast within which to consider the related ironies of the noesis of impiety itself. While a like "internal" dialectical opposition distinguishes the first two from the last two scenes of the *[Prima] Pagina Pastorum*, or the first scene from the other three in the *[Secunda] Pagina Pastorum*, the contrast here, much more ambitious in scope but still evidencing attentiveness to the Gothic stylistic principle of clarification,[10] is formed partly by the two plays separating the *Magnus Herodes* from the shepherds' plays, and partly by the three following and separating the *Magnus Herodes* from the plays of the "Passion group." These latter three, of course, keenly remind the audience that Christ is very much alive, each emphasizing an important moment in His youth and early life—the *Purificacio marie* treating His infancy, [*Christ and the Doctors*], the visit to His "Father's house" in Jerusalem, and *Iohannes baptista*, the baptism. The preceding pair, likewise, assure spectators *before* the fact of the Massacre of the Innocents that, no matter what is planned and carried out in the *Magnus Herodes*, all is for nought as far as Herod is concerned. The *Fugacio Iosep et marie in egiptum*'s placement in the collection directly before the *Magnus Herodes* removes the Christ child from any harm Herod would inflict upon Him and so establishes an ironic context within which to display the totality of Herodian perversity, noetic and otherwise. Wendy Clein has suggested that the specific placement of this play frees the Wakefield Master to structure the Slaughter of the Innocents as comedy,[11] an effect also partially achieved by the performance order of plays 18 and 19 in the York Cycle.[12] While this argument is made even more convincing by Stevens and Cawley's attribution, on stylistic grounds, of the *Fugacio* to the Wakefield Master,[13] the modification of the play performance order through inclusion of the *Oblacio Magorum* directly before the *Fugacio*, and directly after the shepherds' plays, further constrains the characterization of Herod within the confines of parody, a fact noted by David Staines, who has convincingly argued how the placement of the *Oblacio Magorum* offers the Towneley collection a contrastive view of kingship and proper homage,[14] a distinction underscoring the connection between the Herod of the *Magnus Herodes* and the traditional anxious Herod in the sources.[15]

The reduction of Herod to the insignificance of parody assures the conventional typology of this biblical figure, one noticeable effect of which is to put in relief the collateral didactic function of Herod's "character" as exemplum of wrath and ire.[16] However, while doing this, the transformation also invites formal examination of the constituent features or condition—as well as irony—of the wrathful impious mind itself, for, at the very least, it alerts spectators to the fact that the process by which the medieval tragic figure falls into the order of justice by subjecting himself to Fortune has already begun.[17]

II

Elucidation of the wrathful impious mind through dramatic allegorizing of its condition or constituent features, origin, and effect—that is, through consideration of structures of reference presented anterior to each part of the play and from which the totality of the play is seen to emerge as if organically[18]—occupies the attention of the nine-stanza induction as well as each of the play's three scenes.[19] Nuncius as he begins the play by relating the "sondys" sent by Herod, for example, offers an instructive introduction to the particular elements of the rational soul's condition of degradation as they will be developed in the play's first scene. Directing his remarks at the audience and thereby initiating the first methexis in the play,[20] Nuncius commands everyone to become dispirited by renouncing the rational soul—by surrendering, as it were, command over each feature of the speculative creaturely triune mind. The first of these qualities or "faculties" to be relinquished, so announces Nuncius, is the will. This is to be demonstrated by all through their bowing at Herod's bidding and expressing a love for him that emphasizes their loyalty:

> Heroude, the heynd kyng—
> By grace of Mahowne—
> Of Iury, sourmontyng
> Sternly with crowne
> On lyfe that ar lyfyng
> In towre and in towne,
> Gracyus you gretyng,
> Commaundys you be bowne
> At his bydyng.
> Luf hym with lewté;
> Drede hym, that doughty!
> He chargys you be redy
> Lowly at his lykyng. (16/14–26)

The next feature of mind or rational soul to be compromised is reason. The delimiting of cognition is to be demonstrated by all principally through disregarding the birth of the boy king, the source of Herod's anger, and also by considering Herod alone their king:

> Carpys of no kyng
> Bot Herode, that lordyng,
> Or busk to youre beyldyng,
> Youre heedys for to hyde. (16/49–52)

The final feature of mind or rational soul to be relinquished is memory. This is to be done through simple acceptance of the official view of Herod's "renowne," a view that only Herod's cousin Mahomet has the eloquence to express. Suppression of this last feature of mind or rational soul is perhaps the most difficult act of renunciation for the Corpus Christi pageant spectator, not only because of the reputation in the Middle Ages of Mahomet as pseudo-prophet, braggart, sensualist, magician, and type of Antichrist,[21] but also because of the conspicuous irony in the expressions used by Nuncius to convey Herod's greatness—expressions appearing in the New Testament and reserved to describe Christ in His majesty:

> He is kyng of kyngys,
> Kyndly I knowe,
> Chefe lord of lordyngys,
> Chefe leder of law. (16/53–56)

While the illusion of this initial methexical moment is nearly dispelled by this irony and its implicit absurdity, attention is suddenly refocused on the degradation of the rational soul as Nuncius himself, in anticipation of Herod's imminent arrival, acts out the commands he has just delivered to all in attendance. His genuflexion—which is more like the act of prostration since, as he says, he will

> knele for his sake
> So low;
> Downe deruly to fall (16/99–101)

—enacts the renunciation of the will, while his description of Herod as "the worthyest of all" (16/103), one he will welcome "worshipfully" (16/96), reveals acceptance of an obviously narrow or official view of the king of Judea. His adding that he welcomes Herod while "Laghyng with lake" (16/97) suggests reason may also have been compromised, if not abjured, upon his leader's approach. But such is not entirely the case, nor is it so in regard to the other features of the rational soul or mind, since Nuncius seizes the opportunity in the waning moments of the induction to explain that, despite his efforts, rumors concerning a newborn king have continued to spread and are now the cause of ceaseless "chateryng" (16/115). Separating the message from the messenger in this way may diminish the effectiveness of the self-abnegation ordered and demonstrated by Nuncius, but it constitutes a means of self-preservation, of which he is not loath to take advantage since he knows his master better than most.

The command to bereave oneself of the Image of God within one's own rational soul, coupled with the subsequent enactment of such total bereavement through a praxis of obsequiousness, is enough perhaps to strain the patience of even the most credulous Corpus Christi spectator, but this brief performance by Nuncius in the metadramatic space and time between stage and audience nevertheless readies the audience, by simple preliminary demonstration, for the degradation of the constituent features of the rational soul that is about to be evoked dramatically through elaborate allegorizing in each of the following scenes' episodes. Also readying the audience for this aesthetic experience is the Wakefield Master's manipulation of inorganic dramatic form in such a way as to insure the general abstract quality of the play's action, partly by deploying dramatic irony through play order, as we have seen, and partly by creating in the play a comic structure lacking comic decorum—the critical element of sympathy between audience and principal character being conspicuously absent.[22] This "distancing" of play content and theme from the audience has the practical hortatory effect of enabling the audience, ultimately, to see the horror of the Slaughter of the Innocents as cause for celebration within the greater context of Christian salvation history, the object of the Corpus Christi celebration itself. But it also has the more immediate practical dramaturgical effect of allowing the Wakefield Master to explore in several ways, through extended dramatic *allegoria*, the condition of mind that exists when the soul is bereft of the life it derives from God.

The first and perhaps most noticeable of these ways to be brought to the audience's attention has to do with memory. When Herod enters, picking up on what Nuncius has just said concerning rumors about the Christ child, he extends the initial methexis by haranguing the audience with "tame-talkyng" threats and threats of excoriation and other physical harm to get their attention and obedience. However, it is neither this initial forgetting of why he is onstage, nor even his subsequent articulation of the perceived need to remind everyone of his identity and reputation as the "doughtiest," that introduces the matter of the degradation of memory in the speculative creaturely triune mind. Rather, it is the emergence in this scene of *phantasma* involving the Christ child that alerts the audience to the corruption of this part of the rational soul. Ordinarily, within the context of Christian salvation history, the *phantasia* or recollected image of the Christ child affords solace or joy. In the case of Herod, however, the *phantasia* of "that lad," coupled with insecurity over his rule, becomes the source of grievous disturbance both in and to his thought process. Of course, the Wakefield Master would not have regarded these strange combinations of recollected images or *phantasiae* as manifestations of paranoia, but he would not have had trouble identifying them as evidence in Herod's thinking of either delusions of grandeur or delusions of persecution. The first of the latter to be presented in the play is the first of all the paranoiac *phantasmata* to which Herod himself calls attention. In this initial delusional fear of persecution involving the image or *phantasia* of the boy king, Herod claims the resultant *phantasma*—just the thought of "that lad"—has had a deleterious impact on both his physical and his emotional self. He observes, for example, that his "myrthes are turned to teyn" and his "mekenes into ire," all of which has engendered suffering "within" as if from "fyre" (16/144–47).

Two other *phantasmata* involving the combination of delusional fear of persecution and the "lad" appear in this scene. The more elaborate of the two occurs at the moment when Herod discovers he has been duped by the Magi. Their action toward him—promising to return and then breaking that promise to seek out the Christ child to give Him the "offeryng that they broght" (16/172–80)—is perceived by Herod as an insult to both his person and his prestige. Even though the "lad" does not directly cause physical or emotional distress in this instance, his being the object of the Magi's quest is enough for Herod to perceive Him as party to the persecution, a perception that makes Herod so agitated he does not hesitate to say how he would enjoy breaking the child's neck. As neither the Magi nor the "lad" is physically present, this *phantasma* of delusional persecution should end as quickly as other like *phantasmata*. But the Wakefield Master, attentive to any dramatic opportunity before him, extends this *phantasma* by means of displacement, turning the soldiers who guard their leader into the object of Herod's continued wrath. When he denounces these characters as "losels" and "thefys," they challenge his delusion of persecution and his ranting, with Tertius Miles saying:

> Why put ye sich reprefys
> Withoutt cause?
> Thus shuld ye not thrett vs,
> Vngaynly to bete vs;
> Ye shuld not rehett vs
> Withoutt othere sawes. (16/229–34)

The final *phantasma* of the fear of persecution involving the "lad" arises near the end of the scene as Herod calls, a second time, for vengeance:

> My guttys will outt thryng
> Bot I this lad hyng;
> Withoutt I haue a vengyng,
> I may lyf no langer. (16/348–51)

This *phantasma* has about it the urgency of exasperation, which the previous call for vengeance does not. The reason is that it comes directly after the consultant scholars, having done research at Herod's request, not only affirm the existence of the Christ child but explain His function. That the "lad" is more real in Herod's thinking after this scholarly report than He has ever been before does not alter Herod's desire to "kyll him downe stryght" (16/344) and destroy this cause of mental anguish. But it does lead Herod to call attention to his delusion of persecution in the novel way of asking rhetorically how it is that a knave in a crib, an infant no more than one year of age, can afflict him—can make him "rafe"—as this one has done.

The recollected image or *phantasia* of the "lad" is also combined with delusions of grandeur and so becomes part of a second kind of *phantasma* created by the degraded condition of memory in Herod's mind. This kind of *phantasma* is more complicated than the first in that the *phantasia* of the "lad" now functions not simply as the perceived cause of affliction but rather as the perceived impediment to the delusion of grandeur itself. The most instructive example of this occurs when Herod, distinguishing himself as the "doughtyest" that "euer ran with spere" and as "lord and kyng ryall" (16/157–60), interrupts his litany of self-praise to lament and ponder how contingent his rule actually is upon defeating the "lad" who is ready to usurp his power—to seize his "stall" (16/162). This perception of the boy as challenge to the regal authority Herod believes he enjoys also arises two other times in the first scene. In one of these *phantasmata* Herod sees a direct correlation between the destruction of the "lad" and the maintenance of his own reputation as feudal leader. To do nothing in response to this child, in fact, is perceived by Herod as a direct threat to his political control as well as an invitation to ridicule:

May I se hym with eyn,
I shall gyf hym his hyre;
Bot I do as I meyn,
I were a full lewde syre
In wonys. (16/148–52)

In the final example, which arises directly after he discovers the Magi have eluded him, Herod acknowledges his rule is threatened by the "lad" since it is the latter, and not Herod himself, who has been called king by the Magi. Herod cannot brook the thought of another enjoying the "mastry" that is rightfully his. The perceived threat of the "lad" to his grandeur is so profound in this instance that he actually condemns himself if he does not prevent this competitor from getting the better of him:

The dewill me hang and draw,
If I that losell knaw,
Bot I gyf hym a blaw
That lyfe I shall hym reyfe. (16/192–95)

The second way in which the degradation of the rational soul is evinced through dramatic *allegoria* in the *Magnus Herodes's* first scene involves the corruption of the will. This is brought to the audience's attention through the dramatization of sequential expressions—that is, serialities—of distinct "affeciounes" or emotional conditions revealing different intensities of agitation, in a repeated pattern consisting of three stages involved in the loss and regaining of a conditional ataraxia. (Such a claim concerning time might be objected to since it involves seriality.[23]

But using temporal sequence or seriality, in this instance, to elucidate a feature of a tragic flaw in "character," since *time* in late-medieval thinking was associated with *illusion*,[24] may be regarded as a deliberate distortion to achieve an intended dramatic effect.) The first instance of this pattern is introduced as soon as Herod has joined Nuncius in threatening the audience to get his "will in this stede" (16/138) obeyed. The expressed "affecioun" of mild agitation or discontent, Herod's initial conditional "easse," becomes apparent shortly afterward as he acknowledges his "myrthes" have "turned to teyn" and his "mekenes into ire" (16/144–45). This condition is elaborated as he articulates a prepensive malice toward the singular object of his consideration—the "lad." But this unsettled state of mind is not a condition over which he has relinquished complete control. Indeed, as he acknowledges his discomfiture, Herod also reveals the reason for feeling as he does. What has put him in this bad way, he indicates, is not only the elusive "lad" whom he later would "byrken all his bonys" with a "steyll brand" if he had him in hand, but also, as we have seen, the poor reputation he would gain as feudal lord were he to do nothing to counter this apparent—though apparently insignificant—threat. Though decidedly affected by this condition, in other words, Herod still has enough presence of mind to identify and explain the source of his disquiet—and to include in that explanation two metaphors, the first likening his troubled inner state to a conflagration, and the second painting the retributive justice against the "lad" to which he believes he is entitled as an instance of the proper feudal custom and practice of wage payment:

> My myrthes ar turned to teyn
> My mekenes into ire,
> And all for oone, I weyn,
> Within I fare as fyre.
> May I se hym with eyn,
> I shall gyf hym his hyre;
> Bot I do as I meyn,
> I were a full lewde syre
> In wonys. (16/144–52)

Change to a more intense state of disquiet or disorder follows directly in stanza 13, however, as Herod, reaffirming his kingship, acknowledges the beginning of volitional errancy by announcing he has started to "anger" (16/165). The rational certainty that has helped him keep his initial emotional display of agitation in check—that certainty enabling him to metaphorize his condition seemingly effortlessly in the previous stanza—no longer is evident as he now observes he does not immediately know the source of this new emotional distress:

> I wote not what dewill me alys. (16/166)

While concluding that this confused response is the effect of having heard all the stories about the "lad" who would "sesse" his "stall," Herod suggests in summary pronouncement—"I wyll peasse no langer" (16/169)—that this loss of peace has already begun to affect his will as well as his reason. The loss of both is further evidenced ironically by two truths about salvation history that Herod himself inadvertently makes as he tries to come to grips with the troubled, wrathful condition of his mind. As he acknowledges he has been made uncomfortable by the stories about the "lad," he emphasizes the loss of his equanimity with the blasphemous anachronistic oath "by Gottys dere nalys" (16/168). And just before, as he reaffirms his right to the crown, Herod inadvertently suggests prophetically that the boy must suffer, which is what He will eventually have to do at the time of the Crucifixion.

The most intense state of disorder—the moment, in other words, when the loss of will is complete, if only temporarily—follows directly after the admission of this anger at the beginning of stanza 14. Here Herod, having cursed the loss of his conditional "easse" or initial equanimity, suggests he now is about to burst from the anger and annoyance he has been forced to suffer:

> What dewill! Me thynk I brast
> For anger and for teyn. (16/170–71)

While this first clangorous expression of volitional errancy is short-lived as the change of states of mind begins its return to a condition like that of his initial "easse," Herod nevertheless continues to demonstrate the symptomatology of the erratic will. One way this is revealed, again, is in an expressed willingness to act out the violence of a prepensive malice in harming the "lad," as he exclaims, by breaking "his nek in two" (16/182). Another example of this continued lack of volitional equilibrium arises in his repeated willingness to engage in chance, something he feels he must do if the Magi have, in fact, eluded him (16/185–86).[25] Even when it appears he has regained rational control of the situation in stanza 15, the moment he turns to the soldiers to receive their report, his need to describe boastfully the pain the Magi will suffer at his own hands evidences a will that is still partially misdirected or not fully under control. While Herod opines that the Magi will endure grievous, unspeakable pain—

> For and thay be so bold,
> By God that syttys in trone,
> The payn can not be told
> That thay shall haue ilkon,
> For ire.
> Sich panys hard neuer man tell,
> For-vgly and for-fell,
> That Lucyfere in hell
> Thare bonys shall all to-tyre (16/200–208)

—what he fails, ironically, to comprehend is that the pain he believes must be the Magi's punishment, the eternal torment of the second death, is the very pain reserved for one like himself, the exemplar or personification of spiritual intransigence and wrath caused by a disordered will.[26]

The next introduction of this tripartite pattern, this seriality, of volitional errancy in the play follows once the dialogue between Herod's soldiers and Herod has begun. This instance of the pattern is of greater consequence than the first, since it is at this point in the play that Herod discovers he has been tricked. Accordingly, the first stage of the pattern to unfold has the same emotional intensity as the high point—that is, the moment of the complete, though only temporary, loss of will—in the first display of volitional errancy. So when Herod begins this response in stanza 19, nearly all of what he first says is characterized by an exclamatory urgency—

> Fy, losels and lyars,
> Lurdans ilkon!
> Tratoures and well wars! (16/235–37)

And earlier, when he turns to Primus Miles in stanza 18, Herod begins indiscriminately savaging his own knights, calling them, among other things, "losels" and "thefys" (16/223). His subsequent belief that his body and soul may sever comes as no surprise as it reasserts the idea of bursting from wrath. But this reassertion also introduces the artistic problem of how an even greater intensity of volitional errancy can be presented, since the most intense appears already to have been demonstrated. The solution offered by the Wakefield Master not only reveals his dramatic genius but also challenges, as elsewhere in the Towneley collection and in this play's induction and part of the first scene,[27] the audience's relation to the events on the stage as well as to the stage itself. But it should be remembered here that while the intensity is now greater, it is still part of a sequence of analogies.

While the intense anger persists in his answer to the questioning by Secundus Miles and Tertius Miles of his accusations' logic, Herod this time does not limit himself to the predictable name-calling, blaming, and threatening that appeared in the first instance of volitional disequilibrium. He does, with the same dedicated purpose, introduce new pejoratives for the knights—"losels," "lyars," and "lurdans"—and new threats, including that he would break every bone of the Magi if he caught them. What changes here is the object of his ire. By allowing Herod to turn momentarily from the knights to an imagined "Fyrst vengeance" against the Magi, the Wakefield Master seizes the dramatic opportunity in stanza 19 for a subsequent contingent action: The reintroduction of the second-person-plural pronouns "ye" and "you" directly following the digression does not return attention to the soldiers, who are still beside Herod, but now includes the audience as well as object or part-object of the harangue:

> Fyrst vengeance
> Shall I se on thare bonys;
> If ye byde in these wonys,
> I shall dyng you with stonys—
> Yei, ditizance doutance! (16/243–47)

The introduction of an innovative methexis of this sort is partly suggested by Herod's next remark, at the beginning of stanza 20, consciously acknowledging the disequilibrium caused by the new intensity of his emotion:

> I wote not where I may sytt
> For anger and for teyn. (16/248–49)

It is also suggested by the unusual usage of the verb "to ding." As Herod threatens to strike now with stones, he extends the prior threat of taking vengeance on the "land-lepars'" bones to include the implicit bones of the audience. Multiple advantages accrue, of course, from such a breach in the dramatic continuum of the play's thematic development. For one thing, the introduction of this shift in focus enables the audience, through participation, to realize their affinity, not with the soldiers who will soon engage in the most famous biblical pogrom of all, but rather with the Magi,[28] who have successfully eluded the aggressive tyranny of volitional errancy. What is more, the verbal assault inflicted upon them as surrogate elusive Magi enables the audience, in this metadramatic condition of participatory analogy, to appreciate anew the Providential design delimiting the effect of Herod and his ilk, while permitting insight into how such errancy calls attention to itself and, ironically, reveals its own limitations and inherent perversity. Here that self-revelation involves the myopia of pretentiousness, a myopia revealed in the sudden misunderstanding of the audience as consisting solely of members of the authority culture like Herod himself who, victimized by their own lack of self-knowledge, tend to use undemotic French expressions such as "ditizance doutance" to emphasize a point.

The return to a state of conditional "easse" ending this second instance of volitional errancy in stanza 20 follows directly, as before, with Herod doing two things to demonstrate the regaining of control of the will. First, he asks how it is things have gotten out of hand, an assertion including an expostulation (16/250–52). Second, he reasserts his royal prerogative as well as the purpose—to give the Magi "start"—that originally galvanized his will, disordered as it may have been:

> As long as I haue eyn,
> I thynk not for to flytt,
> Bot kyng I will be seyn
> For euer.
> Bot stand I to quart,
> I tell you my hart:
> I shall gar thaym start,
> Or els trust me neuer. (16/253–60)

The final instance of serial volitional errancy presented in this scene introduces yet another moment of analogy, occurring as soon as Herod has dismissed the soldiers he has just berated to pursue a more learned approach to solving the problem of the "lad." As in the second instance, the intensity of agitation displayed here is great even at the outset, in stanza 26. As this example of volitional errancy begins to unfold, Herod angrily accuses the learned counselors of having misled him. The obligatory name-calling occupies a noticeable part of the initial verbal assault here. Then, after he tells the scholars to throw their books in the brook, since their unwelcome findings have ignored the narrow research protocol he himself set,[29] Herod acknowledges he is raving or going out of his mind:

> With sich wylys and crokys
> My wytt away rafys. (16/337–38)

At this point the dramatic problem of reintroducing the initial Herodian response in an already frenzied state of mind is again presented to the Wakefield Master. And again a solution, which turns out to be quite effective dramatically, is worked out by the Master—yet another instance of the singular creative genius working within the stylistic conventions of the Gothic and the practical constraints of dramatic production. While it seems impossible to conceive dramatically of a frenzy more intense than frenzy itself, and while the artistic option of representing this condition of mind through *re-presentation* or the incorporation of methexis cannot now be repeated for obvious reasons, the Master dramatizes anew the febrile delirium of this frenzied, wrathful condition of errancy in stanza 27 by giving it this time a recognizable physiological dimension. In other words, the fever pitch of the anger, the complete lack of control, is made readily identifiable as Herod, now in a towering, murderous rage, has to break off from the contemplated killing of the "lad" to regain his breath:

> Nay, he shall on-slant;
> I shall kyll hym downe stryght.
> War! I say, lett me pant. (16/343–45)

Sudden breathlessness at such a critically dramatic moment cogently images, in a manner like Eliot's objective correlative in the modernist poetic line, not only the loss of will but also the bereavement of spirit that results from such a loss. The latter is suggested as the Herodian dyspnea momentarily dramatizes, by means of the conventional association between the divine or creative spirit and the act of breathing—a symbolic association with an obvious biblical source as well as a complex history[30]—the loss of divine *inspiration* or *in-spiriting*. The loss of will, on the other hand, is not as readily evident, though it is no less symbolically complex. The dyspnea in this case dramatizes turbulence of mind, what now would be called "the loss of one's wits." This particular condition of mental disequilibrium, the dramatization of which is characterized, at least in part, by volitional errancy and subsequent impairment of basic physiological process, implies prior loss of the "intellectuals" or "spirits," images conventionally identified with the "breath" as metaphor of the *tertium quid*, the subtle *gumphus*, or the nexus between the body and the soul, an idea traceable to the *Timaeus* and widely known in the Middle Ages owing to its treatment by Apuleius, Chalcidius, pseudo-Dionysius, and Alanus.[31] Thus, as the breath is lost, so also is the proper order of the will and of the other features, by implication, of the speculative creaturely triune mind, as we have seen and as we shall shortly see.

Herod's shift to the interrogative form at the beginning of stanza 28, the final stanza treating this instance of serial volitional errancy as well as the last instance of *phantasma* involving delusions of grandeur, suggests that a return to conditional "easse" is occurring yet again. But unlike the previous two instances, this return is interrupted, as the consultant scholars, to protect themselves, offer the strategy of pogrom or the "nobyll gyn." This distracts the king of Judea so much that, for the first time in the play, he appears actually to experience a genuine rather than a conditional "easse." The immediate acceptance of this strategy, while affording a distinct peace of mind to Herod as well as an effective conclusion to the first scene, reveals the degree to which Herod's reason has also been corrupted as the result of the wilful impiety that has led to the bereavement in his rational soul of the life it derives from God. This revelation, of course, is not the only evidence in the first scene pointing to such degradation. In fact, this corruption of the reason, like that of the will and that of the memory before it, is evinced extensively throughout the play's first twenty-nine stanzas. This form of corruption is heard perhaps most loudly and startlingly as Herod orders the consultant scholars to throw their books in the "brookys," or as he joyously accepts the strategy of pogrom without considering the horror of such an act or even the cost/benefit consequences of annihilating an entire generation. But a more systematic dramatization of defective reason is also incorporated in the very first scene, with the matter of the play's action organized according to a modified form of *concordantia*, or what Panofsky has identified as the second controlling principle of Scholasticism[32]—the technique, that is, of reconciling the seemingly irreconcilable through presentation of a preliminary set of propositions or *videtur quod,* presentation of a second set of contrary propositions or *sed contra,* and presentation of a reconciliation of the irreconcilables or *respondeo dicendum,* the technique that in the later Middle Ages determined the form of academic instruction, of public *disputationes de quolibet,* and even of argumentation in the Scholastic writings themselves.

The formal incorporation in the play's first scene of *concordantia* as *discordantia* or defective *disputatio* enables the Wakefield Master to demonstrate repeatedly the ineffectuality of impaired reason. The dramatizations of irrationality consist of varied but consistent disavowals of "inventive" or hermeneutical responses to any kind of challenging interpretive *circumstantiae*. First, at the beginning of the induction, Nuncius startles all within earshot by disrupting the aesthetic distance between spectator and stage through the introduction of methexis, as has been mentioned. While the monologue then proceeds according to the formal pattern of Scholastic argumentation, no reconciliation of irreconcilables occurs. In other words, even though the *videtur quod*'s "sondys" presented by Nuncius—three in all, including the announcements of Mahowne's wanting everyone to be happy (stanza 1) and Herod's wanting everyone to love and dread him (stanza 2), and the reminder not to cross Herod (stanza 3)—are countered by the introduction of a brief *sed contra* concerning the "boy" whose destiny, rumor has it, is to be "kyng" (16/38–40), no synthesis or solution is offered as this first irreconcilable is summarily dismissed at the beginning of the induction's first *respondeo dicendum:*

> And that we deny;
> How shuld it so fall,
> Greatt meruell haue I;
> Therfor ouerall
> Shall I make a cry
> That ye busk not to brall
> Nor lyke not to ly
> This tyde.
> Carpys of no kyng
> Bot Herode, that lordyng. (16/41–50)

What is more, as this *respondeo dicendum* of sorts is elaborated in the rest of the induction (stanzas 5–7), it becomes clear that it has little other dramatic function than to reassert the "sondys" already set forth in the *videtur quod*. Even though the form of the Scholastic method is employed here to introduce the fundamental matter of the play, it is manipulated to produce the opposite of what is intended. This establishes the first dramatic irony in the play by breaking the plane, as it were, of the play-performance reality and realienating the audience, who moments before were invited, through the direct discourse of methexis, to respond empathically to the action they were about to witness.

Another feature of this formal pattern's incorporation that contributes to this alienation—to this redistancing of the audience—is the collateral irony that results from the inability to respond "inventively" to challenging interpretive *circumstantiae*, an inability demonstrated as this first *disputatio* is undermined. As the *sed contra* of the boy who would be "kyng" is introduced and almost as quickly denied, Nuncius reveals he can comprehend neither the "unknown literal" of the boy nor the "unknown figurative" of the boy's destined role as king. This insurmountable interpretive challenge is avoided, as noted, by the summary act of denial. But as soon as the faulty *respondeo dicendum* is introduced to reassert the "sondys" of the *videtur quod*, evidence of Nuncius's inability to comprehend the "ambiguous literal" and the "ambiguous figurative" also becomes noticeable. This failing on Nuncius's part is not as easily dismissed. In fact, it is elaborated for the purpose of introducing yet another consonant irony—this time through anachronism. As Nuncius sings Herod's praises, his glorification reveals the inability to comprehend the "ambiguous literal" through his inclusion, as we have seen, of expressions conventionally used for Christ—expressions such as "kyng of kynges" and "lord of lordyngys." This confusion establishes the basis for introduction of like confusion, one instance of which is similar and one more complex. The first follows in the bathetic geographical anachronism of Nuncius's reference to "Kemptowne,"[33] a reference that functions as part of the geographical expression of the scope of Herod's fame:

From Paradyse to Padwa
To Mownt Flascon,
From Egyp to Mantua

> Vnto Kemptowne,
> From Sarceny to Susa
> To Grece it abowne,
> Both Normondy and Norwa
> Lowtys to his crowne. (16/66–73)

The second is found in Nuncius's subsequent claim that only Herod's "cosyn Mahowne" can speak of Herod's fame. Introducing this ineffability topos as he does to praise Herod, Nuncius inadvertently and ironically achieves the opposite end—that is, he offers an antiphrasis of sorts[34]—by revealing the uncertainty of public report about Herod. He transforms the fame, a fact or "known literal," in other words, into an "ambiguous figurative," a challenging interpretive circumstance to which no one can respond but Mahomet, a figure in conventional medieval artistic representations who, along with his other defects, was not known for his interpretive ability.[35]

A second dramatic irony completes the induction and, as its elaboration continues into the first scene, links the induction to what follows. This irony inheres in the contrast between the purpose and the effect of the *disputatio* form used yet again to present content. The *videtur quod* consists of three stanzas of predictable praise of Herod, as well as acknowledgment of the disturbing development caused by the rumor of the new "kyng." The *sed contra* that follows, the beginning of scene 1, challenges this development through Herod's violent threat of talk-taming and hanging. As in the previous incorporation of the *disputatio* form in the induction, the deployment of this patterned response here again does not reconcile irreconcilables, since the two-stanza *respondeo dicendum* merely reasserts the *videtur quod* by demonstrating anew, through many threats, that Herod is one who must be obeyed.

This debasement of the *disputatio* form is not the only source of humor at this point in the play. As he begins his initial rant, Herod calls attention to the fact that he, like Nuncius, cannot make sense of any challenging interpretive circumstance. This incapacity is revealed in two ways. In the first complete stanza of the *respondeo dicendum*, or stanza 10, Herod acknowledges he is incapable of engaging in analysis by examination—in the first, that is, of the two intellectual habits of mind promoted by Hugh of St. Victor as essential to explicating signs or a text.[36] While violating the aesthetic distance between spectator and stage by continuing the play's initial methexis of direct address, now in the form not of a warning but of a threat, he reveals metaphorically that, for him, the process of opening up things that are hidden is not a means of arriving at truth but rather a way of punishing by silencing those who do not "harkyn" to what he offers as rede:

> Stynt, brodels, youre din—
> Yei, euerychon!
> I red that ye harkyn
> To I be gone;
> For if I begyn,
> I breke ilka bone,
> And pull fro the skyn
> The carcas anone—
> Yei, perdé!
> Sesse all this wonder,
> And make vs no blunder,
> For I ryfe you in sonder,
> Be ye so hardy. (16/118–30)

This incapacity is elaborated by the next stanza as Herod demonstrates he is incapable of engaging in analysis through separation. While continuing his rant by warning everyone to remain quiet, he reveals that, for him, the process of sorting out things that are mingled together is not a means of arriving at the truth but, again, a way of punishing by silencing those who "Styr" without "lefe" (16/141). This revelation is conveyed through the metaphor of the cut-up stew meat or "small... flesh to pott" (16/143) into which Herod threatens to turn everyone who forgets that he has the power of "lyfe and dede" (16/134). Such threatened butcherly separation into parts of anyone opposing him, in keeping with the tenor of the previous threat of excoriation (16/124–25), suggests the degree to which meaning will be slaughtered by the butchery of the Herodian literal-mindedness to follow.[37]

The audience does not have to wait long for this demonstration. The remaining two instances of *discordantia*, or the defective *disputatio* form, in the first scene combine to form an ironic dramatic *allegoria* of the disavowal of the "inventive" speculative creaturely triune mind. The dramatic irony of this disavowal is again evoked here by the use to which is put the habit of mind associated with the Scholastic method. But while the action's order of presentation does not lead to the reconciliation of opposites, also contributing to the irony in this portion of the play is the way the same action demonstrates the inability to respond "inventively" to the challenging interpretive *circumstantiae* of both the "unknown literal" and the "unknown figurative."

The "unknown literal," evidenced in a new *videtur quod* in the next five stanzas (12–16), is the aggravated suspicion occupying Herod's attention. This is no ordinary feeling; it is evoked by a complex of related things. The most important of these is the "lad" or "losell" about whom rumor is now flying and whose bones Herod would break, if given the chance, with an anachronistic "steyll brand" (16/155). But also part of this complex are two other things, one of them another "unknown literal" and the other an "unknown figurative." The former consists of the unknown "kyngys" who have sought out the "lad" and managed to escape Herod unscathed. The latter is the baffling source of the emotion of anger, of which Herod finds himself suffering repeated bouts, one now practically after another. This last feature of Herod's suspicion reveals the limit of his self-knowledge and the effect of pride, a condition for which Herod is conventionally identified as a principal type.[38]

The *sed contra* in stanzas 17–20 repudiates the *videtur quod*'s unfounded suspicion in two factual ways. First, it introduces information about the Magi's departure. Primus Miles does this, pleading for Herod not to be angry at the messenger over the content of the message, which is that the "kyngys" have left by "Anothere way in hy" (16/213). Secondly, the *sed contra* challenges the conjectural by laying bare Herod's "hart," a revelation more important than the finding of fact. What Herod discloses about the "inner" man is that he remains suspicious and wrathful even when the object of his suspicion and wrath has been removed. In other words, his anger and unsettled state of mind are voluntary and habitual, not an accident or an aberration, and so he embodies what Aquinas identifies as "sinful madness."[39] This fact of Herod's character is enunciated by Tertius Miles as he objects, after Herod calls his knights "thefys," to Herod's rebuking without justification (16/229–34). It is also revealed strikingly by Herod himself as he rejects Tertius Miles's objection and continues to berate his men. In this impassioned, wrathful moment, as he denounces his cohort by calling all of them "losels and liars, / Lurdans ilkon!" (16/235–36)—terms usually reserved for those in opposition to the status quo—Herod inadvertently introduces the methexis of direct discourse in the violent conjecture concerning what he would do to the "kyngys" or "land-lepars" if he could get his hands on them. Proclaiming he will exact retribution on their "bonys," he follows this threat with another—

If ye byde in these wonys,
I shall dyng you with stonys (16/244–45)

—which momentarily turns the audience themselves, as we have noted, into the "land-lepars" whose bones Herod would like to break. This act of discovering or identifying the object of his suspicion, described by at least one critic as a significant metatheatrical moment,[40] has the effect of drawing the audience "closer" to the action onstage. But it also serves to remind everyone who may be thrilled by the imminent danger evoked by such a threat that the cause of Herod's wrath is not something extrinsic to Herod himself.

While the conjectural is countered by the factual in the presentation of the "unknown literal" and "unknown figurative" of rancorous suspicion, the *respondeo dicendum* that follows here, comprising the three knights' replies (stanzas 21 and part of 22), does not reconcile irreconcilables but, contrary to Scholastic method, introduces a new conjectural—to wit, what the soldiers would have done had they caught the Magi themselves. If what the soldiers proclaim sounds much like what Herod earlier announced he would do under similar circumstances, it should not come as a surprise. The similitude—this manifestation of the mystery of Herod by way of analogy[41]—allows the soldiers to declaim against the "kyngys" and thereby turn attention away from themselves. What is more, this braggadocio has a salutary effect. By appearing to be Herodian in their speculative response to the flight of the "kyngys," the soldiers actually elicit approbation from Herod himself. The embodiment of *ira* and *superbia*,[42] Herod cannot denounce in his men traits fundamental to his own persona, since to do so would be a denunciation of himself.

Herod's inability to respond "inventively" to either the "ambiguous literal" or "ambiguous figurative" occupies the attention of the first scene's final episode, as Herod turns to his "preuey counsell" to discover the meaning of the "wonderfull talkyng" that has come to his ear.[43] In this instance, the incorporated *disputatio* form is used properly, but even this anomaly turns out to be ironic. In the *videtur quod* (stanzas 23–25)

Herod prescribes the method for inquiring into the nature of the "wonderfull talkyng," as he allows only irrelevant texts or sources, prohibiting pertinent works such as "legende," "pystyls and grales," "Mes," and "matyns" (16/295–99). While he permits Homer, he also includes Virgil, a choice conspicuously suggesting lack of familiarity with the Messianic Eclogue.[44] This oversight notwithstanding, Primus Consultus and then Secundus Consultus ignore the prohibition and offer an explanation for the "talkyng," the combination of which completes the *videtur quod*. The first contribution from Primus Consultus concerns the "ambiguous literal" and is an explication of "Isay" 7:14, the prophecy of the Virgin Birth, a miracle with a long tradition in medieval drama, which has its origin in the pseudo-Augustinian sermon *Contra Judaeos*:[45]

> *Virgo concipiet*
> *Natumque pariet*
> *Emanuell* is hete. (16/309–11)

While Primus Consultus paraphrases the earlier part of the famous quotation—

> We rede thus by Isay:
> He shal be so kynde
> That a madyn, sothely,
> Which neuer synde,
> Shall hym bere (16/304–8)

—he makes certain to include as precise a translation as he can of the line's final word, "*Emanuell*," concluding, "'God is with vs' / That is for to say" (16/313–14). In a sense, then, he offers an explanation for the "wonderfull talkyng" by performing a linguistic analysis by separation, an analysis in which the more important part of the line is deconstructed to distinguish it from the other parts of the sentence with which it is mingled syntactically as well as grammatically. Secundus Consultus offers a complementary explanation, performing an analysis by examination of the "ambiguous figurative" of the "wonderfull talkyng" by turning to and explicating Micheas 5:2—that is, by opening up what is "hidden" or implicit in the verse—then combining or fulfilling the Michean line with the idea of rule or captaincy found in the Matthean version of it (2:6) to reveal the "sentence" of the original verse. Thus, while his gloss begins by identifying the "gracyus / Lord" with Bedlem, it concludes by emphasizing the social order of those who will obey Him and over whom He shall rule for eternity:

> Of Bedlem a gracyus
> Lord shall spray
> That of Iury myghtyus
> Kyng shal be ay,
> Lord myghty;
> And hym shall honoure
> Both kyng and emperoure. (16/317–23)

The *sed contra* that follows, Herod's reply, begins at the end of stanza 25 and concludes three lines into stanza 28. As anti-intellectual in its tone as the explications by Primus and Secundus Consultus are intellectual, the *sed contra* here denounces both literal and figurative meaning. The denunciation of the literal arises in stanza 26 as Herod calls the counselors liars, and has two parts. Herod begins by impugning the motives of each advisor, first singling out Primus Consultus and claiming he spoke as he did only to anger him, Herod (16/327–28), and then denigrating the intelligence of Secundus Consultus (16/330–32). In the second part of the denunciation of the literal, at the end of the stanza, Herod, having called his counselors a number of insulting names, orders them to throw the literal away by casting their "bookys . . . in the brookys" (16/335–36).

The denunciation of the figurative, the remainder of the *sed contra*, occupies the entirety of stanza 27 plus three lines and takes the form of a literalization of the figurative, the interpretive response of taking a sign for a thing, the act Saint Augustine indicates constitutes the death of the soul.[46] The first part of this literalizing consists of the dismissal of the miracle of the "lad" as nothing more than a "trant," as something incredible. The next part of the literalizing consists of the threat against the "lad" by means of a brief methexis consisting of the interjection "War! I say" (16/345), as if the child, the counselors, and the audience were directly before him. The final part of the literalizing occurs at the end of the *sed contra* in the first three lines of stanza 28 as Herod dismisses the miracle of the "lad" by questioning how it is that "a carll in a kafe / Bot of oone yere age" (16/352–53)—that is, how a vulnerable infant—could anger him as much as this one has.

The *respondeo dicendum* that completes the episode, as well as the scene, actually reconciles the irreconcilables of the prophetic revelation and the summary dismissal of meaning through the positing of a plan of action. While Primus Consultus quiets Herod and reminds him the child is only a year old, Secundus Consultus introduces the stratagem of killing all the "knaue-chyldren" under the age of two. This sweeping approach reveals that little consideration has been given to the relationship between the cost in terms of the next generation and the benefit in terms of killing the one "lad," a fact that, though historically determined, undermines the credibility and intellectual standing of both scholars. But while these two should know better because of their demonstrated ability to engage in analysis by separation and analysis by examination, they nevertheless put their own preservation before the prophecy whose significance they themselves have so eloquently expounded.

III

Further elucidation of the impious mind's condition through a dramatic allegorizing of its principal cause—the vitiation of innocence—informs the iconic logic of the second scene's action. This is done in two ways. The first of these, the more humorous of the two, presents this corruption as the result of ignorance as Nuncius, in the scene's second episode, anachronistically engages in summoning the feudal host. Instructed to gather the "flowre of knyghthede" to demonstrate "legeance," Nuncius misconstrues the interpretive *circumstantia* of this particular metonymy by literalizing the "ambiguous figurative" of the flower in terms of a readily identifiable quality of appearance. As a result, he insists the feudal host assemble "In armowre full bright; / In youre best aray" (16/405-6), an incongruity remarked even by one of the knights (16/415). Nuncius does not want to do wrong, to fall in his master's estimation, especially since he has been addressed as "Bewshere," and since the promise of advancement made to him is contingent upon his carrying out his duties to Herod's satisfaction. Yet his desire not to err leads directly to his doing wrong. That this mistake is not perceived by Herod becomes yet another of the scene's ironies, as does, eventually, the ceremonial armor's monstrous inappropriateness to the act of baby-killing in which the knights agree to engage.[47]

Vitiation of innocence as the result of malevolence, or the intentional will to do harm, is also brought to the audience's attention twice in the second scene. The first instance is in the brief opening episode as Herod, now fully convinced of the "nobyll gyn's" efficacy, declares he will proceed to take vengeance. While he has called for vengeance previously in *phantasma*-induced exasperation over the "lad," the deliberateness now of the declaration, the result of the perceived practical ease with which the plan can be carried out, alerts the audience that retribution is being sought, to satisfy Herod's feelings, for a wrong against him that, of course, has not occurred. The distortive quality of this unreasonableness is also suggested just moments before in the conception of grace Herod articulates in return for the "nobyll gyn." What for Herod is perceived to be sacred is nothing more than the profanation of the ideal in the form of materialistic reward, the most pleasing recompense consisting of

Markys, rentys, and powndys,
Greatt castels and groundys.(16/387–88)

The second instance of innocence's vitiation through malevolence occurs in the scene's final and longest episode, "The Massacre of the Innocents." Recent critical response to this passage has singled out two distinct features of the account of the event in the Towneley play distinguishing it from treatments elsewhere. First, the staging of the slaughter is far more formal than in other Herod plays, where the brawl is usually emphasized. Second, the mothers fight more like chivalric knights than do the knights themselves, a distinction emphasized especially by the difference in language used by the two combatant groups.[48] This is not to say that the mothers turn out to be "mothers of invention." The emphasis on the formalistic matriarchal response in each representation of the struggle that results from the combination of these two salient features, rather, provides the dramatic opportunity to *re-present* the historical event of the Slaughter of the Innocents as the allegorized tropological event of the slaughter of innocence. Such modification of the slaughter's purpose requires demonstration of the degradation of each feature of the speculative creaturely triune mind as well as the expression of the cause leading to that corruption. In addition, because the degradation of the rational soul cannot occur without the soul's having been bereft of the life it derives from God, each *re-presentation* of degradation likewise cannot be complete without some form of acknowledgment of divine abandonment.

First evidence of such extensive allegorizing in this part of the play arises in the initial encounter between Prima Mulier and Primus Miles.

As the action of the massacre begins, the threat to the will is brought to the audience's attention. The way in which this threat is imaged or suggested is through a series of attempts on Prima Mulier's part not to be contained. The first occurs as Primus Miles, in carrying out his orders, tries to diminish the heinousness of the act he is about to commit by asking Prima Mulier, simply, not to take amiss her child's impending death. Primus Miles, however, obviously does not know the nature of his adversary. Prima Mulier immediately replies that it is her will to protect her infant—that Primus Miles will not be able to carry out what he has come to do if she can help it:

> *1 Miles.* Dame, thynk it not yll,
> Thy knaue if I kyll.
> *1 Mulier.* What, thefe, agans my wyll?
> Lord, kepe hym in qwarte! (16/478–481)

In the second attempt at containment, Prima Mulier chafes under physical restraint as Primus Miles stops her, prohibiting her flight. Her intention is to put as much distance between the soldier and her child as she can, but because she is held in check, she uses the only nonviolent means left her by challenging her adversary with the threat of making "nose" or quarreling—that is, of verbally calling attention to what is happening so as to secure her child's and her own liberty while revealing the guilt of her assailant. Her initial and subsequent identifications of Primus Miles as "thefe" (16/480 and 484) and then, pleonastically, as "fals thefe" (16/490), are further examples of this linguistic strategy, the hope of which lies in the faulty assumption that the greater force of language through redundancy will act as a deterrent.

The final act of containment, the event intended to circumscribe Prima Mulier's response and will, is the actual killing, which occurs as soon as Primus Miles declares it is his comrades' and his purpose to carry out the pogrom. The finality of this act does eventually halt Prima Mulier's exercise of control through exercise of deliberate purpose rather than impulse, but not before her attempt to throw off one last time such constraint born of malevolence. In this final volitional response, Prima Mulier makes a thrust at her son's murderer. Not only is this an act of defiance, it is a successful one. To clear the way for the lethal blow she means to deliver, Prima Mulier gets Primus Miles to drop his guard, as it were, by suggesting that her intended target is the soldier's genitalia. Telling Primus Miles to protect his groin—

> Tyd may betyde,
> Kepe well thy nose,
> Fals thefe (16/488–90)[49]

—she takes advantage of the deception to land a crushing blow to the skull. That the stratagem achieves its end—that Prima Mulier manipulates her adversary's response and momentarily contains the one who would contain her—is attested by his sudden outburst of anger in the first of many pejoratives used to describe the mothers. But Prima Mulier's success is at best a Pyrrhic victory; her son is dead, and the expression of will has proved ineffectual against Herod's malevolence.

As the second encounter between soldier and mother begins, a change in substance of response alerts the audience to the second aspect of the vitiation of innocence through the Massacre of the Innocents—the degradation, that is, of memory. This outcome is resisted as long as possible by Secunda Mulier's repeated efforts not to let matters of significance be forgotten. This "mnemonic" resistance first arises as Secunda Mulier encounters Secundus Miles and learns immediately his homicidal purpose. As she engages Herod's soldier, Secunda Mulier attempts to insure the remembrance of two things. By begging for "mercy," she tries to get Secundus Miles to recollect a disposition of mind other than the one driving him to complete his grim task. The other thing not to be forgotten is that the victim is someone near and dear to her, an individual upon whom she places a face by identifying and singling him out as her "awne dere son" (16/507).

A second attempt not to let matters of significance be forgotten follows as soon as it is obvious the initial plea has fallen on deaf ears. This too consists of two parts, which now take the form of threats. One intimidatory announcement calls attention to memory itself by focusing on the actual anatomical site with which medieval authorities associated this mental faculty[50]—"Then thi skalp shall I clefe!" (16/510)—which is ironic, of course, in that Secunda Mulier threatens to end Secundus Miles's memory in order to get him to remember what he is doing. The other threat, following logically from the first, demands that Secundus Miles recollect the painful physical experience of being scratched to drive home the danger he now faces at the hands of his chosen matriarchal adversary:

> Lyst thou be clawd?
> Lefe, lefe, now bylefe! (16/511–12)

The final instance of "mnemonic" resistance comes suddenly after Secundus Miles has brutally struck down Secunda Mulier's child. The two parts of this response consist of the rebuke of her child's murderer. The first part, the ethical, calls attention to the "interior" man by asking Secundus Miles to recollect what he has just done and feel shame:

> Fy, fy, for reprefe!
> Fy, full of frawde—
> No man! (16/514–16)

This attempt to stir in Secundus Miles's consciousness some awareness of guilt attempts to stimulate remembrance of the murder as well as the fraud or misrepresentation of his chivalry that has enabled him to get close to the mother and child to carry out the deed. The second part of the rebuke, the practical, turns attention to the "exterior" man by identifying his tabard as the target of Secunda Mulier's lunge. This reminds the audience of the tabard's mnemonic sociopolitical function, which is the identification and remembrance not only of officialdom but usually also of some pronouncement coming from officialdom, since the garment was more often than not associated with the office of herald.[51] By thrusting as she does at the tabard, then, Secunda Mulier engages the audience's sympathy temporarily, but her action nevertheless introduces a discrepancy since the blow to Secundus Miles's mid-section implies an attempted destruction of this sociopolitical "mechanism" of remembrance, this emblem of official memory. That Secunda Mulier engages in pejoration like Primus and Secundus Milites as she calls Secundus Miles "Harlot and holard" (16/518), and that she concludes the rebuke with "I cry and I ban!" (16/520), furthers the discrepancy by demonstrating, on the one hand, how she has become like her adversary and, on the other, how she has forgotten, in invoking destruction or punishment on her adversary, the divine injunction concerning vengeance itself. While laudable, her defiance has led to her forgetting that it is her purpose not to forget.

The final part of "The Massacre of the Innocents" introduces, through the encounter between Tertia Mulier and Tertius Miles, the last aspect of the allegorized slaughter of innocence—the degradation of reason. This consequence is challenged by Tertia Mulier's repeated resistance to victimization by force motivated by irrationality. This distinction becomes apparent in Tertia Mulier's initial response to the beckoning of her by Tertius Miles at the outset of the encounter. As she answers Herod's soldier, she asks him straightforwardly whether it is his intention to do her or her child any harm. The directness of her question leaves no room for evasion:

> Wyll ye do any dere
> To my chyld and me? (16/538–39)

A second way she tries to put a stop to victimization by irrationality is through appeal to higher authority. This appeal follows her initial question when it is clear her child has been singled out to be murdered and she has been singled out to witness the act. Not much time is permitted Tertia Mulier to make this appeal, with dramatic events accelerating at this point to heighten the suddenness and tragic effect of the killing. In the fleeting moment afforded her, however, Tertia Mulier begs God for deliverance through the exclamation "God forbede!" (16/542).

The final way Tertia Mulier attempts to forestall her victimization at the hands of irrationality involves two actions, one concerning herself and the other Tertius Miles. The former occurs as the horror of her child's murder nearly makes her lose her reason. While she exclaims in response to the killing, she maintains control, difficult as this is for her under such circumstances, by explaining aloud the cause of her distress, and by consciously limiting, also by means of explanation, the expression of that distress:

> Out, I cry! I go nere wood!
> Alas, my hart is all on flood,
> To se my chyld thus blede. (16/544–46)

The second action she takes to forestall her inevitable victimization at the hands of irrationality is to remind Tertius Miles that he must suffer the consequence of his actions:

> By God, thou shall aby
> This dede that thou has done. (16/547–48)

This is something to which Tertius Miles gives little heed. As a result, he is so caught off guard that Tertia Mulier has time to deliver two thrusts at his person. The first hits him on an undisclosed part of his body as Tertia Mulier exclaims, "Take the ther a foyn!" (16/552). The "ther" of the second blow is more specific as Tertia Mulier thrusts again, this time at Tertius Miles's genitalia (16/554). The attempt at emasculation by this second strike reinforces Tertia Mulier's determination not to be victimized by the lack of reason informing Tertius Miles's actions. But as with the previous two encounters, nothing Tertia Mulier does can alter the course of history. While undaunted to the end, she finally reveals degradation of reason—"I cry and I rore" (16/558)—as she responds more now as if out of impulse than out of reason.

Further evidence in the third episode of the allegorizing of the Massacre of the Innocents as the massacre of innocence is also made apparent by identification of the cause leading to the degradation of the rational soul, and by the concomitant acknowledgment in each engagement, or expressed condition of corruption, of the distance separating humankind from God. The former consists of the soldiers' repeated demonstration of the vitiated reason, the condition of spirit in which the spirit suffers not from the body but from itself in adjusting itself to the body.[52] This corrupt condition of reason is partly suggested by their desire for worldly things—a desire motivating them to function as the militant agency of Herod's malevolence in order to reap the pecuniary reward implicit in his promise to be "freyndly" (16/467)—and partly by their callousness in approaching their task as a "dulfull lake" (16/466). But it is most evident in the "excessive, intensifying pejoration" in which they find themselves engaging as each meets with an unanticipated resistance mounted by a mother to save her child.[53] Such reliance upon contumely alerts the audience to the absence of the *verbum Dei* as informing principle of each soldier's "interior" man.

The repeated demonstration of the separation between humankind and God that completes the second scene's allegorizing of the massacre of innocence is articulated in the final part of each mother's response to the murder of her child. This demonstration, often identified as the cry for vengeance, is part of a formalized expression of emotion in each section of "The Massacre" that verisimilitudinously represents the profundity of personal loss by each woman. While this emotionalism is designed to engage audience sympathy to an extent, the successive expressions of grief also provide the dramatic opportunity to construct a progression of increasing specificity of accusation, beginning at the level of class distinction, moving next to generic distinction, and concluding with distinction according to species. In the first part of this telescoping progression, the response to the murderer calls attention to the shamefulness of the act—"Outt, for reprefe!" (16/494)—while the cry for vengeance reflects the perception of the act as "syn," or transgression against divine law:

> Veniance for this syn
> I cry both euyn and morne. (16/501–2)

In the next part, the response to the murderer now identifies him as a "morder-man" (16/521) or murderer—that is, as one who has engaged in manslaughter through the prepensive desire to do harm—while the cry for vengeance identifies Herod and his knights as the objects of divine and natural retribution. In the final part of the progression, the response to the murderer singles him out as the exact or specific person who has committed the unlawful and heinous act—"Out on the, mans mordere!" (16/559)—while the cry for vengeance, now an expression of abject distress, calls attention not to the "son" or "chyld" but to the child's "body...all to-rent," the material evidence of Herod's culpable brutality. This final emphasis—upon exact identification of the victim as well as assailant—suggests, on looking back at the less exact identifications of culpability, that a greater distancing is occurring between sufferer and God, whose name, to bridge that ever-widening gap, is repeatedly invoked to carry out retribution.

IV

The elucidation of the wrathful impious mind also occupies the attention of the *Magnus Herodes*'s final and shortest scene, which demonstrates—since the Corpus Christi performance was meant to be therapeutic on an individual and a civic level—the distortive and injurious effect such a mind has on both the "interior" and the "exterior" man. One instance of the latter effect is evidenced in the first brief episode, "The Readying for the Triumph," as the soldiers quickly decamp from the field of carnage to bring news to Herod of the thorough success of their murderous mission. As they prepare to make their report, their interaction vitiates the presumed sodality of a brotherhood in arms. Secundus and Tertius Milites agree they should hurry to Herod to "tell of this lott" (16/577), and Tertius Miles, commending Secundus Miles on his fine work, suggests he be the one to convey the "tayll" to their commander. The emphasis on camaraderie in Tertius Miles's commendation is echoed when he concludes, moments later, that if Secundus Miles conveys the news, Herod's response will be nothing short of praise. But Primus Miles's interruption spoils the effect of harmony as he presumptuously claims precedence:

> I am best of you all
> And euer has bene;
> The deuyll haue my saull
> Bot I be fyrst sene!
> It syttys me to call
> My lord, as I wene. (16/586–91)

This act of wilful severance, the result of an energetic and anarchic arrogance,[54] shows how tenuous the immediate cohesion of social order is when those asserting or maintaining that order align themselves with a mind that wilfully arrogates power to itself and thereby permits the Image of God within it to be destroyed through a self-serving insolent impiety.

Another effect the wrathful impious mind has on the "exterior" man, the final scene suggests, is the degradation of feudal reciprocity, the system of mutual support that binds social and political order, from the highest point of the hierarchal structure to the lowest. The demonstration of this corruption, the subject of the scene's second episode, "The Seeking of Reward," is presented two ways. The first of these consists of Herod's two-part ridicule of the soldiers. As they approach him with news of the slaughter's completion, he derides them by offering a "lady" for each to wed. In other words, for services rendered, each knight is rewarded with the opportunity to be again with the very adversary he has just had great difficulty in defeating. As the soldiers stolidly press for "greatt plenté," they are again mocked by Herod, but this time the derision consists of being tantalized with the illusion of fabulous reward while being given actually only pennies:

> As I am kyng crownde,
> I thynk it good right;
> Ther goys none on grownde

That has sich a wyght.
A hundreth thowsand pownde
Is good wage for a knyght,
Of pennys good and rownde,
Now may ye go light
With store. (16/638–46)

The insincerity of this second act of ridicule is repeated in Herod's parting words to the soldiers, in which he commends them to "Mahowne" in the hopes that they will be brought to where that false god is "lord freyndly"—that is, to the very epicenter of perdition itself, or even the Muslim paradise, which also costs him nil.

The second way feudal reciprocity is shown to be vitiated by the influence of the wrathful impious mind involves the soldiers' credulous response to the two instances of ridicule directed at them. In the one instance, they appear not to understand the offer at all and are unresponsive. In the other, they first accept as promise merely the estimation of a hypothetical wage, and when a promise of future liberality, indeed in perpetuity, follows—

And ye knyghtys of oures
Shall haue castels and towres,
Both to you and to youres,
For now and euermore (16/647–50)

—they accept, imprudently, without any surety. For feudal reciprocity to exist and be a functional means of informing social order, reasonable response from both parties engaged in the relation of mutual support has to be forthcoming. For the soldiers to misconstrue the mocking tantalization and subsequent promise not only as compensation but also as money in the bank is as grievous an error of omission as Herod's derisive—even sadistic—joy in deceiving the soldiers is an obvious error of commission.

The injurious influence of the wrathful impious mind on the "interior" man is reserved for the scene's final episode, "The Daemonic Sermon," for obvious dramatic as well as hortatory effect. This is not to say the social consequences of such a mind are unimportant, especially in a performance art form, the principal civic therapeutic purpose of which is the reassertion of social order through sacramental understanding. But how the "interior" man is affected by such a mind's contagious influence does have direct bearing on how the "exterior" man affects others and the world about him since, in medieval thinking, the proper or improper order of one's interiority—that is, of the microcosm—influences the proper or improper order of one's exteriority, or the macrocosm. Accordingly, consideration of this effect, for aesthetic as well as philosophical reasons, is chosen as the most effective way to conclude the play, because through this final dramatization the audience is permitted to see clearly what the effect is when the divine influence acting in man or the Light of Truth[55] is irrevocably extinguished.

To frame the dramatic evocation of this condition through Herod's last monologue, the Wakefield Master organizes the play's final action according to a modified version of the basic plan of the late-medieval "artistic sermon," an instructive example of which can be found in Thomas of Salisbury's *Summa de arte praedicandi*. The modification in this instance combines the sections of the Division—that is, the statement of parts of the theme—with the Development (*prosecutio*) of elements named in the Division. The rest of the incorporated structure is left more or less intact: the Opening Prayer, the introductory Protheme or Antetheme, the Theme itself—that is, the statement of scriptural quotation preceding the Division and Development—and the Conclusion.[56]

The beginning of the final episode takes the form of the Opening Prayer, though it is less an entreaty for divine aid than a thanksgiving to "Mahowne" for helping restore "peasse" to Herod's mind. This transformation is apparently so profound that, as part of his thanksgiving prayer, Herod even states with uncharacteristic generosity that he is ready to give of his land in appreciation:

> Now in peasse may I stand—
> I thank the, Mahowne—
> And gyf of my lande
> That longys to my crowne. (16/664–67)

This "peasse"-induced largesse, while startling, is also functional as it affords a transition to more pertinent matter, which, taking the form of a Protheme or Antetheme of sorts, introduces the sermonic monologue's theme. While the subject matter that follows has specifically to do with the promise of material reward, the thematic issue of the absence of truth is raised even before Herod has completed half of his introductory remarks. This is done by insertion of a final methexis, as Herod asks everyone to draw near. Though the multitude he has in mind or the newly established cohort he must now face—a cohort of spectators armed with the knowledge of the primary dramatic irony created by the play performance order enframing the *Magnus Herodes*, as well as with knowledge of secondary dramatic ironies resulting from the many acts of deception and self-deception thus far witnessed in the play—is not as ready as Herod's soldiers to accept the promise of a future liberality, still the direct address allows Herod to demonstrate, to the delight of all who are now perforce part of the action,[57] the audacity for which he is known, an audacity that instructively clarifies how he, like Guido da Montefeltro in the *Inferno*, is long on promise and short on performance.[58]

The introduction of the theme of truth's absence through the dramatic innovation of the prothemic methexis of direct discourse here sets the stage, as it were, for the introduction of yet another, even more startling, dramatic innovation as what Herod next says turns attention to the theme proper or the statement of scriptural quotation. While the audience has been drawn "closer" to the stage—has now, in effect, become part of Herod's daemonic cohort—through the methexical promise of a fabulous future liberality, Herod now, in considering the result of the Massacre of the Innocents, the "statement of scriptural quotation," turns from them without distancing himself from them to begin to explain how his "hart is at easse" (16/678)—a combined maneuver and disclosure that introduces complete soliloquy form, more subjective perhaps than expository, in which, for a brief time, the audience becomes even more than before a "part of the experience enacted on stage."[59] The experience, however, is still that of a conceptual reality more than it is an imitation of external life in time and space, and so the form might perhaps better be described as being more subjectively expository than its Elizabethan descendants.[60]

Whatever nomenclature is ultimately used to describe this singular dramatic innovation, its incorporation at this point in the final monologue allows for the development of the theme of the absence of truth in two distinct ways. First, Herod denies the significance of the slaughter. This is a remarkable refusal to make, since the account of the killing includes an exaggerated description of the carnage as a "flode" of blood "From the fote to the nese" (16/681–82). The absence of truth in Herod's attitude lies in his inability or lack of desire to recognize that a pogrom of this magnitude is a horribly grave event. The second way soliloquizing develops the theme of the absence of truth is by showing how Herod, known for deceiving others, readily deceives himself. What he asserts as truth at the end of stanza 53—

> I may do what I shall,
> And bere vp my crowne (16/688–89)

—is nothing more than illusion, ironically obscuring the fact that, because of the very pogrom he himself ordered, he now is irrevocably part of salvation history, and so may not do as he wishes, but rather must do as the sequence of events in that history dictates. His two callous remarks, about laughing to the point of wheezing over the slaughter, and about the lightness of his soul leading to the sweetening of his gall, also ironically resonate the absence of truth. While he takes these two symptoms, one behavioral and the other spiritual/physiological, as signs of good fortune, they suggest the opposite. Breathing with an audible friction suggests a corruption of the inaudible breath, the image of the soul, by the presence of material obstruction, a variation on Herod's previous loss of breath through panting,[61] while the lightness of the "saull" suggests an absence or the bereavement in the soul of the life it derives from God.

Another thing incorporation of the soliloquy form permits here is the prosecution of the two principal implications of the theme—namely, the absence of truth in perceived things exterior to Herod himself, and the absence of truth in things perceived within Herod's own mind. Pursuit of the former involves the two ways Herod employs evidence to convince himself of the pogrom's efficacy. First, he asserts the "lad" must be dead because the carnage indicates the impossibility of anyone's having escaped:

> Bot I thar not dyspare,
> For low is he layd
> That I most dred are,
> So haue I hym flayd;
> And els wonder war—
> And so many strayd
> In the strete—
> That oone shuld be harmeles
> And skape away hafles,

Where so many chyldes
Thare balys can not bete. (16/692–702)

The description reveals a horrific, brutal thoroughness, but the direct evidence offers no proof of the "lad's" demise. And the second consideration of evidence, the actual body count with its obvious ironic apocalyptic implications, functions the same way: though a great deal of evidence is to be seen, none of it, either in its grisly detail or in its specific numbers, makes the truth any more apparent.

Pursuit of the theme's second implication—the absence of the Light of Truth in Herod's mind—draws the soliloquy to a close. This demonstration of absence takes the form of Herod's boastful speculation that he would be the subject of much talk and even legend if he had had the opportunity to give the child "bot oone bat" (16/709). The presumption that an audience would see Herod as having thus been "wrokyn" or avenged certainly does not take into consideration the thinking of the actual audience, who are now more part of his experience since he has begun to explain his "hart" in the dramatic way he has chosen. Nor does it take into consideration the thinking of anyone who remembers the multiple ironies in practically everything Herod has thus far said and done. There may be a truth to Herod's speculation—credulous simpletons like his soldiers might actually be in agreement with him—but no factual evidence is available to support it.

The successful prosecution and demonstration by Herod himself of the absence of any truth whatsoever in his experience reveals, finally, the tragedy he both embodies and exemplifies. But the profundity of that tragedy becomes clear only in the two-stanza conclusion that completes the play, as Herod not only repeats that he still believes in the lie of his success, but also now sees the need to promulgate that lie as the basis of a new exemplarism. The perception of this need—the expression, in a sense, of his irrevocable tragic alienation, which would now perhaps be diagnosed as his paranoid suspicion but which the Middle Ages would understand as the condition of *duritia cordis*—reasserts the chilling effect the wrathful impious mind has been shown to have upon the order and cohesion of society. As the direct address of methexis is reintroduced here, an indication of the final incorporation of the "artistic sermon" structure in the final lines of the monologue, the audience as cohort— that is, as potential soldiers in Herod's cause—is suddenly transformed from potential followers deserving of a promised future liberality into potential "knauys" or adversaries who must, like the "lad," be subdued. The implied perception of the audience as "knauys" here has a reassuring effect on spectators, ironically, through the association it obviously implies. But it also introduces the opposite effect, ultimately, of the conclusively demonstrated fact that no reciprocity is possible, or will ever come about, where the only truth is that no truth exists. The subsequent dreary and predictable threats and commands that obedience be shown and that no questioning of anything occur reveal further this truth about truth's absence through the implied expectation of absolute compliance with any tyrannical demand. Herod's final words, thus, offer closure of sorts, not by concluding the action of the play, but rather by introducing a test of this expected kind of compliance hereafter to be demonstrated unconditionally. His final counsel not to be too cruel, an articulation of "staggering impudence,"[62] challenges anyone who might remember how he has delighted in or been callous to others' pain, or who might recall how bogus is the evidence he has adduced to prove his success. And his final deliberate misconstruing of the valedictory "Adew" as the curse "to the deuyll" reveals a like arbitrariness in interpretive understanding, as well as a kind of cruelty, since commending one in such a way implies the expectation of pain. That such an arrogant attitude would finally be dismissed by Herod himself as nothing more than speaking "Franch" no doubt provides a final moment of jingoistic delight for the entire Corpus Christi audience now fully aware, historically, of their rival and adversary across the Channel. But like other instances of verbal legerdemain before it in the play, it too fails to distract attention, finally, from the fact that no good can come from the mind bereft, through wilful and impious perversity, of the life it derives from God.

6

The Repudiation of the Eschatology of Labor in Two "Passion Group" Revisions and the *Coliphizacio*

A final permutation of the axiomatic idea of serving God cooperatively by serving the self through the technological mastery and practical use of nature arises in the remaining works attributed to the Wakefield Master—that is, in the *Coliphizacio*, the sixth and last of his entire plays, and in certain "Passion group" play revisions involving such memorable characters as Pilate and Tutivillus.[1] What distinguishes this permutation, set as it is in the latter part of the sixth age or the time of reconciliation, is that it principally explores the idea of cooperation through its inverse, or the repudiation of the eschatology of labor. This emphasis—if not startling, then certainly unanticipated, given the late-medieval conception of labor as positive preliminary means to salvation—is a conception most memorably imaged in medieval literature by Piers the Plowman preparing to set himself to plow, and most instructively articulated by the transformation of the idea of the working saint into the saintly worker.[2] But this disparity, appearing at this point in the Towneley *regenall*, is no accident. The emphasis provides the Wakefield Master with the artistic opportunity to awaken his audiences to the perilousness of their moral condition, much the same way contemporary medieval homilists do through sermon, by exploring imaginatively, yet again through deft dramatic allegoresis, the tragic implications of such spiritual and practical obstinacy from the two instructive perspectives of abuse, at the institutional and the individual level.

I

Exploration of individual abuse involves the characters of Pilate and Tutivillus—characters appearing in revisions attributed to the Wakefield Master in the *Conspiracio, Flagellacio, Processus Talentorum,* and

Iudicium. In the case of Pilate, the most memorable and consistently developed villain in all of British medieval drama,[3] this sort of repudiation is allegorized as two forms of abuse: that having to do with legal procedure or "mastry," and that having to do with legal rule or "sovereigntée." The latter receives attention at least twice in two of the four works in which Pilate is treated by the Master.[4] First, Pilate's signature ranting, which is found at the beginning of the *Conspiracio* and the *Processus Talentorum*, evokes dramatically the abuse of the *techne* or practical art of rule by the "nakedest form of oppression, the unscrupulous use of absolute power."[5] In the *Conspiracio* Pilate brandishes a sword and, engaging in the verbal swagger expected of *Os Malleatoris*,[6] which includes an initial methexis of direct address to the audience,[7] warns all within earshot that he is not the kind of ruler who is averse to breaking bones:

> I am kyd, as men knawes,
> Lef leder of lawes;
> Seniours, seke to my sawes,
> For bryssyng of youre bonys. (20/10–13)

In addition, he points out how well dressed he is and how his caste distinction, one at least partially based upon appearance,[8] should inspire in the "carles" or the "Vnconand," both onstage and in the audience, respect for him as "A rewler of great renowne" (20/17). Though he is only a Roman procurator, what is clear about Pilate in the feudal anachronizing of him by the Wakefield Master is that none of the principles associated with the idealistic late-medieval political conception of *rex pius et justus* has made its way into his characterization. Not only is Pilate self-absorbed and menacing, his way of rule is also openly contemptuous of those whom he governs. This is heard initially in the *Conspiracio* when he proclaims the ignorant should learn obedience, as might an animal, from the brandished sword before them. Such abuse of sovereignty is also made apparent at the beginning of the *Processus Talentorum* as Pilate, now using the language of authority culture as a weapon to inspire conformity, begins his signature harangue exclusively in Latin, and then continues it macaronically in Latin and English. The menacing gesture of satrapic absolutism is thus effectively supplanted by the razor-sharp intellectual edge of a polyglottal linguistic dexterity. But the bluster and swagger, not to mention the threat by raised fist, are not completely abandoned here as Pilate, having completed his report on the Crucifixion's completion, announces, once more in an intimidating Herodian way,

> Bot ye youre hedys
> Bare in thies stedys,
> Redy my swerde is
> Of thaym to shere now. (24/49–52)[9]

Regardless of the language used to express it, no reciprocity, feudal or otherwise, has a place in this legal order of rule. Those who are governed, in fact, have no option but to obey and conform to Pilate's command. As the final words given Pilate by the Wakefield Master indicate, order will exist provided all, in general as well as individually, remain silent:

> *Silete,*
> *In generali*
> *Sic speciali;*
> Yit agane byd I,
> *Iura tenete!* (24/61–65)

The tragedy of perverse "mastry" is also evidenced by Pilate in at least three of the four plays in which he appears or is referred to.[10] In the *Conspiracio* this is deftly achieved in the fourth stanza as the Wakefield Master, employing a brief methexis, allows Pilate to recruit directly from the audience a large force to deal with the "lurdan ledyr" Christ, who, according to Pilate, has threatened the stability of the sociopolitical order:

> More nede had I neuer
> Of sich seruand now, I say you—
> So can I well consider
> The trowth, I most displeas you—
> And therfor com I hedyr;
> Of peas, therfor, I pray you.
> Ther is a lurdan ledyr
> I wold not shuld dysmay you,
> Abowtt:
> A prophete is he prasyd,
> And great vnright has rasyd;
> Bot, be my banys her blasid,
> His deth is dight no dowtt. (20/40–52)

This direct appeal alerts everyone to the danger posed to the law by Christ, but also puts everyone, fellow characters as well as audience, within earshot of the explanation, on alert as to how the problem of the "lurdan ledyr" will be dealt with. For those of Pilate's way of thinking, the orientation is reassuring; for those who see this as a dangerous precedent, it quickly becomes clear that Christ will suffer the abuse of judicial process, being victimized by the bearing of false witness, as Pilate openly admits:

> And yit I stand in fere:
> So wyde he wyrkys vertus,
> No fawt can on hym bere,
> No lyfand leyde tyll vs.
> Bot sleyghtys
> Agans hym shall be soght,
> That all this wo has wroght;
> Bot on his bonys it shall be boght,
> So shall I venge oure rightys. (20/57–65)

A like abuse of judicial procedure is heard indirectly at the end of the *Coliphizacio*. Caiaphas, upset that Christ has been sent to Pilate for final judgment, suggests that procedure will be disregarded if Pilate is offered an attractive enough bribe:

> *Cayphas.* Alas, now take I hede!
> *Anna.* Why mowrne ye so?
> *Cayphas.* For I am euer in drede,
> Wandreth and wo,
> Lest Pylate for mede
> Let Iesus go.
> Bot had I slayn hym indede
> With thise handys two
> At onys,
> All had bene qwytt than.
> Bot gyftys marres many man;
> Bot he deme the sothe than,
> The dwill haue his bonys! (21/625–37)

This matter is of so much concern to Caiaphas that, at the end of the play, he informs Annas that he and his men, which may again include the audience by means of a methexical imperative,[11] will continue to watch Pilate to insure that Christ not be set free.

It is, however, in the last work in which the Wakefield Master's Pilate appears that the tragedy of perverse "mastry" is demonstrated most extensively and instructively. In the *Flagellacio*, the Pilate of the civil courts, "our old friend ... the unjust Judge," as Gerald R. Owst describes him,[12] has to maneuver legally in such a way as to avoid being blamed for Christ's execution. When the Passover offer to free the felon results in the call to liberate Barabbas instead of Christ, Pilate's most telling manipulation of judicial procedure follows. At first, he tries to elicit a response from Christ through leading questions and statements. His intention is to get Christ to acknowledge the reality of temporal rule's power:

Thou man that suffurs all this yll,
Why wyll thou vs no mercy cry?
Slake thy hart and thi greatt wyll,
Whyls on the we haue mastry.
Of thy greatt warkes shew vs som skyll;
Men call the kyng, thou tell vs why;
Wherfor the Iues seke the to spyll,
The cause I wold knowe wytterly,
Perdee. (22/248–56)

When this form of interrogation and manipulation fails, Pilate then searches for the technicality that will enable him to avoid censure when the execution of Christ, which is now a foregone conclusion, is completed. Interestingly enough, he discovers the answer he is looking for in the definition of legal rule or "sovereigntée" that is embraced by the people of Judea themselves. After Secundus Consultus confirms that Christ has identified himself as "a kyng in euery place" (22/265) and is about to undermine their laws, a fact to which Primus Consultus has previously testified (22/131–39), Pilate does not use the "machinery of the courts like a whip,"[13] which all too often, lamentably, was the case in late medieval England,[14] but rather introduces the possibility of the sociopolitical order's being predicated upon the late-feudal idea of multiple homage.[15] This possibility permits him to observe that the people of Judea, as represented vocally by the Consulti and actively by the Tortores, practice only a simple or direct homage and do not include in their political conception of order the idea of a liege lord or rear or border vassalage:

> Now, certys, this is a wonder thyng
> That ye wold bryng to noght
> Hym that is youre lege lordyng;
> In faith, this was far-soght. (22/274–77)

As a result, Pilate deftly presents himself with the opportunity to ask the most important question of all—that is, who it is the people consider to be the supreme head of the power structure informing their culture. If Christ has called Himself king and the people do not recognize that kingship, since they do not accept the idea of multiple homage, then it is the people, not Pilate, who will ultimately decide Christ's fate. And this is what happens. When Pilate, after an artful statement about the nature of the political order the people espouse, puts his leading question—

> Bot say, why make ye none obeyng
> To hym that all has wroght? (22/278–79)

—the people, through Tertius Tortor, identify their supreme and only lord, the person to whom they do homage directly, as "Syr Cesar":

> Sir, he is oure chefe lordyng,
> Syr Cesar, so worthyly wroght
> On mold. (22/280–82)

Thus it is the people, not Pilate, who assert that Christ's identification of Himself as king presents a competing idea of kingship or rule that is outside of—and thereby inimical to—the legal order giving stability to the current regime in Judea. Through this maneuver, Pilate has not had to use the law as a weapon, nor has he had to wrestle with conscience as Pilates in other medieval pageants must do;[16] rather, he has simply had to find within procedure the technicality that would free him from blame. He avoids engaging not only in "wycked warkys" but also "warkes wylde" (27/24), to use a term introduced in the *Perigrini* by Lucas, another of the Wakefield Master's creations, and so subtly and adroitly absolves himself of all guilt in connection with Christ's crucifixion.

The second character through whom the Wakefield Master allegorically explores dramatically the implication of the repudiation of the eschatology of labor at the level of the individual is the *Iudicium*'s

Tutivillus, the Towneley collection's version of the famous recording devil, the fiend that informs Jacobus de Vitriaco:

> I bere in my sacche sylablys & woordys,
> ouerskyppyd and synkopyd, & verse & psalmys
> þe whiche þese clerkys han stolen in þe qweere,
> & haue fayled in here seruyse.[17]

In some ways he resembles other versions, especially in his swagger and his use or abuse of language. As he introduces himself here, for example, he demonstrates, as Martin Stevens has noted, the "abuse which he was designed to guard against—that is, the incoherent and excessive utterance of words"[18] through the Latin gibberish he appends to the expression or motto with which he is traditionally associated:

> Mi name is Tutiuillus;
> My horne is blawen.
> *Fragmina verborum,*
> *Tutiuillus colligit horum;*
> *Belzabub algorum*
> *Belial belium doliorum.* (30/363–68)[19]

But under the Wakefield Master's imaginative pen he assumes the new identity of Judgment Day's infernal tax collector.[20] This innovative identity allows for presenting the "anti-swynke" attitude—that is, the refusal to serve God cooperatively through labor as preliminary means to salvation—as a response to an apocalyptic levy, a compulsory payment that includes the resonant irony of the act of censure, the principal etymology of the word "tax" itself. This allegorized presentation of transgression as tax, an association that would have been ironically pleasing to an audience whose members were no strangers to excessive levies,[21] introduces the opportunity for Tutivillus to provide a job self-assessment, which he does so thoroughly that Primus Demon—that is, Satan—has to pronounce that none, in the history of the infernal cohort, has ever rivaled this accomplishment.[22] But more important, this metaphoric association between transgression and tax allows Tutivillus to reveal how the effect of the psychology of sloth on labor[23] manifests itself in three distinct ways.

The first of these, from the "roll of ragman / Of the rownde tabill" (30/326–27), involves the repudiation of the eschatology of labor by means of the abuse of the *techne* of good husbandry through acts either of omission or of commission. The abuse of this practical art through omission is dramatized in an *allegoria* of the foppish layabout. This type, who has obviously spent all of his wages on his "Gay gere" and entertainment, ignores his responsibility as head of household, which leaves his children destitute and the family without order or hope:

> Gay gere and witles,
> His hode set on koket,
> As prowde as pennyles,
> His slefe has no poket,
> Full redles
> With thare hemmyd shoyn;
> All this must be done,
> Bot fyre is out at hye noyn
> And his barnes bredeles. (30/343–51)

The abuse of the *techne* of good husbandry through commission is dramatized in an *allegoria* of the deception practiced by women who lead "men to foly." This art, which involves "paynt" to make the woman appear like a "saynt," conceals a truth about its practitioner, that she is "wars then the deyle" (30/390), the discovery of which fact can only have a deleterious effect on domestic management and marital tranquility.

The next way the effect of the psychology of sloth on labor is revealed by Tutivillus is through elaboration, in the manner of the sermonic exemplum, of the expression of contrariety or the disordered will in a variety of social situations. Those who do not "gete [their] lyfe wyth swynke, and put away all ydylnes and slewth," to quote John Mirk again,[24] may, as Tutivillus now indicates is the custom, "breke thare wedlake" (30/401), act as "fals swerars" (30/406), or misrepresent themselves by means of false "gise" (30/421). While those who abuse the *techne* of good husbandry, through either commission or omission, are "mysdoers" (30/436), many others evidencing a similarly disordered will can be found among the "kyrkchaterars":

> Yit of thise kyrkchaterars
> Here ar a menee,
> Of barganars and okerars

And lufars of symonee,
Of runkers and rowners. (30/430–434)

Tutivillus calls attention one last time to the consequence of the repudiation of the eschatology of labor by innovatively recasting the Seven Deadly Sins through the formal combination of dramatized *allegoria* and sermonic exemplum—through, in other words, a "Somthyng speciall / Now nately to neuen" (30/444–45).[25] The audience is reminded of all the sins, and, in customary fashion, initial emphasis first comes to pride, the most important sin of all, as evidenced by the parvenu whose outfit makes his "luddokkys . . . lowke / Like walk-mylne cloggys" (30/456–57), and Nell, whose "Gill knaue" getup of an open-backed "smok" is wickedly vulnerable to the "west wynde" (30/480). The something special that is introduced, however, is the explanation for all the sinful behavior, both by the tavern-frequenting "howndys of hell" (30/493) and by the "Ianettys of the stewys / And lychoures on lofte" (30/508–9). The reason given for the conspicuous downturn in moral probity is sloth, but not indolence in the general sense. The sloth Tutivillus says has enabled him to bring record numbers of "saules" to the demons, "Mo then x m / In an howre of a day" (30/315–16), is the sloth in which malefactors do not do "Goddys warkys" (30/496)—the sloth, in other words, resulting from the rejection of labor or "lyfe wyth swynke" as cooperation and means to salvation.

II

The second imaginative exploration of the tragic implications of the spiritual and practical obstinacy leading to the repudiation of the eschatology of labor, one limited this time to the *Coliphizacio* alone, is elaborated by means of abuse at the level of institutional activity, which involves a complex dramatic allegorizing of Christ's Trial and Buffeting in terms of the principal features of judicial procedure in the days before jury standard of proof. The event, as recounted in its gospel sources,[26] lends itself readily to such allegorization because such procedure, that of Roman-canon law of proof or the *ius commune*,[27] involves the same array of characters, more or less, as appears in the gospel accounts of the Trial—that is, examiners, eyewitnesses, torturers, and the accused.[28] As a result of this congruency, the four-scene *Coliphizacio*,[29] under the artistic direction of the Wakefield Master, evokes dramatically the tragedy of this particular kind of repudiation allegorically through several demonstrations of procedural irregularity or, in other words, through repeated demonstrated abuse of the *techne* of legal procedure.

Before considering how the *Coliphizacio* dramatizes the biblical events of the Trial and Buffeting in terms of this intentional procedural error, it is necessary to understand how and why the play's biblical sources are appropriated and modified. A cursory review of scripture recalls to mind that two trial sequences do, in fact, exist. The first, the "Jewish," involves an initial hearing before Annas (John 18:12–14, 19–23), an informal trial before Caiaphas and the Sanhedrin (Matthew 26:57–68, Mark 14:53–65, Luke 22:54, 63–65, and John 18:24), and a formal trial by the Sanhedrin that leads to execution (Matthew 27:1, Mark 15:1, and Luke 22:66–71). The second, the "Gentile," involves initial interrogation by Pilate (Matthew 27:2, 11–14, Mark 15:1–5, Luke 23:1–5, and John 18:28–38), further interrogation by Herod (Luke 23:6–12), and final questioning by Pilate again (Matthew 27:15–26, Mark 15:6–15, Luke 23:13–25, and John 18:39–40). Aware of the differences between these two accounts of the Trial and Buffeting, the Wakefield Master imaginatively combines them in a way that not only creates a manageable sequence of events for his play but also permits modification of narrative opportunities within that sequence to emphasize the thematic implications of the particular kind of tragedy the *Coliphizacio* is designed to present. Three things result from this trial-sequence conflation. The first part of the "Jewish" trial sequence is combined with that of the "Gentile" sequence to provide partial subject matter for the *Conspiracio*, the play directly preceding the *Coliphizacio* in the Towneley collection. Likewise, the third part of the "Jewish" sequence is combined with that of the "Gentile" sequence to provide partial subject matter for the *Flagellacio*, the play directly following the *Coliphizacio*. While a linkage among the first three plays in the "Passion group" is thus established by these imaginative combinations, an even more profound effect results from the combination of the informal trial before Caiaphas and the Lukan interrogation of Jesus by Herod. This combination, which provides the subject matter of the *Coliphizacio*, "Herodifies" the informal inquisition, which not only transforms Caiaphas's character or *mentalité* but also alerts the audience, given what they have already witnessed in the *Magnus*

Herodes, to perceive demonstrations of procedural irregularity or abuse as the consequence of cognitive deficiency.

An instructive example of this perceptual effect of the "Herodified" informal interrogation is presented in the first scene by the torturers themselves. Their function in the play, which for some time has remained misunderstood,[30] is defined by their identification *as* torturers, an identification that distinguishes them from Malcus and the two Milites who, at the end of the *Conspiracio*, are assigned the task of accompanying Christ to "Cayphas hall."[31] However, despite this distinction, these two torturers fail to do anything remotely associated with the *techne* of torture itself. The discrepancy arises not because the late-medieval English system of jurisprudence did not present an occasion for torture, nor because it did not, like continental judicial procedure, develop institutions to conduct torture.[32] Nor is it because the general imposition of the "discipline of chivalry" in the feudal setting precluded such activity.[33] Indeed, nor is it even because the late Middle Ages, unlike the sixteenth, seventeenth, and eighteenth centuries, did not see a need to preserve information about this particular dreary art.[34] Rather, the *Coliphizacio*'s torturers do not torture—that is, do not inflict pain for the purpose of extracting confession or information contributing to full proof[35]—because they are cognitively incapable of exercising or even comprehending the art or procedural technique of which their identification *as* torturers indicates they should have mastery.

Evidence of the torturers being allegorized exemplars of the "uninventive" speculative creaturely triune mind, as well as of the rational soul bereft of any life it might derive from God, is presented first in their response to the prisoner—to Christ Himself, the Incarnation of the Word. They have enough presence of mind or rudimentary cognition to remember why Christ is now in their charge: as the play begins, they generalize about His deeds, ironically providing a brief survey of part of Christ's public ministry. Secundus Tortor, for example, observes, while accusing Him, that Christ has gotten the people to forsake the old law and embrace the new:

Sich wyles can thou make,
Gar the people farsake
Oure lawes and thyne take. (21/23–25)

Primus Tortor then points out that Christ has brought about these conversions through eloquence and the ability to articulate the new principles by which to live:

> Fare wordys can thou paynt,
> And lege laws newe. (21/31–32)

But neither torturer knows who Christ is; neither realizes the Incarnation of the Word is standing directly before him. Their initial response thus allows the audience to behold the inability to comprehend even the most obvious of interpretive *circumstantiae*, what Saint Augustine in *De doctrina christiana* denotes as the "unknown literal."[36]

This interpretive inability is demonstrated by the torturers several other times in the same episode. In one instance Primus Tortor, telling Christ to move forward, challenges Him to pick up the pace, as if Christ were a horse:

> Do io furth, io!
> And trott on apace!
> To Anna will we go
> And Syr Cayphas. (21/1–4)

Such treatment, like the subsequent treatment of Christ as if He were a criminal, reveals Primus Tortor's own brutality, as well as his inability to comprehend the "double humanity necessary for salvation: [his] own as sinful [creature] raised above the rest of creation, and Christ's as divinity descended to mankind."[37]

The torturers' inability to comprehend the Incarnation of the Word or the "unknown literal" standing directly before them can also be heard toward the end of the first episode as their mode of address to their prisoner changes from direct discourse employing the second-person-familiar "thou" to an account of Christ in the third person. This change in orientation toward Christ suggests a further distancing from Him, and of Him—one even more extreme than the distance shown earlier in the episode in the torturers' inability to hear the silent speech articulated by Christ through His presence alone before them.

This tendency to move away from the embodiment of the interpretive *circumstantia* they should be trying to comprehend is evidenced one further time at the end of the play's first episode as the torturers reveal that the only concern they have about their prisoner is how He has made them work hard by walking:

> He has done vs greuance;
> Therfor shall he drynk.
> Haue he mekill myschaunsce
> That has gart vs swynke
> In walkyng,
> That vnneth may I more. (21/57–62)

The acknowledgment of such self-centeredness, as well as the absurdity of equating labor with walking, demonstrates not only how profoundly difficult it will be for them to begin the process of gaining salvation through work, but also how distant in their thinking they now are from understanding their function in the process of establishing full proof through the extraction of confession. Most torturers deal with the accused; these torturers appear to be concerned only with themselves.

The ignorance precluding the torturers' ability to engage effectively in their art is further revealed to the audience in this and the next episode through their repeated lack of comprehension of the "unknown figurative"—an irony since their language now, especially in many of their exclamations, is more figurative than before. This inability is evinced two ways. The more noticeable is the language they use to describe their own inconvenience, a language that in its original context is used to educate the auditor to the gravity of the divine sacrifice about to be made through Christ's suffering. As they lead Christ forward toward "Cayphas hall," Secundus Tortor observes that the duty of accompanying Christ has caused great "hart-stangyng" (21/17) and "hart-lanyng" (21/19). Secundus Tortor is encouraged by the fact that he will have to suffer no further once his prisoner has several times been promised a hanging—that is, has been bullied and threatened into submission. The "heart-stinging" or "heart-longing," of course, are terms used to describe Christ's great agony suffered for humanity in the Crucifixion, an agony poignantly described in fourteenth-century Crucifixion lyrics such as this example attributed to Friar William Herebert:

> Þer he was wounded and
>   Vurst y-swunge,
> With sharpe spere to herte y-stonge.[38]

Primus Tortor reveals a like obliviousness to the significance of an expression he uses at the beginning of the second episode. Once they have arrived at "Cayphas hall," the two torturers enter into a dialogue with the two high priests, Annas and Caiaphas. As Primus Tortor recounts his difficulty with Christ, or the "tratoure," he tells Annas the ordeal was so strenuous that he completely missed his rest:

> Sir, as I am true knyght,
> Of my dame sen I sowked
> Had I neuer sich a nyght;
> Myn een were not lowked
> Togeder right
> Sen morowe. (21/82–87)

While this lack of sleep has caused Primus Tortor great discomfort, it pales in comparison with the sleeplessness suffered by Christ in Gethsemane. The language that would otherwise convey the profundity of divine sacrifice is thus appropriated by the torturers to describe their self-centered peevishness and temporary distress, a language the meaning of which would be understood by the audience.

Another way the torturers demonstrate inability to comprehend the "unknown figurative" is by incomprehension of things about Christ's person. The first of these, toward the end of the opening episode, is Christ's demeanor. As they approach "Cayphas hall," Primus Tortor observes that Christ appears about to "wynk" or fall asleep—or maybe it is just that His countenance "falys" (21/54–55). Neither observation comprehends the profundity of suffering that has caused the change in Christ's expression—the same profundity of suffering, indeed, that has come from his knowing fully what the agony of the cross would mean when his soul would be made an offering for sin.

Similarly in the second episode Primus Tortor recounts the capture of Christ at Gethsemane and explains that, while Christ taught many and had a following, all fled when he, Primus Tortor, and others approached. Primus Tortor suggests that Christ's disciples abandoned their leader when they beheld the menacing sword Primus Tortor himself was brandishing:

> When we toke hym,
> We faunde hym in a yerde;

Bot when I drew out my swerde,
His dyscypyls wex ferde,
And soyn thay forsoke him. (21/100–104)

Primus Tortor's account does not mention Peter's swordplay and the injury to the ear of Malcus. What it also ignores—and cannot possibly include—is an understanding of the event as the fulfillment of divine prophecy.

The most remarkable lack of any rational intelligence, however, is demonstrated by the torturers as they actually attempt to engage in procedural response by providing Annas and Caiaphas with eyewitness testimony and circumstantial evidence or *indicia* relating to Christ's alleged crime. While each offers examples of the latter by calling attention to different features of Christ's public ministry—Primus Tortor describing, for instance, how Christ raised Lazarus (21/144–47), and Secundus Tortor pointing to Christ's healing of the sick and lame (21/118) and His forgiving of the woman caught in adultery (21/140–43)—neither one comprehends the figurative meaning of these works or miracles, condemning and dismissing each as nothing more than "lyes" and "fals wyles," "soceres" and "wychcraft." What is more, while Secundus Tortor goes so far as to impute a mercenary motive for Christ's works—

Thus he gettys many fees
Of thym he begyles (21/120–21)

—neither torturer appears aware of, much less concerned about, the legal fact that this kind of evidence does not constitute, in pre-jury standard of proof, an adequate basis for "conviction and condemnation, no matter how compelling."[39] The only thing consistent with judicial procedure about the kind of evidence they adduce—which, through the process of repetition, they heap on as they make their case before Annas and Caiaphas to get these authorities to act—is, as they appear to understand, that circumstantial evidence of sufficient gravity may constitute at least a half proof and so open the door, as it were, to torture.[40] This does not, however, explain why Secundus Tortor offers two instances of eyewitness testimony concerning Christ, the first having to do with the destruction and rebuilding of the temple—

Sir, I hard hym say he cowthe dystroew
Oure tempyll so gay,

And sithen beld a new
On the thrid day (21/105–8)

—and the second having to do with the insignificance of temporal authority—

Yit is ther anothere thyng
That I hard hym neuen:
He settys not a fle-wyng
Bi Syr Cesar full euen;
He says thus. (21/135–39)

In pre-jury standard of proof, the testimony of *two* eyewitnesses to the gravamen of a crime was sufficient to convict and condemn,[41] while the testimony of one eyewitness was enough to establish half proof and so make possible the application of torture.[42] Two instances of testimony by one eyewitness might justify torture, but the redundancy, even perhaps as an act of judicial hedging, does not change half proof into sufficient grounds to convict and condemn.

This confusion over the difference between two eyewitnesses giving testimony and Secundus Tortor's giving eyewitness testimony twice, while providing yet another irony in the first scene, appears at least to clarify one matter concerning the play's production. While Stevens and Cawley suggest Froward should appear with Primus and Secundus Tortores in the first scene, in order to reassert the character symmetry established by Malcus and Primus and Secundus Milites at the end of the *Conspiracio,* and to reassert other character symmetries appearing previously in the *Magnus Herodes* and the two shepherds' plays,[43] the Wakefield Master's course—having Christ suffer the ignominious treatment He does at the hands of only two torturers who do not know enough about their own practical art of extracting confession, or enough about the judicial procedure of which their art is an instrumental part, to offer at least the kind of eyewitness testimony that would convict and condemn—appears to be a more satisfactory way of dramatizing procedural irregularity or abuse, while reminding the audience also of the torturers' conspicuous cognitive deficiency.

III

Consideration of the tragic repudiation of the eschatology of labor through the allegorization of the Trial and Buffeting as abuse of judicial procedure receives further treatment in the play's middle two scenes as Caiaphas and Annas respond to the torturers' plea to put an immediate halt to Christ's "warkys." Because no torture is performed by the torturers themselves, and because the torturers, before being abruptly dismissed, provide enough circumstantial evidence and eyewitness testimony to constitute at least half proof, the task of "torturing" the prisoner Christ to extract confession devolves upon the two high priests themselves. This is not to say either one tortures Christ, though both, as it ironically turns out, are better suited to the task than are the torturers themselves—a fact that may reveal a hitherto unremarked embedded instance of anti-Semitism in the play. But neither one, despite his efforts and ability, can secure the confession that would both convict and condemn. The interrogation that occurs, under the direction first of Caiaphas and then of Annas, only provides further demonstrations of procedural error through abuse in several ways, inviting consideration once again of cognitive deficiency as explanation for that abuse.[44]

The most obvious procedural abuse committed by Caiaphas as torturer has to do with the mode and object of his initial interrogation or "examynyng" of Christ. As the questioning begins, Caiaphas does not appear to understand that, as a practitioner of the *techne* or practical art of torture, he must employ his skill in such a way that Christ will confess to details of his alleged crime—will provide information, that is, no innocent person can know.[45] Instead, all Caiaphas wants is an abject confession of guilt. Consequently, his approach to Christ consists of little more than a simplistic attempt to coerce confession by derision bolstered by threat:[46]

> Harstow, harlott, of all?
> Of care may thou syng!
> How durst thou the call
> Aythere emperoure or kyng?
> I do fy the!
> What the dwill doyst thou here?
> Thi dedys will do the dere.

> Com nar and rowne in myn eeyr,
> Or I shall ascry the. (21/187–95)

The lack of mental agility implicit in this demonstration of bullying or full-frontal assault is anticipated by Caiaphas's inability to make sense of the first eyewitness testimony given him by Secundus Tortor, a testimony distinguished in several gospel accounts of the Trial and Buffeting, ironically, as "false witness." When Secundus Tortor tells Caiaphas that he heard Christ say He could destroy the temple and rebuild it on the third day (21/105–8), Caiaphas's predictable reply indicates he is incapable of comprehending figurative expression. In fact, as he considers the proposition, the "sign" given the Pharisees in John 2:19–20, he dismisses it as an impossibility, seeing in the temple not a metaphor of the Body of Christ but only a literal, material structure:

> How myght that be trew?
> It toke more aray!
> The masons I knewe
> That hewed it, I say,
> So wyse,
> That hewed ilka stone. (21/109–14)

This pharisaical literalizing of the figurative, this mental habit of taking a sign for a thing, evidences, in Saint Augustine's words, "a miserable servitude of the spirit."[47] The trenchant irony here results not only from Caiaphas's being a high priest, one of the spiritual leaders of his people, but also from the fact that, as one now functioning in the role of torturer, he should be sensitive to nuance.

Caiaphas's inability to decipher either the "ambiguous literal" or the "ambiguous figurative" is brought to the audience's attention two other times in the second scene in order to emphasize the paucity of his wit. One happens immediately after—and as a direct result of—the first confrontation with Christ. Once it is clear Christ will not make the abject confession of guilt that Caiaphas would like Him to make, Caiaphas begins the first of his Herodian rants, one lasting for five stanzas (21/196–260).[48] The predictable name-calling, ridicule, exclamation, and obscenity are included here; at this point, all that is missing is the Herodian wrath. But another thing is different as well. As the Wakefield Master presents this verbal chaos, the emphasis in each part of the rant remains on procedural irregularity or the abuse of the *techne* of torture. After his initial mistake of seeking a full confession and not the details, Caiaphas, having come up empty-handed, makes the subsequent error of peremptorily judging and convicting Christ, not even on the basis of the *indicia* provided by the torturers, but now only on what he perceives to be an impertinence on Christ's part. When Christ does not whisper as requested in Caiaphas's ear, Caiaphas becomes exasperated, suggesting this is the work of insult and trickery:

> This is a great skorne
> And a fals trane;
> Now wols-hede and outhorne
> On the be tane,
> Vile fature! (21/200–204)

The tortuous logic of his response is easily remarked, as the object of his attention shifts quickly from Christ to himself and back again to Christ, and the exclamations and interrogatives begin to cascade. But amid these histrionic expostulations and argumentative volte-faces, the arbitrary judgments begin to be heard. At first they are simply name-calling, as in Caiaphas's identifying Christ as "fature" or imposter. But they soon become more complicated and accusatory. As Caiaphas quotes canonical proverbial lore—"*Et omnis qui tacet / Hic consentire videtur*" (21/207–8)—he attempts adroitly to indicate indirectly Christ's culpability. But when this strategy of implication does not elicit even "oone word" of response, then the condemnatory conclusions become more pronounced and vindictive. In one, Caiaphas calls Christ a bastard who lives by larceny:

> Fy on the, fundlyng!
> Thou lyfys bot bi brybré. (21/220–21)

In another he addresses Christ as Sir Sybré, perhaps an allusion to a local malefactor, perhaps a mocking reference to the obscurity of Christ's birth.[49] His identification of Christ as "Kyng Copyn," or the king of fools, again suggests Christ's fraudulence. And lastly, probably out of exasperation as much as anger, Caiaphas declares Christ must be deaf and dumb, this being the only conclusion that remains to him—and certainly one that shows the audience which of them, he or Christ, has neither ears to hear nor eyes to see.

The final demonstration of Caiaphas's lack of cognitive agility comes in the second scene's closing episode, or the first postexamination interlude. While he abuses judicial procedure in his first Herodian rant by moving to convict Christ solely on the perception of behavior he himself cannot comprehend, Caiaphas's next, even more remarkable, abuse of procedure involves repeated attempts to punish or even execute the accused simply on the basis of the anger aroused by his own incomprehension. As Annas tries to calm Caiaphas, a flurry of threats from the irascible high priest calls attention to his desire to inflict physical pain on Christ—that is, to impose an "afflictive sanction" on his prisoner.[50] In a predictable Herodian way, Caiaphas claims his heart will "brist" if he cannot actually hit Christ (21/276–77). Shortly afterward he proclaims he will thrust out Christ's eyes (21/279–80). But such threats give way to intimidatory announcements concerning Christ's imminent death. No clear or logical progression from threat of bodily harm to threat of physical death can be perceived here: one moment, Caiaphas wants to behead Christ (21/289); the next, he says he will fast until Christ has been put in the "stokys" (21/293–95). This variability of mind, however, is precisely what the Wakefield Master wants as a way of revealing the disordered quality of Caiaphas's "Herodified" *mentalité*. When Caiaphas eventually declares it is his desire and intention "to murder" Christ "with knokys" (21/299), Annas is hard pressed to contain his fellow priest by reminding him of his position and responsibility as "man of holy kyrk," one who should remember his role as "techere," whose purpose it is "Mekenes to wyrk" (21/300–303).

This intervention, the first of a two-part strategy pursued by Annas to get Caiaphas, quickly, to stop thinking and expressing himself in a "bustus" way, consists of encouraging the high priest to gain control of the "exterior" man or the public self. While other examples of this strategy arise during their exchange—examples even calling attention to the need to engage the public, tactical self or the self dedicated to upholding the law—the majority of encouragements Annas directs toward Caiaphas involves the latter's need to gain control of the "interior" man or the subjective self. These encouragements include Annas's telling Caiaphas not to be upset with Christ's silence, and to calm himself. He even points out that Caiaphas is too "vexed" over the matter and should pursue a course of moderation, a point he expresses aphoristically when suggesting a calm approach to the matter at hand will reap the benefits desired:

"All soft may men go far" (21/306). Like his attempts to get Caiaphas to change the "exterior" man, however, these attempts to pacify the "interior" man, buttressed though they are by Annas's formal and polite address in response to Caiaphas, an address beginning repeatedly with the vocative "Sir," come to nought. Ultimately, Annas has to restrain Caiaphas:

> Syr, do away!
> For if ye thus thrett hym,
> He spekys not this day.
> Bot herys:
> Wold ye sesse and abyde,
> I shuld take hym on syde,
> And inquere of his pryde
> How he oure folke lerys. (21/318–25)

The anger that motivates Caiaphas to ignore even this attempt leads to two more exchanges between Annas and Caiaphas before Annas, finally, cuts off his colleague to begin his own examining of the accused in the opening lines of the next brief episode, "The Second Examination." Like Herod's before him, Caiaphas's distemper thus appears to be an example of "sinful madness," as it is voluntary and habitual, and not accidental or aberrant.[51]

IV

Annas, as it turns out, is much more able than Caiaphas to fulfill the role of de facto torturer. The first notable difference is in what Annas emphasizes as important to the process of interrogation. As he tries, toward the end of the second scene, to persuade Caiaphas to control both the "interior" and "exterior" man, Annas explains to his fellow high priest that such a change in behavior will provide the opportunity for Christ to say a word:

> *Anna.* It is best that we trete hym
> With farenes.
> *Cayphas.* We, nay!
> *Anna.* And so myght we get hym
> Som word for to say. (21/312–16)

Annas does not seek, nor does he want, an abject confession of guilt. All he wants is a detail, a word, for if he can receive that much, and the word turns out to be something no innocent would know, then he will have the cogent incriminating evidence he needs to establish full proof. The importance Annas ascribes to this strategy is attested by its articulation two more times before the end of the episode:

> Wold ye sesse and abyde,
> I shuld take hym [Christ] on syde,
> And inquere of his pryde
> How he oure folke lerys (21/321–24)

and

> Sir, the law will not he gang
> On no kyn wyse
> Vndemyd.
> Bot fyrst wold I here
> What he wold answere. (21/332–36)

Annas's effectiveness as de facto torturer is demonstrated a second way in the interrogation strategy he employs to extract confession from Christ. As he approaches the accused at the beginning of the third scene, Annas does two things. First, he asks Christ a series of loaded questions.[52] These are not "suggestive" questions, the type that supply the accused with details the interrogating torturer would like to hear, for to ask such would invalidate the confession.[53] But, in terms of their intention, they are very close. In fact, they are questions so framed that any answer, any at all, would perforce demonstrate a knowledge no innocent person could have:

> Say, dyd thou oght this yll?
> Can thou oght excuse the?
> Why standys thou so styll
> When men thus accuse the? (21/354–57)

Annas understands the law of criminal evidence, and the function of torture as a tool. When this part of the strategy fails to elicit a response, however, the second thing Annas does is to ask a direct question of fact, a direct question, in this case, pertaining to the fact of Christ's divine nature:[54]

> Say, art thou Godys son of heuen,
> As thou art wonte for to neuen? (21/361–62)

Annas knows this question must be answered, as it is a truth that cannot be left unaffirmed.[55] And his procedural resourcefulness indeed elicits a response, the only words spoken by Christ in the entire play.

But getting Christ to speak is a qualified achievement, for what Christ has to say consists of both an "ambiguous literal" and an "ambiguous figurative." In the first part of His reply to Annas, Christ makes use of an adverbial conjunctive expression—as in "as the tree falls, so shall it lie"—which, by making His reply an expressed extension of the question, identifies Annas as being as much the author of the answer as Christ Himself:

> So thou says by thy steuen,
> And ryght so I am. (21/363–64)

The second part of Christ's reply, the "ambiguous figurative," involves the eschatological promise of judgment, the understanding of which is precluded by Annas's adamant conformity to the old law, and by Caiaphas's previously demonstrated Herodian wrathful ignorance:

> For after this shall thou se
> When that [I] com downe
> In brightnes on he,
> In clowdys from abone. (21/365–68)

So a reply is made, but it does not include any cogent incriminating evidence. The legal condition of there being a half proof, a condition warranting torture to extract confession, thus remains in effect, though obviously not for lack of tactical ability on Annas's part.

The procedural error—that is, the abuse of the *techne* of judicial process—that arises in this scene does not involve Caiaphas's reception of either the ambiguity of authorial coefficiency or Christ's eschatological warning as a literal, though this feature of Caiaphas's response does remind the audience once again of the severe limitations under which he is compelled to function owing to the carnality of his spirit and the resultant deficiency of his reason. What introduces the abuse here, rather, is that once Caiaphas believes Annas and he have received the detail of cogent incriminating evidence that transforms the half proof obtained from *indicia* and eyewitness testimony into full proof justifying conviction and condemnation, he announces that there is no need to investigate and verify to a feasible extent[56] the information that Christ has provided in answer to Annas's question concerning His divine nature:

> *Cayphas.* A, ill myght the feete be
> That broght the to towne!
> Thou art worthy to de.
> Say, thefe, where is thi crowne?
> *Anna.* Abyde, syr!
> Let vs lawfully redres.
> *Cayphas.* We nede no wytnes;
> Hysself says expres. (21/369–76; emphasis mine)

V

The immediate consequence of this abuse of judicial procedure, coupled with the ambiguity of Christ's response, is the preclusion of the possibility of a plea, which makes it impossible for the prosecution to proceed. This ironic result, the prevention of a trial in a play at least partly about a trial, introduces a perplexing legal situation that often, apparently, did exist in late-medieval England, and for which a legal remedy under English law was established—a practice with which torture, coincidentally, was often confused. Until the eighteenth century, the accused under English law had three legal options upon arraignment for trial. They could either plead guilty and waive adjudication, which left only sentencing to the court, or controvert the indictment with a not-guilty plea and so go to trial, or not plead at all and thereby prevent trial. In the last case, the remedial practice was to incarcerate until such time as a plea should be made. This practice was originally known as *prison forte et dure,* though the reality of this type of incarceration, which often involved physical coercion so terrible that it killed the accused, soon corrupted the phrase to *peine forte et dure.*[57] Such physical coercion, it would appear, provides the compromise solution sought by Annas to stay within the law with regard to the prisoner Christ and yet to appease Caiaphas who, unable rationally to grasp the complexity of the legal dilemma facing both Annas and himself, only wants to execute Christ in the most grimly barbaric way. This is why, in the second postexamination interlude or the third scene's second episode, Annas seems, after repeated attempts to get Caiaphas to control at least the "exterior" man, to contradict his own advice, on the one hand by informing his fellow high priest that Christ should be sent to Pilate to be sentenced under temporal law, and on the other by allowing the buffeting to occur with the sole condition that the violence inflicted on Christ be tempered:

> Ye ar bot to skar.
> Good syr, abat
> And here:
> What nedys you to chyte?
> What nedys you to flyte?
> If ye yond man smyte,
> Ye ar irregulere. (21/436–42)

Annas knows it is impossible to kill Christ, but he at least can make Him suffer in the interim, before sending Him back to Pilate, by putting Him to *peine forte et dure*, which satisfies the immediate bloodlust of those like Caiaphas while enabling himself, through a legal technicality, to save face and elude responsibility. That Caiaphas views the buffeting more as *peine forte et dure* than does Annas can be heard repeatedly in the closing lines of the third scene as he encourages the torturers to strike hard when hitting Christ. As the torturers first ask for Caiaphas's blessing, Caiaphas promises reward to the one whose blow hurts Christ most:

> Now he shall haue my blyssyng
> That knokys hym the best. (21/493–94)

VI

The legal maneuver of transforming the Buffeting into *peine forte et dure*, an effective combination of Roman canon law of proof with torture-free law of proof,[58] allows for capital punishment without conviction, but in doing so also provides the opportunity for further abuse of judicial procedure. The *allegoria* of this abuse is evoked dramatically by the Wakefield Master in three ways. The most obvious of these involves Primus and Secundus Tortores' interrupting of themselves, which keeps postponing and eventually minimizing the severity of the punishment or affective sanction they have been ordered to carry out. This nearly comic turning of the Buffeting as *peine forte et dure* into the Buffeting as *peine ni forte ni dure* begins once the torturers, the same who in the first scene demonstrate they know nothing about either the *techne* or the technology of torture, hold off from engaging in the Buffeting because they decide the prisoner should be seated on a stool (21/500). This interruption is extended, first, by the request having to be made a second time (21/507), and next by an explanation for the request having to be given to Froward, the torturers' servant,[59] who was asked in the first place to fetch the piece of furniture in question:

> Sir, we do it for a skawnce.
> If he [Christ] stode vpon loft,
> We must hop and dawnse
> As cokys in a croft. (21/511–14)

Once the stool has been procured, another interruption follows as the torturers, experiencing difficulty in getting Christ to sit, again neglect their task to discuss the prisoner's fate and apparent abandonment by family and followers:

> 2 Tortor. Ther is none in this towne,
> I trow, be ill payde
> Of his sorow,
> Bot the fader that hym gate.
> 1 Tortor. Now, for oght that I wate,
> All his kyn commys to late
> His body to borow. (21/527–33)

Secundus Tortor's inadvertent condemnation of pharisaical thinking with regard to the expression of sorrow provides an unexpected irony, as does Primus Tortor's inadvertent moment of insight concerning the Body of Christ, the basis of the new sacramentalism about to be established through the Crucifixion.

When the torturers realize how dilatory they have become—Secundus Tortor even remarks, "I wold we were onwarde" (21/534)—they interrupt themselves yet again to send Froward after a blindfold with which to cover Christ's eyes:

> 1 Tortor. Bot his een must be hyd.
> 2 Tortor. Yei, bot thay be well spard,
> We lost that we dyd.
> Step furth thou, Froward! (21/535–38)

This interruption would not last as long as it does were Froward not so annoyed when ordered to retrieve the veil. But the command, as seemingly unreasonable as the previous one, provides him with an opportunity to express his grievance over exploitation and unfair labor practices, an opportunity he is not loath to seize. The simple stating of his case would not prolong the interruption much, either. What delays the torturers further from setting themselves to the task is the argument that erupts over Froward's perception of his being exploited, an argument revealing as much annoyance on the side of the torturers as on Froward's:

2 Tortor. Thou must get vs a vayll.
Froward. Ye ar euer in oone tayll.
1 Tortor. Now ill myght thou the!
            Well had thou thi name,
            For thou was euer curst.
Froward. Sir, I myght say the same
            To you, if I durst.
            Yit my hyer may I clame;
            No penny I purst.
            I haue had mekyll shame,
            Hunger, and thrust
            In youre seruyce.
1 Tortor. Not oone word so bold!
Froward. Why, it is true that I told!
            Fayn preue it I wold.
2 Tortor. Thou shal be cald to peruyce. (21/544–59)

Froward does eventually procure the blindfold, but even that concession is not enough to end the interruptions. As he gives it to the torturers, yet another altercation breaks out over who is going to secure the blindfold over Christ's eyes. The torturers want Froward to do it, but he is unwilling, since he fears Christ's curse, a curse apparently suffered by the one who last has dealings with a prisoner about to be executed. As a result, he begins the tying of the blindfold but leaves it to be completed by his masters. He may be a servant, but, as far as he is concerned, he is not stupid:

Froward. How shuld it be bon?
2 Tortor. Abowte his heade cast.

> *1 Tortor.*   Yei, and when it is well won,
> Knyt a knot fast,
> I red.
> *Froward.* Is it weyll?
> *2 Tortor.*   Yei, knaue.
> *Froward.* What, weyn ye that I rafe?
> Cryst curs myght he haue
> That last bond his heade! (21/564–73)

Then the actual Buffeting begins, but not before seventy-seven lines of a one-hundred-four-line episode have passed.

A less obvious—but by no means less important—way in which abuse turns the Buffeting into *peine ni forte ni dure* arises also from the torturers' treatment of their task as sport rather than earnest. The *allegoria* of this is evoked dramatically in two distinct ways. The first involves a metaphor, of the kind the torturers use in thinking of the nature of the activity in which they are ordered to engage. At the beginning of the episode, for example, Primus Tortor refers to the buffeting that is about to be inflicted on Christ as, simply, a "new play of Yoyll" (21/498). This conceiving of physical violence in terms of the children's game of Hot Cockles, which ritualizes and makes acceptable a barbarous action, is reintroduced later as the blindfold is requested, and again at the episode's end when each of the torturers asks whether Christ knows who, Primus Tortor or his colleague, has struck last. Another game metaphor used by Primus Tortor, which has the same effect as the first, involves the Shrovetide game of Cock-Throwing, an allusion introduced in the explanation to Froward of the need to procure the stool for Christ to sit on during the buffeting.[60]

The torturers also reveal their treatment of the buffeting as a game through their actions once they finally start to inflict punishment on Christ. As soon as they begin to hit their prisoner with their fists, they turn their attention from Christ, the object of their violent activity, to comment on each other's technique.[61] At first their evaluation is constructive, professional:

> *1 Tortor.*   Now sen he is blynfeld,
> I fall to begyn;
> And thus was I counseld
> The mastry to wyn.

> 2 *Tortor.* Nay, wrang has thou teld;
> Thus shuld thou com in. (21/573–78)

But as they strike Christ a second time, the evaluation degenerates into a disagreement of sorts, each turning on the other, denigrating the other's ability. Secundus Tortor, for example, accuses Primus Tortor of being, literally, limp-wristed:

> There is noght in thi nefe,
> Or els thi hart falys. (21/588–89)

Primus Tortor, likewise, suggests Secundus Tortor will be more effective if he digs in all his nails together as he strikes the prisoner:

> Godys forbot ye lefe,
> Bot set in youre nalys
> On raw. (21/592–94)

The only thing that seems to matter to the torturers, finally, is whether Christ knows who struck him last. Each, in other words, is concerned more about the superstition of Christ's curse than about the actuality of having harmed Christ Himself.

The final way the first episode of the *Coliphizacio*'s last scene presents the Buffeting as *peine ni forte ni dure* is through Froward's function as foil to the action of which he is a part. This function has two principal modalities. The first involves Froward's response as servant/participant in the Buffeting. As the torturers' subordinate, he is ordered to do a number of things: to procure the stool, to get the blindfold, and finally to knot it in place. As a participant in the action, Froward's increasingly irritable reluctance to comply with each successive request by his masters serves to remind the audience, once again, of how many times the actual act of buffeting is postponed. In the first instance, when asked to get the stool, for example, Froward exclaims the prisoner Christ should be treated the opposite of the way the torturers are treating Him, so as to make His suffering more acute:

> We, dote!
> Now els wer it doyll
> And vnnett;
> For the wo that he shall dre,
> Let hym knele on his kne (21/501–5)

and

> Why must he sytt soft—
> With a mekill myschaunce!—
> That has tenyd vs thus oft? (21/508–10)

Forward's objection, in other words, reveals that the basic setting of the Buffeting has not even been agreed on by the torturers. When next asked to get the blindfold, Froward shows even greater annoyance over being summoned a second time and over the fact that the torturers apparently have no one else to help them. His reluctance to do as requested is evidenced by his lengthy protest over unfair labor practice, which in this case involves withholding of wages (21/551–55).

This objection, more combative in tone and content than the first, indicates that basic buffeting technique or procedure is still being worked out, while reminding the audience of other ways in which the torturers are given to delay. Froward's final response as servant/participant, refusing to finish tying the blindfold's knot, suggests again that all of the details of the procedure have not been fully taken care of. What is more, it allows Froward to demonstrate he is not as ignorant as his station as servant may lead one to believe.

The second modality of Froward's function as foil involves his role as observer/participant. This role, actually consisting of two observer/participant modes of response, one the emotional and the other the disinterested, enables Froward to remind the audience how much the act of buffeting, which should be treated with earnestness, has been ritualized into a game. The emotional observer/participant mode—what would now be called the response of the enthusiastic fan or spectator—is evidenced several times before and during the Buffeting, keeping attention on the gamelike quality of the punishment. Before the Buffeting, this response is heard once the need for the stool has been explained. As the torturers do not want to appear foolish in relation to Christ, who apparently is much taller than they are,[62] Froward readies himself to watch a satisfying beating as punishment, even expressing the enthusiasm of anticipation:

> Now a veniance
> Com on hym!
> Good skill can ye shew
> As fell i the dew. (21/515–18)

Once the actual Buffeting begins, Froward again expresses the emotional response of excited observation. The first instance can be heard as he remarks that Secundus Tortor has hit his mark and raised a welt:

> Yei, that was well gone to;
> Ther start vp a cowll. (21/584–85)

Another instance, the most memorable part of his response as excited spectator, involves Froward's observation, in the middle of the torturers's spat over whose technique is the more effective, that he himself could probably knock the dandruff from Christ's head:

> I can my hand vphefe
> And knop out the skalys. (21/590–91)[63]

The disinterested observer/participant mode of Froward's response—what would now be identified as the response of the referee or officiating participant—is also heard during the Buffeting and serves to remind the audience of the continuing gamelike quality of the torturers' endeavor. This particular response is manifested as soon as the first punch is thrown. Cognizant of his role as disinterested observer, Froward remarks carefully, in response to the first blow directed at Christ, that the strike is ineffective:

> I stode and beheld—
> Thou towchid not the skyn
> Bot fowll. (21/579–81)

The second instance of Froward's response to the Buffeting as disinterested observer comes at the end of the activity, short as it is, when he reassures the torturers that Christ cannot know who landed the last strike, a reassurance that opens the door to drawing a parallel between the present action and Matthew 26:22.

> 2 Tortor. Who smote the last?
> 1 Tortor.   Was it I?
> Froward. He wote not, I traw. (21/597–99)

Given his perspective, Froward suggests he knows more than either of the torturers can know, and more than even Christ Himself, when he responds with the admonishment not to lie, not in response to Primus Tortor's request to Christ to identify who of the two torturers has hurt

Him the more, but to Christ Himself as part of the game. Cawley's observation that Froward participates as a torturer at this moment, throwing a punch and following that with the admonition against lying,[64] provides yet another dimension of the disinterested or professional response, but one qualitatively different from that of referee or officiating participant. Striking Christ as he might, and then calling for the articulation of truth, is the first act in the entire play that legitimately resembles an act of torture conducted to extract confession. This irony, however, is actually eclipsed by another of even greater subtlety, which directly results from the transformation of the Buffeting into *peine forte et dure*. Even if the *peine forte et dure* led to Christ's death, an outcome that would certainly have satisfied Caiaphas, Christ's estate, the Kingdom of Heaven—that is, the choicest of tropological real estate—would still descend to His heirs, since killing a prisoner without conviction, the often lamentable result of *peine forte et dure,* always presupposed indemnification that protected the entirety of the decedent's estate.[65]

VII

The potential for yet another abuse of judicial procedure, a final reminder of the repudiation of the eschatology of labor at the institutional level, is voiced by Caiaphas in the closing lines of the play, after he has ordered the torturers to accompany Christ to Pilate. As the torturers lead Christ away, again as if He were an animal, Caiaphas castigates himself for having agreed to let the temporal authorities make the final judgment concerning the disposition of Christ. What worries him most is that Pilate will let the prisoner go, not because no full proof to convict and condemn Him exists, but rather because the reality of judicial procedure includes the probability of abuse in the form of a bribe:

> I am euer in drede,
> Wandreth and wo,
> Lest Pylate for mede
> Let Iesus go. (21/627–30)

The likelihood of this abuse occurring is so great, at least in his thinking, that Caiaphas prepares to oversee the torturers, and blames Annas angrily for the way the matter has been dealt with, reminding the audience one last time of his close kinship to Herod. The suggestion with which the audience is left as Caiaphas leads his men away, a suggestion that may involve the members of the actual audience if Cawley is correct about the final methexis in the play,[66] is that if judicial procedure is abused, then that abuse will be corrected by yet another abuse—Caiaphas's taking the matter of Christ's execution into his own hands by stabbing Him "To the hart full wan / With [his] dagger so keyn" (21/642–43).

Conclusion

The Wakefield Master's contribution to the Towneley collection is a remarkable artistic feat of unrivaled proportions. At least six plays, as well as numerous revisions always including the innovative poetic "thirteener," the signature stanza, can be attributed to him with certainty, and in nearly all of these examples of his redactive or creative dramatic art in the *regenall* the performance proves unequaled in its creative imagination and in the consistency of the dramatic illusion it creates. The dedication of purpose implicit in the quality of such artistic achievement allows the Master to investigate imaginatively biblical events in the time of erring, renewal, and reconciliation, the first three of the four periods of history as set forth, for example, in Jacobus de Voragine's outline of history in the prologue to the *Legenda Aurea*,[1] and this creative rendering of the past provides the artistic opportunity, in this the most literary of all play collections found in medieval British drama,[2] to consider fully the principal implications of the axiomatic idea informing the Master's approach to the dramatic works he creates—the idea, that is, that serving God cooperatively can and should vigorously be achieved by the serving of the self through the technological mastery and proper use of nature in all of its infinite variety. The *Mactatio Abel* and the *Processus Noe cum filiis* present the question of what is to be mastered technologically and used practically. What is revealed here is that time and space can be easily misunderstood or even abused if a proper attitude toward these two dimensions of nature is not initially established. Part of this orientation, of course, includes the realization of how *techne* or practical art can either aid or impede this comprehension and its ultimate consequence, the collaborative effort with God that leads to salvation.

The Master's artistic efforts in depicting the time of renewal, the largest portion of his contribution to Towneley and also the portion of his redactive art that includes perhaps the most famous dramaturgic creation in all of medieval British drama, again turns attention to this axiomatic idea, but this time by showing how—and how not—to serve the self by means of the relation between technological mastery and practical use. If one knows that nature is to be used as a means to the greater end of loving God, then it becomes imperative to discover how mastery of nature can be effected by means of *techne*. At its most rudimentary level, this discovery might involve the application of some basic practical art to alter nature in some predictable way, as the construction of a weir to trap fish in a river leads to proper alimentation and physical nourishment. A more sophisticated form of such technological mastery would, however, have to be the object of such speculative endeavor, since the technological serving of the self, ultimately, has to be analogous with the cooperative serving of God. In this regard, the attainment of a hermeneutic ability in response to nature and convention is the desired end, since the effect of spiritual understanding informs any kind of mastery and provides practical explanation of any kind of proper *use*. Possessing the totality of mind suggested by the combination of the two shepherds' plays—that is, the combination of the "inventive" speculative creaturely triune mind and the "inventive" empirical creaturely triune mind, or *sapientia* and *scientia*—establishes and assures the ideal hermeneutic ability that enables one to possess the tropological insight subjectively predisposing one to appreciate fully the religious metaphysics of the age. As if this were not enough, the *Magnus Herodes*, yet another work set in the time of renewal, reminds everyone what it is like to be bereft of any semblance of hermeneutic ability leading to tropological insight.

In this way, the audience is prepared for the Master's final artistic statement in the "Passion group" about the need to achieve mastery and gain from the practical use of nature in the period of reconciliation. This is the moment in history when one can say, without equivocation, that the serving of self technologically is coefficient with the serving of God. The temptation, as the *Coliphizacio* demonstrates, is to err in believing that *techne*—in this case, the practical legal art of pre-jury standard of proof—can actually be treated as an end in itself and not as a means to the greater end of loving God. This misapprehension of *techne's* role, as revealed also in Pilate's misapplication of the legal principles of "mastry" and "sovereigntée," has tragic consequences, since the favoring of the art as an end in itself, through wilful and deliberate, not accidental, rejection of spiritual understanding's value in favor of a false or specious understanding buttressed merely by artifice alone, precludes, ultimately, any possibility of salvation.

This abuse, the use of art merely for the sake of advancing one's own ambitions in the world, introduces one more concern to which the Wakefield Master addresses his attention. In the final age of the world—that is, in the time of pilgrimage, to return to Jacobus de Voragine's historical design one last time[3]—it is necessary to be prepared against all manner of assault on one's regained innocence after the fortunate fall from innocence into experience. Equipped with the "armor" of the proper understanding of nature, which implies an appreciation of nature's inherent beauty; and with the proper comprehension of hermeneutic response to all manner of interpretive *circumstantiae*, including those involving the things or *signa* that one might encounter in the journey of life; and having the proper appreciation of the function of all *technae* as being means, ultimately, to the greater end of loving God, and not as ends in themselves, no matter how intricately beautiful or sophisticated they may intrinsically or extrinsically appear to be—so equipped, each spectator is readied to venture forth as a Christian soldier, as it were, in the time of pilgrimage, the current time of spiritual "warfare," to "resist in the evil day," as Saint Paul says in Ephesians 6:13, "and to stand in all things perfect."

Such a conservative view of the purpose of the Wakefield Master's dramatic art is consistent with the civic, therapeutic dimension of the Corpus Christi drama in general. Should the majority of the Master's audience realize the importance of wearing the "armor of God" as a consequence of the works he has contributed to the Towneley collection—and it is not conceivable the majority would not, especially given the fact that the collection has the most obvious sacramental design of all play collections or cycles[4]—then the idealistic order of the community, now understood in terms of the Body of Christ, is asserted anew, exactly the same way one's idealistic commitment to God is reasserted sacramentally at the very moment of the taking of the Eucharist. Such a sacramental outcome, the preferred consequence of the drama for obvious reasons, would also reap one other important civic benefit: as the Body of Christ is asserted through the drama of this kind of spiritual understanding, so the city of man, once again, is replaced by the City of God in the world.

Notes

Preface

1. Camille, *Mirror in Parchment*, 47.
2. Paxson, "(Re)Facing Prosopopeia and Allegory," 12.
3. *The Towneley Plays*. The entire play collection first appeared in 1836 in the edition of Gordon and Hunter, *The Towneley Mysteries*. Second, in 1897, came the edition of England and Pollard, *Towneley Plays*.
4. Stevens and Cawley, *The Towneley Plays*, 1:i.
5. In this study, manuscript or Latin play titles will be used.
6. Panofsky, *Early Netherlandish Painting*, 1:181.

Introduction

1. Patterson, in *Negotiating the Past*, 3–74, and in his most recent corrective, "Chaucer's Pardoner on the Couch," 656–80, makes the case for such diligent historical reconstruction and avoidance of anachronism while acknowledging the obvious political nature of critical discourse.
2. Stevens and Cawley, *The Towneley Plays*, 1:293, line 189, 1:13, line 58, 1:111, line 182, 1:414, lines 456–57, 1:67, lines 109–10, and 1:339, lines 113–15, respectively. Hereafter, reference to this edition of the plays will appear in text, play numbers preceding line numbers.
3. The acknowledgment, identification, or discussion of realism in the Towneley plays can be found in a number of studies by several twentieth-century scholars, including Cady, "Wakefield Group," 257; Carey, *Wakefield Group*, 47–48, who emphasizes that the plays make use of local allusions and are "packed with realism"—especially in terms of references to contemporary life; Davidson, *Technology, Guilds* and, previously, "Unity," 499, where he points out that the "real is a part of the pattern of the drama, and to exclude it would certainly be foreign to the spirit of the Corpus Christi festival at which the whole Wakefield cycle was originally produced"; Gayley, *Plays of Our Forefathers*, 173–79; Kahrl, *Traditions*, 72–74; Prosser, *Drama and Religion*, 76–83, who finds the comic realism in the mystery plays, as she describes it, "annoying if not blasphemous"; Robinson, *Stagecraft*, 53 (a special

expression of gratitude is in order for Professor Thomas Bestul, who saw Professor Robinson's manuscript through to completion and publication after Professor Robinson's untimely death); and Swart, "The Insubstantial Pageant," 133, who observes that the "Plays' realism [is] concerned with everyday life," with the "essentials as the Middle Ages saw it."

4. Kolve, *Corpus Christi*, 104. In emphasizing the unselfconscious quality of this kind of anachronism, Kolve reminds the reader of what Nelson says in "'Sacred' and 'Secular' Currents," 399, about Noah—namely, that he "is a medieval man acting out the story of the Flood without discarding everything he knows from having lived after the Flood. He does not dissociate himself from his knowledge of Christ and His fulfillment of the prophecies."

5. Kolve, 112, points out—and no one has yet convincingly demonstrated otherwise—that no other medieval playwright "was more consistent in anachronism and anglicization than the Wakefield Master."

6. Ibid., 110.

7. Paxson, "Structure of Anachronism," 335, provides a helpful and instructive summary of the types of anachronism found in the medieval mystery plays.

8. Kolve, 104–5 and 109. On this more complicated form of anachronism, also see Stevens, *Mystery Cycles*, 77–79.

9. Kolve, 116.

10. Ibid.

11. Ibid.

12. Robertson, "Question of 'Typology,'" 173. While Davidson, in *Technology, Guilds,* does not address the subject of anachronism in the entire monograph except to acknowledge, in a discussion of biblical characters, that "identification of Joseph with present-day [medieval] craftsmen from the city was not something to be ignored" (67), his examination of the many technologies needed to produce the mystery plays inadvertently supports the notion that something more than civic pride—that is, the comprehension of the ethical implications of technology itself—inspired artisans and actors to recreate biblical history in a way most meaningful to and congruent with their collective spiritual outlook.

13. Kolve, 116–23. Helterman, *Symbolic Action,* 21–23, also appears to approach this understanding of anachronism, without using the actual term, as he discusses the timelessness of action transformed into symbol or symbolic gesture in the Wakefield Master's works.

14. Robertson, 172. Stevens, "Illusion and Reality," 457, suggestively calls attention to this feature of the tropological in the plays as he makes the case for the audience being drawn into the plays' action by the combination of realism and symbolism, much like participants in a ritual rather than spectators at a play. Davidson, "Space and Time," 46 and 49, argues, in his discussions of spatial and temporal orientation in the drama, for the resultant condition of ontological, *imaginative* participation. This distinct form of participation is consonant with the dramatic function of anachronistic tropological verisimilitude.

15. On the identity and character of this elusive playwright, see Cady, "The Maker of Mak"; Cargill, "Authorship"; Cawley, *Wakefield Pageants*, xxx–xxxi; Foster, "Gilbert Pilkington"; Fowler, *Bible*, 36–44; Gayley, *Plays of Our Forefathers*, 160–90; Lester, "The Wakefield Master"; and Stevens and Cawley, 1:xxvi–xxxi.

16. While still a matter of conjecture, the contributions to the Towneley collection now attributed to the Wakefield Master on the basis of his signature stanza and other internal and stylistic evidence, according to Stevens and Cawley, 1:xxviii–xxxi, include six entire plays, viz., *Mactatio Abel* (2), *Processus Noe cum filiis* (3), *[Prima] Pagina Pastorum* (12), *[Secunda] Pagina Pastorum* (13), *Magnus Herodes* (16), and *Coliphizacio* (21), and the stanza form and even portions of at least nine other plays, viz., *Fugacio Iosep et marie in egiptum* (15), *Conspiracio* (20), *Flagellacio* (22), *Processus Crucis* (23), *Processus Talentorum* (24), *Peregrini* (27), *Ascencio Domini* (29), *Iudicium* (30), and *Lazarus* (31). In other words, the Wakefield Master appears to have had a hand as either author, redactor, or both in nearly half of the plays as they exist in manuscript. This is, more or less, the agreed-on authorship of plays and revisions since the beginning of the twentieth century. For further discussion, see Cady, "Wakefield Group," 244–45; England and Pollard, *Towneley Plays*, xxii; Gardner, *Construction*, 130, 138–39; Helterman, *Symbolic Action*, 4–5; Robinson, *Stagecraft*, 17; Stevens, *Mystery Cycles*, 130. For purposes of critical consistency, this study accepts Stevens and Cawley's authorship identifications.

17. Stevens and Cawley, 1:xxii, make the point that the Master's work was probably begun after midcentury, basing this date partly on demographic evidence offered by Dobson, "Yorkshire Towns," 1–21, and by Rimmer, "The Evolution of Leeds," 274–81. Further support for this demographic argument can be found in Moorman, introduction to *Place-Names*, xxxiii–xxxiv. For phonological argument that supports demographic evidence, see Trusler, "Language."

18. While an academic dustup over whether the Towneley plays were ever collected and performed as a "cycle" by members of Wakefield's craft guilds appears to have erupted after the publication of Palmer's "'Townelye Plays' or 'Wakefield Cycle' Revisited," Stevens and Cawley's argument that "references make it clear that the pageants were collectively called a Corpus Christi play and that craft guilds performed them on pageant wagons" (1:xxii) remains more convincing than Palmer's conjectures. The argument Stevens and Cawley make is based on authentic external evidence including the Diocesan Court of High Commission document of 1576 and three references in the Wakefield Burgess Court Rolls for 1556 and 1559, references published and discussed earlier by Cawley, Forrester, and Goodchild in their "Wakefield Burgess Court Rolls"; see especially 99. Mills, "'The Towneley Plays' or 'The Towneley Cycle'?" 96, in quoting Benson on romance cycles (*Malory's "Morte Darthur,"* 8), makes the interesting and instructive point about the idea of "cycle" that it may be more helpful to consider the term "not as a controlling literary structure but as a mental frame of reference."

19. Stevens and Cawley, 1:xix–xxiii.

20. For general discussions of Wakefield, see Aikin, *Description of the Country*,

579, who quotes Leland describing Wakefield as a market town, the "whole profit of which standeth by coarse drapery," and Leland, *Itinerary,* 41–43. For more specific discussions of Wakefield's economic prosperity in the fifteenth century, see Frampton, "Flourishing," 657–58, who argues that by the mid-fifteenth century, despite the Wars of the Roses, Wakefield was growing dramatically. Gardner, *Construction,* 139, presents the same argument, adding that Wakefield was "booming" at this time, as evidenced by the costly improvements being made to All Saints. Heaton, *Woollen and Worsted,* 77–78, Pevsner, *Yorkshire: The West Riding,* and Robinson, *Stagecraft,* 21, elaborate on the improvements to which Gardner refers, reiterating that the fifteenth and sixteenth centuries were, as Pevsner aptly puts it, a "period of great prosperity in districts connected with wool and cloth ... [when] ... a number of large and important churches went up in the principal towns" (531)—churches such as Rotherham (1410), Wakefield (1420), and Halifax (1430–35), and unique religious structures, such as the Wakefield Bridge Chapel, one of the last four of its kind in England yet standing today. Cawley, *Wakefield Pageants,* xvii, arrives at the same conclusion when he says the guilds of Wakefield were prosperous enough by the end of the century "to bring forth" the "cycle." Similar but briefer characterizations of the town at midcentury are offered by Chambers, *English Literature,* 35; Swart, "The Insubstantial Pageant," 131; Williams, *Drama of Medieval England,* 72–73; and Woolf, *The English Mystery Plays,* 310–11. Stevens, *Mystery Cycles,* 112, demurs, arguing that Wakefield did not become a commercial center until the early sixteenth century; even then it remained under seigneurial control (126). Hey, *Yorkshire from AD 1000,* 96, however, makes the point that while the York wool trade was in decline in the fifteenth century, cloth making, especially the production of cheap kerseys, flourished in the West Riding in towns like Wakefield. Bartlett, "Expansion and Decline," 29, goes so far as to argue that the growing competition from cloth making in the West Riding "intensified" or hastened the waning of York's prosperity. West Riding merchants, Bartlett adds, not only knew that people wanted to wear country cloth, they also understood that by avoiding the markets of York and Hull, they could dispatch most of their cloth to London for sale or export (32). Power, *Wool Trade,* 16–19, explains the principal economic reasons for the shift from exporting wool to making cloth. Others presenting similar arguments include Carus-Wilson, *Medieval Merchant Venturers,* 280–81; Lipson, *Woollen and Worsted Industries,* 19–26; and Sigsworth, *Black Dyke Mills,* 1. Hartley and Elliot, *Life and Work,* 2:13, 27–29, also offer the reminder that the fifteenth century was a time when England carried on extensive foreign trade, especially as the result of Henry IV's 1407 charter supporting merchant ventures.

21. Hey, 85. The soke mill of the manor, located "just above the bridge" over the Calder, would also have been part of this activity. See Frampton, 645, and Robinson, *Stagecraft,* 54. It should be remembered that the Domesday Book records ninety-two mills in Yorkshire, of which forty were located in the West Riding alone. In *Mills,* 31, Holt observes that three windmills had appeared at the eastern end of the

vast manor of Wakefield by 1270. Fulling mills also made their appearance in the vicinity, one of the first in England in Newsham in Yorkshire (153).

22. Carus-Wilson, "Industrial Revolution," 60, argues quite convincingly and instructively that the region became known for its various kinds of broadcloth—for its Kendals, Ludlows, Cotswolds, Mendips, Castlecombes, Stroudwaters, and Westerns.

23. Hey, 83.

24. Hey, 84; also see Aikin, *Description of the Country*, 96.

25. Pevsner, *Yorkshire: The West Riding*, 31, includes the fact that a number of "large and important churches went up in the principal towns" of the area during this time. These can be seen in Rotherham, Wakefield, and Halifax, as mentioned before, and also in Sheffield, Bradford, Tadcaster, and Doncaster. As for All Saints, the west tower was added in 1429, and the chancel was under construction from 1458 to 1475. This is the time of Thomas Rogers's incumbency as Vicar of Wakefield, a period in Wakefield (1462–1502) when the Perpendicular Style was introduced as part of the ambitious rebuilding program of All Saints. See Allen, *Wakefield Cathedral*, 6–9.

26. Pevsner, 19, provides a description of how the Grand Trunk linked Doncaster (Danum), Castleford (Legiolium), Aldborough (Isurium), and Newton Kyme. He also points out that there were other roads crisscrossing the area. One of these is the Lancashire Road to Aldborough via Ilkeny (Olicana). Another is the road that linked Manchester with York. Closer to Wakefield, Hey points out, the "Wakefield Gate" linked the "vaccaries on the moorland edges of the upper Calder Valley with the manorial centre" and "must at the time have been a busy drove road, for all the cattle were taken to Wakefield to be marketed and sold" (73–74). Aikin, *Description of the Country*, 109, also observes that the Aire and Calder were navigation routes that experienced a great deal of traffic.

27. Walker, *Wakefield*, 1:52–54, indicates—although how accurate his account may be remains a matter of conjecture—that a charter for a Wakefield fair was first granted by King John in 1202. A second charter was granted to John, the seventh earl de Warenne, by Henry III in 1258. The Woodkirk or Lee Fair, in the time of Edward II, was "reckoned to be one of the most famous in the country," as merchants from as far away as France, Germany, Spain, Italy, and the Low Countries would come there to sell their horses, cattle, and produce (1:46).

28. Chenu, *Nature, Man, and Society*, 39–40, provides the translation; the manuscript can be found in MS London Lambeth Palace 36D, fol. 32rb.

29. Ibid., 40–41. For further discussion of this "vision," also see Curtius, *Latin Middle Ages*, 544–46, and Jordan, *Shape of Creation*, 35. The mythological foundation of this view can be found in early representations of the maker of tools, *homo faber*, who strives to imitate divine models. On this mythological source, see Eliade, *Forge and the Crucible*, 100–101.

30. For a thorough discussion of the agricultural revolution, see White, *Social*

Change, 39–78. Gimpel, *The Medieval Machine*, 29–58, arrives at similar conclusions.

31. White, *Medieval Religion and Technology*, 145.
32. Ibid., 251.
33. Ibid., 250–51. See also Hattinger, *Book of Hours*, plates 3 and 6–10; Stern, "Poésies et représentations" and *Le calendrier de 354*, 356–57; and Webster, *Labors of the Months*.
34. Chenu, *Nature, Man, and Society*, 44–45; Forbes, "Power," 2:606; Sambursky, *Greeks*, 241.
35. White, *Medieval Religion and Technology*, 146.
36. Ibid., 89.
37. Ibid., 235–37. White elaborates this point, partly by paraphrasing Ernst Benz's thesis that "Western technology is closely connected with the specifically Christian premises of our Western culture"; see Benz's "Christian Expectation," 121.
38. White, *Medieval Religion and Technology*, 320.
39. Ibid., 328–29.
40. Ibid., 137–44.
41. Ibid., 186.
42. Ibid., 65; also see 239. This iconography could be found in Yorkshire in the fifteenth century. God as Master Craftsman holding the compass may be seen, for example, in a window in York Minster.
43. Blunt, "Blake's 'Ancient of Days,'" 53 n. 4. For the image of God as Master Craftsman, also see Hassall, *Holkham Bible Picture Book*, 56, fol. 2.
44. White, *Medieval Religion and Technology*, 244, provides an instructive introduction to this important figure in the history of technology.
45. Theophilus, *On Divers Arts*, 62.
46. Ibid., 62–63. The "proof," which involves seven "virtues" or exercises of "spirit," leads to "greater deeds of skill," whose purpose it is to reveal "divine mysteries" and to support the "service of the Offices."
47. *S. Bernardi vita prima*, 285 (2.5.31).
48. *Descriptio positionis*, 570–71; the gloss is provided by White, *Medieval Religion and Technology*, 245.
49. Ibid., 246.
50. Ibid., 247–48.
51. Hugh of Saint Victor, *Didascalicon*, 74–75.
52. Ibid., 75–77. The elevation in importance of the *quadrivium*, and even the modification of the *quadrivium* and the seven liberal arts, can be seen in works by thinkers influenced by the Victorine school. Peter Alfonso, for example, retains all four arts of the *quadrivium* in his *Disciplina clericalis*, but keeps only logic in the case of the *trivium*, and omits rhetoric entirely, substituting physics and necromancy for it and grammar. Al-Farabi, in his *The Rise of the Sciences*, emphasizes the importance of natural science, adding its eight parts to the *quadrivium*. He points

out that a science—that is, an applied science—is needed to deal with changes in nature. In *De ortu sive divisione scientiarum*, Robert Kilwardby alters Hugh's division of the mechanical arts, reorganizing the *trivium* to consist of earth culture, food science, and medicine, and the *quadrivium* to consist of costuming, armor making, architecture, and business courses. See Thorndike, *History of Magic*, 2:72, 80–81, 82–83, respectively.

53. Ibid., 79.

54. Haskins, *Renaissance of the Twelfth Century*, 93–193.

55. See Jeffrey, *Franciscan Spirituality*, 83–118, and White, *Medieval Religion and Technology*, 37.

56. It should come as no surprise, within the actual and historical context in which the Wakefield Master wrote and revised, that the culmination of mechanical precision's evolution would be embodied in the horologium or clock, and that this particular mechanism would be associated with the virtue of self-restraint and Christ Himself (see White, *Medieval Religion and Technology*, 181–204, and Cipolla, *Clocks and Culture*, 40–47). Nor is it startling that praise would be sung to the invention of invention in a variety of ways and to innovation itself. Remarkable among examples of the latter is the passage in *De secretis operibus* (533) when Roger Bacon prophesies an age of automated land, water, and air transportation:

> Machines for navigation can be made without rowers so that the largest ships on rivers or seas will be moved by a single man in charge with greater velocity than if they were full of men . . . cars can be made so that without animals they will move with unbelievable rapidity . . . flying machines can be constructed so that a man sits in the midst of the machine revolving some engine by which artificial wings are made to beat the air like a flying bird . . . [also] a machine small in size [can be constructed] for raising or lowering enormous weights, than which nothing is more useful in emergencies . . . [also] a machine can be made by which one man can draw a thousand to himself by violence against their wills . . . [and] machines can be made for walking in the sea and rivers, even to the bottom without danger.

Equally remarkable among instances of the invention of invention is the instructive principal sentiment of a sermon preached in 1306 by the Dominican Fra Giordano of Pisa, in which the invention of eyeglasses is identified as the discovery of a new art and presented as evidence that "we shall never see an end of finding" the arts (White, *Medieval Religion and Technology*, 221).

57. Thorndike, *History of Magic*, 2:536–37. Others make the same observations about the Gothic. In discussing late medieval painting, Dvořák, for example, makes the point, in *Idealism and Naturalism*, 138, that van Eyck's great contribution is "the total victory of that subjective discovery of the world in its infinite variety," which becomes "a world view formulating a source of art based upon its own principles." Mâle also discusses the careful *re-presentation* of nature through the Gothic style in *The Gothic Image*, 27–64. Panofsky, *Early Netherlandish Painting*, 1:181, echoes Dvořák's point about the Gothic in relation to van Eyck when he observes

that van Eyck's works are "reconstructions" rather than "representations." Simson, *The Gothic Cathedral*, 39, reemphasizes the rediscovery of nature in the Gothic when he says the style "embodies the vision that the Platonists at Chartres had unfolded." In other words, the Gothic was not a style that imaged the truth but rather was an artistic "realization of its laws." The effect of this was to bring about a change from a "mystical to a rational approach to truth drawn from Christian metaphysics." This idea is suggested by Mumford in his *Technics and Civilization*, 28–29.

58. White, *Medieval Religion and Technology*, 240–41.
59. Le Goff, *Time, Work, and Culture*, 114–21.
60. Mirk, *Festival*, 2.
61. Robertson, *A Preface to Chaucer*, 65–113, especially 65.
62. Robertson, "Question of 'Typology,'" 173.
63. John of Garland provides this definition of invention in *Parisiana poetria*, 8–9.
64. White, *Machina ex deo*, 101.
65. Copeland, *Rhetoric, Hermeneutics, and Translations*, 151.
66. Augustine, *On Christian Doctrine*, 7, implies these interpretive moves at the beginning of his study of sacred rhetoric when he suggests "invention" is the "discovery of things which are to be understood."
67. Copeland, 158.
68. Thorndike, *History of Magic*, 2:29–30. Adelard of Bath, for example, calls for the use of the telescope and microscope to aid in the scrutiny of nature. Interestingly, precise description of experimental procedures as well as the recording of findings was also advocated, as is illustrated by the preface of Hugh of Santalla's *De spatula* or the prefaces of the later, popular books of "experiments" or "secrets" (2:87). This emphasis reminds us of the importance Saint Augustine assigns to the *modus proferendi* or the dissemination of what is understood, the pedagogical focus of *De doctrina christiana*'s fourth book.
69. Sypher, *Literature and Technology*, 86.
70. Copeland, 80–81. Also see Russell, *Allegoresis*, xi–xv, and the provocatively insightful afterword, in which Wasserman clarifies the latent and sophisticated nature of *allegoria*. This feature of the play may explain why Craig insists, in his *English Religious Drama*, 15, that "medieval religious drama existed primarily to give religious instruction, establish faith, and encourage piety" even when the plays contained matter not relevant to biblical themes.
71. Copeland, 81.
72. Jacobus de Voragine, in *The Golden Legend*, 1:3, offers the historical designation of the time of renewal. The idea of the sixth age, as Kolve, *Corpus Christi*, 89, points out, is a conception of history offered by Saint Augustine. Accordingly, the first group of plays is set in the time of erring or Augustine's second and third ages, and the final group, according to Jacobus, occupies the historical period known as the time of reconciliation.

73. On the shepherds' being "priestlike," see Stevens and Cawley, 2:490, line note 478, and Edminster, "Foolish Shepherds," 63–67.

74. Peter Lombard, *Sententiae*, PL, 192:701–6. For further explanation of the distinction between these two notions, also see Robertson, *A Preface to Chaucer*, 74–75.

75. See, for example, Woolf, *The English Mystery Plays*, 192.

76. While this conjecture has not yet made its way into print, the argument for it offered anecdotally by Jergens-Forsythe and later by Roney has merit. Only so many plays can be performed during each performance day of the Corpus Christi celebration, even though these are the longest days of the year. Continuity between the end of the first and the beginning of the second performance day would be insured if the shepherds' plays were performed at these two times.

77. Stevens and Cawley, 2:521.

78. Herod's ranting and raving, as will be shown shortly, frequently tests the "distance-limit"—that is, the perilous margin between mimesis and methexis—that Sypher, *Literature and Technology*, 88, defines in his discussion of Edward Bullough's conception of "psychical" objectivity (see *Aesthetics*, 93–130). For further discussion of this dimension of the Master's art, see Diller's analysis of "address to the audience" in *Mystery Play*, 122–59, especially 129–31, 135–40.

79. Copeland, 80.

80. On the empirical temper of sacramentalism in the late Middle Ages, including its influence on the development of medieval drama, see Hardison, *Christian Rite*, 205–18, and Rubin, *Corpus Christi*, 213–87. White, *Medieval Religion and Technology*, 34, observes that this is the time in which the elevation of the consecrated host first appears (between 1196 and 1208), the time in which the altar had to support the monstrance, the time in which the dogma of transubstantiation was first defined (1215), the time in which the feast of the Corpus Christi was first instituted (1264), and the time in which the procession in honor of the host was first held (1279).

81. On Corpus Christi drama's establishing social wholeness, as well as projecting a community of equals, see James, "Ritual, Drama," 19.

Chapter 1. The Abuse of Time and Space in the *Mactatio Abel*

1. On the play-collection thematic function, see Boone, "Skill of Cain," 112, who points out that Cain and Abel plays are of interest because "of their position as first moral action in history." Stevens, *Mystery Cycles*, 127–28, elaborates this idea, saying that the playwright sets the stage, as it were, with this play, and that the play "must be read as a typological forecast, [as] a kind of map for the full dramatic action to unfold." On the unusual comic element in the play, see Prosser, *Drama and Religion*, 80, who argues the comic element of farce in the play is "not sufficiently integrated with the scriptural story," and so distracts the audience, a fact Carey, *Wakefield Group*, 258, also notes. Brockman, "Comic and Tragic Counterpoint," 331, on the other hand, argues that the comic in the play "establishes the play's deepest human and theological meaning." Speirs, *Medieval English Poetry*, 320, concurs,

adding that not only is the farce integrated but Garcio and Cain are "the perennial pair of quarreling clowns." On the extensive editing, stanza forms, and versification, see Stevens and Cawley, *The Towneley Plays*, 2:441.

2. The story was as well known to medieval as to original audiences. For a discussion of its principal source other than the Bible, St. Ambrose's fourth-century treatise *De Cain et Abel*, see Bernbrock, "Slaying of Abel," 317. Other sources and treatments increasing the story's popularity include *Salomon and Saturnus, Cursor Mundi, De Lyff of Adam and Eue* (1375), the Hegge play of Abel, the Cornish play *Creation*, and a Breton play (1550). For a discussion of these and other parallels, see Bonnel, "Cain's Jaw Bone," 141–42, and Carey, 9–12. On the relation of the play to the plow-play, see Reiss, "Symbolic Plow," 12–14.

3. On Cain's wrath, see Hartnett, "Cain," 26, who argues it is a function of Cain's isolation; Helterman, *Symbolic Action*, 26–46, who maintains it is the result of an inability to grasp the logic of charity; and Stevens, *Mystery Cycles*, 129, who points out that it reflects a social dislocation. On the various relationships, feudal and otherwise, see Gardner, *Construction*, 25–27, and "Theme and Irony," 515–16, and Meyers, *A Figure Given*, 27. On stewardship, see Jeffrey, "Stewardship," 70–73. On poor and wicked plowmanship, see Brockman, "Comic and Tragic Counterpoint," 337, and Reiss, 7.

4. By and large, critics and scholars agree that the play is about the tragedy of obdurate impenitence. See, for example, Bernbrock, "Slaying of Abel," 321; Hanks, "*Mactatio Abel*," 52; Hartnett, 21; Reiss, 17–18; Robertson, "Question of 'Typology,'" 167.

5. The play's structure is symmetrical, consisting of four parts or "scenes" and an induction. The induction, in which Garcio makes his initial proclamation, lasts for twenty-four lines. There follows scene 1, "The Fraternal Encounter and Interview," involving the initial exchange between Cain and Abel (2/25–171). The next scene, "The Tithing" (2/172–305), shows both brothers making their offerings, beginning with their arrival at the tithing area and ending with Cain's denunciation of God. The third scene, "The Killing of Abell," begins with Abel's assessment of Cain's mistithing and ends with the reentry of Garcio at line 387. The fourth scene, "The Cover-Up," occupies the final eighty-nine lines of the play.

I have chosen to identify scenes, and often episodes within scenes, by descriptive titles in the discussion of the plays in this study. These identifications, some will argue, introduce an interpretive bias. While such lack of critical disinterestedness cannot be denied, the desire to establish clarity is the reason for the identifications. Such scene designations, of course, do not occur in the *regenall* (see Cawley and Stevens, *The Towneley Cycle*).

6. Sypher, *Literature and Technology*, 76.

7. *Machina ex deo*, 148. The other means of controlling matter and space, White contends, is transport.

8. Keen, *Chivalry*, 134–140, describes the function of the medieval herald. By the end of the fourteenth century, the herald, Keen points out, is an important member

of the aristocratic household. He is usually an expert in armory and in all matters of secular ceremony. As Garcio begins the play, it is obvious that, while the formulaic quality of his language implies a knowledge of ceremonial function, he is nothing more than a parody of what a herald should be.

9. Hartnett, "Cain," 23, describes the ranting merely as an instance of bombast often used to quiet a medieval audience. Hamelius, "Character of Cain," 338, observes that such jesting and sneering was not out of place, and Helterman, *Symbolic Action*, 27, identifies the ranting as conventional mockery. However, Robertson's observation in "Question of 'Typology,'" 166, that the opening speech in the *Mactatio Abel* calls attention to the play's tropological relevance by identifying the audience as members of the generation of Cain appears to be closer to the mark. The rant, vulgar as it is, demonstrates the limitation of those who would be like Cain. While not as specific, Brockman appears to support this idea with his observation in "Comic and Tragic Counterpoint," 335, that Garcio's rant moves from "meaninglessness to meaningful laughter" by suggesting the kind of person Cain is. If Happé's observations in "Vice," 183, are accurate about Garcio's being a type of folk-play presenter whose settling of the audience has a controlling influence in a play, then the inability to control space is further emphasized by this association.

10. Axton, *European Drama*, 177–78, maintains that the team consists of nine animals. Reiss, "Symbolic Plow," 12, is probably more accurate when he concludes that most evidence from the Middle Ages suggests four beasts of burden usually comprised the team. Richardson, "The Medieval Plough-Team," 287–96, arrives at the same conclusion. The latest to weigh in to the number debate is Morey, who agrees with Axton but emphasizes the folly of the team's being mixed, though such (apparently) was the custom in late medieval England; see "Plows, Laws, and Sanctuary," 53–54. Symbolic and practical applications of the medieval plow receive careful treatment also in Barney, "Ploughshare of the Tongue," Langdon, *Horses, Oxen*, and Passmore, *The English Plough*.

11. Robertson, "Question of 'Typology,'" 166.

12. White, *Machina ex deo*, 84, and *Medieval Religion and Technology*, 138–39.

13. Being alienated from God as he is, Cain cannot, as Reiss, "Symbolic Plow," 5, points out, make the earth bear fruit.

14. The correlative image of the master-servant relationship is discussed by several critics of the play. See Hanks, "*Mactatio Abel*," 49–50, who characterizes Garcio as a type of the "impudent servant"; Meyers, *A Figure Given*, 25, indicates that Garcio is to Cain as Cain is to God. Cain is also both a false lord and a false servant, as Gardner argues in "Theme and Irony," 517. This falsity, Helterman argues in *Symbolic Action*, 28–29, results from Cain's desire "to be master among servants." The master-servant relationship between the two, Gardner argues later in *Construction*, 31, may also suggest the lack of feudal reciprocity.

15. A dramatic irony perhaps missed by contemporary audiences would be perceived by initial onlookers in response to the substance here of Garcio's threat. When he refers to using the same "mesure and weght," Garcio is reminding his

immediate Corpus Christi celebrants of one of the principal ways in which medieval people defrauded each other. On the use of false weights and measures, see Hartley and Elliot, *Life and Work*, 1:20, 71, plate 20a.

16. White, *Machina ex deo*, 148. Davidson's argument in "Space and Time in Medieval Drama," 40–58, concerning the spatiotemporal dimension of medieval drama as an ontological *imaginative* participatory perceptual experience precluding seriality and causation is certainly true of much of the early liturgical drama. But in the case of an artist like the Wakefield Master, whose employment of an anachronistic verisimilitude may actually have involved the driving of a real plow, and possibly even a real plow team, into the performance area, such prohibitions appear to be too delimiting. This is not to say the Master's purpose is to reject the worldview fundamental to liturgical drama. Rather, it is to suggest that the Master is using the very materiality of created reality—the stuff with which people engaged in labor on a daily basis—to enable his audiences to relearn the principles undergirding that worldview.

17. Helterman, *Symbolic Action*, 27, calls attention to Cain's driving a two-man team alone, saying the playwright thus symbolically conveys that Cain must choose a proper friend. Reiss, "Symbolic Plow," 8, observes that Cain's action, in light of peasant/farming ideals, makes him a "grotesque parody of the proper, good plowman."

18. See British Library, Add. MS. 42130, fol. 170. For another pictorial representation of proper or efficient plowing procedure, see Hassall, *Holkham Bible Picture Book*, 68; also see, for further discussion of proper procedure, Camille, "Laboring for the Lord" and "When Adam Delved."

19. Critics have overlooked the function of the lead animal, regardless of the team's size. When dealing with large plow teams, farmers would normally call out to one or perhaps two animals, depending on the size of the team. My informant, Kenneth L. Ferguson, whose father plowed with large horse teams in turn-of-the-century Nebraska, also pointed out—a commonplace notion among farmers—that this procedure, so far as he knows, has always been followed with regard to plow animals. In fact, the lead animal in this arrangement would always walk the furrow, the other animals off to the unplowed side to insure furrow symmetry.

20. Jeffrey, "Stewardship," 68, points out that, as a plowman, Cain does not get the animals to pull as a team because he goes after individual animals. If the team is large, then the greater the confusion. If the team consists of only four animals, then the confusion is perhaps not as dramatic, but it is no less apparent since the call is not to the lead animal. And even if Rogerson, "Plough-Team on Stage," 182, and Davidson, *Technology, Guilds*, 3–5, are correct about there being only two animals, confusion is still the likely effect. In this case, while one of the animals is the dominant one, calling both animals by a variety of names increases the likelihood of unproductive response.

21. Most agree it is a mixed team and that a precedent for such did, in fact, exist in England in the late Middle Ages (see Reiss, "Symbolic Plow," 10, and Robertson,

"Question of 'Typology,'" 167). Reiss, 10–11, also indicates that Cain is associated with a mixed team in *The Holkham Bible Picture Book,* and that evidence for such teams can be found in the anonymous *Seneschaucie* and *Fleta.*

22. White, *Social Change,* 62.

23. Hanks, "*Mactatio Abel,*" 51, makes this point.

24. The biblical injunction is found in Deuteronomy 22:10. See Jeffrey, "Stewardship," 69. The reality of the mixed team in medieval England, of which there are illustrations, may actually have been iconographic rather than agricultural.

25. Henley, *Walter of Henley's Husbandry,* 13–15, 23–25.

26. Ibid., 19.

27. Brockman, "Law of Man," 699, states the play's "most striking reference to medieval English judicial process occurs in Cain's efforts to persuade Pickeharnes [Garcio] to aid in disposing of Abel's body."

28. Ibid.

29. Brockman, "Comic and Tragic Counterpoint," 345, observes that the decree "satirizes the administration of justice in fifteenth-century England by associating contemporary society with the egocentric ethos of Cain's city of man." In his "Law of Man," 702, Brockman also indicates that this moment in the play "reminds the audience of the abuse of royal prerogative." While both of these points may be valid, they appear to overlook the ethical issue of the more sinister—practically malicious—dimension of Cain's strategy.

30. Bernbrock, "Slaying of Abel," 320, observes that Cain kills and then "compounds sin by defending it." In other words, he kills first by weapon and then proceeds to "kill" again with words.

31. On the corrective, mocking voice of Garcio, see Gardner, *Construction,* 38, and Helterman, *Symbolic Action,* 37.

32. Reiss, "Symbolic Plow," 18, points out that a tradition of associating the plow with the Crucifixion had a great deal of currency in medieval thinking. Gardner's point in *Construction,* 122, that the favorite threat of hanging is unique to the Towneley collection not only underscores Gardner's conclusion that such a threat is "traceable to the poet's interest in social satire and realism"; it also emphasizes the fact that the playwright's keen awareness of and interest in the ethics of technology include the dismal carceral arena of penal execution.

33. White, *Medieval Religion and Technology,* 116–18.

34. Morey, "Plows, Laws, and Sanctuary," 53.

35. Harrison, "Discovery, Invention, and Diffusion," 1:59.

36. On the Englishness of the ass jawbone used by Cain, see Bonnel, "Cain's Jaw Bone," 141. Interestingly, Bonnel adds that there is "no doctrinal force in making [the jawbone] the instrument of Abel's death." This fact increases the likelihood of the Wakefield Master's wanting the audience to associate other meaning—especially that of invention—with the mandible-turned-weapon. For further discussion of Cain's weapon, see Guilfoyle, "Staging," 45–47.

37. Brockman, "Law of Man," 704.

38. Stevens and Cawley, 2:445, line note 334.

39. For this particular usage, see, for example, Chaucer's *Romaunt of the Rose* (B 2154), *Book of the Duchess* (1102), and *Troilus and Criseyde* (2.854 and 3.1287), in *The Riverside Chaucer*, 710, 343, 501, 530, respectively.

40. The moment occurs when Jonah says: "At alle peryles . . . I aproache hit no nerre; / I wyl me sum oþer waye þat he ne wayte after; / I schal tee in-to Tarce and tary þere a whyle, / And lyȝtly when I am lest he letes me alone" (Anderson, *Patience*, 33–34, lines 85–88).

41. Helterman, *Symbolic Action*, 35–36.

42. Hartnett, "Cain," 25. Hartnett argues that a distinguishing feature of Cain is that he changes from "a scurrilous boor to a complex and artful human sinner." This ability to steal God's thunder would seem to support her conclusion.

43. While several who have commented on this most unusual geographical identification have tried to find symbolic or other meaning in Cain's choice of burial location (see, for example, Guilfoyle, "Cain, Lamech," and Robinson, *Stagecraft*, 53), it is important to remember, as Gimpel points out in *The Medieval Machine*, 59, that "Stone quarrying was by far the most important mining industry in medieval Europe, more important possibly than all the others combined." In other words, Cain's final resting place is very valuable real estate, especially given its location in Goodybower, a close in Wakefield, and so not far from All Saints and the famous Bridge Chapel, two principal building sites requiring a great deal of quarried stone in the fifteenth century.

44. Helterman, *Symbolic Action*, 37.

45. Hartnett, "Cain," 29, and Carey, *Wakefield Group*, 31, make the claim that these responses by Cain are motivated by his dissatisfaction with his hard lot in life. The claim is not without merit, as Cain reviles his brother with a "seemingly inexhaustible and certainly inspired fund," to quote Hanks, "*Mactatio Abel*," 51, "of earthly profanity and obscenity." However, the purpose of this unique complaining, it should be noted, is to avoid accountability rather than to give an accurate accounting of former misfortunes.

46. White, *Medieval Religion and Technology*, 263.

47. Ibid., 264–76, provides a number of instructive examples, the most memorable of which perhaps include his discussion of alcohol, the "fun medicine," and Islam's opposition to the printing press. The example of Edward III included here is also from White's collection (266–67). A brief sampling of other instances of technology assessment in the Middle Ages should convince even the most skeptical that the Middle Ages, like our own, was a period of intense assessment, especially of many practical technologies. On how the late medieval East appropriated gun technology but ignored printing press technology, see Ayalon, *Gunpowder and Firearms*; on the identification of Bologna as the principal location in the Middle Ages to purchase paper more cheaply than anywhere else, see Briquet, *Les filigranes*, 2:317; on the end of the trébuchet as a weapon of war and on the "anathema directed by the Lateran Council of 1139 against archers and cross-bowmen using their detestable

weapons in wars between Christians," see Contamine, *War in the Middle Ages*, 193–97 and 274–75, respectively; on the replacement of the longbow by firearms in the English army, see Esper, "Replacement"; on the effect of firearms on naval combat, see Guilmartin, *Gunpowder and Galleys*; on Langland's assessment of the chimney, see *The Vision of William*, 148, passus X, lines 93–98; on Hugh Latimer's assessment of games, see his *Sermons*, 197; on games and sporting activities, also see Poole, "Recreations," 625; on eyeglasses, see Rosen, "The Invention of Eyeglasses"; and on the effect of the poor laws on society, see Tierney, *Medieval Poor Law*, 44–67.

48. While Robertson in "Question of 'Typology,'" 169, and Helterman, *Symbolic Action*, 42, call attention to the potentially obscene gesture here resulting from a possible wordplay on "farthing," what appears to be more important to Cain is that the process of the payment of debts has been interrupted by the priest. Boone's observation in "Skill of Cain," 118, that Cain tacitly denies his original debt to God and "explicitly converts the transaction into a purely material exchange" would seem to support this emphasis.

49. White, *Medieval Religion and Technology*, 139.

50. Gardner, *Construction*, 34.

51. Langland, *Vision of Piers Plowman*, 66, lines 201–11:
"I'm well avenged on vagabonds by virtue of you.
But I pray you, before you part," said Piers to Hunger,
"With beggars and street-beadsmen what's best to be done?
For well I know that once you're away, they will work badly.
Misfortune makes them so meek now,
And it's for lack of food that these folk obey me.
And they're my blood brothers, for God bought us all.
Truth taught me once to love them every one
And help them with everything after their needs.
Now I'd like to learn, if you know, what line I should take
And how I might overmaster them and make them work."

52. On Cain's materialism being more important than his spirituality, see Boone, "Skill of Cain," 123; Robertson, "Question of 'Typology,'" 169; and Hartnett, "Cain," 27.

53. Helterman, *Symbolic Action*, 38.

54. The characterization of the counting as a model of disorder can be found in Bernbrock, "Slaying of Abel," 320; as bad ring-giving, in Gardner, *Construction*, 34–35; as a sleight of hand, in Helterman, 38–39, and also in Bernbrock, 319. Also see Crowther, "Bad Tither."

55. Panofsky, *Gothic Architecture and Scholasticism*, 64.

56. Boethius, *The Consolation of Philosophy*, 107.

57. On the *computus*, see White, *Medieval Religion and Technology*, 333–34, and Thorndike, *History of Magic*, 2:444.

58. An instructive parallel—though involving the model, as it were, of the proper vassalic relationship—can be found in the fourteenth-century poem *Patience*, as

Jonah, in his "Whale's-Belly Prayer" to God, acknowledges his own inadequacy, contrasts God's omnipotence and omnipresence to his own weak and limited condition, and bids God to intervene on his behalf and extricate him from cetological confinement. See Anderson, *Patience*, 41–42, lines 305–36.

59. On the *compotus* being this kind of perceived reality, see Saul, *Scenes from Provincial Life*, 138.

60. Brockman's observation in "Comic and Tragic Counterpoint," 339, that Cain becomes "increasingly convinced by his own rhetoric and his indignation builds until he condescendingly offers to tithe," adds support to this transformation occurring in Cain's character.

61. Meyers, *A Figure Given*, 51, indicates Cain is the earthly counterpart of Lucifer; Reiss, "Symbolic Plow," 4, states Cain is the "offspring of Satan and [is] the first disciple of the devil"; Brockman, "Comic and Tragic Counterpoint," 337, argues that the plowman, who in traditional iconography represents the persevering Christian, now personifies the contrary in the character of Cain.

62. On this usage of the application of the practical art, see Boone, "Skill of Cain," 113.

63. Hartnett, "Cain," 26, argues counting repetitions occur because Cain cannot let go of his worldly possessions; Boone, 126–27, says that Cain "does not divide properly"; Gardner, "Theme and Irony," 519, says Cain cannot "give up part of a skimpy profit to a lord he has never seen"; Helterman, *Symbolic Action*, 38–39, identifies Cain as a "short-change expert."

64. Helterman, 38–39, for example, implies this when he says God gets "one tenth" of the corn; when discussing line 234, Stevens and Cawley, 2:444, say Cain lays down "the second ten sheaves."

65. The tally stick was the chief register of work done or payments made on the medieval manorial farm. That "tally" implies "counterpart" is important visually as well as arithmetically. On this two-part, two-column, or either-side-of-the-tally feature of the tally, see Hartley and Elliot, *Life and Work*, 3:31.

66. For the definition of "thrafe," see Cawley, *Wakefield Pageants*, 177.

67. On Cain's being the personification of *possessio*, see Brockman, "Cain and Abel," 171.

68. The reeve needed the ability, as Bennett, "Reeve and the Manor," 364–65, points out, to think quickly, especially during the annual manorial audit when auditors might cross-question him regarding unusual details in the *compotus*. The reeve would have to anticipate questions about the accounts information he had gathered and offer explanations and justifications for expenditures, etc. Saul's characterization of the audit as a lengthy business, as well as a battle of wits involving many hours of difficult negotiations between auditors and the reeve (*Scenes from Provincial Life*, 125–26), attests to the reeve's need for a powerful intelligence and memory. Dyer, *Standards of Living*, 28, also concludes the reeve must possess this degree of intellectual acumen.

69. Jeffrey, "Stewardship," 76.

70. Ibid., 71. Jeffrey argues the smoke and stench are reminiscent of hell itself.

71. Hartnett, "Cain," 25.

72. The effect of ecological crisis was well known to fifteenth-century England, the result of two centuries of deforestation and reliance on sooty, smoke-producing blast furnaces. On the extent of this crisis, see Gimpel, *The Medieval Machine*, 78–79.

73. Boone, "Skill of Cain," 126, points out that the smoke is a manifestation of Cain's prior condition.

74. Robertson, "Question of 'Typology,'" 166, calls the individual in this condition the "perennial Cain."

Chapter 2. The Abuse and Use of Time and Space in the *Processus Noe cum filiis*

1. Stevens and Cawley, *The Towneley Plays*, 1:xxiv, and 2:447. Also see Stevens, *Mystery Cycles*, 133, for an instructive discussion of the innovative stanza.

2. On the principal sources of this play, see Helterman, *Symbolic Action*, 48, who points out that the Wakefield Master combines the two York Noah plays; Schless, "Comic Element," 230, who observes that the unified effect of the play results from the merging of folkloric comedy and biblical narrative; and Stevens, *Mystery Cycles*, 100 and 125. Secondary sources for this and other plays include the *Holkham Bible Picture Book* and the *Vita Christi* of Ludolphus. On the former, see Kolve, *Corpus Christi*, 38, and Woolf, *The English Mystery Plays*, 132 and passim. On the latter, see Robinson, *Stagecraft*, 30–31.

3. Daniels, "Uxor Noah," 24, suggests that Noah's speaking first, a peculiarity of the Towneley *Processus Noe*, gives his speech "more human relevance and meaning." Nelson, "'Sacred' and 'Secular' Currents," 394, emphasizes the fact that the innovative treatment of the biblical text does not alter the force of the biblical narrative. It does, however, underscore the importance of responsibility.

4. White, *Medieval Religion and Technology*, 236, makes the point that this presupposition is fundamental to the Judeo-Christian view of reality and destiny. Among the many treatments of Noah in scholarship concerning the play, two distinct views of the patriarch/mariner arose during the latter half of the last century. The first of these emphasizes the typic or figural dimension of Noah's characterization. See, for example, Gardner, "Imagery and Allusion," 7–8; Helterman, *Symbolic Action*, 7; Jeffrey, "Stewardship," 75; Kolve, 71 and passim; J. Lewis, *Noah and the Flood*, 156–80; Meyers, *A Figure Given*, 18–19; Nelson, "'Sacred' and 'Secular' Currents," 398; and Robinson, *Stagecraft*, 56–57. The other view of Noah calls attention to his all-too-human nature. See, for example, J. Campbell, "Idea of Order," 81; Hirshberg, "Noah's Wife," 32; and Sachs, "Raven and the Dove," 200. Bevington, *Medieval Drama*, 290, like Stevens and Cawley, 2:447, suggests a compromise by pointing out that Noah, while a "believably imperfect man with whom the audience can identify," is also a "type of Christ." Considering Noah as an exemplar of the

mind that serves God cooperatively by serving itself in the technological mastery and practical use of nature seeks to further this compromise view of Noah.

5. The structure of the Towneley *Processus Noe* has been the subject of debate for a considerably long time. Gayley, *Plays of Our Forefathers,* 168, argues the play has five scenes, each of which is associated with a distinct location—namely, the forest, Noah's house, the forest, Noah's house, and the Ark. Another proposal, from Helterman, 53, limits the play to a tripartite structure, beginning with the dialogue between Noah and God, continuing with the battle between Noah and Uxor Gill, and ending with harmony on the Ark. This arrangement suggests a correspondence between the play and medieval sermon structure. The present chapter also argues for a symmetrical three-scene structure, though with a few alterations that find at least part of their inspiration in the scheme offered by Gayley.

The structure proposed here is this: The first scene, "The Problem," can itself be divided into three parts or episodes. The first episode, lines 1–104, is "Noah's Monologic Prayer." The second, "God's Monologue," ends at line 169, when God turns to Noah to give the human the divine blueprint for saving the remnant and the world. The final episode, lines 170–262, is the "Dialogue" between God and Noah.

The second scene, "The Solution," also has three episodes, though the first and last might more precisely be identified as interludes. The opening interludial episode begins at line 263, as Noah turns from his interview with God and prepares himself to inform his wife of what has just befallen him, and ends at line 360. The concluding interludial episode begins not long afterwards at line 417 and continues until line 607. Between these two interludes unfolds "The Construction of the Ark," an episode of 56 lines.

"The Application," the 199-line final scene, also has three episodes. The first, "The Mensuration," begins at line 608, as soon as Noah and Gill agree to follow their sons' advice and stop fighting. After the three lowerings of the plumb line and the discovery that the waters have receded, the next part begins at line 677. This episode, "Mensuration II," in which a centrosymmetry is established by means of an avian survey and the application in a real-world setting of planimetric principles, concludes at line 755, as soon as the sons realize that all the waters have receded. "The Disembarkation," the last episode, ensues, ending with the assertion of a reorganization of the world, a new order that recognizes humanity's proper relationship to God modeled on the friendship Noah initially experienced with God.

6. Eliade, *Cosmos and History,* 22–23, explains the importance of such a summoning by pointing out that it puts the individual contemporary with the cosmogony and anthropogony. Noah, in other words, contributes to the recreation of the world, an observation made by Helterman in *Symbolic Action,* 71, when pointing out that Noah's task is a "kind of creation." By virtue of this initial act, then, Noah establishes himself as an analogue of God the Master Craftsman—an apprentice of sorts, to be sure, but one whose mind is fundamentally ready to serve God cooperatively.

7. J. Campbell, "Idea of Order," 79, identifies this moment in the play as being one of the most important, since it is at this juncture that the strength of this and every subsequent relationship is determined to be based upon love and its resulting "commitment to act upon that love." Robinson, *Stagecraft*, 26, observes that God's descent to stand alongside Noah at this moment is an expression of humility not demonstrated in any of the other Noah plays.

8. This conspicuous anachronism serves to remind the audience that the new age of religious subjectivism and the importance of preparing the mind to receive God's message are fundamental to the Wakefield Master's thinking. This point may not prove Stevens's observation, in "Language as Theme," 105, and in *Mystery Cycles*, 163, that the Master was a Wycliffite, but it adds support to the notion advanced by Kolve, *Corpus Christi*, 58, and others of viewing the Towneley collection's famous "play doctor" as a cleric with strong leanings toward reform.

9. Though Noah has much to learn, it is not inaccurate to describe him at this point in the play as a good husbandman, as several have. Jeffrey, "Stewardship," 73, for example, elaborates Noah's good qualities of praying, being concerned with repentance, being a prelatical figure, and acting like a trustworthy feudal vassal.

10. Noah's prayer—that is, Noah's acknowledging and defining of God's relationship to himself and to all creation—is the means by which the Wakefield Master establishes the master-servant, lord-vassal, God-believer relationships that introduce and develop the theme of obedience in the play. For discussion of these relationships and theme, see J. Campbell, "Idea of Order," 77; Gardner, "Imagery and Allusion," 4–5; Meyers, *A Figure Given*, 31; and Nelson, "'Sacred' and 'Secular' Currents," 395.

11. Unger, *Art of Medieval Technology*, 74 and 76–77, observes that this kind of "anointing," while a maritime reality, may have "taken its inspiration from art." Be that as it may, its inclusion here further develops the idea of preserving time in terms of space since the sacramental and healing overtone implied by "annointing," as Watson suggests in "The Wakefield Noah," 6, leads to a proper use of the spatial. Meyers's observation, 38, regarding the limitation of Noah's knowledge of the Oil of Mercy at this point in the play is correct. However, knowing that some kind of help is available implies the beginning of an orientation that will use rather than abuse the spatial.

12. The emphasis upon exactness of spatial detail here is expected, given the Ark's conventional metaphoric and typological significance. On the former, see Helterman, *Symbolic Action*, 70; Speirs, *Medieval English Poetry*, 322; and Watson, 6. On the latter, see Gardner, "Imagery and Allusion," 7–8. But it should be remembered that, as J. Campbell points out in "Idea of Order," 78, this blueprint also pertains to building relationships between man and God, man and community, man and family, and man and nature.

13. Panofsky, *Gothic Architecture and Scholasticism*, 64.

14. On Noah's careful summarizing and refocusing of history, see Meyers, *A Figure Given*, 27–29.

15. On this paradoxical condition, elaborated by Saint Augustine, see my "Pardoner's Old Man," 337–40.

16. The implication of this change in punishment increases in importance the idea of responsibility as the motivation behind cooperation and avoidance of sin.

17. Noah's subsequent use of "alod" at line 81 to describe at this point the widespread nature of sin in the world has been glossed a number of ways, as Stevens and Cawley indicate, 2:448, line note 79–82. The similarity of "alod" to "allodium" (see, for example, Besserman, "*Noah*, Lines 55–56") suggestively introduces a deviation from the spatial allotment within the system of feudal tenure. Since no "repentance" is forthcoming from those engaged in this "allodial" or "free" or liberated sinning, however, Noah, aged though he may be, hurriedly begs mercy of God to avert the same kind of punishment suffered in the previous two accounts of spatial disruption. Noah may not have complete technological mastery of space or time at this point in the play, but he knows enough to recognize the abuse of each and to distinguish his "fry" and himself from those who do not.

18. Helterman, *Symbolic Action*, 60, identifies these interludes as the fabliau matter in the play. Gayley, *Plays of Our Forefathers*, 144, claims that the incorporation of this matter represents an aesthetic advance in dramatic art. Nelson, "'Sacred' and 'Secular' Currents," 393–400, reminds us that, aesthetic advance or not, the farcical or fabliau is an integral part of the play in which "natural human reactions to character and situation" are examined.

19. Gardner, "Imagery and Allusion," 3, points out that the comedy here, novel as it may be, is nevertheless thoroughly medieval and functional.

20. Helterman, *Symbolic Action*, 48, argues that the Stafford blue connotes the "henpecked" husband. Stevens and Cawley, 2:450, suggest on philological grounds that it means to be "beaten black and blue," another way of considering the husband who is dominated by his wife. For further discussion of this textile color, see Sarah Stanbury Smith, "'Game in Myn Hood,'" 4–5, where the figurative meaning of this color and its relation to certain articles of clothing suggest, among other things, deception, folly, and faithlessness. Further, a qualitative insult may be implicit in the reference to the color blue as it suggests the alliance of Noah with the cloth of a geographic competitor.

21. Noah, argues J. Campbell, "Idea of Order," 81, can hardly be seen as a paradigm of virtue in view of his violence, both physical and verbal. Britton, "Language and Character," 6, notes the dramatic change in Noah's language between the first and second scenes of the play. Stevens, *Mystery Cycles*, 156, also makes this point in his discussion of the Master's concern with the use and abuse of language in many of the Towneley plays.

22. Carey, *Wakefield Group*, 96, says that Noah's thought of Uxor Gill "arouses misgivings in his breast. He is the craven husband, pure and simple, terrified of his formidable wife." Gardner, "Imagery and Allusion," 8, adds that Noah "shudders" to think of what Uxor Gill will say and do. While Garvin, "Noah's Wife," calls attention to Uxor Gill's inveterate testiness, more important than this personality trait or even

Noah's diffidence, for the audience, is the fact that Noah has forgotten the divine injunction against tarrying, delivered just moments before.

23. Helterman, *Symbolic Action*, 66, points out that, in this first greeting, Uxor Gill's association with Eve and the sin of gluttony is established. The abuse of the spatial through the aside, and the concomitant loss of mastery of time, affirm this association, as does Noah's later characterization of Gill as the "Begynnar of blunder" (3/587). For further discussion of disobedience and the association between Uxor Gill and Eve, see Evans, "Feminist Re-enactments"; Hodges, "Noe's Wife," 30–36; Nelson, "'Sacred' and 'Secular' Currents," 393; and Schless, "Comic Element," 233. Stevens, *Mystery Cycles*, 170, argues that this characterization introduces the first "tyrant figure" in the collection.

24. Daniels, "Uxor Noah," 27, makes the point of there being so much discord in this first encounter that Noah does not have a chance to inform Uxor Gill of what he has learned from God. In other words, communication—which White in *Machina ex deo*, 148, calls one of the two principal ways of mastering and properly using space—is effectively disabled. Uxor Gill's garrulity, as Stevens points out in *Mystery Cycles*, 170, also impedes communication.

25. J. Campbell, "Idea of Order," 81.

26. Sypher, *Literature and Technology*, 86–91.

27. See, for example, chap. 1, sec. 5.

28. Stevens and Cawley, 2:451, line note 477. This continued lack of clarity on Noah's part is even more pronounced when one recalls that "garn on the reyll," the first of Noah's evasions, was possibly considered a figurative expression for wrangling. On this association, see Revard, "Tow on Absalom's Distaff."

29. Of all the Uxors, the Towneley Uxor Gill is the most stubborn, according to de Bruyn, *Woman and the Devil*, 133. Robinson, *Stagecraft*, 54, and Swart, "The Insubstantial Pageant," 133, note that, as a distinct feature of this recalcitrance, the Towneley Uxor Gill is the only spinner. It is now a demonstration of scholarly wisdom to associate the "rok" in this instance with this particular technology, which, according to White, in *Medieval Religion and Technology*, 47, makes its first appearance at Speyer around 1280. Hirshberg, "Noah's Wife," 30, and Cawley, *Wakefield Pageants*, 97, line note 364, for example, contend that the term "rok" has to do with the distaff, the staff used for supporting flax while spinning. The iconographic association between the distaff or "rok" and the punishment of Eve following the Fall has also been made. Helterman, *Symbolic Action*, 65, building on this particular association, adds that the act of spinning introduces a concern for things of this world rather than for the things of salvation. Hodges, "Noe's Wife," 37–38 n. 13, calls attention to the technological advance of the "seat" arrangement commonly affixed to the bottom of the distaff, or even a bench arrangement that made Uxor Gill's sitting on her "rok" such an evocative bit of theatrical business. The fact that the Wakefield Master identified this particular clothing manufacturing technology as a means of putting off salvation may have had a distinct, ironic meaning for the immediate late-medieval audience comprised of textile workers from Wakefield and the surrounding

West Riding area. What is more, another irony may have been initially apparent to Corpus Christi audiences since cloth-making technology is being portrayed as less valuable than shipbuilding.

30. See Curry, *Chaucer and the Mediaeval Sciences,* chap. 6, and Cawley, *Wakefield Pageants,* 97, line note 345.

31. This repeated lack of explanation sheds light on the issue of responsibility with regard to Uxor Gill. While she is slow to change, she may not be as culpable as she has previously appeared to a number of critics, such as Gardner, who in "Imagery and Allusion," 11, interprets her reluctance as representing "late repentance"; Helterman, *Symbolic Action,* 67, who views the delay as a manifestation of "rebellious humanity"; and Jeffrey, who observes in "Stewardship," 75, that the refusal to enter the Ark reminds us of the battle we "all face with the 'old man' in us."

32. See Sutherland, "'Not or I See More Neede,'" 189. The fact that it is an empirical experience that motivates Uxor Gill to change her venue reminds the audience, once again, of the playwright's interest in actuality and the relationship between ethical conduct and the treatment of space and time.

33. On the final altercation, see J. Campbell, "Idea of Order," 82, who points out that this is the refusal to leave the known for the unknown. To an extent this is true, but the fault appears, once again, to lie in the fact that the technological mastery of space is impaired by an impediment to communication.

34. It is important to remember that, as Nelson points out in "'Sacred' and 'Secular' Currents," 400, the farcical in these two interludes is the means by which Noah and Uxor Gill are eventually reunited. Related, too, as J. Campbell observes, 84, is the irony implicit in the paradox here in which the loss of the individual struggle for dominance, or the establishment of cooperation, leads ultimately to a victory for humankind.

35. Speirs, *Medieval English Poetry,* 322, argues that shipbuilding here is not just a realistic element but also an "intrinsic part of the performance" to demonstrate pride of craft—that is, pride in "the craft of carpentry or boat-building." Demonstrated mastery of the various technologies used to build ships, in actual performance, it should also be remembered here, establishes for the audience an exact visual association between the tropological anachronism of technology and the act of the cooperative serving of God through the serving of self in the mastery and practical use of nature.

36. On the noiseless ax motif, see Mill, "Noah's Wife Again," 625–26.

37. The Ark, though divinely inspired and designed, is still an invention, according to Harrison's definition in "Discovery, Invention, and Diffusion," 1:59, since it is the product of the "discovery and material application of what is latent in nature for the purpose of technologically fulfilling the divine will in the world." Davidson, in *Technology, Guilds,* 13–14, points out that the Wakefield Master is "amusingly vague about the matter of ark-building" when compared to the York Shipwrights' play. Davidson elicits the anecdotal support of Palmer in a footnote (104, n. 57) to give ballast to this position by repeating her observation about God's "not [having]

a clue, from the lines, on how to build a ship." Both Davidson and Palmer are correct about the vagueness here. But both miss the point of the Wakefield Master's shifting the responsibility for ark-building to Noah to "discover and engage in the material application of what is latent in nature for the purpose of technologically fulfilling the divine will in the world." Noah, in other words, has to participate in the act of material invention, with a little help from his "freend," before he takes on the responsibility of making meaning or responding "inventively" in the sense of engaging in the *modus interpretandi*, which he does toward the end of the ark-building endeavor as he observes, in reference to the construction, "This is a nobull gyn" (3/400) and

> Therof am I paide,
> Forwhy
> It is better wroght
> Then I coude haif thoght.
> Hym that maide all of noght
> I thank oonly. (3/411–16)

38. J. Campbell, "Idea of Order," 79, argues the exercise of the collaborative spirit here is analogous to the working out of the idea of love.

39. Theophilus, *On Divers Arts*, 62–63.

40. This oddity of measuring after the fact is explained by Stevens and Cawley, 2:451, line note 365–409, as being a function of prefabrication construction. Another explanation, however, is that proper building procedure here is less important than acknowledgment of invention. This postconstruction mensuration, thus, confirms the miracle of "discovery and material application of what is latent in nature for the purpose of technologically fulfilling the divine will in the world." What is more, it reminds the audience of the integral relationship between space and time, and provides a contrastive point of reference for the next time mensuration is employed in the play, the event in history when mensuration precedes the act of fabrication.

41. Hirshberg, "Noah's Wife," 32, points out that the play is about work. From the moment God addresses Noah, he argues, the emphasis is upon work, the preliminary activity required for directing one successfully toward the goal of salvation.

42. This knowledge and the consequent ordering effect it has on the individual is reminiscent of the emphasis on "good entent" (2/180) and acting with "stedfast thoght" (2/182) articulated by Abel in the *Mactatio Abel* through the tithing prayer he models for the purpose of Cain's instruction and (much hoped-for) tithing reform.

43. The name of Gill given to Uxor earlier in the play, according to Stevens and Cawley, 2:450, line note 318, may be a pejorative. It is no longer associated with Uxor after this point as she is now referred to, first, as Wife (3/613) and, later, as Dame (3/683). See Hirshberg, 36, who observes that Uxor undergoes a dramatic change through the process of learning. Now that she is actively engaged in the cooperative effort and is serving herself as well as the family in the same way Noah served God, she no longer deserves the name of Gill; in fact, she has earned the appellation of

Dame or Wife (on other names used for Gill, see Utley, "Names"). This change—which reveals Gill's pragmatism, as David suggests in "Noah's Wife's Flood," 106—corresponds with a like change that occurs in representations of Mary. White points out in *Medieval Religion and Technology*, 37, that early medieval representations of Mary depict her as a spinner engaged in her practical art. In post-thirteenth-century representations, however, Mary is shown at prayer or in a contemplative posture—in a posture, in other words, that reveals her as disposed intellectually to receive the divine message, as in Jan van Eyck's early-fifteenth-century "Mystic Lamb" altarpiece, with Mary as Sapience crowned with lilies and roses. For further discussion of this change in representations of Mary, see Prampolini, *L'Annunciazione*. An active or working Mary may also be seen in representations of her work in cloth-making activities and knitting. See Turnau, "Knitting," 382–84, and also Hodges, "Noe's Wife," 31 and 37 n. 10.

44. Helterman, *Symbolic Action*, 71, observes that everyone's taking of his or her proper place on the Ark symbolizes the unity of the household, the new social harmony that has emerged. In other words, the social microcosm now reflects the natural macrocosm, the new order of creation about to emerge from the destruction wrought by the Flood.

45. J. Campbell, "Idea of Order," 83.

46. Sutherland, "'Not or I See More Neede,'" 190, makes the point that the Towneley Uxor "plays a more important role during the Flood itself than do her Chester and York counterparts."

47. Meyers, *A Figure Given*, 30, observes that the 350 days pass in a little over eleven lines. The effect is of time passing quickly. This is a feature of what Meyers identifies as "syncopation" in the play. What has been overlooked, however, is that the 350-day year—the only kind of year, according to Carey, *Wakefield Group*, 64, in the "cycle" plays—is the lunar or feminine year. As the sun, or the image of the masculine principle, emerges in the east after this period of time, so a new social/familial unity is forged involving an analogous balance and harmony between masculine and feminine principles through the calendrical valorization of the feminine.

48. Schless, "Comic Element," 240, calls attention to the fact that Noah's answer is a "brilliant example of paronomasia," a wordplay whose implied comparison offers a rhetorical analogy of the reciprocity inherent in the collaborative relationship.

49. The planimetric dimensions of creation here are simplistic. Nevertheless, the aesthetic implications of the presence of a planimetry, even as rudimentary as this one may be, suggest the conception of dramatic mimetic art as being an inorganic material, a veil. Such a suggestion serves to remind the audience of the nature of the Wakefield Master's aesthetic and the importance that the Gothic style places on an empirical interest in nature. On planimetry, see Jordan, *Shape of Creation*, 1–9.

50. Hirshberg, "Noah's Wife," 36, makes the point that Uxor's choice demonstrates the "incomplete state of her education."

51. White, *Medieval Technology and Religion*, 86, observes that in the new intellectual revolution of the later Middle Ages "Aristotle's qualitative-metaphysical

physics was assaulted by means of a new quantitative-empirical physics." At first this occurs by ingenious analysis, but the realization of the necessity for experimentation soon supplants rational, pure science. The early fifteenth century's interest in mechanical technology, as White also points out in *Machina ex Deo*, 164–65, no doubt contributed to this growing interest in the verifying of truth through actual experiment and through trial and error.

52. Schless, "Comic Element," 238, concludes Uxor's character is allowed to develop in a state of harmony, which is demonstrated by her navigational competence and command of rudimentary planimetrics.

Chapter 3. *[Prima] Pagina Pastorum* and the "Inventive" Speculative Creaturely Triune Mind

1. The inspiration for this approach to the Shepherds' plays owes much to Roney's "Complements," and to a point made by Diller in "Craftsmanship," 251, where, in discussing the difference between the Chester and Towneley playwrights, Diller points out that in Chester we observe the result, whereas in Towneley we observe the process of thought, an idea like that of Mills in "The Towneley Plays" 102, when he distinguishes between Towneley and Chester by pointing out that Towneley's plays are a drama of experimental diversity.

2. The three plays set in the time of renewal or the sixth age that are revised by the Wakefield Master are the *[Prima] Pagina Pastorum*, the *[Secunda] Pagina Pastorum*, and the *Magnus Herodes*. Stevens and Cawley, in *The Towneley Plays*, 2:482, make the point that no satisfactory explanation has been offered for "why the Towneley cycle should have two shepherds' plays," in a way echoing Meyers's observation in *A Figure Given*, 62, that the two plays pose one of the cycle's most vexing problems—having two plays that cover the same material. The conclusion at which all three arrive—that "the author of the First Shepherds' Play realized he could improve on his own handiwork, and did so in the Second"—provides only a partially satisfactory answer.

Munson, "Audience and Meaning," 54, suggests, on the other hand, the *[Pagina] Prima Pastorum* is "moving away from traditional, holiday art and becoming more self-conscious." It is the purpose of this and the next chapter to offer a number of explanations in support of this idea of artistic self-consciousness, though from a different point of view. The first of these has to do with why there are two shepherds' plays in this play collection, and why both would have been performed, as is contended by Rose, *The Wakefield Mystery Plays*, 19–34. The next has to do with why both plays are equally aesthetically sophisticated, thematically important, and dramatically pleasing. The final explanation has to do with why these two plays should be considered in relation to the *Magnus Herodes*.

3. Stevens and Cawley, 2:482. Cawley, "Wakefield *First Shepherds' Play*," 118, adds that the play's raw ingredients also include "proverbial lore, economic grievance, folk-lore, disputes of commons rights, burlesque Yule feast, traditional wassail, Christianized spells, secular and religious songs, a pseudo-Augustinian sermon,

Virgil's Messianic Eclogue, the influence of liturgical and Magi plays, New Testament stories of the nativity, and stories of the wool trade and woollen industry." For further discussion of a possible source related to Jak's "fools of Gotham" remark, see Eaton, "Source." For a source for the encounter between the shepherds that elicits the "fools of Gotham" remark from Jak, see A. B. of Phisike Doctour, *Merie Tales,* x and 1–2.

4. As should be clear from this particular choice of wording, the following argument, while doing intellectual homage to Robertson and heeding his caveat concerning the rigorously nonpsychological nature of medieval literary as well as plastic art, suggests that the objective scheme of moral values as they appear in a sustained and dramatized figural allegory possesses a durational continuity much like that of the motion picture, which allows for presentation or at least evocation, limited though it may be, of the "motion" or action of the soul.

5. For the distinction between the Christian as seeker and as passive recipient, see White, *Medieval Religion and Technology,* 37.

6. On the creaturely triune mind, see the brief but illuminating discussion offered by Trinkaus, "Dignity of Man," 4:138B. For a more detailed discussion of the triune mind, see Saint Augustine, *De Trinitate,* 298–99, 403. For *De Musica,* see *Of Music,* 337–38, and also Robertson, *A Preface to Chaucer,* 68; for the "Letter to Nebridius," see Saint Augustine, *Letters, 1–82,* 14–19, and Robertson, *A Preface to Chaucer,* 69. The first three books of *De doctrina christiana* must also have been of fundamental interest to the Wakefield Master: see these in *On Christian Doctrine.* Finally, for an instructive discussion of the distinction between these hermeneutical and pedagogical *technae,* see Copeland, *Rhetoric, Hermeneutics, and Translations,* 158.

7. On the popularity of this mode of artistic expression, see Mâle, *The Gothic Image,* 14–22; Robertson, *A Preface to Chaucer,* 33–38; and Seznec, *Pagan Gods,* 84–121; this quotation is from p. 90. Study of this mode of medieval artistic expression has recently received renewed treatment in Russell, *Allegoresis.*

8. White, *Medieval Religion and Technology,* 37–38, reminds us of the Gothic insistence that the eye of the spirit must be supplemented by the eye of the flesh in this new age of religious subjectivism and emotionalism, and that this fact is nowhere better illustrated than in the actual dramatization of the scene at Bethlehem, which begins the popularization of the crèche especially during the Christmas or Nativity season. The combination of the eye of the spirit and the eye of the flesh is remarked by Diller, "Craftsmanship," 250–51, when he observes that the emphasis in Towneley appears often to be on the process of thought.

9. Meyers, *A Figure Given,* 113, makes the point that, if he is not another Shakespeare, we have certainly found "in the Wakefield Master ... the equal of a Jonson or Wycherly." It is the purpose of this chapter and the following two to demonstrate further the Master's uniqueness, which makes this playwright an artistic rival, not of Shakespeare, but of his medieval near-contemporary Geoffrey Chaucer.

10. Panofsky, *Gothic Architecture and Scholasticism,* 64. Also see Roney,

"Complements," 701, where she discusses this feature of Gothic art in terms of binary oppositions, and Adams, "Egregious Feasts," 100, who discusses how the use of scriptural dictionaries influenced the Wakefield Master to incorporate sudden juxtapositions and stark contrasts.

11. While Stevens and Cawley, 2:482–83, suggest the play possesses a tripartite scene structure, the play actually has four scenes. This structure helps explain a number of emphases in the play that have hitherto been overlooked or misunderstood.

The first scene, "The Shepherds' Convocation," consists of four episodes: the initial "Pastoral Complaints" (12/1–117), the "Pastoral Encounter/Quarrel" (12/118–82), and "Slawpase's Arrival and Pastoral Lesson" (12/183–256), ending with "Garcio's Denunciation" (12/257–75).

In the second scene, "The Shepherds' Celebration," the episodes are "The Grotesque Feast" (12/276–347), "The Drinking Bout" (12/348–404), and "The Act of Odd Charity" or almsgiving (12/405–12), ending with the even odder "Evening Prayer" (12/413–25).

The third scene, "The Annunciation" (12/426–659), consists of three episodes. The first, "The Annunciation" itself, involves the angelic prophecy and song (12/426–38). The second, "The Pastoral Intellectual Response," and the third, "The Preparation for the Pastoral Way of Teaching," are longer and more complex.

"The Pastoral Intellectual Response" consists of two parts, one barely half the length of the other. The first part, "The Pastoral Speculative Response to the Unknown," itself consists of two sections. The first of these (12/439–77) involves simple intellectual/mnemonic response to the "unknown literal" by means of a rudimentary *disputatio* methodology consisting of supposition followed by corrective refutation; the other (12/478–503) involves a more complicated *sic et non* methodological response to the "unknown figurative," this time with memory affecting intellect. The second part, "The Pastoral Speculative Response to the Ambiguous," consists of two sections as well. In each of these, the combination of supposition and corrective refutation is more elaborately developed than in either section of the second episode's first part. The supposition of the first section here, inviting this time an even more advanced mnemonic/intellectual and intellectual/mnemonic response to the "ambiguous literal," begins at line 504. The corrective refutation picks up at line 532 and ends at line 555. While the second section's supposition turning attention to the "ambiguous figurative" consists of only eleven lines (12/556–66), its corrective refutation occupies fifty-four (12/567–620). What is more, this corrective refutation changes from a mnemonic/intellectual to a volitional/intellectual response by employing two related but different kinds of analysis. One, in lines 567–85, introduces analysis by examination. The other, continuing to the end of the episode at line 624, introduces analysis by separation and ends in song, followed by a brief response.

The third episode of the third scene, "The Preparation for the Pastoral Way of Teaching," involves the readying of the self for the demonstration of wisdom. This readying, the result now of the action of the intellect upon the will, consists of five elements (12/625–59) culminating in travel to Bethlehem. The first of these elements (just the two lines 12/625–26) is the display of pastoral resolve. The second (12/627–33) is the use of technology to determine direction, the third (12/634–46) is the demonstration of humility, the fourth (12/647–49) is prayer, and the fifth, the demonstration of civility, comprises the episode's last ten lines.

The final scene, "The Adoration," begins as soon as the shepherds approach the Christ Child, and consists of three brief episodes. The first, "The Gift-Giving" (12/660–98), is perhaps the most memorable part of the play. The second brings "Mary's Response" (12/699–711), then the "Pastoral Promise" (12/712–24) completes the play and ends with yet another song.

12. Munson, "Audience and Meaning," 59, makes the point that the interaction between Gyb and John gives so much of a sense of character that the "audience's social response to a type recedes in favor of its seeing psychological traits of an 'individual.'" The distinction here between "inventive" and "uninventive" mind should not be misconstrued as a "psychological" reading of the play as the term is now conventionally used.

13. One is reminded of the function of such inventive deceptiveness in accounts of "fantasie" in Chaucer's *Miller's Tale*, lines 3191–92 and 3611–13, and *Merchant's Tale*, lines 1577–1610; see *The Riverside Chaucer*, 68, 73, and 158, respectively. Also see Jehan le Bel, *Li ars d'amour*, 1:201–3, for an equally amusing and instructive demonstration of the dangers of "imaginacioun."

14. Saint Augustine describes in *De musica* (6.5.13) how this diminishment occurs: "For the spirit should be ruled by a superior and should rule an inferior. Only God is superior to it, and only the body is inferior to it, if you consider every spirit as a whole. Just as it cannot be complete without its Lord, it cannot excel without its servant. Just as its Lord is greater than it is, so also is its servant less than it is. This is the reason that when it is attentive to its Lord, it is both greater in itself and its servant is greater through it. But when its Lord is neglected, and it is intent upon its servant which is led by carnal concupiscence, it perceives the motions which that servant communicates to it, and it is lessened" (translated in Robertson, *A Preface to Chaucer*, 68). For further discussion of this process of diminishment, also see Lottin, "La doctrine morale," 51–53.

15. Robertson, *A Preface to Chaucer*, 68.

16. Ibid., 69.

17. Power, *Wool Trade*, 6.

18. The clichés that reaffirm a sense of helplessness start to cascade as soon as each shepherd recognizes the other. Gyb first opines that he is always the same, though he cannot identify the cause, concluding no one fares worse than a shepherd. John answers that poor men are in dire straits and often perish. Gyb next sounds the misogynous note by affirming the accuracy of the expression

> A man may not wyfe
> And also thryve,
> And all in a yere. (12/141–43)

And John concludes that we must creep before we walk. The hackneyed expressions here do not contradict Speyser's point in "Dramatic Illusion," 3–4, that the complaints introduce the need for a miracle—in this case a linguistic one to introduce active, vigorous language—as solution to the shepherds' troubles, one of the major themes of the play.

19. While much debate about what the props here actually consist of occupies scholarship devoted to this scene of the play, it would seem that the sack has to be actual to demonstrate the foolishness of waste and contamination, especially before an audience who are members of communities that still face the ever-present threat of famine. For a different but equally compelling reason, it would seem that the "Grotesque Feast" should be imaginary. There are just too many items on the menus for the shepherds to carry onstage. What is more, having actual food would contradict the physical as well as spiritual hunger suffered by the shepherds. Having actual bottles of drink, it would seem, is necessary, as the following pages in this chapter will demonstrate, to reveal how clever the two older shepherds are. And having actual sheep, a logistical nightmare on any stage, would contradict the emphasis the Wakefield Master places on various *phantasmata* in the early scenes of the play.

20. The typification of the rich man by this figure can be found in the *Coliphizacio* when Caiaphas, reprimanding the torturers, exclaims

    Perdé, if thou were a kyng,

    Yit myght thou be ridyng. (12/218–19)

This image of the rich man's loss of wealth also figures prominently in the famous instructional debate poem *Þe Desputisoun bitwen þe Bodi and þe Soule*; see Linow's edition, lines 1–30.

21. Nitecki, "Sacred Elements," 235, observes that Slawpase's emptying of his bag to show the others the emptiness of their wits demonstrates an emptiness of his own. Speyser, "Dramatic Illusion," 10, concurs, pointing out there is little wisdom in wasting grain, especially in a society that can readily suffer the effects of famine. Zumwalt, "Irony," 38, underscores the fact that Slawpase "renders his wisdom questionably." In a word, as Munson indicates in "Audience and Meaning," 56–57, Slawpase is deficient in wit, even though he is presented as the one of the three who has great intellect.

On the other hand, Helterman, *Symbolic Action*, 83, sees this moment as a turning point, one in which the second shepherd says he will "sup on wisdom." Jeffrey, "Pastoral Care," 213, like Robinson, *Stagecraft*, 97, points out that the shepherds have not achieved *sapientia* but at least are turning to bare "wysdom for to know."

22. Munson, 59, says of John's denigration of Slawpase that it "extricates him from the game while maintaining the 'reality' of the sheep."

23. Cawley, "'Grotesque' Feast," 213, says the meal is "Grotesque only in the sense that the author achieves humor of incongruity by mixing together aristocratic and plebeian dishes." For others who view the meal in much the same way, see Carey, *Wakefield Group*, 162, and Hemingway, *English Nativity Plays*, 281, line note 212 ff.; Jeffrey, "Pastoral Care," 212, calls it the Feast of Fools.

24. The "Grotesque Feast" has elicited considerable critical interest and response. Most agree that the feast itself is imaginary for a number of practical and thematic reasons. Cawley, "Wakefield *First Shepherds' Play*," 116, says the scene possesses a poetic truth because it is imaginary. Furnish, "Metatheatre," 144–45, argues the scene is improvised to achieve a degree of figural meaning and self-reflexivity. Munson, "Holiday," 108, points out that the mock feast provided a means of alluding to guild regulations among other things. He adds, in "Audience and Meaning," 60, that the imaginary feast establishes a sense of what is playful and imaginary, an idea also acknowledged by Furnish, 144, when the latter says the set of gestures calls attention to the act of representation itself. Nitecki, "Sacred Elements," 231, makes the case that the enactment of the feast restores the figural and thematic relation between the first and second halves of the play. Roney, "Complements," 718, reminds us of staging practicalities—namely, that the actors would not have had time to put out all of the foods to which they refer. Speirs, *Medieval English Poetry*, 329, makes the point that the imagined jollity and abundance prefigure the promise and abundance of spring. Speyser, "Dramatic Illusion," 13, quoting Cawley ("'Grotesque' Feast"), Morgan ("High Fraud," 679), and Kolve (*Corpus Christi*, 302–3, n. 67), concludes the feast is imaginary much the same way the sheep episode is. One who disagrees is Helterman, *Symbolic Action*, 86–87. He makes the point that something has to be there.

Another observation made about the feast is that it is a turning point in the play. Helterman, 84, argues that it represents the moment in the play when the audience is made aware of the shepherds' creative vision for the first time. It is there that they reveal they have achieved what he calls the "aesthetic imagination" (86), a conspicuously unmedieval notion if one accepts arguments made since the late 1930s for an Augustinian influence on the fundamental aesthetic principles undergirding medieval literature and drama in general, and the plays and revisions by the Wakefield Master in particular. Nitecki, 230, points out that the event marks the completion of the secular action as the shepherds achieve a degree of peace and establish a collective brotherhood for the first time. In this way, the feast is a central and didactic element in the play (229).

The importance attached to this event reminds us of the many instances in the criticism where scholars have called attention to the figurative and parodic function of the shepherds' mealtime activity. In this regard, most are in agreement that the feast's function is to provide a farcical treatment of the Eucharistic act to prepare the audience for the Nativity and its Eucharistic implications in the play's second half. For discussion of this feature, see J. Campbell, "Farce as Function," 339; Gardner, *Construction*, 81; Helterman, 83; Nitecki, 231–32; Speyser, 14–15; and Robinson, *Stagecraft*, 100.

The possible pagan source for the feast (see Cawley, "Wakefield *First Shepherds' Play*," 115), as well as its analogue in the Chester cycle (see Carey, 163), have been a subject of interest, though not as much as the function of the feast, as dramatic means of precipitating social disintegration. J. Campbell, 339, argues that the episode provides the opportunity to turn social order upside down. Speyser, 14, makes the point that the feast ends in quarreling and comic disorder. If the gallimaufry of dishes the shepherds produce is, in fact, a repetition of the medieval burlesque recipe for restoring to a woman her lost maidenhead, as is suggested in Wright and Halliwell, *Reliquae Antiquae*, 1:250–51, then yet another farcical figural dimension can be seen to exist in the play. As the parodic Eucharistic meal restores virginity in the play's first half, a miracle to say the least, the immaculate conception and birth of Christ in the play's second half leads to yet another miracle, the restorative function of the Eucharistic meal itself.

25. Cawley, "'Grotesque' Feast," 213.

26. Cawley, "Wakefield *First Shepherds' Play*," 115, makes the point that the illusion of aristocratic fare is not consistently developed, the menu being interlarded with humble dishes.

27. Cawley, "'Grotesque' Feast," 216.

28. As might be expected, the "good ale" and subsequent drinking bout, like other moments in this scene, have elicited an energetic critical response. Part of this response involves the identification of "Hely." Cawley, "Wakefield *First Shepherds' Play*," 116, observes the ale is not of Ely but probably of Healy in the West Riding near Orsett and Wakefield. Robinson, *Stagecraft*, 53, concurs. Another part of this response involves consideration of the drink's symbolic implication. Helterman, *Symbolic Action*, 85, suggests the conjuring up of drink is related to the imbibing of wisdom. Jambeck, "'Ayll of Hely' Allusion," identifies the ale as Elijah's ale, and suggests that, because of Elijah's twofold eschatological role, allusion to it marks a significant advance in the play's doctrinal structure. Speirs, *Medieval English Poetry*, 332, reminds us of the association between ale and divinity by pointing out that the boar and ale were sacred to the Teutonic peoples. Speyser, "Dramatic Illusion," 15–16, makes the point that since the cup is not drained, its replenishment betokens a miracle.

29. This is a comic use of the phrase normally used with reference to Christ. See Stevens and Cawley, 2:488, line note 357.

30. The drinking song as expression of conviviality is found in literature of every age. See Baugh, *Literary History*, 222–23. What is interesting about this instance is the unexpected association within it: those who have drunk the most demonstrate more precise memory, while the one who has drunk the least is still outwitted and deprived of his share of the ale. Sobriety, in other words, may actually have disadvantages.

31. While some have viewed the drinking as a miracle, it should be remembered that Gyb and John were ready to drink when they first came onstage, and so probably have several bottles ready for consumption.

32. Von Simson, 54, points out that a principal feature of the Gothic style is the idea that the degree to which something "resembles God determines its place in the hierarchy of things." As a result, all things, even the grotesques appearing on the façade, have meaning and have to be "read" or interpreted. For further discussion of

the function of the iconographic programs involving fantastic bestial or creaturely exemplifications, see Mâle, *The Gothic Image*, 59–63, and Robertson, *A Preface to Chaucer*, 195.

33. Cawley, "'Grotesque' Feast," 214.

34. See Lepow, "'What God Has Cleansed,'" 280–82, who observes that the theological point of the menu reveals how the Old Law is superseded by the New, and Nitecki, "Sacred Elements," 233, who considers the feast to be a type and parody of the Eucharist.

35. Helterman, *Symbolic Action*, 85, underscores how the feast shows the shepherds' "imagination" at work. While he sees this as a positive effect (a reading of the text that would appear to misunderstand medieval wariness of "imaginacioun"), his observation about the activity of the imagination—that is, its excessive engagement—is nevertheless accurate.

36. Speyser, "Dramatic Illusion," 16.

37. Stevens and Cawley, 2:489–90, and see also Anderson, "Towneley Shepherds," 317–19. But Saint Augustine, it should be remembered, observes in *De doctrina christiana* (2.20.30) that such superstition amounts to nothing more than idolatry; see *On Christian Doctrine*, 55.

38. On the de Warenne family, their holdings, and the Wakefield Manor, see Walker, 1:60–62. Monastic houses and holdings in the region were also quite extensive in the fifteenth century. A sampling affirms this fact. Directly to the west of Wakefield, in Normanton Newland, was a Hospitallers house, and in Kirklees a Cistercian nunnery. To the southwest, in Monk Britton, was a Cluniac house. Directly south, in Beauclief, could be found a Premonstratensian abbey. To the southeast, in Nostell, Hampole, Doncaster, and Tickhill, were Augustinian, Cistercian, Franciscan, and Austin houses, respectively. South of Tickhill, too, was the location of the well-known Cistercian house Roche Abbey. To the east of Wakefield were Carmelites, Dominicans, Cluniacs, Benedictines, Augustinians, and Templars in Pontefract, St. Lawrence, Templehirst, and Drax. To the northeast were the Cistercians, Benedictines, and Augustinians at Nunappleton, Selby Abbey, and Bolton Percy. Directly north of Wakefield were the Cistercians at Kirkstall and, much further north, more Cistercians at the very famous Fountains Abbey. To the northwest of Wakefield, in Esholt, and far to the west-northwest, in Sawley, were more members of the same order.

39. Stevens, *Mystery Cycles*, 129.

40. This is a *phantasma* by definition because, by his own admission in the initial complaint, Gyb has no sheep, the result of the murrain. The image, or *phantasie* in memory, of sheep is recalled and combined with images and *phantasiae* of many other sheep to create the large flock of a "hundreth togedyr." This substantial flock, one whose size is probably double that of any Gyb ever shepherded, is truly a fantasy in the Augustinian sense of the word.

41. The ovine *phantasma* as theatrical exploration of the resiliency of mimetic representation of the diminished spirit's deceptive mnemonic creative capacity sug-

gests the Wakefield Master's interest in the theoretic implications of the distinction between the medieval *technae* of dramatic mimesis and dramatic methexis. This artistic exploration functions, not by drawing the audience "in" or "closer" to the action as do the interludial asides in the *Processus Noe*, but rather by engaging the audience members intellectually in an innovative dramatic mimesis in which they must discover and respond to—that is, take on the responsibility for making meaning of—the fact they are being duped by a *phantasma* of which, possibly unbeknownst to them, they are participants through their willingness to continue watching the play's action.

42. The source of humor for those members of the audience involved in shepherding or who just know of the reality of sheep herding would be the apparent lack of logic implicit in the action of making animals go around in circles when the purpose of herding is to get them to go in one particular direction, usually from one run or pasture to another.

43. See Guillaume de Lorris and Jean de Meun, *Romance of the Rose*, 61, lines 2233 ff., where the God of Love, or desire, gives the dreamer ample instruction in how to engage in the "delightful thought" of the *phantasma* of the beloved.

44. This fact of the play's action alone provides an argument against having actual sheep onstage during the production.

45. Two things about Slawpase noted in the criticism of the play support this interpretation of function. The first, as Gardner points out in *Construction*, 81, is that while Slawpase is limited, and his wisdom may be nothing more than the specious wisdom of words (as Munson observes in "Audience and Meaning," 57), he is nevertheless associated with the reason, one part of the rational soul. He is, in other words, the pastoral "intellect," or at least thinks he is. The other thing about Slawpase that would make his presence inimical to the performance reality of the ovine *phantasma* is that he appears, as Munson argues in "Holiday," 111, to inhabit, even more than the other two shepherds, "a physical space with a good deal [of] separate definition." This is the functional space of the mare, the sack of grain, and the mill, the location of which Robinson, *Stagecraft*, 53, identifies as being actually either in Horbury or Wakefield.

46. The substance of this observation is reminiscent of the various *phantasmata* created by the artful philosopher in the *Franklin's Tale*. His fantastic images ironically revive ailing Aurilius, whose *delectatio cogitationis* in response to the beloved Dorigen has brought him to the brink of despair, very much in the same way that the desire for a flock of sheep has transformed Gyb. See *The Riverside Chaucer*, 184, lines 1189 ff.

47. On the story, its principal sources, and its popularity in England by the fifteenth century, see Gerould, "Moll."

48. Dunn, "Prophetic Principle," 121, identifies the corrective as a rebuke, a use of earthly language to reduce the shepherds another rung in their pride and self-assertiveness.

49. Helterman, *Symbolic Action*, 80, suggests the corrective is less judgmental,

the allusion serving as an instructive don't-count-your-chickens-before-they-hatch lesson. The reason is that the Wakefield Master's treatment of the story alters the fact that something is left after the pitcher is broken: though without milk, the Towneley Moll still has one sheep.

50. Cawley, "Jak Garcio," 169–72, provides a careful summary of critical response to Jak in the first half of the last century, as well as a discussion of the possibility of Jak's being Tercius Pastor, the result possibly of a misunderstanding on the part of the copyist. Cooper, "Wakefield *Prima Pastorum*," 326, reasserts Cawley's argument on the grounds of consistency of speech order, role, and dramatic technique.

51. Current critical response to Jak's presence and function is more or less in agreement, and directly or indirectly supports the point made here about putting the shepherds' fantastic imaginings in perspective. Axton, *European Drama*, 66, says Jak shows up the foolery of the shepherds; Gardner, *Construction*, 81, suggests Jak is a messenger of light, calling attention to the fact that things are better than imaginings; Helterman, *Symbolic Action*, 79–80, identifies Jak's role as "choreic figure" introducing a note of skepticism; Jeffrey, "Pastoral Care," 211, indicates that one function of Jak's remarks is to demonstrate how far out of touch with the flock the shepherds really are; Kolve, *Corpus Christi*, 158, observes that Jak is presented to introduce a dramatic mood; Robinson, *Stagecraft*, 96, suggests the import of Jak's denunciation is to underscore the shepherds' foolishness; Roney, "Complements," 720, introduces the possibility of Jak's remarks revealing the "wise foolishness" of the shepherds since they eventually will become the bellwethers of the flock; and Speyser, "Dramatic Illusion," 9–12, points out that Jak's arrival alters the chaotic mood of the scene's end, calling to the audience's attention the idea that "one's perception of reality is at least in part a matter of will." One other function Jak's presence has is to bring the scene to a close.

52. On the story of the "wise fools of Gotham," see Eaton, "Source," 265–66, and A. B. of Phisike Doctour, *Merie Tales*, 1–2. Helterman, 76, suggests the allusion raises the issue of the relation between folly and wisdom.

53. Jeffrey, "Pastoral Care," 211, suggests that this fiction is a way of showing the shepherds' sloth.

54. Helterman, 79, suggests this reference marks the end of the spiritual winter suffered by the shepherds, a parallel of which can be found in the *Cursor Mundi* and the *South English Legendary*.

55. See Hill and Rotelle, 299.

56. Saint Augustine makes this point in *De Musica* (6.16.51); see *Of Music*, 372.

57. Trinkaus, "Dignity of Man," 4:138B, emphasizes this distinction. Also see Thomas P. Campbell, "Why Do the Shepherds Prophesy?" 146, who makes the point that the shepherds, at this moment, are both prophets and participants in the congregation—that is, intermediaries between expectation and fulfillment—and Travis, *Dramatic Design*, 128, who identifies this moment in the play as the objectification of "an inner process of growth."

58. Hugh of Saint Victor, 150.

59. Augustine, *On Christian Doctrine*, 43–50. Dunn, "Prophetic Principle," 123, makes the point that the shepherds are now in a dialogue and have assumed, in a sense, "La Voix de l'Église."

60. This methodology is expected in light of the emphasis placed by Saint Augustine in *De doctrina christiana* (2.33.51) on the importance and utility of *disputatio*; see *On Christian Doctrine*, 69–70. Also, the elevation in style and dignity of language at this point offers a striking contrast, as Dunn notes, 123, to the linguistic joviality preceding it. Roney's observation, "Complements," 709, that the action of grace upon the shepherds is intellectual is borne out by the stylistic and substantive changes in what is said by the shepherds. As Kolve points out in *Corpus Christi*, 172, it is at this point that these shepherds begin to become learned pastors charged with a divine calling. Accordingly, the interaction between the shepherds from this moment on betrays the mental habit of the age, informing and informed by the process of argumentation found in Scholastic writings. In other words, the technique of reconciling irreconcilables is employed here so that each topic to be discussed in response to the angelic Annunciation is formulated as a *quaestio* of sorts, the consideration of which, as Panofsky in *Gothic Architecture and Scholasticism*, 68, indicates, "begins with the alignment of one set of authorities (*videtur quod* . . .) against the other (*sed contra* . . .), [and so] proceeds to the solution (*respondeo dicendum* . . .)."

61. Robinson, *Stagecraft*, 103.

62. Stevens, "Language as Theme," 112.

63. Stevens and Cawley, 2:490, line note 449–50.

64. For Saint Augustine's discussion in *De doctrina christiana* (2.1.1–2) of natural and conventional signs, see *On Christian Doctrine*, 34.

65. Ibid., 50–78.

66. Dunn, "Prophetic Principle," 122–23. Dunn also underscores the fact that this *processus* is modified, since the shepherds are not prophets. Carey, *Wakefield Group*, 120, observes that a "close association in the liturgical drama of the *Prophetae* and *Pastores* created a tradition which could entirely account for what at first sight seems quite out of place: the detailed citation of the prophecies in the *Prima Pastorum*." On the other hand, Meyers, *A Figure Given*, 63, ignores this distinction, calling the sequence a "miniature" *Processus Prophetarum*.

67. Helterman, *Symbolic Action*, 73–74, argues that this part of the play examines the growth of "imagination" as it learns how to read symbolic meanings. While he is right to say the shepherds are becoming more adept at interpretation, he is inaccurate here in characterizing the growth of the mind as a function of imagination. Such a view of growth is a post-Romantic notion that would have been contrary to the Wakefield Master's conception of proper creaturely noesis, which consists of the full, vigorous activity of the memory, intellect, and will, freed from the deceptive effect of any *phantasma* or creation of the "imaginacioun."

68. Young, *Drama*, 2:143.

69. Augustine, *On Christian Doctrine*, 78–83.

70. See Stevens and Cawley, 2:491, line note 506, and Young, 2:130.

71. Nitecki, "Sacred Elements," 235, characterizes this overcoming of doubt as the revelation of the possibility of changed perception. Meyers, *A Figure Given*, 63, observes the three rough shepherds "do some competent Scriptural interpretation of their own."

72. Stevens and Cawley, 2:491, line note 553, quote Coverdale to explicate "hym" in the line as reference to God. The sense of the previous line with its emphasis on Christ in the subject as well as the predicate nominative, however, dictates that the pronominal "hym" refer, in this instance, to Christ.

73. Augustine, *On Christian Doctrine*, 83–117.

74. Ibid., 83.

75. Stevens and Cawley, 2:492, line note 563–64.

76. See Hugh of Saint Victor, 147; also see Miller, *Chaucer: Sources and Backgrounds*, 58–65, for instructive excerpts.

77. See Robertson, *A Preface to Chaucer*, 256.

78. The shepherds have become "types" of the clergy by this point. On this distinction, see Robertson and Huppé, *Piers Plowman and Scriptural Tradition*, 152–53. Also see Kolve, *Corpus Christi*, 158–59.

79. Carpenter, "Music," 699, and Cutts, "'Wee happy heardsmen here,'" 268.

80. Dutka, *Music*, 109–10. Also see Palmer, *Early Art*, 269–77, for further discussion of musical iconography.

81. Characterization of this squabble and consequent song as "grisly parody," as Gardner suggests in *Construction*, 83, is perhaps too severe, though his prior remark about the shepherds' joyousness appears to be accurate.

82. One is reminded here of the aesthetic sobriety so characteristic of medieval Christian poetics as imaginatively portrayed in Umberto Eco's *The Name of the Rose*. If it had been available to him, the Wakefield Master, no doubt, would have been very much interested in Aristotle's discussion of comedy. But even with this knowledge, his interest in the weightier matter of the relationship between hermeneutics and ethical reform, so anchored in traditional Augustinian principles, would still remain the foremost concern of his dramatic art.

83. Dutka, *Music*, 111.

84. On the parodic nature of pastoral musical response to the Annunciation in other mystery plays and cycles, see Kolve, 169–72.

85. Leonard, "The School for Transformation," 190, points out that a transformation is occurring as the shepherds try to recreate the angelic song: "at the beginning they are still old men marked by ignorance and error; at the end they are born anew." On this kind of transformation, also see Robertson, *A Preface to Chaucer*, 65.

86. Augustine, *On Christian Doctrine*, 7. Also see book 4.

87. Jeffrey, "Pastoral Care," 214.

88. Augustine, *On Christian Doctrine*, 117–69. Also see Copeland, *Rhetoric, Hermeneutics, and Translation*, 154.

89. Augustine, *On Christian Doctrine*, 162–63.

90. Ibid., 162.

91. Even the terms "swetyng" and "praty mytyng" convey this last sense here. A "sweet one" or the "beloved" suggests the possibility of cosmogonic renewal. And the "praty mytyng" is the metaphoric embodiment itself of that regeneration or recreation of the universe.

92. Augustine, *On Christian Doctrine*, 163.

93. Ibid.

94. Stevens and Cawley, 2:494, line note 668. For the humorous touch, see Robinson, *Stagecraft*, 106, who calls attention to Slawpase's belief that the ridiculously large bottle he offers is in keeping with the tenor of the celebration. For a sampling of iconographic and allegorical interpretations, see Blanch, "Gifts of the Shepherds in the *Prima Pastorum*," 70–72, who suggests the coffer's wood is emblematic of Christ's death and resurrection, the ball of the Creator's omnipotence, perfection, and eternal nature, and the bottle of faith and salvation; Cantelupe and Griffith, "Gifts," 329, who argue the coffer, ball, and bottle are symbolic of the Trinity; Helterman, *Symbolic Action*, 91–92, who interprets the coffer to mean sacrifice and resurrection, the ball Christ's reign, and the bottle the condition of being inebriated with wisdom; and Roney, "Complements," 721, who equates the ball with Christ, and the coffer and bottle with containers for the body and blood of the Eucharist.

95. Cantalupe and Griffith, 335, indicate, for example, that the *Prima Pastorum* is preparation for the *Secunda Pastorum*. Gardner, *Construction*, 85, argues the *Secunda Pastorum* is a revision of the *Prima Pastorum*. Stevens, *Mystery Cycles*, 174–75, concurs, suggesting this revision is in the direction of making things more explicit. Williams, *Drama of Medieval England*, 73, says of the two plays that they are alternate versions, while Woolf, *The English Mystery Plays*, 192, suggests the *Prima Pastorum* was performed, while the *Secunda Pastorum* was reserved for sophisticated audiences.

96. Jeffrey, "Pastoral Care," 220–21.

Chapter 4. *[Secunda] Pagina Pastorum* and the "Inventive" Empirical Creaturely Triune Mind

1. *The Mediaeval Stage*, 2:146.

2. On the plays being alternate versions, see Williams, *Drama of Medieval England*, 73. Although the play's principal source is Luke 2:8–20, as Stevens and Cawley suggest (*The Towneley Plays*, 2:494–95), the introduction of Mak and the parodic subplot of the play increases the likelihood of inclusion of, and artistic modification by, a variety of folktale matter. Critics over the years have pursued this line of inquiry through the identification and examination of analogues to the Mak story. For discussion of this feature of the play, see Baugh, "The Mak Story"; Cook, "Another Parallel"; Cosbey, "Folklore Analogues"; W. Johnson, "Origin," 47–48; Parrott, "Mak and Archie Armstrong"; Roberts, "Another Parallel"; Smyser, "Analogues"; Stroup, "Analogues" and "Another Southern Analogue"; Wann, "French Farce," 360–68; and Whiting, "Analogue."

3. Roney, "Complements."

4. The argument that follows, one building upon Cleland's observation concerning the play's emphasis on sentiency or the metaphysics of what is actual in life ("*Second Shepherds'* and *Homecoming*," 46), should put to rest, once and for all, the notion that the second of the shepherds' plays somehow evolved out of the first, as is suggested by Cantelupe and Griffith, "Gifts," 335; Gardner, *Construction*, 85; and Stevens, *Mystery Cycles*, 174–75, and "Language as Theme," 114. What is more, while physical evidence in the *regenall* indicates frequent handling of the *[Secunda] Pagina Pastorum*, the argument that follows should also demonstrate, beyond a reasonable doubt, that both plays were performed as is maintained by Rose, *The Wakefield Mystery Plays*, 28–29, and that neither was reserved for an audience consisting of a particular social stratum, an argument made by Woolf, *The English Mystery Plays*, 192. On the heterogeneity of the Corpus Christi audience, it is important to remember Kolve's observation in *Corpus Christi*, 4, concerning this fact. Also see the argument by Taft, "Surprised by Love."

5. Three critical perspectives have arisen concerning the structure of the play. Those who argue for a binary structure include Marshall, "Sacral Parody"; Ross, "Symbol and Structure"; and H. Watt, "Dramatic Unity." Those dissatisfied with the idea of a "dramatic diptych" structure and more inclined to emphasize the play's sequential continuity include Mack, "The *Second Shepherds' Play*"; Schell, "Seeing Through a Glass Darkly"; and Stevens, "Language as Theme," 114–16. Those arguing for a tripartite structure include Carpenter, "Music"; Gardner, "Structure and Tone"; Longo, "Symmetry and Symbolism"; Schmidt, "'Vides Festinare Pastores'"; F. Thompson, "Unity"; and Vaughan, "Three Advents" and "Proportions," 358–59. The structure proposed here leans in the direction of sequence, but also embraces the ideas of the play's having a binary as well as a triadic structure. Thus this chapter will demonstrate that, like the *[Prima] Pagina Pastorum* before it, the *[Secunda] Pagina Pastorum* possesses a four-scene structure.

The first scene, "The Convocation," consists of two episodes. The opening one includes the first three pastoral complaints (13/1–212). The next episode involves Daw's defiant response and his eventual silencing by his pastoral colleagues (13/213–73). The second scene, "The Pastoral Perscrutations," is perhaps the most famous dramatic moment in all of medieval British drama. This scene also has two episodes. "The Pretentious Impersonation" (13/274–379) introduces a preliminary perscrutation. The succeeding episode, "The Parodic Nativity," introduces a more complicated perscrutation consisting of five parts: an initial "Set-Up" (13/380–502) occurring in the sheep run, a continuation of the "Set-Up" (13/503–81) that moves the action to Mak and Gill's dwelling, a completion of the "Set-Up" (13/582–646) with the characters again in the sheep run, an "Encounter" (13/647–821) back in the dwelling, and a "Discovery" (13/822–919), set before and within the dwelling. The third scene, "The Annunciation," occupies lines 920–1023. And the fourth, "The Adoration," completes the play by modifying the act of gift-giving that occurs at the end of the *[Prima] Pagina Pastorum*.

6. Panofsky, *Gothic Architecture and Scholasticism*, 64.

7. In the *[Prima] Pagina Pastorum*, the first two scenes are devoted to the presentation of the "uninventive" speculative creaturely triune mind. Here, only the first scene is devoted to presenting the noetic contrast. Stevens, *Mystery Cycles*, 125, points out that the Wakefield Master adapts and reshapes his material much the way Chaucer does. On economizing of plot material, especial from contemporary French farce, Woolf, *The English Mystery Plays*, 190, reveals how careful the Master is in the emphases he places upon his sources as he appropriates matter from them. Zumwalt, "Irony," 43, makes the point that the shepherds "who are open to grossness and delusion are at least instrumental in discovering the central truth of Christianity." Such a result, this chapter will demonstrate, occurs when the mind changes from being "uninventive" to "inventive" in its response to challenging interpretive *circumstantiae*.

8. Panofsky, *Gothic Architecture and Scholasticism*, 31.

9. On Coll, see, for a sampling of views, Gardner, *Construction*, 93, who offers the observation that Coll introduces a stabilizing tendency; Jeffrey, "Pastoral Care," 215, who suggests Coll may embody the "prelatical Christian"; Mack, "The *Second Shepherds' Play*," 79, who states "Coll enacts for his fifteenth-century viewers the condition of hopelessness"; Roney, "Complements," 713, who says his complaint introduces the ideas of domination, oppression, resentment, and deceit; and Robinson, *Stagecraft*, 116–20 and 135, who examines the actual and symbolic implications of the shepherd's old age.

10. While Robertson, "Question of 'Typology,'" 163, argues that the complaints at the beginning of this play are about the "reign of the Old Law with its attendant inversions in contemporary society," his interpretation can be made more specific if it is considered in terms of the effect of the diminished soul upon the creaturely triune mind. This narrowing of focus is in keeping with his thesis, as the complexity of the creaturely triune mind and its relationship to the divine mind is one of the principal considerations of Saint Augustine in *De Trinitate* and other works.

11. Hassall, *Holkham Bible Picture Book*, 89, fol. 13, presents a picture of three shepherds in the field. One of the shepherds is depicted with his legs "folded" beneath him. While a coincidence, what is especially interesting about this picture is the fact that the seated shepherd is also the only shepherd not wearing gloves.

12. Robertson, *A Preface to Chaucer*, 68.

13. On these and other misfortunes visited upon all of the Yorkshire Ridings, see Hey, *Yorkshire from AD 1000*, 86–87.

14. On the violence and lawlessness of the times, also see Hey, 97.

15. Ibid.

16. On purveyance, see Bloch, *Feudal Society*, 1:278–79, Coulton, *Medieval Village*, 342–44, and Salzman, *Mediaeval Byways*, 127–28, who instructively describe the conditions suffered by the manor farm workforce at the hands of the "gentlerymen," the stewards, bailiffs, and other minor members of officialdom.

17. Robinson, *Stagecraft*, 120, points out that one thing is consistent about the shepherds' entry onstage: none is aware of the one who may be there before him.

18. The laboring shepherd, the only one of the three shepherds in the *Holkham Bible Picture Book*'s illustration "Shepherds in the field" (Hassall, 89, fol. 13) to be wearing heavy work gloves and sturdy work boots, is foregrounded by the illustrator. It is clear from the picture that this laborer is not going to suffer from his feet freezing to his shoes. A suggestion may also be here that a shoe technology propriety exists and if that order is conformed to, then the effect will be comparable to the apparent comfort experienced in the picture book by the barefoot patriarchs, angels, saintly types, and Christ.

19. Jeffrey, "Pastoral Care," 216, suggests this relationship between hen and cock parallels that between parishioner and priest. Such an interpretation, while intriguing, ignores the purpose the anecdote serves with regard to Gyb's "character" itself—which is to reinforce the idea of passivity.

20. Stevens and Cawley, 2:497, line note 118–26, argue that the lines call attention to serial monogamy; that the "Second Shepherd speaks of men remarrying after becoming widowed." The lack of any reference to remarriage or widowhood, as well as the Wakefield Master's inclusion of the expression "In store" (13/126) to describe the number of wives some will have, however, appears to support Holthausen's belief in "Das zweite Hirtenspiel," 218, that the new "wonder" to behold is, in fact, polygamy, apparently a demographic reality of the age.

21. On this metatheatrical dimension of the performance reality of the Wakefield Master's plays, see Furnish, "Metatheatre," 139. For a discussion of the difference between mimesis and methexis, see Sypher, *Literature and Technology*, 86. Skiffington, *English Soliloquy*, 37, calls the shepherds' complaints here "embrionic beginnings, possibly the birth, of character-soliloquy, skillfully leavened by comedy."

22. *The Riverside Chaucer*, 108–10, lines 235–378.

23. On Alys's monologic dialogue, see my "Alys's Formulation of Intent," 198–201.

24. Stevens and Cawley, 2:497, line note 144.

25. Robinson, *Stagecraft*, 120, argues that the hyperbole here is merely for the audience's enjoyment. While that may be one of its functions, it appears the hyperbole also demonstrates the power of the *phantasma*.

26. Jeffrey, "Pastoral Care," 216. Shurgot, "*Puer Senex* Topos," 421–22, observes that Daw evidences greater wisdom than the other shepherds from the moment of his introduction.

27. On the relationship between Daw and Noah, see Jeffrey, "Pastoral Care," 217, and Robinson, 121.

28. Stevens and Cawley, 2:498, line note 196 ff.

29. On this definition of fear, see, for example, Saint Augustine, *De Trinitate*, (11.2.7).

30. For an instructive discussion of this feature of the Wakefield Master's dramatic art, see Furnish, "Play-within-the-Play."

31. It should be remembered that Saint Augustine in *De doctrina christiana* describes the diminished soul as being "emptied" and thus "hungry"; see *On Christian Doctrine*, 89.

32. Stevens and Cawley, 2:499, line note 259.

33. Traver, "Musical Terms," 1, and Dutka, *Music*, 99 and 104.

34. Much has been written on Mak. For a sampling of the various interpretations of this character, see J. Campbell, "Farce as Function," 340–41, who argues that Mak, who either possesses magic or is all too human, maneuvers us into the farcical world; Helterman, *Symbolic Action*, 19, who concurs with Campbell's conclusion concerning Mak's nimiety of humanness, even if he is parodically satanic; Jeffrey, "Pastoral Care," 217–18, who suggests he is symbolic of the human soul; Longo, "Symmetry and Symbolism," 75–76, who suggests Mak is an analogue of the false messiah; Mack, "The *Second Shepherds' Play*," 80–81, who discusses Mak's creative role-playing; Robinson, *Stagecraft*, 127–30 and 141, who suggests a number of things about Mak, including the etymology of his name that associates him with Cain, the language he uses, his attitude toward the lie he tells, his thievery, his satanic likeness, his likeness to the Antichrist, etc.; and Zumwalt, "Irony," 39–40, who remarks Mak's occult powers as well as the irony of his psychology and behavior.

35. For this distinction, see White, *Medieval Religion and Technology*, 39.

36. On the concept, see Thorndike, *History of Magic*, 3:103–18, wherein he discusses Perscrutator or the Dominican Robert of York and his principal work of eighteen chapters, *Correctorium alchimiae* or *Correctio fatuorum*, a work often erroneously ascribed to a Master Bernard. What establishes a distinctive point of connection between the thinking fundamental to Perscrutator and that fundamental to the *[Secunda] Pagina Pastorum* is the emphasis Perscrutator notes at the outset of his treatise when, treating alchemical processes, he says that "art may augment nature . . . but it must ever consider and conform to nature" (107). Manion, "Reinterpretation," 50–56, argues that this part of the play incorporates the Harrowing of Hell motif. Such an idea, that of *extraccio*, suggests the action of perscrutation.

37. The emphasis in the *[Prima] Pagina Pastorum* is in the third scene since the "divinity" of the "inventive" speculative creaturely triune mind is experienced by means of the Annunciation. When the Image of God is within one, then the integrity of the "inventive" speculative creaturely triune mind is assured. Here, however, the emphasis is in the second scene because the "inventive" empirical creaturely triune mind achieves its "divinity" through practice in created reality.

38. On this feature, see *Secunda Pastorum* in Hemingway, *English Nativity Plays*, 286, line note 190. Also see Jungman, "Seven Names," and F. Thompson, "Unity," 304, who suggests that the seven names refer to the Deadly Sins.

39. Hugh of Saint Victor, 150. On Mak's costume, which is in violation of sumptuary law, see John H. Smith, "Another Allusion to Costume," 901.

40. Hugh of Saint Victor, 150.

41. On the inclusion of Southernisms here, see Irace, "Mak's Sothren Tothe."

42. Stevens and Cawley, 2:501, line note 291–309, make the point that there are only just enough of these Southernisms to suggest a dialectical distinction.

43. In order to be prepared for interpreting all manner of *circumstantiae*, Saint Augustine says, knowledge of things and signs is preliminary to the interpretive act. For an instructive illustration of such preparation, see *On Christian Doctrine*, 50–53.

44. Gardner, *Construction*, 91, sees Mak and Gyll, their relationship, as an exaggeration of the common human situation.

45. Clark, "Liturgical Influences," 69–70.

46. Stevens and Cawley, 2:502, line note 384–85.

47. Manly, "Shepherds and Prophets," 155, suggests the blasphemous parody here associates Mak with the Antichrist.

48. Thorndike, *History of Magic*, 3:608–10.

49. Ibid., 3:608. It should also be noted that, prior to the suffumigation, Mak describes the roundness of the circle in terms of the lunar, thereby contradicting fundamental necromantic practice of identifying the circle with the prime mover, the true source of power to be invoked by the exorciser of the spell.

50. J. Campbell, "Farce as Function," 340–41, suggests the sheep stealing, a pivotal point in the play, acts out the tensions presented in the three opening laments or complaints. It is at this moment that the play, in her estimation, "comes alive." For this reason, the act of theft can be considered a "hinge," as the introduction of the farcical shapes the style and content of the rest of the play.

51. While the distinction here is obviously Aristotelian, it appears the Wakefield Master sees the value, in relation to the events of the play's action at this moment, in the contention articulated in *Physica* I.1 that human cognition first comprehends the generic features of physical things and only later comes to the specific *differentiae*. This does not mean, however, that he rejects the notion of understanding the essence of a thing through the process of regressive discovery as posited by Aristotle in *De Anima* II. See Weinberg, "Abstraction," 1:2, 2A–2B.

52. C. S. Lewis, *The Discarded Image*, 64.

53. Gyll, for example, says she will swaddle the sheep, place it in her cradle, and lie beside it, groaning as if she has just given birth to it. Mak, likewise, says he will further the "gyse" by saying that Gyll has become mother to a "knave-childe," a notion he has already partially introduced into the shepherds' thinking earlier in the scene by means of abstraction when attempting to elicit a sympathetic response from Coll, who, having inquired about Gyll's whereabouts, has clarified the "unknown figurative" by identifying the uxorial "thing-ness" associated with Mak's "mak-ness." Sturges, "Spectacle and Self-Knowledge," 28, makes the point, in reference to the *[Secunda] Pagina Pastorum*, that "theater in its own indirect way can bring its audience into the presence of grace." Attainment of the ability to comprehend all interpretive *circumstantiae*, in other words, readies one for the experience of the Light of Truth.

54. The construction of the form or idea of a birth in the shepherds' cognition is sequentially and incrementally wrought by Mak. The expostulation here is, in a sense, a finishing touch, completing the sequence.

55. Jeffrey, "Pastoral Care," 219, suggests the sound the two make together is the Old Song, the one that is soon to be obscured by the New Song sung by the shepherds.

56. Fiondella, "Derrida, Typology," 445, argues that "Mak's gesture succeeds in positing the truth of his discourse, tacitly confirming the baby's reality and construing the oaths to signify 'impossibility.'"

57. That Gyll is responsible for contributing to the actual makes sense given the conventional iconographic association between the flesh and the feminine. On this association, see Robinson, *Stagecraft*, 132.

58. C. S. Lewis, *The Discarded Image*, 63.

59. Kolve, *Corpus Christi*, 209–13.

60. Stevens and Cawley, 2:489, line note 400–402.

61. Ibid., 2:482.

62. Augustine, *On Christian Doctrine*, 83.

63. Ibid., 88. Also see Gardner, "Structure and Tone," 5; K. Johnson, "Rhetoric of Apocalypse," 40; Remly, "*Deus Caritas*," 747–48; Shurgot, "*Puer Senex* Topos," 426–27; and Strauss, "Grace Enacted."

64. Jambeck, "'Day Star' Allusion," 303, suggests the allusion is a figure signifying the tropological "middle advent," the "time of judgment in which the redemptive work accomplished by the Savior is itself fulfilled within the souls of the faithful, each individual realizing personally and in time what will occur for all at the end of time." That Daw articulates this figure indicates that the engagement in charity has already wrought a tropological change in him.

65. While much has been made of this discovery—from discussion of the unity in the play that the false or pseudo-nativity creates in anticipation of the true Nativity, as H. Watt, "Dramatic Unity," 276, has argued, to the diabolical implications of the sheep's snout and horns, to which Stevens and Cawley call attention (2:509, line note 867)—what has been overlooked in this critical response to the discovery of the swaddled sheep is the image the event also offers of the ideological dismissal, through the acts of infantilization on the one hand and of the *osculatio* on the other, of the pre-Christian or pagan religion as embodied by the horned one.

66. Mâle, *The Gothic Image*, 230–35. Also see K. Johnson, "Rhetoric of Apocalypse," 39; Robinson, *Stagecraft*, 136; Stearns, "Gyll"; and Zumwalt, "Irony," 40, who makes the point that, though a creature of illusion, Gyll is roughly analogous to Mary by virtue of her pretended birth.

67. Augustine, *On Christian Doctrine*, 86.

68. Whether the Wakefield Master read Aristotle's *Poetics* may not be ascertainable, though his incorporation of events eliciting fear and sympathy suggests he might have. If in fact he did, it would make sense that the two emotions identified by Aristotle as having a principal function in tragedy would shape this

portion of the scene, for it is here that Mak and Gyll are attempting to make the literal appear the figurative and the figurative as the literal, which is a tragedy in that as it is idolatry within Christian metaphysics. Many of Aristotle's works would have been available to the playwright in York, Rievaulx, and Durham. On the availability of Aristotle's works, see J. Thompson, *The Medieval Library*, 298–99.

69. Stevens and Cawley, 2:509. On cowardice, see Hirsh, "Mak Tossed," 118; on humiliation as punishment for the staged pseudo-nativity, see Jambeck, "Canvas-Tossing Allusion," 50–51. Jambeck, 53, also makes the point that the toss provides a metaphor of the Last Judgment through the act of sifting, for which canvas was used in the Middle Ages. Ashley, "The Guiler Beguiled," 136, suggests, while acknowledging Chambers's contribution to the discussion (*The Mediaeval Stage*, 1:156–58), that the toss banishes harmful elements at such seasons as Christmas and Shrovetide; Chidamian, "Mak and the Tossing," 187, observes that the punishment echoes a folk method of hastening childbirth; Helterman, "Satan as Everyshepherd," 525, suggests that, while the canvas toss casts out all the attitudes Mak has symbolized, it is the shepherds who groan as if in response to punishment; and Vaughan, "Tossing Mak Around," 148, asks where Mak goes and what Mak does after the toss. While the text partially answers both of these last two questions as Coll, before falling asleep a second time in the play, asks if he can lie down *on* the "thefys" (13/917), the fact that Mak and Gyll are lying down raises the possibility that Mak's former condition of "unevenness" has been flattened out or, finally, made even. For discussion of a possible analogue of the blanket toss, see Withington, "Mak, Op-Signorken, and Mr. Hardwick."

70. Thorndike, *History of Magic*, 3:379.

71. On the musical structure of the play and the function of music in the play, see Collins, "Music," 616; Evitt, "Musical Structure"; and Ingram, "Use of Music," 63.

72. Withington, "'Thre Brefes to a Long,'" suggests that the sound created by this musical arrangement is like the celebrated phrase of Beethoven's Fifth Symphony. Most who are familiar with that work understand how wilful this musical phrase can sound.

73. *Oxford English Dictionary*, compact ed., s.v. "sad," def. 2.

74. On the gift-giving in general, with specific treatment of each gift, see Blanch, "Symbolic Gifts"; Cutts, "Shepherds' Gifts"; Guilfoyle, "Riddle Song"; Longo, "Symmetry and Symbolism," 81–84; Meyers, *A Figure Given*, 69; Robinson, *Stagecraft*, 124; Ross, "Symbol and Structure," 126–33; and Roney, "Complements," 721.

75. On the dissemination of the Cherry Tree motif, see Carr, "Nativity Cherry Tree."

76. On the child as puppet or dolly, see Oosterwijk, "Of Mops and Puppets."

77. Russell, "*Sub Specie Aeternitatis*," 205, makes the point that the "second shepherd knows an amazing amount of doctrine: this nine-line hymn is a veritable Athanasian Creed in little, including references to the doctrine of redemption [l. 1037], creation *ex nihilo* [ll. 1040–1042], the hypostatic union [ll. 1046–1047], and the Eucharist [l. 1048]."

78. On the tennis ball, see Gillmeister, "Gift," and Lepow, "Daw's Tennis Ball."

Chapter 5. *Magnus Herodes* and the Degradation of the Rational Soul

1. On this feature of the play, see Stevens and Cawley, *The Towneley Plays*, 2:521–22, and, specifically, on the absence of Herod Antipas in Towneley, see Williams, *Characterization of Pilate*, 61–62 n. 25. On the distinctions between, and conflations of, Herod Ascalonita and the other Herods (his son and grandson), see Hussey, "How Many Herods," 257; Parker, "Reputation of Herod"; Perowne, *Herod the Great*; Tomlinson, *Herodes-Charakter*, 35–41; and Valency, *Herod and Mariamne*, 32–34.

2. Helterman, *Symbolic Action*, 115–31. Also, for discussion of Herod as Antichrist, see T. Campbell, "Eschatology and the Nativity," 312–17; for discussion of Herod as figure of the Antichrist, see Furnish, "Technique *versus* Feeling," 41, and Stemmler, "Typological Transfer," 138.

3. Helterman, *Symbolic Action*, 115. Also see Gardner, *Construction*, 98.

4. Meyers, *A Figure Given*, 72.

5. On the relationship between the Antichrist and thinking like the Antichrist, see Gregory I, *Moralia*, 75:484.

6. Saint Augustine, *City of God*, 510, makes this distinction when defining the death of the soul or mortal sin, physical death or the "first death," the "death of the whole man" or the cessation of physical life when the soul is said to be dead, and the consequent "second death," which is said to be the death that does not die, and the death in which the soul and body are recombined for the purpose of eternal torment.

7. On presumption, see Robertson's discussion of Chaucer's Pardoner, in *A Preface to Chaucer*, 270.

8. For Saint Augustine's discussion of such debasement, see *Of Music*, 337–38.

9. Mills, *The Chester Mystery Cycle*, 100, anticipates this point when he suggests Herod has no self-knowledge.

10. Panofsky, *Gothic Architecture and Scholasticism*, 40.

11. Clein, "Towneley *Magnus Herodes*," 55–56.

12. See Lucy Toulmin Smith, *York Plays*, 138–55.

13. Stevens and Cawley, 1:xxxi.

14. Staines, "To Out-Herod Herod," 45.

15. Furnish, "Technique *versus* Feeling," 39–40. This anxiety may or may not also suggest that Herod is an example of an improper French king—that is, an example of the *dominium regale*—if this idea had currency in the fifteenth century. On this possible dimension of Herod's characterization and its implications, see Jungman, "Analogue in Fortescue," 2.

16. T. Campbell, "Eschatology and the Nativity," 320, observes that, liturgically, "to prepare for the celebration of Christ's birth was also to prepare for His return as Judge"; to celebrate the Nativity, in other words, was to prepare for the end of history. Given this penitential tone in the celebration of the Advent season, inclusion of the dramatized personification of impiety offered a polar opposite to the embodi-

ment of the promise of salvation, the emphasis suggested by the dramatic allegorizing of the mind of the active seeker of the divine in the pattern of creation as conveyed by the two shepherds' plays earlier in the collection.

17. On the *Magnus Herodes* being a tragedy, see Gardner, *Construction*, 104.

18. On this feature of *allegoria*, see Copeland, *Rhetoric, Hermeneutics, and Translation*, 81.

19. The play's structure is symmetrical, consisting of three scenes as Clein, "Towneley *Magnus Herodes*," 55–56, suggests. Each scene has three episodes, the whole preceded by a nine-stanza induction. Scene 1, the play's longest, begins with a partial or "linking" episode, "The Harangue," occupying the end of stanza 9 and the next two. Its second episode, "The Confused Blustering," runs through stanza 22. The final episode, "The Strategy of Pogrom," ends partway through stanza 29, with the end of the stanza providing a link to the succeeding scene.

Scene 2 opens with "The Nobyll Gyn," a "linking" episode developed in the next stanza and a half. The second episode, "The Summoning of the Feudal Host," follows at line 400 and continues through stanza 36. The final episode, "The Massacre of the Innocents," the scene's most significant in that the action of the massacre begins here, occupies stanzas 37–44.

The first episode of scene 3, "The Readying for the Triumph," comprises stanzas 45 and 46. The second episode, "The Seeking of Reward," runs to the end of stanza 51. The scene, and the play, conclude with the six-stanza episode of "The Daemonic Sermon."

20. Sypher, *Literature and Technology*, 86.

21. Paull, "Figure of Mahomet," 189.

22. Clein, "Towneley *Magnus Herodes*," 62.

23. Davidson, "Space and Time," 57, makes the point in his meditation on temporality and medieval drama that understanding a play such as the *Magnus Herodes* "in terms of seriality . . . involves a serious critical error," for medieval drama is "founded on a different view of reality." While this may be true, especially for the earlier liturgical drama, it does not seem to pertain to the works of the Wakefield Master, whose creatively innovative approach to dramatic representation includes consideration of temporal sequence as well as causation.

24. Poteet, "Time, Eternity," 240.

25. Like Christ's executioners, Herod's choice of game at this juncture introduces the diversion of attention, another way of representing the continued lack of will. For further discussion of this game's function, see Kolve, *Corpus Christi*, 190–91.

26. On Herod's being a likely candidate to suffer the "second" or "undying" death, see my "Pardoner's Old Man," 339–40.

27. See, for example, previous instances of methexis in *Mactatio Abel*, *Processus Noe cum filiis*, *[Prima] Pagina Pastorum*, and *[Secunda] Pagina Pastoum*.

28. Kolve, 206–36, argues quite convincingly how the condition of "natural" man—that is, the *wilful*, anarchic self—is often represented in the drama. In this instance, however, it appears the Wakefield Master wants the audience to under-

stand what it is like to be the opposite of wilful through the association with the elusive Magi.

29. Staines, "To Out-Herod Herod," 46, points out that the catalogue of books Herod offers has "no relevance to the subject of the investigation."

30. On the breath's being an analogy of the spirit, see Neumann, *Consciousness*, 22.

31. For the most accurate and instructive discussion of the *tertium quid*, see C. S. Lewis, *The Discarded Image*, 166–67.

32. Panofsky, *Gothic Architecture and Scholasticism*, 64.

33. Steinberg, "*Kemp Towne*," 260.

34. Augustine, *On Christian Doctrine*, 103–4. Augustine earlier makes the point that the "ambiguities of figurative words . . . require no little care and industry" as one responds interpretively to complex signs. It would appear the inadvertent confusion and antiphrasis resulting here from the ineffability topos would remind the initial Corpus Christi audiences of the "miserable servitude of the spirit" suffered by one who is not "able to raise the eye of the mind above things that are corporal and created to drink in eternal light" (84).

35. Mahomet's love of violence and promiscuity, as well as the association between him and the rule of ignorance and appetite, was well known to medieval audiences. Staines, "To Out-Herod Herod," 45, points out that Herod's ignorance, the source of comedy, is presented in direct contrast to the wisdom of the Magi. Paull, "Figure of Mahomet," 189–90 and 192, calls attention to Herod's other less desirable characteristics. For further discussion of these and related associations, also see Leshock, "Representation of Islam," 196; W. M. Watt, "Encounters with Medieval Europe"; and White, *Medieval Religion and Technology*, 276, who reminds us how slow Islamic culture was to accept the new printing technology of book culture and the dissemination of information through the written word.

36. Hugh of Saint Victor, 150.

37. Ibid. For further discussion of the stew-meat metaphor, see Robinson, "'As Small as Flesh to Pot.'" Also see, for a different view on the violence, Hennequin, "'Byrkyn many bonys.'"

38. Doob, *Nebuchadnezzar's Children*, 98. Also see Robertson, *A Preface to Chaucer*, 385.

39. Doob, 102.

40. Furnish, "Technique *versus* Feeling," 40–41.

41. This response can be viewed as an instructive instance of what Panofsky identifies as elucidation or clarification—that is, *manifestatio*—in *Gothic Architecture and Scholasticism*, 30–31.

42. Kolve, *Corpus Christi*, 222–23, and Doob, 115.

43. This "wonderfull talkyng" may be viewed as a parody of the "wonderfull talkyng" that occurs during the Annunciation. This can be seen in the Towneley *Annunciacio* as Maria learns from Gabriell that "all shall hald" (10/142). What is intriguing about this connection is that it anticipates the play's end by offering an

explanation for the symbolic detail of the flower Herod holds to his nose while flippantly surveying the carnage of the Massacre of the Innocents. In many late-medieval representations of the Annunciation, such as miniatures, manuscript illustration, and at least three windows at Laon, Sens, and Bourges, the presence of the "marvelous flower," the image of Christ, between Mary and the approaching angel can be seen. Herod's holding of the flower as he comments on the slain innocents would certainly have reminded some in the audience of this iconographic tradition. For discussion of this symbolic detail, see Mâle, *The Gothic Image*, 244–45.

44. Stevens and Cawley, 2:526, line note 293.

45. Young, *Drama*, 2:126.

46. Augustine, *On Christian Doctrine*, 84.

47. Woolf, *The English Mystery Plays*, 205.

48. On the formality of the encounters, see Helterman, *Symbolic Action*, 128, where he makes the observation that the killings are so formalized as to give the impression of being ritual. On the difference between the mothers' and soldiers' language, see Clein, "Towneley *Magnus Herodes*," 59, who points out that the language of the "noble art of war" reveals the cowardice of the soldiers' "depraved chivalry with language of jousting knights." Skey, "Iconography," 69, makes the point that in earlier representations of the killing the soldiers play the most important part. She also observes in "Herod the Great," 342–43, that the violence here is consistent with violence found in the European tradition of the Herod plays.

49. Gardner, *Construction*, 102, suggests the reference here to "nose" introduces an expression that is a "sexual euphemism."

50. Thorndike, *History of Magic*, 1:660–61.

51. Stevens and Cawley, 2:528, line note 517; see also Frampton, "Flourishing," 632.

52. Robertson, *A Preface to Chaucer*, 68.

53. Elliott, "Language and Theme," 352.

54. Kolve, *Corpus Christi*, 209.

55. On the absence of grace in one like Herod, see Wenzel, *Fasciculus Morum*, 119.

56. Murphy, *Rhetoric*, 325, offers a concise summary of this plan. Stevens and Cawley, 2:529, line note 664, incorrectly characterize the last monologue simply as a "harangue." Helterman, *Symbolic Action*, 130–36, interestingly enough, sees in this part of the play a parody of the mass.

57. Staines, "To Out-Herod Herod," 51.

58. On this particular feature of "character," see Wasserman and Purdon, "Sir Guido and the Green Light," 647–61.

59. van Laan, *The Idiom of Drama*, 32. On the distinction between these two fundamental kinds of soliloquies, see Schücking, *Character Problems*, 29. Skiffington, *English Soliloquy*, 35, identifies this rant as "ranting soliloquy" but does not set it in the context of methexis. In fact, of all the instances of methexis in

the Wakefield Master's dramatic art, this is the closest in form to the Elizabethan soliloquy.

60. Robertson, *A Preface to Chaucer*, 272, underscores the distinction about the Gothic style when he points out that it is always more conceptual than imitative.

61. See note 30.

62. Stevens and Cawley, 2:530, line note 739.

Chapter 6. The Repudiation of the Eschatology of Labor in Two "Passion Group" Revisions and the *Coliphizacio*

1. These revisions from the "Passion group" include *Conspiracio* (20/1–77, 624–75), *Flagellacio* (22/53–351), *Processus Crucis* (23/345–502), *Processus Talentorum* (24/1–65, 378–429), *Perigrini* (27/19–31), *Ascencio Domini* (29/362–87), *Iudicium* (30/131–559, 706–822), and *Lazarus* (31/139–52). The other revision attributed to the Wakefield Master possibly includes *Fugacio Iosep et marie in egiptum* (15).

2. Le Goff, *Time, Work, and Culture*, 115, and White, *Medieval Religion and Technology*, 237–41.

3. Williams, *Characterization of Pilate*, 16.

4. The total number of plays here, to avoid confusion, includes Caiaphas's reference to Pilate at the end of the *Coliphizacio*.

5. Williams, *Characterization of Pilate*, 39. Also see Maltman, "Pilate—Os Malleatoris," 310.

6. The expression "Pilatus qui os malleatoris interpretur" was an exegetical commonplace. See Walahfrid Strabo (Walafridus Strabus), *Glossa Ordinaria*, 114:173 (Evang. Matt. 27).

7. Sypher, *Literature and Technology*, 86.

8. In Hassall, *Holkham Bible Picture Book*, 99, fol. 30v, Herod wears rather stylish shoes. This snappy feature of his appearance suggests caste distinction, as the shepherds are simply shod or wearing boots, and also ethical distinction, as Christ and the angels always appear barefoot. The illustrations suggest that the closer one is to the sartorial cutting edge, as it were, the further one is from ethical and spiritual righteousness (on this feature of the shoe image, see especially Mellinkoff's discussion of the shoe in terms of the "shape-and-drape principle" in her *Outcasts*, 1:39). The shoe transformation that occurs in the sequence of illustrations in Hassall depicting Noah's life demonstrates most instructively this symbolic feature of apparel. Starting with Lamech's killing of his son and the warning to Noah, Noah is presented in shoes (fol. 7). Building the Ark (fol. 7v), Noah is still well shod. In the illustration concerning the dove and the raven, Noah's shoes are obscured (fol. 8). Once at the altar, however, Noah no longer wears shoes (fol. 8v). Noah is still shoeless as he descends from the Ark and has a bit too much wine (fol. 9).

9. Clopper, "Tyrants and Villains," 15, argues the Towneley Pilate is modeled on Herod.

10. Williams, *Characterization of Pilate*, 39.

11. Cawley, *Wakefield Pageants*, 123, line note 450.

12. Owst, *Preaching in Medieval England*, 495–96.

13. Williams, *Characterization of Pilate*, 39.

14. Jolliffe, *Constitutional History*, 410, observes the Parliament rolls during the reigns of Edward III, Richard II, Henry IV, Henry V, and Henry VI "show that the honesty of provincial courts was declining, that the law itself was coming to be a weapon in the hands of the unscrupulous, and that open violence was on the increase."

15. This reality of late medieval feudal culture, including what is identified as border vassalage and rear vassalage, is most instructively elaborated by Nicholas in her examination of feudal structures in the Low Countries in the late twelfth and thirteenth centuries, "When Feudal Ideals Failed." Also see Ganshof, *Feudalism*, 75–95.

16. For an instructive discussion of the tradition of the good Pilate, see Williams, *Characterization of Pilate*, 2–9.

17. Brandeis, *Jacob's Well*, 114–15. For further discussion of Tutivillus in Towneley, see Jennings, "Tutivillus," 58–64.

18. Stevens, "Language as Theme," 107. Tutivillus, in a sense, functions thus as an "effective sign," though the obverse of the typical effective sign, the parable, in conventional medieval homiletic art. On this dimension of hortatory instruction, see Kelly and Irwin, "Meaning."

19. The motto's first line is adapted from the Latin phrase *Fragmina psalmorum colligit horum*. See Wright, *Collection of Latin Stories*, 44.

20. Davidson, "Interpretation," 111–12, points out in one of the few essays written about this play that the "Wakefield Tutivillus has expanded duties, though these still include taking note of verbal lapses in the liturgy." Apparently, however, he overlooks Tutivillus's reference to being a "chefe tollare" (30/309), one who carries a "roll of ragman" (30/326). The complexity of this metaphoric treatment of Tutivillus's character here argues against McAlindon's specific view of Tutivillus as a "chuckling terrorist" in "Comedy and Terror," 324, and his general view of devils as "buffoons" in his "Comic Type," 365. McClure, "Eschatological Themes," 25, while offering just a brief analysis of the Towneley *Iudicium*, remarks the innovative quality of Tutivillus.

21. On the unpopularity of excessive taxation in late medieval England, see Spek, *Church and the Churchman*, 6.

22. Matheson, "Linguistics and Hierarchy," 210, suggests that pronominal usage establishes an infernal hierarchy in the play, at the top of which is Primus Demon.

23. Wenzel, *The Sin of Sloth*, 150.

24. Erbe, 2.

25. The relationship between Tutivillus and homiletic tradition is noted by Robert Withington in "Braggart, Devil and 'Vice,'" 125–26.

26. The principal literary sources for the play are the gospel narratives, specifically Matthew 26:57, 59–68; Mark 14:53, 55–65; Luke 22:54, 63–71; and John 18:13–

14, 19–24. Stevens and Cawley, *The Towneley Plays*, 2:555, point out: "Some details may go back to the account of the accusation of Christ before Herod in the apocryphal Nicodemus" and some may be traceable to the account of the Buffeting found in the vernacular *Northern Passion*. Also see Lyle, *Original Identity*, 18–19, and Robinson, *Stagecraft*, 177.

27. Helterman, *Symbolic Action*, 140, observes that the conception of the court in this play is "ecclesiastical rather than Jewish." This perceived transformation is in keeping with the Wakefield Master's desire, like that of other playwrights, to make, as Kolve suggests in *Corpus Christi*, 116, "the guilt of Christ's death and the blessing of His sacrifice . . . be felt as local." Also see Velz, "Fox, Bull, and Lion," 2–3, who suggests the need to consider the legal dimension of the play.

28. On this distinction, see Langbein, *Torture*, 4.

29. Stevens and Cawley, 2:554, suggest the play has two major scenes, with the break coming at line 494, or between the examinations of Christ and the actual buffeting, which continues until nearly the end of the play. An alternative order appears to be implicit in the play's action, however, giving the play a four-scene structure.

The first scene in this order, "To Cayphas Hall," consists of the play's first fourteen stanzas. It includes two episodes, "Christ and the Torturers" (stanzas 1–5), and "The Arrival at Cayphas Hall."

Scene 2, "The First Examination," runs from stanza 15 until halfway through stanza 27. Its first episode, Caiaphas's interrogation of Christ, occupies the scene's first six stanzas. A postexamination interlude follows.

The third scene, "The Second Examination," follows the same two-episode pattern. Annas's examination begins halfway through stanza 27 and ends abruptly halfway through stanza 29. The second postexamination interlude runs from the second half of stanza 29 through stanza 38.

The play's final scene, "The Buffeting," also contains two episodes. The actual buffeting occupies stanzas 39 through 46, while the report concerning the disposition of Christ runs to the end of stanza 50.

30. Diller, "Torturers," 57–65, provides a helpful introductory view of the torturers' function. What follows builds on and adds to several of his observations.

31. Confusion concerning the characters in the Towneley collection assigned the task of controlling, torturing, and executing Christ has persisted in the criticism of the collection's plays in general, and of the Wakefield Master's plays in particular. The most obvious demonstration of this tendency in either kind of study is usually the description of the torturer as a "tormentor," the less specific denotation of the Latin *tortor*. This is seen, for example, in Rossiter's brief analysis of the *Coliphizacio* in *English Drama*, 69–70, when he discusses the "cruelly humorous delight" experienced by the "tormentors," whom he then likens to the York *Crucifixion* "executioners," who in the actual York text are not distinguished as *tortores* but rather as *milites* (see Lucy Toulmin Smith, *York Plays*, 350, lines 37 ff.). The latter certainly prove to be as inept as the Towneley *tortores*, and that ineptness offers a grisly

humor nearly as horrifying in its implications as the "fiendish delight [taken by the more villinous of Towneley] in inflicting," as Rossiter notes, "savage pain" (70). But the stupidity demonstrated by the York soldiers as they prepare Christ for the cross in no way qualifies them as torturers. This distinction is quite important. The Wakefield Master's labeling of these characters as *tortores* reveals that he is thinking of them not as *vexatores*, the usual Latin term for tormentors, but specifically as the type of individuals engaged in the practical art of physical coercion. This specific identification, furthermore, is limited to Towneley alone. York, as we have just seen, uses *milites*, while Chester uses *Iudeus* and its plural form (see Mills, *The Chester Mystery Cycle*, 287 and passim) and N-Town uses specific characters identified by such names as Gamalie, Rewfyn, Judas, and Leyon (see Bevington, *Medieval Drama*, 500 and passim).

32. Langbein, *Torture*, 78.

33. Contamine, *War in the Middle Ages*, 290–91.

34. While the *techne* and technology of torture flourished on the Continent in the sixteenth, seventeenth, and eighteenth centuries, and are preserved in such works as the *Constitutio Criminalis Carolina* (1532) and Damhouder's *Praxis Rerum Criminalis* (1554), not much is heard in the preceding centuries from proponents and practitioners of this art. Only those endowed with an overabundance of sadism and the desire to bequeath to future generations their singular talents and genius for hatred preserved their art or technique in manuscript. One of these few, a true anomaly, was the medieval German engineer Conrad Keyser of Ausbeck, who recorded in his *Bellifortis* an instrument designed for the purpose of slow castration. See White, *Medieval Religion and Technology*, 306–7, especially n. 29, for further discussion of Keyser's other, more salutary achievements.

35. Langbein, *Torture*, 74 and 76–77.

36. Augustine, *On Christian Doctrine*, 43–49. Other matters involving the Wakefield Master's concern about interpretive ability can be found in the rest of book 2 and book 3.

37. Helterman, *Symbolic Action*, 144.

38. Brown, *Religious Lyrics*, 16; also see 18 and 223–24.

39. Langbein, *Torture*, 4.

40. Ibid., 5.

41. Ibid., 4.

42. Ibid., 5.

43. Stevens and Cawley, 2:555, line note 1.

44. Clopper, "Tyrants and Villains," 12, calls the motivation here an instance of "judicial maliciousness."

45. This distinction appears in Article 54 of the *Constitutio Criminalis Carolina* of 1532, an English translation of which is available in Langbein, *Prosecuting Crime*, 282:

> When there is employed the aforementioned questioning of a confession secured with or without torture, the judge shall send to the places and shall

(with all diligence appropriate to the circumstances which the person examined told of in confessing the crime to the extent useful to precise knowledge of the truth) have it inquired whether the confession of the aforementioned circumstances is or is not true; because when someone declares the extent and mode of a crime as explicated in part above, and when just these circumstances are discovered, then it can be firmly established that the person committed the crime confessed, particularly when he discloses such circumstances as occurred in the event and which no innocent can know.

46. Lepow, *Enacting the Sacrament*, 106.

47. Augustine, *On Christian Doctrine*, 84.

48. Sanders, "Who's Afraid of Jesus Christ?" 98–99, characterizes the rant as "verbal chaos."

49. For other implications of this allusion's meaning, see Stevens and Cawley, 2:558, line note 217.

50. Langbein, *Torture*, 77.

51. Doob, *Nebuchadnezzar's Children*, 102.

52. Helterman, *Symbolic Action*, 150, observes that Annas employs an indirect legal strategy.

53. Langbein, *Torture*, 15, and *Prosecuting Crime*, 282–83, and Fiorelli, *La tortura guidiziaria*, 2:67.

54. Robinson, *Stagecraft*, 186.

55. Helterman, *Symbolic Action*, 156, points out that Annas understands Christ's role but refuses to believe it and so demonstrates ultimate misunderstanding.

56. Langbein, *Torture*, 5.

57. Ibid., 74–75.

58. Pollack and Maitland, *History of English Law*, 2:659, indicate that the invention of *peine forte et dure* predates jury standard of proof.

59. Froward is not a *tortor* per se, as the torturers themselves indicate when they distinguish him as their servant. Indeed, since he vexes the torturers themselves with his obstinacy, he is perhaps more accurately described as a "tormentor" or *vexator*, the term frequently used erroneously in criticism of the Towneley collections's Passion plays to describe the torturers themselves. See *Oxford English Dictionary*, compact ed., s.v. "froward," def. 1.

60. Sanders, "Who's Afraid of Jesus Christ?" 97, suggests other games are included in the play, games such as Ninepins and Skittles. Stevens and Cawley's gloss of Froward's "skalys" remark, 2:563, line note 591, reduces Sanders's number of game allusions to Blind Man's Buff or Hot Cockles and Cock-Throwing. For further discussion of this game presence in the play, see Kolve, *Corpus Christi*, 185. For visualization of the game of Hot Cockles as metaphor of the Buffeting, see Hildburgh, "Alabaster Carvings," plate 17a.

61. See Davidson, "Jest and Earnest," 73.

62. Stevens and Cawley suggest a tall man played the part of Christ. See 2:561, line note 512.

63. On "skalys" being dandruff rather than the game of Skittles, see Stevens and Cawley, 2:563, line note 591. Professor Laura Hodges has reminded me in a note that "skalys" may also have been a reference to the "form of leprosy called alopicia," or syphilis, or scabies, as listed in Janette Richardson's "headnotes" treating Chaucer's Summoner (*The Riverside Chaucer*, 822). If this is the case, the use of such a term, as Professor Hodges adds, would be "a highly insulting thing for the torturer to say about Christ." What is intriguing about this possible implication, Professor Hodges concludes, is that this is a disease that was viewed as being potentially curable either by faith or by "Veronica's veil." The calling for the veil at this point in the play may therefore introduce yet another irony.

64. See Furnish, "Audience," 244. Following Cawley, Furnish adds on 245 that Froward gets so caught up in the action that he accidentally adopts the role of torturer by stepping forward and striking Christ in his turn.

65. Langbein, *Torture*, 75–76.

66. Cawley, *Wakefield Pageants*, 123, line note 450.

Conclusion

1. Jacobus de Voragine, *The Golden Legend*, 1:3–4.
2. Dunn, "Literary Style."
3. Jacobus de Voragine, 1:4.
4. Lepow, "Drama of Communion," 412.

Bibliography

1. Primary Works, Anthologies, and References

A. B. of Phisike Doctour. *Merie Tales of the Mad Men of Gotam.* Edited by Stanley J. Kahrl. With R. I., *The History of Tom Thumbe,* edited by Curt F. Bühler. Evanston, Ill.: Northwestern University Press, 1965.

Aikin, John. *A Description of the Country from Thirty to Forty Miles round Manchester.* 1795. New York: A. M. Kelley, 1968.

Anderson, J. J., ed. *Patience.* Manchester: Manchester University Press; New York, Barnes & Noble, 1969.

Arnold of Bonneval. *S. Bernardi vita prima.* In vol. 185 of *Patrologiae cursus completus, . . . Series latina,* edited by J.-P. Migne, 221 vols. Paris, 1844–64.

Augustine, Saint, Bishop of Hippo. *Concerning the City of God against the Pagans.* Translated by Henry Bettenson. New York: Penguin, 1972.

———. *De Trinitate.* Translated by Edmund Hill. Edited by John E. Rotelle. Brooklyn: New City Press, 1991.

———. *Letters, 1–82.* Translated by Sister Wilfrid Parsons. Vol. 9 of *Writings of Saint Augustine,* edited by Roy Joseph Deferrari. New York: Fathers of the Church, 1951.

———. *Of Music.* Translated by Robert Catesby Taliaferro. Vol. 2 of *Writings of Saint Augustine,* edited by Ludwig Schopp. New York: CIMA Publishing, 1947.

———. *On Christian Doctrine.* Translated by D. W. Robertson Jr. New York: Liberal Arts Press, 1958.

Bacon, Roger. *De secretis operibus.* In *Fr. Rogeri Bacon Opera quaedam hactenus inedita,* edited by J. S. Brewer. London, 1859.

Bevington, David, ed. *Medieval Drama.* Boston: Houghton Mifflin, 1975.

Boethius, Anicius Manlius Severinus. *The Consolation of Philosophy.* Translated by Richard Green. Indianapolis: Bobbs-Merrill, 1962.

Brandeis, Arthur, ed. *Jacob's Well: An English Treatise on the Cleansing of Man's Conscience.* Part 1. EETS o.s. 115. London: K. Paul, Trench, Trübner, 1900.

British Library. Add. MS. 42130, fol. 170.

Brown, Carleton, ed. *Religious Lyrics of the XIVth Century*. Oxford: Clarendon, 1924.
Cawley, A. C., ed. *The Wakefield Pageants in the Towneley Cycle*. Manchester: Manchester University Press, 1958.
Cawley, A. C., and Martin Stevens, eds. *The Towneley Cycle: A Facsimile of Huntington MS HM 1*. Leeds: University of Leeds, Department of English, 1976.
Chaucer, Geoffrey. *The Riverside Chaucer*. Edited by Larry D. Benson. 3d ed. Boston: Houghton Mifflin, 1987.
Descriptio positionis seu situationis monasterii Claravallensis. In vol. 185 of *Patrologiae cursus completus, . . . Series latina*, edited by J.-P. Migne, 221 vols. Paris, 1844–64.
England, George, and Alfred W. Pollard, eds. *Towneley Plays*. EETS e.s. 71. London: K. Paul, Trench, Trübner, 1897.
Gordon, James, and Joseph Hunter, eds. *The Towneley Mysteries*. Surtees Society, 1836.
Gregorius Magnus, Saint, Pope. *Moralia*. Vols. 75–76 of *Patrologiae cursus completus, . . . Series latina*, edited by J.-P. Migne, 221 vols. Paris, 1844–64.
Guillaume de Lorris and Jean de Meun. *The Romance of the Rose*. Translated by Charles Dahlberg. 3d ed. Princeton: Princeton University Press, 1995.
Hassall, William Owen, ed. *The Holkham Bible Picture Book*. 2d ed. London: Dropmore, 1954.
Hattinger, Franz, ed. *The Duc de Berry's Book of Hours*. Berne: Hallwag, 1962.
Hemingway, Samuel B., ed. *English Nativity Plays*. New Haven: Yale University Press, 1909.
Henley, Walter de. *Walter of Henley's Husbandry*. Translated by Elizabeth Lamond. London: Longmans, Green, 1890.
Hugh of Saint Victor. *Didascalicon: A Medieval Guide to the Arts*. Translated by Jerome Taylor. New York: Columbia University Press, 1971.
Jacobus de Voragine. *The Golden Legend: Readings on the Saints*. Translated by William Granger Ryan. 2 vols. Princeton: Princeton University Press, 1993.
Jehan le Bel. *Li ars d'amour*. Edited by J. Petit. 2 vols. Brussels: V. Devaux, 1867–69.
John of Garland. *The Parisiana poetria of John of Garland*. Edited and translated by Traugott Lawler. New Haven: Yale University Press, 1974.
Langland, William. *The Vision of William Concerning Piers Plowman: The "Crowley" Text; or Text B*. Edited by W. W. Skeat. EETS 38. London, 1869.
———. *Will's Vision of Piers Plowman*. Translated by E. Talbot Donaldson. Edited by Elizabeth D. Kirk and Judith H. Anderson. New York: Norton, 1990.
Latimer, Hugh. *Sermons*. Vol. 1 of *The Works of Hugh Latimer*, edited by G. E. Corrie. Cambridge: Cambridge University Press, 1844.
Leland, John. *The Itinerary of John Leland*. Part 1. Edited by Lucy Toulmin Smith. London: G. Bell, 1907.
Linow, Wilhelm, ed. *Þe Desputisoun bitwen þe Bodi and þe Soule*. Amsterdam: Rodopi, 1970.

Migne, J.-P., ed. *Patrologiae cursus completus, . . . Series latina.* 221 vols. Paris, 1844–64.
Mills, David, ed. *The Chester Mystery Cycle.* East Lansing: Colleagues Press, 1992.
Mirk, John. *Mirk's Festival: A Collection of Homilies.* Edited by Theodor Erbe. EETS e.s. 96. London: K. Paul, Trench, Trübner, 1905.
Peter Lombard. *Sententiae.* Vol. 192 of *Patrologiae cursus completus, . . . Series latina,* edited by J.-P. Migne, 221 vols. Paris, 1844–64.
Rose, Martial, ed. and trans. *The Wakefield Mystery Plays.* London: Evans Bros., 1961.
Saints. *See under* respective Christian names.
Smith, Lucy Toulmin, ed. *York Plays.* New York: Russell & Russell, 1963.
Stern, Henri, ed. *Le calendrier de 354.* Paris: P. Geuthner, 1953.
Stevens, Martin, and A. C. Cawley, eds. *The Towneley Plays.* 2 vols. EETS s.s. 13. Oxford: Oxford University Press, 1994.
Theophilus. *On Divers Arts.* Edited and translated by John G. Hawthorne and Cyril Stanley Smith. Chicago: University of Chicago Press, 1963.
Walahfrid Strabo. *Glossa Ordinaria.* Vols. 113–14 of *Patrologiae cursus completus, . . . Series latina,* edited by J.-P. Migne, 221 vols. Paris, 1844–64.
Wenzel, Siegfried, ed. and trans. *Fasciculus Morum: A Fourteenth-Century Preacher's Handbook.* University Park: Pennsylvania State University Press, 1989.
Wright, Thomas, ed. *A Collection of Latin Stories.* London: T. Richards, 1842.
Wright, Thomas, and James Orchard Halliwell, eds. *Reliquiae Antiquae.* 2 vols. London: J. R. Smith, 1845.

2. Historical and Critical Studies

Adams, Robert. "The Egregious Feasts of the Chester and Towneley Shepherds." *Chaucer Review* 21 (1986): 96–107.
Allen, John. *Wakefield Cathedral.* Wakefield: n.p., 1989.
Anderson, J. J. "The Towneley Shepherds and the York Primer." *Neophilologus* 75 (1991): 317–20.
Ashley, Kathleen M. "The Guiler Beguiled: Christ and Satan as Theological Tricksters in Medieval Religious Literature." *Criticism* 24 (1982): 126–37.
Axton, Richard. *European Drama of the Early Middle Ages.* London: Hutchinson, 1974.
Ayalon, David. *Gunpowder and Firearms in the Mamluk Kingdom: A Challenge to a Medieval Society.* London: Vallentine, Mitchell, 1956.
Barney, Stephen A. "The Plowshare of the Tongue: The Progress of a Symbol from the Bible to *Piers Plowman.*" *Medieval Studies* 35 (1973): 261–93.
Bartlett, J. M. "The Expansion and Decline of York in the Later Middle Ages." *Economic History Review,* 2d ser., 12 (1959): 17–33.
Baugh, Albert C., ed. *A Literary History of England.* New York: Appleton-Century-Crofts, 1948.

———. "The Mak Story." *Modern Philology* 15 (1918): 729–34.
Bennett, H. S. "The Reeve and the Manor in the Fourteenth Century." *English Historical Review* 41 (1926): 358–65.
Benson, Larry D. *Malory's "Morte Darthur."* Cambridge: Harvard University Press, 1976.
Benz, Ernst. "The Christian Expectation of the End of Time and the Idea of Technological Progress." In *Evolution and Christian Hope,* translated by Heinz G. Frank, 121–42. Garden City, N.Y.: Doubleday, 1966.
Bernbrock, John E. "Notes on the Towneley Cycle Slaying of Abel." *Journal of English and Germanic Philology* 62 (1963): 317–22.
Besserman, Lawrence L. "The Wakefield *Noah,* Lines 55–56." *Papers on Language and Literature* 15 (1979): 82–84.
Blanch, Robert J. "The Gifts of the Shepherds in the *Prima Pastorum:* A Symbolic Interpretation." *Cithara* 13 (1974): 69–75.
———. "The Symbolic Gifts of the Shepherds in the *Secunda Pastorum.*" *Texas Studies in Literature* 17 (1972): 25–36.
Bloch, Marc. *Feudal Society.* Translated by L. A. Manyon. 2 vols. Chicago: University of Chicago Press, 1961.
Blunt, A. "Blake's 'Ancient of Days': The Symbolism of the Compass." *Journal of the Warburg Institute* 2 (1938–39): 53–63.
Bonnel, John K. "Cain's Jaw Bone." *Publications of the Modern Language Association* 39 (1924): 140–46.
Boone, Blair W. "The Skill of Cain in the English Mystery Cycles." *Comparative Drama* 16 (1982): 112–29.
Briquet, C.-M. *Les filigranes.* 2d ed. Leipzig: Hiersemann, 1923.
Britton, G. C. "Language and Character in Some Late Medieval Plays." *Essays and Studies* 33 (1980): 1–15.
Brockman, Bennett A. "Cain and Abel in the Chester *Creation:* Narrative Tradition and Dramatic Potential." *Medievalia et Humanistica* 5 (1974): 169–82.
———. "Comic and Tragic Counterpoint in the Medieval Drama: The Wakefield *Mactatio Abel.*" *Medieval Studies* 39 (1977): 331–49.
———. "The Law of Man and the Peace of God: Judicial Process as Satiric Theme in the Wakefield *Mactatio Abel.*" *Speculum* 49 (1974): 699–707.
Bullough, Edward. *Aesthetics: Lectures and Essays.* Edited by Elizabeth M. Wilkinson. Stanford: Stanford University Press, 1957.
Cady, Frank W. "The Maker of Mak." *University of California Chronicle* 29 (1927): 261–72.
———. "The Wakefield Group in Towneley." *Journal of English and Germanic Philology* 11 (1912): 244–62.
Camille, Michael. "Laboring for the Lord: The Ploughman and Social Order in the Luttrell Psalter." *Art History* 10 (1987): 423–54.
———. *Mirror in Parchment: The Luttrell Psalter and the Making of Medieval England.* Chicago: University of Chicago Press, 1998.

———. "When Adam Delved: Laboring on the Land in English Medieval Art." In *Agriculture in the Middle Ages: Technology, Practice, and Representation*, edited by Del Sweeney, 247–76. Philadelphia: University of Pennsylvania Press, 1995.
Campbell, Josie P. "Farce as Function in the Wakefield Shepherds' Plays." *Chaucer Review* 14 (1980): 336–43.
———. "The Idea of Order in the Wakefield *Noah*." *Chaucer Review* 10 (1975): 76–86.
Campbell, Thomas P. "Eschatology and the Nativity in the English Mystery Plays." *American Benedictine Review* 27 (1976): 297–320.
———. "Why Do the Shepherds Prophesy?" *Comparative Drama* 12 (1978): 137–50.
Cantelupe, Eugene, and Richard Griffith. "The Gifts of the Shepherds in the Wakefield 'Secunda Pastorum': An Iconographical Interpretation." *Medieval Studies* 28 (1966): 328–35.
Carey, Millicent. *The Wakefield Group in the Towneley Cycle*. Baltimore: Johns Hopkins Press, 1930.
Cargill, Oscar. "The Authorship of the *Secunda Pastorum*." *Publications of the Modern Language Association* 41 (1927): 810–31.
Carpenter, Nan C. "Music in the *Secunda Pastorum*." *Speculum* 26 (1951): 696–700.
Carr, Sherwyn T. "The Middle English Nativity Cherry Tree: The Dissemination of a Popular Motif." *Modern Language Quarterly* 36 (1975): 133–47.
Carus-Wilson, E. M. "An Industrial Revolution of the Thirteenth Century." *Economic History Review* 11 (1941): 41–60.
———. *Medieval Merchant Venturers: Collected Studies*. 2d ed. London: Methuen, 1967.
Cawley, A. C. "The 'Grotesque' Feast in the *Prima Pastorum*." *Speculum* 30 (1955): 213–17.
———. "Jak Garcio of the *Prima Pastorum*." *Modern Language Notes* 68 (1953): 169–72.
———. "The Wakefield *First Shepherds' Play*." *Proceedings of the Leeds Philosophical and Literary Society* 7 (1955): 113–22.
Cawley, A. C., Jean Forrester, and John Goodchild. "References to the Corpus Christi Play in the Wakefield Burgess Court Rolls: The Originals Rediscovered." *Leeds Studies in English*, n.s. 19 (1988): 85–104.
Chambers, E. K. *English Literature at the Close of the Middle Ages*. Oxford: Clarendon, 1945.
———. *The Mediaeval Stage*. 2 vols. London: Oxford University Press, 1903.
Chenu, M.-D. *Nature, Man, and Society in the Twelfth Century*. Translated by Jerome Taylor and Lester K. Little. Chicago: University of Chicago Press, 1968.
Chidamian, Claude. "Mak and the Tossing of the Blanket." *Speculum* 22 (1947): 186–90.
Cipolla, Carlo M. *Clocks and Culture, 1300–1700*. New York: Norton, 1978.

Clark, E. M. "Liturgical Influences in the Towneley Plays." *Orate Fratres* 16 (1941): 69–70.

Clein, Wendy. "The Towneley *Magnus Herodes* and the Comedy of Redemption." *Renascence* 38 (1985): 54–63.

Cleland, John H. "*Second Shepherds'* and *Homecoming*: Two Dramatic Imitations of Life." *Faith and Reason* 3 (1977): 46–64.

Clopper, Lawrence M. "Tyrants and Villains: Characterization in the Passion Sequences of the English Cycle Plays." *Modern Language Quarterly* 41 (1980): 3–20.

Collins, Fletcher, Jr. "Music in the Craft Cycles." *Publications of the Modern Language Association* 47 (1932): 613–21.

Contamine, Philippe. *War in the Middle Ages.* Translated by Michael Jones. New York: Basil Blackwell, 1984.

Cook, A. S. "Another Parallel to the Mak Story." *Modern Philology* 14 (1916): 11–15.

Cooper, Helen. "A Note on the Wakefield *Prima Pastorum*." *Notes & Queries* 20 (1973): 326.

Copeland, Rita. *Rhetoric, Hermeneutics, and Translation in the Middle Ages: Academic Traditions and Vernacular Texts.* Cambridge: Cambridge University Press, 1991.

Cosbey, Robert C. "The Mak Story and Its Folklore Analogues." *Speculum* 20 (1945): 310–17.

Coulton, G. G. *Medieval Village, Manor, and Monastery.* 1925. New York: Harper, 1960.

Craig, Hardin. *English Religious Drama of the Middle Ages.* Oxford: Clarendon, 1955.

Crowther, J. D. W. "The Wakefield Cain and the 'Curs' of the Bad Tither." *Paregone* 24 (1979): 19–24.

Curry, Walter Clyde. *Chaucer and the Mediaeval Sciences.* 2d ed. New York: Barnes & Noble, 1960.

Curtius, Ernst Robert. *European Literature and the Latin Middle Ages.* Translated by Willard R. Trask. New York: Pantheon, 1953.

Cutts, John P. "The Shepherds' Gifts in *The Second Shepherds' Play* and Bosch's 'Adoration of the Magi.'" *Comparative Drama* 4 (1970): 120–24.

———. "'Wee happy heardsmen here': A Newly Discovered Shepherds' Carol Possibly Belonging to a Medieval Pageant." *Comparative Drama* 18 (1984): 265–73.

Daniels, Richard J. "Uxor Noah: A Raven or a Dove?" *Chaucer Review* 14 (1979): 23–32.

David, Alfred. "Noah's Wife's Flood." In *The Performance of Middle English Culture: Essays on Chaucer and the Drama in Honor of Martin Stevens*, edited by James J. Paxson, Lawrence M. Clopper, and Sylvia Tomasch, 97–109. Cambridge: D. S. Brewer, 1998.

Davidson, Clifford. "An Interpretation of the Wakefield *Iudicium*." *Annuale Mediaevale* 10 (1969): 104–19.

———. "Jest and Earnest: Comedy in the Work of the Wakefield Master." *Annuale Mediaevale* 22 (1982): 65–83.

———. "Space and Time in Medieval Drama: Meditations on Orientation in the Early Theater." In *Word, Picture, and Spectacle*, 39–93. Kalamazoo: Medieval Institute Publications, 1984.

———. *Technology, Guilds, and Early English Drama*. Kalamazoo: Medieval Institute Publications, 1996.

———. "The Unity of the Wakefield *Mactatio Abel*." *Traditio* 23 (1967): 495–500.

de Bruyn, Lucy. *Woman and the Devil in Sixteenth-Century Literature*. Tisbury, Wiltshire: Compton Press, 1979.

Diller, Hans-Jürgen. "The Craftsmanship of the 'Wakefield Master.'" *Anglia* 83 (1965): 271–88. Reprinted in *Medieval English Drama*, edited by Jerome Taylor and Alan H. Nelson, 245–59. Chicago: University of Chicago Press, 1972.

———. *The Middle English Mystery Play: A Study in Dramatic Speech and Form*. Translated by Frances Wessels. Cambridge: Cambridge University Press, 1992.

———. "The Torturers in the English Mystery Plays." *Middle English Theatre* 11 (1989): 57–65.

Dobson, R. B. "Yorkshire Towns in the Late Fourteenth Century." *Thoresby Society Publications* 18 (1985): 1–21.

Doob, Penelope B. R. *Nebuchadnezzar's Children: Conventions of Madness in Middle English Literature*. New Haven: Yale University Press, 1974.

Dunn, E. Catherine. "The Literary Style of the Towneley Plays." *American Benedictine Review* 20 (1969): 481–504.

———. "The Prophetic Principle in the Towneley *Prima Pastorum*." In *Linguistic and Literary Studies in Honor of Helmut A. Hatzfeld*, edited by Alessandro S. Crisafulli, 117–27. Washington, D.C.: Catholic University of America Press, 1965.

Dutka, JoAnna. *Music in the English Mystery Plays*. Kalamazoo: Medieval Institute Publications, 1980.

Dvořák, Max. *Idealism and Naturalism in Gothic Art*. Translated by Randolph J. Klawiter. Notre Dame, Ind.: University of Notre Dame Press, 1967.

Dyer, Christopher. *Standards of Living in the Later Middle Ages*. Cambridge: Cambridge University Press, 1989.

Eaton, H. A. "A Source for the Towneley *Prima Pastorum*." *Modern Language Notes* 14 (1899): 265–68.

Edminster, Warren. "Foolish Shepherds and Priestly Folly: Festive Influence in *Prima Pastorum*." *Medieval Perspectives* 15 (2000): 57–73.

Eliade, Mircea. *Cosmos and History: The Myth of the Eternal Return*. Translated by Willard R. Trask. New York: Harper & Row, 1959.

———. *The Forge and the Crucible*. Translated by Stephen Corrin. New York: Harper & Row, 1962.

Elliott, Charles. "Language and Theme in the Towneley *Magnus Herodes*." *Medieval Studies* 30 (1968): 351–53.

Esper, Thomas. "The Replacement of the Longbow by Firearms in the English Army." *Technology & Culture* 6 (1965): 393.

Evans, Ruth. "Feminist Re-enactments: Gender and the Towneley *Uxor Noe*." In *A Wyf Ther Was: Essays in Honor of Paule Mertens-Fonck*, edited by Juliette Dor, 141–54. Liège: English Department, University of Liège, 1992.

Evitt, Regula Meyer. "Musical Structure in the *Secunda Pastorum*." *Comparative Drama* 22 (1988–89): 304–22.

Fiondella, Maris. "Derrida, Typology and the *Second Shepherds' Play:* The Theatrical Production of Christian Metaphysics." *Exemplaria* 6 (1994): 429–58.

Fiorelli, Pièro. *La tortura guidiziaria nel diritto comune*. 2 vols. Milano: Giufré, 1953–54.

Forbes, R. J. "Power." In *A History of Technology*, edited by Charles Singer et al., 2:589–628. Oxford: Clarendon, 1956.

Foster, Frances A. "Was Gilbert Pilkington Author of the *Secunda Pastorum*?" *Publications of the Modern Language Association* 43 (1928): 124–36.

Fowler, David C. *The Bible in Middle English Literature*. Seattle: University of Washington Press, 1984.

Frampton, Mendel G. "The Date of the Flourishing of the 'Wakefield Master.'" *Publications of the Modern Language Association* 50 (1935): 631–60.

Furnish, Shearle. "Audience in the Text of the Wakefield *Buffeting*." *Mediaevalia* 14 (1988): 231–58.

———. "Metatheatre in the *First Shepherds' Play*." *Essays in Theatre* 7 (1989): 139–48.

———. "Play-within-the-Play in the Dramas of the Wakefield Master." *Medieval Perspectives* 14 (1999): 61–69.

———. "Technique *versus* Feeling in the Wakefield Master's *Magnus Herodes*." *Kentucky Philological Association Bulletin*, n.v. (1984): 36–43.

Ganshof, F. L. *Feudalism*. Translated by Philip Grierson. London: Longmans, Green, 1952.

Gardner, John. *The Construction of the Wakefield Cycle*. Carbondale: Southern Illinois University Press, 1974.

———. "Imagery and Allusion in the Wakefield Noah Play." *Papers on Language and Literature* 4 (1968): 3–12.

———. "Structure and Tone in the *Second Shepherds' Play*." *Educational Theatre Journal* 19 (1967): 1–8.

———. "Theme and Irony in the Wakefield *Mactatio Abel*." *Publications of the Modern Language Association* 80 (1965): 515–21.

Garvin, Katherine. "A Note on Noah's Wife." *Modern Language Notes* 49 (1934): 88–90.

Gayley, Charles Mills. *Plays of Our Forefathers and Some of the Traditions Upon Which They Were Founded*. New York: Duffield, 1907.

Gerould, G. H. "Moll of the *Prima Pastorum*." *Modern Language Notes* 19 (1904): 225–30.

Gillmeister, Heiner. "The Gift of a Tennis Ball in the *Secunda Pastorum:* A Sports Historian's View." *Arete: Journal of Sports Literature* 4 (1986): 105–19.
Gimpel, Jean. *The Medieval Machine: The Industrial Revolution of the Middle Ages.* New York: Holt, Rinehart & Winston, 1976.
Guilfoyle, Cherrell M. "Cain, Lamech, and the 'Quarell Hede.'" *English Language Notes* 25 (1987): 13–18.
———. "'The Riddle Song' and the Shepherds' Gifts in *Secunda Pastorum,* with a Note on the 'Tre callyd Persidis.'" *Yearbook of English Studies* 8 (1978): 208–19.
———. "The Staging of the First Murder in the Mystery Plays in England." *Comparative Drama* 25 (1991): 42–51.
Guilmartin, John Francis, Jr. *Gunpowder and Galleys.* London and New York: Cambridge University Press, 1974.
Hamelius, Paul. "The Character of Cain in the Towneley Plays." *Journal of Comparative Literature* 1 (1903): 324–44.
Hanks, Dorrel T., Jr. "The *Mactatio Abel* and the Wakefield Cycle: A Study in Context." *Southern Quarterly* 16 (1977): 47–57.
Happé, P. "The Vice and the Folk Drama." *Folklore* 75 (1964): 161–93.
Hardison, O. B., Jr. *Christian Rite and Christian Drama in the Middle Ages: Essays in the Origin and Early History of Modern Drama.* Baltimore: Johns Hopkins Press, 1965.
Harrison, H. S. "Discovery, Invention, and Diffusion." In *A History of Technology,* edited by Charles Singer et al., 1:58–84. Oxford: Clarendon, 1954.
Hartley, Dorothy, and Margaret M. Elliot. *Life and Work of the People of England: A Pictorial Record from Contemporary Sources.* 6 vols. London: B. T. Batsford, 1926–31.
Hartnett, Edith. "Cain in the Medieval Towneley Play." *Annuale Mediaevale* 12 (1971): 21–29.
Haskins, Charles Homer. *The Renaissance of the Twelfth Century.* Cambridge: Harvard University Press, 1927.
Heaton, Herbert. *The Yorkshire Woollen and Worsted Industries, From the Earliest Times Up to the Industrial Revolution.* Oxford: Clarendon, 1920.
Helterman, Jeffrey. "Satan as Everyshepherd: Comic Metamorphosis in *The Second Shepherds' Play.*" *Texas Studies in Language and Literature* 12 (1971): 515–30.
———. *Symbolic Action in the Plays of the Wakefield Master.* Athens: University of Georgia Press, 1981.
Hennequin, M. Wendy. "'Byrkyn many bonys': The Breaking of Bones in the *Magnus Herodes.*" *Early Drama, Art and Music Review* 23 (2000): 49–61.
Hey, David. *Yorkshire from AD 1000.* London: Longman, 1986.
Hildburgh, W. L. "English Alabaster Carvings as Records of the Medieval Religious Drama." *Archaeologica* 93 (1949): 51–101.
Hirsh, John C. "Mak Tossed in a Blanket." *Notes & Queries* 28 (1981): 117–18.
Hirshberg, Jeffrey Alan. "Noah's Wife on the Medieval English Stage: Iconographic

and Dramatic Values of Her Distaff and Choice of Raven." *Studies in Iconography* 2 (1976): 25–40.

Hodges, Laura. "'Noe's Wife': Type of Eve and Wakefield Spinner and 'Recalcitrant Wife' in the Ramsey Abbey Psalter." In *Equally in God's Image: Women in the Middle Ages,* edited by Julia Bolton Holloway, Constance S. Wright, and Joan Bechtold, 30–45. New York: Peter Lang, 1990.

Holt, Richard. *The Mills of Medieval England.* Oxford and New York: Basil Blackwell, 1988.

Holthausen, F. "Das zweite Hirtenspiel der Wakefielder Spiele." *Englische Studien* 63 (1929): 193–219.

Hussey, S. S. "How Many Herods in the Middle English Drama?" *Neophilologus* 48 (1964): 252–59.

Ingram, R. W. "The Use of Music in English Miracle Plays." *Anglia* 75 (1957): 55–76.

Irace, Kathleen. "Mak's Sothren Tothe: A Philological and Critical Study of the Dialectical Joke in the *Second Shepherds' Play.*" *Comitatus* 21 (1990): 38–51.

Jambeck, Thomas J. "The 'Ayll of Hely' Allusion in the *Prima Pastorum.*" *English Language Notes* 17 (1979): 1–7.

———. "The Canvas-Tossing Allusion in the *Secunda Pastorum.*" *Modern Philology* 76 (1978): 49–54.

———. "The 'Day Star' Allusion in the *Secunda Pastorum.*" *Modern Language Quarterly* 50 (1989): 297–308.

James, Mervyn. "Ritual, Drama and Social Body in the Late Medieval Town." *Past and Present* 98 (1983): 3–29.

Jeffrey, David L. *The Early English Lyric and Franciscan Spirituality.* Lincoln: University of Nebraska Press, 1975.

———. "Pastoral Care in the Wakefield Shepherds' Plays." *American Benedictine Review* 22 (1971): 208–21.

———. "Stewardship in the Wakefield *Mactatio Abel* and *Noe* Plays." *American Benedictine Review* 22 (1971): 64–76.

Jennings, Margaret. "Tutivillus: The Literary Career of the Recording Demon." *Studies in Philology* 74 (1977): 1–95.

Johnson, Kenneth E. "The Rhetoric of Apocalypse in Van Eyck's 'Last Judgment' and the Wakefield *Secunda Pastorum.*" In *Legacy of Thespis: Drama Past and Present,* edited by Karelisa V. Hartigan, 31–41. Lanham, Md.: University Press of America, 1984.

Johnson, Wallace H. "The Origin of the *Second Shepherds' Play:* A New Theory." *Quarterly Journal of Speech* 52 (1966): 47–57.

Jolliffe, J. E. A. *The Constitutional History of Medieval England, From the English Settlement to 1485.* London: Black, 1937.

Jordan, Robert M. *Chaucer and the Shape of Creation: The Aesthetic Possibilities of Inorganic Structure.* Cambridge: Harvard University Press, 1967.

Jungman, Robert E. "An Analogue in Fortescue to the Wakefield *Magnus Herodes.*" *American Notes and Queries* 14 (1975): 2–3.

———. "Mak and the Seven Names of God." *Lore and Language* 3 (1982): 24–28.
Kahrl, Stanley J. *Traditions of Medieval English Drama*. London: Hutchinson, 1974.
Keen, Maurice. *Chivalry*. New Haven: Yale University Press, 1984.
Kelly, T. Daniel, and John T. Irwin. "The Meaning of *Cleanness:* Parable as Effective Sign." *Medieval Studies* 35 (1973): 232–60.
Kolve, V. A. *The Play Called Corpus Christi*. Stanford: Stanford University Press, 1967.
Langbein, John H. *Prosecuting Crime in the Renaissance: England, France, Germany*. Cambridge: Harvard University Press, 1974.
———. *Torture and the Law of Proof: Europe and England in the Ancien Régime*. Chicago: University of Chicago Press, 1977.
Langdon, John. *Horses, Oxen, and Technological Innovation: The Use of Draught Animals in English Farming from 1066 to 1500*. Cambridge: Cambridge University Press, 1986.
Le Goff, Jacques. *Time, Work, and Culture in the Middle Ages*. Translated by Arthur Goldhammer. Chicago: University of Chicago Press, 1980.
Leonard, Frances M. "The School for Transformation: A Theory of Middle English Comedy." *Genre* 9 (1976): 179–91.
Lepow, Lauren. "Daw's Tennis Ball: A Topical Allusion in the *Secunda Pastorum*." *English Language Notes* 22 (1984): 5–8.
———. "Drama of Communion: The Life of Christ in the Towneley Cycle." *Philological Quarterly* 62 (1983): 403–13.
———. *Enacting the Sacrament: Counter-Lollardy in the Towneley Cycle*. Rutherford, N.J.: Fairleigh Dickinson University Press, 1990.
———. "'What God Has Cleansed': The Shepherds' Feast in the *Prima Pastorum*." *Modern Philology* 80 (1983): 280–83.
Leshock, David. "The Representation of Islam in the Wakefield Corpus Christi Plays."*Medieval Perspectives* 11 (1996): 195–208.
Lester, G. A. "The Wakefield Master." In *Great Writers of the English Language: Dramatists*, edited by James Vinson and D. L. Kirkpatrick, 592–93. London: Macmillan, 1979.
Lewis, C. S. *The Discarded Image: An Introduction to Medieval and Renaissance Literature*. Cambridge: Cambridge University Press, 1964.
Lewis, Jack Pearl. *A Study of the Interpretation of Noah and the Flood in Jewish and Christian Literature*. Leiden: E. J. Brill, 1968.
Lipson, E. *The History of the Woollen and Worsted Industries*. London: Black, 1921.
Longo, Joseph A. "Symmetry and Symbolism in the *Secunda Pastorum*." *Nottingham Medieval Studies* 13 (1969): 65–85.
Lottin, O. "La doctrine morale des mouvements premiers de l'appétit sensitif aux XIIe et XIIIe siècles." *Archives d'histoire doctrinale et littéraire du moyen âge* 6 (1931): 49–173.
Lyle, Marie C. *The Original Identity of the York and Towneley Cycles*. Minneapolis: University of Minnesota, 1919.

McAlindon, T. "Comedy and Terror in Middle English Literature: The Diabolical Game." *Modern Language Review* 60 (1965): 323–32.

———. "The Emergence of a Comic Type in Middle English Narrative: The Devil and Giant as Buffoon." *Anglia* 81 (1963): 365–71.

McClure, Hazel Dean. "Eschatological Themes in English Medieval Drama." *Emporia State Research Studies* 14 (1965): 14–28.

Mack, Maynard, Jr. "*The Second Shepherds' Play:* A Reconsideration." *Publications of the Modern Language Association* 93 (1978): 78–85.

Mâle, Emile. *The Gothic Image: Religious Art in France of the Thirteenth Century.* Translated by Dora Nussey. New York: Harper & Row, 1958.

Maltman, Sister Nicholas, O.P. "Pilate—*Os Malleatoris*." *Speculum* 36 (1961): 308–11.

Manion, F. P., S.J. "A Reinterpretation of the *Second Shepherds' Play*." *American Benedictine Review* 30 (1979): 44–68.

Manly, William M. "Shepherds and Prophets: Religious Unity in the Towneley *Secunda Pastorum*." *Publications of the Modern Language Association* 78 (1963): 151–55.

Marshall, Linda E. "'Sacral Parody' in the *Secunda Pastorum*." *Speculum* 47 (1972): 720–36.

Matheson, Lester M. "Linguistics and Hierarchy: The Demons in the Judgment Play." *Neuphilologische Mitteilungen* 91 (1990): 209–13.

Mellinkoff, Ruth. *Outcasts: Signs of Otherness in Northern European Art of the Late Middle Ages.* 2 vols. Berkeley and Los Angeles: University of California Press, 1993.

Meyers, Walter E. *A Figure Given: Typology in the Wakefield Plays.* Pittsburgh: Duquesne University Press, 1969.

Mill, Anna J. "Noah's Wife Again." *Publications of the Modern Language Association* 56 (1941): 613–26.

Miller, Robert P., ed. *Chaucer: Sources and Backgrounds.* New York: Oxford University Press, 1977.

Mills, David. "'The Towneley Plays' or 'The Towneley Cycle'?" *Leeds Studies in English,* n.s. 17 (1985): 95–104.

Moorman, F. W. *The Place-Names of the West Riding of Yorkshire.* Leeds: The Thoresby Society, 1910.

Morey, James H. "Plows, Laws, and Sanctuary in Medieval England and in the Wakefield *Mactatio Abel*." *Studies in Philology* 95 (1998): 41–55.

Morgan, Margery M. "'High Fraud': Paradox and Double Plot in the English Shepherds' Plays." *Speculum* 39 (1964): 678–89.

Mumford, Lewis. *Technics and Civilization.* New York: Harcourt, Brace, 1934.

Munson, William F. "Audience and Meaning in Two Medieval Dramatic Realisms." *Comparative Drama* 9 (1975): 44–67.

———. "Holiday, Audience Participation, and Characterization in the Shepherds'

Plays." *Research Opportunities in Renaissance Drama* 15–16 (1972–73): 97–115.

Murphy, James J. *Rhetoric in the Middle Ages*. Berkeley and Los Angeles: University of California Press, 1974.

Nelson, Alan H. "'Sacred' and 'Secular' Currents in *The Towneley Play of Noah.*" *Drama Studies* 3 (1964): 393–401.

Neumann, Erich. *The Origins and History of Consciousness*. Translated by R. F. C. Hull. New York: Pantheon, 1954.

Nicholas, Karen S. "When Feudal Ideals Failed: Conflicts between Lords and Vassals in the Low Countries, 1127–1296." In *The Rusted Hauberk: Feudal Ideas of Order and Their Decline,* edited by Liam O. Purdon and Cindy L. Vitto, 201–26. Gainesville: University Press of Florida, 1994.

Nitecki, Alicia K. "The Sacred Elements of the Secular Feast in *Prima Pastorum.*" *Mediaevalia* 3 (1977): 229–37.

Oosterwijk, Sophie. "Of Mops and Puppets: The Ambiguous Use of the Word 'Mop' in the Towneley Shepherds' Plays." *Notes & Queries* 44 (1997): 169–71.

Owst, G. R. *Preaching in Medieval England*. Cambridge: Cambridge University Press, 1926.

Palmer, Barbara D. *The Early Art of the West Riding of Yorkshire*. Kalamazoo: Medieval Institute Publications, 1990.

———. "'Townelye Plays' or 'Wakefield Cycle' Revisited." *Comparative Drama* 21 (1987–88): 318–48.

Panofsky, Erwin. *Early Netherlandish Painting: Its Origins and Character*. 2 vols. Cambridge: Harvard University Press, 1953.

———. *Gothic Architecture and Scholasticism*. Latrobe, Pa.: Archabbey Press, 1951.

Parker, Roscoe E. "The Reputation of Herod in Early English Literature." *Speculum* 8 (1933): 59–67.

Parrott, T. M. "Mak and Archie Armstrong." *Modern Language Notes* 59 (1944): 297–304.

Passmore, J. B. *The English Plough*. Oxford: Oxford University Press, 1930.

Patterson, Lee. "Chaucer's Pardoner on the Couch: Psyche and Clio in Medieval Literary Studies." *Speculum* 76 (2001): 638–80.

———. *Negotiating the Past: The Historical Understanding of Medieval Literature*. Madison: University of Wisconsin Press, 1987.

Paull, Michael. "The Figure of Mahomet in the Towneley Cycle." *Comparative Drama* 6 (1972): 187–204.

Paxson, James J. "(Re)Facing Prosopopeia and Allegory in Contemporary Theory and Iconography." *Studies in Iconography* 22 (2001): 1–20.

———. "The Structure of Anachronism and the Middle English Mystery Plays." *Mediaevalia* 18 (1995 for 1992, guest coeditors, Martin Stevens and Milla Riggio): 321–40.

Perowne, Stuart. *The Life and Times of Herod the Great*. New York: Abingdon Press, 1959.

Pevsner, Sir Nikolaus. *Yorkshire: The West Riding.* 2d ed., revised by Enid Radcliffe. Harmondsworth: Penguin, 1967.

Pollack, Sir Frederick, and Frederic William Maitland. *The History of English Law Before the Time of Edward I.* 2d ed. 2 vols. Cambridge: The University Press, 1898.

Poole, Austin Lane. "Recreations." In *Medieval England,* rev. ed., 624–30. Oxford: Clarendon, 1958.

Poteet, Daniel P., II. "Time, Eternity, and Dramatic Form in *Ludus Coventriae* 'Passion Play I.'" In *The Drama of the Middle Ages,* edited by Clifford Davidson, C. J. Gianakaris, and John H. Stroupe, 232–48. New York: AMS Press, 1982.

Power, Eileen. *The Wool Trade in English Medieval History.* Oxford: Oxford University Press, 1941.

Prampolini, Giacomo. *L'Annunciazione nei pittori primitivi italiani.* Milano: U. Hoepli, 1939.

Prosser, Eleanor Alice. *Drama and Religion in the English Mystery Plays: A Reevaluation.* Stanford: Stanford University Press, 1961.

Purdon, Liam O. "Alys's Formulation of Intent—or Her Killing Us Softly with Her Siren Song." *In Parentheses: Papers in Medieval Studies* 1 (1999): 188–204.

———. "The Pardoner's Old Man and the Second Death." *Studies in Philology* 89 (1992): 334–49.

Reiss, Edmund. "The Symbolic Plow and Plowman and the Wakefield *Mactatio Abel.*" *Studies in Iconography* 5 (1979): 3–30.

Remly, Lynn. "*Deus Caritas:* The Christian Message of the *Secunda Pastorum.*" *Neuphilologische Mitteilungen* 72 (1971): 742–48.

Revard, Carter. "The Tow on Absalom's Distaff and the Punishment of Lechers in Medieval England." *English Language Notes* 17 (1980): 168–70.

Richardson, H. G. "The Medieval Plough-Team." *History,* n.s. 26 (1942): 287–96.

Rimmer, W. G. "The Evolution of Leeds." In *The Early Modern Town: A Reader,* edited by Peter Clark, 273–91. New York: Longman, 1976.

Roberts, Ian. "Another Parallel to the Mak Story?" *Notes & Queries* 15 (1968): 204–205.

Robertson, D. W., Jr. *A Preface to Chaucer: Studies in Medieval Perspectives.* Princeton: Princeton University Press, 1962.

———. "The Question of 'Typology' and the Wakefield *Mactatio Abel.*" *American Benedictine Review* 25 (1974): 157–73.

Robertson, D. W., Jr., and Bernard F. Huppé. *Piers Plowman and Scriptural Tradition.* Princeton: Princeton University Press, 1951.

Robinson, J. W. "'As Small as Flesh to Pot.'" *Folklore* 80 (1969): 197–98.

———. *Studies in Fifteenth-Century Stagecraft.* Kalamazoo: Medieval Institute Publications, 1991.

Rogerson, Margaret. "The Medieval Plough-Team on Stage." *Comparative Drama* 28 (1994): 182–200.

Roney, Lois. "The Wakefield First and Second Shepherds' Plays as Complements in Psychology and Parody." *Speculum* 58 (1983): 696–723.

Rosen, Edward. "The Invention of Eyeglasses." *Journal of the History of Medicine and Allied Sciences* 11 (1956): 13–46, 182–218.

Ross, Lawrence J. "Symbol and Structure in the *Secunda Pastorum*." *Comparative Drama* 1 (1967): 122–49.

Rossiter, A. P. *English Drama from Early Times to the Elizabethans: Its Background, Origins, and Development.* London: Hutchinson, 1950.

Rubin, Miri. *Corpus Christi: The Eucharist in Late Medieval Culture.* Cambridge: Cambridge University Press, 1991.

Russell, J. Stephen, ed. *Allegoresis: The Craft of Allegory in Medieval Literature.* New York: Garland, 1988.

———. "*Sub specie aeternitatis:* Time, Sequence, and Cycle in Medieval Popular Literature." *Medieval Perspectives* 3 (1988): 200–210.

Sachs, Arieh. "The Raven and the Dove: An Iconographic Comparison between the Holkham and Towneley Noahs." In *Studies in the Drama*, 199–206. London: Oxford University Press, 1967.

Salzman, L. F. *Mediaeval Byways.* Boston: Houghton Mifflin, 1913.

Sambursky, Samuel. *The Physical World of the Greeks.* Translated by Merton Dagut. London: Routledge & Paul, 1956.

Sanders, Barry. "Who's Afraid of Jesus Christ? Games in the *Coliphizacio*." *Comparative Drama* 2 (1968): 94–99.

Saul, Nigel. *Scenes from Provincial Life: Knightly Families in Sussex, 1280–1400.* Oxford: Clarendon, 1987.

Schell, Edgar. "Seeing Through a Glass Darkly: The Action Imitated by the *Secunda Pastorum*." *Modern Language Quarterly* 37 (1976): 3–14.

Schless, Howard H. "The Comic Element in the Wakefield *Noah*." In *Studies in Medieval Literature: In Honor of Professor Albert Croll Baugh*, edited by MacEdward Leach, 229–43. Philadelphia: University of Pennsylvania Press, 1961.

Schmidt, Gary D. "'Vides Festinare Pastores': The Medieval Artistic Vision of Shepherding and Manipulation of Cultural Expectation in the *Secunda Pastorum*." *Neophilologus* 76 (1992): 290–304.

Schücking, Levin L. *Character Problems in Shakespeare's Plays.* New York: Holt, 1922.

Seznec, Jean. *The Survival of the Pagan Gods.* Translated by Barbara F. Sessions. New York: Pantheon, 1953.

Shurgot, Michael W. "The *Puer Senex* Topos in the Wakefield *Secunda Pastorum*." *Papers on Language and Literature* 27 (1991): 419–29.

Sigsworth, Eric M. *Black Dyke Mills.* Liverpool: Liverpool University Press, 1958.

Simson, Otto Georg von. *The Gothic Cathedral.* New York: Pantheon, 1956.

Skey, Miriam Anne. "Herod the Great in Medieval European Drama." *Comparative Drama* 13 (1979–80): 330–64.

———. "The Iconography of Herod in the Fleury Playbook and the Visual Arts." *Comparative Drama* 17 (1983): 55–78.

Skiffington, Lloyd A. *The History of English Soliloquy: Aeschylus to Shakespeare.* Lanham, Md.: University Press of America, 1985.

Smith, John H. "Another Allusion to Costume in the Works of the 'Wakefield Master.'" *Publications of the Modern Language Association* 52 (1937): 901–2.

Smith, Sarah Stanbury. "'Game in Myn Hood': The Traditions of a Comic Proverb." *Studies in Iconography* 9 (1983): 1–12.

Smyser, H. M. "Analogues to the Mak Story." *Journal of American Folklore* 47 (1934): 378–80.

Speirs, John. *Medieval English Poetry: The Non-Chaucerian Tradition.* London: Faber and Faber, 1957.

Spek, Cornelis van der. *The Church and the Churchman in English Dramatic Literature before 1642.* Amsterdam: H. J. Paris, 1930.

Speyser, Suzanne. "Dramatic Illusion and Sacred Reality in the Towneley *Prima Pastorum.*" *Studies in Philology* 78 (1981): 1–19.

Staines, David. "To Out-Herod Herod: The Development of a Dramatic Character." *Comparative Drama* 10 (1976): 29–53.

Stearns, Mary. "Gyll as Mary and as Eve: Order and Disorder in the *Secunda Pastorum.*" *Fifteenth-Century Studies* 15 (1989): 295–304.

Steinberg, Clarence B. "*Kemp Towne* in the Towneley *Herod* Play: A Local Wakefield Allusion?" *Neuphilologische Mitteilungen* 71 (1970): 253–60.

Stemmler, Theo. "Typological Transfer in Liturgical Offices and Religious Plays of the Middle Ages." *Studies in Literary Imagination* 8 (1975): 123–43.

Stern, Henri. "Poésies et représentations carolingiens et byzantins des mois." *Revue archéologique* 46 (1955): 164–66.

Stevens, Martin. *Four Middle English Mystery Cycles: Textual, Contextual, and Critical Interpretations.* Princeton: Princeton University Press, 1987.

———. "Illusion and Reality in the Medieval Drama." *College English* 32 (1971): 448–64.

———. "Language as Theme in the Wakefield Plays." *Speculum* 52 (1977): 100–117.

Strauss, Jennifer. "Grace Enacted: The *Secunda Pastorum.*" *Paregone* 14 (1976): 63–68.

Stroup, Thomas B. "Analogues to the Mak Story." *Journal of American Folklore* 47 (1934): 380.

———. "Another Southern Analogue of the Mak Story." *Southern Folklore Quarterly* 3 (1939): 5–6.

Sturges, Robert S. "Spectacle and Self-Knowledge: The Authority of the Audience in the Mystery Plays." *South Central Review* 9 (1992): 27–48.

Sutherland, Sarah. "'Not or I See More Neede': The Wife of Noah in the Chester, York, and Towneley Cycles." In *Shakespeare and Dramatic Tradition,* edited by

W. R. Elton and William B. Long, 181–93. Newark: University of Delaware Press, 1989.

Swart, J. "The Insubstantial Pageant." *Neophilologus* 41 (1957): 127–41.

Sypher, Wylie. *Literature and Technology: The Alien Vision.* New York: Random House, 1968.

Taft, Edmund M. "Surprised by Love: The Dramatic Structure and Popular Appeal of the *Wakefield Second Shepherds' Pageant.*" *Journal of Popular Culture* 14 (1980): 131–40.

Thompson, F. J. "Unity in the *Second Shepherds' Play.*" *Modern Language Notes* 64 (1949): 302–6.

Thompson, James Westfall. *The Medieval Library.* Chicago: University of Chicago Press, 1939.

Thorndike, Lynn. *A History of Magic and Experimental Science.* 8 vols. New York: Macmillan, 1923–58.

Tierney, Brian. *Medieval Poor Law.* Berkeley and Los Angeles: University of California Press, 1959.

Tomlinson, Warren E. *Der Herodes-Charakter im englischen Drama.* Leipzig: Mayer & Müller, 1933.

Traver, H. "The Relation of Musical Terms in the Woodkirk Shepherds' Plays to the Dates of Their Composition." *Modern Language Notes* 20 (1905): 1–5.

Travis, Peter W. *Dramatic Design in the Chester Cycle.* Chicago: University of Chicago Press, 1982.

Trinkaus, Charles. "Renaissance Idea of the Dignity of Man." In *Dictionary of the History of Ideas,* edited by Philip P. Wiener, 4:136–47. New York: Scribner's, 1973.

Trusler, Margaret. "The Language of the Wakefield Playwright." *Studies in Philology* 33 (1936): 15–39.

Turnau, Irena. "The Diffusion of Knitting in Medieval Europe." In *Cloth and Clothing in Medieval Europe: Essays in Memory of Professor E. M. Carus-Wilson,* edited by N. B. Harte and K. G. Ponting, 368–89. London: Heineman, 1983.

Unger, Richard W. *The Art of Medieval Technology: Images of Noah the Shipbuilder.* New Brunswick, N.J.: Rutgers University Press, 1991.

Utley, Francis Lee. "The One Hundred and Three Names of Noah's Wife." *Speculum* 16 (1941): 426–52.

Valency, Maurice Jacques. *The Tragedies of Herod and Mariamne.* New York: Columbia University Press, 1940.

van Laan, Thomas F. *The Idiom of Drama.* Ithaca: Cornell University Press, 1970.

Vaughan, Mícáel F. "Mak and the Proportions of the *Second Shepherds' Play.*" *Papers on Language and Literature* 18 (1982): 355–67.

———. "The Three Advents in the *Secunda Pastorum.*" *Speculum* 55 (1980): 484–504.

———. "Tossing Mak Around." In *Approaches to Teaching Medieval English*

Drama, edited by Richard K. Emmerson, 146–50. New York: Modern Language Association, 1990.

Velz, John W. "Fox, Bull, and Lion in the Towneley *Coliphizacio.*" *Early Drama, Art and Music Review* 14 (1991): 1–10.

Walker, J. W. *Wakefield: Its History and People.* 2 vols. Wakefield: West Yorkshire Printing Co., 1934.

Wann, Louis. "The Influence of French Farce on the Towneley Cycle of Mystery Plays." *Transactions of the Wisconsin Academy of Sciences, Arts, and Letters* 19 (1918): 356–68.

Wasserman, Julian N. Afterword to *Allegoresis: The Craft of Allegory in Medieval Literature,* edited by J. Stephen Russell, 215–28. New York: Garland, 1988.

Wasserman, Julian N., and Liam O. Purdon. "Sir Guido and the Green Light: Confession in *Sir Gawain and the Green Knight* and *Inferno* XXVII." *Neophilologus* 84 (2000): 647–66.

Watson, Thomas Ramey. "The Wakefield *Noah.*" *Explicator* 40 (1982): 5–7.

Watt, Homer A. "The Dramatic Unity of the *Secunda Pastorum.*" In *Middle English Survey: Critical Essays,* edited by Edward Vasta, 271–82. Notre Dame, Ind.: University of Notre Dame Press, 1965.

Watt, William Montgomery. "Encounters with Medieval Europe." In *Muslim-Christian Encounters: Perceptions and Misperceptions,* 74–88. London: Routledge, 1991.

Webster, J. Carson. *The Labors of the Months in Antique and Medieval Art to the End of the Twelfth Century.* Evanston, Ill.: Northwestern University Press, 1938.

Weinberg, Julius. "Abstraction in the Formation of Concepts." In *Dictionary of the History of Ideas,* edited by Philip P. Weiner, 1:1–9. New York: Scribner's, 1968.

Wenzel, Siegfried. *The Sin of Sloth: Acedia in Medieval Thought and Literature.* Chapel Hill: University of North Carolina Press, 1967.

White, Lynn, Jr. *Machina ex deo: Essays in the Dynamism of Western Culture.* Cambridge: MIT Press, 1968.

———. *Medieval Religion and Technology: Collected Essays.* Berkeley and Los Angeles: University of California Press, 1978.

———. *Medieval Technology and Social Change.* Oxford: Clarendon, 1964.

Whiting, B. J. "An Analogue to the Mak Story." *Speculum* 7 (1932): 552.

Williams, Arnold. *The Characterization of Pilate in the Towneley Plays.* East Lansing: Michigan State College Press, 1950.

———. *The Drama of Medieval England.* East Lansing: Michigan State University Press, 1961.

Withington, Robert. "Braggart, Devil and 'Vice': A Note on the Development of Comic Characters in the Early English Drama." *Speculum* 11 (1936): 124–29.

———. "Mak, Op-Signorken, and Mr. Hardwick." *Notes & Queries* 194 (1949): 530–31.

———. "'Thre Brefes to a Long.'" *Modern Language Notes* 58 (1943): 115–16.

Woolf, Rosemary. *The English Mystery Plays.* Berkeley and Los Angeles: University of California Press, 1972.
Young, Karl. *The Drama of the Medieval Church.* 2 vols. Oxford: Clarendon, 1933.
Zumwalt, Eugene E. "Irony in the Towneley Shepherds' Plays." *Research Studies of the State College of Washington* 26 (1958): 37–58.

Index

Abel, 29, 31, 23; as voice of the divine will, 30; asked by Cain to participate in his tithing, 39; at tithing place, 37; being threatened, 40; expression of fear by, 36; request of, 36; silencing of, 30; steadfast thought of, 41; tithing prayer of, as procedural model, 37; tithing steadfastness of, 38
Aberration, 19
A. B. of Phisike Doctour, 251–52n.3, 260n.52
Abraham and Isaac, 2
Absolute compliance, 190
Adams, Robert, 252–53n.10
"Address to audience," 235n.78
Adoration, 98–99, 149
The Adoration of the Magi, 143
Advent season, 271–72n.16
Aesthetic distancing, 14
"Aesthetic imagination," 256n.24
Age of Renewal, 67
Agricultural cooperative, 6, 23, 35; ethos of, 30
Agricultural revolution, 6
Aikin, John, 229–30n.20, 231n.24
Alanus ab Insulis, 167
Alcohol, 240–41n.47
Ale of Healy, 75, 257n.28
All Saints, 4; tallest spire in Yorkshire, 105, 230n.20, 231n.25
Al-Farabi, *The Rise of the Sciences*, 232n.52
Alienation of audience, 169
Allegoresis, 15, 68, 191

Allegoria of abuse of "sovereigntée," 192–93
Allegoria of Christ's Trial and Buffeting in terms of judicial procedure, 199
Allegoria of the disavowal of the "inventive" speculative creaturely triune mind (rational soul), 171–76
Allegoria of the foppish layabout, 198
Allegoria of hermeneutical pastoral response, 84–85, 104
Allegoria of the "inventive" empirical creaturely triune mind, 119; *circumstantia* confronting, involving "ambiguous literal" in terms of calculated risk, 131; *circumstantia* confronting, involving "ambiguous literal" in terms of dream-vision, 128–29; *circumstantia* confronting, involving "ambiguous literal" in terms of direct performative contribution, 129–30; *circumstantia* confronting, involving "ambiguous literal" in terms of impersonation, 128–29; *circumstantia* confronting, involving "ambiguous literal" in terms of feigned fraternal solidarity, 132; *circumstantia* confronting, involving "ambiguous literal" in terms of Gyll, 132–33; *circumstantia* confronting, involving "ambiguous literal" in terms of Mak, 106–7, 124–25; distinguished from "inventive" speculative creaturely triune mind, 119, 267n.37; response of, engaging in *modus proferandi*, 150–51; response of, to "am-

biguous figurative," 140–44; response of, to "ambiguous literal," by disencumbering prejudice and senses, 141–42; response of, to "ambiguous literal," by deconstructing illusion, 142–43; response of, to "ambiguous literal," evidencing prejudicial purblindness, 139–40; response of, to "ambiguous literal," using dream-vision authority, 135–36; response of, to "ambiguous literal," using assumption-based conclusion (hypothesis), 136–37; response of, to "ambiguous literal," using artful indirection, 137–39; response of, to Annunciation, 145–48; response of, to "unknown figurative" of Mak's "mak-ness" in terms of yeomanry, 121–22; response of, to "unknown figurative" of Mak's "mak-ness" through knowledge of the thing, 123–24; response of, to "unknown figurative" of Mak's "mak-ness" through *modus interpretandi*, 121; response of, to "unknown figurative" of Mak's "mak-ness" through sense of hearing, 120; response of, to "unknown figurative" of Mak's "mak-ness" through sense of sight, 120–21; response of, to "unknown literal" of Mak's faulty reasoning, 120; response of, to "unknown literal" of Mak's invoking of the Rabbinical tradition, 119–20

Allegoria of the "inventive" speculative creaturely triune mind, 83; the degradation of, 153; the divine faculties of, 83; as "Image of God," 84; intellect of acting upon volition, as in *modus proferandi*, 96–101; memory of acting upon intellect, 84; memory of acting upon intellect, in addressing the "ambiguous literal," 88–91; memory of acting upon intellect, in addressing the "unknown figurative," 87–88; memory of acting upon intellect, in addressing the "unknown literal," using a *disputatio* methodology, 85–86; no *phantasmata* of, 84; ready for intellectual and volitional rigor, 84; volition of, acting upon intellect, in addressing the "ambiguous figurative," 91–96; as "La Voix de l'Église," 261n.59

Allegoria of perverse "mastry," 193–96

Allegoria of repudiation of the eschatology of labor, in terms of the abuse of judicial procedure, 207–23; in terms of Pilate's actions, 191–96; in terms of Tutivillus's actions, 196–99

Allegoria of the "uninventive" empirical creaturely triune mind, 104–5; condition of passivity in, 105–6, 113; condition of passivity associated with marriage in, 110–11; feature of memory of unpleasant sensation in, 105; feature of *phantasma* in, 107–9; feature of *phantasma* of abuse of purveyance in, 108; feature of *phantasma* of coercion and absurdity in, 107–8; feature of *phantasma* of defiance in, 116–17; feature of *phantasma* of suffering in, 116; feature of *phantasma* of "yong-men" in, 11–12; feature of role playing of "gentlery-men" in, 115–16; feature of sensation in, 113–14; feature of undoing the *phantasma* of defiance in, 117–18; feature of unpleasant sensation in, 109–10

Allegoria of the "uninventive" speculative creaturely triune mind, 69; actions of torturers demonstrative of, 201; condition of lethargy in, 71–72; condition of passivity in, 70; condition of passivity as expressed through language in, 71; function of memory in, 72–76; memory in, as means of requital, 75–76; memory of Jak Copé in, 72–73; *phantasmata* of, 77–83

Allegoria of the wrathful impious mind, 155; debasement of the rational soul in, 183–90; debasement through loss of reason, 167–68; debasement through memory, 157–60; debasement through volitional errancy, 160–67; vitiation of innocence in, through degradation of memory, 179–80; vitiation of innocence in, through degradation of reason, 180–85; vitiation of innocence in, through degradation of will, 176–79

Allen, John, 231
"Alod," 52
"Allodium," 246n.17
Alopicia, 280n.63
Ambrose, Saint, *De Cain et Abel*, 236
Anachronism, ix, 2–9, 47, 68, 169
Analogy, function of, 149
Anderson, J. J., 242n.58, 258
Angelic song, 262n.85
Anglicization, 2
Animal organics, 149
Annas, 20, 194, 210–15, 222
Annunciacio, 273–4n.43
Annunciation, 90, 94, 96, 98, 145–46, 261n.60, 262n.84, 273–74n.43
Anointing, 245n.11
Anthropogony, 244n.6
Antichrist, 152, 267n.34, 268n.47, 271n.2, 271n.5
Anti-Semitism, 3, 207
"Anti-swynke," 196
Antonius de Monte Ulmi, *De occultis et manifestis*, 126
Apuleius, 167
Aquinas, Saint Thomas, 172
Archery, 33
Aristotle, 12, 14, 250–51n.51; *De Anima* and *Physica*, 268n.51; discussion of comedy, 262n.82 *Poetics*, 269–70n.68
Ark, 49, 248n.37, 275n.8; construction of, 60–62; door of, 49; hull, waterproofing of, 49; proper use of postponed, 57; purpose of, 57; seaworthiness of, 50; seven-day construction deadline of, 50; unrealized potentiality of, 54
Armor of God, 226
Artful philosopher, 259n.46
Artistic difference, 95
Artistic sermon, 186
Ascencio Domini, 275
Ashley, Kathleen M., 270n.69
Ataraxia, 160
Athanasian Creed, 270n.77
Audience, Corpus Christi: as community, 20; as daemonic cohort, 187–90; heterogeneity of, 264n.4; as "knavys," 190; as Magi, 165, 173

Augustine, Saint, Bishop of Hippo, 14, 68; *City of God*, 271; *De doctrina christiana*, 14, 68, 83–85, 91, 119, 123, 140–41, 143, 175, 202, 208, 234n.66, 258n.37, 261–2, 267n.31, 268n.43, 269, 273n.34, 274, 278n.36, 279; *De Musica*, 68, 254n.14, 260, 271n.8; *De Trinitate*, 68, 84, 265n.10, 266n.29; "Letter to Nebridius," 68; on the mind, 252n.6; on style, 98–99, 263n.90, 263n.92; on the Trinitarian soul, 67
Augustinians, 258n.38
Aurelius, 259n.46
Avian search modality, 125
Axiality, directional, 64–65
Axiom of the age, 5
Axton, Richard, 237n.10, 260n.51
Ayalon, David, 240n.47

Baby killing, 176
Bacon, Roger, *De secretis operibus*, 233n.56
Barabbas, 194
Bare feet, 275n.8
"Barnard, Seynt," 12
Barney, Stephen A., 237n.10
Bartlett, J. M., 229–30n.20
Bathos, 169
Baugh, Albert C., 257n.30, 263
Beauty, medieval doctrine of, 13
Bedtime prayer, 77–78
Beethoven, Ludwig von, Fifth Symphony, 270n.72
Beggary, 36
Bellifortis (Keyser), 278n.34
Benedictines, 258n.38
Bennett, H. S., 242n.68
Benson, Larry D., 229n.18
Bernbrock, John E., 236n.2, 241n.54
Besserman, Lawrence L., 246n.17
Bestul, Thomas, 227–28n.3
Bethlehem, 69, 147, 174–75, 254n.11
Bevington, David, 243–4n.4, 278n.31
Bible Moralisée, 8
Binary structure, 264n.5
Birth, 269n.64. *See also* Childbirth
Black Death, 106
Blanch, Robert J., 263n.94, 270

Blazing star, 98
Blindfold, 216
Bloch, Marc, 265n.16
Blunt, A., 232
"Bob of cherys," 149
Boccaccio, *Des cas des Nobles Hommes et Femmes*, 8
Boethius, Ancius Manlius Severinus, *The Consolation of Philosophy*, 37, 241n.56
Bolton Priory, 4
Bonnel, John K., 236n.2, 239n.36
Bonneval, Abbot Arnold of, 9, 232n.47
Books, 273n.29
Book culture, 273n.35
Book of the Duchess (Chaucer), 240n.39
Booke of Nurture (Russell), 74
Boone, Blair W., 235n.1, 241n.48, 241n.52, 242n.62, 242n.63, 243n.73
"Borrowing," 127
Bottle, 263n.94
Brandeis, Arthur, 276
Breath, as image of *tertium quid*, 167, 188; as analogy of spirit, 273n.30. See *tertium quid* Breathlessness, as image of loss of divine inspiration, 167; physiological dimension of frenzy, 166
Bribe, 222
Bridge Chapel, 240n.43
Briquet, C.-M., 240n.47
British Library. Add. Ms. 42130, fol. 170, 238n.18
Britton, G. C., 246n.21
Broadcloth, 4
Brockman, Bennett A., 235n.1, 236n.3, 237n.9, 239n.27, 239n.29, 239n.37, 242n.60, 242n.61, 242n.67
Brown, Carleton, 278n.38
Buffeting, 20, 199, 215–16; as game, 218–20; as *peine forte et dure*, 215–18; as *peine ni forte ni dure*, 219–20
Bullogh, Edward, 235n.78
Burning Bush, 89
Byzantium, 6

Cady, Frank W., 227–28n.3, 229
Caesar, Julius, 2, 196
Caiaphas, 19, 194, 205, 207–11, 213–15, 222–23; condemning Christ peremptorily, 209; as de facto torturer, 207
Cain, 21; abuse of innovation, 30, 37; abuse of linguistic act, 31; abuse of tithing prayer, 38, 41; acquisitiveness of, 40, 43, 242; "amend," 30; anger and wrath of, 28, 236n.3; argument against tithing, 35–36; bad "entent" of, 39, 44; belligerence of, 40; cost-benefit analysis of, 35–36, 57; cost-benefit argument of, 34–35; counting repetions of, 41; crisis of spiritual ecology of, 44; curse of, 32, 240n.42; defiance of, 40; defiance as skill of, 41; *duritia cordis* of, 38, 44; "entent" of, 38; dissatisfaction of, 240n.45; estrangement of, 30; exploitiveness of, 18; false husbandry of, 43; the farthing of, 34–35; found in arrears, 44; God's judgment of, 32–33; illusion of distance of, 31; improper care of plow-team of, 24–25; improper plow maintenance of, 25; ineffectuality of, 23; innovative accounting strategy of, 33; inventive lingual/physical and lingual abuse, 31–32; lack of conscience of, 39; malice prepense of, 28; "mastry," as an abuse of, 30–33; materialism of, 36, 241n.52, 242n.63; methexis of direct discourse, use of, 30; mixed plow-team of, 239n.21; modification of obedience of, 39–40; obdurate wilfulness of, 38, 242n.60; obscenities of, 44; parody of good plowman, 238n.17, 242n.61; perennial, 44–45, 243n.74; profit incentive of, 36; as protective sign, 32; pudding-in-the-pot remark of, 2; ranting of, 237n.9; relationships of, 237n.14; as satanic figure, 39; "sawe" of, 33; skill of, 42–43; stewardship of, at annual audit, 42; "thrafe" of, 41, 242n.66; tithing hypothetical of, 39; use of vigesimal arithmetic progression, 41; voice of, 22
Cain and Abel: improper master/servant relationship between, 23
Calculator, 144. See also Swineshead, Richard
Calculationes (Swineshead), 144
Calendar: illustrated, 6; lunar, 2

Camille, Michael, ix, 227, 238n.18
Campbell, Josie P., 243, 245n.7, 245n.10, 245n.12, 246n.21, 247, 248n.33, 248n.34, 249n.38, 250, 256n.24, 267n.34, 268n.50
Campbell, Thomas P., 260n.57, 271n.2, 271–72n.16
Cannibalism, 134
Cantelupe, Eugene, and Richard Griffith, 263n.94, 263n.95, 264n.4
Canvas, 270n.69
Canvas toss, 144–45, 270n.69
Carey, Millicent, 227–28n.3, 235n.1, 236n.2, 240n.45, 246n.22, 250n.47, 255n.23, 256n.24, 261n.66
Cargill, Oscar, 229
Carmelites, 258n.38
Carpenter, Nan C., 94, 262, 264n.5
Car, medieval, 233n.56
Carr, Sherwyn T., 270n.75
Carus-Wilson, E. M., 229–30n.20, 231n.22
Castration, 278n.34
Cataclysm, 52
Cattle plagues, 106
Causation, 272n.23
Cawley, A. C., 229, 229–30n.20, 242n.66, 247n.29, 248n.30, 255n.23, 256n.24, 257, 258, 260n.50, 276n.11; and Martin Stevens, 236n.5
Censure, 196
Centrosymmetry, cosmological, 65
Chalcidius, 6, 167. *See also* Timaeus
Chambers, Sir E. K., 103, 229–30n.20, 263, 270n.69
Chance, 50, 162. *See also* Fortune
Changeling, 143
Character-soliloquy, 266n.21
Character symmetry, 206
Charity, 13–14, 140
Chaucer, Geoffrey, 43, 81, 11–12, 252n.9, 254; *Book of the Duchess*, 240n.39; *Franklin's Tale*, 259n.46; *Merchant's Tale*, 254n.13; *Miller's Tale*, 254n.13; the Pardoner, 271n.7; Reeve Osewold, 43; *Romaunt of the Rose*, 240n.39; *Troilus and Criseyde*, 240n.39; *Wife of Bath's Prologue*, 111–12

Chenu, M.-D., 231n.28, 232
Cherry Tree motif, 270n.74
Chester cycle, 256n.24
Chester playwrights, 251n.1
Chidamian, Claude, 270n.69
Childbearing, suffering of, 110
Childbirth, 270n.69
Chimney, 240–41n.47
"Choreic figure," 260n.51
Christ, Jesus, 3, 194–96, 199–223, 262n.72; barefoot, 275n.8; as child, 69, 158; curse of, 217, 219; examining of, 207; "Gentile" version of trial of, 200; "Jewish" version of trial of, 200; as "Kyng Copyn," 209; as "lurdan ledyr," 194; public ministry of, 205; only words of, 213; as a tall man, 220; trial of, 199
Christ and the Doctors, 154
Christmas season, 252n.8
Cipolla, Carlo M., 233n.56
Cistercians, 258n.38
City of God (Saint Augustine), 271
City of God in the world, 226
Civic pride, 228n.12
Clairvaux, 9
Clarification, 154, 273n.41. *See also* Gothic
Clark, E. M., 268
Clein, Wendy, 154, 271, 272n.19, 274n.48
Cleland, John H., 264n.4
Clichés, 254n.38
Clock, 233n.56. *See also* Horologium
Clopper, Lawrence M., 275n.9, 278n.44
Cloth manufacturing, 229–30n.20
Cluniacs, 258n.38
Cock, 266n.19
Cock-throwing, 218, 279n.60
Coliphizacio, x, 15, 19, 119, 191, 194, 199–223; modified placement of, 200; structure of, 199, 277n.29
Coll (Primus Pastor), 105–9, 268n.53, 270n.69; assuming role of "gentleryman," 115; bereft of voice, 108; coercing Daw, 117; coldness of, 105; concluding need to travel, 146; demanding proof, 148; dullness of, 105; emphasis upon sentiency, 148; giving of, 149; having to be toady, 108; identifying source of coer-

cion, 107; interrogating Mak, 122–24; loss of will, 106; lying next to Mak, 124; sources of, 199, 276–7n.26; napping, 105; oppression of, 107; passivity of, 106; prejudging Mak, 139; questioning strange sound, 120; remarking child's deformities, 141; remarking qualities of mind, 147–48; threat of vengeance from, 143; voice of, 136–37

Collaborative spirit, 47; as new social order, 62; collective experience of, 65; experiencing of, through communication, 65; labor as dramatic expression of, 62–64; lack of, 57–59; like good "entent" and steadfast thought, 249n.42; loss of, 53; social order of family in, 62–63; transformative effect of, 62, 64–65

Collins, Fletcher, Jr., 270
Comedy, 246n.19
Comic decorum, 157
Commercium, 37
Community, 20, 226, 235n.81
Compass, 8
Compliance, social, 107
Compotus, 38, 41–43, 242n.59, 242n.68
Computus, 14, 37; distinguished from *compotus*, 38
Concordantia, 37, 50, 69, 104; as *discordantia*, 168; modified form of, 167. See also Gothic
Confessor manuals, 12
Confusion, agricultural, 25
Consecrated Host, 235n.80
The Consolation of Philosophy (Boethius), 38
Conspiracio, x, 191, 192, 193, 200, 201, 206, 275
Constitutio Criminalis Carolina, 278n.34, 278–79n.45
Consultant scholars, 159, 166–7
Consultus, Primus and *Secundus*, 194
Contamine, Philippe, 240–1n.47, 278
Contemptus mundi, 113
Cook, A. S., 263
Cooper, Helen, 260n.50
Cooperation, 23, 47; as communication, 48; dedication fundamental to, 60; following guidelines of, 60; image of, in shipbuilding, 248n.35; spirit of, 18

Cooperative farming, 6
Copeland, Rita, 234, 235, 252n.6, 262, 272
Correctorium alchimiae or *Correctio fatuorum* (Robert of York), 267n.36
Corruption, 19
Coseby, Robert C., 263
Cosmogony, 244n.6
Coulton, G. G., 265n.16
Coverdale, Miles, 262n.72
Cover-up, 26–27; 236n.5
Cradle, 268n.53
Craig, Hardin, 234n.70
Crane, medieval, 233n.56
Creation, *ex nihilo*, 270n.77
Creation, the Cornish, 236n.2
Creative role-playing, 267n.34
Creator's omnipotence, 263n.94
Crêche, 252n.8
Criminal evidence, 212
Crosby, Bing, 75
Crossbowmen, 240–41n.47
Crowther, J. D. W., 241
Crucifixion, 162, 193, 203, 216
Cupidity, 13, 14
Curry, Walter Clyde, 248n.30
Cursor Mundi, 236n.2, 260n.54
Curtius, Ernst Robert, 231n.29
Cutts, John P., 262, 270

Damhouder, *Praxis Rerum Criminalis*, 278n.34
Daniels, Richard J., 46, 243n.3, 247n.24
Dante Alighieri, *Inferno*, 187
David, Alfred, 249–50n.43
David, King, 87–8
Davidson, Clifford, 227–28n.3, 228n.14, 238n.16, 238n.20, 248–49n.37, 272n.23, 276n.20, 279
Daw (Tercius Pastor), 16, 113–18; assumption of, 136; calling Mak, 123; charity of, 141; conclusion of, 137; *contemptus mundi* of, 113; dismissal of, 118; on "eere marke," 143; empty handed, 139; exploitive servitude of, 117; flight of, 114; frustration of, 142; hunger pangs of,

116; identifying Mak and Gyll as thieves, 136; "in dowte," 114; inquiring about Mak's whereabouts, 135; insisting Mak be close, 124; interrogating Mak, 124; memory of, 146; as one who raves, 115; opportunism of, 147; passivity of, 113; on *phantasma*, 114; ready to accuse, 135; relationship to Noah, 113, 266n.27; remembering angelic song, 146; request for food, 115; seeing Mak, 137; sensation of, 113; silencing of, 117; sixpence of, 148; "sodan syght" of, 114; threat of, 116–7; tropological change in, 269n.64; "trouth" of, 116; wisdom of, 266n.26

Daydreaming, 82
Dead reckoning, 97. *See also* Navigation
Dead soul, 153. *See* Soul
Death, paradox of undying, 51
de Bruyn, Lucy, 247
De Cain et Abel (Saint Ambrose), 236
Deceit, idea of, 265n.9
De diversis artibus (Theophilus), 8, 9, 60, 232, 249
De doctrina christiana (Saint Augustine), 14, 68, 83–85, 91, 119, 123, 140–41, 143, 175, 202, 208, 234n.66, 258.37, 261–62, 267n.31, 268n.43, 269, 273n.34, 274, 278n.76, 279
De Grammatica (Hugh of St. Victor), 10
"Delightful thought," 259n.43
Delusion, 158
De Lyff of Adam and Eue, 236
De Musica (Saint Augustine), 68, 254n.14, 260, 271n.8
De occultis et manifestis (Antonius de Monte Ulmi), 126
Demographic changes, 106
Des cas des Nobles Hommes et Femmes (Boccaccio), 8
Descriptio positionis, 232
De secretis operibus, 233n.56
Despair, 259n.46
Þe *Desputisoun bitwen þe Bodi and þe Soule* (Linow), 255
De Trinitate (Saint Augustine), 68, 84, 265n.10, 266n.29
Devils, 3

de Warrenne, seventh earl, 231n.27, 258n.38
Dice, 50
Didascalicon, 10, 84
Diller, Hans-Jürgen, 235n.78, 251n.1, 252n.8, 277n.30
"Ding," 164
Diminished or enfeebled spirit, 70, 119, 254n.14
Diocesan Court of High Commission, 229n.18
Disciplina clericalis (Peter Alfonso), 232–33n.52
Discordantia, 168. *See also Disputatio*, defective form of
Disinformation, 27
Disputatio: defective form of, 17; debasement of the form of, 170; methodology of, 85, 253n.11
Disputationes de quolibet, 168
"Distance limit," 235n.78. *See also* "Psychical objectivity"
Divine will, 30
Divinity, 267n.37
Dobson, R. B., 229
Doctrine of redemption, 270n.77
Doll. *See* Puppet
Domesday Book, 230n.21
Domination, idea of, 265n.9
Dominicans, 258n.38
Dominium regale, 271
Doob, Penelope B. R., 273
Dove, 275n.8
Drama, spatiotemporal dimension of, 238n.16
Dramatic anachronism, 2–3
Dramatic diptych, 264n.5
Dramatic irony, 134, 153, 170, 237–38n.15
Dream-vision, 128–29
Drinking prayer, 75
Dullness, 73
Dunn, E. Catherine, 87, 259n.48, 261n.59, 261n.60, 261n.66, 280
Durham, 269–70n.68
Duritia cordis, 189
Dutka, Joanna, 94, 95, 262, 267
Dyer, Christopher, 242n.68
Dvořák, Max, 233n.57

Eadiwi Gospel Book, Winchester, 8
Eaton, H. A., 251–52n.3, 260
Eco, Umberto, 262n.82
Ecological crisis, 44
Edminster, Warren, 235
Edward II, King of England, 231
Edward III, King of England, 33; 276n.14
"Eere-marke," 143
Eliade, Mircea, 231n.29, 244n.6
Elijah, 257n.28
Eliot, T. S., 166
Elliott, Charles, 274
England, George, and Alfred W. Pollard, 227, 229
Empirical temper of the Middle Ages, 69, 252n.8
Empty-sack exemplum, 72, 73, 76
Enjoyment, incorrect, 21
Epitome (Hugh of St. Victor), 10
Epochal time frame of plays, 15, 234n.72
Erbe, Theodor, 276
Errancy, volitional, 17. *See also* Will, disordered
Erythraean Sibyl, 88
Eschatology of labor, repudiation of, 19
Esper, Thomas, 240–41n.47
Estrangement, spiritual, 120
Eucharist, 270n.77
Eucharist, farcical treatment of, 256n.24, 258n.34
Evitt, Regula Meyer, 270
Executions, 272n.25
Experimentation, 250–51n.51
Evans, Ruth, 247
Eye of mind, 273n.34
Eye of the spirit, 252n.8
Eyeglasses, 233n.56, 240–41n.47

Fabliau, 246n.18
Fairs, 5
False messiah, 267n.34
False witness, 194, 208
Famine, 255n.19, 255n.21
Father, figure of, 99
Fatigue, 124
Fear, 114, 266n.29, 269–70n.68
Feast of Fools, 255n. 23

Feet, image of bare, 266n.18
Feminine, 269n.57; calendrical valorization of, 250n.47
Ferguson, Kenneth L., 238n.19
Feudal host, 176
Feudal reciprocity, degradation of, 184
Field rotation, 35
Fifth Symphony (Beethoven), 270n.72
Figural and personification allegory, dramatization of, 68
Fiondella, Maris, 269n.56
Fiorelli, Pièro, 279
Flagellacio, x, 191, 194, 200, 275
Fleta, 238–39n.21
Flood, the, 228n.4. *See also* Cataclysm
Flower, 273–74n.43
Flying machines, medieval, 233n.56
Fools of Gotham, 83, 251–52n.3, 260n.52
Forbes, R. J., 232
Forges, 4. *See also* Furnaces
Foster, Frances A., 229n.15
Forrester, Jean, 229
Fortune, 155. *See also* Chance
Fountains Abbey, 4
Fourth Virgilian Messianic Eclogue, 91. *See also* Messianic Eclogue
Fowler, David C., 229n.15
Fra Giordano of Pisa, 233n.56
Frampton, Mendel G., 229–30n.20, 274
Franciscans, 258n.38
Franklin's Tale (Chaucer), 259n.46
Fratricide, 27; as abuse of invention, 29
Friars' Latin, 92
Friendship, 47, 145, 248–49n.37
Froward, 119, 206, 216–18, 220, 222, 279n.59; as de facto torturer, 222; as foil, 219; as officiating participant, 221
Fugacio Iosep et marie in egiptum, 17, 154, 275
Fulling mills, 4
Furnaces, 243n.73. *See also* Forges
Furnish, Shearle, 256n.24, 266n.21, 267n.30, 271, 273, 280n.64

Gallimaufry, 74, 256–57n.24
Games and sporting activities, 240–41n.47
Ganshof, F. L., 276

Garcio, 22; accessory after the fact, 26, 239n.27, 239n.31; compared to Uxor and Noe in their interludes, 54; faulty plowing of, 26; as folk-play presenter, 237n.9; as impudent servant, 237n.14; induction proclamation of, 22; legal jeopardy of, 26; the pardon of, 26–27; as parody of herald, 237n.8

Gardner, John, 229–30n.20, 236n.3, 237n.14, 239n.32, 241n.54, 242n.63, 243, 245, 246n.19, 246n.22, 248n.31, 256, 259n.45, 260n.51, 262n.81, 263n.95, 264, 265n.9, 268n.44, 269, 271, 272, 274n.49

Garvin, Katherine, 246–47n.22

Gayley, Charles Mills, 227, 229, 244n.5, 246n.18

"Gentlery-men," 106–7, 122, 265n.16; enacted, 112–13; *phantasma* of, 108

Gerould, G. H., 259

Gethsemane, 204

Gift giving, 98, 99–100, 263n.94, 149–50, 270n.74, 271n.78

Gilbert de la Porrée, *Notae super Johannem secundum magistrum Gilbertum*, 5

Gillmeister, Heiner, 271

Gimpel, Jean, 231–32, 240n.43, 243n.72

Gloria, 94, 95, 118, 145

Glossa Ordinaria (Walafrid Strabo), 275n.6

Gloves, 265n.11, 266n.18

Gluttony, 247n.23

God: blessing of, 48; degradation of the image of, 17; descent of, 245n.7; as friend, 47, 145; great work of, 5; as "Hob," 31; justification for destruction of creation, 52; as master craftsman, 8, 38, 232n.42, 232n.43; monologue of, 48–49; saving space through the preservation of time, 60; saving time through the preservation of space, 49; as sole author, 5

Godhead, 150

Golden Age, new, 93

Goodchild, John, 229

Goodybower, 240n.43

Gordon, James, and Joseph Hunter, 227

"Gossyppys," 140

Gothic, 11, 12, 69, 233–34n.57, 250n.49, 252n.8, 257–58n.32

Governance, divine, 5

Grace, 18, 65–66; absence of, 188–90

Grand Trunk (A1), 4

Gregorius Magnus, Saint, Pope, 271n.5

"Grotesque Feast," 73, 77, 118, 140, 255n.19; pagan source of, 256–57n.24

Ground-meal-sack exemplum. *See* Empty-sack exemplum

"Gudeboure," 32, 240n.43. *See also* Goodybower

Guido da Montefeltro, 187

Guild regulations, 256n.24

Guilfoyle, Cherrell M., 239n.36, 240n.43, 270

Guillaume de Lorris and Jean de Meun, *Romance of the Rose*, 80, 259n.43

Guilmartin, John Francis, Jr., 240–41n.47

Gun, 240–41n.47

Gyb (Primus Pastor), 16, 254n.18, 259n.46; alluding to story of children of Judah, 88–89; assumption about child, 87; assumptive doubt of, 89; a bellwether fool, 72; bereft of "wyttys," 73; congratulating John, 76; contribution to feast, 74; corrective refutation of, 92; declaiming, 76; denouncing of menu, 75; desire to drink, 74; despairing words of, 71; dullness of, 70; encouraging Slawpase, 95; explanations of, 87; exposition on, 93; fear of, 85; gift of, 99; on Golden Age, 93; on "gramery," 75; greeting child, 99; indolence of, 70; initial response to angelic song, 85; irony of, 76; Jack Copé reference made by, 72; lack of mental acuity, 73; lack of perspicacity, 71; language of feudatory rank, 98; litany of woe, 72; lost imaginary flock of, 71; on "Saturne," 93; on stylistic feature of angelic song, 94; outfoxing Slawpase, 75–76; overcoming doubt, 90; ovine *phantasma* of, 78–81, 83; passivity of, 71; prophetic affirmation of "Greatt meruell," 91; quarreling of, 78; ready to gamble, 71; recognition of value of faith, 90; remembrance of unhappiness of, 72–74; response to acoustical dimension of experience, 86; sedentary condition of, 71; subdued style of, 99; surmise of, 89; threat made by, 95; typological interpretation made by, 89; wanting to see child, 87; with John, 73

Gyb (Secundus Pastor), 109–15; apology of, 132; assuming role of "gentlery-men," 115; bleak marital situation of, 112; complaint of, concerning "sely wedmen," 110; denunciation of marriage, 111; dismissing Daw's complaint, 117–18; examining infant, 139; examining song, 146; fabulous notion of, 112; frozen feet of, 109; giving gift, 149; "hee frawde," 132; identifying likeness of infant to lost sheep, 141; identifying Mak, 121; identifying Mak and Gyll as culprits, 137; on "imaginacioun," 112; labeling Daw, 115; lack of "divine" intellect, 109; learning to "abyde," 110; marriage as incarceration, 110; memory of sensation, 109; on polygamy, 111; passivity of, 110; putting down Daw, 117; remembering angel spoke of God's son, 146; reminding brethren of Mak's reputation, 123; reminding brethren to go to Bethlehem, 147; response to Mak's impersonation, 122; sleeping near Mak, 124; suffering of, 110; threat made by, 123

Gyll, 123; "bowrde" of, 128; cannibalism of, 134; chastised by Mak, 131; disguise of sheep by, 133; exclamations of, 133–34; as false Madonna, 142–43; found out, 144; identified as thief, 136, 138; impersonation, 131; innocence maintained by, 142; Mak instructed by, 129; Mak known in terms of, 123; "mayllease" of, 130; postparturiency of, 131; rejoinder of, 134; reluctance to open door, 127; victim of changeling, 143

Halifax gibbet, 106
Hamelius, Paul, 237n.9
Hanging, 28–29, 170
Hanks, Dorrel T, Jr., 236, 237n.14, 239n.23, 240n.45
Happé, P., 237n9

Harangue, 274n.56
Hardison, O. B., Jr., 235n.80
Harrison, H. S., 239, 248n.37
Harrowing of Hell motif, 267n.36
Hartley, Dorothy, and Margaret M. Elliot, 229–30n.20, 237–38n.15, 242n.65
Hartnett, Edith, 236n.3, 237n.9, 240n.42, 240n.45, 241, 242n.63, 243
Haskins, Charles Homer, 233
Hassall, William Owen, *Holkham Bible Picture Book,* 232n.43, 238n.18, 265n.11, 266n.18, 275n.8
Hattinger, Franz, 232n.33
Healy, 257n.28
Heaton, Herbert, 229–30n.20
"Hee frawde," 142
Hegge Play of Abel, 236
Hell, 243n.70
Hell's mouth, 8
Hen, 266n.19
Helterman, Jeffrey, 152, 228n.13, 229, 236n.3, 237n.9, 237n.14, 238n.17, 239n.31, 240, 241n.48, 241n.54, 242n.63, 242n.64, 243n.2, 244n.5, 245n.12, 246n.18, 246n.20, 247n.23, 247n.29, 248n.31, 250n.44, 255n.21, 256n.24, 257n.28, 258n.35, 259–60n.49, 260n.51, 260n.52, 260n.54, 261n.67, 263n.94, 267n.34, 270n.69, 271, 274n.48, 274n.56, 277n.27, 279n.52, 279n.55
Hemingway, Samuel B., 255n.23, 267n.38
Hennequin, M. Wendy, 273n.37
Henry III, King of England, 231n.27
Henry IV, King of England, 229–30n.20, 276n.14
Henry V, King of England, 276n.14
Henry VI, King of England, 276n.14
Herald, 236–37n.8
Heraldry, 180
Herebert, Friar William, 203
Herod, 17, 235n.78; Antipas, absence of, 271n.1; Ascalonita, 152; audacity of, 187; culpable brutality of, 183; exemplum of wrath and ire, 154, 271–72n.16; as feudal leader, 160–61; inability to engage in analysis by examination or separation, 170–71; lack of self-knowledge, 172; lar-

gesse of, 186; mind of, 159; ridicule of soldiers by, 184; self-deception of, 188; shoes of, 275n.8; soliloquy of, 187; the three, 152; tragedy of, 189; un-demotic French of, 165

"Herodification," 200, 208, 210

Hey, David, 229–30n.20, 230–31n.21, 231, 265n.13, 265n.14

High Gothic, stylistic principles of, 105

High style, 98–99

Hill, Edmund, and John E. Rotelle, 260

Hinge, 268n.50

Hipperholme, 4

Hirsh, John C., 270n.69

Hirshberg, Jeffrey Alan, 243, 247n.29, 249n.41, 249–50n.43, 250n.50

History: inability to alter course of, 182; making of, ix; preparing for end of, 271–72n.16

Hodges, Laura, 247, 247–48n.29, 249–50n.43, 280n.63

Holkham Bible Picture Book (Hassall), 8, 238–39n.21, 243n.2

Holt, Richard, 230–31n.21

Holthausen, F., 266n.20

Holy Spirit, 99, 153

"Holy Vyrgynyté," 89

Homage, 2, 154, 194, 196

Homer, 174

Homiletic tradition, 276n.25

Homo artifex, 6, 8

Homo faber, 231n.29

Hope, Bob, 75

Horn, John [Iohn Horne] (Secundus Pastor), 16; accosting Gyb, 71; adoration of child, 99; ale cup of, 75; analytical process of, 94; civility of, 95; clarifying angelic message's import, 85–86; complaint of, 70–71; complimenting Slawpase, 96; conclusion of, 87; contemptuous jibe of, 95; contribution to feast, 74; corrective refutation of, 85; declaiming against brawling, 76; denunciation of Latin, 92; desiring drink, 74; duping Slawpase, 75–76; encouraging others to take heed, 87; explaining *unknown* sign, 86; fear of, 85; figural interpretation of, 89; gift-giving, 99; humiliation of, 76; identifying angelic voice as that of a man, 85; identifying infant as part of tradition, 97; identifying proof of miracle; indolence of, 71; lack of mental acuity, 73; obscenity of, 92; offering modified *Processus Prophetarum*, 90; participating in ovine *phantasma*, 79–82; praising superficially, 73; praying to God, 71; quarreling, 78; quoting Isaiah, 87; on remembrance, 90; role playing, 75; running to Bethlehem, 97

Horologium, 233n.56. *See also* Clock

Hospitallers, 258n.38

Hot cockles, 279n.60

Household, unity of, 250n.44

Hugh of St. Victor, 10–11, 93, 121, 141, 170, 232, 260, 262, 267, 273; *De Grammatica*, 10; *Didascalicon*, 10, 84; *Epitome*, 10

Human soul, degradation of, 17

Humility, articulation of, 97

Hunger, 116, 267n.31

Huntington MS 1 (HM 1), x, 21

Huntington, Henry E., Library and Art Gallery, x

Husbandry (Walter of Henly), 25, 239n.25

Hussey, S. S., 271n.1

"Hye noyne," 198

"Hyllys of Armonye," 64

Hyperbole, 266n.25

Hypostatic union, 270n.77

Hypothermia, 105

Idolatry, 258n.37

"Imaginacioun," 16, 80, 107, 112, 116, 140, 254n.13; inventive deceptiveness of, 70; not part of "inventive" speculative mind, 84; *phantasmata* created by, 16

Impenitence, 37; theme of obdurate, 21

Incantatory suffumigation, 125

Indicia (circumstantial evidence), 205, 213

Indirect legal strategy, 279n.52

Indolence, 70–71

Ineffability topos, 170, 273n.34

Infantilization, 269n.65

Inferno (Dante), 187

Ingram, R. W., 270
Innocence, destruction of, 18
Innovation, 121; abuse of, 29, 37; praise of, 233n.56
Innovative stanza, 224, 243n.1. *See also* "Thirteener"
Insight, tropological, 13
Institutional thinking, corruption of, 19–20
Intellect, 14, 84, 91, 96
Intellectual grotesqueries, feast of, 118–20
Intellectual revolution, 250–51n.51
Interpretation: of "ambiguous figurative," 91–96, 140, 143–45; of "ambiguous literal," 88–91, 125–42; of "unknown figurative," 87–88, 121–24; of "unknown literal," 85–87, 119–21
Inventio, as *heuresis* (discovery), 13; distinguished from meaning-making *inventio* (invention), 14, 84
Invention: abuse of, 29, 39–41; active seekers of understanding associated with, 13; definition of, 30; distinguished from *inventio* or *heuresis*, 13–14, 234n.63; invention of, 233n.56; relation of, to mimesis, 14; Saint Augustine's definition of, 234n.66, 234n.67
Invention, linguistic: abuse of, 32
"Inventive" empirical creaturely triune mind, 16, 103
"Inventive" speculative creaturely triune mind, 15, 83–98, 101
Iohannes baptista, 154
Irace, Kathleen, 268
Irony, 30, 280n.63
Irresponsibility, 23
Isaiah, 87, 88
Iudicium, x, 1, 3, 192, 196, 275, 276n.20
Ius commune, 199, 215. *See also* Roman-canon law of proof

Jack Copé, 72
Jacobus de Vitriaco, 196
Jacobus de Voragine, *Legenda Aurea*, 224, 226, 234n.72
Jak Garcio, 71, 82–83; current views of, 260n.51; denunciation of Shepherds' *phantasmata*, 82; enigmatic denunciation of shepherds, 83; source of "fools of Gotham" remark of, 252n.3; as Tercius Pastor, 260n.50
Jambeck, Thomas J., 257n.28, 269n.64, 270n.69
James, Mervyn, 235n.81
Jawbone, 29, 239n.36
Jeffrey, David L., 102, 233, 236n.3, 238n.20, 239n.24, 242, 243n.70, 245n.9, 248n.31, 255n.21, 255n.23, 260n.51, 260n.53, 262, 263, 265n.9, 266n.19, 266n.26, 266n.27, 267n.34, 269n.55
Jehan le Bel, *Li ars d'amour*, 254n.13
Jennings, Margaret, 276n.17
Jergens-Forsythe, Elizabeth, 17, 235n.76
Jesse, 88
John, King of England, 231n.27
John of Garland, *Parisiana poetria*, 234n.63
Johnson, Kenneth E., 269
Johnson, Wallace H., 263
Joliffe, J. E. A., 276n.14
Jonah, 31; "Whale's-Belly Prayer" of, 242n.58
Jonson, Ben, xi, 252n.9
Jordan, Robert M., 231n.29, 250n.49
Judgment, 213
Judicial maliciousness, 278n.44
Jungman, Robert E., 267n.38, 271n.15

Kahrl, Stanley J., 227
Keen, Maurice, 236–37n.8
Kelly, T. Daniel, and John T. Irwin, 276n.18
"Kemptowne," 169
Kerseys (cheap broadcloth), 229–30n.20
Keyser, Conrad, of Ausbeck, *Bellifortis*, 278n.34
Kilwardby, Robert, 232–33n.52
King's peace, proclamation of, 27–28
Kingship, 154
Kirkstall Abbey, 4
Knitting, 250n.43
Kolve, V. A., 2–3, 137, 228n.4, 228n.5, 234n.72, 243n.2, 256–57n.24, 260n.51, 261n.60, 262n.78, 262n.84, 264n.4, 269, 272n.25, 272–73n.28, 273, 274, 277n.27
"Kyng Copyn," 209
"Kyrkchaterars," 198

Labor: Benedictine affirmation of, 7; Benedictine idea of, 61–62; Benedictine motto *Laborare est orare*, 7, 62; deserving compensation, 12; disavowal of the eschatological value of, 19; expressed in terms of "swynke," 12, 203; as means to salvation, 12; as penitential act, 12; positive attitude toward, 7; refinement of attitude toward, 12; view of, in Classical Antiquity, 7
Lamech, 275n.8
Langbein, John H., 277n.28, 278, 278–79n.45, 279, 280
Langdon, John, 237n.10
Langland, William, *Piers Plowman*, 240–41n.47, 241n.51
Language, 178; degeneration of proclamative, 22; manipulation of, 123–24
Last Judgment: metaphor of, 270n.69; sermon on, 12
Lateran Council (1139), 240–41n.47
Latimer, Hugh, 240–41n.47
Latin, denunciation of, 91–92
Lawlessness, 265n.14
Lazarus, 205
Lazarus, 275
Lazy servant, 115
Lead, for construction, 4
Learned pastors, 261n.60
Legal procedure, practical art of, 26
Legenda Aurea (Jacobus de Voragine), 224, 280
Le Goff, Jacques, 234, 275
Legs, "folded," 265n.11
Leland, John, 229–30n.20
Leonard, Frances M., 262n.85
Lepow, Lauren, 226, 258n.34, 271, 279, 280
Leshock, David, 273n.35
Lester, G. A., 229
"Letter to Nebridius" (Saint Augustine), 68
Lewis, C. S., 268, 269, 273n.31
Lewis, Jack Pearl, 243
Li ars d'amour (Jehan le Bel), 254n.13
Liber exceptionem (Richard of St. Victor), 10, 11
Light of Truth, 186, 268n.53
Lingual acts, 32

Linow, Wilhelm, 255n.20
Lipson, E., 229–30n.20
Liturgy, 276n.20
Liturgical drama, 87
Logical discourse, language of, 90
Longbow, 33
Longo, Joseph A., 264, 267n.34, 270
Lottin, O., 254n.14
Lucas, 196
Lucifer: associated with Cain, 242n.61; associated with Herod, 152; suffering of, with cohort, 51; undermining angelic hierarchy, 50. *See also* Satan
Ludolphus, *Vita Christi*, 243n.2
Lunar calendar, 3
Lunar year, 63
Luttrell Psalter, ix, x
Lyle, Marie C., 276–77n.26

Mack, Maynard, Jr., 264n.5, 265n.9, 267n.34
Mactatio Abel, x, 15, 18, 21–45, 54, 57, 69, 111; induction of, 22; structure of, 236n.5; theme of improper family relations in, 21; theme of lack of feudal reciprocity in, 21
Madonna, seated, with Christ child, 142–43, 150–51
Magi, 158, 160, 162–63; imagined vengeance against, 164; wisdom of, 273n.35
Magi plays, 251–52n.3
Magic circle, 126–27
Magnus Herodes, x, 15, 17, 152–90, 200–1, 206, 251; induction of, 155–57; structure of, 155, 272n.19; tragedy of, 155, 272n.17
Maidenhead, 256–57n.24
Mahomet, 156, 170, 272, 273n.35
Mahowne, 170, 185; thanksgiving prayer to, 186
Mak, 118–45; associated with enfeebled spirit, 120; magic spell of, 126–27; "makness" of, 120; as part of the Pharisaic problem, 125; prayer of, 124–26; unevenness of, 123; unevenness of flattened out, 144–45, 270n.69
Mak and Gyll, 16, 127–45; their "gyn," like the ovine *phantasma*, 140

Malcus, 205
Mâle, Emile, 233n.57, 252n.7, 257–58n.32, 269, 273–74n.43
Malice prepense, 27, 161
Maltman, Sister Nicholas, O. P., 275n.5
Man, proper condition of, 38
Manifestatio, 173, 273n.41. *See also* Gothic; Clarification
Manly, William M., 268n.47
Manslaughter, 32
Margins, x
Marlowe, Christopher, xi
Marshall, Linda E., 264n.5
Martha, 12
Marvel, 83
"Marvelous flower," 274n.43
Mary, 100–1, 150, 250n.43, 269n.66, 273n.43
Mass, 274n.56
Massacre of Innocents, 154, 176–83, 187; as *allegoria* of massacre of innocence, 176–83. *See also* Slaughter of Innocents
Master Bernard. *See* Robert of York
Masters of Chartres, 6
"Mastry," abuse of, 19, 193–96
Mathematical physics, 144
Matheson, Lester M., 276n.22
Matter, utilization of, 18
Matter and space, conquest of, 22
Meaning, role of audience in, 14
Meaning-making, "inventive," 14, 19, 68
Measures and weights, 237–38n.15
Mechanic arts, 10; *trivium* and *quadrivium* of, 10, 11
Mechanical crank, 8
"Medillerd," destruction of, 52
Mellinkoff, Ruth, 275n.8
Memory, 114; degradation of, 17; physical location of, 179, 274n.50; of sensation, 105; workings of, 72–76
Mendicant confessor manuals, 12
Mensuration, 63–64
Mentalité, "Herodified," 210; of dead soul, 153
Merchant's Tale (Chaucer), 254n.13
Messianic eclogue, 252n.3
Metadrama, 111

Metadramatic space: location of, 157; manipulation of, 169
Methexis, 14, 15, 17, 55, 22, 28, 111, 115, 155, 164–65, 170–71, 172–73, 175, 187, 189, 192–94, 223, 272
Meyers, Walter E., 236n.3, 237n.14, 242n.61, 243–44n.4, 245n.11, 245n.14, 251n.2, 252n.9, 261n.66, 262n.71, 270, 271
Micheas, 174
"Middle advent," 269n.64
Mill, Anna J., 248n.36
Miller, Robert P., 262
Miller's Tale (Chaucer), 254n.13
Mills, 230n.21
Mills, David, 229n.18, 251n.1, 271n.9, 277–78n.31
Mimesis, 258–59n.41
Mind, late-Gothic, xi; *allegoria* of the totality of, 17; bereft of "inventive" ability, 69; dysfunction of, 18; repudiation of, 17; triune, 15–16, 252n.6;
Mining, 4
Mirk, John, 198, 234
Misogyny, 254n.18
Mixed team, 239n.21
Modus interpretandi, 14, 86–91, 91–96, 120–24
Modus proferandi, 70, 98–101
Moll, 81–82, 259n.47
Monastic houses of the Yorkshire Ridings, 258n.38
Monsters, 12
Moorman, F. W., 229n.17
"Mop," 99. *See* Puppet
Morey, James H. 237n.10, 239
Morgan, Margery M., 256–57n.24
"Mothers of invention," 177
Mumford, Lewis, 234n.57
Munson, William F., 251n.2, 254n.12, 255n.21, 255n.22, 256–57n.24, 259n.45
Murphy, James J., 274n.56
Murrain, 106, 258n.40
Musical iconography, 262n.80
Musket, 34
Muslim paradise, 185
Myopia of pretentiousness, 165

"Mystic Lamb" altarpiece (Van Eyck), 250n.43
McAlindon, T., 276n.20
McClure, Hazel Dean, 276n.20

The Name of the Rose (Eco), 262n.82
Nature: attitudes toward, 18; use and abuse of, 21
Natural man, 272–73n.28
Natural theology, 11
Nativity, 98–101, 149–50, 269n. 65, 271–72n.16
Navigation, 97
Nebuchadnezzar, 88
Necromantic arts, 125
Nell, 199
Nelson, Alan H., 228n.4, 243n.3, 245, 246n.18, 247
Neumann, Eric, 273n.30
Nexus: achieved through prayer, 63; the unfolding moment of, 45
Nicholas, Karen S., 276n.15
Nicodemus, 276–77n.26
Night spell, 125
Ninepins, 279n.60
Nitecki, Alicia K., 255n.21, 256–57n.24, 258n.34, 262n.71
Noah, 1, 2, 46–66, 113, 228n.4; abuse of time leading to loss of space, 54; "alod," use of, 246n.17; alternative avian search modality of, 64; anger of, 63; aside of, 55–56; ax of, 60, 248n.36; "charité" of, 48; civility of, 47; cooperation of, in following guidelines, 60–61; daughters-in-law of, 59; disrobement of imaged, 62; evasiveness of, 247n.28; exemplarism of, 46–47, 61–63; forestalling suffering, 52; "freend," identified by God as, 49; friendliness of, 47; furthering spirit of cooperation, 49; good husbandman, 245n.9; humanity of, 243n.4; in *Holkham Bible Picture Book*, 275n.8; incomplete cost/benefit analysis of ark, 57–58, 58–59, 59–60; initiator of nexus, 46; material invention of, 249n.37; measuring after, not before, construction, 61, 249n.40; measuring innovation, 63; miraculous project completion of, 61; misogamy and misogyny of, 56; monologic prayer of, 47–50, 245n.10; new social order of family of, 62–63; paronomasia of, as analogy of cooperative spirit, 250n.48; plummet of, 63; sons of, 59; sons of, articulating ethical norm, 63; time of Flood, 113; typic or figural view of, 243n.4; using spatio-temporal properly, 65–66; violence of, 246n.1
Noah and Uxor, planimetry developed by, 64, 250n.49
Noesis of impiety, 153
Noesis of modernity, 119, 267n.35
Noesis of tradition and authority, 119, 267n.35
Noetic dysfunction, 18
Noiseless ax motif, 248n.31
Northern Passion, 277n.26
Notae super Johannem secundam magistrum Gilbertum (Gilbert de la Porrée), 5
Notre-Dame de la belle verrière, 143
Nose, 274n.49
Nose flower as parody of "marvelous flower," 274n.43
Nuncius, 155, 161, 168, 169, 170, 176

Objective correlative, 166
Oblacio Magorum, 17, 154
Obscenity, 92, 123
Officialdom, 121–22
Old age, 265n.9
Old Dispensation, 93
Old Law, 265n.10
Old Man, figure of, 246n.15
Oosterwijk, Sophie, 270n.76
Oppression, idea of, 265n.9
Opus Creatoris, ix, 6, 8
Opus naturae, 6
Os malleatoris, 275n.6
Osculatio, 269n.65
Outwood, 4
Ovine *phantasmata*, 79–82, 140
Owst, G. R., 92, 194, 262n.75
Oxford English Dictionary, 279n.59

Pagan animism, rejection of, 7
Pagan religion, dismissal of, 269n.65
Palmer, Barbara D., 229n.18, 248–49n.37, 262n.80
Panofsky, Erwin, xi, 167, 227, 233–34n.57, 241, 245, 252, 261n.60, 265, 271, 273, 273n.41
Paper, 240–41n.47
Paradise, 51
Pardoner, 271n.7
Parisiana poetria (John of Garland), 234n.63
Parker, Roscoe E., 271n.1
Parliament rolls, 276n.14
Parody, 124, 154
Parrott, T. M., 263
Parvenu, 71, 199
"Passion group," 15, 19, 154, 191, 200
Passivity, 110–13
Passmore, J. B., 237n.10
Pastoral directional commands, 79–81
Pasturage-rights disputes, 78
Patience, 31, 240n.40, 241–42n.58
Patterson, Lee, 1, 227
Paull, Michael, 272, 273n.35
Paxson, James J., 3, 227
Peine forte et dure, 20, 214, 215, 279n.57, 279n.58
Peine ni forte ni dure, 216, 218
Pejoration, 179, 182
Penal execution, 239n.32
Pennine sheep runs, 78
Perceptual change in attitude toward nature and technology, 6
Perigrini, x, 196, 275
Perowne, Stuart, 271
Perpendicular style, 231n.25
Perscrutator, 267n.36. *See* Robert of York
Perscrutation, 119
Perversion of reason, memory, and will, 153
Peter Alfonso, *Disciplina clericalis*, 232–33n.52
Peter Lombard, *Sententiae*, 16–17, 235n.74
Pevsner, Sir Nikolaus, 229–30n.20, 231n.25
Phantasiae, creation of, 70
Phantasma, 70, 72; gastronomic, 77; illusory reality of, 140; ovine, 79–82; performance reality of, 116–18

Pharisees, 208
Physica (Aristotle), 268n.51
Piers the plowman, 191, 241n.1
Piers Plowman (Langland), 36, 241n.51
Piety, medieval, 68
Pilate, Pontius, x, 19, 125, 191–92, 195–96, 215, 222, 225; the good, 276n.16; polyglottal linguistic dexterity of, 192
Platonists of Chartres, 234n.57
Play performance order, 154, 187
Play-within-the-play structure. *See Rahmenerzahlung*
Plebeian fare, 74
Pliny, 12
Plow, 6, 23; four-ox, illustration of, 24; as gallows, 29, 239n.32; stalled, 24, 28, 35; "streeking" of, 29
Plowing procedure, faulty, 24
Plowmanship, 21
Plow team, 23; calling lead animal of, 238n.19, 238n.20; choke harness of, 25; figurative injunction against mismatched, mixed team, 25; management of, 24; mismatched, mixed, 237n.10; question of its being real, 238n.16; size of, 23, 25
Poetics (Aristotle), 269–70n.68
Pogrom, 167, 178–83, 187–88
Pollack, Sir Frederick, and Frederic William Maitland, 279n.58
Polygamy, 110, 266n.20
Pontefract, 4
Poole, Austin Lane, 240–41n.47
Poor laws, 240–41n.47
Postexamination interlude, 210, 214
Postparturiency, 129–31
Poteet, Daniel P., II, 272n.24
Power, Eileen, 229–30n.20, 254
Prampolini, Giacomo, 249–50n.43
"Praty mytyng," 263n.91
Praxis Rerum Criminalis (Damhouder), 278n.34
Prayer, 71
Pre-jury standard of proof, 199, 205, 225
Premonstratensians, 258n.38
Presumption, 153
Prime mover, 268n.49

Prima Mulier, 177
[Prima] Pagina Pastorum, x, 1, 15, 16, 67–102, 111, 124, 140; as self-conscious art, 251n.2; source of, 67, 251–52n.3, 256n.24; structure of, 69, 272n.27
Primus Consultus, 174
Printing press, 240–41n.47
Prison forte et dure, 214
Processus Crucis, 1, 275
Processus Noe cum filiis, x, 15, 18, 46–66, 67, 69, 81, 111, 272; cataclysmic flood in, 62–64; conjugal conformity in, 65; cooperation in, 248n.34; fabliau element in, 53; farcical element as uniting force in, 248n.34; interludes of, 53–57, 79, 258–59n.41; interludial asides in, 79; raven and the dove in, 64; simultaneous abuse of time and space in, 57–60; sources of, 45, 243n.2; space becomes place in, 65; structure of, 47, 244n.5; "syncopation" in, 250n.47; theme of obedience in, 245n.10; theme of work in, 249n.41
Processus Prophetarum, 1, 87, 88, 90; modified form of, 147
Processus Talentorum, x, 191, 192, 275
Promiscuity, 273n.35
Proof, 119, 129, 148; half, 205, 213; full, 212
Prophetae play of Limoges, 88, 261
Prosser, Eleanor Alice, 227–28n.3, 235n.1
"Prow," 39
Pseudo-Dionysius, 167
"Psychical objectivity," 235n.78
Psychology of sloth, 197–98
Purdon, Liam O., 246n.15, 266n.23, 272n.26
Purificacio marie, 154
Puppet, 270n.76
"Purveance," 107, 265n.16; in action, 108
Pyrotechnical cloud, 44. *See also* Smoke

Quadrivium, 232n.52

Rahmenerzählung (play-within-the-play structure), 115, 267n.30
Rational soul, renunciation of, 155–57
Rarefaction, 144
Raven, 64, 275n.8
Realism, 1–2, 227–28n.3

Recklessness, 43–44
Reeve, 242n.68
Reeve Osewold, 43, 48
Reform, civic and moral, 44, 225–26
Regenall, Towneley, 264n.4
Reiss, Edmund, 26, 236n.2, 237n.13, 238n.17, 238–39n.21, 239n.32, 242n.61
Remembrance, 86–87
Remly, Lynn, 269
Remnant, 49
Renunciation of rational soul, 155–57
Res cogitans, 33, 35–36
Resentment, idea of, 265n.9
Res extensa, 33, 36
Responsibility, 51, 246n.16, 248n.31
Resurreccio Domini, 1
Revard, Carter, 247n.28
Rex pius et justus, 192
Richard II, King of England, 276n.14
Rich man, typification of, 255n.20
Richard of St. Victor, *Liber exceptionem*, 10, 11
Richardson, H. G., 237n.10
Richardson, Janette, 280n.63
Rievaulx, 269–70n.68
Rimmer, W. G., 229n.17
Ripon Cathedral, 4
The Rise of the Sciences (Al-Farabi), 232n52
Ritual, 228n.14, 274n.48
Road movies, 75
Roads, 231n.26
Robert of York (Perscrutator), *Correctorium alchimiae* or *Correctio fatuorum*, 267n.36
Roberts, Ian, 263
Robertson, D. W., Jr., 3, 13, 228n.12, 234, 235n.74, 236, 237n.9, 237n.10, 238–39n.21, 241n.48, 243n.74, 252n.4, 252n.6, 252n.7, 254n.14, 257–58n.32, 262n.85, 265n.10, 271n.7, 273, 274, 275n.60
Robertson, D. W., Jr., and Bernard F. Huppé, 262n.78
Robinson, J. W., 227–28n.3, 229, 229–30n.20, 240n.43, 243n.2, 245n.7, 247n.29, 255n.21, 256–57n.24, 257n.28, 259n.45, 260n.51, 261n.60, 263n.94,

265n.9, 266n.17, 266n.25, 267n.34, 269n.57, 270, 273n.37, 277, 279
Roche Abbey, 4
Rogers, Thomas, 231n.25
Rogerson, Margaret, 238n.20
Roman-canon law of proof, 199, 215. *See also Ius commune*
Romance of the Rose (Guillaume de Lorris and Jean de Meun), 80, 259n.43
Romaunt of the Rose (Chaucer), 240n.39
Roney, Lois, 103, 251n.1, 252–53n.10, 256–57n.24, 261n.60, 263n.94, 264, 265n.9, 270
Rose, Martial, 251n.2, 264n.4
Rosen, Edward, 240–41n.47
Ross, Lawrence J., 264n.5
Rossiter, A. P., 277–78n.31
Russell, J. Stephen, 234n.70, 252n.7, 270n.77
Russell, John, *Booke of Nurture*, 74

Sachs, Arieh, 243–44n.4
Sacramental design, 226
Sacramentalism, 20, 216, 235n.80
Sacred center, x
Sacred rhetoric, 14
Sadism, 278n.34
Saintly worker, 12, 191
Salomon and Saturnis, 236n.2
Salvation history, 188
Salzman, L. F., 265n.16
Sambursky, Samuel, 232
Sanctuary, 30
Sanders, Barry, 279n.48
Sanhedrin, 200
Sapientia, 151
Satan, 196. *See also* Lucifer
Satrapic absolutism, 192
Saturn, 93
Saturn's reign, 93
Saul, Nigel, 242n.59, 242n.68
Savior, 269n.64
Scabies, 280n.63
Schell, Edgar, 264n.5
Schless, Howard H., 243n.2, 247, 250n.48, 251n.52
Schmidt, Gary D., 264n.5

Scholastic writings, 261n.60
Scholasticism: as mode of thinking, 18; rise of, 11; second principle of, 167–68
Schücking, Levin L., 274–75n.59
Scientia, 119
Scots invasions, 106
Scriptural dictionaries, 252–53n.10
Scuba diving, medieval, 233n.56
Second death, 272n.26, 271n.6
Secunda Mulier, 179
[Secunda] Pagina Pastorum, x, 15, 16–17, 82, 103–51, 272n.27; beginning of comic subplot in, 119; structure of, 104, 264n.5
Secundus Consultus, 174, 176
Selby Abbey, 4
Self-knowledge, 271n.9
"Sely Copyle," 110
Seneschaucie, 238–39n.21
Sensation, 70; creation of, 153; of hunger, 113–14, 116; memory of, 109
Sententiae (Peter Lombard), 16–17, 235n.74
Sentiency, 119
Serial monogamy, 266n.20
Serial volitional errancy, 162–68
Seriality, 160, 272n.23
Sermo contra Judaeos, 89, 262n.70
Sermonic exemplum, 198
Seven deadly sins, 199
Seznec, Jean, 252n.7
Shakespeare, William, xi, 252n.9
"Shape-and-drape principle," 275n.8
Sheepherding, 259n.42; art of medieval, 15, 68
Shepherds: gifts of, 100, 149–50; priestlike qualities of, 235n.80; as types, 93, 262n.78;
Shepherds' plays: as *débat*, 102; difference between, 103–4, 206
Shurgot, Michael W., 269
Shipbuilding, 58
Shoe technology, 266n.18, 275n.8
Sifting, 270n.69
Signs, natural and conventional, 86, 261n.64, 273n.34
Sigsworth, Eric M., 229–30n.20
Sinful madness, 172, 211, 279n.51
"Skalys," 221, 280n.63

"Skaunce," 27
Skepticism, 82
Skey, Miriam Anne, 274n.48
Skiffington, Lloyd A., 266n.21, 274–75n.59
Slander, 137
Slapstick, 95
Slaughter of the Innocents, 18, 154, 157, 177
Slaughter of meaning, 171
Slawpase (Tercius Pastor), 16, 73, 259n.45; accusing shepherds, 76; acknowledging traditions of prophets, 97; almsgiving of, 97; bedtime prayer of, 77–78; contribution of, to "Grotesque Feast," 74; demonstrating learning, 99; deprived of "holsom ayll" of Healy, 75; excluded by shepherds, 76; giving of gift, 99; "gramery" of, 75; ground-meal-sack, exemplum of, 73, 255n.21; interpreting, 86, 93; "lawe" of, 73; logical discourse language of, 90; memory of angelic song, 95; Moll story told by, 82; own intellect questionable, 73; perception of other shepherds, 73; *phatasiae* of, 83; response of, to *Gloria*, 85; skepticism of, 82; synthesizing of pastoral responses, 86
Sloth, 19, 199
Smith, John H., 267n.39
Smith, Lucy Toulmin, 271n.12
Smith, Sarah Stanbury, 246n.20
Smoke, 44
Smyser, H. M., 263
Sobriety, 257n.30, 262n.82
Social engineering, 65
Soldiers (Primus, Secundus, Tercius Milites), 159; arrogance of, 184; credulity of, 185; decamping of, 183; desire of, for worldly reward, 182; object of mockery, 184; pejoration of, 182; Primus, 163; Primus fighting Prima Mulier, 177–79; Secundus fighting Secunda Mulier, 179–80; Secundus and Tercius, 164; Tercius, objecting, 172; Tercius fighting Tercia Mulier, 180–82
Soliloquy, 266n.21; Elizabethan, 274–75n.5; ranting, 274–75n.59
Soliloquy form, 187

"Sondys," 168
Soul, motion of, 69
South English Legendary, 260n.54
Southernism, 122, 268n.41, 268n.42
"Sovereigntée," abuse of, 19, 192–93
Space, abuse of, 22; conquest of, 22; improper use of, 23; temporal transformation of, through mensuration, 64
Spatial transformation of time, 64–65
Spectator: bereavement of will and intellect of, 112; privileged point of view of, destabilized, 53–54
Spek, Cornelius van der, 276n.21
Speirs, John, 235–36n.1, 245n.12, 248n.35, 256–57n.24, 257n.28
Speyser, Suzanne, 254–55n.18, 255n.21, 256–57n.24, 260n.51
Spirit, diminished or enfeebled, 70, 119, 254n.14
Spiritual life, active, 12
Spirituality, revolution in, 6–7
Sports banned by King Edward III, 33
St. Alban's, 106
St. Peter, 205
"Stafford blew," 53, 246n.20
Staines, David, 154, 271, 273n.29, 273n.35, 274
Steadfastness, illusion of, 41–42
Stearns, Mary, 269
Steinberg, Clarence B., 273
Stern, Henri, 232
Stevens, Martin, 228, 229, 229–30n.20, 235n.1, 236n.3, 243n.2, 246n.21, 247n.23, 247n.24, 258, 261, 263n.95, 264n.4, 265n.7, 276n.18
Stevens, Martin, and A. C. Cawley, x, 78, 85, 140, 154, 206, 227n.2, 229n.16, 235n.73, 235–36n.1, 240, 242n.64, 243n.1, 243n.4, 246n.20, 247n.28, 249n.40, 249–50n.43, 251n.2, 251–52n.3, 253n.11, 257n.29, 258n.37, 261, 262n.72, 263n.2, 266n.20, 267, 268n.42, 269n.65, 270n.69, 271n.1, 274n.56, 275, 276–77n.26, 277n.29, 278, 279n.49, 279n.62, 280n.63
Stew meat, 171, 273n.37
Stewardship, improper, 24–25, 238n.20
Stone, quarried, 4

Stool, 216
Strauss, Jennifer, 269
Stroup, Thomas B., 263
Stupidity, 277–78n.31
Sturges, Robert S., 268n.53
Stychomythia, 27–28
Subdued style, 99–100
Subjectivism, 69, 252n.8
Subsistence farming, 106
Suffering, 110, 115–18, 203; function of consciousness of, 51; Herod's physical, 158; marriage-induced, 110–11; spiritual, 71
Suffumigation, 266n.49
Summa de arte praedicandi (Thomas of Salisbury), 186
Sumptuary laws, 267n.39
Sutherland, Sarah, 248n.32, 250n.46
Sympathy, 269–70n.68
Syphilis, 280n.63
Swart, J., 227–28n.3, 229–30n.20, 247–48n.29
"Swetyng," 263n.91
Swineshead, Richard, *Calculationes*, 144. *See also* Calculator
"Swynke," 12, 198, 203
Symmetry, 69
Sypher, Wylie, 234, 235n.78, 236, 247, 266n.21

Taft, Edmund M., 264n.4
Tally, 41, 242n.65
"Tame-talkyng," 158, 170
Taxation, 196, 276n.21
Tax collector, 196
Taylor, Jerome, 267
Techne of legal process, 26, 30
Technology, 3; anachronistic verisimilitude of, 22; cost/benefit analysis, 3; ethics of, 239n.32; of the gallows, 29; positive attitude toward, 7; tropological anachronistic verisimilitude of, 47
Technology assessment, 33–34, 240–41n.47; abuse of, 57
Telecommunications, medieval, 233n.56
Templars, 258n.38
Temporal sequence, 272n.23

Temporal transformed by space, 63–64
Tennis ball, 150, 271n.78
Tertium quid, 167, 273n.31
Testimony, 206
Theatrics as nourishment, 11
Theme of the absence of truth, 187–88
Theophilus, *De diversis artibus*, 8, 9, 60, 232, 249
Thinking as physically taxing act, 124
"Thirteener," 224, 243n.1. *See also* Innovative stanza
Thomas of Salisbury, *Summa de arte praedicandi*, 186
Thompson, F. J., 264n.5, 267n.38
Thompson, James Westfall, 269–70n.68
"Thoner-flone," 86
Thorndike, Lynn, 11–12, 126, 232–33n.52, 234n.68, 241n.57, 268, 270, 274
"Thre brefes to a long," 146
Three-field rotational planting system, 6
Tierney, Brian, 240–41n.47
Timaeus, 6, 167
Time: as artifact, 3; associated with illusion, 161; of erring, 46; improper use of, 23; of reconciliation, 191; of renewal, 67, 152
Time and space: improper mastery of, 24; proper use of, 18, 46
Tokening, 65
Tomlinson, Warren E., 271n.1
Tormentor, 277n.31
Torture, 214
Torture-free law of proof, 215
Torturers (Totores), 19, 277–78n.31; distinguished from soldiers (milites), 277–78n.31; incapable of torturing, 201–6, 215–22
Towneley play collection (*regenall*), 1, 3; drama of experimental diversity, 251n.1; editions of, x; historical focus of, 46; possible cycle in sixteenth century, 4
Translation projects, 11
Transubstantiation, 235n.80
Traver, H., 267
Travis, Peter W., 260n.57
Trébuchet, 240–41n.47
Trespass, 118
Trinitarian soul, 67, 68–69

Trinity, 98–99, 263n.94; invocation of, 60–61
Trinkaus, Charles, 252n.6, 260n.57
Trivium, 232n.52
Troilus and Criseyde (Chaucer), 240n.39
Trusler, Margaret, 229n.17
Turnau, Irena, 249–50n.43
Tutivillus, x, 19; as effective sign, 276n.18; as infernal tax collector, 197; job self-assessment of, 197; Latin gibberish of, 197; on the psychology of sloth, 197; as recording devil, 197; sermonic exemplum of, on contrariety, 198; sermonic exemplum on the foppish layabout, 198; sermonic exemplum on the parvenu and naughty Nell, 199

Unevenness, 120, 128
Unger, Richard W., 245n.11
"Uninventive" empirical creaturely triune mind, 107–8, 265n.7
"Uninventive" speculative creaturely triune mind, 77–83
Universities, rise of, 11
"Unknown figurative," 87
"Unknown literal," 85
Upward social mobility, 73
Use, idea of, 13, 18–19, 22, 26, 225
Utley, Francis Lee, 249–50n.43
Utrecht Psalter, 7
Uxor Gill, 53, 123, 246n.22; aside of, 54–55; calling Noah "husband," 64; command of rudimentary planimetry, 251n.52; compared to Eve, 247n.23; contrariety of, 58; difference between her and York and Chester counterparts, 63, 250n.46; error of, in choosing raven, 64; garrulity of, 247n.24, 247–48n.29; happiness of, 64; incisive interpretation of "trew tokyn," 67; interpreting true tokening, 65; name of, as possible pejorative, 249–50n.43; navigational competence of, 251n.52; now "Dame," 249n.43; reluctance of, 248n.31; "rok" of, 58, 247n.29; spinning of, 58; wanting exact explanation, 58; as "wife" and "Dame," 249–50n.43
Uxorial "thing-ness," 268n.53

Valency, Maurice Jacques, 271n.1
Van Eyck, Jan, "Mystic Lamb" altarpiece, 233–34n.57, 250n.43
Van Laan, Thomas F., 274–75n.59
Vassalage, 196, 276n.15
Vaughan, Mícéal F., 264n.5, 270n.69
Vegetable organics, 149
Velz, John W., 277n.27
Verbal chaos, 279n.48
Verbal lapses, 276n.20
Verbum Dei, 182
Verisimilitude, tropological, 3
"Veronica's veil," 280n.63
Villard de Honnecourt, 11
Violence, 273n.35, 276n.14
Virgil, 174, 252n.3
Virgin, 88–89, 174
Virgin birth, 89
The Virgin of the Portal, 143
Vita Christi (Ludolphus), 243n.2
Voice, bereavement of, 111–12
Volition, 91, 94, 95, 120; dramatized loss of, 112
Volitional equilibrium, 162
Voluntarist theology, 7
Von Simpson, Otto, 234n.57, 257n.32

Wadworth Chapel, 4
Wage, 185
Wage payment, 161
Wakefield, 3, 4, 230n.20
Wakefield Bridge Chapel, 230n.20
Wakefield Burgess Court Rolls, 229n.18
"Wakefield Gate," 4
Wakefield Master, 2, 3, 228n.5, 229n.15; as artistic rival of near-contemporary Geoffrey Chaucer, 252n.9; revisions of Shepherds' plays by, 67; signature stanza of, 46, 243n.1; as Wycliffite, 245n.8
Wakefield Manor, 4, 258n.38
Walafrid Strabo, *Glossa Ordinaria*, 275n.6
Walker, J. W., 231n.27, 258n.38
Walter of Henley, *Husbandry*, 25, 239n.25
Wann, Louis, 263
Wars of the Roses, 106
Wasserman, Julian N., 234n.70

Wasserman, Julian N., and Liam O. Purdon, 274n.58
"Watling Street," 3
Watson, Thomas Ramey, 245n.11, 245n.12
Watt, Homer A., 264n.5, 269n.65
Watt, William Montgomery, 273n.35
Webster, J. Carson, 232
Weinberg, Julius, 268n.51
"Wenyand," 44
Wenzel, Siegfried, 274n.55, 276
West Riding of Yorkshire, 3
Western Voluntarist theology, 7
White, Lynn, Jr., 6, 7, 8, 22, 231–32n.30, 232n.48, 233n.56, 234, 236n.7, 237, 238n.16, 239, 240, 241n.57, 243n.4, 247n.24, 247–48n.29, 249–50n.43, 250–51n.51, 252n.5, 252n.8, 267n.35, 273n.35, 278n.34
Whiting, B. J., 263
Wife of Bath's Prologue (Chaucer), 111–12
Wilful impiety, 153
Will, 17, 38
Williams, Arnold, 229–30n.20, 263n.95, 263n.2, 271n.1, 275, 276n.16
Windmills, 230–31n.21
"Wise foolishness," 260n.51
Withington, Robert, 270n.69, 270n.72, 276n.25

"Wonderfull talkyng," 173–74, 273–74n.43
Woodkirk or Lee fair, 5, 231n.27
Wool and cloth manufacture, 4
Woolf, Rosemary, 229–30n.20, 235, 243n.2, 263n.95, 264n.4, 265n.7, 274
Work boots, 266n.18
Wrath, 21
Wright, Thomas, 276n.19
Wright, Thomas, and James Orchard Halliwell, 256–57n.21
"Wrytys," 27
Wycherly, William, 252n.9

York, 269–70n.68; wool trade of, 229–30n.20
York *Crucifixion*, 277n.31
York cycle, 154
York *Horae*, 78
York Minster, 105, 232n.42
York Noah play, 46
York shipwrights' play, 248n.37
Yorkshire, West Riding of, 3
Young, Karl, 261, 274
Yule feast, 251n.3

Zumwalt, Eugene E., 255n.21, 265n.7, 267n.34, 269n.66

Liam O. Purdon is professor of English at Doane College in Crete, Nebraska. He is coeditor, with Cindy Vitto, of *The Rusted Hauberk: Feudal Ideals of Order and Their Decline* (University Press of Florida, 1994).

Juliette Benzoni

Juliette Benzoni est née à Paris. Fervente lectrice d'Alexandre Dumas, elle nourrit dès l'enfance une passion pour l'histoire. Elle commence en 1964 sa carrière de romancière avec la série des *Catherine*, traduite en plus de 20 langues, série qui la lance sur la voie d'un succès jamais démenti jusqu'à ce jour. Elle a écrit depuis une soixantaine de romans, réunis notamment dans les séries intitulées *La Florentine* (1988-1989), *Les Treize Vents* (1992), *Le boiteux de Varsovie* (1994-1996) et *Secret d'État* (1997-1998). Outre la série *Catherine* et *La Florentine*, *Le Gerfaut* et *Marianne* ont fait l'objet d'une adaptation télévisuelle.

Du Moyen Âge aux années 30, les reconstitutions historiques de Juliette Benzoni s'appuient sur une documentation minutieuse. Vue à travers les yeux de ses héroïnes, l'Histoire, ressuscitée par leurs palpitantes aventures, bat au rythme de la passion. Figurant au palmarès des écrivains les plus lus des Français, elle a su conquérir 50 millions de lecteurs dans plus de 20 pays.

DU MÊME AUTEUR
CHEZ POCKET

DANS LE LIT DES ROIS
DANS LE LIT DES REINES
LE ROMAN DES CHÂTEAUX DE FRANCE (1 et 2)
UN AUSSI LONG CHEMIN
DE DEUX ROSES L'UNE
LA PERLE DE L'EMPEREUR
REINES TRAGIQUES

LE GERFAUT
(4 tomes)

MARIANNE
(6 tomes)

LE JEU DE L'AMOUR ET DE LA MORT
(3 tomes)

SECRET D'ÉTAT
(3 tomes)

LE BOITEUX DE VARSOVIE
(4 tomes)

LES TREIZE VENTS
(4 tomes)

LES LOUPS DE LAUZARGUE
(3 tomes)

LA FLORENTINE
(4 tomes)

LES DAMES DU MÉDITERRANÉE-EXPRESS
(3 tomes)

CATHERINE
(7 tomes)

JULIETTE BENZONI

La Florentine

✷✷

FIORA
ET LE TÉMÉRAIRE

PLON

Le Code de la propriété intellectuelle n'autorisant, aux termes de l'article L. 122-5, (2° et 3° a), d'une part, que les « copies ou reproductions strictement réservées à l'usage privé du copiste et non destinées à une utilisation collective » et, d'autre part, que les analyses et les courtes citations dans un but d'exemple et d'illustration, « toute représentation ou reproduction intégrale ou partielle faite sans le consentement de l'auteur ou de ses ayants droit ou ayants cause est illicite » (art. L. 122-4).
Cette représentation ou reproduction, par quelque procédé que ce soit, constituerait donc une contrefaçon sanctionnée par les articles L. 335-2 et suivants du Code de la propriété intellectuelle.

© Plon, 1988.
ISBN 2-266-14747-1

Première partie

CEUX DE BRÉVAILLES

CHAPITRE I

UNE TOMBE ABANDONNÉE...

Fiora regardait l'échafaud.

Les yeux durs et secs, les mains nouées ensemble et serrées si fort que les jointures en blanchissaient, elle détaillait du regard le vieux bâti de pierre et de bois. Dépouillé du dérisoire habit de drap noir qu'il revêtait pour les exécutions importantes, il montrait sa carcasse, de poutrelles et de planches écaillées brunies par le sang, dont aucun lavage à grande eau n'effacerait jamais les traces, tachées et brûlées par le contact du fer rouge ou de l'huile bouillante, et témoignait ainsi de la cruauté humaine...

Sous la plate-forme, la jeune femme pouvait même voir les coffres où le « carnacier » rangeait ses outils de travail et la grande marmite dans laquelle il arrivait que l'on mît des faux-monnayeurs à bouillir cependant que, sur le plancher, s'érigeaient la potence, la roue et, au pied d'une haute croix, signe de l'ultime miséricorde, le billot de bois rugueux, verni, noirci, révélant des traces de coups d'épée ou de doloire anciennes. C'était, en vérité, une parfaite image de l'enfer qu'offrait cet échafaud de la prévôté de Dijon et, pourtant, c'était là qu'un matin d'hiver étaient tombées les têtes de Marie et de Jean de Brévailles, les jeunes parents de Fiora, exécutés pour crimes d'inceste et d'adultère, cinq jours après sa naissance... Au prochain mois de décembre, le dramatique épilogue de cet amour condamné serait vieux de dix-huit années. Tout comme Fiora elle-même...

Le dégoût, l'horreur et la colère gonflaient son cœur en face de cette machine à supplicier où s'étaient brisés ces parents inconnus dont le miroir seul pouvait lui donner un reflet. Elle eût aimé y porter le feu purificateur. Pourtant, le vieil échafaud exerçait sur elle un attrait morbide, une sorte de fascination dont elle ne pouvait se déprendre. Son esprit recréait l'affreuse scène. Elle entendait monter en elle le glas et les murmures de la foule. Le ciel azuré de cette belle journée de juin s'effaçait devant un autre chargé de neige, gris comme la robe de Marie et le pourpoint de Jean, gris comme leurs yeux et le seul froid soleil de ce jour de malédiction brillait alors dans les cheveux blonds de la condamnée... Dans un coin de la place, il y avait aussi un jeune homme venu de Florence dont le cœur s'était élancé vers cette belle jeune femme qui allait mourir et ne s'était jamais repris. Francesco Beltrami, à cet instant suprême, avait voué sa vie à celle qui allait la perdre, qui ne le connaîtrait jamais et à l'enfant qu'elle venait de mettre au monde. La petite fille abandonnée avait été par lui sauvée d'un assassinat, recueillie, adoptée, élevée comme si elle était née sur les marches d'un trône et non d'un échafaud...

Dans ce même coin du Morimont, il y avait des mules chargées de riches étoffes, des valets qui en prenaient soin et leur chef, ce Marino Betti qui, en dépit d'un vœu de silence juré sur un autel, avait, au début de ce printemps 1475, trahi son serment, tué le maître qui s'était fié à lui et arraché de la sorte Fiora au doux paradis de sa jeunesse pour la réduire, proscrite, et privée de sa fortune à fuir la ville de son enfance. Aujourd'hui, Marino Betti, massacré par un ordre de Lorenzo de Médicis, avait payé d'un juste prix son parjure et son crime mais sa complice, celle pour laquelle il s'était damné, Hieronyma Pazzi, courait encore, enfuie vers on ne savait quel horizon...

Contrainte elle-même à l'exil, Fiora avait dû laisser cette femme disparaître, mais sans perdre l'espoir de la retrouver un jour et de lui faire enfin payer ses crimes.

Cependant, il y avait pour elle, dans ce pays de Bourgogne où elle venait d'arriver, une tâche sacrée à accomplir : tirer vengeance de ceux qui avaient conduit ses parents à cet échafaud. Et ils étaient trois : d'abord Regnault du Hamel, l'époux de Marie qui, par ses mauvais traitements, l'avait contrainte à s'échapper avec le frère qu'elle aimait trop, et qui avait poursuivi le couple d'une haine impitoyable. Puis Pierre de Brévailles, le père qui, pour une sordide question d'argent, avait obligé sa fille à un mariage dont elle avait horreur et qui, le drame venu, n'avait rien fait pour tenter de sauver ses enfants. Enfin, le duc Charles de Bourgogne dont Jean de Brévailles était l'écuyer au temps où celui-ci n'était que comte de Charolais et qui, par orgueil blessé et parce que le jeune homme avait quitté son service sans autorisation, ne sut pas accorder la clémence qui sied à un prince, surtout envers un compagnon d'armes...

Ces trois hommes, Fiora les avait condamnés à mort, de compte à demi, pour le Téméraire, avec son vieil ami Démétrios Lascaris, le mage-médecin de Byzance qui tenait, de son côté, à venger la mort de son jeune frère Théodose, exécuté par les Turcs pour avoir cru ingénument au serment de ce prince... Et l'heure était venue, à présent, de se mettre à l'œuvre.

S'arrachant soudain à son amère réflexion, la jeune femme tourna les talons et fit face au trio silencieux que formaient, avec Démétrios et son serviteur Esteban, dame Léonarde Mercet, la vieille fille que Francesco Beltrami avait jadis emmenée, de cette même ville de Dijon, pour servir de seconde mère au bébé abandonné. Ce fut à elle que Fiora s'adressa :

— Où se trouve la maison du bourreau ?

— Pourquoi cette question ?

— Ne m'avez-vous pas dit que mon père, avant de quitter cette ville, avait remis à cet homme de l'or pour qu'il donne une sépulture décente à ma mère et... à son frère ?

— Ce frère était votre vrai père, reprocha doucement Léonarde.

— Je ne le considérerai jamais comme tel. Il m'a seulement donné le souffle de la vie mais mon père véritable sera toujours et à jamais celui qui repose sous les dalles de l'église d'Or San Michele, à Florence. Néanmoins, je veux voir cette tombe.

— Ce pourrait être difficile, voire impossible. L'exécuteur de l'époque, Arny Signart, était un homme déjà âgé. Il n'est peut-être plus de ce monde et, de toute façon, il n'exercerait certainement plus...

— Eh bien, son successeur nous apprendra ce qu'il en est. Allons le voir!

Sans attendre d'autre réponse, elle se dirigeait vers les chevaux qu'Esteban avait attachés à l'anneau de fer d'une maison mais Démétrios arrêta son élan :

— Laisse-moi y aller! Ta place n'est pas dans ce genre d'endroit. L'homme, le tourmenteur qui manie ces instruments, ajouta-t-il en désignant l'échafaud et ses accessoires, est tenu à l'écart par tous les autres. Il est une sorte de lépreux que l'on évite...

— Et lorsqu'il se rend au marché, car il faut bien qu'il vive, renchérit Léonarde, il est muni d'une baguette à l'aide de laquelle il doit désigner ce qu'il veut acheter.

— Et son argent? On n'en veut pas? demanda Fiora, sarcastique.

— Il est tenu de porter des gants. Mais beaucoup préfèrent lui donner plutôt que d'accepter des pièces qui sont le prix du sang. Jadis, le duc Jean de Bourgogne que l'on disait Sans Peur, a causé un scandale à Paris, lors des troubles de 1413, en serrant la main de Capeluche, le bourreau de la ville.

— Tout ceci ne me concerne pas, coupa Fiora. Merci de ta sollicitude, Démétrios, mais cette visite fait partie de la tâche que je me suis imposée et je dois l'accomplir tout comme j'accomplirai encore bien d'autres choses déplaisantes. Où habite cet homme?

— Comme vous voudrez! soupira Léonarde, sachant bien qu'il était inutile d'insister. Suivez-moi! Ce n'est pas loin d'ici. Inutile de prendre les chevaux...

Laissant les montures à la garde d'Esteban, Léonarde guida sa compagne et le médecin grec vers le fond de la place où coulait un ruisseau, le Suzon, près duquel s'élevait le moulin des Carmes. Une maison apparut sur l'arrière de ce dernier, appuyée au rempart et sans qu'aucune autre lui fît face ou se tînt à ses côtés ; une maison solide et solitaire dont la porte rouge était peinte de neuf. Un guichet grillagé permettait aux habitants de reconnaître le visiteur avant de lui ouvrir.

A l'appel du marteau de fer, un visage barbu apparut derrière les minces barreaux :

— Que voulez-vous ? fit une voix sèche.

— Êtes-vous le bourreau de cette ville ? demanda Fiora, je voudrais vous parler.

— Qui êtes-vous ?

— Une voyageuse, une étrangère et mon nom ne vous dirait rien. Mais je paierai si vous répondez à mes questions.

— Chez moi, on paie plus volontiers pour que je n'en pose pas.

Le guichet se referma mais la porte s'ouvrit. Un homme vêtu de cuir et qui devait être d'une force peu commune se montra. Il pouvait avoir quarante ans mais, de sa figure envahie par des moustaches et une barbe brune, on ne distinguait qu'un nez court et des yeux sombres profondément enfoncés sous d'épais sourcils qui se rejoignaient. Il tenait un livre à la main.

Sans prier ses visiteurs d'entrer plus avant que le couloir sur lequel ouvrait sa porte, le bourreau croisa les bras :

— Écoutons vos questions en attendant de voir votre argent.

— Je voudrais vous parler de votre devancier, maître...

— Arny Signart, souffla Léonarde.

— Maître Signart n'est pas mon devancier. Celui-là se nommait Jean Larmite et, avant lui, c'était Étienne Poisson. Et moi, je suis Jehan du Poix. Il y a dix ans que

Signart a reposé l'épée de justice. Après trente-cinq ans de service !

— Il est mort ?

— Pas encore que je sache mais il est fort âgé...

— Sauriez-vous me dire où je peux le trouver ? s'enquit Fiora en portant la main à l'escarcelle retenue par une châtelaine à sa ceinture.

Les yeux de l'homme suivirent son geste avec intérêt :

— Il avait amassé quelque bien qui lui a permis d'acheter un petit clos, hors les murs, près du prieuré de Larrey. On dit qu'il s'entend avec les moines qui seront ses héritiers... Si vous voulez le voir, c'est là que vous le trouverez... à moins qu'il ne soit mort dans la nuit.

— Ce qu'à Dieu ne plaise ! Merci de m'avoir répondu...

Elle tendit trois pièces d'argent et il avança la main pour les recevoir sans quitter des yeux cette jeune femme vêtue de fin drap gris dont le visage se dissimulait derrière le voile qui couvrait sa tête. Mais elle semblait belle et, d'après son allure, on pouvait supposer qu'elle était une noble dame. Il s'attendait à ce qu'elle cherchât des yeux un meuble quelconque pour y déposer cet argent mais, sans hésiter, elle le plaça dans la paume ouverte.

— Vous ne craignez pas de toucher la main d'un bourreau ?

— Pourquoi non ? Vous faites au grand jour et sur ordre ce que d'autres font en secret ou sous le couvert de la nuit. Beaucoup d'entre nous sont des exécuteurs – et nous n'en savons rien... Adieu, Jehan du Poix. Dieu vous garde !

Il ouvrit la porte devant elle et, cette fois, s'inclina quand la jeune femme la franchit :

— S'il peut entendre la prière d'un misérable, c'est vous qu'il gardera, noble dame...

En silence et sans prêter même attention aux yeux ronds d'une commère qui les regardait passer, les trois voyageurs rejoignirent leurs chevaux. Léonarde, qui était entrée chez l'exécuteur avec une certaine répugnance, s'était hâtée de dire une prière dès qu'elle en fut sortie.

Elle l'achevait quand Fiora, un pied sur l'étrier, lui demanda :

– Vous savez, j'imagine, où se trouve ce prieuré ?

– A une demi-lieue environ de la porte d'Ouche. Voulez-vous donc y aller maintenant ?

– Bien sûr. La journée n'est pas encore avancée. Est-ce que cela vous contrarie ?

– Non, mon agneau. Je suis d'ailleurs la seule à pouvoir vous montrer le chemin. Il faut néanmoins nous hâter si nous voulons revenir avant la fermeture des portes.

Hors de la ville, on franchit l'Ouche, une jolie rivière ombragée d'aulnes et de saules. Au bord, des lavandières frappaient leur linge à grands coups de battoirs sans arrêter un seul instant de rire et de bavarder car le temps était beau, doux et incitait à la gaieté. Le long du coteau au sommet duquel se profilaient les bâtiments et la tour d'un vieux couvent, quelques arpents de vigne se chauffaient au soleil...

– Qui pourrait croire, soupira Démétrios, que ce pays est en guerre ? Tout y respire la paix et la prospérité...

Depuis des mois, en effet, le duc Charles de Bourgogne, toujours à la poursuite du rêve qui le hantait de reconstruire l'antique royaume lotharingien en réunissant par de nouvelles terres ses domaines flamands à son duché proprement dit et à la Franche-Comté, assiégeait, près de Cologne, la forte ville de Neuss dont il ne pouvait venir à bout. Et cela indépendamment du fait qu'il avait donné rendez-vous, en ce même été 1475, au roi d'Angleterre Édouard IV pour l'aider à conquérir la France, cette France dont il haïssait le roi, Louis, onzième du nom, et avec laquelle la trêve, conclue depuis trois ans, venait de s'achever sans autre espoir de prorogation. Le Téméraire méritait bien son surnom...

– La guerre est loin, fit Léonarde, et le duc ne peut tirer de ses provinces que ce que lui accordent, en hommes et en argent, les États de Bourgogne pour ce pays-ci, les États de Flandres pour ceux de par-delà... Et il faut, tout de même, bien des bras à cette terre...

— Mais le duc commence à manquer d'or à ce que l'on dit, reprit le Grec avec une sombre joie. Alors qu'il était le prince le plus riche de toute la chrétienté... S'il cherche à contracter des emprunts...

Il se tut brusquement, conscient de ce qu'il était en train de dire. Rappeler les besoins en argent frais du Téméraire au moment où Fiora s'obligeait à ce pénible pèlerinage ne pouvait qu'être douloureux à la jeune femme. C'était ramener à la surface le souvenir cuisant de l'étrange mariage conclu en trois jours, l'hiver précédent, entre l'héritière du riche Francesco Beltrami et le comte Philippe de Selongey, l'ambassadeur envoyé par le Téméraire auprès de Lorenzo de Médicis pour tenter de négocier un emprunt. Emprunt que le Magnifique avait refusé par fidélité à son alliance avec le roi de France. La dot royale de Fiora avait alors rejoint les coffres du duc de Bourgogne cependant que sa vie d'épousée se réduisait à la seule nuit de noces. Et puis Philippe s'en était reparti, à l'aube, pour aller se faire tuer, ayant, pensait-il, souillé son nom par cette union avec l'enfant de l'inceste. Fiora qui l'aimait avait beaucoup pleuré mais, à présent, il était difficile de deviner quels étaient au juste ses sentiments envers son fugitif époux. L'aimait-elle encore ou l'avait-elle ajouté au nombre de ceux dont elle entendait se venger ? Il est vrai que Selongey avait reparu discrètement à Florence au moment où s'écroulait la fortune des Beltrami, mais qu'il en était reparti encore plus vite sans chercher à savoir ce qu'était devenue sa jeune femme. Voulait-il la revoir ou bien tenter de procurer à son maître de nouveaux subsides ?

Conscient du silence qui avait suivi ses derniers mots, Démétrios, après un bref coup d'œil à Fiora qui chevauchait, impavide, à son côté, reprit la parole mais se contenta de vanter le charme du paysage et la beauté opulente de cette ville de Dijon où les ducs de Bourgogne avaient accumulé œuvres d'art et bâtiments prestigieux. Telle cette Sainte-Chapelle couronnée d'or où se tenaient les grands chapitres de la Toison d'or, l'ordre de chevalerie fondé par le père du Téméraire et dont Selongey était honoré.

En fait, Fiora n'entendait guère ses propos. La violence des drames qu'elle avait vécus, ce dernier printemps, s'atténuait en elle pour laisser place au souvenir de celui vécu jadis par ses jeunes et imprudents parents. Était-ce la magie propre à cette terre de Bourgogne vers laquelle, depuis l'instant où elle y avait posé le pied, elle se sentait attirée ? Toujours est-il que Jean et Marie de Brévailles lui devenaient plus proches et plus chers à mesure qu'elle remontait le temps pour rejoindre leur drame.

Aux abords du prieuré de Larrey, se trouvait un petit clos dont les murs bas jouxtaient ceux du couvent. C'était un minuscule domaine composé d'une vigne, d'un grand carré potager avec quelques arbres fruitiers et d'une maison basse, abritée sous un toit à deux pentes. Un homme en sarrau de toile bise, ses longs cheveux blancs dépassant d'un bonnet de laine, y travaillait, courbé sur les ceps couverts de feuilles vertes. C'était un homme âgé mais, quand il se redressa, soutenant de ses mains ses reins qui devaient lui faire mal, on put voir qu'il était grand et encore vigoureux.

— C'est lui, dit Léonarde. Voulez-vous que je lui parle ?

— Non, merci, répondit Fiora. Je préfère y aller moi-même. Si vous voulez bien m'attendre un moment ?

Elle sauta à terre, marcha vers la barrière faite de grosses branches qui fermait l'étroit domaine, la poussa et se dirigea vers le vieillard qui, une main en auvent au-dessus des yeux, la regardait venir à lui dans un rayon du soleil.

— Pardonnez-moi d'entrer chez vous sans y être invitée, dit-elle. Vous êtes maître Arny Signart, n'est-ce pas ?

Peu habitué à des visites de cette qualité, l'ancien bourreau salua gauchement :

— Si vous savez mon nom vous savez donc aussi ce que j'étais ?

— Je le sais. C'est à ce titre que j'ai désiré vous voir...

— Je n'aime guère me rappeler ces années-là mais... à votre service, madame! Voulez-vous vous asseoir un peu devant la maison?

— Ne pouvons-nous marcher? Vous avez là une belle vigne...

Sous la barbe blanche qui donnait à ce solitaire l'air d'un patriarche, naquit un timide sourire :

— Et qui donne de bon vin... Marchons donc puisque c'est votre désir...

Ils firent quelques pas entre les rangées régulières de plants que le vieil homme caressait au passage d'un geste affectueux.

— Il y aura dix-huit ans en décembre prochain, dit Fiora, un inconnu, un riche marchand florentin, vous a donné de l'or pour accomplir une mission qu'il vous avait confiée et qui lui tenait à cœur. C'est de cela que je suis venue vous parler...

Maître Signart s'arrêta et Fiora, qui marchait devant lui, se retourna. Elle vit que son visage était devenu très pâle :

— Qui êtes-vous, fit-il d'une voix soudain enrouée, pour évoquer ce terrible jour dont j'implore chaque jour le Tout-Puissant de m'ôter le souvenir?

Lentement, Fiora fit glisser le voile blanc qui enveloppait sa tête pour mettre son visage à découvert :

— Regardez-moi!... Je suis « leur » fille, celle que le marchand florentin avait adoptée...

Vivement, le vieillard se signa comme devant une apparition puis cacha sa figure dans ses mains que la jeune femme put voir trembler.

— Que... que voulez-vous? balbutia l'ancien bourreau. Quelle vengeance voulez-vous exercer sur un vieil homme?

— Je leur ressemble donc à ce point?

— Au point de réveiller mes cauchemars. Vous n'imaginez pas combien de fois je les ai revus, tous les deux! Ils étaient jeunes... ils étaient beaux, ils se souriaient... et moi j'ai dû les abattre...

— C'est peut-être le meilleur service que vous ayez pu leur rendre parce qu'ils sont partis ensemble. Je hais ceux qui les ont conduits à l'échafaud mais, si on les avait enfermés, séparés l'un de l'autre et jusqu'à ce que la mort les prenne, je crois qu'ils auraient été infiniment malheureux. Quand on s'aime, il doit y avoir une douceur à partir ensemble, même par ce chemin-là...

Le vieil homme avait laissé retomber ses mains et contemplait cette belle jeune femme qui, de toute évidence, l'avait oublié et se parlait à voix haute. Il la regardait avec étonnement mais non sans une sorte de soulagement...

— Vous pensez vraiment ce que vous dites ?

Elle lui sourit sans la moindre arrière-pensée. Ce vieillard déplorant le crime qui n'était pas le sien, qui même en était obsédé la touchait. Lui, le malheureux, n'avait été qu'un instrument et il demeurait hanté par le souvenir de ces deux êtres qu'il lui avait fallu décapiter. Ceux qui avaient voulu, ordonné cette double mort avaient-ils connu, eux aussi, les mauvais rêves et les obsessions ? Fiora en doutait beaucoup. Regnault du Hamel était un homme sans cœur, Pierre de Brévailles ne devait pas en avoir davantage. Quant au duc de Bourgogne, le souvenir d'un jeune frère d'armes assassiné ne devait pas peser beaucoup auprès de ses royales ambitions.

— Je pense chacun des mots que je dis, reprit Fiora, et je ne suis pas venue vous tourmenter mais uniquement vous demander où se trouve cette tombe que mon père avait souhaitée pour eux. Je voudrais pouvoir y prier...

Tout en disant ces mots et se souvenant de ce qui s'était passé chez Jehan du Poix, elle porta la main à son escarcelle mais le vieillard l'arrêta :

— Surtout, ne m'offrez rien ! Votre père a royalement payé la tâche qu'il m'a confiée : c'est à lui que je dois de posséder cette maison qui me rapproche du ciel, moi qui vivais dans la fange. La tombe que vous cherchez est tout près d'ici...

— Vous allez pouvoir m'y conduire, alors ?

— Non, car il vaut mieux que l'on ne nous voie pas ensemble. Mais vous trouverez facilement : en sortant d'ici et en prenant le chemin à main gauche, vous verrez, près du petit bois qui couronne ce coteau, une fontaine. Elle appartient au prieuré comme les terres qui l'entourent et s'appelle la fontaine Sainte-Anne. Le sol en est sacré. C'est à côté de la fontaine que je les ai enterrés et j'ai planté dessus une aubépine qui est en fleur plus tôt et plus longtemps que les autres. Les gens de la région ont vu, dans sa floraison, une sorte de miracle et, au printemps, les filles viennent y cueillir quelques brindilles comme porte-bonheur...

— Quand avez-vous fait cela ?...

— Trois jours après l'exécution, il n'y avait plus de neige et il valait mieux ne pas attendre que la terre soit trop tassée. C'était la lune nouvelle et il faisait très noir mais je suis comme les chats et j'y vois dans l'obscurité. Et puis, j'ai eu de l'aide...

— Qui donc ? L'un de vos valets ?

— Oh non ! Je n'avais pas assez confiance. C'est le vieux prêtre qui m'a donné la main. Il n'a pas voulu repartir pour Brévailles avant d'avoir accompli avec moi ce qu'il considérait comme un devoir pieux. Pauvre brave homme ! Il n'était pas très solide mais il m'a été tout de même bien utile. Et il a pu au moins bénir la terre... Voyez-vous, madame, ce m'est une douceur de savoir que ces malheureux enfants reposent là, dans la paix d'un sol béni et tout près de moi. Même si mes nuits restent pénibles. Ma paix à moi, je ne l'ai trouvée que lorsque j'ai abandonné le métier et suis monté ici pour n'en plus redescendre. Et c'est pourquoi, tout à l'heure, j'ai eu si peur en vous reconnaissant...

— Vous voyez bien qu'il n'y avait aucune raison. Je suis certaine qu'ils vous ont pardonné eux-mêmes depuis longtemps. Sans doute depuis l'instant où vous avez frappé. Adieu, maître Signart ! Nous ne nous reverrons sans doute jamais. Sachez pourtant que je vous remercie du fond du cœur...

Le laissant rentrer dans sa maison, peut-être pour y prier mais plus certainement pour y boire un verre de son vin afin de se remettre, Fiora rejoignit ses compagnons.

– Les savoir en paix et dans une terre sainte change-t-il quelque chose à tes projets de vengeance ? demanda Démétrios.

– Cela n'atténue en rien les fautes des coupables. J'irai jusqu'au bout...

– Hormis le duc Charles, les autres sont peut-être morts ?

– C'est ce qu'il faudra découvrir. Seule la justice de Dieu peut leur éviter la mienne. Mais voici, je crois, la fontaine.

La description de l'ancien bourreau avait été parfaite et l'endroit paraissait charmant. A l'orée d'un joli bois de pins, un filet d'eau coulait dans un petit bassin fait de grosses pierres veloutées de mousse et, tout auprès, un gros buisson d'aubépine poussait ses branches vigoureuses, ses feuilles finement découpées et la neige parfumée de ses fleurs délicates qui poudraient déjà le sol et tremblaient sur l'eau de la fontaine. Mais ce que n'avait pas prévu le vieux Signart, c'était une présence : quelqu'un priait devant l'aubépine.

C'était un jeune homme pauvrement vêtu et si grande était sa ferveur qu'il n'avait pas entendu le pas des chevaux. Du regard, Fiora interrogea Démétrios. Le médecin haussa les épaules :

– Si l'on vous a dit que cet arbuste passait pour miraculeux, cela s'explique. Il suffit de laisser ce garçon achever sa prière...

Ce ne fut pas long. Sentant peut-être qu'il était observé, le paysan – car tout indiquait que c'en était un – termina bientôt son oraison sur un ample signe de croix puis, se penchant vivement, il baisa la terre, se redressa, cassa une petite branche qu'il enfouit sous sa blouse, enfin, se retournant, enfonça son bonnet sur sa tête d'un geste rageur et jeta aux nouveaux venus :

— Que venez-vous chercher céans ? Si c'est pour faire boire vos chevaux, sachez que cette fontaine est sainte.

— Nos chevaux n'ont pas soif, répondit Fiora et nous ne souhaitons rien faire d'autre que ce que vous faisiez vous-même : prier. Y voyez-vous quelque empêchement ?

Le jeune homme ne répondit pas mais s'avança lentement vers les cavaliers qui, d'ailleurs, mettaient pied à terre. C'était un garçon qui pouvait avoir vingt-cinq ou trente ans, assez grand mais, en dépit de ses habits grossiers, d'une complexion plus délicate et, pour tout dire, plus élégante que l'on ne pouvait s'y attendre. Son visage sans beauté avait des traits rudes et un peu brouillés mais qui, pourtant, semblèrent curieusement familiers à Fiora. Pour sa part, le paysan avait fixé sur elle son regard sans plus s'occuper des autres personnages. Il vint droit à elle :

— Marie ! murmura-t-il, trompé par le voile blanc qui cachait la chevelure noire de la jeune femme, Marie ! Ce n'est pas toi ?... Ce ne peut pas être toi ?... et pourtant...

— Non, dit Fiora, je ne suis pas Marie. Mais je suis sa fille. Et vous, qui êtes-vous ? L'avez-donc connue pour reconnaître son visage après tant d'années ?

— Je suis son jeune frère, Christophe. J'avais dix ans lorsque... et je les aimais tant, tous les deux ! Vous ne pouvez pas savoir : ils ont été la seule lumière de ma vie et voilà bientôt dix-huit ans que cette lumière s'est éteinte. Depuis, je n'ai pas cessé d'être malheureux...

Un sanglot lui noua la gorge. Alors, il se détourna et, arrachant son bonnet, courut s'agenouiller de nouveau sous l'aubépine comme il aurait couru vers un refuge :

— Regarde, murmura Démétrios. C'est un prêtre.

En effet, dans la masse broussailleuse des cheveux châtains, une tonsure découpait la rondelle blanchâtre qui est le signe du sacerdoce...

— Il n'a pas dû avoir d'autre alternative ! fit Léonarde avec un regard plein de compassion sur la maigre silhouette secouée par le chagrin. Fiora le rejoignit et récita une courte prière. Puis, prenant le jeune homme aux épaules elle l'aida à se relever, offrant son mouchoir pour qu'il essuie son visage inondé de larmes.

— Je me croyais sans famille, dit-elle doucement, et voilà que je trouve un jeune oncle ! Peut-être puis-je vous aider à être moins malheureux. Je m'appelle Fiora et je viens de Florence... Et vous, vous êtes d'Église, n'est-ce pas ?

Il eut un geste de dénégation violente puis, comprenant que sa tonsure l'avait trahi, enfonça rageusement son bonnet jusqu'aux sourcils :

— Je ne le suis plus... Hier je me suis enfui du monastère de Cîteaux où j'étouffais depuis dix-sept ans et je ne sais pas encore où je vais, mais loin, le plus loin possible !... Avant, pourtant, j'ai voulu venir prier ici, voir leur tombe au moins une fois...

— Qui vous l'a indiquée ?

— Notre vieux chapelain, le Père Antoine Charruet, qui les avait accompagnés jusqu'au bout et qui est venu mourir dans mon couvent après que mon père l'eut chassé comme un valet malhonnête à cause de ce qu'il avait fait. Mon père est un monstre. Il n'a ni cœur ni entrailles... J'ai été conduit à Cîteaux trois jours après l'exécution tandis que l'on menait ma petite sœur Marguerite chez les Bernardines de Tart... où elle est morte l'hiver dernier...

— Et... votre mère ? Est-elle encore vivante ?

— Malheureusement, car sa vie est un enfer. Elle vit autant dire recluse dans notre château, enfermée avec ce vieux démon qui n'a jamais assez d'injures pour les maudire, elle et les fruits de ses entrailles. Elle, si bonne et si douce, elle qui a tant souffert et qui doit encore endurer ce calvaire dont il semble que Dieu se complaise à prolonger la durée. Oh, si je pouvais la délivrer !...

— Pourquoi ne pas chercher ensemble le moyen d'y parvenir ? dit Fiora, émue par la profonde douleur de ce garçon aux yeux hagards de bête traquée...

— Que voulez-vous dire ? Et d'abord, pourquoi êtes-vous revenue par ici ? N'étiez-vous pas heureuse auprès de ce marchand florentin dont le Père Charruet m'a tant vanté la générosité ?

— Oh si... mais mon père est mort et je suis venue ici pour payer de vieilles dettes. Si vous ne savez où aller, venez avec nous ! Je prendrai soin de vous...

— Vous êtes bonne... mais ce que je veux, c'est faire la guerre, c'est aller me battre. C'est le seul moyen d'en finir honorablement avec une vie qui me fait horreur...

Démétrios s'avança et posa sa grande main sur l'épaule de Christophe :

— Vous ne trouvez pas que cela fait déjà assez de morts dans la famille ? Pourquoi ne pas chercher plutôt à vous faire une vie plus conforme à vos goûts et digne d'un gentilhomme ?

— D'un gentilhomme ? Je n'ai même plus de nom ni de prénom. A Cîteaux j'étais le frère Anthime, rien d'autre. Mon père entend qu'il ne reste aucune trace de notre famille...

— Eh bien, faites-vous un autre nom ! Soyez un ancêtre au lieu d'être un descendant ! De toute façon, votre départ pour la guerre pourra tout de même attendre jusqu'à demain ? Et je crois que, d'ici là, vous aurez encore beaucoup de choses à apprendre à... votre nièce ? Venez avec nous ! Il se fait tard et les portes de la ville vont bientôt fermer...

A la lueur qui s'était allumée dans les yeux de l'ex-moine — ces yeux gris des Brévailles si semblables aux siens ! — Fiora comprit qu'il mourait d'envie d'accepter et elle insista gentiment :

— Venez, je vous en prie ! Vous n'imaginez pas combien je suis heureuse que le destin nous ait fait rencontrer...

— Moi aussi je suis heureux et pour la première fois depuis bien longtemps ! J'avais oublié ce que c'était !

Et, sans plus se faire prier mais en refusant le cheval que Fiora lui offrait dans l'intention de partager celui de Léonarde, il sauta joyeusement en croupe d'Esteban.

La jeune femme, cependant, retournait vers la tombe cachée, et, s'agenouillant :

– Je suis venue ici pour tirer vengeance de ceux qui vous y ont mis, murmura-t-elle. Lorsque ma tâche sera accomplie je reviendrai vous en rendre compte mais, en attendant, je vais faire en sorte que les autres victimes, votre mère et votre frère, retrouvent au moins la paix du cœur. Je suis votre enfant et je vous aime...

Se courbant tout à fait, elle baisa la terre sous l'herbe verte et se releva, emportant sur ses cheveux un semis de pétales blancs. Comme l'avait fait Christophe, elle cassa une brindille et revint vers ses compagnons :

– Nous pouvons aller, fit-elle avec un sourire.

Après un dernier signe de croix, les cavaliers quittèrent la fontaine Sainte-Anne dans l'eau claire de laquelle le soleil jetait des étincelles. Ils redescendirent en silence vers la ville.

C'était à présent au tour de Léonarde d'aller à la rencontre de ses souvenirs...

Quand elle franchit la porte Guillaume, qui ouvrait la ville au nord-ouest, le cœur battait à la vieille fille un peu plus vite que de coutume en dépit de ses allures imperturbables. Elle avait vécu près de dix ans dans cette auberge de la Croix d'Or dont on pouvait déjà apercevoir la belle enseigne peinte et découpée et elle ne l'avait pas revue depuis dix-huit années. Elle y était venue peu de temps après la mort de sa mère quand sa cousine Bertille, la maîtresse du lieu, lui avait proposé de l'y aider dans ses tâches quotidiennes. Et, en vérité, Léonarde s'était trouvée bien dans cette opulente auberge, réputée par tout le duché – et même au-delà – pour le confort de ses chambres et la perfection de sa cuisine. On y voyait beaucoup de monde, beaucoup de riches voyageurs et, souvent aussi, de grands personnages. Il était même arrivé au duc Philippe en personne de venir avec quelques gentilshommes de son entourage souper à la Croix d'Or. Inutile de dire que, ce soir-là, maître Huguet, le propriétaire, avait vidé son auberge pour la consacrer uniquement à son seigneur.

Oui, Léonarde Mercet se plaisait bien chez ses cousins. Pourtant, il avait suffi qu'un soir on mît entre ses bras un bébé maigre, une petite fille abandonnée, pour qu'elle sentît s'éveiller en elle ce qu'elle n'espérait plus ressentir : l'instinct maternel, le besoin de se dévouer, d'étreindre et de se donner de tout son être sans même envisager qu'un jour cela lui soit rendu. Et, dès le lendemain, elle tournait délibérément le dos à tout ce qui avait été sa vie jusque-là pour s'en aller à l'aventure, avec un inconnu dont elle pressentait seulement qu'il était aussi généreux qu'elle-même. Aussi, dans la litière que Francesco Beltrami avait achetée tout exprès pour ce voyage, la petite Fiora, baptisée la veille dans la chambre même du négociant, reposait entre les bras d'une Léonarde infiniment heureuse...

En revenant de la sorte à son point de départ et tandis que sa monture descendait la rue Porte-Guillaume, Léonarde pensait qu'elle avait fait le bon choix en dépit du drame par lequel s'était achevé son séjour à Florence[1] et que, si c'était à refaire, elle recommencerait sans la moindre hésitation, car elle avait vécu dix-sept années de vrai bonheur dans le palais des bords de l'Arno. De ce bonheur, il ne restait plus aujourd'hui de réel que ce qu'elle avait connu en quittant Dijon jadis : sa tendresse pour Fiora et le devoir de veiller sur elle.

Évidemment, c'était à présent moins facile. Fiora était une femme et une femme qui connaissait la souffrance, une femme altérée de vengeance qui avait rencontré son semblable en Démétrios et qui n'aurait trêve ni repos jusqu'à ce que tout soit accompli. Léonarde s'était alors donné pour tâche essentielle de veiller à ce que l'enfant de son cœur ne sorte pas de ce dangereux chemin plus blessée encore qu'elle ne l'était en s'y engageant.

Quand les cavaliers arrivèrent devant l'auberge, Léonarde pensa que rien n'avait changé, du moins en appa-

---

1. Voir *Fiora et le Magnifique*.

rence. C'était toujours la même impeccable propreté, les mêmes rutilances de cuivres et d'étains briqués à grand renfort de son et d'huile de coude ainsi que le montraient les fenêtres ouvertes dont les petits carreaux brillaient autant qu'autrefois, les mêmes effluves gourmands qui débordaient jusque dans la rue et les mêmes dallages de belles pierres blanches du pays que l'on récurait chaque jour à grande eau. Par contre, le ventre de maître Huguet, le propriétaire qui vint à leur rencontre, était plus rebondi qu'autrefois et son haut bonnet blanc, bien amidonné, laissait dépasser des mèches grises...

Impressionné par l'allure de Fiora et de Démétrios qui allaient en tête du groupe, le digne homme fit tous ses efforts pour se plier en deux – sans grand résultat d'ailleurs – et informa les « nobles voyageurs » que sa maison comme lui-même étaient tout à leur service si toutefois ils voulaient bien lui confier ce qu'ils désiraient de lui.

– Savoir si la maison est toujours aussi bonne, mon bon cousin, déclara gaiement Léonarde qui s'était avancée auprès de la jeune femme. Nous sommes des voyageurs fatigués et... affamés !

La stupeur arrondit les yeux et la bouche de Donatien Huguet et il dut faire appel à ses besicles pour s'assurer qu'il n'avait pas la berlue :

– Par tous les saints du paradis ! Léonarde ! Est-ce bien vous ?

– C'est bien moi, en chair et en os ! Plus d'os que de chair, d'ailleurs comme autrefois mais vous, que vous voilà gras et fleuri ! L'image même de la prospérité ! Pour ne pas dire de l'abondance !

– Je ne me plains pas, je ne me plains pas ! La maison marche à souhait et nous gardons notre réputation...

Sur ce, les deux cousins s'embrassèrent avec toute effusion que l'on met quand on ne s'est pas vus depuis longtemps. Les baisers claquaient à la bonne franquette. Léonarde, cependant, les interrompit pour demander :

– Et ma cousine Bertille ? Où est-elle ? J'ai hâte de l'embrasser.

Le bon visage épanoui de maître Huguet parut se recouvrir de brume et même une larme monta à ses yeux :

— Ma pauvre femme nous a quittés il y aura quatre ans à la Saint-Fiacre et je n'en suis pas encore consolé. C'est ma jeune sœur Magdeleine qui m'aide à présent mais, bien qu'elle ait beaucoup de bonne volonté, elle n'est pas si entendue que ma Bertille...

On se réembrassa avec des larmes des deux côtés car Léonarde était de ceux qui savent garder leur affection au chaud sans que le passage des années y change quoi que ce soit. Elle aimait bien Bertille et, à présent, elle la pleurait d'un cœur sincère. Mais, cette fois, ce fut l'aubergiste qui rompit l'embrassade :

— Mais nous sommes là à parler famille, à nous attendrir, et nous faisons languir ces nobles personnes qui vous accompagnent...

— Il y en a une encore que vous connaissez, fit Léonarde en glissant son bras sous celui de Fiora. Vous souvenez-vous de messire Beltrami, mon cousin ?

— Comment aurais-je pu l'oublier ? Un seigneur si généreux, si aimable... et qui aimait tellement mon coq au vin de Beaune ! Par exemple, il y a belle lurette que nous ne l'avons vu...

— Et vous ne le reverrez plus, hélas, car lui aussi a quitté ce monde mais voici donna Fiora, sa fille, dont je suis toujours la gouvernante...

En face de cette belle jeune femme dont les grands yeux gris lui souriaient, maître Huguet joignit les mains avec un étonnement plein de ferveur mais qui pourtant ne sonnait pas très juste.

— La... petite fille qui a été baptisée ici ? Doux Jésus ! Qu'elle est belle !... comme ma Bertille aurait été heureuse de la voir !

— Quant à ce seigneur, ajouta Léonarde, c'est messire Démétrios Lascaris, médecin personnel de Mgr Lorenzo de Médicis que celui-ci envoie au roi de France. Il y a aussi son écuyer et... un ami. A présent, tâchez de nous bien loger et de nous bien nourrir !...

Escorté de l'aubergiste qui avait retrouvé sa bonne humeur, tout le monde pénétra dans l'auberge où Magdelaine, qui ressemblait fort à son frère de par son tour de taille et son bon visage épanoui, embrassa Léonarde et offrit à Fiora sa meilleure révérence. Puis elle les précéda dans l'escalier pour les conduire à la plus belle chambre de la maison, une grande pièce blanchie à la chaux mais réchauffée d'une tapisserie de laine, à personnages, meublée d'un grand lit à courtines de velours vert et de quelques beaux meubles bourguignons luisants de bonne santé et de cire fine dont le parfum embaumait plus encore que le grand bouquet de genêt qui mettait un éclaboussement de soleil sur un coffre de chêne sculpté.

Léonarde la reconnut aussitôt car, en dépit des années écoulées, cette chambre, grâce au plus soigneux entretien, était celle-là même où Francesco Beltrami avait rapporté l'enfant arrachée à la fureur haineuse de Regnault du Hamel, le mari de sa mère, et où la petite Fiora avait reçu le baptême. Elle l'apprit à cette grande Fiora qui regardait autour d'elle avec des yeux pleins d'émotion et choisit de l'y laisser seule un moment pour redescendre à la cuisine où elle était certaine de rencontrer maître Huguet. Tout à l'heure, en effet, elle lui avait trouvé un son de voix bizarre quand il avait constaté que Francesco Beltrami n'était pas venu à la Croix d'Or depuis longtemps, un peu comme s'il en éprouvait de la satisfaction. Il aurait aussi bien pu ajouter, du même ton : « Dieu en soit loué ! » Et la vieille demoiselle tenait à savoir pourquoi.

Elle surprit son cousin occupé à mesurer les précieuses épices qu'il destinait à un pâté de veau dont un de ses marmitons avait entrepris la confection. Sachant l'importance d'une telle opération, elle attendit qu'il en eût terminé puis l'entraîna à part dans la petite pièce où l'aubergiste faisait d'ordinaire ses comptes :

— Tirez-moi d'un doute, mon cousin ! Tout à l'heure, lorsque vous avez dit n'avoir pas vu messire Beltrami depuis longtemps, il m'est apparu que vous n'en étiez pas autrement désolé ?

— Comment pouvez-vous penser cela, Léonarde ? C'était un si bon client...

— ... et un client qui, la dernière fois, vous a laissé une belle somme en paiement des petites choses inhabituelles qu'il vous avait demandées. Les... folies de ce brave homme vous ont rapporté pas mal d'or. Cela pourrait justifier pour le moins un regret ?

Les joues vernies de maître Huguet passèrent au rouge ponceau et il jeta un rapide regard à la cuisine en pleine activité pour s'assurer que personne n'écoutait :

— Pas mal d'or, en effet mais aussi pas mal d'ennuis. Avez-vous l'intention de séjourner ici longtemps ?

— Eh bien, fit Léonarde estomaquée, vous pouvez vous vanter d'avoir une curieuse façon de comprendre l'hospitalité, sans parler de votre sens du commerce ! Nous pouvons payer largement, vous savez ?

— Je n'en doute pas mais vous comprendrez mieux tout à l'heure qu'en disant cela je ne pense pas seulement à moi mais aussi à vous et surtout à cette belle jeune femme. Qui pourrait imaginer, à lui voir cette allure de reine, qu'elle est la même que ce pauvre petit être...

— Vous célébrerez la beauté de donna Fiora plus tard ! Dites-moi plutôt ce qui s'est passé ici après notre départ !

La voix de l'aubergiste baissa de plusieurs tons au point que sa compagne dut se pencher pour mieux l'entendre :

— Une véritable catastrophe ! On avait négligé de nous dire que la petite fille « trouvée » était, en réalité, l'enfant de ces deux malheureux exécutés le jour même... Et nous ne savions pas davantage que messire Beltrami avait abandonné le sire du Hamel, ligoté et bâillonné, dans l'ancien hospice des pestiférés où il a failli mourir de froid...

— Failli seulement ? C'est bien dommage ! Quant au reste, je ne vois pas pourquoi on vous en eût fait part. Messire Francesco était homme à savoir ce qu'il faisait et ne jugeait pas utile de le crier sur les toits. Ainsi du Hamel en a réchappé ? Qui est l'auteur de ce joli coup ?

— Un paysan qui passait par là en allant aux tanneries et qui a entendu des gémissements. C'est lui qui a appelé à l'aide. Mais vous étiez déjà partis depuis plus de vingt-quatre heures...

— C'est encore heureux! Et comment cela s'est-il passé?

— Assez mal. Messire Regnault, une fois réchauffé et réconforté, a jeté feu et flammes. On a fouillé cette maison, en dépit de mes protestations, pour retrouver l'homme qui « avait osé s'opposer à la justice du prince » et, bien sûr, on ne l'a pas retrouvé.

— C'eût été étonnant! fit Léonarde avec un demi-sourire.

— Moi, j'ai dit uniquement ce que j'étais censé savoir : le marchand florentin avait quitté Dijon la veille et à l'aube, sans doute pour se rendre à Paris où il avait affaires. De l'enfant, ni moi ni ma femme n'avons touché mot, bien que le sire du Hamel soit fort acharné à la retrouver. Nous n'avons rien su dire non plus de ce qu'était devenu le Père Charruet sinon qu'il était parti en même temps que son nouvel ami. C'était d'autant plus facile que nous ne savions absolument rien de ses intentions.

— Et votre parent, le chanoine de Saint-Bénigne qui vous a vendu au poids de l'or sa vieille litière? Il n'a rien dit?

— Encore aurait-il fallu que l'on sût l'affaire. Personne n'a même songé à lui...

— Et votre personnel qui a néanmoins vu certaines petites choses, à commencer par mon départ, n'a-t-il pas été interrogé?

— Si fait mais, ajouta maître Huguet d'un air de dignité offensée, vous devriez savoir, ma cousine, que n'entre pas ici qui veut. Je suis très difficile sur le choix de mes gens et, une fois qu'ils font partie de la maison, ils se feraient hacher menu plutôt que de risquer d'en être chassés. On aurait pu penser qu'ils étaient tous sourds, muets et aveugles. Ils ont juré en chœur que messire Beltrami était parti pour Paris où il comptait confier à quelque couvent l'enfant qu'il avait trouvée...

— N'a-t-on pas couru après nous ?

— Si. Le prévôt de la ville a envoyé des hommes à vos trousses... mais dans la mauvaise direction...

— Eh bien, mais... tout est pour le mieux ? Pourquoi donc avez-vous si grande hâte de voir nos talons ? D'autant que l'histoire ne date pas d'hier – ni même d'avant-hier !...

— Pour certains, tel messire Regnault, elle est toujours actuelle et s'il venait à apprendre qu'une jeune femme du nom de Beltrami est à la Croix d'Or...

— Je ne vois pas comment il pourrait l'apprendre ? Il habite Autun et ce n'est pas la porte à côté...

— Il habitait Autun quand il était conseiller dans cette juridiction. A présent il est conseiller du duc et « lieutenant » du chancelier au siège de Dijon. C'est un personnage important !

— Diantre ! C'est pour le consoler d'avoir été si fort cocu qu'on l'a ainsi honoré ? En vérité, on croit rêver ! Et, si je vous ai bien compris, il habite donc ici ?

— Pas dans cette maison mais pas très loin. Il a acheté, rue du Lacet, près de la Vieille Poissonnerie, la maison d'un ancien chevaucheur du duc Philippe le Hardi. C'est là qu'il vit depuis près de dix ans et, hormis pour se rendre à la chancellerie, il n'en sort pour ainsi dire jamais...

— En ce cas, pourquoi vous en inquiéter ?

— Parce qu'il est très lié avec le fonctionnaire chargé des auberges et des étrangers. Ce n'est pas à vous que je vais apprendre que nous tenons registre des voyageurs ? Je ne me vois pas du tout y inscrivant le nom de Beltrami.

— Eh bien, ne l'écrivez pas ! répondit vivement Léonarde. Et comme le mien, si modeste qu'il soit, pourrait peut-être aussi vous compromettre... prenez plutôt celui du docteur Lascaris ?... Oui, c'est cela : vous avez reçu ce soir messire Démétrios Lascaris, médecin grec au service de Mgr Lorenzo de Médicis, sa nièce, la gouvernante de celle-ci, autrement dit moi, son écuyer et... son secrétaire ? Cela vous convient ?

Une tombe abandonnée

— Le secrétaire, c'est celui qui était en croupe de l'autre et qui a l'air d'un paysan ?

— Soyez certain que, dès demain, il aura tout à fait l'allure de l'emploi, fit Léonarde goguenarde. Pour l'instant, évidemment...

— Qui est-il ? Je lui trouve un drôle d'air...

— Ne vous souciez donc pas de cela ! Si je vous le disais, vous seriez capable de vous évanouir dans votre marmite et cela gâterait la soupe. Au fait, on vous réclame là-bas si j'en crois les bruits que j'entends.

— Je viens, je viens ! cria maître Huguet qui ajouta, plus bas : Qu'avez-vous décidé ?

— Je vous le dirai demain. Vous m'avez appris des choses fort intéressantes dont je dois discuter avec donna Fiora et nos compagnons... Ah ! pendant que j'y pense : veillez à nous servir dans notre chambre et tous ensemble. Vous redoutez par trop les curiosités. Et puis, nous serons plus tranquilles !

— Moi aussi, approuva maître Huguet qui ne put cependant s'empêcher de ronchonner, en homme qui se méfie d'instinct de l'exotisme, qu'un médecin grec cela ne faisait pas très sérieux. Du coup Léonarde se fâcha :

— Le roi de France s'apprête bien à le prendre au sérieux, lui ? Pourquoi pas vous ? Mais si vous tenez tellement aux honneurs, vous pouvez toujours l'appeler Monseigneur, parce que j'ai négligé de vous spécifier qu'il est aussi prince, descendant d'un empereur de Byzance.

Et, sur cette flèche du Parthe qui laissa son cousin sans voix, Léonarde, abandonnant la cuisine d'où montait, avec des fumets délectables, le joyeux tintamarre du coup de feu, s'en alla rejoindre Fiora mais ne la mit pas tout de suite au fait de ce qu'elle venait d'apprendre, préférant s'accorder un temps de réflexion. Elle savait en effet que, sur la liste de ceux dont la jeune femme entendait purger la terre, Regnault du Hamel venait en première place. Comment allait-elle réagir en apprenant que son ennemi se trouvait si près d'elle quand elle pensait devoir le chercher à Autun ?

La tentation de ne rien dire était grande pour la vieille demoiselle qui craignait profondément de voir son « agneau » s'engager dans le chemin du crime, mais, d'autre part, si elle la laissait faire le voyage d'Autun pour y apprendre finalement que du Hamel se trouvait à Dijon, cela ne ferait que retarder l'inéluctable. Elle connaissait trop bien la jeune femme pour entretenir la moindre illusion : Fiora irait jusqu'au bout de la tâche qu'elle s'était assignée, quelles qu'en puissent être les conséquences.

Léonarde se borna donc, sur le moment, à dire qu'elle avait demandé que l'on servît le souper dans leur grande chambre et s'en alla en informer leurs compagnons.

Le repas que l'on prit en commun fut excellent car maître Huguet y avait apporté un soin tout particulier et se déroula dans une atmosphère joyeuse. Fiora était heureuse d'avoir pu accomplir le pèlerinage qu'elle souhaitait et plus encore d'avoir rencontré ce jeune oncle vers lequel se penchait instinctivement son cœur compatissant. Elle voyait dans ce hasard heureux un signe du destin.

Assis en face d'elle, Christophe de Brévailles n'était pas loin de se croire en paradis. Les deux nuits précédentes, il les avait passées, dans un bois d'abord, puis dans un trou de haie, mangeant le pain qu'il avait emporté du couvent et quelques fruits sauvages, buvant de l'eau des ruisseaux. Il n'avait pas été malheureux parce que la saison était belle et qu'il était soutenu par ce désir accroché en lui depuis tant d'années : voir la tombe près de la fontaine Sainte-Anne et y prier car, s'il fuyait le couvent, il n'avait pas perdu pour autant la foi. Et voilà qu'au moment où il allait devoir décider de son avenir et se choisir un chemin – mais dans quelle direction ? – le ciel avait suscité cette belle jeune fille qui était l'image identique de ceux qu'il avait tant pleurés. Et le même sang coulait dans leurs veines. Grâce à elle, sa vie misérable venait de prendre un tour nouveau et il ne pouvait s'empêcher de trouver amusant, lui qui n'avait jamais rencontré que des gens de son terroir, de partager la même table avec un médecin venu de Byzance, un Espagnol de Castille, sans compter cette ravissante nièce tombée du ciel qui se voulait florentine, bien qu'elle ait vu son premier jour de douleur sur la paille d'une prison bourguignonne... Elle avait vraiment les plus beaux yeux du monde et que ce prénom de Fiora était donc joli !... Sans compter que ce repas était bien le meilleur qu'il eût jamais dévoré de toute sa vie !

De son côté, en vrai philosophe volontiers épicurien, Démétrios se contentait de goûter l'instant de chaude convivialité autour d'une table agréable. Il était satisfait que Fiora eût commencé sa quête tragique par un succès et en tirait les meilleurs augures pour ce qui leur restait à accomplir même si le but final pouvait, d'ici, apparaître démentiel : abattre Charles le Téméraire, l'homme qui était peut-être le plus puissant d'Europe et cela, selon toute vraisemblance, au milieu de l'armée qu'il ne quittait plus depuis qu'il s'était mis en tête de devenir roi. Mais Démétrios croyait fermement aux miracles et, plus encore, à son inflexible volonté...

En fait, autour de cette table, Esteban était à peu près le seul à trouver la vie vraiment belle. Il avait goûté pleinement, en amoureux des grands horizons, le voyage depuis Florence, au long du rivage méditerranéen puis à travers la Provence pour rejoindre les vallées du Rhône et de la Saône. A présent, il découvrait, après quelques autres libations en chemin, la magnificence des vins de Bourgogne... et y prenait un plaisir extrême. Les yeux mi-clos et la mine épanouie il ne voyait pas plus loin, pour l'instant, que son gobelet empli d'un chaleureux vin de Chambertin...

Léonarde ne s'était guère mêlée à la conversation dont Démétrios avait heureusement fait les frais en homme qui a beaucoup vu et beaucoup retenu. Elle attendit que le dernier plat eût été emporté et la table débarrassée à l'exception d'une ultime bouteille. Elle avait conscience, en effet, de ce que pouvait représenter d'exceptionnel cette réunion avec le jeune Brévailles. Fiora souriait et c'était quelque chose qui importait fort à sa gouvernante.

Néanmoins, quand la porte de la chambre se fut refermée sur le dernier valet, elle se leva, marcha vers la cheminée où l'on avait allumé un feu en raison de la fraîcheur du soir, lui tendit ses mains qu'elle frotta un instant l'une contre l'autre. Puis, se retournant, elle fit face à ses compagnons. Esteban étant précisément en train de constater que cette auberge de la Croix d'Or était sans aucun doute la meilleure de toute la chrétienté :

— C'est certainement vrai, le coupa-t-elle. Le malheur est que nous ne puissions guère y séjourner longtemps. J'ai un certain nombre de choses à vous dire...

Tous parurent se figer : Fiora assise au pied du lit, Démétrios sur la bancelle près de la cheminée, Christophe sur un escabeau. Seul Esteban alla remplir son verre une dernière fois mais il ne souriait plus. Tous avaient conscience que l'instant privilégié venait de prendre fin...

CHAPITRE II

LA MAISON SUR LE SUZON

La décision de Fiora fut instantanée : puisque Regnault du Hamel habitait Dijon, elle y resterait tout le temps qu'il lui faudrait pour débarrasser cette terre de l'homme qui avait martyrisé sa mère et tenté de massacrer un bébé. Mais l'appréhension justifiée que montrait maître Huguet à garder chez lui des voyageurs compromettants posait un cas de conscience car la peur est mauvaise conseillère. Dans une autre auberge, d'ailleurs, le risque encouru serait le même :

— La meilleure solution, suggéra Démétrios, me paraît de louer, si cela est possible, une maison pas trop éloignée de celle qui vous intéresse. Pour une affaire de ce genre, il faut savoir prendre son temps, étudier les habitudes de l'ennemi, épier... et patienter.

La patience ! Elle était l'arme préférée du médecin grec et il s'efforçait inlassablement d'inculquer cette rare vertu à celle dont il faisait, jour après jour, à l'aide d'une infinité de petites leçons, la meilleure des élèves... Ce qui n'était pas le cas d'Esteban.

— Nous n'allons tout de même pas nous installer ici ? protesta-t-il. Ne devons-nous pas aller à Paris ?

— Chaque chose en son temps. Nous avons largement celui de rejoindre le roi, qui d'ailleurs n'est pas à Paris. Et, pour l'heure présente, c'est ici que nous avons à faire. Est-il possible de nous trouver un logis convenable pour quelques semaines, dame Léonarde ?

— C'est toujours possible. Reste à savoir si nous en trouverons un bien situé !

C'est le problème qu'elle alla, dès le matin, soumettre à Magdelaine, la jeune sœur de maître Huguet qu'elle avait connue lorsqu'elle avait l'âge de Fiora et qui avait témoigné, en la revoyant, d'une joie sans arrière-pensée. Il y aurait, de ce côté-là, une aide assurée sans qu'il soit besoin, peut-être, de nombreuses explications.

Magdelaine, en effet, était une âme simple. Elle écouta sagement Léonarde lui exposer que ses « maîtres », séduits par la beauté de la ville et de la région, souhaitaient séjourner quelque temps à Dijon et donc y découvrir une maison agréable à habiter, au centre si possible, pour n'être pas trop éloignés des halles, etc. Elle se montra enchantée d'une idée qui allait lui permettre de rencontrer pendant quelque temps cette chère Léonarde mais lui fit remarquer, avec un brin d'amour-propre froissé, que l'auberge de son frère était malgré tout et sans conteste l'endroit le plus agréable pour tout séjour, fût-il long.

— A condition d'être en bonne santé, riposta Léonarde. Or donna Fiora est souffrante ce matin. Le long voyage depuis Florence l'a fatiguée. Elle a besoin de repos et de calme. En outre, messire Lascaris, qui est un savant, n'aime pas séjourner trop longtemps dans une hostellerie, même aussi bonne que la nôtre. Il a en cours d'importants travaux et il lui faut le silence d'une pièce bien à lui...

— Mais, objecta Magdelaine qui, bien qu'étant une âme simple, ne manquait ni de logique ni de mémoire, je croyais que ce grand médecin se rendait auprès du roi de France ?

Démétrios prévoyait cette objection lorsqu'il fit remarquer à Léonarde qu'elle avait eu la langue trop longue...

— Le roi est aux armées en ce moment et ne nous attend qu'à l'automne. Nous le rejoindrons alors en son château du Plessis-lès-Tours sur le fleuve de Loire...

Ainsi éclairée, Magdelaine se déclara satisfaite et ajouta même qu'elle aurait peut-être le moyen de contenter rapidement cette amie d'autrefois :

— Avez-vous gardé souvenance, lui dit-elle, de la noble dame Symonne Sauvegrain qui est veuve de l'ancien gouverneur de la Chancellerie, messire Jehan Morel?
— Celle qui fut autrefois la nourrice du Téméraire et qui, en échange de son lait, a reçu un titre de noblesse?
— Plus récemment encore, elle a donné, pendant près de trois ans, ses soins à la jeune princesse Marie, fille unique de notre duc, ce dont Monseigneur lui garde de la reconnaissance.
— Si je me souviens bien, feu Jehan Morel avait fait construire un grand et bel hôtel rue des Forges?
— Un hôtel devenu trop grand pour dame Symonne. Elle y vit seule avec son fils Pierre depuis le mariage de sa fille Ysabeau et je suppose qu'elle louerait volontiers le bâtiment qui est voisin du Suzon. Voulez-vous que j'aille voir son intendant?
— Allons-y ensemble! Le temps de m'habiller pour sortir et de demander à donna Fiora si elle serait d'accord...

C'était d'ailleurs façon de pure révérence car Fiora n'avait aucune raison de refuser une maison située presque en face de celle de son ennemi et, donc, à un emplacement stratégique inespéré.

La maison que Jehan Morel avait construite, quarante ans plus tôt, pour sa femme à laquelle il vouait une vraie dévotion, était, avec ses fenêtres en double accolade, ses vitraux de couleur et l'élégant balustre sculpté qui soulignait son toit de tuiles brillantes, l'une des plus belles de la ville. Construite en U, son bâtiment arrière avait vue sur le Suzon, et possédait une installation indépendante qui permettait de l'isoler du reste de l'hôtel. Ce pavillon se composait d'une salle commune, d'une cuisine et de quatre petites chambres. Ce n'était certes pas immense mais c'était commode, bien meublé et, surtout, l'orientation de certaines des fenêtres permettait d'observer les allées et venues du logis appartenant à du Hamel. Seule la largeur du Suzon qui, à cet endroit, disparaissait sous la rue du Lacet séparait les deux maisons. Quant à l'entrée, elle donnait sur la rue des Forges ce qui la laissait hors de vue puisque, pour atteindre la porte, il fallait traverser par un couloir toute la largeur de l'hôtel Morel-Sauvegrain et une cour que l'on franchissait sous galerie.

Pensant que c'était vraiment là un présent du ciel, Léonarde se hâta de conclure engagement et versa trois mois de location à Jacquemin Hurtault, l'intendant des Morel qui fournissait en outre une servante pour l'entretien... Le prix était au demeurant raisonnable compte tenu du fait que la maison, confortable, ne manquait de rien.

Pendant ce temps, dans sa chambre, Fiora causait avec Christophe qui avait souhaité lui parler. Grâce à Esteban qui avait couru la ville dès potron-minet pour lui procurer des vêtements convenables, le jeune homme avait à présent meilleure allure avec son costume gris foncé, ses bottes noires et le chaperon drapé qui cachait sa tonsure. Esteban, pour qui un homme sans arme est un homme incomplet, avait ajouté une dague d'une facture un peu archaïque mais en bon acier de Tolède. Elle avait fait sourire l'ancien moine :

— Je n'ai jamais appris à me servir de cela, dit-il. On en porte rarement au monastère...

— L'épée demande un long apprentissage mais, en cas de danger, on se sert de la dague presque instinctivement, lui répondit le Castillan. En outre, n'avez-vous pas dit que vous vouliez être soldat ? L'armée vous enseignera...

Christophe venait donc remercier Fiora de tous ses bienfaits et la saluer avant de s'éloigner car il ne voulait pas être à sa charge plus longtemps.

— Vous voulez nous quitter déjà ? dit celle-ci. Je vous assure que, si charge il y a, elle est bien légère et j'étais heureuse d'avoir, auprès de moi, quelqu'un de ma famille. Mais je comprends que vous ayez hâte d'aller vers un nouveau destin. Quel chemin comptez-vous prendre ? Hier vous sembliez hésiter ?

— Je n'hésite plus. J'ai beaucoup réfléchi cette nuit et je crois que je vais rejoindre l'armée du duc Charles !

Fiora eut un haut-le-corps :

— Vous semble-t-il donc un maître tellement souhaitable alors que votre mère, jadis, a vainement imploré sa pitié ?

— Je sais, mais votre ami grec, hier, m'a dit une chose qui m'a donné à réfléchir. Je voulais chercher la mort, il m'a conseillé de chercher plutôt la vie et d'essayer de me faire un nom. Or, je suis bourguignon quoi qu'il en soit et, ce nouveau nom, j'aimerais qu'il soit de Bourgogne. Hier, après souper, je suis descendu avec Esteban dans la salle d'auberge et j'ai écouté parler des marchands. Ils disaient qu'un légat du pape s'est entremis pour faire cesser le trop long siège de Neuss. Le duc songerait à ramener son armée en Lorraine afin de punir le jeune duc René II qui a rompu leur alliance. On dit aussi que le roi de France fait marcher ses troupes sur l'Artois d'une part et sur la Comté Franche de l'autre. Il va y avoir de la besogne pour défendre le pays. Je veux en être. Vous, vous allez partir pour la France, n'est-ce pas, puisqu'un plus long séjour vous mettrait en danger ?

Christophe ignorait en effet que Fiora avait décidé de rester à Dijon. La veille au soir, le jeune homme s'était retiré avec Esteban pour aller boire dans la salle un dernier gobelet de vin. C'était alors que la jeune femme avait avisé Léonarde et Démétrios de ce qu'elle pensait faire. Bien qu'il lui eût inspiré une instinctive sympathie, elle estimait qu'elle ne connaissait pas suffisamment Christophe pour lui faire part de tous ses projets. Mais comme elle crut déceler de l'inquiétude dans son regard, elle lui sourit gentiment :

— Je n'aime pas quitter un endroit sous prétexte que je pourrais y craindre quelque chose. D'autant que j'ai envie de mieux connaître cette ville que mon père aimait. Il se peut que je reste encore quelques jours.

— C'est de la folie ! Vous avez entendu dame Léonarde hier au soir ? Ce misérable Regnault du Hamel vit ici et il est toujours aussi mauvais. S'il allait vous rencontrer ? Vous ressemblez tellement à ma douce Marie !...

— C'est peut-être là ma grande différence avec ma mère. Elle était infiniment douce, tendre et vulnérable — ce que je ne suis pas... ou, plutôt, ne suis plus ! Si le sire du Hamel s'en prend à moi — et je ne vois pas sous quel prétexte valable il pourrait m'attaquer — soyez sûr que je serai sur mes gardes. D'ailleurs j'ai de bons défenseurs. Partez tranquille ! Un jour peut-être nous nous reverrons...

L'entrée tumultueuse de Léonarde lui coupa la parole. La vieille demoiselle rayonnait littéralement de satisfaction et, n'ayant pas vu Christophe, lança du seuil :

— J'ai ce qu'il nous faut ! Une maison juste en face de celle qui nous intéresse...

S'apercevant que la jeune femme n'était pas seule, elle s'arrêta court et devint toute rouge, ce qui amusa Fiora : C'était la première fois qu'elle voyait à sa vieille Léonarde les couleurs de la confusion. Mais il y eut soudain un silence gênant. Christophe de Brévailles regarda tour à tour les deux femmes. Ses épais sourcils s'étaient froncés mais il avait pâli :

— Et pour mieux visiter Dijon, articula-t-il lentement, vous avez besoin d'une maison voisine de celle de du Hamel ? C'est bien cela, n'est-ce pas ?

Fiora se leva et s'avança vers le jeune homme dans les yeux de qui elle planta son regard :

— C'est bien cela mais je vous prie de ne pas vous en soucier.

— Vous me demandez trop. Qu'avez-vous dans l'idée ?

— Je pourrais vous répondre que c'est là mon affaire mais, après tout, vous avez peut-être le droit de savoir. Hier, je crois vous avoir dit que je venais payer de vieilles dettes ? Regnault du Hamel en est la plus criarde. J'allais me rendre à Autun pour l'y chercher mais le ciel — ou l'enfer — a décidé de m'épargner du chemin puisqu'il est ici. Et je ne quitterai cette ville qu'après l'avoir purifiée de sa présence...

— Vous voulez... le tuer ?

— Vous traduisez à merveille mon intention.
— C'est insensé...
— Je ne crois pas. De toute façon, et quoique vous puissiez objecter, vous ne me ferez pas changer d'avis.

Avec effroi, Christophe la regarda, droite et fière en face de lui, si mince dans cette robe noire qui la faisait plus longue encore, avec ses grands yeux gris où semblaient voyager les nuages et cette allure d'altesse... Elle paraissait plus inflexible qu'une lame d'épée et le jeune homme comprit qu'il ne parviendrait pas à la faire céder. Alors, éperdu sans qu'il comprît vraiment pourquoi cette jeune femme comptait tellement pour lui à présent, il se tourna vers Léonarde et chercha son regard, espérant un secours de ce côté-là, mais elle hocha la tête...

— Vous pensez bien que j'ai déjà essayé...
— En ce cas, décida Christophe, je reste. Je vous aiderai et ne partirai que lorsque ce sera fait. Et si quelqu'un doit frapper, ce sera moi !

Sans lui répondre, Fiora prit les deux mains du jeune homme et les retourna pour en considérer la paume comme si elle tentait d'en déchiffrer le réseau de lignes puis releva les yeux :

— Avez-vous reçu les ordres majeurs ? demanda-t-elle doucement.

Sous ce regard qui interrogeait sans dureté, Christophe rougit.

— Oui... mais je ne le voulais pas.
— Néanmoins, cela est ! Ces mains ont été consacrées. Vous ne pouvez les souiller de sang...
— Et que ferai-je d'autre à la guerre ?
— C'est différent. Il y eut, il y a encore des moines-soldats. En outre, vous engagerez votre vie dans les combats.
— Mais je ne veux plus être moine du tout, ni soldat ni autrement. Je veux être un homme libre de choisir son sort...
— Il en sera comme vous voudrez, mon ami, mais du

moins ne serez-vous pas souillé d'un crime froidement prémédité. En outre, je ne laisserai à personne le bonheur de frapper à ma place... Enfin, après ce meurtre, il y en aura d'autres qui me conduiront peut-être un jour à l'échafaud. Je refuse de vous y entraîner car voilà dix-sept ans que vous souffrez. Vous avez le droit de vivre comme vous l'entendrez et cela me sera doux. Ne m'enlevez pas cette consolation qui sera peut-être ma dernière bonne action !

– Je vous en supplie, laissez-moi rester ! Je veillerai sur vous, je vous protégerai...

– Nous sommes là pour cela, intervint la voix grave de Démétrios qui venait d'entrer. Donna Fiora a raison : vous devez aller vers votre destin et nous laisser décider du nôtre. Partez sans arrière-pensée !

– Croyez-vous que ce soit possible à présent ?

– J'en suis certain. Cela est même nécessaire car il faut qu'un jour vous vous trouviez en un certain lieu, à une certaine heure, pour payer la dette que vous avez contractée aujourd'hui.

– Que voulez-vous dire ?

– Il arrive que le voile de l'avenir se lève, par moments, devant moi. Il viendra un jour où il vous sera donné de rendre ce que vous avez reçu.

– Il faut le croire ! assura Fiora. Il ne se trompe jamais... Quittons-nous à présent... et priez pour nous !

Sans un mot, Léonarde prit le manteau noir que Christophe avait déposé sur un escabeau en pénétrant dans la chambre et le disposa sur ses épaules. Il se laissa faire en fixant Fiora comme s'il ne pouvait plus en détacher son regard. Mais il tressaillit quand Démétrios glissa dans son escarcelle quelques pièces d'or puis le poussa vers la jeune femme :

– Allez l'embrasser ! Il en est temps. Esteban vous attend dans la cour avec un cheval. Dirigez-vous sur la Lorraine où les troupes bourguignonnes commencent à se reformer. On parle de Thionville...

pénétra dans le bel hôtel des Morel-Sauvegrain et gagna la chambre qui lui était réservée, l'une des deux donnant sur l'arrière de la maison.

Cette chambre, dont la porte lui fut ouverte courtoisement par l'intendant Hurtault, était tout éclairée par un grand bouquet de pivoines disposées dans un pot d'étain auprès d'un drageoir rempli de fruits confits.

— Ma maîtresse, dit-il, souhaite la bienvenue à Votre Seigneurie, et espère, lorsque sa santé sera meilleure, avoir le plaisir de venir la saluer...

Fiora répondit, d'une voix faible, par quelques remerciements auxquels Démétrios ajouta qu'il serait heureux, pour sa part, d'être admis à l'honneur de présenter ses devoirs à une hôtesse dont le renom et le mérite étaient venus jusqu'à lui...

— Je n'y manquerai pas, confia-t-il à Léonarde une fois la porte refermée sur l'intendant. Elle peut sûrement nous apprendre des choses fort utiles...

— Je me charge, moi, de questionner les servantes, répondit celle-ci. C'est encore par les cuisines que les commérages vont le meilleur train...

Fiora n'écoutait pas, ayant déjà sauté à bas du lit où Esteban l'avait étendue pour courir à la fenêtre. La maison de Regnault du Hamel était bien là où Léonarde l'avait indiquée... Elle était aussi telle que la jeune femme l'imaginait : sombre et sinistre, comme dut l'être la maison d'Autun où Marie de Brévailles avait gravi son calvaire avant de s'enfuir.

C'était une demeure presque aussi solitaire que celle du bourreau. Encadrée sur trois côtés par la rue de la Tonnellerie, la rue du Lacet et le Suzon, un maigre jardin mal entretenu tenait le quatrième à distance des habitations voisines. Un soubassement de pierre qui n'offrait d'autre ouverture qu'une porte de bois sombre armée de pentures de fer soutenait deux étages d'encorbellement à croisillons noircis par le temps, le tout sous un grand toit abritant le pignon pointu. Deux fenêtres à l'étage noble, une ouver-

Fiora fit la moitié du chemin vers le jeune homme qui, soudain, la prit dans ses bras. Elle l'éloigna doucement mais l'embrassa sur les deux joues avec une tendresse fraternelle :

— Dieu vous garde, mon bel oncle ! Où que vous alliez, vous lui appartiendrez toujours...

Il la baisa au front puis, se détournant brusquement, partit en courant suivi de Démétrios. On l'entendit dégringoler l'escalier. Les deux femmes sortirent sur le balcon de bois qui régnait tout autour de la cour pour assister à son départ. Elles le virent sauter en selle comme s'il n'avait fait que cela toute sa vie au lieu d'user ses genoux sur les dalles d'un couvent, serrer les mains de Démétrios et d'Esteban puis, ôtant son chaperon d'un geste empli d'élégance naturelle, en saluer les dames avant de rendre la main à son cheval et de s'engouffrer sous la voûte de l'auberge.

— Vous avez bien fait de l'éloigner, fit Léonarde.
— Pourquoi ? Est-ce qu'il ne vous inspirait pas confiance ?

— Pauvre garçon ! Bien sûr que si... mais il était en train de tomber amoureux de vous, mon agneau... et vos affaires de famille sont bien assez compliquées comme cela. A présent, venez vous préparer à emménager dans votre nouveau logis. J'espère qu'il vous plaira.

— C'est sans importance. Si ses fenêtres offrent la vue que j'espère, le reste peut être aussi délabré qu'il voudra...

— Heureusement, il n'en est rien ? Voilà bien l'égoïsme de la jeunesse ! Pensez un peu à moi, Fiora, qui suis passée de cette belle hostellerie à l'élégance du palais Beltrami. J'ai de mauvaises habitudes, que voulez-vous ?...

Léonarde, d'accord en cela avec ses compagnons, avait loué la maison au nom du médecin Démétrios Lascaris voyageant avec sa nièce Fiora, son secrétaire et la gouvernante de la jeune femme. C'est donc en tant que princesse Lascaris que Fiora, étroitement voilée et portée dans les bras d'Esteban comme la malade qu'elle était censée être,

ture fermée de volets de bois et une lucarne donnant sur le ruisseau ne devaient pas procurer beaucoup de jour. Il est vrai que, de son observatoire, Fiora ne pouvait voir la façade côté jardin mais, telle qu'elle était, cette maison était aussi triste qu'une prison... ou qu'un tombeau car, en dépit du beau temps, aucune vitre n'était ouverte, aucune vie ne s'y manifestait...

Démétrios, qui avait choisi l'autre chambre arrière, celle qui faisait l'angle de la maison, à pic, à cet endroit, sur le Suzon, et qui avait la meilleure vue sur l'entrée, vint rejoindre Fiora :

— Il faudrait savoir, lui dit-il, comment se présente le côté jardin. Cette nuit, j'enverrai Esteban en reconnaissance...

— C'est trop tôt, remarqua Fiora. Notre arrivée, saluée si aimablement par notre hôtesse, a dû faire quelque bruit dans ce quartier. Mieux vaut ne pas risquer de se faire remarquer trop tôt...

Avec un sourire amusé, le Grec applaudit silencieusement :

— Bravo ! Je vois que mes leçons de sagesse ont porté leurs fruits. J'espérais que tu me répondrais cela, sans trop oser y croire. Et tu as raison. Tu es une jeune femme malade, moi un vieux savant qui ne quitte guère la compagnie de ses livres et on se fera vite à cette paisible image. Cependant, Esteban n'a aucune raison de se priver de courir les tavernes. Il n'a pas son pareil pour s'y faire des amis et délier les langues. Et dame Léonarde pourra peut-être tirer quelque chose de cette servante que l'on nous a donnée...

La servante en question se nommait Chrétiennotte Yvon. C'était une solide commère d'une trentaine d'années à l'œil rond mais vif, à la figure épanouie et avenante, à qui ne faisaient peur ni le travail ni les longs bavardages. Comme les autres servantes de la nourrice ducale elle était, sur sa personne comme dans son ouvrage, d'une propreté flamande. Mais ce qui n'appartenait qu'à elle seule, c'était l'heureux caractère qui la poussait à chanter du matin au soir. Elle rappelait un peu à Léonarde la grosse Colomba, son amie florentine [1] qui était toujours la femme la mieux renseignée de la ville. Elle se retint néanmoins de se laisser aller à témoigner trop de sympathie à Chrétiennotte en pensant que dame Morel-Sauvegrain leur avait peut-être dépêché une servante aussi loquace avec une idée de derrière la tête : celle d'être parfaitement renseignée de son côté sur les faits et gestes de ses nouveaux locataires.

— Parlez-lui le moins possible, conseilla-t-elle à Fiora, et laissez-moi faire. Je saurai bien lui tirer les vers du nez !

La vie, dans la maison sur le Suzon, s'organisa, paisible et silencieuse, rythmée par les coups de maillet que « Jacquemart et sa femme Jacqueline » frappaient sur une cloche, à l'église Notre-Dame voisine pour marquer les heures [2]. Fidèle à ses anciennes habitudes, Léonarde se rendait chaque matin à la première messe puis, le reste du temps, veillait à l'entretien de la maison. Démétrios compulsait les ouvrages emportés de Florence et rédigeait le traité sur la circulation sanguine qu'il avait entrepris. Esteban courait la ville. Quant à Fiora, au bout de deux jours, elle ne supportait plus que difficilement ce personnage de malade si contraire à sa nature mais auquel la contraignait son extrême ressemblance avec ses parents : elle risquait d'être reconnue. Sa seule distraction, en dehors de la broderie que Léonarde lui avait placée dans les mains et d'un livre grec prêté par Démétrios, était d'épier la maison d'en face.

Assise durant des heures dans la cathèdre garnie de coussins qu'elle ne quittait que pour son lit, elle observait obstinément ce qui se passait de l'autre côté du ruisseau. Et, en vérité, ce n'était pas grand-chose : par deux fois,

---

1. Voir *Fiora et le Magnifique*.
2. En 1383, après le sac de Courtrai, le duc Philippe le Hardi avait, selon l'usage, décapité le beffroi de la ville rebelle, en avait ôté l'horloge à deux personnages et en avait fait don à sa ville de Dijon en remerciement de son aide militaire.

elle vit sortir ou entrer, avec des paniers, l'un ou l'autre des deux valets qui, au dire d'Esteban, constituaient tout le personnel du conseiller ducal. Mais lui-même, elle ne l'avait pas encore aperçu car il s'était rendu pour quelques jours dans une terre qu'il possédait près de Vergy, dans l'arrière-côte.

Elle se morfondait tellement qu'au matin du troisième jour, elle ne résista pas à l'envie d'interroger Chrétiennotte :

— Cette maison, de l'autre côté du pont, qui n'ouvre jamais ses fenêtres et rarement sa porte, à qui donc appartient-elle ?

La servante roula des yeux plus ronds que jamais et se signa précipitamment deux ou trois fois et, comme Fiora s'étonnait, elle soupira :

— Demoiselle, vaudrait mieux qu'on vous change de chambre si vous devez vous intéresser à cette bicoque...

— Une bicoque ? il me semble que c'est une assez belle maison, solide et bien construite...

— Oui, bien sûr, mais mal habitée. Moi qui vous parle, j'aime guère à passer devant quand la nuit tombe.

— Vous voulez dire que c'est... un mauvais lieu ?

— Pas vraiment, mais le maître est un mauvais homme. Il est riche, pourtant, et de belle position, mais ladre comme un juif. Et il déteste les femmes pour lesquelles il a toujours un mauvais regard ou même un mot méchant. Il n'a pas de servante d'ailleurs, mais deux valets, deux lourdauds qui grognent comme des chiens hargneux et qui mordent au besoin. Malheur au mendiant qui oserait frapper à cette porte : il ne récolterait que des coups de bâton...

— Il n'est pas marié ?

— Messire du Hamel ? Marié ? Si riche qu'il soit, aucune femme ou fille, même miséreuse, ne voudrait de lui. Faut dire qu'il a déjà eu une épouse jadis, quand il habitait par ici. Une jeune demoiselle dont on dit qu'elle était belle comme tous les anges et il l'a si fort maltraitée qu'elle s'est enfuie de chez lui pour rejoindre son frère. Le malheur a voulu que, ce frère et elle, ils s'aimaient plus qu'il aurait fallu et ça a mal fini. Le mari les a retrouvés et les a fait exécuter par le bourreau... alors, vous pensez si ça donne envie à d'autres !... Tenez, vous voyez ! Voilà un des valets qui sort pour aller aux provisions...

Un homme de forte corpulence, le visage inexpressif sous les cheveux gris coupés au carré, vêtu d'une livrée gris et noir assez propre et portant au bras un grand panier, quittait en effet la maison dont il refermait soigneusement la porte derrière lui avant de mettre la clé dans sa poche.

— Celui-là, c'est le Claude, l'aîné. L'autre, le Mathieu, son frère, est un peu plus jeune. Ils ne sortent jamais ensemble. Quand y en a un qui s'en va, on peut être sûr que l'autre reste à la maison. C'est le maître qui veut ça...

— En tout cas, si le maître est avare, le valet n'a pas l'air si mal nourri...

— Le maître est pas fou. Il sait bien qu'il faut donner à manger à des molosses si on veut pas qu'ils vous dévorent. On dit que les deux frères lui sont tout dévoués. Ils sont peu causants... N'empêche que j'ai idée qu'y doit se passer des choses pas catholiques dans cette maison si bien gardée !

— Pourquoi cela ?

Chrétiennotte parut hésiter et regarda Fiora comme si elle se demandait jusqu'à quel point elle pouvait lui faire confiance. Puis, finalement se décida :

— Bon, je vous raconte encore ça et puis j'vais à mon travail. Sans ça, votre dame Léonarde va gronder. C'était y a deux ans à peu près, au temps où mon défunt Janet était encore sur cette pauvre terre. Un soir qu'y rentrait un peu tard de son travail – il était maçon – il est revenu chez nous tout sens dessus dessous parce que en passant par la rue du Lacet il avait entendu pleurer et gémir quelqu'un et ce quelqu'un c'était une femme qu'avait l'air de souffrir beaucoup... Comme c'était un gars courageux, mon Janet, il a cogné à la porte en demandant si on avait besoin d'aide mais personne n'a répondu...

— Il y avait peut-être une femme à ce moment-là ?

— Ça se serait su ! D'ailleurs, mon pauvre Janet est pas seul à avoir entendu des bruits du même genre, mais on pense dans le quartier que c'est peut-être l'âme de sa pauvre petite femme qui revient le tourmenter : c'est ici, au Morimont, qu'elle a été mise à mort... et le Morimont, c'est pas loin.

— Si je comprends bien, conclut Fiora, ce... du Hamel... a bien tort de se donner tant de mal pour faire garder une maison où personne n'a envie d'entrer ?

— C'est ça tout juste ! fit Chrétiennotte avec satisfaction. Moi j' sais bien qu'y faudrait me payer, et cher, pour que j'y aille. Et encore, ça serait pas sûr !

Ayant ainsi donné son opinion catégorique, la veuve de Janet reprit son balai, ses torchons et, avec une espèce de révérence à Léonarde qui franchissait la porte au même instant, elle disparut dans le couloir en fredonnant un cantique.

Mais l'histoire qu'elle venait de raconter laissait Fiora songeuse. Que la maison eût mauvaise réputation et qu'elle passât pour hantée lui convenait tout à fait – et même lui donnait une idée pour la façon dont elle pensait attaquer Regnault du Hamel. Dès son arrivée à Dijon, en effet, elle avait refusé tout net la proposition radicale d'Esteban :

— Vous voulez la mort de cet homme ? lui avait dit le Castillan. C'est la chose la plus facile du monde. Je l'attends un soir à son entrée ou sa sortie de chez lui et je vous l'étrangle.

C'était simple, en effet, trop simple même et surtout trop rapide. Elle ne voulait pas que le bourreau de sa mère tombât soudainement dans la mort, frappé d'un coup qu'il n'aurait pas vu venir et sans savoir qui l'avait ordonné. Fiora voulait être l'instrument de la vengeance ; elle entendait savourer le trépas de son ennemi. En digne fille de la subtile et cruelle Florence, elle était décidée à dépenser le temps et l'or qu'il faudrait afin que cette mort atteignît à la perfection d'une œuvre d'art...

Elle y songea longuement ce soir-là, les yeux perdus dans l'azur pâlissant du ciel où se poursuivaient des bandes d'oiseaux, écoutant les bruits de cette ville où elle était née et que, cependant, elle ne connaissait pas. Contrairement à Florence si animée au coucher du soleil, Dijon, à la fin du jour, paraissait s'endormir sous ses toits dont les tuiles de couleur jaune, rouge ou noire, dessinaient des tapisseries entre les bouquets verts des jardins... Dans chaque quartier, le bourgeois le plus considérable se rendait auprès du vicomte-mayeur [1] afin de lui remettre les clés de la porte dont il avait la garde. Ces hommes, pour qui c'était un fief viager, avaient la responsabilité de ces portes dont ils entretenaient les défenses à l'aide d'une part des droits de vivres et de marchandises. Ils se rendaient toujours en cérémonie à la maison de ville, mettant un point d'honneur à conserver cet usage un peu solennel dans une cité que ses ducs désertaient le plus souvent. Et Fiora savait que Pierre Morel avait la charge d'une de ces clés.

Quand elle l'eut entendu rentrer et que les marguilliers de Saint-Jean eurent sonné le « crève-feux » après lequel les rues devenaient désertes hormis pour les amateurs d'aventures, Fiora descendit dans la salle où Léonarde achevait de ranger après le souper auquel la jeune femme n'avait pas voulu participer. Démétrios et Esteban, assis auprès d'une fenêtre, profitaient des derniers instants de lumière pour disputer une partie d'échecs mais tous levèrent des yeux surpris en constatant que Fiora portait le costume de garçon dans lequel elle avait quitté Florence et tenait à la main un chaperon d'homme destiné à cacher ses cheveux.

— Doux Jésus! s'écria Léonarde. Où prétendez-vous aller à cette heure, mon agneau?

---

1. Le maire de la ville.

— Pas très loin. Je voudrais aller voir de près la maison de du Hamel, dès qu'il fera nuit tout au moins. Si Esteban veut bien m'accompagner...

— Naturellement, dit le Castillan qui se leva aussitôt. Mais pour quoi faire ? Le maître n'est pas encore rentré...

— C'est la raison pour laquelle je veux y aller. Quand il sera revenu, cela ne sera plus possible...

— Qu'as-tu derrière la tête ? demanda Démétrios qui avait pris le roi d'ivoire et l'examinait comme s'il s'agissait d'un objet rare.

— Je te le dirai plus tard. Pour l'instant, je désire voir le jardin et, si possible, y pénétrer.

Démétrios rejeta la pièce d'échecs et fronça les sourcils :
— C'est de la folie ! A quoi cela t'avancera-t-il ?

Sans répondre, Fiora alla jusqu'à un dressoir où se trouvait une corbeille de cerises, en prit une poignée et se mit à les croquer tout en regardant le ciel s'obscurcir lentement :

— Dans ces conditions, j'irai aussi, soupira Démétrios.

— Je préfère que tu restes avec Léonarde. Je n'en aurai pas pour longtemps et on remarque moins deux personnes que trois...

Le Grec n'insista pas. Il savait qu'il était inutile de discuter avec la jeune femme quand elle employait un certain ton. Pour en atténuer le côté péremptoire, elle ajouta gentiment :

— Sois sans crainte, tu sauras tout. Je t'expliquerai à mon retour.

Quand la nuit fut complète, Fiora et Esteban quittèrent l'hôtel en évitant de faire le moindre bruit et gagnèrent l'angle de la rue du Lacet où ils restèrent un instant cachés dans l'ombre épaisse fournie par l'encorbellement d'une maison, observant celle de du Hamel. Esteban avait conseillé cette halte :

— Mieux vaut attendre. Les valets sortent régulièrement, chacun à son tour, quand les rues sont désertes.

— Où vont-ils ?

— Rue du Griffon, dans une maison de filles. Reste à savoir s'ils y vont aussi quand le maître est là ! Tenez ! En voilà un qui sort.

En effet, le même homme que Fiora avait observé dans l'après-midi venait d'apparaître et fermait soigneusement la porte dont il mit la clé dans sa poche avant de s'éloigner d'un pas tranquille.

— Je me demande pourquoi ils ne sortent pas tous les deux, remarqua Fiora. Puisque la maison est vide ?

— Si le maître est avare, il doit être riche. Il tient sans doute à ce que sa demeure soit gardée. Allons-y à présent !

Sans faire plus de bruit que des chats, les deux compagnons d'aventures s'avancèrent sur le petit pont qui enjambait le ruisseau. Ils avaient tous deux la légèreté de la jeunesse et leurs pieds, chaussés de cuir souple, n'éveillaient aucun écho. Parvenue devant la porte, Fiora l'examina soigneusement. La nuit d'été était claire et la jeune femme avait de bons yeux mais elle acquit très vite la certitude qu'à moins de l'attaquer avec un bélier, cette porte se révélerait impossible à forcer. Comme elle représentait la seule ouverture du rez-de-chaussée, la maison était donc inviolable de ce côté.

— Allons voir le jardin ! souffla Fiora.

Il s'étendait sur l'arrière de la bâtisse, entre le Suzon et la rue de la Vieille-Poissonnerie. Le quatrième côté donnait sur une ruelle étroite et noire mais des murs assez élevés le défendaient.

— Si j'ai bien compris, fit Esteban, vous voulez entrer là-dedans ? Je vais passer le premier...

La vie de soldat de fortune menée si longtemps avait entraîné le Castillan à tous les exercices du corps. Escalader le mur fut pour lui un jeu d'enfant. Il s'y installa à califourchon puis se pencha pour aider Fiora. Il saisit les mains qu'elle lui tendait et la hissa auprès de lui. Après quoi tous deux examinèrent les lieux.

— C'est bien la peine d'avoir un jardin pour le laisser dans un état pareil ! marmotta Esteban. En effet, de leur observatoire, les visiteurs n'entrevoyaient qu'une masse confuse de buissons et d'herbes folles dans laquelle on ne pouvait distinguer le moindre sentier. La maison elle-même montrait une tourelle percée d'étroites ouvertures qui devait renfermer l'escalier mais les fenêtres étaient aussi rares que sur la façade rue : deux à l'étage dont l'une était ouverte sur les ténèbres intérieures et une sous le toit fermée par des volets.

— Restez là ! ordonna Fiora. Je reviens...

Et avant que son compagnon ait pu la retenir, elle avait glissé de l'autre côté du mur où elle resta accroupie un instant pour laisser se dissiper le bruit des feuillages froissés. La voix étouffée d'Esteban lui parvint comme de très loin :

— Faites attention, je vous en prie ! Vous n'avez même pas d'armes !

— J'ai un couteau, cela devrait suffire en cas de besoin, répondit-elle en posant la main sur la gaine de cuir qui pendait à sa ceinture. Puis, sans plus attendre, en prenant la maison comme point de repère, elle se faufila, toujours courbée, à travers la végétation sauvage du jardin. Elle allait lentement, un pas après l'autre, écartant les branches de ses mains gantées de cuir épais et les jambes bien protégées par des bottes souples qui lui montaient jusqu'aux genoux. Un bruit de fuite dans l'herbe l'immobilisa, le cœur arrêté, mais un miaulement aigu vint la rassurer presque aussitôt : c'était un matou que les approches de la pleine lune mettaient en émoi.

Elle arriva enfin au pied de la maison et toucha de la main le bois d'une porte découpée dans la tourelle, mais cette porte-là était aussi solide, aussi bien armée que l'autre. La seule possibilité d'entrée était offerte par cette fenêtre ouverte à l'étage mais l'encorbellement en rendait l'accès impossible à moins que de posséder une échelle.

Déçue, Fiora allait rebrousser chemin quand un nouveau bruit suspendit son mouvement. Cette fois, ce n'était plus le cri d'un chat mais des sanglots qui semblaient monter du sol. Écartant doucement les grandes herbes qui croissaient contre le soubassement, elle aperçut soudain un étroit soupirail défendu par un croisillon de fer. Il y avait là une cave, très certainement, et, dans cette cave, quelqu'un pleurait...

Se jetant à genoux, Fiora se courba pour essayer d'apercevoir quelque chose mais ses yeux ne purent fouiller l'obscurité.

— Qui pleure ici ? murmura-t-elle, bouleversée par cette invisible douleur qui évoquait celle d'une âme en peine. Puis-je vous aider ?

Les sanglots cessèrent sur un reniflement. Fiora allait renouveler son appel quand un vacarme de verrous tirés parvint jusqu'à elle, suivi d'une voix rude qui grondait :

— Assez pleuré comme ça ! Tu m'empêches de boire !... J' veux plus t'entendre, t'as compris ?

Le silence retomba, à peine coupé par un petit gémissement. La créature enfermée là s'efforçait sans doute de contenir ses sanglots. L'homme qui devait être le second valet ne bougeait pas. Et soudain, Fiora entendit :

— Tu peux pas dormir ?... Pas étonnant avec c't'attirail !... Tiens ! bois un coup... et si t'es gentille t'en auras encore...

Il y eut un bruit de chaînes puis un lappement semblable à celui d'une bête qui boit. L'homme éclata de rire :

— Là ! Tu vois ? Ça va mieux !... Allez, laisse-toi faire ! Autant s'amuser un peu, pas vrai ? Tant qu' le vieux est pas là !

Fiora, épouvantée, n'eut aucune peine à identifier les bruits qui suivirent. Lentement, se retenant même de respirer, elle s'éloigna du soupirail et rejoignit le mur sur lequel Esteban se morfondait. A nouveau il l'aida à grimper jusqu'à lui.

— Alors ? Vous avez trouvé quelque chose ?

Elle appuya vivement sa main sur la bouche de son compagnon.

— Oui, mais ce n'est pas l'endroit pour en parler. Rentrons ! souffla-t-elle.

Quelques minutes plus tard ils étaient de retour et Fiora faisait le récit de son aventure avec la passion qu'elle mettait toujours lorsque son cœur était touché :

— Il y a une femme dans cette cave, une femme enchaînée sans doute et qui sert de jouet à ces misérables. Il faut faire quelque chose !

— Je ne demande pas mieux, fit Démétrios, mais quoi ? Pénétrer dans cette maison par la force ? Tu as pu constater toi-même que c'est impossible. Dénoncer le sire du Hamel aux autorités ? Nous ne sommes que des étrangers : on ne nous écouterait même pas et avant qu'une enquête, si nous l'obtenions, soit entamée, cette malheureuse aurait sans doute disparu. De toute façon, si l'histoire que t'a racontée Chrétiennotte est véridique, c'est une situation qui dure depuis pas mal de temps...

— Est-ce une raison pour qu'elle s'éternise ? Il faut que j'entre dans cette maison, il le faut à tout prix. Sinon, comment atteindre du Hamel ?

— Quand il sera là nous aviserons...

— Il faut aviser avant et nous préparer. D'ailleurs, j'ai une idée, risquée sans doute, mais c'est notre seule véritable chance.

— Laquelle ?

— Je t'expliquerai. En attendant, il me faut trois objets.

— Qui sont ?

— Une robe de velours gris dont je donnerai le modèle, de faux cheveux blonds... et la clé de la maison du Hamel. Il doit être possible de la voler à l'un des valets quand il sort la nuit pour aller chez les filles.

— Ça doit pouvoir s'arranger, approuva Esteban. J'aurai cette clé... mais il faudra agir dès qu'elle sera en notre possession.

— Une heure devrait suffire, dit Fiora mais peut-être, ensuite, serons-nous obligés de quitter la ville...

Le lendemain, comme il avait été dit, dame Morel-Sauvegrain se présenta chez sa jeune locataire pour faire sa connaissance et prendre des nouvelles de sa santé.

Fidèle à son rôle, Fiora la reçut avec un empressement qui n'était pas exempt d'une certaine curiosité car cette dame connaissait bien l'homme contre lequel Démétrios et elle-même s'étaient unis par un lien de sang.

L'ancienne nourrice ducale était une grande femme de plus de soixante ans mais qui conservait de la fraîcheur et dont les cheveux argentés se souvenaient qu'ils avaient été blonds. Elle portait avec élégance le deuil, jamais quitté, d'un époux mort depuis trente-sept ans, mais ce deuil était de soie brodée et sa haute coiffe s'ornait de précieuses dentelles.

Une immédiate sympathie rapprocha les deux femmes. Fiora remercia son hôtesse des attentions qu'elle avait eues pour elle et dame Symonne déplora qu'une si jeune créature soit contrainte au repos.

— Est-ce que la campagne ne serait pas meilleure pour vous? lui dit-elle. J'y possède plusieurs manoirs et je pourrais facilement mettre l'un d'eux à votre disposition?...

— Vous êtes infiniment bonne, répondit Fiora, et j'ai honte de vous avouer que... la campagne m'ennuie. J'aime à sentir, autour de moi, l'animation d'une ville et celle-ci me plaît...

— Notre cité est belle, sans doute, soupira dame Symonne, mais voilà bien longtemps qu'elle ne connaît plus guère d'animation. Songez qu'elle ne voit jamais plus ses princes! Le duc Charles est venu l'an dernier, en février, et il n'avait pas vu Dijon depuis douze ans. Encore était-ce dans une circonstance funèbre...

— Funèbre? Quelqu'un de sa famille était-il mort?

— Non. Il venait recevoir les corps de son père et de sa mère, le duc Philippe et la duchesse Isabelle, ensevelis auparavant à Bruges et à Gosnay, dans les pays de par-deçà, afin qu'ils reposent auprès de leurs parents, à la chartreuse de Champmol qui est nécropole des ducs de Bourgogne... C'était jour de grande froidure sous un ciel lourd de neige et pourtant j'étais heureuse parce que ma chère duchesse, à qui j'étais si fort dévouée, revenait ici, près de moi, pour y attendre la résurrection...

Pour elle-même plus encore peut-être que pour sa silencieuse auditrice, dame Symonne laissa sortir de sa mémoire le long et fastueux cortège qui entra dans Dijon ce jour-là, mené par le seigneur de Ravenstein et le connétable de Saint-Pol montés sur des chevaux couverts de velours noir, la pompeuse ordonnance des insignes du duc défunt : le pennon armorié, le cheval de guerre que menaient les frères de Toulongeon, l'épée à la garde étincelante de pierreries, puis l'écu, le heaume, la bannière portés par les plus hauts seigneurs, enfin la cotte aux symboles de la Toison d'or, que le roi d'armes de l'ordre tenait déployée entre ses mains, et toute la noblesse des différents pays du grand-duc d'Occident en habits de deuil suivant le duc Charles tout de noir vêtu qui accueillait les deux cercueils en présence des archevêques de Cologne, de Besançon et d'Autun, des ambassadeurs d'Aragon, de Bretagne, de Venise et de Rome. Et puis tous les chevaliers de la Toison d'or portant les lourds colliers de l'Ordre...

A cet instant, quelque chose bougea dans le cœur de Fiora. Doucement, elle interrompit la narratrice :

— L'hiver dernier, à Florence, nous avons vu venir l'un de ces chevaliers envoyé en ambassade auprès de Mgr Lorenzo de Médicis. Il se nommait... le comte de Selongey. Vous le connaissez peut-être ?

L'émotion qui avait vibré dans la voix de dame Symonne fit place à un rire amusé :

— Messire Philippe ? Qui ne le connaît à la cour de Bourgogne ? Mgr Charles, auquel il est dévoué corps et âme, l'aime beaucoup. Et pas seulement lui !

— Que voulez-vous dire ?

— Qu'il est fort apprécié par ses compagnons de combat car il est d'une grande bravoure, mais aussi par beaucoup de dames et de damoiselles. Il a du charme et je gage que les dames florentines lui ont volontiers souri ?...

— Elles n'en ont guère eu le temps car il n'est resté que peu de jours, dit Fiora furieuse de sentir que sa voix tremblait et qu'elle avait peine à cacher sa colère. Ainsi, il a beaucoup de belles amies ?

— On le dit mais je ne saurais vous répondre avec certitude car je vis éloignée d'une cour qui nous boude et nous réduit à l'état de cité provinciale, nous qui sommes pourtant ville capitale. Les bruits en sont lointains pour nous et tout ce dont je suis certaine c'est que, là où est le duc Charles, là est aussi le seigneur de Selongey. Or le duc ne cesse de guerroyer. Cela laisse peu de temps pour les amours. Mais vous-même, ma chère, comment avez-vous trouvé cet ambassadeur-là ?

— Il m'a paru... séduisant, encore que je ne l'aie guère rencontré. Mais laissons ce sujet, et si vous le voulez bien, parlez-moi du duc ! Quel homme est-ce ?

Fiora s'attendait à une explosion d'enthousiasme et cependant il n'en fut rien. Dame Symonne resta un moment silencieuse, contemplant les bagues d'or, de perles et d'améthystes qui ornaient ses doigts :

— Comment vous le dépeindre au plus près de la vérité, cette vérité qui change suivant les regards ? Le mien est sans doute celui de la tendresse puisque je l'ai nourri de mon lait et il est vrai que je l'aime infiniment, mais j'avoue qu'à présent il me fait un peu peur à cause de cet orgueil sans mesure auquel se joint une étrange propension à la mélancolie. Cela m'a frappée lorsque je l'ai vu l'an passé et tient, je pense, à son sang portugais...

— Portugais ?

— Mais oui. Sa mère nous est venue de Portugal. Elle était la sœur de ce prince Henri le Navigateur qui prétendait conquérir les mers et elle lui a donné ses rêves de gloire et d'infini. Monseigneur Charles n'est heureux que dans l'action et, cependant, depuis toujours il craint la mort et la brièveté de la vie lui est insupportable. Pourtant il ne recule jamais devant le danger et, même, il aime à le rechercher. Jeune homme, lorsqu'il vivait à Gorcum, il aimait s'embarquer seul sur une barque à voile et affronter ainsi la tempête. D'ailleurs, la tempête est comme la guerre son élément naturel. Elle trouve en lui des résonances car il a de terribles accès de fureur. Je redoute que ce vieux rêve qu'il poursuit de reconstituer l'antique royaume bourguignon ne le mène plus loin qu'il ne faudrait. Il cherche à unir par la conquête les pays de par-deçà aux pays de par-delà [1] où nous sommes, et mieux vaudrait sans doute qu'il songe d'abord à protéger ce qu'il possède. Ce n'est pas un mince ennemi que le roi de France et il surveille notre duc comme l'araignée guette sa proie du fond de sa toile...

— Comment est-il physiquement ?

— Que voilà une question bien féminine! fit dame Symonne en riant. Sachez donc, jolie curieuse, que c'est un bel homme, moins grand que n'était son père, mais de belle stature et bien proportionné... et très vigoureux, ce qui le rend endurant à la fatigue et aux privations. Il a le visage large et coloré au menton puissant, aux yeux sombres et dominateurs. Ses cheveux sont noirs et drus. Il sourit rarement, beaucoup moins qu'autrefois et c'est dommage car cela lui conférait un grand charme...

— On dit que son père aimait fort les dames. Lui ressemble-t-il à ce sujet?

— En aucune façon car il tient beaucoup plus de sa mère et se plaît d'ailleurs à dire : « Nous autres, Portugais... », ce qui faisait enrager le duc Philippe en son temps. Celui-là a eu des maîtresses sans nombre et sa femme en a trop souffert pour que le fils ne prît pas la débauche en horreur. Charles a aimé, profondément, Isabelle de Bourbon, sa défunte épouse qui lui a donné la princesse Marie, et je crois qu'il est attaché à Marguerite d'York, la duchesse actuelle, mais son cœur s'est arrêté là et il ne se laisse jamais entraîner par ses sens. Il se méfie des femmes, leur préfère de beaucoup ses compagnons

---

1. Pays-Bas et Flandres d'une part et Bourgogne proprement dite de l'autre.

d'armes — en tout bien tout honneur car il est chaste. Comme il préfère la guerre aux fêtes, lui le prince le plus fastueux d'Europe, il déteste les grands banquets et les bals que son père aimait tant...

— N'aime-t-il donc pas se distraire ?

— Si, mais à sa manière. Il aime lire et, surtout, il adore la musique et passe des heures à écouter les chantres de sa chapelle que dirige maître Antoine Busnois. Ils le suivent partout et il lui arrive de chanter avec eux... C'est un étrange prince, n'est-ce pas, que je vous décris là ?

— C'est, je crois, le fait des princes de n'être pas comme tout le monde. Le duc est-il aimé de ses peuples ?

— Je n'en suis pas certaine. On le craint et, d'ailleurs, il a dit un jour aux Flamands : « Je préfère votre haine à votre mépris. » Mais il dédaigne ce qui est bourgeois ou populaire. En outre, il peut être d'une impitoyable cruauté. Les gens de Dinant et les Liégeois dont il a rasé les villes en savent quelque chose, ceux tout au moins qui sont encore vivants pour s'en souvenir...

Sur leur tourelle, Jacquemart et sa femme sonnèrent quatre coups et dame Symonne se leva aussitôt.

— Vous ne partez pas déjà ? s'exclama Fiora.

— Si, il est tard et j'ai à faire... Alors, vraiment, vous tenez à rester ici, à contempler les eaux du Suzon et cette maison aux volets clos ?

— Elle est un peu mélancolique, sans doute...

— Dites qu'elle est sinistre. Et autrefois elle paraissait si charmante et si gaie ! Le jardin en été semblait un bouquet de fleurs. La maîtresse en était une lingère de la duchesse Marguerite de Bavière, grand-mère de notre duc, et elle adorait toutes les plantes. Il en poussait le long de tous ses murs...

— On dit que le maître en est absent ?

— Qu'il soit là ou non ne change rien. Si mes bavardages ne vous fatiguent pas, je vous en parlerai à ma prochaine visite. Mais c'est un assez vilain oiseau...

Tout en parlant, dame Symonne s'était approchée de la

fenêtre pour jeter un regard machinal à la maison en question et, soudain, son œil s'anima :

— Vous allez pouvoir en juger par vous-même, ma chère, car le voilà qui rentre.

Fiora jaillit de ses coussins avec une vivacité qui eût sans doute surpris sa visiteuse si le regard de celle-ci n'avait été retenu ailleurs. Un homme, en effet, descendait péniblement d'une belle mule devant la porte de la maison d'où venait de surgir l'un des valets.

S'efforçant de rester à l'abri du meneau qui partageait la fenêtre, Fiora dévora des yeux le nouveau venu avec une haine dont la violence la surprit. C'était un vieillard maigre qui semblait courbé par le poids du riche manteau ourlé de fourrure qu'il portait en dépit de la chaleur. Entre les cheveux gris et ternes qui pendaient de l'épais chaperon de velours, la jeune femme aperçut un long visage couleur de vieil ivoire, un nez pointu, une barbe clairsemée mais ne put voir les yeux sous le bourrelet proéminent des sourcils broussailleux...

— Dieu qu'il est laid! fit-elle, sincère.

— L'âme n'est pas plus belle, croyez-moi!

— Et... il vit seul dans cette maison?

— Avec deux valets, deux frères qui ressemblent davantage à des reîtres qu'à d'honnêtes serviteurs.

— Aucune femme? Pourtant, on m'a soutenu avoir, un soir, entendu des plaintes et des gémissements...

Dame Symonne se mit à rire :

— Ça, c'est du Chrétiennotte tout pur! Elle est persuadée la maison du Hamel est hantée et raconte son histoire à qui veut bien l'entendre. Mais, vous savez, elle est comme beaucoup de filles de la campagne et voit du merveilleux partout...

— Elle se dit, en effet, persuadée qu'un fantôme est attaché à cette triste maison... Celui de...

— La malheureuse qui a jadis été mariée à ce triste personnage? dit dame Symonne qui ne riait plus. Après tout, c'est peut-être vrai, car elle aurait toutes les raisons pour cela... Mais assez parlé! Le marguillier de Notre Dame doit déjà m'attendre pour parler de la procession de dimanche. Je vous souhaite le bonsoir!

Elle s'éclipsa dans un grand bruit de soie froissée, laissant après elle une agréable odeur d'iris. La rue du Lacet était vide à présent. Du Hamel, sa mule et son valet avaient disparu. Fiora retourna s'asseoir dans ses coussins et resta là un long moment à réfléchir, le menton dans sa main. L'heure d'agir n'allait plus tarder...

CHAPITRE III

MARGUERITE

Minuit venait de sonner et le cœur de Fiora battait lourdement dans sa poitrine, lui donnant parfois l'impression d'étouffer. La chaleur avait sévi toute la journée sans que le crépuscule annonçât de fraîcheur. La nuit était pesante, orageuse, opaque, mais le roulement lointain du tonnerre laissait prévoir de la pluie avant l'aube. Fiora espérait néanmoins que la tempête ne viendrait pas trop tôt : ces ténèbres vaguement menaçantes lui convenaient tout à fait pour accomplir ce qu'elle avait décidé : l'heure était venue pour Regnault du Hamel, d'expier ses forfaits...

Debout devant le miroir que dame Symonne avait fait installer dans sa chambre, Fiora se regardait et ne se reconnaissait pas : ce pâle visage blanchi à l'aide d'une pâte, ces cheveux blonds qu'un barbier avait procurés à Démétrios !... Seul lui était familier le petit hennin de dentelle taché de sang que Léonarde avait réussi à sauver, avec quelques objets précieux, du désastre du palais Beltrami et qu'elle avait épinglé, de ses mains tremblantes, sur la tête de « son agneau ». La robe de velours gris moucheté d'or était lourde et pénible à porter par cette température, pourtant Fiora ne transpirait même pas. Cette manifestation humaine lui était refusée comme si l'âme de Marie de Brévailles était entrée en elle pour assumer sa vengeance et l'eût désincarnée. Comme si elle n'était plus qu'une apparence...

Derrière elle, Fiora entendit Léonarde gémir. La vieille fille était terrifiée par ce qu'elle voyait et plus encore, peut-être, par ce qui allait se passer. Elle avait lutté de toutes ses forces pour détourner la jeune femme de son dangereux projet...

– La haine de cet homme n'est pas éteinte, mon agneau. S'il allait vous tuer ou seulement vous blesser ?

– On ne tue, on ne blesse pas un fantôme ! Et je ne serai pas seule. Démétrios tient à entrer avec moi pour s'occuper du valet de garde...

– Cette vengeance vous tient donc tellement à cœur ? L'homme est vieux, il ne vivra plus très longtemps...

– Trop longtemps de toute façon pour la malheureuse qu'il retient captive. Je vais prendre une vie mais en libérer une autre...

Démétrios frappa à la porte et pénétra sans attendre d'y être prié mais s'arrêta net à l'entrée de la chambre, considérant la jeune femme qui se tournait vers lui.

– Comment me trouves-tu ?

– Impressionnante... même pour moi ! N'oublie pas le voile blanc et, auparavant, laisse-moi parfaire notre œuvre !

S'approchant de la jeune femme, il lui passa, autour du cou, un mince ruban rouge puis, prenant des mains de Léonarde une grande pièce de mousseline blanche, il la jeta sur la tête de Fiora dont le personnage devint brumeux à souhait sans toutefois cesser d'être reconnaissable...

– Il faut me laisser ma liberté de mouvements, dit-elle en désignant la dague qu'elle portait attachée à sa haute ceinture mais dissimulée dans les plis de la robe...

Le cri d'un oiseau de nuit, répété trois fois, se fit entendre par la fenêtre ouverte :

– C'est Esteban, dit Démétrios, il nous attend. Viens à présent si tu es toujours décidée !

– Plus que jamais !

Elle s'enveloppa d'une ample et légère mante de soie

noire destinée à la rendre invisible dans la nuit et suivit Démétrios. Bien graissée, la porte de l'hôtel s'ouvrit sans bruit et, un instant plus tard, Fiora et Démétrios rejoignaient Esteban.

— Tu as la clé ? demanda le Grec.

— Sinon je n'aurais pas sifflé, mais faites vite tout de même, le gros Claude qui a bu comme une éponge dort dans les bras d'une fille de la rue du Griffon mais il pourrait se réveiller.

— De toute façon, dit Fiora, s'il ne retrouve pas sa clé ce sera sans importance. La maison sera ouverte...

— Je tiens tout de même à la lui rapporter. Pour le bon ordre et pour que les hommes du prévôt ne se posent pas trop de questions demain quand ils découvriront le cadavre.

En deux sauts légers, le Castillan fut à la porte qui s'ouvrit sous sa main sans le moindre grincement. L'obscurité de la maison engloutit les trois amis qui restèrent immobiles un moment pour habituer leurs yeux aux ténèbres environnantes. L'absence de fenêtres ne rendait pas la chose aisée mais ils aperçurent finalement un charbon qui rougeoyait, probablement dans une cheminée, et Esteban alla y allumer la chandelle qu'il avait dans sa poche. Ils virent alors qu'ils se trouvaient dans une cuisine au fond de laquelle apparaissait la spirale d'un escalier et la porte donnant sur le jardin. Personne n'était en vue.

Fiora abandonna sa mante noire et disposa son voile blanc de façon à garder l'usage de sa main droite. Esteban marchant en tête, ils se dirigèrent vers l'escalier qu'ils montèrent aussi silencieusement que possible et ils atteignirent ainsi la grande salle qui était parfaitement vide.

— Ils doivent être en haut, chuchota Esteban.

Effectivement, quand sa tête émergea au ras du second étage il aperçut Mathieu, le second valet, qui dormait profondément, étendu devant une porte, sur une simple couverture. Il n'était pas difficile de deviner qui reposait derrière cette porte...

— Reste là ! souffla Démétrios à l'oreille de Fiora. Il faut que nous nous en débarrassions...

Esteban, souple et silencieux comme un chat, se glissait déjà vers le dormeur qui, du fond de son sommeil dut deviner son approche car il remua, grogna et changea de position. A genoux à deux pas de lui le Castillan retenait sa respiration. Mais, avec un soupir de contentement, Mathieu se rendormait. Alors, d'un maître coup de poing, asséné avec la rapidité et la force de la foudre, Esteban l'assomma. Ensuite, aidé par Démétrios, il tira sur la couverture lui servant de couche pour éloigner l'homme de la porte. Le chemin était libre à présent pour Fiora qui vit un mince rai de lumière filtrer à l'endroit où le valet avait été couché.

Laissant son serviteur ficeler et bâillonner Mathieu, Démétrios revint vers Fiora et doucement, tout doucement, ouvrit la porte dont le loquet joua sans bruit. La zone lumineuse s'élargit et la jeune femme aperçut enfin son ennemi. Assis plutôt qu'étendu dans son lit comme font les asthmatiques, Regnault du Hamel lisait à la lueur d'une chandelle posée à son chevet. Un bonnet de nuit était enfoncé sur ses oreilles et son buste disparaissait sous une camisole de laine grise. Des besicles chaussaient son long nez. Il ressemblait à une gargouille de cathédrale, si laid que Fiora eut envie de bondir sur lui et de frapper tout de suite. Mais elle se retint. Ce qu'elle voulait voir, sur cette figure jaune, c'était la peur. Très lentement, elle s'avança dans la chambre, glissant plus qu'elle ne marchait sur le plancher en espérant qu'il ne grincerait pas, mais ses pieds trouvèrent un tapis et elle se sentit plus assurée. Du Hamel ne l'avait pas encore aperçue. Il lisait toujours.

Alors elle fit entendre une faible plainte, puis une autre... Le vieillard leva les yeux et vit, à quelques pas de son lit, une ombre blanche. Le livre s'échappa de ses mains et tomba à terre avec un bruit sourd, mais l'ombre s'approchait toujours... A présent Regnault pouvait distinguer un visage, des cheveux blonds, un cou qui semblait porter la trace sanglante de l'épée du bourreau... Une folle épouvante envahit sa figure. Il essaya de reculer dans son lit et voulut crier mais, comme dans les cauchemars, aucun son ne sortit de sa bouche aux lèvres violettes. Il tendit ses deux bras devant lui pour repousser l'apparition et réussit à souffler :

— Non... non!...

— Tu vas mourir, chuchota la voix basse du fantôme. Tu vas mourir de ma main...

Fiora ébauchait déjà le geste de tirer la dague pour frapper quand, soudain, du Hamel porta ses deux mains à sa gorge. Sa bouche qui cherchait désespérément l'air s'ouvrit sur un râle, ses yeux parurent jaillir de leurs orbites. Un spasme secoua tout son maigre corps qui glissa sur le côté et ne bougea plus. Son visage était devenu violet comme si une main invisible l'avait étranglé.

Stupéfaite, Fiora demeura un moment immobile puis, enlevant son voile, se pencha sur l'homme inerte et appela :

— Démétrios! Viens voir!

Le médecin grec accourut, prit la main abandonnée sur le drap, posa son oreille à l'emplacement du cœur puis, considérant la bouche ouverte sur un cri qui ne serait jamais poussé, les yeux qui ne verraient plus rien de ce monde, il soupira :

— Il est mort, Fiora... mort d'épouvante.

— Est-ce que cela est possible?

— La preuve! Néanmoins, il ne devait pas avoir le cœur bien solide... Viens à présent, et surtout ne touchons à rien. On dirait que le ciel t'a évité de faire couler le sang. Il faut qu'on trouve le corps tel qu'il est... Esteban va libérer le valet et reporter la clé à l'autre.

Il avait pris son bras pour l'entraîner mais elle résista :

— Tu oublies quelque chose, Démétrios. Cet homme est mort et je suis satisfaite mais il y a ici quelqu'un à délivrer, cette femme que j'ai entendue pleurer et je ne partirai pas sans elle...

Rassemblant ses robes qui la gênaient dans ses mouvements, Fiora s'élança dans l'escalier après avoir pris la chandelle des mains du Grec. Elle alla ouvrir la porte qui donnait sur le jardin dans l'espoir de mieux y voir mais la referma aussitôt car le vent se levait. Le tonnerre d'ailleurs s'était rapproché et grondait sur sa tête. Elle cherchait encore une porte descendant à la cave quand Esteban et Démétrios la rejoignirent.

— Ce n'est pas une porte qu'il nous faut trouver, dit le Castillan, c'est une trappe... et vous avez les pieds dessus.

En effet, à cet endroit, le dallage cédait la place à des planches épaisses mais il y avait tellement de poussière que Fiora n'avait pas vu la différence. Les muscles solides d'Esteban eurent tôt fait de soulever l'abattant qui révéla un escalier de pierre plongeant dans les entrailles de la maison. Une bouffée d'odeur infecte sauta au visage de Fiora quand elle mit le pied sur la première marche. Démétrios la retint en arrière :

— Laisse-moi passer le premier. Je t'éclairerai...

Il commença à descendre puis tendit une main à Fiora :

— Prends garde! Les marches sont glissantes. Cela pue l'humidité...

— Mais au moins on n'étouffe pas, déclara Esteban qui suivait. Il fait nettement moins chaud que dans le reste de la maison.

Au bas des marches, ils se trouvèrent dans une sorte de caveau à voûte ronde sur lequel donnaient deux portes faites de vieilles planches vermoulues :

— C'est celle-ci qu'il faut ouvrir, indiqua Fiora. Le soupirail du jardin doit donner de ce côté. Mais nous n'en avons pas la clé...

— Pas besoin de clé pour ouvrir ça! fit Esteban. Et, d'un magistral coup de pied, il enfonça le battant qui n'était tenu que par une mauvaise serrure. Un gémissement pitoyable fit écho au vacarme qu'il déclencha. La prisonnière devait craindre de nouveaux sévices. Mais Fiora s'était déjà précipitée par l'ouverture en se baissant pour ne pas s'assommer. Ce qu'elle entrevit grâce à la chandelle de Démétrios qui l'avait suivie lui arracha un cri d'horreur : au fond d'une sorte d'*in pace* où il était impossible de se tenir debout, une femme vêtue d'une robe en loques était étendue sur une litière de paille à demi pourrie. Des bracelets et des chaînes de fer la rattachaient à un gros anneau pendu au mur. Fiora ne vit pas son visage mais une longue, une immense chevelure blonde, sale comme l'étaient les haillons de la malheureuse.

Entendant pénétrer dans son cachot, celle-ci se tourna péniblement, révélant une petite figure maigre qui portait des égratignures et des traces de coups, comme ses membres menus et sans doute tout le reste de son corps. Les larmes aux yeux, Fiora se jeta à genoux près d'elle sans souci de souiller sa robe, cherchant déjà comment lui retirer ses chaînes :

— N'ayez pas peur, dit-elle doucement. Nous venons vous délivrer. Votre bourreau est mort... Dites-nous seulement qui vous êtes.

La prisonnière ouvrit la bouche mais ne réussit à produire que des sons inarticulés en dépit de l'effort pathétique qui fit perler des larmes à ses yeux pâles mais sans couleur définie.

— Mon Dieu ! soupira Fiora. Est-ce qu'elle serait muette ?

— Peut-être, fit Démétrios, mais écarte-toi et laisse-moi faire. N'essayez pas de parler ! ajouta-t-il pour la prisonnière. Nous allons vous emmener d'ici, vous soigner... Nous sommes des amis. Il faudrait briser ces fers ou les ouvrir, ajouta-t-il pour Esteban qui repartit en courant. La clé doit bien en être quelque part...

Le Castillan revint heureusement peu après, tenant la clé qu'il avait retrouvée, avec d'autres, dans la chambre du mort. Les bracelets de fer tombèrent révélant de cruelles ecchymoses.

— Nous allons la ramener chez nous, n'est-ce pas ? pria Fiora qui, d'une geste plein de douceur, avait enveloppé la jeune femme qui ne devait guère avoir plus de quinze ou seize ans – dans le grand voile blanc qu'elle avait porté tout à l'heure.

Pour toute réponse, Esteban se courba, l'enleva dans ses bras et se dirigea vers la porte, sans négliger de se courber pour la franchir. Fiora et Démétrios le suivirent et remontèrent dans la cuisine dont le Grec laissa retomber la trappe. Le bruit s'en confondit avec un violent coup de tonnerre. Cependant Démétrios ouvrait la porte avec précaution pour voir si la rue était vide. Les éclairs qui se succédaient sans interruption montraient qu'il n'y avait pas une âme. Fiora ramassa la mante noire qu'elle avait abandonnée tout à l'heure et s'en couvrit. Ils allaient sortir quand Démétrios se tourna vers Esteban qui ne semblait guère peiner sous son fardeau :

– Donne-la-moi ! fit-il. Toi, tu devrais aller t'assurer que le valet est toujours évanoui...

– C'est sans importance, il est ficelé et n'a rien vu.

– Comme tu voudras... Quant à son frère, après tout, il est inutile de lui restituer la clé. Donne-la-moi. Je vais la jeter dans la rivière...

Comme ils atteignaient le coin de la rue des Forges, la pluie s'abattit sur eux avec une telle violence qu'ils furent instantanément trempés bien qu'ils n'eussent plus que trois pas à faire. Les vannes du ciel s'étaient ouvertes, précipitant des trombes d'eau qui en quelques secondes transformèrent les rues en autant de ruisseaux et gonflèrent le paisible et modeste Suzon à l'importance d'un torrent... Tonnerre et éclairs se succédaient sans interruption et leur vacarme couvrit le bruit, léger il est vrai, de la rentrée du groupe.

Fiora décréta d'emblée que l'on donnerait son lit à l'inconnue mais Démétrios ayant obligeamment décidé de partager le sien avec son « secrétaire », c'est finalement dans la chambre d'Esteban que l'on porta la rescapée auprès de laquelle Léonarde s'empressait déjà. Elle envoya le Castillan faire chauffer de l'eau à la cuisine, pendant qu'aidée de Fiora elle délivrait la malheureuse de ses haillons infects. Le corps qui leur apparut était maigre, couvert de marques pénibles mais plus formé toutefois que ne le pensait Fiora qui, jusque-là, n'avait pas attribué plus de quinze ou seize ans à la prisonnière.

— Elle doit avoir une vingtaine d'années, apprécia Léonarde, qui ajouta, examinant le ventre légèrement gonflé : Je me demande si elle n'est pas enceinte...

— Cela n'aurait rien d'étonnant d'après ce que j'ai perçu par le soupirail, dit Fiora. L'une de ces brutes s'amusait d'elle et peut-être bien les deux...

Démétrios qui était allé prendre chez lui ce dont il pouvait avoir besoin rentra à cet instant mais infirma le diagnostic de Léonarde...

— Je ne pense pas. Mais je me demande qui elle peut être et pourquoi ces misérables la tenaient séquestrée ?

L'inconnue ne disait toujours rien. Elle tenait ses yeux fermés et se laissait faire comme si elle n'avait plus la force d'accomplir le moindre geste. Entre les mains de Démétrios qui l'examinait, elle était aussi molle qu'une poupée de chiffons.

— Elle a dû être battue souvent car certaines de ces traces sont anciennes et elle a sans doute manqué de nourriture, mais elle devrait être en assez bonne santé...

— Tu as oublié qu'elle semble muette ? dit Fiora. On lui a peut-être coupé la langue ?

Démétrios s'assura aussitôt qu'il n'en était rien puis déclara que la terreur et les mauvais traitements pouvaient priver quelqu'un de la parole, parfois pour un temps et parfois pour toujours.

— Lorsqu'elle sera en meilleur état, nous tenterons une petite expérience, ajouta-t-il. Pour l'instant c'est trop tôt...

Léonarde et Fiora lavèrent de leur mieux la rescapée avant de lui passer l'une des chemises de Fiora. On enduisit de baume ses poignets que les fers avaient mis à vif et on les banda de fine toile. Puis on s'attaqua au visage que l'on avait gardé pour la fin. On le débarrassa de la crasse et des traces de sang que l'on y voyait mais on ne put estomper les bleus qui dénonçaient les coups reçus.

— Quels beaux cheveux! soupira Fiora en maniant la longue chevelure blonde. Quel dommage qu'ils soient si sales! Il faudrait les laver!

— Soyez sûre que nous n'y manquerons pas quand elle sera assez forte pour cela... Oh! voyez, mon agneau, elle ouvre les yeux!

Les deux femmes et le Grec se penchèrent sur le lit où l'inconnue venait, en effet, de soulever ses paupières, révélant des prunelles d'un bleu pâle tirant légèrement sur le vert. Elle regarda les trois visages et s'efforça de sourire sans y parvenir réellement.

— Vous êtes en sûreté ici, dit doucement Fiora. Personne ne vous fera plus de mal et nous veillerons sur vous...

— Nous allons commencer par vous donner quelque chose à manger, fit Léonarde, et un peu de lait à boire...

— Avec ce temps orageux votre lait a dû tourner, dit Démétrios. Faites-lui plutôt une tisane de tilleul bien sucrée au miel dans laquelle vous mettrez une pincée de ceci, ajouta-t-il en lui tendant une petite boîte de bois peint.

Demeuré seul avec Fiora, Démétrios revint vers le lit et considéra le jeune visage douloureux qui ressortait sur la blancheur de l'oreiller. Soudain, il se pencha et prit le chandelier qui brûlait au chevet pour l'élever au-dessus du lit.

— Sais-tu, murmura-t-il, que cette malheureuse te ressemble ?

— A moi ?

— Oui... pas beaucoup d'ailleurs. En fait, c'est surtout à ce garçon qu'elle ressemble, ce jeune moine échappé que nous avons envoyé à la guerre.

— Christophe ? Tu penses qu'elle pourrait être de la famille ?

Léonarde revenait avec sa tisane et, tandis que celle-ci

refroidissait assez pour être buvable, Fiora lui fit part de l'idée de Démétrios en ajoutant qu'elle ne voyait pas très bien qui la jeune femme pouvait être. Mais Léonarde, elle, voyait. Après avoir considéré de plus près le visage aux yeux clos, elle rappela à Fiora le récit en forme de confession qu'un soir de printemps Francesco Beltrami avait fait à sa fille :

— Souviens-toi ! Il nous a dit que ta mère avait donné une fille à Regnault du Hamel. Je jurerais que c'est elle. En ce cas, elle devrait bien avoir vingt ans comme je le pensais...

— Sa fille ? Il aurait traité sa fille de cette manière ignoble ? Et cela depuis des années ? C'est impossible : elle serait morte depuis longtemps ?...

— Non, dit Démétrios, cela n'a rien d'impossible. On a vu des prisonniers, même des femmes, s'obstiner à vivre dans des conditions affreuses. La résistance humaine peut se révéler stupéfiante, surtout lorsqu'il s'agit d'êtres jeunes et, à présent, je suis certain d'avoir raison : cette jeune femme est ta sœur, Fiora !

— Ma... sœur ?

Le mot et plus encore l'idée cheminèrent lentement dans l'esprit de la jeune femme cependant si vif. Elle n'avait guère jusqu'ici arrêté sa pensée à cette péripétie du récit de son père et jamais songé, surtout pas comme à une sœur, à l'unique enfant que Marie de Brévailles avait eu de son mariage. Elle n'avait pas non plus posé de questions à ce sujet parce qu'elle n'imaginait pas qu'un père, fût-ce un du Hamel et si abject soit-il, pût se faire le bourreau de son propre enfant. Selon elle, la fille du conseiller avait dû être confiée, après la fuite de sa mère, à quelque couvent, à moins que sa grand-mère ne l'eût réclamée, ce qui eût été normal. Mais elle découvrait à présent que l'infâme personnage avait reporté sur l'enfant la haine qu'il vouait à Marie. Il en avait fait son souffre-douleur, lui infligeant un long martyre qu'il dut se complaire à observer. La tuer aurait été trop rapide, moins délectable sans doute, mais qu'il eût poussé l'ignominie jusqu'à la livrer aux entreprises de ses valets... cela passait l'entendement et toute tolérance ! Tremblante de colère, Fiora pensa qu'il était bien dommage que du Hamel fût mort si vite. Quelques secondes à peine de folle terreur alors qu'il eût largement mérité une lente agonie subie dans les plus cruelles tortures !

Lentement, elle s'en revint vers le lit où Léonarde faisait boire cette sœur dont elle ne savait même pas encore le nom et se sentit envahie par une immense pitié. Elle prit doucement une des mains si maigres qu'elles ressemblaient à des griffes et la conserva dans la sienne. Léonarde lui jeta un rapide coup d'œil :

— Vous pensez, n'est-ce pas, que ce misérable n'a pas payé assez cher ? Sur cette terre, sans doute. Encore que je remercie Dieu qu'il vous ait évité de tremper vos mains dans ce sang pourri ! Mais je ne crois pas que l'enfer soit un lieu si délectable et vous pouvez être certaine qu'à cette heure messire du Hamel en a déjà franchi le seuil brûlant.

Spontanément, Fiora vint entourer de son bras le cou de sa vieille gouvernante et l'embrassa :

— Vous savez toujours trouver les mots qu'il faut me dire, n'est-ce pas, ma chère Léonarde ? Faites-moi penser à vous rappeler plus souvent que je vous aime beaucoup !

— C'est bien agréable à entendre. Et puisque vous trouvez que mes discours ont quelque à-propos, écoutez donc celui-là : il est affreusement tard et vous tombez de sommeil. Allez dormir ! Demain il fera jour et nous verrons à mettre un peu d'ordre dans nos idées. Je sais en tout cas que les miennes en ont le plus grand besoin !...

Le lendemain matin, le quartier était en révolution et son vacarme montait à l'assaut des nobles demeures et des ateliers d'armuriers de la rue des Forges. Trouvant la porte de la maison du Hamel largement ouverte, une voisine poussée par une curiosité ancienne s'y était hasardée non sans avoir, tout de même, lancé quelques appels dans le vide. Elle en était ressortie peu après en poussant d'affreux hurlements qui avaient réveillé en sursaut tout ce qui dormait encore et attiré sur-le-champ une foule excitée au premier rang de laquelle on pouvait remarquer Chrétiennotte, tenant de grands discours avec des airs de tête superbes et racontant à qui voulait l'entendre l'aventure nocturne de son défunt Janet, agrémentée de quelques trouvailles de son cru.

— D'ici qu'elle nous mêle à ses histoires il n'y a pas loin ! grogna Démétrios en constatant que, par trois fois, la bavarde avait désigné leurs fenêtres. Et il expédia Esteban chercher Chrétiennotte pour la rappeler à une plus juste compréhension de ses devoirs domestiques. Celle-ci se laissa ramener sans résistance mais ne s'occupa pas pour autant du ménage. Penchée jusqu'à mi-corps à la fenêtre de Fiora, elle ne fit que changer de poste d'observation. En effet, elle ne voulait à aucun prix manquer l'arrivée du prévôt et de ses gens qui s'en venaient constater les dégâts. Ce que voyant, Léonarde haussa les épaules, s'empara d'un panier et s'en alla faire le marché après avoir pris, toutefois, la précaution de fermer à double tour la chambre où reposait la malheureuse que Fiora avait tirée de l'enfer.

Naturellement généreuse, Léonarde n'aimait pas beaucoup cependant l'intrusion de ces successifs rappels, dans la vie de Fiora, à un passé qu'elle souhaitait lui voir oublier. Christophe de Brévailles avait pris, grâce à Dieu, son propre chemin et, la nuit dernière, il avait été épargné à Fiora de faire couler le sang – ce dont Léonarde avait éprouvé un grand soulagement. Du Hamel était mort de peur, tué par sa propre conscience et c'était très bien ainsi mais, à présent, il y avait cette fille, muette et peut-être idiote, qu'il fallait cacher, ce qui ne serait pas facile, et qui représentait une charge bien lourde pour des épaules de dix-huit ans à peine...

Au retour du marché, Léonarde semblait plus inquiète encore qu'au départ. Partout on ne parlait que de la mort du conseiller ducal et de celle de son valet Mathieu que l'on avait trouvé poignardé à quelques pas de sa chambre. Quant au second valet, Claude, il avait disparu, et ce n'était qu'une voix pour l'accuser du double crime bien que le corps de du Hamel ne portât aucune marque de sévices quelconques. En revanche, ses coffres et armoires avaient été scrupuleusement fouillés et vidés...

Ce qui s'était passé n'était pas difficile à imaginer. Rentrant tard dans la nuit, et sans doute bien soulagé de trouver la porte ouverte, Claude, craignant peut-être d'être accusé de la mort de son maître, avait trouvé plus simple de prendre la fuite avec tout ce qu'il avait pu ramasser après avoir assassiné son propre frère pour éviter de partager avec lui. Quant à la prisonnière, personne n'en parlait, sa présence étant ignorée de tous, mais elle n'en constituait pas moins un danger permanent par les bavardages que son sauvetage et son hébergement chez le médecin étranger pouvaient susciter. Ces bavardages, ces cancans... la grande spécialité de Chrétiennotte! Bien sûr, Esteban avait fait une défense expresse à la brave femme d'entrer dans sa chambre, prétextant un travail délicat qu'il y avait entrepris, mais pendant combien de temps pourrait-on la tenir à distance?

Aussi, à peine rentrée, Léonarde posa son panier à la cuisine, alla tirer d'autorité Chrétiennotte de son observatoire — où il n'y avait d'ailleurs plus rien à voir — en lui intimant l'ordre d'éplucher les légumes pour la soupe. Puis elle s'en vint conter ses angoisses à Démétrios qu'elle trouva dans sa chambre en train d'écrire.

Le Grec l'écouta sans rien dire suivant son habitude mais quand elle eut fini, il se leva et se mit à marcher de long en large, d'un bord du tapis à l'autre.

— Qu'allons-nous faire? demanda Léonarde. Dieu m'est témoin que j'ai pitié de cette pauvre fille, mais nous ne pourrons pas la cacher éternellement, pas plus que nous ne resterons toujours ici. Alors?

— Honnêtement, je ne sais pas moi non plus comment il faut agir. La meilleure solution serait encore de confier cette malheureuse une fois guérie à un couvent du voisinage. Mais un couvent exige une dot, et c'est une telle dépense! Nous ne pouvons pas nous la permettre. Nous verrons assez vite le bout de l'or remis par Lorenzo de Médicis et il faudra bientôt songer nous-mêmes à rejoindre le roi Louis. D'autre part, si cette fille est vraiment celle du triste sire qui est mort cette nuit, elle devrait être aussi son héritière?

– Le moyen de réclamer l'héritage en son nom sans risquer de nous faire accuser du meurtre?

– Ce serait possible, à la rigueur, mais encore faut-il être assurés qu'elle est vraiment ce que nous pensons?

– Comment faire? Elle est muette.

– Ce n'est pas tout à fait certain car elle émet des sons. Jadis, en Égypte, j'ai vu une femme qui avait perdu l'usage de la parole à la suite d'une grande frayeur. Un imam, dont je suivais alors l'enseignement, la lui a rendue. Étant donné ce qu'elle a enduré, cela pourrait être le cas de notre rescapée. Dès qu'elle pourra le supporter, je tenterai une expérience. En tout état de cause, soyez certaine, dame Léonarde, que j'entreprendrai tout pour que nous partions d'ici le plus tôt possible. Il n'est pas bon, pour Fiora, de se retremper dans l'atmosphère malsaine de ces anciens drames...

– Vous l'encouragez pourtant à poursuivre ces vengeances qui lui empoisonnent le cœur?

– L'impunité des coupables le lui empoisonnerait bien plus encore. En outre, je n'ai aucun pouvoir sur sa volonté qui est inflexible. Je crois voir revivre en elle ces princesses de la Grèce antique, Antigone, Hermione ou Médée, qui allaient implacablement au bout de leurs desseins quel qu'en soit le prix à payer...

– Libre à vous! Moi j'aimerais revoir en elle l'enfant qu'elle était, l'adolescente tendre et joyeuse qui courait dans le jardin de Fiesole...

– De toute façon, et même si le drame n'était intervenu, cette enfant-là ne pouvait subsister. Il vient toujours un moment où la fillette fait place à la femme. Fiora en est une, à présent, et une femme robuste, forgée au feu du malheur : ce sont les meilleures... ou les pires ! Mais c'est là leur secret.

— Tâchez au moins de ne pas trop la pousser dans cette seconde catégorie !

Ayant parlé, Léonarde s'en alla voir si Chrétiennotte s'était enfin décidée à se remettre au travail.

Démétrios n'était pas le seul à vouloir découvrir avec certitude l'identité de la prisonnière. Fiora, qui s'était instituée son infirmière, avait entrepris de connaître au moins son nom et, deux jours après son arrivée, voyant que la santé ne demandait qu'à revenir et que sa protégée progressait presque à vue d'œil, elle lui mit dans les mains du papier et une plume préalablement trempée dans l'encre :

— Puisque vous ne pouvez dire votre nom, lui proposa-t-elle doucement, écrivez-le.

Mais la jeune malade, devenue soudain toute rouge, lui rendit ces objets en hochant la tête d'un air si désolé que Fiora, émue, passa un bras autour de ses épaules fragiles et l'embrassa :

— Vous ne savez pas écrire ? C'est peu de chose et vous apprendrez vite. Mais nous allons essayer de connaître au moins votre nom de baptême. Je vais dire des noms et vous m'arrêterez lorsque j'aurai trouvé le vôtre...

L'inconnue approuva avec un sourire. Le jeu devait l'amuser mais Fiora s'aperçut vite qu'elle avait besoin d'aide car elle connaissait surtout des prénoms florentins qu'il lui fallait traduire. Aussi trouva-t-elle plus facile d'aller chercher Léonarde, mieux au fait qu'elle-même des prénoms portés en Bourgogne.

— Cela ne devrait pas être trop compliqué, fit celle-ci. Dans les familles nobles, on donne souvent aux filles le nom des duchesses, présentes ou passées. Lorsque cette enfant est née, la duchesse s'appelait Isabelle. Vous appelez-vous Isabelle ?

C'était non. Fiora émit l'hypothèse que ce pouvait être Marie ? Mais ce n'était pas non plus Marie...

— Continuons avec les princesses, reprit Léonarde. C'est assez simple : la mère, la grand-mère et l'épouse du duc Charles se recommandent toutes les trois de la même patronne : Marguerite...

Léonarde tombait juste. La jeune femme battit des mains cependant qu'un semblant de sourire éclairait son visage :

— Marguerite... répéta Fiora. C'est une très jolie fleur, toute blanche avec un cœur doré. Cela vous convient bien : vous êtes toute blanche et vous avez des cheveux couleur de soleil...

Démétrios félicita vivement la jeune femme de son initiative et ajouta que l'on pouvait peut-être même tenter d'aller plus loin. Quand vint le soir, tout le monde se réunit dans la chambre de Marguerite, dont, en dépit de la chaleur, on ferma soigneusement les fenêtres et les volets. La pièce ne fut plus éclairée que par un chandelier posé sur un coffre assez loin du lit et par une chandelle posée à son chevet.

Le Grec prit Fiora par la main et la conduisit au chevet pour que Marguerite se sentît plus en confiance. Puis il se pencha sur la jeune femme :

— Je voudrais d'abord que vous répondiez à une question afin que je sache s'il m'est possible de vous aider. Avez-vous toujours été muette ?

Marguerite hocha la tête négativement.

— Donc, il y a eu un moment, dans votre vie, où vous parliez ?

— Oui...

— Avez-vous perdu la parole à la suite d'un accident ?

— Non...

— A la suite d'une grande peur ou d'une violente émotion ?

— Oui...

— Bien. Alors, il est possible que je parvienne à vous la

rendre. Si toutefois vous avez confiance en moi et m'obéissez. Je vous assure que je ne cherche que votre bien et que vous n'avez absolument rien à craindre de moi. Je ne vous ferai aucun mal et ne vous toucherai même pas...

— Il faut faire ce qu'il dit, Marguerite, murmura Fiora en lui prenant la main. Il va essayer de découvrir le mal dont vous avez souffert et dont vous souffrez encore...

Au regard apaisé que Marguerite posa sur elle, Fiora comprit qu'elle lui faisait confiance. Démétrios alla souffler l'une après l'autre les bougies du chandelier, ne gardant que celle du chevet qu'il prit dans sa main et éleva un peu au-dessus de la tête posée sur l'oreiller, de façon à ce que Marguerite n'eût qu'à garder ses yeux ouverts pour la voir.

— Il faut fixer attentivement la flamme, dit le médecin avec une ferme douceur. Et il fut obéi : les yeux clairs reflétèrent la lumière dorée et la considérèrent avec un calme absolu. Marguerite lâcha Fiora, croisa ses mains sur sa poitrine et attendit sans manifester la moindre crainte.

— Bien! approuva Démétrios qui, aussitôt, ordonna : A présent, regardez bien la lumière et ne la quittez surtout pas des yeux... pas des yeux... pas des yeux... pas des yeux...

La voix profonde, incantatoire du Grec entraînait avec elle une sorte de paix, un calme auquel furent sensibles les trois spectateurs. Cependant les paupières de Marguerite frémissaient comme si elles souhaitaient se fermer et que sa volonté seule les retînt.

— Vous avez sommeil, très sommeil... Vos paupières sont si lourdes... Ne luttez pas contre le sommeil qui vous envahit. Laissez-vous aller... dormez, dormez! Tous vos membres sont détendus, votre corps est infiniment las; il réclame le repos... Abandonnez-vous à ce repos... Dormez... dormez... dormez!...

A présent, les paupières étaient complètement fermées.

Les mains étaient retombées, sans force, le long du corps. La respiration devint régulière. Un instant, le silence régna dans la chambre paisible. Chacun retenait son souffle. Démétrios alors reprit :

— Je sais que vous dormez, Marguerite, mais m'entendez-vous ?

Lentement, celle-ci approuva de la tête...

— Bien... Maintenant votre esprit se trouve libéré de votre corps et les influences mauvaises sont repoussées. Nous allons ensemble remonter dans votre vie jusqu'à votre enfance. Considérez-vous, Marguerite. Vous avez dix ans... Vous parlez alors ?

Des larmes montèrent instantanément aux yeux de la dormeuse. Elle fit signe que oui mais aussitôt eut le réflexe de protéger sa tête contre d'invisibles coups. Fiora serra ses mains l'une contre l'autre si fort que ses ongles lui meurtrirent les paumes...

— Vous étiez une enfant malheureuse et cependant vous parliez. Que s'est-il passé ensuite ? Regardez votre vie de façon à revenir vers le drame où vous avez laissé votre voix. Égrenez les années...

Soudain, le corps de Marguerite commença à s'agiter. Les draps furent rejetés cependant que, de ses deux bras, la dormeuse cherchait à repousser quelque chose qui l'horrifiait. Elle faisait des efforts terribles pour garder ses jambes jointes et, malgré tout, quelque chose les écartait irrésistiblement. Elle pleurait, elle gémissait... et tout ceci était d'une clarté incroyable :

— Dios ! souffla Esteban : elle a été violée...

Puis tout s'apaisa et Marguerite demeura inerte, comme privée de vie. Démétrios lui accorda un moment de repos puis revint vers elle.

— Est-ce au moment de cette affreuse épreuve que vous avez perdu l'usage de la parole ?

Marguerite hocha lentement la tête de droite à gauche.

— Donc c'était après. Souvenez-vous de ce qui s'est passé ensuite. Il faut que vous reveniez à l'instant où votre voix s'est éteinte... Est-ce si douloureux ?

Marguerite, en effet, se tordait à présent sur son lit. Elle tenait ses mains au-dessus d'elle comme si elle soutenait un ventre devenu beaucoup plus gros et elle poussait d'affreux gémissements.

– On dirait, fit Léonarde d'une voix blanche, qu'elle est en train d'accoucher ?...

Et, se laissant tomber à genoux, elle se mit à prier...

– Ne pourrait-on pas, murmura Fiora, l'empêcher de revivre toute cette souffrance ?

Démétrios posa ses mains sur celles de la jeune femme en appuyant doucement...

– A présent, dit-il, l'enfant est né... vous êtes délivrée.

Instantanément, Marguerite s'apaisa. Un sourire émerveillé illumina son visage. On put la voir tendre ses mains vers un bébé imaginaire, le prendre contre sa poitrine, le bercer doucement, l'embrasser. Ce bonheur serein, étendu sur ce petit visage émacié, avait quelque chose de poignant... Mais, soudain, ce fut le drame. Épouvantés, les spectateurs virent Marguerite serrer ses bras contre sa poitrine avec une expression terrifiée et farouche tout à la fois, comme si une affreuse menace s'abattait sur elle. On la vit lutter de son mieux mais elle était sans doute vaincue d'avance. Et tout à coup, elle cria d'une voix enrouée, comme rouillée :

– Mon fils ! Rendez-moi mon fils !... Vous ne pouvez pas le prendre ! C'est mon enfant... ayez pitié !

Elle ouvrait la bouche pour pousser un cri qui aurait dû être inhumain, mais déjà Démétrios avait imposé ses mains sur la tête de la malheureuse et ordonnait :

– Ne criez pas, Marguerite ! Tout est fini... Ne pensez plus à cet instant où vous avez atteint le sommet de la souffrance humaine. Vous n'avez pas eu ce cri... Vous pouvez encore parler... N'est-ce pas que vous pouvez encore parler ?

Encore haletante et couverte de sueur, la jeune femme ressemblait à une naufragée qui vient d'atteindre une plage après une lutte épuisante. Fiora voulut la prendre dans ses bras mais, d'un geste, Démétrios la cloua sur place...

— Répondez-moi, Marguerite! Pouvez-vous parler?... Dites : Je le peux...

— Je... le peux...

La voix était faible, rocailleuse, mais cependant nette.

— C'est bien, dit Démétrios. A présent, reposez-vous! Vous avez fourni un effort terrible mais le mal est vaincu... Dans un instant je vais vous réveiller. Vous ne vous souviendrez plus d'avoir revécu ce martyre et vous pourrez maintenant parler tout à votre aise à ceux qui vous entourent et qui vous aiment. Vous m'avez entendu?

— Oui... j'ai entendu.

— Alors, je vais donc vous rappeler parmi nous. Vous vous éveillerez quand je prononcerai votre nom. Attention! Marguerite, ouvrez les yeux!

Et les yeux s'ouvrirent en effet sur un regard un peu égaré qui se tourna d'abord vers le visage attentif du médecin puis ceux émerveillés de Fiora et de Léonarde que la lumière jaune découpait sur l'obscurité de la chambre. Un peu plus loin, Esteban, d'une main qui tremblait, rallumait le chandelier. Fiora s'approcha de Marguerite et l'embrassa :

— Vous êtes guérie, mon amie. Votre voix est revenue.

— Ma voix?... C'est vrai... Oh! que s'est-il passé? Il me semble que je viens de faire un rêve... un rêve effrayant...

— Ce n'était qu'un rêve mais les forces maudites qui tenaient votre voix prisonnière ont été vaincues. Désormais vous êtes et serez comme tout le monde et nous pourrons parler ensemble!

Esteban qui s'était absenté un instant revint avec un pot et des gobelets.

— Après ce que nous venons de vivre, je pense que nous avons tous grand besoin d'un peu de vin. Vous êtes aussi exténué que votre patiente...

S'étant laissé tomber sur une bancelle auprès du lit, Démétrios en vérité semblait infiniment las, et son visage était d'une pâleur de cire. Aussi accepta-t-il volontiers le gobelet que lui tendait son serviteur et le but lentement, presque voluptueusement. Léonarde s'empressait auprès de Marguerite pour changer sa chemise trempée car elle ne demandait qu'à dormir, Fiora s'approcha de son vieil ami :

— Tu as accompli un miracle, Démétrios... D'où tires-tu cette étonnante puissance que je t'ai déjà vu employer par deux fois, sur la Virago et sur cette misérable Hieronyma ? Tu les endormais pour leur donner des ordres mais, cette fois, tu as obtenu que Marguerite retrouve la parole...

— Elle l'avait perdue à la suite d'un terrible choc. Il fallait donc lui faire revivre cette épreuve. Par l'effet de ma volonté, j'y suis parvenu, mais j'admets volontiers que je suis épuisé...

— N'était-ce pas dangereux... pour elle ?

Le médecin leva vers Fiora ses yeux sombres que de larges cernes bleus marquaient durement puis il soupira :

— Si. Elle pouvait en mourir.

— Et tu l'as fait tout de même ?

— Pourquoi pas ? fit-il rudement. Qu'avait-elle à perdre ? Sa vie est à jamais brisée. On ne saurait la guérir de tout ce qu'elle a subi durant des années ! Elle peut parler à présent et, dans peu de jours, elle sera sur pied. Mais pour quel avenir ? Penses-tu te charger d'elle ?

— Toi qui peux lever le voile qui nous cache les temps futurs, pourrais-tu m'aider à répondre à cette question ?

— Non... non, je n'ai rien vu. Sans doute ne m'intéresse-t-elle pas assez ? N'oublie pas que nous avons une tâche importante à accomplir ensemble...

— Je n'oublie pas, lui accorda Fiora. Quant à Marguerite, si elle est vraiment ma sœur...

— Rien ne l'assure, qu'une vague ressemblance... fit Démétrios avec agacement.

— Si vague... qu'elle vous a néanmoins frappés, Léonarde et toi ! Si, donc, elle est vraiment la fille de ma mère

– si tu préfères cette formule – je crois que j'ai quelque idée de ce que nous pourrions en faire...

– Ne pourriez-vous parler moins fort ? reprocha Léonarde qui était en train de clore les courtines autour du lit de Marguerite. D'ailleurs, il serait peut-être temps d'aller dormir, nous aussi ?

Démétrios se leva et s'étira puis, avec un soupir, alla vers la porte suivi de Fiora, silencieuse. Parvenu dans le couloir qui desservait les chambres, ils marchèrent lentement jusqu'à celle de la jeune femme.

– Ne me diras-tu pas à quoi tu penses ? demanda le Grec.

– Je pense, répondit Fiora, que nous quitterons bientôt cette maison. Nous n'avons plus rien à y faire...

– Et pour aller où ? Rejoindrons-nous le roi Louis ?

– Pas encore, s'il te plaît ! Je n'oublie pas ce que nous a raconté Christophe. Il y a encore, non loin d'ici, une femme qui gravit elle aussi un calvaire par la faute de son époux. Regnault du Hamel a payé sa dette, mais nous devons examiner à présent celle de Pierre de Brévailles... Et peut-être qu'en la lui réclamant, je réussirai à procurer un peu de bonheur à deux êtres qui en ont le plus urgent besoin...

Et, sans vouloir s'expliquer davantage, Fiora posa un baiser furtif sur la joue barbue de Démétrios, puis disparut dans sa chambre dont la porte se referma, sans bruit.

Ce soir-là, Fiora, toutes lumières éteintes, demeura longuement accoudée à sa fenêtre, contemplant cette ville qu'elle habitait depuis un certain temps déjà, mais qu'elle allait devoir quitter et qu'elle ne connaîtrait peut-être jamais mieux. La nuit d'été était chaude, sans excès, le ciel pur, plein d'étoiles – et aucun nuage annonciateur d'orage n'en troublait l'immensité bleue : un ciel presque florentin... Négligeant la maison muette et désormais silencieuse où sa vengeance s'était accomplie dans de si étranges circonstances, elle laissa son regard suivre le mince ruban moiré du Suzon qui plongeait sous la rue Musette pour reparaître au chevet de l'église des Jacobins. La petite rivière entrait dans la ville par le nord et c'était au nord que se trouvait Selongey, le domaine de Philippe...

Elle s'accorda le loisir de penser à lui, – ce qu'elle s'était refusé le plus souvent jusqu'à présent pour ne pas se laisser distraire de ses projets – mais la mort de du Hamel avait rapproché le temps où, enfin, elle pourrait aller vers lui pour tenter de connaître la vérité de son cœur. Était-ce par amour pour elle et pour la revoir qu'il était venu secrètement à Florence et en avait parcouru les rues sous un déguisement ? Ou bien souhaitait-il seulement chercher, auprès de Francesco Beltrami, une nouvelle aide financière pour les guerres de son maître ?... Léonarde penchait pour la première hypothèse que partageait le cœur de Fiora, mais la jeune femme s'avouait qu'en fait elle ne connaissait pas son époux et qu'elle ignorait tout de ses pensées et de ses réactions. Un coureur de jupons ? C'était le portrait hâtif tracé par dame Symonne, un coureur qui ne devait pas avoir besoin de beaucoup courir pour attraper sa chance. S'il était à ce point entouré et couvert de femmes, quelle place elle-même pouvait-elle espérer tenir dans un cœur ainsi assiégé ?

Pourtant, devant Dieu et devant la loi florentine – à défaut de celle des hommes – devant l'amour aussi, elle était bien réellement sa femme, et le lourd anneau d'or aux armes des Selongey pendait toujours entre ses seins, au bout de sa chaîne d'or. Fiora tira sur le mince lien précieux pour prendre la bague dans sa main. Elle était pesante, chaude de sa propre chaleur, presque vivante... Fiora la baisa comme elle eût baisé la bouche de Philippe...

Où était-il à cette heure ? Quelque part en Luxembourg où le gros de l'armée se réunissait dans l'intention d'occuper la Lorraine ? A Bruges, où l'on disait que le duc

Charles réunissait les États de Flandres pour en obtenir une aide de guerre en hommes et en argent ? Quoi qu'il en soit, il n'était pas, il ne pouvait pas être à Selongey où, cependant, Fiora savait bien qu'aucune force humaine ne l'empêcherait de se rendre une fois qu'elle en aurait fini avec ceux de Brévailles...

En les évoquant, sa pensée revint tout naturellement à Marguerite et s'interrogea : qu'éprouvait-elle au juste pour cette demi-sœur tombée du ciel ou, plutôt, remontée des Enfers ? De la pitié, bien sûr, et aussi de la sympathie, toute la compassion du monde, mais, à vrai dire, cela n'allait pas beaucoup plus loin. La voix du sang ne s'était pas encore manifestée alors qu'elle avait plaidé hautement, spontanément, en faveur de Christophe.

Honnête avec elle-même, Fiora se reprocha cette tiédeur qui venait peut-être du fait qu'il avait été impossible, jusque-là, de communiquer réellement avec la prisonnière libérée. Etait-ce à cause de ce long nez pointu signant son unique ressemblance avec un père qui n'en méritait pas le titre ? De toute façon, qu'elle l'aimât ou non était de peu d'importance : elle n'était pas destinée à vivre avec Marguerite, et, à cela au moins, Fiora était bien déterminée.

Aux approches de l'aube vint la fraîcheur. Otant ses vêtements, la jeune femme alla s'étendre sur son lit pour se laisser baigner par elle. Sa tête était un peu lourde, d'avoir sans doute respiré trop longtemps l'odeur délicieuse d'un tilleul qui s'épanouissait dans un jardin voisin. Elle découvrait que cette terre de Bourgogne pouvait être enivrante et qu'il devrait être doux d'y vivre à la condition d'être deux...

Un instant, Fiora caressa l'idée d'aller s'installer à Selongey pour y attendre patiemment le retour de Philippe. L'expression de son visage au moment où il la reverrait répondrait sans doute à toutes ses questions. Mais comment subsister là-bas ? Comment y arriver aussi démunie qu'une pauvresse, elle que Philippe avait connue si riche ? Démétrios n'était pas seul à se tourmenter pour les jours à venir. L'or du Magnifique fondait à vue d'œil. Bientôt s'imposerait une visite rue des Lombards, à Paris, au comptoir qu'Agnolo Nardi tenait pour son frère de lait et où, si Lorenzo de Médicis n'avait pas trompé Fiora, des fonds seraient déposés à son nom. Et puis, il y avait le serment qui la liait à Démétrios, ce serment qu'ils avaient sacralisé en mêlant leur sang. Fiora pouvait d'autant moins le transgresser qu'elle jalousait et haïssait le Téméraire presque autant que l'ancien médecin de Byzance. Seule, sa mort pourrait libérer Philippe du sortilège qui le retenait captif et, peut-être, le ramener à Fiora... s'il ne s'était pas fait tuer avant pour la plus grande gloire de son prince! Mais elle chassa cette idée funeste. Si Philippe ne respirait plus quelque part sous le ciel, un pressentiment l'en aurait avertie. Elle aurait senti qu'une partie d'elle-même avait cessé de vivre...

– Dès que Marguerite sera suffisamment remise, décréta-t-elle, nous partirons pour Brévailles...

Et, forte de cette résolution, elle tomba d'un seul coup dans le sommeil tandis que résonnait au loin le premier chant du coq...

CHAPITRE IV

LA VENGEANCE APPARTIENT AU SEIGNEUR

« Renonce, Fiora ! », dit soudain Démétrios en rapprochant son cheval de celui de la jeune femme. Ils allaient en tête de la petite troupe qui se dirigeait vers Brévailles. Léonarde et Marguerite venaient derrière sur des mules bien dociles et Esteban, armé jusqu'aux dents contre les infortunes de la route, fermait la marche.

— A quoi veux-tu que je renonce ? A conduire Marguerite à sa grand-mère ?

— Tu sais très bien ce que je veux dire. Même sans Marguerite tu serais venue ici pour y abattre ton grand-père... Ne proteste pas ! Que tu le veuilles ou non, il l'est ?

— Il ne le serait que s'il avait d'abord été un père mais il est à l'origine de tous les malheurs de ma mère. Non seulement il l'a mariée de force à ce misérable du Hamel mais il n'a rien fait pour la sauver quand l'heure en est venue. Tu voudrais que je lui pardonne ?

— Non, mais je voudrais que tu t'épargnes toi-même. Laisse-moi conduire Marguerite avec Léonarde et retourne avec Esteban à l'hôtellerie de Verdun[1] où nous avons dormi. Il vaut mieux que tu ne pénètres pas dans cette maison, ajouta-t-il en désignant de sa houssine le château dont les tours semblaient flotter sur la nappe de brouillard blanc qui montait de la rivière.

---

1. Verdun-sur-le-Doubs.

Ce n'était pas un grand château mais, avec ses trois tours, son donjon et ses hautes courtines habillés de hourds visiblement en parfait état, il offrait un aspect redoutable et il ne devait pas être facile d'en forcer l'entrée. Campé au-dessus du Doubs dont les eaux tumultueuses emplissaient ses fossés et l'isolaient quand le pont-levis était relevé, il ressemblait à quelque guerrier obstiné qui, sans se soucier de se mouiller les pieds, surveille et commande la rivière...

— Que crains-tu ? demanda Fiora avec une pointe de dédain.

— Ton visage !

— Mon voile le cache.

— Mais tu seras bien obligée de le découvrir. Quel accueil crois-tu que l'on va te réserver dans une demeure où le maître fait régner une discipline qui ressemble à la terreur ? Souviens-toi de ce que t'a dit Christophe ! C'est un homme dur, impitoyable et qui, non seulement n'a pas tenté de sauver ses enfants coupables, mais a aidé le mari à obtenir le châtiment. Si tu entres ici, j'ai grand-peur que tu n'en sortes pas...

— C'est ce que nous verrons ! Et puis qu'ai-je à craindre en ta compagnie ? Aurais-tu perdu ce pouvoir qui te permet de dominer les gens au moment d'une forte émotion ? Tu pourrais l'exercer ! La vue de ma figure a toutes les chances de provoquer cette réaction.

— C'est toujours plus difficile sur un homme et je redoute que ce Brévailles ne soit un vieux dur à cuire imperméable à tout état émotionnel.

— L'occasion est d'autant plus belle de tenter une expérience intéressante ! D'ailleurs, je ne vois pas comment on pourrait refuser de recevoir une petite-fille on ne peut plus légitime ? Marguerite, elle, n'est pas née dans le péché ! ajouta-t-elle avec une pointe d'amertume. Je n'ai pas le droit de lui refuser cette chance.

— En admettant que ce soit une chance ! Je ne sais pas si ce château est l'endroit idéal pour oublier des années de souffrances.

La vengeance appartient au Seigneur 93

Marguerite, en effet, avait réussi à leur raconter peu à peu ce qu'avait été sa vie dans les demeures successives de son père. Quatre ans de relative douceur aux mains d'une nourrice qui l'avait quittée pour un monde meilleur, puis le quasi-abandon auprès de domestiques indifférents et, pour la plupart du temps, loin des yeux d'un père qui ne celait pas son aversion. Ses seules sorties la conduisaient à l'église voisine, sous la garde d'une servante bigote qui ne trouvait jamais assez longues les stations que l'on faisait, à genoux, sur des dalles froides. Elle avait fini par penser qu'un couvent ne serait pas plus pénible que sa vie dans la maison paternelle et, un jour, elle avait osé demander qu'on lui permît d'entrer en religion.

Du Hamel avait refusé sèchement. Il n'avait aucune envie de payer une dot pour une fille qui lui économisait déjà une servante de cuisine. Et puis, quand l'adolescence avait formé le corps de Marguerite, elle avait dû subir les violences d'un palefrenier qui l'avait odieusement forcée dans la paille de l'écurie. La suite, les nouveaux amis de la malheureuse – elle ignorait toujours le lien de sang qui l'unissait à Fiora car Démétrios, prudent, l'avait exigé – en avaient appris le plus noir durant la transe où la jeune femme avait été plongée : l'accouchement dans la cave où du Hamel l'avait séquestrée après l'avoir cruellement frapée quand son état était devenu visible, la naissance d'un petit garçon qu'on lui avait arraché et froidement étranglé sous ses yeux...

C'était alors l'époque où du Hamel avait été nommé à Dijon. Il en avait profité pour réduire son train de maison à deux valets ; deux frères qui avaient su gagner son entière confiance à défaut de plus amples gages et il avait emmené Marguerite enfermée dans une litière à rideaux hermétiquement clos, qui contenait aussi la plupart des bagages et ne s'était ouverte que de nuit, devant la maison de la rue du Lacet. La malheureuse enfant avait été alors enchaînée dans la cave, pour la nuit tout au moins car, le jour, elle travaillait dans la maison, mal nourrie, maltraitée souvent. Seul, le gros valet Claude lui témoignait quelque compassion quand du Hamel n'était pas au logis. Il lui apportait un peu de nourriture, du vin aussi dont il lui avait donné le goût, mais il lui faisait payer ses bienfaits de la seule monnaie que la pauvre enfant eût à sa disposition. Fort heureusement, ces infâmes et brèves étreintes n'avaient jamais eu de conséquences extrêmes.

En dépit de cette aide intéressée, Marguerite s'affaiblissait et, surtout, désespérait. L'envie de vivre – si l'on pouvait appeler cela vivre! – l'avait quittée et elle en était venue à souhaiter ardemment une fin prochaine quand le secours, enfin, lui fut porté...

Elle allait bien mieux à présent. Les forces lui revenaient et ses joues reprenaient couleur mais elle ressemblait plus à un être mécaniquement animé qu'à une femme naturellement vivante. A ses sauveurs, elle montrait beaucoup de reconnaissance mais elle ne semblait guère s'intéresser à l'avenir. Elle était douce, plutôt silencieuse, bien que l'usage de la parole lui fût revenu tout à fait. Avec elle, Fiora avait l'impression de se trouver en présence d'une ombre...

– J'ai bien peur, dit Léonarde, que son âme ne s'en soit allée avec celle de son enfant... Peut-être lui reviendrait-elle si quelqu'un lui apportait beaucoup, beaucoup d'amour? Nous n'avons à lui offrir quant à nous que de l'amitié.

Arrêtée au bord du chemin qui suivait le cours de la rivière, Fiora songeait à tout cela. Le château, il est vrai, n'avait pas un air très engageant avec ses murailles noircies par le temps. Marguerite n'allait-elle pas troquer un cachot contre un autre genre de prison? Fiora se détourna pour apercevoir la jeune femme restée un peu en retrait avec Léonarde, profitant de l'arrêt pour s'isoler. Elle lui avait dit qu'elle l'emmenait chez sa grand-mère en négligeant tout à fait de parler du grand-père. Comment celui-ci accueillerait-il la fille de Marie, la réprouvée même née dans le mariage? Cette sombre demeure à l'abord hostile ne lui inspirait pas grande confiance.

Davantage par acquit de conscience que pour apaiser cette troublante suspicion, Fiora héla un paysan qui, faux sur l'épaule, se dirigeait vers un champ.

– C'est bien Brévailles?

L'homme ôta poliment le bonnet qui bâchait sa tête et approuva:

– Sûr que c'est Brévailles! Mais... c'est-y qu'vous voudriez y aller? ajouta-t-il avec un intraduisible mélange d'inquiétude et de curiosité. N'entre pas qui veut, vous savez?

– Pourtant, je voudrais voir dame Madeleine. Je suppose qu'elle est chez elle?

– Où qu'vous voulez qu'elle aille? Elle sort jamais et, d'puis qu' le seigneur est malade, on voit plus personne qu' l'intendant et une fille de cuisine qu'est à peu près aussi causante qu'une carpe.

– Il est malade? intervint Démétrios. A merveille! Je suis précisément médecin. Et de quoi souffre-t-il?

Le paysan se gratta le crâne, fit un effort suprême et méritoire de réflexion et, finalement, hocha la tête avec une moue significative:

– J'crois ben qu'personne en sait rien par ici. Quand on d'mande des nouvelles, on vous répond qu'y va pas mieux. En tous les cas, médecin ou pas, ça m'étonnerait ben qu'on vous ouvre.

– Pourquoi? demanda Fiora.

– Parc'qu'on n'ouvre jamais à personne: ni moine, ni mendiant, ni baladin, ni voyageur attardé... C't'une mauvaise maison qu'celle où on n'donne pas l'hospitalité chrétienne... Faut dire quand même qu'y a eu d'grands malheurs par ici...

Visiblement, l'homme ne demandait qu'à bavarder, mais Fiora en savait autant que lui et sinon plus sur les épreuves qui s'étaient abattues sur les hôtes de ce château. Elle remercia le paysan au moyen d'une pièce d'argent et, le restant de la troupe l'ayant rejointe, elle guida résolument son cheval vers les tours solitaires. Démétrios la rattrapa, prétendant poursuivre sa mise en garde, mais Marguerite le suivait de près et il était impossible de discuter devant elle.

Le brouillard matinal se levait sur le Doubs, laissant voir les tourbillons qui agitaient l'eau verte. Puis le chemin dévia aux abords du château pour s'engager dans un petit bois au-delà duquel on peut apercevoir quelques simples maisons recouvertes de chaume, le petit clocher d'une église... Un sentier envahi d'herbes folles qui ne portait guère de traces de passage s'ouvrait à gauche et permettait de rejoindre la petite forteresse. Fiora y dirigea son cheval et trouva rapidement le pont dormant que le pont-levis devait atteindre pour peu qu'on l'abattît. Mais dans l'instant présent, celui-ci se dressait, telle une infranchissable muraille, de l'autre côté d'un large fossé broussailleux que l'eau de la rivière emplissait presque à ras bord. En face, refermé comme un poing serré, muet et silencieux comme un tombeau, Brévailles érigeait ses pierres moroses et fières qui semblaient défier le clair soleil de ce jour d'été...

Sans mettre pied à terre, Esteban emboucha la trompe de corne et d'argent qui pendait à sa ceinture et lança un son prolongé qui fit s'envoler une famille de martins-pêcheurs. On attendit mais rien ne vint.

— Est-ce vraiment là le château de ma grand-mère ? questionna Marguerite qui se tenait au côté de Fiora.

— Oui, pour ce que j'en sais, répondit celle-ci, qu'en pensez-vous ?

— Rien, sinon que cela semble bien triste. Notre maison d'Autun ne l'était pas autant. Pourquoi donc ma mère ne s'y plaisait-elle pas ?

— Peut-être parce que l'époux qui l'y faisait entrer n'avait pas su gagner son cœur. Une chaumière vaut mieux qu'un palais si c'est l'amour qu'elle héberge.

— Elle aurait pu m'aimer, moi ? Mais elle ne m'aimait pas, sinon elle ne m'aurait pas abandonnée...

C'était la deuxième fois, depuis qu'elle avait été

recueillie, que Marguerite faisait allusion à Marie. La première, c'était en parlant avec Léonarde qui semblait lui inspirer une confiance toute particulière, mais la vieille demoiselle n'avait pas insisté car elle avait cru s'apercevoir que Marguerite détestait Marie presque autant que son époux. La cruauté de Regnault du Hamel n'avait épargné à l'enfant aucun détail affreux ou sordide et, pour elle, sa mère n'était qu'une femme perverse et dépravée qui n'avait délaissé son foyer que pour assouvir de bas instincts dont elle avait été fort justement punie. Fiora avait tenté un jour de modifier ce jugement sans concessions mais Marguerite avait fermé les yeux en affirmant que cela ne l'intéressait pas... Là était peut-être la raison primordiale pour laquelle Fiora ne réussissait pas à s'attacher réellement à sa demi-sœur.

Elle arrêta le bras d'Esteban qui s'apprêtait à renouveler son appel.

— Souhaitez-vous que je vous conduise plutôt dans quelque couvent ? demanda-t-elle.

Mais Marguerite secoua sa tête dont les magnifiques cheveux blonds, à présent propres et sagement tressés, brillaient dans le soleil :

— Non... Puisque ma famille habite ici, je n'ai aucune raison de souhaiter vivre ailleurs. C'est une maison noble et peut-être que l'on m'y aimera...

C'était prononcé d'une petite voix tranquille, unie, presque sans intonation et cependant le cœur de Fiora se serra. Du geste, elle fit signe à Esteban de reitérer et, pour la seconde fois, la corne lança son mugissement dans l'air calme du matin.

Son insistance fut récompensée. Une tête surmontée d'un casque apparut au créneau cependant qu'une voix rude criait :

— Qui va là et que voulez-vous ?

— Que l'on baisse ce pont car nous avons à faire ici, lança Esteban avec une morgue digne d'un grand d'Espagne qui ne parut d'ailleurs pas produire tout l'effet escompté.

— Passez votre chemin. On n'entre pas!

A son tour, Démétrios prit la parole :

— Il le faudra bien pourtant. Allez dire à la dame de Brévailles que son gendre, messire Regnault du Hamel, est mort et que nous lui amenons céans damoiselle Marguerite, sa petite-fille!

Sur son chemin de ronde, l'homme parut hésiter un instant sur ce qu'il convenait de faire puis, finalement, cria :

— Je vais voir!

Et il disparut...

L'attente qui suivit parut interminable. Campée sur son cheval qui grattait la terre d'un sabot impatient, Fiora allait prier Esteban de sonner une troisième fois quand une sorte de grondement se fit entendre à l'intérieur du château et lentement, lentement, le grand pont-levis s'abaissa vers eux tandis que la herse se relevait en grinçant.

— Eh bien, allons! fit Démétrios avec un soupir qui semblait monter de la terre tant il était profond. Fiora lui sourit :

— Tu vois que nous avons réussi à entrer?

— Espérons seulement que nous sortirons aussi aisément. Ce castel ressemble comme un frère à une prison.

L'intérieur, cependant, était plus aimable. En pénétrant dans la cour dont le haut donjon occupait le centre, les voyageurs virent qu'un logis de deux étages, éclairé par de belles fenêtres à meneaux sculptés, dont les plus hautes s'ornaient de gables fleuronnés, était adossé à la muraille donnant sur la rivière. Un perron de trois marches y menait sur lequel un vieil homme tout vêtu de noir se tenait debout dans une attitude pleine de dignité.

Les nouveaux arrivants mirent pied à terre, laissant leurs brides aux mains d'un valet d'écurie. De toute évidence, leur venue constituait un événement de taille et, près des cuisines, trois servantes les regardaient avec des mines effarées en frottant leurs mains à leur tablier. Un gamin qui poursuivait des poules accourut et resta planté là, un doigt dans la bouche, en contemplation muette.

Fiora avait tiré son voile sur son visage autant que le permettait la bienséance, néanmoins ce fut elle que le vieux serviteur regarda d'abord :

— Pouvons-nous voir la dame de céans ? s'enquit-elle doucement. Voici sa petite-fille, damoiselle Marguerite, que nous nous sommes chargés d'amener jusqu'à elle...

Le vieillard salua en homme qui sait son monde mais il redemanda :

— Me direz-vous enfin qui vous êtes ?

— Nos noms ne vous diront rien, intervint Démétrios, car nous sommes des voyageurs étrangers et seul le hasard nous a permis d'apporter une aide à damoiselle Marguerite, que voici. Cette jeune dame, ajouta-t-il en désignant Fiora qu'une émotion soudaine étreignait au moment de pénétrer dans cette maison qui avait vu grandir ses jeunes parents et s'éveiller leur passion fatale, cette jeune dame est une noble florentine, donna Fiora Beltrami, et voici dame Léonarde Mercet, sa gouvernante. Quant à moi, je me nomme Démétrios Lascaris, prince et médecin, et je viens de Byzance.

Le vieux serviteur approuva de la tête et fit signe aux arrivants de le suivre dans un bel escalier de pierre parfaitement entretenu et qui menait à une grande salle où, entre une cheminée sans feu et une étroite fenêtre donnant sur la rivière, une dame en deuil était assise dans une grande chaise à bras, un chapelet entre les doigts. Elle avait dû être très belle et gardait quelque reflet de cette beauté passée mais, sous la haute coiffe noire, ses cheveux et son visage étaient d'une blancheur diaphane. Le bord de ses yeux était rougi par trop de larmes. Elles avaient décoloré les prunelles dont le bleu ne se percevait plus guère. L'expression habituelle de ce visage devait être empreinte de tristesse et cependant, à cet instant, il semblait animé par un rayon de lumière. Elle se leva pour accueillir ses visiteurs et Fiora s'aperçut qu'elle était presque aussi grande qu'elle-même... et qu'elle tremblait comme une feuille, bouleversée par une émotion qu'elle ne parvenait pas à dominer.

— On me dit, fit-elle d'une voix émue dont la douceur frappa Fiora, que ma petite-fille, Marguerite, se trouve parmi vous ?... Mais comment est-ce possible ?... Voici des années que je ne sais plus rien d'elle. J'avais même fini par la croire morte...

— C'est sans doute ce que souhaitait son père, dit Démétrios de sa belle voix grave, mais, à présent, messire du Hamel n'est plus. Il est mort il y a maintenant trois semaines et nous avons eu le bonheur, étant de ses proches voisins, de recueillir demoiselle Marguerite qu'il retenait en sa maison comme en une étroite prison. Elle n'a plus que vous au monde et nous avons pensé qu'il était de notre devoir de vous l'amener...

— Et vous avez bien fait. Comment vous en remercier ?... Marguerite... ne veux-tu pas venir jusqu'à moi ?

Mais, déjà, la jeune femme s'était précipitée à genoux devant elle. Son étrange indifférence venait de s'évanouir d'un seul coup et elle versait d'abondantes larmes sur les mains tremblantes qui s'étaient tendues vers elle et qui la relevaient. Un moment, les deux femmes restèrent étroitement embrassées. Debout à quelques pas, Fiora les contemplait avec un peu d'amertume. L'envie soudaine lui venait de se jeter, elle aussi, dans ces bras affectueux, d'embrasser ce visage pâle. Car cette femme était sa grand-mère plus encore peut-être que celle de Marguerite et elle pensait à présent qu'il devait être bien doux d'être la petite-fille de Madeleine de Brévailles...

Mais celle-ci dominait son émotion. Sans quitter la main de Marguerite, elle offrit à ses hôtes inattendus un sourire charmant.

— Vous me rendez la vie et je ne vous accueille même pas comme je le devrais ! Prenez place, je vous en prie et racontez-moi tout ce que vous savez de cette enfant. Je vais faire servir des rafraîchissements en attendant l'heure du repas. On préparera aussi vos chambres...

Mais Fiora émit de vives objurgations :

— N'en faites rien, dame, je vous en prie. Nous voyageons, mes compagnons et moi-même, et ne souhaitons pas nous attarder car la route est encore longue qui s'étend devant nous.

— Si longue soit-elle, elle supportera bien une halte ? Vous avez tant de choses à m'apprendre...

— Sans doute... mais l'on nous a dit que le maître de ce château était malade et nous ne voudrions pas...

Au prix de sa vie, Fiora eût été incapable de dire pourquoi, parvenue dans ce château avec la décision bien arrêtée d'y abattre Pierre de Brévailles, elle souhaitait à présent s'en éloigner le plus vite possible. Elle pensait y entrer en libératrice mais la femme qu'elle avait devant elle ne semblait pas avoir besoin d'un quelconque secours. Elle en eut même la certitude quand dame Madeleine déclara paisiblement :

— Mon époux est malade, en effet, mais je vous assure que votre présence ne saurait le déranger. Ne vous tourmentez donc pas pour lui et causons...

Tandis que Démétrios faisait pour leur hôtesse le récit — un peu arrangé — du sauvetage de Marguerite, Fiora qui avait choisi à dessein de s'asseoir le dos à la luminosité de la fenêtre ne l'écoutait que d'une oreille. Elle scrutait cette salle aux meubles sévères mais admirablement entretenus. Elle regardait la table que deux servantes étaient en train de dresser, la nappe d'une éclatante blancheur qu'elles étendaient et les différents objets qu'elles y disposaient, tous rutilants. Elle considérait aussi son hôtesse, assise sur une bancelle garnie de coussins, Marguerite dont elle tenait toujours la main assise auprès d'elle et ne la quittant pas des yeux. Toutes deux goûtaient évidemment un moment d'ineffable bonheur. Elles se souriaient, riaient même de temps en temps comme deux fillettes bien que le récit du Grec ne fût guère récréatif et leur rire sonnait bizarrement dans une atmosphère que Fiora trouvait de plus en plus lourde... Elle se sentit sur le point presque d'étouffer et laissa glisser légèrement son voile. Une des servantes, la plus âgée lâcha brusquement les couteaux qu'elle tenait et qui résonnèrent sur les dalles cependant que ses yeux s'agrandissaient de stupéfaction. Dame Madeleine lui jeta un coup d'œil agacé, puis tourna les yeux vers Fiora et lui dit à mi-voix, d'un ton futile :

— Nos servantes campagnardes sont d'une grande maladresse. Êtes-vous mieux servie à Florence ?

— Dame Léonarde vous répondrait mieux que moi à ce sujet mais je n'ai jamais eu à me plaindre de nos serviteurs...

— Quelle chance vous avez !

Puis, revenant à Démétrios dont l'œil, entre les paupières resserrées, s'était fait soudain aigu, enchaîna :

— Ainsi, vous disiez que...

La vue du visage de Fiora qui venait de frapper de stupeur une simple servante ne lui causait apparemment aucune émotion. Il en fut ainsi durant tout le repas qui suivit. Démétrios tenait le dé de la conversation et avait entrepris de raconter par le menu quelques-uns de ses voyages aux deux interlocutrices ravies qui bavardaient joyeusement avec lui. Marguerite semblait avoir complètement oublié ses deux compagnes et ne tournait jamais les yeux vers Fiora ou vers Léonarde qui, silencieuses, mangeaient du bout des dents. L'idée de passer la nuit dans cette demeure était insupportable à la jeune femme et elle en voulait un peu à Démétrios de tous les frais qu'il déployait. Était-ce le même qui, tout à l'heure, la suppliait presque de renoncer à ses projets ?

Qu'en restait-il, d'ailleurs, de ces fameux projets à cette heure où, assise à la table d'un aïeul détesté, elle n'en mangeait pas moins son pain ? La mort brutale d'un homme qui semblait tenir si peu de place dans l'esprit de sa femme — elle éludait chaque fois que le Grec tentait d'en savoir plus sur la maladie de Brévailles — serait-elle de nature à améliorer la situation ? Elle semblait parfaitement maîtresse d'elle-même et de cette maison où chacun lui obéissait sans faillir...

Le repas s'achevait sur d'exquises confitures accompagnées de belles tranches d'un boichet[1] qui embaumait, lorsque le vieil homme qui avait accueilli les voyageurs et devait être l'intendant reparut à l'entrée de la salle :

— Le maître, dit-il cérémonieusement, désirerait recevoir personnellement la jeune dame étrangère qui a ramené damoiselle Marguerite...

Et comme tous les autres convives se levaient d'un même mouvement, il ajouta :

— Il désire la voir seule !

— Montrez-moi le chemin, consentit Fiora. Je vous suis.

Sans songer seulement à s'excuser auprès de son hôtesse mais avec une sorte de soulagement, elle quitta la table pour se diriger vers l'escalier. A son étonnement, au lieu de monter celui-ci vers l'étage supérieur, on le descendit. Derrière l'intendant, Fiora traversa la cour et pénétra dans le donjon. En dépit de la chaleur extérieure, une chape de froid et d'humidité lui tomba sur les épaules dès la porte franchie, mais elle y prit à peine garde car son esprit était agité de questions... De quelle maladie pouvait bien souffrir le seigneur de Brévailles pour qu'on l'installât dans ce donjon antique ?

Toujours précédée de son guide, elle gravit un étage et pénétra dans une salle ronde qui lui parut d'autant plus immense qu'elle était sombre et dégarnie de meubles à l'exception d'un lit isolé parmi des ombres denses et de deux ou trois tabourets. Mais le spectacle qui l'y attendait n'en était pas moins impressionnant : près d'une ouverture à peine plus large qu'une meurtrière, un homme barbu aux longs cheveux gris était assis dans une haute cathèdre de bois noir, une couverture sur les genoux et totalement immobile. Auprès de lui et presque aussi rigide, presque aussi âgé d'ailleurs, un homme d'armes se trouvait debout tenant d'une main un pennon voilé de noir et, de l'autre, une épée dégainée. Saisie, Fiora s'arrêta au seuil de la porte que l'intendant avait ouverte devant elle :

[1]. Ancien nom du pain d'épice.

— Approchez ! intima une voix qui semblait émaner des profondeurs mêmes des fondations.

Fiora s'avança et, derrière elle, l'huis se referma sans bruit. Elle avançait comme dans un rêve. Était-ce donc, là, cet aïeul dont elle avait juré la perte ? Il ne paraissait pas affaibli le moins du monde. Au contraire et bien que la lumière fût incertaine, ce que la barbe et les cheveux laissaient transparaître de son visage trahissait la santé... Machinalement, elle chercha, à sa ceinture, la dague que les plis de sa robe dissimulaient et s'arrêta à quelques pas des deux hommes...

— Approchez encore, dit Brévailles. Je vous vois mal !

Elle atteignit la tache de soleil que l'étroite ouverture plaquait sur le dallage au bout d'un rayon lumineux où dansaient des myriades de grains de poussière. Et resta là sans plus bouger, consciente de ce regard presque immobile qui la scrutait intensément...

— Justine a raison, dit le vieux seigneur comme pour lui-même, c'est étonnant...

Puis, sèchement, il ordonna :

— Va-t'en, Aubert !

La statue armée qui se tenait à son coude protesta :

— Vous voulez que je m'éloigne, seigneur ? Songez que je suis votre bras, votre force...

— J'estime n'avoir besoin ni de l'un ni de l'autre. Va ! Je te rappellerai plus tard...

— Êtes-vous certain que vous n'aurez besoin de rien ?

— Je n'ai jamais besoin de rien et maintenant moins que jamais, dit le seigneur sans quitter Fiora des yeux. Il attendit que son écuyer ait franchi la porte puis reprit :

— Ainsi, c'est vous qui avez conduit jusqu'ici cette Marguerite que nous croyions perdue ? Où l'avez-vous trouvée ?

— A Dijon, enchaînée dans la cave de l'homme indigne qui était son père, à ce qu'il paraît. Il s'en est fallu de bien peu qu'elle ne soit à jamais perdue, en effet...

— Et lui ? J'ai cru comprendre qu'il est mort ? De quoi ?

La vengeance appartient au seigneur 105

— De peur ! D'avoir vu un fantôme...
— Étrange ! Je ne l'aurais jamais cru émotif à ce point ! Mais tout dépend, évidemment, du fantôme en question. Peut-être vous ressemblait-il ?
— Peut-être...
— C'est ce que je supposais... Vous venez de Florence, m'a-t-on dit ? Quel est votre nom ?
— Fiora... Fiora Beltrami. Je suis, en effet florentine...

Il y eut un silence que troublait seulement la respiration de ces deux êtres qui, du premier regard, s'étaient reconnus comme ennemis. Aucune courtoisie n'atténuait le ton agressif de leur voix. Les paroles tombaient, à la limite de l'insolence, de part et d'autre, tranchantes comme des couteaux. Un duel s'établit dès le premier abord entre ce vieil homme aussi rigide qu'une statue, appuyé sur le dossier de son siège, et cette belle jeune femme dressée en face de lui, refrénant de son mieux une instinctive aversion.

Brévailles émit un petit rire sec et reprit, plus mordant que jamais :

— Florentine ? Allons donc ! Vous êtes « leur » fille ! Croyez-vous que j'ignore ce qui s'est passé après l'exécution de ces deux misérables ? Avant que je ne le chasse d'ici, ce vieux fou d'Antoine Charruet avait eu le temps de tout raconter. Je sais qu'un marchand de Florence a ramassé le fruit désastreux de l'inceste et de l'adultère... Eh bien, vous ne dites plus rien ? C'est bien cela, n'est-ce pas ? J'ai deviné juste ?
— Je suis leur fille, en effet, et figurez-vous que j'en suis fière, parce qu'ils ont été des victimes avant tout : vos victimes ! C'est vous qui êtes la cause première du drame dont je suis issue...
— Moi ? Vous osez ?...
— Oui, j'ose et plus encore ! Rien ne serait arrivé d'irrémédiable si, quand vous vous êtes aperçu de ces liens trop tendres noués entre Marie et Jean, vous aviez choisi pour elle un autre époux que ce du Hamel. Mariée à un

homme jeune, aimable et amoureux, elle aurait oublié son frère. Mais vous avez préféré le pire – et pourquoi ? Parce qu'il était riche ? Malheureusement c'était un monstre ignoble qui n'aura jamais su que martyriser sa femme tout comme il a martyrisé sa fille...

– J'ai pris le premier parti convenable qui s'est présenté. On commençait à jaser sur...

– Jean et Marie ? Vous ne parvenez même pas, encore aujourd'hui, à prononcer leurs noms, n'est-ce pas ? Ils vous empoisonnent la bouche ? Quant à la fortune de du Hamel, vous allez pouvoir la revendiquer à présent que vous avez Marguerite ! Car elle est en droit d'y prétendre ! Cependant, je ne crois pas – et c'est tant mieux ! – que vous en profiterez longtemps...

Il eut un ricanement déplaisant :

– Faites-vous profession de dire la bonne aventure ? En tout cas, vous n'êtes guère logique. Vous me haïssez, n'est-ce pas ? Alors pourquoi avoir mené céans Marguerite et son héritage ?

– Parce que après tant d'années d'oppression et de souffrance, elle a bien droit à un légitime bonheur et j'espère qu'elle le trouvera auprès de sa grand-mère. Quant à vous...

– Quant à moi ? lança-t-il, la défiant avec arrogance.

– Vous n'aurez plus le loisir de la rendre encore malheureuse parce que je suis venue vous tuer...

– Me tuer ? Et comment ?

– Avec ceci.

La dague venait d'apparaître, fermement brandie dans sa main. D'un mouvement rapide, Fiora passa derrière le siège et appuya la lame contre la gorge de Brévailles...

– Surtout n'appelez personne ! Vous n'auriez pas le temps d'achever votre cri...

– Pourquoi appellerais-je ? Tuez-moi donc si vous en avez envie... et si le parricide ne vous fait pas peur !

– Non, car vous n'êtes rien à mes yeux qu'un homme presque aussi méprisable que Regnault du Hamel. Si vous avez quelque prière à dire, dépêchez-vous...

En dépit de sa ferme résolution, la force d'âme de cet homme la confondait : il n'avait même pas remué un bras pour tenter d'écarter la dague de sa gorge. Pourtant, il ne devait pas manquer de force ?

— Je n'ai jamais été diseur de patenôtres. Mais, après tout, vous avez peut-être raison de m'assassiner. La venue inopinée de cette Marguerite ne me cause aucune joie : elle n'est après tout que la fille d'une putain incestueuse et...

Il n'acheva pas. La porte, violemment poussée, venait de frapper contre le mur et Madeleine de Brévailles se précipitait :

— Ne le tuez pas, Fiora ! Vous lui feriez trop de plaisir ! Si vous voulez vraiment venger votre mère, laissez-le vivre et priez même pour qu'il vive encore de nombreuses années !

Stupéfaite, Fiora découvrait cette femme nouvelle et insoupçonnée qui se dressait devant eux, la bouche amère et les yeux brûlants de haine. Plus rien de similaire avec la tendre grand-mère qui il y a peu cajolait Marguerite et riait avec elle. Celle-ci rejetait d'un bloc des années de souffrances et de rancœur et, en face d'elle, l'homme accusé se terrait, muet, bien que son visage ne reflétât qu'une rage impuissante. Il hurla :

— Tue-moi ! Pourquoi as-tu retenu ton bras ? Je n'ai commis que des crimes et j'en suis heureux... Tue-moi, te dis-je !

Immobile entre dame Madeleine et son époux, Fiora les regardait tour à tour sans parvenir à comprendre. Elle ne vit pas ainsi Démétrios entrer et ne s'aperçut de sa présence que lorsqu'elle le vit tout à coup près du malade, soulevant un bras, puis rejetant la couverture afin d'examiner ses jambes...

— Qu'est-ce que cela signifie ? interrogea Fiora.

Démétrios hocha la tête et haussa les épaules :

— Que cet homme est paralysé. Il est même étonnant qu'il puisse encore parler... Comment est-ce arrivé ?

— Une chute de cheval il y a un an environ, déclara la dame d'un ton aussi satisfait que si elle avait été elle-même la cause et la force agissante qui avaient provoqué l'accident. Depuis, je me suis enfin remise à vivre. Finies les années d'esclavage ! Finie l'impitoyable tyrannie qui durant tant d'années a terrorisé ce château ! C'est moi la maîtresse à présent et, puisque, grâce à Dieu et grâce à vous, ma petite-fille m'est rendue, notre vieille demeure va s'ouvrir et s'égayer à nouveau ! Nous avons, désormais, bien des jours de joie devant nous...

— Tu es folle ! Serons-nous moins déshonorés parce que tu as récupéré un être de ton sang ? Mais celle-ci que tu as empêché de me tuer est aussi ta petite-fille !

— Je sais parfaitement qui elle est. Je n'avais pas oublié le nom du marchand florentin dont m'avait parlé le bon père Charruet...

— Et tu n'as pas envie de la garder, elle aussi ? Elle me hait de toute son âme et, un jour ou l'autre, je saurai bien l'amener à me délivrer...

— Ce n'est pas moi qui ne désire pas la garder, dit Madeleine avec une tristesse subite, bien au contraire ! C'est elle qui n'a pas envie de rester... Elle est trop belle et vive pour cette austère demeure... Mais j'espère ardemment qu'elle n'oubliera pas tout à fait une grand-mère qui lui gardera une bonne part de son cœur...

Elle ouvrit les bras et Fiora s'y jeta, les larmes aux yeux.

— Moi non plus je ne vous oublierai pas ! Tout à l'heure... j'enviais Marguerite...

— Touchante scène de famille ! grinça Brévailles. Charmant tableau ! Et moi, serai-je oublié ? On ne m'embrasse pas ? J'ai toujours apprécié qu'une jolie fille me caresse... et j'ai quelquefois regretté de n'avoir pas tenté ma chance avec cette jolie garce de Marie, après tout, puisque ça ne la gênait pas de coucher avec son frère. Pourquoi pas avec moi ?

Démétrios empoigna Fiora qui, emportée par une

colère sauvage, allait se jeter sur lui, la dague haute. Il la lui arracha puis, se tournant vers l'infirme et sans lâcher la jeune femme, il prononça fermement :

— Vous n'y parviendrez pas, messire! Fiora doit admettre qu'en ce qui vous concerne la vengeance appartient au Seigneur. Celle qu'il exerce pour l'heure est terrible mais vous la méritez amplement. Que Son nom soit béni! Viens, à présent, il est temps de partir...

L'un après l'autre, ils quittèrent la salle ronde où le vieil Aubert vint reprendre auprès de l'infirme sa garde fidèle et dérisoire. La dernière image que Fiora emporta fut celle d'un visage barbu aux yeux étincelants de fureur impuissante mais d'où glissaient de lourdes larmes...

Ils repartirent dans la chaleur de cet après-midi de juillet encore pénible bien que le jour fût déjà avancé. L'air vibrait au ras de l'eau dans laquelle glissait une couleuvre. Tout était silence quand, soudain, un éclair zébra le ciel blanc...

— Si seulement nous pouvions avoir un bel orage! soupira Léonarde en s'éventant avec son mouchoir. Rien ne me plairait autant qu'une grosse ondée...

— A vous peut-être mais sûrement pas aux paysans! Cela pourrait gâter leurs foins, s'exclama Démétrios en surveillant Fiora du coin de l'œil.

Depuis leurs adieux à la dame de Brévailles, celle-ci n'avait pas desserré les dents. Elle allait droit son chemin, le regard absent. Quand on fut rendu au coude de la route d'où l'on pouvait apercevoir encore le château veillant au bord de la rivière, elle arrêta son cheval et resta là, figée sur place.

Démétrios respecta sa rêverie durant quelques instants mais, comme Fiora semblait s'éterniser, il s'approcha d'elle :

— Regretterais-tu quelque chose?

— Peut-être... mais pas dans le sens que tu imagines. Je regrette d'être venue...

— Ne nous fallait-il pas ramener Marguerite ?

— J'aurais pu t'en charger et attendre à Beaune, par exemple, que tu reviennes...

— Tu voulais accomplir ta vengeance à tout prix. Souviens-toi comme j'ai essayé de t'en détourner !...

— Je sais... Et je reconnais que tu avais raison puisque Dieu s'en était déjà chargé ! Bien illogique, d'ailleurs, le Seigneur ! Il a frappé ici mais laissait prospérer le monstrueux du Hamel...

— Tout cela signifie-t-il que tu regrettes... de quitter cet endroit ? Après tout, là est ton authentique famille et il serait naturel que tu désires y vivre. En ce cas, tu peux t'en retourner en compagnie de dame Léonarde. Je te délie de ton serment... et je n'en demeurerai pas moins ton ami à jamais.

— Tu ne me comprends pas, Démétrios ! Il est exact que mon cœur était tout près de se donner à Madeleine de Brévailles. Les bras d'une grand-mère sont... infiniment doux. Mais rester ici, non, jamais ! Je crois d'ailleurs que Marguerite ne l'eût pas apprécié, ajouta-t-elle avec un demi-sourire.

En effet, le visage de Marguerite avait soudain pris une expression chagrine quand dame Madeleine, à l'instant du départ, avait embrassé Fiora avec une tendre effusion et ses adieux, à elle, avaient été livrés du bout des lèvres. Elle était visiblement soulagée de quitter cette jeune femme, trop belle peut-être, à qui elle devait la vie.

— Elle est tout de même la fille de du Hamel, remarqua Léonarde qui s'était approchée. Et vous avez bien fait de recommander à dame Madeleine le silence absolu sur votre lien de parenté. Je crois bien qu'elle vous détesterait si elle vous savait sa sœur. Quant à vous, mon agneau, ces regrets vous passeront plus vite qu'ils sont venus ! Votre destin n'est pas ici.

— Je sais ! Mais j'ai voulu regarder encore une fois ces lieux que je ne reverrai sans doute jamais... Même si, un jour, je revenais habiter la Bourgogne... Ce qui peut toujours se faire.

A présent qu'elle était dégagée de ces devoirs de vengeance qu'elle s'était imposés en Bourgogne, Fiora pouvait tout à loisir laisser son esprit, et son cœur, vagabonder sur les pas d'un autre Bourguignon qui était son époux. Elle pouvait se souvenir qu'elle était ici dans son pays, et ce n'était pas sans une douce nostalgie puisqu'elle n'avait toujours pas reçu de réponse à la question qu'en quittant Florence elle se posait : était-ce pour la revoir, en dépit du pacte passé avec Francesco Beltrami, que Philippe était revenu sous un déguisement dans la cité des Médicis ? Et c'était infiniment plus important que la jalousie d'une demi-sœur à laquelle rien ne la liait...

Résolument, elle fit faire demi-tour à son cheval pour reprendre la route et ne permit plus à son esprit de retourner à Brévailles où elle souhaitait que sa grand-mère trouvât enfin un peu de bonheur véritable auprès de la fille de Regnault du Hamel... Il faisait beau, elle n'avait pas dix-huit ans et elle aimait passionnément l'homme dont l'anneau pendait sur sa poitrine, à l'abri de sa robe... Même l'image lointaine et d'ailleurs indistincte de l'impitoyable duc de Bourgogne ne parvenait pas à troubler cette minute de paix heureuse qu'elle s'accordait à elle-même. Pourquoi donc, après tout, le ciel ne se chargerait-il pas de lui comme il avait disposé de Pierre de Brévailles ? Les bruits qu'elle avait entendus depuis son arrivée en Bourgogne pouvaient lui donner à ce sujet quelque espérance car les ennemis acharnés à la perte du Téméraire commençaient à être légion : les Suisses, les princes allemands, le duc de Lorraine et, surtout, surtout, ce roi de France dont on murmurait à juste titre qu'il était le plus habile de tous les diplomates et peut-être le plus puissant de ces ennemis. Les gens hasardaient volontiers qu'entre lui et le Téméraire la haine ne prendrait fin que par la mort de l'un d'eux. Et c'est vers ce souverain énigmatique – car son image différait selon ceux qui en parlaient – qu'elle et Démétrios allaient s'acheminer de concert... non sans un petit détour que Fiora était bien décidée à obtenir...

Ils firent étape à Beaune, dans un relais proche de l'admirable Hôtel-Dieu édifié trente-deux ans plus tôt par le chancelier de Bourgogne, Nicolas Rollin, et son épouse Guigone de Salins. Sans avoir la splendeur architecturale de son voisin, l'auberge du Grand Saint Vincent leur offrit, avec ses lits aux draps soigneusement repassés, sa cuisine abondante et variée et la fraîcheur de la vigne qui revêtait ses murailles, une halte aussi reposante pour le corps que pour l'esprit. Après le souper qu'on leur servit, toutes fenêtres ouvertes sur les grands toits bruns des Halles, dans la chambre que partageaient Fiora et Léonarde, Démétrios s'inquiéta auprès de l'hôte, maître Baudot, du chemin qu'il convenait de prendre pour se rendre à Paris.

Afin de calmer les soupçons de ce brave homme qui, en digne serviteur du duc Charles, commençait à regarder de travers des gens qui souhaitaient se rendre dans la ville capitale de « l'infâme roi Louis XI », Démétrios se hâta de préciser qu'ils devaient rejoindre un cousin, marchand drapier dans la rue des Lombards. Satisfait, Baudot lui exposa que le meilleur chemin sans contredit passait par Dijon et par Troyes, en Champagne, celui qui, après avoir traversé une partie du Morvan et l'Auxois, rejoignait la vallée de l'Yonne n'étant plus praticable.

– On dit, observa maître Baudot, que les troupes du roi Louis, après la rupture de la trêve, se sont ruées sur nos terres et sont arrivées jusqu'à Auxerre où elles dévastent, ravagent, pillent et brûlent tout ce qui leur tombe sous la main. C'est bien le fait d'un mauvais homme, ajouta-t-il, car ce roi sait bien que Mgr Charles, – que Dieu nous veuille garder en santé ! – vient tout juste d'en finir avec le siège de Neuss...

– La ville est-elle enfin tombée ? demanda Fiora qui savait parfaitement à quoi s'en tenir mais tenait à jouer jusqu'au bout son rôle d'étrangère nouvellement débarquée.

– Oui et non. Elle s'est ouverte devant le légat de sa

sainteté le pape Sixte qui en a pris possession au nom de l'Église. Il n'y a ni vainqueur ni vaincu mais notre duc a tout de même perdu beaucoup d'hommes et pas mal d'or... Profiter de cela, c'est indigne!

— Croyez-vous? fit Démétrios d'un air innocent. Des marchands flamands que nous avons rencontrés au-dessus de Lyon nous ont appris que le duc, laissant son armée derrière lui, rejoignait à marches forcées ses possessions de Flandres pour y réunir les États et pour retrouver à Calais son allié le roi d'Angleterre en compagnie duquel il entend entreprendre la conquête de la France. Il voudrait même le faire couronner à Reims...

— Le roi d'Angleterre est frère de Mme la duchesse, repartit dignement Baudot. Lui et Monseigneur peuvent se rencontrer sans qu'il y ait mauvaise intention à l'égard de la France. Mais les gens ont si méchante langue qu'ils sont capables d'aller jusqu'à prétendre que si le roi Louis nous envahit ce serait entièrement de notre faute! Vos marchands me font l'effet de fieffés cancaniers et...

Démétrios mit un terme à l'indignation du brave homme en lui commandant un pichet de son meilleur vin de Beaune puis, quand il fut servi, se tourna vers ses compagnes.

— Notre chemin est tout tracé. Il faut remonter à Dijon mais nous n'entrerons pas dans la ville. Nous la contournerons pour rejoindre la route de Troyes qui se trouve vers le nord...

— Passerons-nous par... Selongey? hasarda Fiora mécontente de se sentir rougir comme si elle était fautive. Lorsque nous étions à Dijon, j'ai appris que cette terre se trouvait aussi au nord...

— Certes, répondit Léonarde avec un regard plein de compassion, mais cela nous détournerait. Nous prendrons par Troyes. Selongey est sur le chemin qui mène à Langres et, de là, aux pays lorrains...

— Le détour serait-il si grand? Je désire vraiment y aller! reprit la jeune femme d'une voix soudain raffermie.

N'est-il pas naturel que je souhaite au moins apercevoir le château dont je devrais porter le nom ?

— Espères-tu y rencontrer messire Philippe ? demanda doucement Démétrios. Tu sais parfaitement qu'il ne quitte jamais le duc Charles. Il doit être en Flandres à l'heure actuelle, à moins qu'il ne soit resté avec l'armée en Luxembourg.

— Il l'a néanmoins quitté deux fois à ma connaissance : la première quand nous nous sommes mariés, la seconde quand il a été reconnu à Florence alors que la populace pillait mon palais ! Je t'en prie, Démétrios : conduis-moi à Selongey ! C'est, je le jure, ma dernière prière...

Les grands yeux gris suppliaient et le médecin crut bien y voir briller une larme. Sa longue main se posa sur celle de sa jeune amie, compréhensive et apaisante :

— Le détour serait-il si grand, dame Léonarde ?

— Je ne sais pas au juste... mais au moins une douzaine de lieues... et par des chemins incertains qui ne vont pas tout droit...

— Une journée de cheval, traduisit Esteban, et nous sommes en été. C'est peu de chose...

— Nous pouvons aussi nous égarer. Je suis née dans cette région mais je ne m'y suis guère promenée...

— Eh bien, nous demanderons notre route ! fit Démétrios avec bonhomie, et nous n'en sommes pas à un jour près ! Nous ne saurions refuser à la dame de Selongey de visiter son domaine. Et nous demanderons même l'hospitalité, si tu le veux, conclut-il en baisant la main de Fiora. Qui peut savoir ce que nous y trouverons ?

Fiora ne répondit pas mais ses yeux, soudain emplis d'étoiles, trahirent l'espoir qui lui était venu. Puisque, pour l'instant, les armes du duc Charles semblaient s'être calmées, pourquoi le comte de Selongey n'en profiterait-il pas pour passer quelques jours chez lui ? A l'idée de le revoir peut-être bientôt, le cœur de Fiora s'affola et elle eut toutes les peines du monde à trouver le sommeil, tandis qu'à côté d'elle, bienheureuse, Léonarde ronflait comme un soufflet de forge...

Vers la fin du second jour, Fiora, le cœur battant toujours au rythme de son espoir, galopait à travers le plateau coupé de bosquets et de masses forestières que l'on avait atteint après Til-Châtel et qui filait droit vers la cité épiscopale de Langres. Un bûcheron du cru, rencontré à une croisée de chemins, avait indiqué celui de Selongey :

— C'est le prochain village : un gros bourg dans la vallée de la Venelle avec une vieille église et un fort château dont vous apercevrez les tours quand vous serez parvenus à cet arbre penché que vous voyez là-bas !

Une pièce avait récompensé le bonhomme de son précieux renseignement et, quelques instants plus tard, Fiora découvrait, en effet, le château de son époux. Son émotion redoubla à cet aspect redoutable : dix tours en poivrière dont les ardoises luisaient sous le soleil, gardées par des hommes d'armes ; de grandes murailles solides et un donjon massif dressé vers le ciel comme le doigt tendu d'un géant. Ainsi, c'était là « sa » maison, là qu'il était né, qu'il avait passé son enfance et quitté les bras tendres d'une mère pour apprendre la rude vie des hommes...

— Mais je ne crois pas qu'il y soit ! soupira Léonarde. Et Fiora s'aperçut alors qu'elle venait de penser tout haut...

— Pourquoi donc ?

— Aucune bannière ne flotte sur le donjon. Cela signifie clairement que le seigneur n'est pas au bercail.

Fiora haussa les épaules, cachant sa déception sous un demi-sourire.

— Tant pis ! Essayons, au moins, de nous faire accorder l'hospitalité pour la nuit.

L'espoir de rencontrer Philippe était faible et Fiora le savait mais n'est-il toujours permis d'espérer...

— Compterais-tu te faire reconnaître comme la dame de ces lieux ? demanda Démétrios.

— Non. Nous sommes de simples voyageurs désorientés. Quand j'entrerai ici en tant que maîtresse, ce sera au bras de mon époux... si j'arrive à le retrouver car j'ai toujours tendance à négliger cet affreux désir qu'il avait de se faire tuer...

— Il était sincère sans doute, coupa Léonarde qui n'aimait pas voir l'esprit de Fiora s'engager dans ces pensées affligeantes, mais, pour ma part, je n'y ai pas vraiment cru...

— Moi non plus, fit Démétrios en écho. Je suis persuadé qu'il est toujours vivant.

Fiora leur adressa, à l'un et à l'autre, un regard chargé de gratitude pour ces paroles encourageantes et pressa un peu l'allure de son cheval. Elle avait hâte à présent d'arriver...

Ils avaient atteint le village et la barbacane d'entrée du château était déjà en vue quand, débouchant de la forêt qui couronnait le coteau, quelques cavaliers apparurent. Les faucons qu'ils portaient sur leur poing ganté de cuir épais disaient assez qu'ils venaient de chasser et quelques oiseaux pendaient au troussequin de la selle de l'un des hommes. Ils étaient six en tout : quatre hommes un peu plus armés peut-être qu'il n'eût fallu pour un divertissement, et deux femmes.

Celle qui allait en tête et qui riait en posant un baiser sur la tête encapuchonnée de son oiseau pouvait avoir une trentaine d'années. Élégamment habillée de soie bleue elle avait de longs cheveux blonds étroitement nattés sous un hennin court de velours assorti à sa robe et où s'attachait un voile azuré. Elle était d'ailleurs très jolie et, à le constater, le cœur de Fiora tressaillit.

A présent les chasseurs qui n'avaient pas remarqué les quatre cavaliers entraient dans le château de l'allure toute naturelle de gens qui reviennent chez eux.

— Qui sont-ils ? fit Léonarde sans cacher sa surprise. Messire Philippe n'avait-il pas dit qu'il n'avait aucune famille ?

— Il peut avoir des invités, dit Démétrios. Même en l'absence du seigneur c'est une chose possible... Le mieux vois-tu, c'est d'entrer à notre tour...

Mais Fiora avait froncé les sourcils et l'arrêta. Elle avisa une lavandière qui, sa corbeille de linge à la hanche, remontait de la rivière et l'appela :

— Pardonnez-moi si je vous parais curieuse, dit-elle gentiment, mais je croyais ce château inhabité. Le comte Philippe n'est pas là, n'est-ce pas ?

La servante ne devait pas être un puits d'intelligence car elle adressa à Fiora son plus béat sourire.

— Pour sûr qu'il est pas là !

— Alors, cette dame qui vient d'entrer ? Savez-vous qui elle est ?

— Bèn... c'est la dame du château. C'est dame Béatrice...

— Béatrice... de Selongey ?

— Ben... oui.

Ce « oui » frappa Fiora comme une gifle. Elle devint soudainement très rouge. Sentant qu'elle allait se mettre à hurler, à sangloter ou à se livrer à toute autre manifestation insensée, elle serra les rênes, fit volter son cheval qui manqua renverser la lavandière puis, enfonçant ses talons dans le flanc de la bête avec un cri sauvage, elle s'élança au triple galop à travers le village qu'elle traversa comme un boulet de canon. L'appel de Démétrios lui parvint de très loin, comme du fond des âges :

— Arrête-toi ! Par pitié...

Pitié pour qui ? Et pour quoi faire ? L'eût-elle voulu, d'ailleurs, qu'il lui était impossible de retenir l'animal emporté. Les yeux fous, les oreilles couchées, l'écume à la bouche, il fonçait droit devant lui mais Fiora, éperdue de douleur et de honte, ne voyait rien, n'entendait rien, attendant passivement que cette course à l'abîme s'achevât dans la mort. Et la mort n'était pas loin car la bête affolée courait droit vers un bois épais dont les branches basses représentaient autant de pièges redoutables.

Esteban s'était élancé derrière Fiora, suivi de Démétrios qui, plus lourd, ne pouvait aller au même train, et de plus loin encore par Léonarde qui, peu familière du grand galop, sanglotait éperdument. Le Castillan était un remarquable cavalier. Couché sur l'encolure de son cheval qu'il ne cessait de cravacher, faisant corps avec lui, il s'efforçait de gagner du terrain dans l'espoir de rejoindre

Fiora avant le bois car il avait pleinement conscience du danger encouru. Il ne criait pas, n'appelait pas, car cela n'eût fait qu'exciter davantage l'animal emballé. Mais il réussit à se rapprocher jusqu'à se trouver botte à botte avec la jeune femme dont il était visible qu'elle ne résistait pas, ne se défendait pas... Alors, mettant sa bride entre ses dents, Esteban se pencha et, saisissant Fiora à bras-le-corps, réussit à l'arracher de sa selle et à la coucher devant lui. A cet instant seulement, il retint sa monture qui freina des quatre fers et finit par stopper, trempée de sueur. Fiora glissa à terre, sans connaissance, tandis que son cheval, libéré de son poids, allait bouler dans un buisson dont il se releva sans autres dommages que des égratignures.

La nuit venait et il leur fallait trouver un abri. Léonarde qui, un peu remise de la peur qu'elle avait éprouvée, les avait rejoints et s'efforçait de ranimer Fiora, proposa le prieuré de Til-Châtel où la maison d'hôtes les recevrait peut-être.

— Si nous pouvons y arriver, c'est la meilleure solution, fit Démétrios. Mais, par tous les diables de l'enfer, j'aimerais étrangler de mes mains ce Philippe de Selongey...

— Je n'arrive pas à comprendre, murmura Léonarde. Si j'ai jamais vu homme amoureux, c'est bien celui-là... lorsqu'il a quitté la chambre nuptiale.

— Allez donc essayer de percer le mystère d'une âme ! Il l'aimait sans doute, à ce moment-là, mais il avait trouvé plus commode à son gré d'oublier qu'il était déjà marié. Je l'avais mal jugé...

En reprenant connaissance, Fiora remercia Esteban puis, sans autre commentaire, remonta sur son cheval que l'on avait laissé reposer un moment. Mais lorsque la porte de la petite chambre qu'elle partageait avec Léonarde au prieuré se fut refermée, elle déclara, les yeux tournés vers cette campagne envahie par la nuit qu'elle avait tant espérée et où elle avait reçu si cruelle blessure :

— J'ai cru en cet homme et je l'ai aimé. Lui s'est moqué

de moi et m'a joué la plus indigne, la plus triste des comédies... Mais un jour viendra où il regrettera de m'avoir seulement rencontrée...

Tout en parlant, elle avait fait passer par-dessus sa tête la chaîne qui soutenait l'anneau de Philippe et le contempla un instant :

— Le gage de sa foi! fit-elle avec amertume. Puis elle tendit la bague à Léonarde : Tenez, vous la donnerez demain au prieur de cette maison pour ses charités... Et, je vous en supplie, ne me parlez jamais... plus jamais de cet homme!...

Deuxième partie

PARIS MENACÉ

CHAPITRE V

UNE GRAND-MESSE A NOTRE-DAME...

Peu après vêpres sonnantes, les voyageurs couverts de poussière et recrus de fatigue descendaient la longue rue Saint-Jacques en direction de la Seine. Le jour d'août, avec son soleil voilé, avait été lourd à supporter mais avec l'approche du soir, un vent humide venu de l'ouest soufflait sur Paris accordant toutes les girouettes qui, en haut des toits, alignaient leurs banderoles de tôle peinte et découpée.

Il y avait beaucoup de monde dehors. C'était l'heure où les grands collèges – Sorbonne, collège du Plessis, collège de Marmoutiers, collège du Mans, collège de Clermont, etc. – lâchaient les troupes turbulentes de leurs étudiants libres qui, par bandes ou isolés, fuyant les subtilités de la scolastique, l'encrier à la ceinture et le chapeau en bataille descendaient vers leurs logis, pour les plus sages ou, pour les plus fous, vers les tavernes de la Cité. Robes et pourpoints étaient plus ou moins riches, plus ou moins propres et plus ou moins effilochés mais tous les yeux brillaient d'une même ardeur à vivre. Ils échangeaient des plaisanteries et certains chantaient. Toutefois rires et chansons cessèrent net quand, d'une rue latérale, déboucha une escorte de gens d'armes à cheval encadrant quelques sergents à pied qui menaient au Châtelet une demi-douzaine de malandrins, mains liées derrière le dos.

Des cris fusèrent. Certains des malfaiteurs étaient

connus des escholiers qui ne se gênaient pas pour leur lancer des encouragements et pour conspuer les soldats du prévôt de la ville.

Quand on atteignit la Cité, passé le Petit-Pont, l'animation fut plus grande encore : hommes, femmes, fillettes, bourgeois, marchands se saluaient, s'arrêtaient, échangeaient des propos tandis que de petits enfants qui s'en allaient quérir du vin ou de la moutarde passaient en agitant leurs pots. Cependant et contrairement aux étudiants, personne ne riait.

— C'est un peu comme à Florence, remarqua Fiora, mais il y manque notre lumière...

— Il n'y a pas du tout de lumière aujourd'hui, dit Démétrios, mais j'ai déjà vu cette ville sous un soleil plus ardent que celui de Toscane. Et nous avons rencontré tant de jardins !

Depuis la porte Saint-Jacques, en effet, Paris s'était montré sous son plus joli jour. Clos, courtils et jardinets, appartenant à des couvents ou à des particuliers, fleurissaient un peu partout cachant les blessures encore visibles subies par la grand-ville pendant une guerre qui avait duré cent ans et, surtout, lors de l'occupation anglaise. Le roi Charles VII qui n'aimait pas Paris n'avait pas fait grand-chose pour une cité qui, selon lui, l'avait rejeté trop longtemps, mais Louis XI, s'il préférait à sa capitale ses châteaux de Loire, n'en avait pas moins compris que Paris méritait d'être défendu et rénové. Les remparts avaient été consolidés, le double fossé recreusé, beaucoup de bâtiments remis en état avec l'aide d'une bourgeoisie que le roi faisait riche et puissante.

Bien qu'il considérât la capitale comme le centre névralgique du royaume, Louis la visitait rarement. Dédaignant l'ancien hôtel Saint-Pol qu'affectionnaient ses grands-parents, il logeait alors au palais des Tournelles dont les ducs d'Orléans avaient fait une sorte d'œuvre d'art avec parc, bois, ménagerie, labyrinthe, galeries, chapelles, cloîtres et bâtiments gracieux, ou plus volontiers encore, à l'hôtel de la conciergerie de la Bastille Saint-Antoine, au cœur des défenses de sa ville.

Il n'était pas rare de rencontrer, à Paris, des voyageurs étrangers. Aussi Fiora et son escorte ne soulevèrent guère de curiosité. D'autant qu'ils n'eurent pas à demander leur chemin : Démétrios, en effet, avait séjourné jadis à l'auberge du Grand Saint-Martin, dans la rue du même nom, lorsque avec son jeune frère Théodose ils avaient fui Byzance en flammes. Sa mémoire infaillible en faisait le guide le plus sûr. Il put même, une fois dans l'île de la Cité, faire un léger détour pour que Léonarde pût contempler tout à son aise la cathédrale Notre-Dame. Elle voulut y pénétrer pour une courte prière à laquelle Fiora ne s'associa pas, préférant attendre, debout sur le petit parvis, contemplant bras croisés la formidable église avec son triple porche, ses statues de rois et ses immenses tours jumelles qui semblaient vouloir lui imposer l'image oppressante de la puissance de Dieu. D'un Dieu envers lequel, plus que jamais, elle se sentait en révolte. D'un Dieu redoutable, impitoyable qui, non content de lui avoir tout arraché, avait encore permis qu'elle donnât son cœur innocent à un homme assez vil et assez pervers pour bafouer le sacrement de mariage, dans l'unique but de posséder son corps et de porter triomphalement à son maître la dot royale qui, à cette heure, devait être engloutie dans les armes d'une injuste conquête... Fiora ne savait plus, ne voulait plus prier, au grand chagrin de Léonarde.

Quand celle-ci ressortit, encore émerveillée de ce qu'elle avait découvert à l'intérieur du saint lieu, Fiora se contenta de remonter en selle et de demander :

— Cette rue des Lombards est-elle encore très éloignée ?

— Non. Quand nous aurons traversé l'autre bras de la Seine nous n'aurons plus guère de chemin. Aimes-tu Paris ?

— Je ne sais pas. C'est sans doute une belle ville mais j'ai un peu l'impression d'y étouffer :

— Le voyage t'a fatiguée et le temps fait le reste.

On quitta l'île par un grand pont de bois, bordé de maisons toutes semblables, le pont Notre-Dame qui était le plus neuf de Paris car il avait été bâti par le roi Charles VI, grand-père de Louis XI. Un vrai tintamarre s'y faisait entendre car il desservait les moulins dont les grandes roues battaient l'eau qu'elles emportaient puis laissaient retomber en longues coulures brillantes... La Seine passée on s'engagea sur une place spacieuse qui venait mourir doucement dans le fleuve. Un imposant bâtiment reposant sur de hautes arcades et couronné de clochetons la bornaient à l'est.

— C'est la Maison aux Piliers, expliqua Démétrios. C'est là que se tiennent les échevins. La Seigneurie, en quelque sorte. On appelle cette place la Grève. Il y a là un monde de négociants, de portefaix, de bateliers, de cabaretiers même qui viennent s'approvisionner en vin aux tonneaux que tu vois sur la berge auprès de ces tas de foin. C'est le lieu le plus animé de Paris, celui des réjouissances... et des exécutions aussi, hélas!

— Seigneur que cela sent mauvais! protesta Fiora en se bouchant les narines.

— Cela provient des tanneries que tu peux voir de ce côté, mais il y a aussi, tout près d'ici, la Grande Boucherie. Néanmoins je te trouve bien difficile tout à coup. Au cœur actif de Florence, cela ne sent pas non plus la rose. Les dames délicates emploient les pommes de senteur ici comme là-bas. Je t'en offrirai une...

On plongea enfin dans un lacis de rues étroites, rendues obscures par les grands toits des maisons en encorbellement qui les bordaient et se rejoignaient presque. En dépit du caniveau creusé au milieu des pavés, des ordures y stagnaient mais, par les fenêtres ouvertes, les relents de cuisine luttaient victorieusement contre ceux des détritus.

La vision séduisante de la rue des Lombards réconforta un peu Fiora. Ses maisons arborant toutes de belles enseignes colorées appartenaient en grande partie à des commerçants génois, milanais, vénitiens et florentins qui s'occupaient de banque, de change ou même d'usure mais qui, en général, étaient riches. L'aspect de leurs maisons s'en ressentait.

Le comptoir d'Agnolo Nardi, frère de lait de Francesco Beltrami et son représentant pour la France septentrionale, s'élevait à l'angle de la rue des Lombards et de la Grande rue Saint-Martin, presque en face du portail de l'église Saint-Merri. C'était une grande et belle demeure dont les trois pignons alignés recouvraient tout à la fois le logis du maître, le dépôt de draps fins et une banque. Le double commerce était à l'exemple de ce qu'avait créé Beltrami à Florence. Les bâtiments étaient soigneusement entretenus et, sur les toits pointus, deux girouettes rouges, telles les langues d'animaux fabuleux, encadraient un fleuron doré du plus bel effet. Les fenêtres largement ouvertes sur la fraîcheur du soir montraient de beaux plafonds aux poutres peintes et enluminées. Enfin, derrière la triple maison, un petit jardin clos de murs la séparait de celle d'un joaillier dont les ouvertures donnaient sur la rue de la Vieille-Courroierie, ce qui assurait à ce petit enclos une tranquillité absolue.

Agnolo Nardi n'était pas tout à fait un inconnu pour Fiora et Léonarde. Elles l'avaient rencontré sept ans plus tôt au cours de la visite qu'il avait faite à sa maison mère et elles en avaient conservé le souvenir d'un petit homme rond, brun comme une châtaigne, vif et gai, ami de la bonne chère comme du bon vin. Un personnage en somme aimable et attachant dont Beltrami vantait tout à la fois la générosité, l'honnêteté et l'habileté en affaires.

Depuis, elles avaient appris son mariage avec une jeune Parisienne, fille d'un des meilleurs drapiers de la ville dont le nom, Agnelle Perrin, les avait beaucoup amusées. Ainsi l'agneau[1] avait trouvé son complément naturel et l'on pouvait espérer qu'il trouverait du même coup son bonheur.

Elles n'en doutèrent plus quand, à peine descendues de

---

1. Agnolo signifie agneau.

cheval, elles le virent accourir, exactement semblable à l'image qu'elles en avaient gardée, ses petits bras courts et dodus grands ouverts avec sur sa bonne figure un sourire qui l'illuminait littéralement :

— Donna Fiora et donna Léonarda! Enfin vous voilà! Vous n'imaginez pas comme j'étais en peine de vous! Je craignais qu'il ne vous fût advenu quelque mauvaise aventure!

Il les embrassa toutes les deux avec l'effusion d'un frère qui retrouve ses sœurs.

— Tu nous a reconnues? s'étonna Fiora, retrouvant instinctivement et avec plaisir la langue toscane et le tutoiement florentin.

— C'est surtout donna Léonarda que j'ai reconnue. Toi, donna Fiora, tu as beaucoup changé. Par Santa Reparata, patronne de notre chère ville, tu es assurément la plus jolie des Florentines!

Et il en profita pour la réembrasser deux ou trois fois avec un plaisir enfantin.

— Est-ce que vous nous attendiez? demanda Léonarde.

— Bien sûr et depuis longtemps déjà! Messer Donati, qui gère à présent les affaires de notre pauvre Francesco, m'a fait tenir un message accompagné d'une lettre de Mgr Lorenzo dont j'ai été fort honoré...

Puis se tournant vers Démétrios qu'il salua courtoisement :

— Messer Lascaris, soyez le bienvenu dans ma modeste maison, vous et votre écuyer.

Agnelle accourait à son tour, ramassant à pleines mains ses jupes de cendal safrané qui bruissaient joliment. Elle formait avec son époux un couple assez peu ordinaire : aussi blonde qu'il était brun, pas plus grande que lui et aussi ronde, elle avait un joli teint un peu doré et ressemblait tout à fait à un pot de miel. Son charmant visage dont les prunelles possédaient le joli bleu des fleurs de lin resplendissait de santé et de belle humeur. Elle embrassa Fiora comme si elle eût été sa petite sœur – elle était nettement plus jeune que son époux – et Léonarde avec une nuance de respect qui séduisit la vieille demoiselle...

– A quoi pense maître Agnolo de vous tenir là, dans la rue, sous les yeux de toutes les commères du quartier, au lieu de vous faire entrer chez nous! Venez, venez! Vous avez grand besoin d'un bon repas, d'un grand repos et nous ne ferons la fête que demain seulement.

– La fête? dit Fiora. Mais pourquoi?

– Pour vous, voyons! Ne faut-il pas célébrer votre arrivée? Voilà des jours et des jours que nous vous attendons!

– Nous avions des affaires à régler en Bourgogne, dit Fiora, et cela nous a retenus plus longtemps que nous ne l'aurions souhaité sans doute. Et puis, nous ignorions que vous nous attendiez.

– Avec impatience! Et nous avons tremblé pour vous. Messer Donati et le seigneur de Médicis ont bien expliqué, dans leurs lettres, les terribles malheurs qui se sont abattus sur vous. Nous ne souhaitons qu'une chose : vous aider...

Ayant ainsi parlé, Agnelle prit ses invitées chacune par un bras, les entraîna vers l'escalier menant aux étages et d'abord à la pièce principale. L'intérieur de la maison ressemblait à l'hôtesse : frais, élégant et d'une propreté flamande. La salle avec sa haute cheminée ornée de statues de saints, sa longue tapisserie à personnages dont était revêtu tout le mur faisant face aux fenêtres, ses dressoirs surchargés de pimpantes majoliques italiennes, de verres dorés et colorés de Venise et de belle argenterie, était digne de celle d'un château. Les sièges de chêne sculpté s'adoucissaient de coussins de velours incarnat bien gonflés de duvet et ornés de franges de soie. De hauts candélabres de bronze supportaient des chandelles de cire blanche et, devant la cheminée sans feu, un brasero en cuivre empli de giroflées et de pivoines blanches apportait une senteur exquise qui évoquait le jardin. Quant aux servantes, vêtues de toile bleue fraîchement repassée, leurs coiffes et leurs devantiers bien nets semblaient tout juste sortis d'une armoire.

Raffinement suprême, la maison possédait une petite salle pour le bain abondamment garnie de brocs, de cuvettes et d'un vaste baquet. Fiora s'y trempa avec délices dans une eau à peine tiède et retrouva la douceur, perdue depuis des mois, des merveilleux savons vénitiens. Deux servantes lui prodiguèrent leurs soins avec un enthousiasme évident mais qui diminua beaucoup quand, après Fiora, elles eurent à s'occuper de Léonarde. Pendant ce temps, enveloppée dans un drap et chaussée de socques légères, Fiora sortait dans le jardin sur lequel ouvrait l'étuve pour rentrer dans la maison par la porte de derrière et remonter dans sa chambre, quand elle se trouva nez à nez avec un jeune homme simplement vêtu de ses chausses et d'un pot de basilic en fleur qu'il serrait tendrement sur sa poitrine. La surprise que la vue inopinée de Fiora lui causa fut si forte qu'il en lâcha son pot. Celui-ci s'écrasa sans que le jeune homme parût autrement s'en soucier. Pétrifié sur place il semblait en extase mais réussit tout de même à articuler :

– Par tous les saints du paradis !... Vous êtes vraie ou pas ?

– Pourquoi ne le serais-je pas ? dit Fiora amusée.

– Vous avez tellement l'air d'une apparition ! Vous êtes belle... belle comme une sainte d'église !

– Rassurez-vous, je n'ai rien de commun avec les saintes et vous me faites beaucoup d'honneur mais, si j'étais vous, je ramasserais ces morceaux et j'irais tout de suite replanter mon basilic dans un autre pot...

Le jeune homme parut redescendre des hauteurs de l'empyrée. La vision de rêve avait vraiment des préoccupations bien terre à terre !

– Vous croyez ?

– J'en suis persuadée. En outre j'aimerais que vous me laissiez passer. Je voudrais monter m'habiller...

– Je... oui, bien sûr. Excusez-moi, ajouta-t-il en s'écartant. Mais prenez garde à ne pas vous blesser avec les morceaux...

Elle lui adressa un sourire puis pénétra dans la maison. Lui ne bougeait pas, se contentant de la regarder. Au moment où elle allait disparaître, il murmura :

– Je m'appelle Florent...

Elle s'arrêta surprise :

– C'est un très joli nom. Je ne l'oublierai pas. Il évoque ma ville de Florence...

Cela aurait dû faire plaisir au garçon mais, au contraire, son visage aigu où les yeux bruns semblaient occuper toute la place sous une tignasse de même couleur s'assombrit.

– Ah... Vous êtes la dame que l'on attendait ? Je ne m'en suis pas rendu compte et je vous demande bien pardon...

– Pardon de quoi ?

– Eh bien... De m'être montré... un peu trop familier... d'avoir osé...

– Vous n'avez rien osé dont une femme puisse être choquée ! Un compliment fait toujours plaisir s'il est sincère. Étiez-vous sincère ?

– Oh oui !

– Alors merci. A présent, je vous en prie, consacrez-vous entièrement à ce malheureux basilic !

La rencontre l'ayant amusée, Fiora apprit plus tard que son admirateur avait été placé chez Nardi par son père, le changeur Gaucher le Cauchois, pour y étudier l'art délicat des tractations bancaires, mais le jeune homme peu attiré par les affaires et très doué pour le jardinage dépensait au service d'Agnelle, aussi bien rue des Lombards que dans son clos de Suresnes, le trop-plein de forces et d'enthousiasme qu'il n'employait pas derrière son pupitre. La chaleur, la taille d'une haie et les besoins de la cuisine expliquaient son costume sommaire et le pot de basilic :

– C'est un gentil garçon, conclut Agnolo, mais très secret, très renfermé et il n'y a guère que ma femme pour deviner ce qui se passe dans sa tête...

Fiora pensa qu'à présent elles étaient deux... puis oublia Florent. L'atmosphère de Paris lui paraissait bizarre. En se rendant chez Nardi, elle et ses compagnons avaient rencontré plusieurs troupes de soldats et, tandis qu'elle se préparait pour le souper, elle entendit sonner l'Angélus et, presque aussitôt, corner la fermeture des portes alors que la nuit était encore assez éloignée.

Démétrios, de son côté, avait fait les mêmes observations et, au souper, quand la maisonnée se retrouva autour d'un cochon de lait rôti et de savoureuses pâtes au fameux basilic — Florent avait fini par approvisionner la cuisine — triomphe d'Agnelle et de l'amour conjugal, le Grec interrogea son hôte :

— Depuis la porte Saint-Jacques où l'on nous a longuement interrogés avant que de nous laisser passer, nous avons croisé beaucoup d'hommes en armes et dame Léonarde a vu, à Notre-Dame, beaucoup de femmes en prière. Les portes ont été fermées de bonne heure. Paris serait-il menacé ?

Un nuage assombrit l'aimable visage d'Agnolo. Il s'arrêta un instant de découper son rôti et regarda tour à tour chacun de ses invités :

— Je suis navré d'être obligé de parler, dès ce soir, de toutes ces choses et j'aurais aimé attendre que soit passée la petite fête que nous projetons pour demain, en votre honneur... Mais, après tout, peut-être vaut-il mieux que vous soyez au courant de la situation...

— Parce qu'il y a bien une situation... dirai-je préoccupante ? dit Démétrios doucement.

— C'est le mot juste. Paris n'est pas menacé dans l'immédiat mais il pourrait l'être bientôt. Nous sommes au début d'une nouvelle invasion anglaise. Et la fameuse guerre de Cent Ans n'est achevée que depuis vingt !

— En chemin, nous avons entendu dire, en effet, que le roi Édouard avait franchi la Manche. Savez-vous où il est, en ce moment ?

— A un peu plus de trente lieues d'ici : à Péronne !

— Si près ? souffla Fiora.

— Oui, madonna, si près. Et il n'y est pas seul : le Téméraire est avec lui.

— Mais, reprit Démétrios, je croyais le duc en Flandres ?

— Il y était en effet, à Bruges, pour essayer d'arracher aux États une aide supplémentaire en argent et en hommes. Grâce à Dieu il n'a pas obtenu tout ce qu'il voulait. Les Flamands sont las de payer pour des guerres incessantes et leur sang leur paraît plus précieux encore. Le duc est reparti alors pour Calais afin d'y joindre son beau-frère [1], lequel, il faut bien le dire, a été fort déçu de le voir déboucher à la tête d'une mince escorte de cinquante hommes alors qu'il escomptait une armée pour l'aider à envahir la France ! Avec une parfaite mauvaise foi d'ailleurs, le Téméraire a contre-attaqué en prétendant qu'Édouard n'avait rien compris, qu'il aurait dû débarquer en Normandie pour faire sa jonction avec le duc de Bretagne, que son armée à lui était en Luxembourg et allait annexer la Lorraine. Et il a même proposé un nouveau rendez-vous : que les Anglais entrent en Champagne et, lui-même venant de Lorraine, ils se rejoindraient à Reims où l'on ferait couronner Édouard roi de France !

— C'est insensé !

— Pas vraiment, mais c'était compter sans le roi Louis. Et le roi Louis, outre sa belle armée, possède une chose que n'a aucun de ses ennemis : son génie. C'est sur ce génie que nous, gens de Paris, comptons, plus que sur les armes, pour vaincre la coalition. Il se dresse entre nous et l'armée anglaise et je le crois capable de brouiller le Téméraire avec Édouard...

— Où est-il en ce moment ? demanda Fiora.

— A Compiègne où il a établi son quartier général.

— Et... L'armée est puissante ?

— Cinquante mille hommes environ, un peu moins du

---

1. Le Téméraire avait épousé Marguerite d'York, sœur d'Édouard.

double de l'armée anglaise, mais le roi est fort ménager du sang de ses soldats. Il préfère payer, ruser, enjôler plutôt que de livrer bataille...

— Est-il donc lâche ? fit dédaigneusement Fiora.

— Aucunement et il en a fourni des preuves, croyez-moi. Oh, certes, il livrera bataille si c'est la seule chance qui lui reste de défendre Paris mais il espère bien ne pas aller jusque-là.

— De toute façon, si son armée est la plus forte...

— Elle ne le serait pas contre les Anglais alliés aux Bourguignons... et à la Bretagne car le duc breton, s'il voyait le roi en mauvaise position, se hâterait de le frapper dans le dos. Il a toujours été un ami des Anglais...

Tout en causant, Agnolo était venu à bout de son porcelet et chacun étant servi, le seul bruit des mâchoires remplaça un moment celui de la conversation. Comme les autres, Fiora mangeait avec plaisir, heureuse de retrouver des saveurs de son pays mais son appétit se ralentit bientôt. Elle reposa son couteau, essuya ses doigts, et dans le silence demanda :

— C'est loin, Compiègne ?

— Un peu plus de vingt lieues, répondit Agnolo.

— Ah !...

Elle n'en dit pas plus mais Démétrios comprit qu'elle se livrait à un petit calcul mental. Trente moins vingt, cela fait dix, et dix lieues ne sont pas grand-chose pour un bon cheval. Pour prévenir une nouvelle désillusion il reprit, se tournant vers le maître du logis :

— Vous disiez que le Téméraire n'avait qu'une cinquantaine d'hommes avec lui, en arrivant à Calais ?

— Oui. Le gros de l'armée est resté à la limite de la Lorraine et du Luxembourg, aux ordres du maréchal de Luxembourg et du comte de Campobasso, un condottiere napolitain, transfuge de l'armée lorraine et que le duc Charles s'est attaché depuis deux ans...

— Transfuge... doux euphémisme ! Cela veut dire traître ? demanda Esteban avec une nuance de mépris qui fit sourire Fiora.

– En quelque sorte, mais pas exactement. Vous qui venez de Toscane, vous devriez savoir qu'un condottiere est plus lié par l'argent que par la foi jurée... Tant qu'on le paie, il marche !

On se leva de table et Agnolo vint prendre le bras de Démétrios :

– Vous souhaitez, je pense, rejoindre rapidement le roi Louis ?

– Sans doute, bien qu'il soit peut-être un peu trop occupé...

– Pour recevoir un habile médecin ? Je puis vous assurer d'une chose : c'est qu'il vous attend et avec impatience.

– Il m'attend ?

– Bien sûr. Vous avez été annoncé là-bas aussi.

– Alors nous partons demain, s'écria Fiora dont un flux de sang venait de rougir soudain les pommettes.

– La place d'une jeune dame, et même d'une dame tout court, n'est pas dans un camp, dit Agnelle. Je serais si heureuse de vous garder quelque temps ici ! Juste le temps de voir comment les choses vont tourner. Notre roi est tout à fait capable d'éviter la guerre mais, pour l'instant, il y a trop de soldats...

– C'est que... nous ne nous sommes jamais séparés !

– La séparation ne sera pas bien longue. Compiègne n'est pas si loin. En outre, le roi serait peut-être mécontent de voir arriver une femme...

– Deux femmes ! rectifia Léonarde. Je ne quitte jamais donna Fiora...

– Agnelle a raison, fit son époux arrivant à la rescousse. Les seules femmes que l'on trouve au camp sont les ribaudes que toute armée traîne après elle. Vous serez mieux ici...

Fiora ne broncha pas : elle n'était pas convaincue. D'ailleurs comment dire à ces braves gens qu'elle avait conclu avec Démétrios le pacte du sang en vue d'abattre à eux deux le grand duc d'Occident ? A Compiègne les deux justiciers se rapprocheraient de leur but et ce qu'elle venait d'apprendre fortifiait la jeune femme dans sa décision. Tuer le Téméraire serait accomplir infiniment plus qu'une vengeance, ce serait sauver Paris, sauver la France du grave danger que représenterait pour elle la jonction des armées anglaises et bourguignonnes. La pensée d'atteindre du même coup Philippe qui, peut-être, accompagnait son duc ne fit que l'effleurer et elle la repoussa avec colère comme importune, la haine comme la passion étant de mauvaises conseillères. Fiora, à cet instant, croyait naïvement haïr Philippe presque autant qu'elle l'avait aimé...

Au matin d'une nuit peu reposante car elle ne dormit guère, Fiora en s'éveillant trouva la chambre vide mais se rappela que Léonarde avait, la veille, demandé à leur hôtesse l'heure de la première messe à l'église voisine. Elle se leva, fit une toilette rapide, le bain de la veille permettant d'écourter les ablutions. Elle en était à hésiter sur ce qu'elle allait revêtir quand un brouhaha de cris et de paroles volubiles l'attira à la fenêtre. Ce qu'elle vit l'épouvanta : un groupe d'hommes portait vers la maison une Léonarde gémissant à fendre l'âme. Fiora alors se jeta sur la première robe qui lui tomba sous la main et, tout en la laçant, se précipita dans l'escalier. Elle arriva juste à temps pour voir le cortège franchir le seuil de la maison.

— N'ayez pas peur ! lui cria Agnelle qui soutenait la tête de Léonarde, elle n'est pas en danger mais je crois qu'elle a une jambe cassée.

— Comment est-ce arrivé ?

— Bêtement, comme toujours en pareil cas : en sortant de l'église, elle a glissé sur le pavé et sa jambe est venue cogner contre la roue d'un tombereau. Elle souffre beaucoup.

La pauvre Léonarde était, en effet, aussi blanche qu'une feuille de papier et de grosses larmes roulaient lentement sans qu'elle pût les retenir. Elle s'accrocha désespérément à la main de Démétrios qui, alors occupé à boucler ses sacoches, était accouru au bruit :

— Vous n'allez pas me couper la jambe, n'est-ce pas ? supplia-t-elle. Vous n'allez pas faire de moi une infirme ?...

— Calmez-vous, je vous en prie. Nous n'en sommes pas là... Il faut que j'examine votre pied.

— Mais vous deviez partir ?

— Je partirai plus tard et voilà tout ! Le roi m'attend depuis assez longtemps déjà. Un peu plus, un peu moins... Vous n'imaginez pas que je vais vous laisser dans cet état ?

On porta Léonarde sur le lit qu'elle partageait avec Fiora. Démétrios jeta à celle-ci un regard rapide :

— Tu vas m'aider. Il faut au préalable la déchausser...

Le pied formait avec la jambe un angle anormal et apparemment très douloureux. Retirer le soulier fut relativement facile, mais il fallut couper le bas blanc taché de sang qu'une mince esquille d'os transperçait. La blessure était mince et saignait peu :

— Le pied n'est que déboîté, diagnostiqua le médecin après avoir promené des doigts agiles sur les os, mais il y a fracture ouverte. Et très douloureuse. Pouvez-vous, dame Agnelle, installer ici même une table recouverte d'un drap...

— Bien sûr. Tout ce que vous voudrez... Je ferai aussi apporter des éclisses de bois doux et des bandes de linge fin...

— Pardieu, c'est une bénédiction d'être malade chez vous, fit Démétrios avec un sourire, car vous en savez plus que beaucoup de nos étudiants. Soyez assez bonne de joindre à tout cela une écuelle pleine de farine, de l'eau... et mon serviteur si vous le trouvez. Il devrait être à l'écurie...

Agnelle disparut comme un petit nuage doré pour s'en revenir peu après avec la moitié de ses servantes et Esteban, tout ce monde chargé de tréteaux, de planches et d'une foule d'objets utilitaires et variés. Pendant ce temps, le Grec avait trouvé dans ses bagages à peu près tout ce dont il allait avoir besoin. Grâce à la princière générosité du Magnifique et aux richesses de son jardin de Fiesole, il possédait un fonds de pharmacopée ambulante qui n'eût pas trouvé certainement son équivalent dans le vieil Hôtel-Dieu parisien dont les vénérables murailles s'élevaient, grises et mélancoliques, auprès de Notre-Dame.

La blessée dont la main tremblante demeurait accrochée à celle de Fiora fut étendue sur la table, la tête soutenue par des oreillers. Elle tremblait de peur autant que de souffrance en dépit des paroles douces et des encouragements que lui procurait la jeune femme. Aussi avala-t-elle avec reconnaissance les deux cuillerées d'opiat au miel que Démétrios lui fit ingurgiter et qui apaisèrent un peu sa douleur. Mais quand le médecin, d'un geste sec et précis, remit son pied en place, elle poussa un cri aigu et s'évanouit...

— C'est ce qui pouvait lui arriver de mieux, fit celui-ci. Profitons-en !

Tandis que deux solides servantes maintenaient Léonarde aux épaules et qu'Esteban se couchait pratiquement sur le milieu de son corps, Démétrios après avoir nettoyé la blessure étira longuement, fermement, la jambe blessée jusqu'à ce que l'os ait repris sa place... Après quoi, avec les attelles et de longues bandes de toile fine qu'il trempait dans de la farine étendue d'eau, il confectionna un appareil qui maintint fermement le membre lésé, au bout duquel il attacha une grosse pierre après que l'infortunée Léonarde eut été ramenée dans son lit. Pendant toute l'opération, la pauvre femme s'était réveillée et réévanouie par deux fois mais, quand tout fut fini, elle s'endormit d'un profond sommeil après avoir absorbé une nouvelle dose d'opiat...

— Vous ne pouvez continuer à partager ce lit, dit Agnelle à Fiora. Je vais en faire monter un autre...

— Donnez-lui ma chambre, fit Démétrios. Je dormirai à l'écurie avec mon serviteur. Pour une nuit...

— Tu penses partir tout de même ? s'enquit Fiora alarmée à l'idée de se séparer de ce solide compagnon...

— Si la nuit a été bonne, je n'aurai aucune raison de rester. Il faudra laisser la nature faire son ouvrage comme elle l'entend.

— Et elle mettra combien de temps à le faire, cet ouvrage ?

— Six semaines environ. Mais rassure-toi, ajouta-t-il en voyant s'allonger le fin visage, je reviendrai avant. Dès que j'aurai soigné le roi, il me laissera sans doute m'éloigner.

— N'y comptez pas trop ! lança Agnolo qui revenait de chez un client à cet instant. Si vous plaisez à notre sire, il ne vous lâchera pas si facilement...

— Je lui expliquerai. Mais, à ce propos, maître Agnolo, vous me semblez bien au fait des habitudes comme de la politique du roi ?

— ... et vous êtes surpris, n'est-ce pas, qu'un simple marchand, étranger de surcroît, vous tienne des discours qu'on attendrait plutôt d'un proche du monarque ?

— Cela ne m'étonnerait pas outre mesure à Florence où chacun se mêle plus ou moins des affaires de l'État mais dans un royaume qui semble gouverné de main de maître...

— Et qui l'est, soyez-en certain. Mais faisons donc quelques pas au jardin, nous y serons au calme et ce sera plus agréable...

En passant auprès de la cuisine, le négociant ordonna à une servante de leur porter du vin frais sous la tonnelle d'aristoloche et de chèvrefeuille qui était l'un des attraits du jardin, l'autre étant les massifs de rosiers auxquels Florent prodiguait des soins de père. Il était justement occupé à couper des fleurs fânées quand les deux hommes pénétrèrent sur son territoire.

— Je vais finir par t'envoyer à mon clos de Suresnes, soupira Nardi. Tu passes dans ce jardin bien plus de temps que devant ton pupitre...

— Cela tient, messire, à ce que j'aime à m'occuper de fleurs beaucoup plus que d'écritures...

— Et que dira ton père ? Il ne t'a pas placé chez moi pour que tu deviennes mon jardinier...

— J'en apprends bien assez pendant la mauvaise saison. Et je suis tellement plus heureux comme cela...

D'un geste affectueux, Agnolo ébouriffa les cheveux du garçon qui n'étaient déjà pas tellement disciplinés :

— Nous verrons cela plus tard. Pour l'instant, fais-moi la grâce d'aller travailler un peu à tes devoirs. Nous avons à parler, ce seigneur et moi.

Florent obéit sur-le-champ et les deux hommes commencèrent à marcher lentement le long des allées sablées où ne se hasardait pas à pousser la moindre mauvaise herbe...

— Contrairement à son père, le défunt roi Charles VII dont Dieu ait l'âme, notre sire Louis fait sa compagnie la plus habituelle et une partie de son conseil de gens comme moi, bourgeois qui sont à même de lui donner l'image véridique de ce que sont les affaires commerciales du pays et de ce qui se passe dans nos villes. Je suis l'un des premiers parmi les marchands étrangers résidant à Paris. J'ai hérité aussi quelque peu de l'amitié que le roi portait à notre pauvre Francesco Beltrami. Il le connaissait bien et il est arrivé que, sur le plan de la banque, Beltrami rendît service au roi de France, en proportions plus modestes que les Médicis, sans doute, mais il n'a jamais eu à le regretter. Moi non plus.

Le vin arrivait, porté par Jeanneton, la plus jeune des servantes de la maison. Elle en emplit deux gobelets qu'elle offrit à chacun des deux hommes puis disparut. La chaleur commençait à se faire sentir et des abeilles bourdonnaient dans le chèvrefeuille. Mais sous la tonnelle il faisait plus frais... Agnolo but une bonne rasade, s'essuya la bouche à la serviette posée sur le plateau et reprit :

— Je n'ai jamais été élevé au rang de conseiller comme mon compère Jean de Paris, mais il est arrivé que l'on me confie quelques missions en accord avec les déplacements qu'implique mon négoce. En outre, j'ai eu l'honneur d'accompagner messire Louis de Marrazin et mon ami Jean de Paris quand, l'an passé, ils se sont rendus auprès de Mgr le duc René II de Lorraine pour rétablir avec lui l'ancien traité d'amitié que le duc de Bourgogne l'avait obligé à rompre...

– Obligé ? Comment cela ?

– Le duc René est jeune – vingt-quatre ans – et très inexpérimenté. Le Téméraire le nomme dédaigneusement « l'enfant », mais c'est un prince aimable et plein de courage qui n'était d'ailleurs pas destiné à régner sur la Lorraine. Seule la mort prématurée de son cousin, le duc Nicolas, il y a trois ans, lui a octroyé la couronne et le roi Louis a tout de suite signé avec lui un traité d'amitié que le Téméraire, il va de soi, n'a pas pu supporter...

– Quels moyens a-t-il employés pour obliger le jeune duc à renier son alliance ?

– Oh, c'était assez facile avec un garçon droit et honnête. Ferry de Vaudémont, son père, et même Yolande d'Anjou, sa mère, devaient beaucoup au duc Philippe, père du Téméraire. Charles a rappelé à René les vieilles créances et René s'est laissé circonvenir. Mais il s'est vite aperçu de ce que pesait l'alliance du grand duc d'Occident. Il a dû laisser à son dangereux allié quatre de ses villes : Épinal, Darney, Preny et Neufchâteau, avec pouvoir d'y tenir garnison et de nommer les gouverneurs. C'était mettre la Lorraine sous la poigne du Bourguignon – et Dieu sait s'il l'a rude ! Les cités gagées en ont crié vers le ciel sans pouvoir se libérer. Quand, après le siège de Neuss dont le Téméraire n'est pas venu à bout, ses troupes ont marché sur le Luxembourg et sur Thionville, le duc René a fait alliance avec les cantons suisses qui avaient, eux aussi, à se plaindre et qui, avec les Alsaciens, tout juste libérés du Landvogt Pierre de Hagenbach, favori du Téméraire, sont entrés dans la Comté Franche. René II était mûr à point pour tomber dans les mains du roi Louis et nul ne s'entend mieux que celui-ci à cueillir les fruits soignés par d'autres...

— Je vois. Que va-t-il se passer à présent ?

— Cela, je n'en sais rien. Vous en apprendrez peut-être davantage au camp de Compiègne ?

— J'espérais que vous me conduiriez. Vous seriez, pour l'étranger que je suis, une bonne introduction...

— Vous n'en avez nul besoin. Quant au chemin, je vous donnerai demain le jeune Florent. Il connaît parfaitement la région et vous mènera à bon port. Je dois, quant à moi, rester ici car demain, à la Maison aux Piliers, messire Robert d'Estouteville, prévôt de Paris, réunit les chefs de corporations et les principaux bourgeois pour délibérer de l'aide qu'ils pourraient apporter au cas où notre cité serait assiégée...

— Un conseil de guerre ? La situation serait-elle plus grave que vous ne l'avez laissé entendre ?

— En aucune façon et je ne vous ai rien caché, de ce que je sais tout au moins, mais un vieil axiome latin enseigne : *Si vis pacem para bellum* — Si tu veux la paix, prépare la guerre. C'est exactement ce que nous allons faire.

Agnolo Nardi et Démétrios devisèrent encore de longues minutes sous la tonnelle du jardin, tout en dégustant leur vin. C'était l'un de ces instants précieux où les hommes venus d'horizons différents s'entendent et se comprennent et où l'existence paraît plus précieuse. Tout était calme dans la maison de la rue des Lombards. Agnelle aidée de Fiora rangeait les pièces d'une lessive nouvellement repassée, Léonarde dormait, toute douleur ensevelie dans le sommeil. Esteban en faisait autant sur la paille de l'écurie et, dans les bureaux du négociant, chacun vaquait à sa besogne : les plumes d'oie grinçaient presque en mesure sur les grands livres reliés de parchemin. Seul, Florent rêvait. Assis sur une marche de l'escalier, il regardait Fiora qui, tout en bavardant, passait à son hôtesse les piles de nappes et de serviettes que celle-ci serrait dans les coffres de la grande salle. Vêtue d'une simple robe de lin blanc bordée d'une mince guirlande de feuilles vertes que Chrétiennotte lui avait confectionnée à

Dijon, la masse lustrée de ses cheveux noirs tordue en une simple natte retombant sur une épaule, elle ressemblait plus que jamais à la princesse de quelque fabliau et le jeune homme la dévorait des yeux. Sans d'ailleurs qu'elle s'en aperçût. Ce fut Agnelle qui remarqua le regard gourmand du garçon et s'en montra irritée :

— N'as-tu rien d'autre à faire qu'à rester assis à bâiller aux corneilles ? Je te croyais au jardin ?

Florent se releva avec une mauvaise volonté évidente et grogna.

— Maître Agnolo y est avec le grand homme noir et m'a signifié de rentrer.

— Sans nul doute avec l'idée de t'envoyer travailler ! Va te laver les mains et te coiffer et puis retourne à ton pupitre. Je commence à regretter de t'avoir confié le jardin...

Florent partit en direction de la cuisine, se tordant le cou pour voir un peu plus longtemps celle qu'il nommait intérieurement sa « belle dame ». Agnelle hocha la tête, haussa les épaules avec un brin de commisération et revint à sa tâche :

— Ce garçon est assotté de vous, ma mie. J'ai bien peur qu'il ne soit plus bon à rien.

— Il m'oubliera dès qu'il ne me verra plus ! Malheureusement la jambe de ma bonne Léonarde va me retenir ici encore quelque temps et nous n'avons pas fini de vous encombrer.

— M'encombrer ? Doux Jésus ! C'est un vrai plaisir de vous avoir et je suis ravie de pouvoir profiter plus longtemps de votre présence. Sans cet accident déplorable, vous partiez ce matin, n'est-ce pas ?

— Oui. Messire Lascaris m'est très proche et nous ne nous séparons jamais. Il a pris pour ainsi dire la place de mon cher père dont le souvenir ne me quitte pas.

— Assurément, mais ne serait-ce pas plutôt à un époux de combler ce vide ? Si jeune, si belle, vous n'êtes pas faite pour courir les grands chemins. Quelque seigneur saura bien, un jour, conquérir votre cœur ?...

— Je ne le crois pas et d'ailleurs je ne le souhaite nullement. L'amour cause plus de blessures qu'il n'apporte de joie. Demandez à ce jeune Florent.

— J'ai grande envie de l'expédier à Suresnes pour lui changer les idées. J'en parlerai ce soir à mon époux...

Mais elle n'eut pas besoin d'en parler, l'état de Léonarde se révélant tout à fait satisfaisant, Démétrios et Esteban prirent dès le lendemain matin congé de la maison Nardi. Et Florent fut chargé de les conduire a Compiègne.

Non sans regrets! Quand vint l'heure du départ, le garçon exhibait des yeux rougis par l'insomnie plus encore que par les larmes. En enfourchant sa mule il enveloppa Fiora d'un regard pitoyable... que la jeune femme ne soupçonna même pas, tout occupée qu'elle était à tenter d'analyser ses propres sentiments. Une chose était certaine : elle avait le cœur gros de voir Démétrios partir sans elle. Sans doute parce qu'il allait se rapprocher assez près de ce duc de Bourgogne dont l'empreinte avait pesé si lourdement sur sa vie mais aussi parce que au fil des jours elle s'était attachée plus qu'elle n'aurait cru à cet homme savant, silencieux et peu communicatif qui était survenu à ses côtés à l'instant où elle désespérait le plus de tout secours humain.

L'idée qu'il pût poursuivre seul sa vengeance ne l'effleurait même pas. Elle savait qu'elle entrait pour une certaine part dans les desseins du Grec mais elle n'ignorait pas non plus que le destin prend parfois un malin plaisir à se mettre en travers des projets les mieux conçus, les plus solidement établis. Il fallait espérer que Démétrios reviendrait au plus vite.

Léonarde, pour sa part, était désolée d'être à l'origine de cette séparation mais elle pensait tout de même secrètement que la volonté de Dieu y avait été pour quelque chose : elle le priait si fort de détourner son « agneau » d'un projet homicide qui avait beaucoup de chance de la jeter entre les mains du bourreau.

— Vous auriez dû partir sans moi ! soupirait-elle avec un rien d'hypocrisie...

— Et vous abandonner ici, seule dans une ville et une maison que vous ne connaissez pas ? Si charmants que soient dame Agnelle et son époux, ils n'en sont pas moins des étrangers. Cessez donc de vous tourmenter et songez seulement à guérir ! Où pourriez-vous être mieux soignée qu'ici ?

En fait, Léonarde était surtout vexée d'avoir été blessée en sortant d'une église. D'autant que l'église en question ne lui inspirait pas une confiance absolue. En effet, elle avait pu constater, comme elle l'expliqua tout en rougissant à Fiora, que les filles publiques semblaient se donner rendez-vous autour de Saint-Merri qui était en quelque sorte leur paroisse. Il n'en fallait pas plus pour que la vieille demoiselle en vînt à concevoir les pires soupçons touchant un saint qui tolérait une pareille promiscuité.

Agnelle à qui Fiora conta l'affaire s'en amusa franchement :

— Ce n'est pourtant pas faute, pour les curés de cette pauvre église, d'avoir protesté au cours des siècles avec des fortunes diverses. Mais, que voulez-vous, mesdames les ribaudes forment de nos jours une véritable corporation, reconnue, qui a ses règlements, ses juges, ses statuts, ses privilèges et qui même, pour la fête de sa sainte patronne, sainte Madeleine, qui a lieu le 22 de juillet, a droit de mener procession. Et une belle procession, croyez-moi, avec riches bannières, nuages d'encens et luminaire généreux...

— Mais alors pourquoi Saint-Merri ?

— Simple question de voisinage : deux des neuf rues de Paris où les ribaudes ont droit de tenir commerce, la rue Brisemiche et la Court-Robert, sont contiguës à l'église. Est-ce que cela vous ennuierait d'aller y entendre la sainte messe dimanche ? ajouta-t-elle plus sérieusement.

Fiora faillit répondre qu'elle avait perdu l'habitude de ses devoirs dominicaux mais craignit, par excès de franchise, de froisser son aimable hôtesse. D'autre part, au désagréable souvenir de son passage chez Pippa, elle ressentit un peu de gêne. Que dirait cette douce, claire et généreuse Agnelle, si elle apprenait cet épisode avilissant qui souillait la vie de celle qu'elle traitait comme une jeune sœur ? Aussi Fiora se hâta-t-elle de la rassurer : elle entendrait la messe du dimanche là où il plairait à Agnelle...

Néanmoins, pour être bien certaine de ne pas froisser la pudeur de celle en qui tout dénotait une noble et pure jeune fille, l'épouse d'Agnolo décida que l'on irait ouïr office à Notre-Dame de Paris et Florent, rentré la veille de Compiègne où il avait tout juste pris le temps de déposer Démétrios et Esteban au logis du roi, reçut l'ordre de préparer des mules afin d'accompagner les dames. Avec l'enthousiasme que l'on imagine !

Le dimanche matin, qui était le 15 août, on se mit en route sous un ciel sans nuages que les hirondelles, rapides et à peine visibles tant elles volaient haut, traversaient comme des flèches noires. Le vacarme des cloches annonçant les offices avait remplacé le tintamarre habituel de la grande cité où, en semaine, on était réveillé, tôt le matin, par le claquement des volets que les marchands rabattaient en ouvrant leurs échoppes et par les cris des garçons d'étuves annonçant que les bains étaient chauds... Pas davantage de ces encombrements rendus inévitables par l'étroitesse et les détours des rues. Les voix fraîches ou puissantes des marchandes de la Halle qui, paniers au bras ou escortées d'un âne, vantaient au chaland le beurre de Vanves, le cresson d'Orléans, les échalotes d'Étampes, l'ail de Gandelu, les oignons de Bourgueil, les œufs de Beauce, les fromages de Brie ou de Champagne, s'étaient tues elles aussi. On ne rencontrait que gens vêtus de leurs plus beaux atours avec lesquels on échangeait un salut ou quelques mots. Certains s'étonnaient de voir Agnelle sans son Agnolo qui, en chrétien scrupuleux, ne manquait jamais l'office du dimanche et il fallut répéter tant de fois que maître Nardi était souffrant que l'on faillit arriver en retard.

— Ne saurait-on vraiment manquer un office religieux sans en donner la raison à toute la ville ? fit Agnelle d'un ton mécontent. Et j'imagine que l'on va par la même occasion se demander pourquoi nous allons à Notre-Dame plutôt qu'à Saint-Merri ?

— Vous voyez bien ! Vous n'auriez rien dû changer pour moi à vos habitudes...

— Mais il m'arrive assez souvent de me rendre à la cathédrale ! C'est si beau ! Et puis c'est aujourd'hui l'Assomption !

Fiora, qui avait refusé d'accompagner Léonarde au jour de leur arrivée dans sa visite de bienvenue, le regretta en pénétrant dans l'immense nef toute rayonnante de centaines de cierges. Il y avait beaucoup de monde autour du maître-autel derrière lequel s'étageaient les châsses et les reliquaires d'or de nombreux saints, mais Agnelle et sa compagne purent trouver place dans les premiers rangs d'une foule que la magie des vitraux jointe à l'éclat du soleil colorait diversement. Et les yeux émerveillés de la Florentine, cependant habitués à la beauté des édifices sacrés, allaient de ces hautes ogives flamboyantes à la grande rosace scintillante au-dessus du portail d'entrée.

Tout le clergé était dans le chœur, en habits rouge et or, entourant le haut siège où avait pris place un hôte de marque : l'aimable cardinal de Bourbon, cousin du roi et primat des Gaules, qui étalait les moires pourpres de sa simarre sous le dais décoré à ses armes sommées d'un chapeau cardinalice. Auprès de sa splendeur, l'évêque de Paris [1] semblait insignifiant...

— Nous avons de la chance, souffla Agnelle. Son Éminence n'est pas souvent à Paris l'été. C'est la période où elle se rend plus volontiers dans sa ville archiépiscopale de Lyon mais le roi a dû l'envoyer pour rassurer les Pari-

---

1. C'est seulement sous Louis XIV que Paris devint archevêché. Il dépendait auparavant de l'archevêque de Sens.

siens. Il appartient en effet aux deux partis en présence : son frère Pierre de Beaujeu ayant épousé il y a deux ans la fille aînée du roi et, par sa mère Agnès de Bourgogne, il est allié aussi au Téméraire. Ce qui, on le conçoit aisément, ne lui facilite pas toujours la vie...

— Chut ! souffla quelqu'un et Agnelle, confuse, opta de cacher son visage dans ses mains pour s'abîmer dans la prière.

Le cardinal d'ailleurs s'était levé et, de sa voix nonchalante de grand seigneur désabusé, adressait quelques mots au peuple de Paris, l'exhortant à garder confiance dans le Seigneur, dans la sagesse de son souverain et dans la solidité de ses murailles. Il l'assura aussi de ses prières et de son soutien en toutes choses. Après quoi, au milieu d'épais nuages d'encens, la messe commença par le chant du *Veni Creator*... Mais Fiora ne voyait plus rien : ni l'imposante silhouette de Mgr de Bourbon, ni les aubes de dentelle, ni les chasubles d'or qui se mouvaient dans le léger brouillard montant des encensoirs de bronze. Ce qu'elle voyait, c'était, agenouillée dans l'une des stalles du chapitre, une robe de moine blanche à demi recouverte d'un scapulaire noir, c'était un crâne en forme de dôme dont la peau olivâtre luisait dans la lumière, c'étaient deux grandes mains sèches dissimulant un visage qu'elle redouta d'apercevoir... Son cœur se mit à battre dans sa poitrine en pulsations plus rapides qui lui montaient à la gorge. Elle essaya de se raisonner, de se persuader qu'elle se trompait et que ce qu'elle croyait voir était impossible... Mais, soudain, le moine laissa retomber ses mains et tourna vers l'autel, en pleine lumière, le grand nez, la bouche serrée et les lourdes paupières de Fray Ignacio Ortega...

Une vague nausée souleva l'estomac de la jeune femme dont les yeux se voilèrent un instant mais, au prix d'un violent effort, elle réussit à surmonter son malaise. Si elle en venait à défaillir, le remous qu'elle créerait attirerait sur elle bien des attentions dont, certainement, celle de son ennemi. Elle se contenta de tirer plus bas sur son visage le voile qui recouvrait le joli hennin de soie blanche, cadeau d'Agnelle qu'elle étrennait ce matin.

Naturellement, elle n'entendit rien, ne vit rien de la grand-messe qui se déroulait sous ses yeux. Les admirables voix des chantres ne représentaient rien d'autre pour elle qu'une rumeur d'orage et une seule pensée occupait son esprit : que faisait à Notre-Dame, au cœur de la France, le dominicain espagnol que le pape Sixte IV avait naguère envoyé à Florence pour tenter de saper la puissance des Médicis ? Aux dernières nouvelles qu'elle en avait eues, Fray Ignacio, ses machinations déjouées, avait été reconduit jusqu'à mi-chemin de Rome par les soldats du Magnifique, et, cependant, il était là, à quelques pas de celle qu'il avait si cruellement persécutée. Pourquoi ? Dans quel but ? Était-ce sa trace à elle qu'il cherchait ?

Fiora secoua la tête comme pour en chasser l'obsédante pensée. Il n'y avait aucune raison pour que le moine sût sa présence à Paris mais, s'il y était venu, on pouvait parier que ce n'était certainement pas pour y accomplir un pèlerinage ou n'importe quelle œuvre pie... Néanmoins, elle frémit quand les yeux de basilic, se tournant vers les fidèles, passèrent sur l'endroit où elle se tenait.

Après que l'Élévation eut courbé toutes les têtes sous le rayonnement de la blanche ostie, Fiora toucha le coude de son amie.

— Ne bougez surtout pas, Agnelle, mais je vais sortir... le plus discrètement que je pourrai...

— Vous n'êtes pas bien ?

— Pas très. J'ai besoin d'air. Ce doit être tout cet encens...

— Nous allons sortir ensemble alors ?

— Non... je vous en prie : restez et suivez la fin de l'office. Je vais rejoindre Florent. Je reviendrai si je me sens mieux...

Il fallait, en effet, échapper à tout prix au danger que pouvait lui faire courir la Communion – à laquelle d'ailleurs elle n'était nullement préparée ne s'étant pas confessée depuis des mois. Qu'elle s'approchât de l'autel pour recevoir le sacrement ou qu'elle demeurât à sa place, mais alors en plein isolement, elle risquait de se faire remarquer. Fray Ignacio avait la vue perçante et, de toute façon, on devait lever son voile pour recevoir l'ostie. Mieux vallait partir au plus vite...

Profitant de ce que tout le monde était debout, elle se glissa dans la foule en appuyant un mouchoir sur sa bouche comme quelqu'un qui se sent mal et on lui fit place. En franchissant les portes rouges ornées de grandes volutes de fer forgé, elle sentit son cœur se desserrer et aspira à pleins poumons l'air doux du matin. Mais la cohorte de mendiants qui assiégeaient toujours la cathédrale aux grandes cérémonies accourut, et elle eut toutes les peines du monde à s'en débarrasser. Avec gentillesse d'ailleurs car elle gardait le souvenir de Bernardino, le mendiant qui l'avait accueillie une terrible nuit dans un palais inachevé. Elle eut le temps d'un éclair, l'envie de prononcer le mot dont il lui avait dit qu'il était compris de tous ses semblables en pays latins : « Mendici ! » — mais c'était là un mot de passe, une sorte d'appel à l'aide dont elle n'avait pas le droit de jouer.

Sa bourse vidée, elle voulut rejoindre Florent qui devait attendre les dames assis auprès de ses mules sur le montoir à chevaux d'un vieil hôtel. Elle l'aperçut en effet mais, tout à coup, une grande joie l'envahit : Florent n'était pas assis mais debout et bavardait avec Esteban.

Elle courut vers le Castillan comme vers un ami perdu que l'on retrouve sans se soucier de perturber l'équilibre de sa coiffure :

— Esteban ! Vous êtes là ?... Alors Démétrios est revenu ?

— Non, il est resté là-bas. Je suis rentré en escortant un seigneur conseiller du roi qui veut vous parler. Mais que vous arrive-t-il, donna Fiora ? Vous semblez bouleversée...

— Il y a de quoi.

Et, tirant Esteban à part sans prendre garde à la mine

assombrie de Florent, elle lui expliqua rapidement ce qui venait de lui arriver. L'écuyer-secrétaire fronça ses épais sourcils :

— Êtes-vous persuadée de ne pas vous tromper ?

— Tout à fait sûre, Esteban, n'en doutez pas. C'est lui ! Comment pourrais-je jamais oublier sa figure ? Mais que vient-il faire ici ? Il ne peut pas savoir que nous sommes à Paris ?

— Si vous voulez mon avis, je pense que nous devons être bien éloignés de son esprit mais il n'en est pas moins urgent de savoir ce qu'il trame ici. Je jurerais qu'il s'intéresse à quelqu'un dans ce pays et, tel qu'on le connaît, ce n'est certainement pas par charité chrétienne...

— Que pouvons-nous faire ?

— Vous, rien. Ce vieux démon serait trop content de remettre sa griffe sur vous. Moi, je vais voir. Où est-il placé dans l'église ?

Elle le lui expliqua. Esteban s'élança alors vers la cathédrale mais, sans cesser de courir, se retourna :

— Quand dame Agnelle vous aura rejoints, rentrez à la maison ! Ne m'attendez pas !...

Fiora le vit traverser les groupes de mendiants et de bateleurs qui se préparaient pour la sortie de la messe et disparaître. Elle vint rejoindre Florent qui, l'air offensé, fit toute une affaire de vérifier les brides rouge et or des mules, mais la jeune femme était trop soulagée pour y prêter la moindre attention. Elle s'assit sur le montoir à chevaux, remit en place le hennin auquel elle n'était pas habituée et dont les épingles lui tiraient les cheveux, puis sortit son mouchoir pour s'en éventer. Encore plus vexé par tant d'indifférence, Florent marmotta, l'œil sombre :

— Vous ne prêtez vraiment aucune attention à moi, n'est-ce pas ?

— Pourquoi ? Je le devrais ?

— Non... non, vous avez raison. Je ne mérite vraiment pas que vous vous intéressiez à mon sort. Que suis-je pour vous ? Rien... moins que rien... Je mourrais à vos pieds que vous ne m'accorderiez pas même un regard...

La volée de cloches qui annonçait la sortie de la messe couvrit ses paroles. Occupée de ses propres soucis, Fiora les avait à peine perçues. Sans un regard pour le jeune homme qui en grinça des dents, elle se leva pour aller au-devant d'Agnelle dont elle apercevait déjà le voile couleur de miel...

CHAPITRE VI

LE SIRE D'ARGENTON

Les cloches sonnaient toujours à la volée pour la plus grande gloire de la Vierge Marie, quand Agnelle et Fiora pénétrèrent dans la salle où l'on achevait de dresser le couvert. Agnolo, apparemment en excellent état, s'y entretenait avec un visiteur, assis tous deux sur une bancelle garnie de coussins en buvant du vin aux herbes dont la fraîcheur embuait leurs gobelets d'étain. A l'entrée des dames tous deux se levèrent et Fiora vit que l'inconnu était un homme jeune – il n'avait certainement pas trente ans – de taille moyenne mais bien prise dans une hucque violette dont les larges manches dentelées tombaient à la hauteur des genoux, les chausses collantes assorties révélant des jambes élégantes. Une large chaîne d'or pendait sur sa poitrine. Les bottes longues et souples étaient poussiéreuses comme il est naturel après une chevauchée. Sur tout cela s'érigeait un visage aimable aux yeux bleus bien fendus, à la bouche charnue, nettement dessinée et volontiers narquoise, au long nez dont les narines sensibles semblaient animées d'une vie propre : des plis profonds partant des ailes du nez rejoignaient presque les maxillaires. Les cheveux d'un blond foncé, très épais encadraient cette figure qui respirait la finesse et l'intelligence. L'inconnu salua les deux femmes avec une aisance toute seigneuriale, à peine plus appuyée pour Fiora qu'il fixa un instant, sourcils relevés, sans même songer à dissimuler son admiration.

— Donna Fiora Beltrami, je suppose ? fit-il avec un demi-sourire.

Sa voix bien timbrée mais souple et caressante aurait pu être celle d'un chanteur et il était évident que l'inconnu savait en jouer avec charme...

— Vous ne vous trompez pas, messire, dit Agnolo, et voici mon épouse, dame Agnelle. Souffrez que je vous présente à elles : voici, chères dames, le conseiller le plus écouté de notre sire le roi, messire Philippe de Commynes, seigneur d'Argenton qui nous est venu voir tout exprès pour s'entretenir avec donna Fiora.

— A moi ? Et de la part de qui, mon Dieu ?

— Mais... du roi, madonna !

— En vérité ? Qui suis-je pour qu'un aussi grand prince prenne souci de moi ?

Le léger persiflage du ton n'échappa pas au seigneur d'Argenton. Son sourire s'accentua tandis que ses paupières se plissaient légèrement :

— La modestie est une vertu qui convient surtout aux laides. Avec une telle beauté, madonna, c'est au moins du temps perdu et, au pire, de l'hypocrisie. Que notre sire s'intéresse à vous n'a rien d'extraordinaire. D'autant qu'il a gardé le meilleur souvenir de feu votre père. Mais peut-être pourrions-nous parler après le repas ? Pardonnez-moi, madame, ajouta-t-il en se tournant vers Agnelle, mais je meurs de faim. Je crois que je pourrais manger un cheval...

Le rire de la jeune femme fusa comme un jet d'eau claire :

— Nous n'en avons pas au menu, messire, mais je crois que notre repas, tout modeste qu'il soit, saura satisfaire votre appétit. Holà, petites ! ajouta-t-elle en frappant dans ses mains, que l'on apporte bassins et serviettes et que l'on voie à nous servir promptement !

Comme si elles n'avaient attendu que ce signal, trois jeunes servantes apparurent portant des cuvettes pleines d'une eau parfumée dans lesquelles les convives lavèrent leurs mains qu'ils essuyèrent à des serviettes fines avant de passer à table. Puis, les servantes disparurent pour faire place à des valets portant les pâtes, tourtes, et « chaircuiteries », très renommées car les glands des chênes nourrissaient de nombreux porcs, qui constituaient le premier service. Vinrent ensuite des poissons, carpes et saumons diversement accommodés, puis des volailles, et un quartier de bœuf rôti accompagnés de fenouil, de carottes, de choux et de raifort; enfin les fromages, les fruits, cerises et prunes, et quelques patisseries. Le tout arrosé des vins de France et d'Italie car Agnolo possédait une cave bien fournie dont il n'était pas peu fier. Il ne cessait de remplir le gobelet de son invité en lui indiquant le cru et l'année que le sire de Commynes avalait avec un enthousiasme flatteur, sans d'ailleurs perdre un coup de dents et sans cesser de parler. Maître Nardi lui rendait raison bravement et les deux hommes discutaient politique avec entrain sans trop se soucier des dames – ce qui ne gênait pas Fiora très intéressée par ce qu'elle entendait, et pas davantage dame Agnelle qui veillait avec vigilance au bon déroulement du festin.

Les nouvelles étaient plutôt bonnes si l'on tenait compte des événements étranges qui se passaient et de ce qui avait failli se passer surtout. Fiora apprit ainsi qu'un certain connétable de Saint-Pol qui était en principe grand chef de l'armée royale mais qui n'en était pas moins « bourguignon » bon teint et vieil ami du Téméraire, avait une conduite fort étrange. Porteur de la grande épée fleurdelisée qui lui donnait le pas sur les princes du sang et marié d'ailleurs avec la belle-sœur de Louis XI, une princesse de Savoie, Louis de Luxembourg, comte de Saint-Pol, n'en était pas moins allé à Péronne offrir ses services au Téméraire et au roi anglais, et leur proposer d'ouvrir devant eux sa ville de Saint-Quentin, mais avait fait tirer ses canons sur eux quand ils se présentèrent devant les remparts de la cité... Étrange, non ?

— J'espère, dit Agnolo, que notre sire ne se fonde pas trop sur la fidélité de ce seigneur ?

— Il le connaît depuis si longtemps ! Saint-Pol, pour autant que j'en puisse juger, ne sait plus à quel saint se vouer ni quel maître lui sera le plus profitable. En attendant, le premier résultat de la canonnade a été le départ de Monseigneur de Bourgogne qui, le lendemain même, plantait là son allié anglais pour se retirer à Valenciennes. Ce que sachant, le roi n'a pas perdu une minute pour entamer des pourparlers avec Edouard IV. Il sait bien que les Anglais sont à court de vivres et que la défection de l'armée bourguignonne a porté un coup fatal à leur moral. Certains d'entre eux pensent que la saison s'avance et qu'il serait peut-être temps de rentrer chacun chez soi en attendant une occasion meilleure mais ils ne veulent pas quitter le camp les mains vides et le roi Louis le sait bien.

— Que demandent-ils pour s'en aller ?

— Disons que leurs prétentions sont allées en décroissant : ils ont d'abord réclamé la couronne de France...

— Ils espéraient vraiment qu'on allait la leur offrir ? fit Agnolo en riant.

— Bien sûr que non mais cela flattait leur vanité. Ensuite ils ont demandé qu'on leur rende la Guyenne et la Normandie qui leur sont toujours chères...

— Mais qui le sont encore plus à la France. Alors ?

— Alors ?... (Commynes avala son bourgogne avec satisfaction et sourit largement à son hôte.) Le roi pense en avoir raison sans trop de peine avec de l'or et des présents... L'or, je suis chargé d'en retirer des caves de la Bastille mais je dois voir aussi avec messieurs les échevins de Paris à quel prix ils estiment leur tranquillité. Et il s'agit d'aller vite. Je repars après-demain...

— Pour Compiègne ?

— Non, pour Senlis où notre sire est revenu. Je dois rapporter l'or sous une escorte que me donnera la ville...

Il se tourna brusquement vers Fiora et ajouta aimablement :

— Ainsi vous n'aurez rien à redouter des dangers de la route, madonna, car j'ai ordre de vous ramener avec moi.

— Le roi veut me voir ? Je pensais qu'il s'agissait seulement d'un message.

— C'est un message, mais verbal. Nous quitterons Paris à l'aube dès l'ouverture des portes. Tenez-vous prête ! A présent, ajouta-t-il en se levant, je dois vous quitter, maître Nardi et vous, dame Agnelle, en vous rendant grâces pour cet excellent repas car je dois rencontrer sans plus tarder messire d'Estouteville, le chancelier Pierre Doriole et le gouverneur de la Bastille, messire Pierre Lhuillier.

Et d'un pas aussi leste que s'il n'eût absorbé qu'une aile de volaille et deux doigts de clairet, le seigneur d'Argenton quitta la maison Nardi avec ses gens qui avaient festoyé à la cuisine, en recommandant à Agnolo d'amener Fiora à la porte Saint-Denis au petit jour du surlendemain. Songeuse, celle-ci monta voir Léonarde pour la mettre au courant de ce qui arrivait. Agnelle la suivit.

— Que peut bien me vouloir le roi Louis ? s'inquiéta Fiora en gravissant l'escalier. J'aurais dû parler de Léonarde à messire de Commynes et lui dire qu'il m'était impossible de l'abandonner.

— Pourquoi donc ? J'en prendrai grand soin, je vous assure, fit Agnelle en souriant. Vous ne serez certainement pas longtemps absente. Et Senlis n'est pas si loin : dix lieues, ce n'est rien. Enfin, un ordre du roi ne se discute pas.

Léonarde en dit tout autant. Elle se sentait parfaitement bien chez les Nardi et prenait son mal en patience :

— Quand il n'y a rien d'autre à faire, c'est la sagesse, fit-elle, et puisque dame Agnelle veut bien nous dire que je ne l'encombre pas trop, je vais attendre ici ma guérison. Allez en paix, mon agneau, vous n'avez rien à craindre du roi Louis.

— J'en suis certaine, renchérit Agnelle. Quant à nous, si la menace anglaise s'éloigne, nous pourrions gagner notre clos de Suresnes. Dame Léonarde y serait beaucoup mieux installée pour poursuivre sa convalescence car la campagne y est belle et nous avons sur la Seine une vue superbe.

Trop émue pour répondre, Fiora embrassa la charmante femme et, négligeant momentanément le roi Louis, tourna son esprit vers d'autres préoccupations : Esteban n'était pas encore revenu.

Il revint à la tombée de la nuit, peu avant le couvre-feu, avec la mine de quelqu'un qui, ayant beaucoup couru, a très faim et très soif. La grande Péronnelle qui veillait à la cuisine chez les Nardi se chargea de lui en dépit de l'heure tardive, l'installa sur un coin de table et lui servit du pâté d'anguille, de la tourte au pigeon, une large tranche de bœuf froid et quelques douceurs, le tout arrosé d'un vin de Bourgueil de nature à réparer les forces les plus amoindries. Le Castillan plaisait fort à la cuisinière à qui, avant de partir pour Compiègne, il rendait maints bons offices tout en s'extasiant, avec une gourmandise non dissimulée, sur les plats qu'il lui voyait accommoder. Ce soir-là, Péronnelle était trop contente de pouvoir gâter Esteban à sa guise et de l'avoir pour elle toute seule. Fiora le comprit et alla attendre dans le jardin que le festin fût achevé.

La nuit était belle d'ailleurs et c'était l'époque des étoiles filantes. Assise sur un banc près d'un grand massif de lis neigeux qui embaumaient, la jeune femme laissa son regard et son esprit se perdre dans le bleu profond du ciel, cherchant à retrouver les constellations qu'à Florence le vieux maître Toscanelli lui avait appris à reconnaître. L'an passé, en ce mois d'août, elle séjournait dans la villa de Fiesole avec son père bien-aimé et se croyait éperdument amoureuse de Giuliano de Médicis. Rien ne manquait alors à son bonheur de jeune fille gâtée, choyée. Sa vie se déroulait aimable et fleurie comme ce satin de la Chine que Francesco Beltrami avait acheté pour sa fille chérie lors d'un de ses voyages à Venise. Et puis, tout avait basculé dans une sorte d'enfer démentiel où s'était abîmée sa vie, un chaos incohérent hérissé d'épines cruelles qui l'avaient déchirée, ne laissant vivre, de son jardin secret, que la grande fleur pourpre, superbe et vénéneuse, de la passion. Ses racines tortueuses et insinuantes étaient armées de griffes puissantes qui ne se laissaient arracher qu'avec des lambeaux de chair et, telle l'hydre de la légende, repoussaient aussitôt, plus impérieuses encore. Quiconque respirait le parfum violent mais suave de cette fleur en demeurait assujetti, esclave et Fiora, ce soir, au creux de ce jardin, osait s'avouer qu'en dépit de tout ce qu'elle avait souffert par lui, elle aimait encore Philippe et sans doute l'aimerait-elle jusqu'à son dernier soupir. La fleur pourpre ne mourrait qu'avec sa vie à elle.

Elle se signait machinalement, chaque fois que, là-haut, un minuscule météore scintillant rayait le velours sombre de la nuit. Certains prétendaient que chaque étoile filante était une âme entrant en paradis. D'autres que c'était signe de bonheur et qu'il convenait de formuler un vœu mais Fiora, en dépit du geste pieux qui lui venait, ne croyait ni à l'un ni à l'autre...

Le sable du jardin crissa sous les pas d'Esteban et, sans souffler mot, il s'assit sur le banc, à la place qu'elle lui indiquait auprès d'elle. Il ne lui laissa pas le temps de poser la moindre question :

— Vous ne vous êtes pas trompée, madonna, c'est bien lui. Je l'ai suivi, guetté suffisamment pour avoir acquis une certitude.

— Où est-il allé ?

— Il a d'abord suivi le cardinal de Bourbon jusqu'en son hôtel qui est proche du Louvre. Il faisait partie des gens qui l'accompagnaient et j'ai même vu, à certain moment, le superbe cardinal se pencher vers le moine pour lui parler comme en confidence. Mais celui-ci a dû seulement prendre, à l'hôtel de Bourbon, le repas du milieu du jour. Je l'en ai vu ressortir et regagner la cathédrale pour y chanter vêpres et complies... auxquelles j'ai assisté en bon chrétien. Ensuite, Fray Ignacio s'est rendu dans un couvent assez voisin de Notre-Dame que l'on m'a appris être celui des Jacobins. Et cette fois, il n'est pas ressorti. Alors je suis rentré, un peu moulu, un peu las, mais dûment sanctifié... Que dois-je faire à présent ?

— Gagner votre lit au plus vite car vous l'avez bien mérité. Et je vous remercie, Esteban, de vous être donné cette peine. Je crois qu'il faut, à présent, abandonner le moine à son destin. Aussi bien, après-demain, je suivrai messire de Commynes. Vous savez sans doute que le roi l'a envoyé me chercher ?

— En effet. Quant à vous dire pourquoi, je n'en sais pas plus que vous. Mais ce ne peut être que dans un but bienveillant si j'en juge l'accueil qu'il a réservé à mon maître. Cependant je ne suis pas de votre avis en ce qui concerne fray Ignacio. Demain, j'irai encore tournailler autour de ce couvent des Jacobins. J'arriverai peut-être à apprendre quelque chose sur ce qu'il vient faire ici.

— Soyez prudent, je vous en prie. Vous savez combien il est dangereux et il est peut-être inutile d'attirer son attention sur nous, que ce soit moi ou votre maître, puisqu'il nous hait autant l'un que l'autre...

— Faites-moi confiance. Il ne soupçonnera même pas ma présence.

Esteban avait son idée. Tôt le matin, vêtu d'une souquenille de toile et armé de deux paniers que Péronnelle lui confia volontiers avec une liste de commissions lorsqu'il lui dit son intention d'aller faire un tour aux Halles, il vint errer aux environs immédiats du couvent des Jacobins jusqu'à ce qu'il en vît sortir un frère convers équipé de paniers assez semblables aux siens. Il lui emboîta le pas et, au bout d'un instant, le rattrapa et le héla, se présentant comme un valet étranger, tout fraîchement débarqué à Paris et encore peu au fait des marchands les plus réputés.

— On m'a donné cette liste, ajouta-t-il en montrant ce qu'il avait écrit lui-même, Péronnelle ignorant tout de cet exercice, et on m'a expliqué le chemin des Halles mais c'est tout.

— Vous avez eu tout à fait raison de vous adresser à moi, mon frère, fit le moine d'un air important. Je connais tous ces marchands et je vous désignerai les boutiques où l'on trouve les meilleures denrées aux plus justes prix.

— Je vous en serai vraiment reconnaissant, mon frère, répondit Esteban avec humilité.

Sa reconnaissance se traduisant de la seule manière qu'il connût. Le Castillan, les paniers une fois remplis, entraîna son guide bénévole dans un cabaret de la rue Coquillière pour l'y régaler de quelques pots de vin frais. Le frère Guyot était un cœur simple qui savait reconnaître et apprécier les bienfaits de Dieu avec un faible pour le jus de la treille, ce divin breuvage sanctifié par le Seigneur lui-même au soir de la Cène. Au bout du troisième pot de vin de Suresnes, Esteban savait ce qu'il était venu chercher : Fray Ignacio Ortega était investi par Sa Sainteté le Pape d'une mission particulière et discrète auprès du roi de France qu'il rejoindrait prochainement — ce dont le couvent tout entier se trouvait honoré.

Ce point acquis, Esteban rappela à son compagnon qu'il était l'heure de rentrer et le remit sur le chemin du retour alléguant, pour ne pas revenir jusqu'à la rue Saint-Jacques, une dernière course à faire dans le quartier. Une demi-heure plus tard, il rapportait à Péronnelle ses paniers pleins et à Fiora ses informations toutes fraîches.

— Sa mission ne devrait pas être d'une importance capitale, estima la jeune femme, sinon le pape en aurait investi quelque cardinal-légat...

— Je ne suis pas de votre avis. Un simple moine passe plus facilement inaperçu que le pompeux cortège d'une simarre pourpre et bien des secrets d'État accompagnent le chemin d'hommes parfois plus modestes encore. De toutes les façons, celui-là se rend où nous allons nous-mêmes. Nous tâcherons, mon maître et moi, de le surveiller. Ne vous mettez plus en peine de lui, donna Fiora !

Cette dernière journée parisienne, Fiora l'avait passée tout entière auprès de Léonarde qu'elle se reprochait d'abandonner comme si la décision en fût venue d'elle-même. Elle ne s'en était écartée qu'un moment, après le déjeuner, pour rejoindre dans son cabinet Agnolo Nardi qui le lui avait demandé.

— N'avez-vous pas besoin d'argent, donna Fiora ? fit le négociant dès qu'elle fut entrée en lui désignant un siège.

— Ne me rendez pas confuse, ser Agnolo ! La générosité avec laquelle vous nous avez reçus, mes amis et moi, m'interdit d'aborder avec vous cette question...

— Per Baccho ! donna Fiora. L'étrange fille de négociant que vous faites ? Vous mélangez tout.

— Je ne crois pas et même je vous demande de ne pas poursuivre car vous me gêneriez fort !

— Dio mio ! Vous ne comprenez rien, mais rien à ce que sont les affaires ! L'hospitalité est un devoir de chrétien qui avec vous se mue en un merveilleux plaisir mais c'est une chose qui ne fait pas partie du commerce ! En ce qui vous concerne, la réalité est ceci : Ser Angelo Donati qui assume, d'accord avec Sa Seigneurie de Médicis, les responsabilités des biens, commerces et propriétés de feu Francesco Beltrami, m'a fait savoir que les bénéfices qui dans mon négoce formaient naguère la part de votre père doivent vous être remis intégralement. Il en est de même pour le comptoir de Bruges où, pour plus de commodité, ser Renzo Capponi a reçu ordre de m'envoyer chaque année ce qui vous revient et je peux dire que, s'il ne s'agit pas d'une richesse comparable à celle de notre cher Francesco, vous êtes tout de même, dès à présent, à la tête d'une gentille fortune qui grossira chaque année et qui vous permet, si aujourd'hui vous le souhaitiez, d'acheter une belle maison en quelque endroit de France qui saurait vous plaire. En pays de Loire par exemple, où la vie est si douce et où le roi réside le plus ordinairement.

— Est-ce que, par pure bonté, vous n'exagéreriez pas un peu ?

— Mais en aucune façon, sur mon honneur ! Il faut songer à l'avenir, donna Fiora, et prendre ce qui vous revient...

— Je ne saurais qu'en faire pour l'instant. Néanmoins j'accepterais volontiers quelque liquidité pour le voyage que je vais entreprendre demain, mais pas plus qu'il n'en faut. Pour le reste, je souhaite que vous le placiez au mieux de nos intérêts communs et je désire que vous préleviez dessus tout ce qui sera nécessaire pour assurer l'entretien et le confort de ma chère Léonarde...

D'un geste désinvolte, Agnolo balaya le dernier article comme quantité négligeable et se dirigea vers l'un des lourds coffres à ferrures qui se trouvaient alignés au fond de sa pièce de travail. Il l'ouvrit et en tira un sac qui semblait d'un bon poids.

— Voilà mille livres pour commencer. Vous pourrez m'en demander chaque fois que vous en aurez besoin mais, puisque vous voulez bien me confier le soin de gérer votre fortune, je veillerai à ce que vous n'ayez jamais à le regretter.

Émue, elle alla vers lui et l'embrassa sur les deux joues.

— J'en suis certaine. En tout cas, merci d'être ce que vous êtes. Si je ne devais partir, je crois que je vous aurais prié de m'initier à ce commerce pour lequel se passionnait mon père...

— Pour cela aussi, je serai toujours à votre disposition. Ce serait bonne chose, en effet, que vous apprissiez les affaires car, si vous êtes en pleine jeunesse, je ne le suis plus guère moi-même. Nous pourrions y songer lorsque vous saurez ce que vous veut le roi notre sire!

Fiora se contenta de sourire et d'embrasser l'excellent homme. Elle n'en avait pas encore fini avec les grands de ce monde, pas plus qu'avec un certain Philippe de Selongey, et sans compter Hieronyma dei Pazzi qu'un véritable miracle avait arrachée à un juste châtiment de ses crimes. Après, il pourrait être passionnant de suivre la trace brillante qu'avait laissée Beltrami. Mais cet « après », quand viendrait-il? Dans combien d'années? Et que serait alors devenue cette jeune Florentine nommée Fiora qui, en dépit de ce qu'elle avait souffert, croyait encore que tout était possible à qui le voulait passionnément?

A l'aube du lendemain, encadrée de Philippe de Commynes et d'Esteban, elle franchissait la barbacane de la porte Saint-Denis. Derrière les trois cavaliers une compagnie montée de francs-archers de la Ville de Paris escortait plusieurs haquets chargés de tonneaux qui faisaient rire les maraîchers alignés le long de la route pour laisser passer le cortège. On s'esclaffait en criant que le malin roi Louis avait grand besoin de bons vins pour donner du cœur au ventre de ses troupes avant la bataille qu'elles allaient livrer à l'Anglais rapace. Les soldats souriaient, répondaient par des plaisanteries. Seul Commynes savait que trois seulement de ces barriques contenaient le vin des coteaux de Loire qu'affectionnait le roi. Les autres étaient remplies d'or, cet or qui, mieux qu'une bataille toujours incertaine chasserait peut-être encore une fois l'Anglais hors du sol de France.

Si la campagne aux environs immédiats de Paris offrait l'image paisible d'un pays occupé à ses récoltes, la route à mesure que l'on avançait vers le nord portait plus de soldats et de charrois militaires que de paysans. Le plus petit village était gardé, le moindre châtel révélait, sur sa tour, l'éclat des casques et des fers de lance. L'épaisse forêt de Senlis où Louis XI se plaisait à chasser en perdait de son silence. L'écho d'un commandement ou de cliquetis d'armes couvraient parfois le chant des oiseaux : le roi, en homme prévoyant, entretenait ses troupes en dispositions belliqueuses alors même que ses émissaires négociaient avec ceux du monarque anglais.

Et soudain ce fut le calme, la divine paix sylvestre peuplée de chants d'oiseaux. On avait quitté le grand chemin au bout duquel se profilaient les remparts de Senlis pour un sentier herbu à peine tracé par les roues de quelques charrettes... A l'interrogation muette de Fiora, Commynes répondit par un sourire.

— Nous arrivons! fit-il.

La forêt venait de s'ouvrir en deux comme un rideau de théâtre devant ce qui semblait être une ville en réduction :

derrière des murs de hauteur moyenne, on apercevait les hautes fenêtres fleuronnées d'un palais surmonté de girouettes d'or et d'azur, la splendeur flamboyante d'une église. Les tours inachevées étaient encore prisonnières d'un lacis d'échafaudages et les ardoises neuves brillaient telles des plaques d'acier bleu. Une grande bannière, longue flamme dont l'outremer fleurdelisé d'or s'écartelait d'une croix blanche bougeait doucement au sommet de sa hampe dorée sur le plus haut pignon de l'édifice.

– L'abbaye de la Victoire, annonça Commynes. Le roi de France aime à y résider...

– Comme c'est beau! soupira Fiora, sincère. Et quel beau nom: la Victoire!

– L'origine en est simple: l'an 1214, alors que, le vingtseptième jour de juillet, le roi Philippe-Auguste venait de l'emporter à Bouvines sur l'empereur allemand Othon, il envoya vers son fils, le prince Louis, un messager porteur de la grande nouvelle. De son côté, celui-ci, encore tout bouillant du succès qu'il avait remporté à la Roche-aux-Moines sur le roi Jean d'Angleterre, dépêchait à son père un messager. Les deux chevaucheurs, se rencontrèrent dit-on à cet endroit précis et, quelques années plus tard, le roi ordonna la fondation d'une abbaye qui fut confiée à douze chanoines réguliers de l'ordre de Saint-Augustin venus de l'abbaye de Saint-Victor à Paris. Richement dotée, elle devint ce que vous voyez: une noble demeure digne du Seigneur Dieu...

– Sont-ce des anges qui la gardent? Aux ailes près, ils ressemblent à une statue de Monseigneur saint Michel que j'ai souvenance d'avoir vue...

Splendides en effet sous leurs armures blanches étincelantes sur lesquelles flottaient les cottes d'armes qui restituaient en plus petit la bannière royale, coiffés de grands bonnets plats que de longues plumes de héron agrafées de médailles d'argent relevaient d'un côté, à pied ou à cheval, les plus beaux soldats que Fiora ait jamais vus montaient, de part et d'autre du haut portail, une garde vigilante. Commynes se mit à rire:

— Ce ne sont pas des anges, loin de là! Vous voyez ici, madonna, la célèbre Garde Écossaise du roi Louis qui compte dans ses rangs quelques-uns des meilleurs guerriers du monde. Ils ne connaissent ici-bas que deux lois : celle du roi auquel ils ont juré fidélité et celle de l'amour susceptible et intransigeant qu'ils vouent à leur honneur et à leur lointaine patrie...

Les voyageurs avaient été aperçus. Un cavalier galopait vers eux et Commynes cria :

— Salut à vous, Robert Cunningham! Je ne vous amène que des amis. Le roi attend cette jeune dame... et les fûts de vin qui nous suivent.

— Les caves sont déjà prêtes à les recevoir. Quant à l'escorte, elle va pouvoir se rafraîchir, et prendre un peu de repos avant de regagner Paris. Mais vous, messire, vous n'avez pas besoin d'introducteur.

Après avoir salué courtoisement Fiora, en tentant toutefois de percer le léger mystère du voile dont elle aimait à s'envelopper la tête pour voyager, l'Écossais fit volter son cheval et prit la tête de la file de haquets. L'un après l'autre, les chariots et ceux qui les gardaient franchirent la porterie du monastère sous l'œil intéressé des archers de garde.

— A nous, à présent! fit Commynes avec enjouement. Je gage que notre sire sera positivement ravi de vous voir, madonna...

Au-delà du haut portail ogival au fronton duquel des anges agenouillés aux ailes immenses semblaient protéger les armes de France, les voyageurs découvrirent un vaste espace couvert d'herbe fraîchement coupée qui formait un joyeux tapis pour les bâtiments abbatiaux et pour le jaillissement d'une admirable église de pierre blanche. Immaculés aussi les grands lévriers aux colliers de cuir cloutés d'or qui s'ébattaient sur la pelouse autour d'un homme qui devait être, selon Fiora, un valet de chiens. Maigre et de taille moyenne, vêtu d'une tunique courte de petit drap gris serrée à la taille par une ceinture de cuir, les chausses disparaissant dans de hautes bottes souples de daim gris, il portait sur un bonnet rouge qui lui cachait les oreilles un chapeau de feutre noir relevé par-derrière et sur la coiffe duquel des médailles étaient fixées.

— Les jolies bêtes! s'exclama Fiora. Elles donnent l'impression de sortir vivantes d'une légende... Et comme elles semblent aimer l'homme qui s'en occupe!

— Elles l'aiment beaucoup en effet, assura Commynes avec un clin d'œil complice à Esteban. Voulez-vous que nous les voyions de plus près?

Il avait déjà mis pied à terre et offrait sa main à la jeune femme pour qu'elle en fît autant. Celle-ci hésita:

— Est-ce bien prudent, pour un instant de plaisir, de faire attendre le roi? On le dit peu patient...

— Venez toujours! Je vous promets que vous aurez droit à toute son indulgence...

Un peu à contrecœur, Fiora se laissa conduire. Esteban demeura sur place, réunissant les trois brides dans ses mains. Sentant l'approche d'étrangers, les lévriers cessèrent de jouer et se figèrent, leurs têtes fines tournées vers les nouveaux venus. Ce que voyant, le valet se retourna. Sous l'œil stupéfait de Fiora, Commynes mit un genou en terre:

— Sire, dit-il me voici de retour ayant accompli les deux missions que le roi avait daigné me confier! Puis, entre ses dents il ajouta: « Saluez, que diable! »

Et Fiora, machinalement, plia les genoux pour une profonde révérence.

— Bien, bien! fit le roi. Vous m'avez, une fois de plus, bien servi, messire Philippe et je vous en remercie. Voulez-vous à présent me laisser seul avec cette jeune dame dont j'espère qu'elle nous fera la grâce d'ôter son voile? Mais ne vous éloignez pas: nous aurons à parler!

Sans quitter son inconfortable position, à demi agenouillée, Fiora rejeta sa mousseline par-dessus le double bourrelet de soie qui lui servait de coiffure, libérant son visage. Mal revenue de sa surprise, elle contemplait ce petit homme sans apparence qui cependant était le roi de France. Il n'était pas bien beau ni jeune — cinquante-deux ans depuis la Saint-Anatole dernière — mais sous le regard dominateur de ses yeux bruns profondément enfoncés dans leurs orbites, la jeune femme se sentit rougir et baissa la tête ayant tout juste eu le temps de remarquer le long nez sardonique, la bouche mince, sinueuse et mobile, mais elle savait déjà que, dût-elle vivre mille ans, elle n'oublierait jamais ce visage. On lui avait dit que cet homme possédait l'intelligence la plus subtile, la plus profonde qui soit et dès ce premier regard elle en avait été persuadée.

Cependant, Commynes s'éloignait sans qu'on ait encore autorisé Fiora à se relever. Et, soudain, elle vit, sous son nez, une longue main sèche qui se tendait vers elle pour l'aider à se redresser tandis qu'une voix aimable prononçait :

— Madame la comtesse de Selongey, soyez la très bien venue.

La stupeur faillit rejeter Fiora à terre. Elle vacilla comme sous l'assaut d'un brusque coup de vent et devint si pâle que le souverain la crut sur le point de s'évanouir :

— Hé quoi ? fit-il d'un ton mécontent, n'est-ce point là votre nom ? Nous aurait-on trompé ?

Comprenant qu'elle avait en face d'elle un redoutable adversaire, Fiora au prix d'un violent effort sur elle-même parvint à se ressaisir.

— Que le roi me pardonne une émotion dont je n'ai pas été maîtresse, fit-elle doucement. C'est la première fois que je m'entends nommer ainsi et je ne suis pas certaine d'avoir droit à ce titre, à ce nom. Messire de Commynes m'est venu dire que le roi voulait voir Fiora Beltrami. C'est elle... et nulle autre qui a l'honneur d'être dès cet instant aux ordres de Votre Majesté...

La révérence, réitérée, fut la perfection même : un miracle de grâce et d'élégance et le dur regard appréciateur s'adoucit d'une pointe de gaieté :

— Ha ha ! Il y a là une sorte de mystère il me semble ?

Voulez-vous, comtesse, que nous marchions un peu pour tirer cela au clair ? Tout beau, les chiens ! Suivez-nous et qu'on ne vous entende pas !

Ils firent en silence quelques pas dans l'herbe encore humide d'une petite pluie qui avait rafraîchi le début de l'après-midi. Désorientée par la brusque apostrophe dont elle avait été l'objet, et cherchant désespérément comment Louis XI pouvait être au courant de son étrange mariage, Fiora se perdait en conjectures. Il était impossible, impensable que Démétrios se fût rendu coupable de bavardages inconsidérés. Alors ? Qui ? Comment ? Pourquoi ? Autant de questions sans réponse possible puisqu'il était défendu d'interroger un roi... Celui-ci d'ailleurs mit fin à ses vaines interrogations en reprenant, sur un ton tout différent :

– Nous avons connu, jadis, messire Beltrami, votre père et nous avions de l'estime pour lui car c'était un homme droit, honnête et généreux, et c'est avec peine que nous avons appris sa fin tragique et les pénibles événements qui l'ont suivie... Nous savions déjà que le seigneur Lorenzo de Médicis possédait un beau talent de poète mais nous ignorions que sa plume pût atteindre à ce degré d'évocation lyrique quand il nous a décrit les malheureux événements dont vous avez été victime, donna Fiora, ajouta le roi avec un mince sourire. En vérité le grand Homère n'eût pas fait mieux !

– Monseigneur Lorenzo m'avait pourtant promis de ne point parler de moi, protesta Fiora qui venait de comprendre d'où Louis XI tenait cette ahurissante possession de ses secrets.

– Sans doute a-t-il changé d'avis. Peut-être dans le but de vous protéger malgré vous ? De toute façon, il nous connaît trop bien pour ignorer qu'en toutes choses nous voulons tout savoir de ceux qui sont appelés à nous approcher. Cette exigence a le mérite d'éclairer les situations, d'éviter les mensonges et de nous épargner des explications aussi filandreuses qu'embrouillées. Nos relations en seront simplifiées. Qu'en pensez-vous ?

— Que le roi a raison, sans conteste, mais que je ne m'en trouve pas moins gênée...

— Pâques-Dieu, madame ! Nous vous parlons franc et clair. Tâchez de nous payer de la même monnaie et faites-nous grâce des minauderies et afféteries féminines. D'après ce que nous savons de vous, vous êtes courageuse. Ne changez pas !... Et ne prenez pas cette mine contrite ! Dites-nous plutôt comment il se fait que vous ne soyez pas sûre d'être Mme de Selongey ?

Un peu soulagée malgré tout de pouvoir s'avancer sur un terrain plus stable, Fiora, aussi simplement que si cet inconnu eût été son confesseur, raconta sa malheureuse visite au château de Philippe et le surcroît de douleur et de colère qu'elle en avait recueilli. Louis XI l'écoutait sans rien dire, marchant la tête un peu penchée et les mains nouées derrière son dos.

— Ainsi donc, fit-il quand elle se tut, messire de Selongey se serait rendu bigame en vous épousant ? C'est là une faute très grave doublée d'un sacrilège et qui mérite l'échafaud.

— Je n'ai aucune raison ni aucune envie de défendre cet homme, sire, mais après la colère m'est venue la réflexion. Peut-être, me croyant morte, n'aura-t-il épousé cette Béatrice que depuis peu ?

Le vif regard que le roi lança à la jeune femme contenait de la surprise et quelque chose qui ressemblait à de la sympathie.

— C'est une qualité rare qu'être capable de raisonner ainsi avec son propre cœur ! Quels sont vos sentiments envers Selongey ?

— En vérité, je n'en sais rien. Il y a des moments où je crois l'aimer encore, d'autres où je le hais autant et plus même que je ne hais son maître, ce duc aux armes duquel il m'a sacrifiée ! cet arrogant Téméraire que nous nous sommes juré d'abattre, Démétrios Lascaris et moi !

Un éclair vite éteint sous la paupière pesante traversa le regard du roi :

— Vous avez juré d'abattre Charles de Bourgogne ? Pourquoi ?

— Si le duc Philippe vivait encore, nous eussions décidé sa perte car le père et le fils sont coupables pour nous à part égale. J'exècre ce duc impitoyable qui n'a pas eu pitié de la jeunesse de mon père, l'authentique, ce duc auquel messire de Selongey m'a sacrifiée. Quant à messire Lascaris, il lui reproche la mort de son jeune frère et la fausse espérance d'un secours entretenue par les Grecs à présent morts ou esclaves...

Louis XI fit demi-tour pour revenir sur ses pas. Les chiens suivirent docilement.

— Selon la règle une femme ne pouvant résider dans cette abbaye, Commynes va vous conduire à Senlis où vous retrouverez votre ami. Je l'ai fort en estime car c'est un grand médecin et je compte me l'attacher ainsi que le souhaitait le seigneur Lorenzo. Mais vous, donna Fiora, si je vous proposais de me servir, accepteriez-vous ?

— Si le roi me permet d'accomplir la vengeance jurée, je n'aurai aucune raison de refuser. Et je serai loyale.

Elle pensait chacun des mots qu'elle prononçait parce que, tout à coup, elle se sentait en confiance. Peut-être parce que le roi, en abandonnant provisoirement le pluriel de majesté, lui paraissait soudain plus proche et plus humain. Il hocha la tête et sourit d'un vrai sourire qui lui ôtait des années et qui, comme toute chose rare, avait beaucoup de charme.

— J'en suis certain. Il suffit pour s'en convaincre de regarder vos yeux... En outre, il serait bon que vous sachiez ceci : Philippe de Selongey est actuellement mon prisonnier... et... en grand danger d'être exécuté. Vous le voyez, je peux déjà vous offrir la moitié de votre vengeance...

Assommée et l'œil agrandi d'épouvante, Fiora parvint péniblement à articuler :

— Mais... pourquoi ? Qu'a-t-il fait ?

— Il a tenté de me tuer. Les magistrats appellent cela un

régicide et si on lui applique la loi, le favori du Téméraire sera mis en quatre quartiers. Mais nous reparlerons de tout cela à loisir n'est-ce pas ? Que Dieu vous ait en sa sainte garde, donna Fiora !

Tournant brusquement le dos à la jeune femme éperdue, Louis XI s'éloigna vers le logis abbatial. Autour de lui, les grands lévriers blancs, las d'une trop longue sagesse, sautaient pour saisir les friandises qu'il élevait à bout de bras. Fiora sentit une immense lassitude. Elle eut envie de s'écrouler là, dans ce moelleux tapis d'herbe, d'y pleurer, d'y dormir... Mais une main solide saisit son bras au moment où ses genoux commençaient à plier :

— Venez, donna Fiora ! Je vais vous conduire auprès de votre ami. Il n'est pas loin : trois quarts de lieue au plus...

Sans rien objecter, Fiora se laissa emmener. Le coup qu'elle venait de recevoir était si rude qu'il lui ôtait jusqu'à la faculté de penser. L'idée de retrouver Démétrios était la seule qui surnageât. Elle s'y raccrocha comme à une branche...

Le château de Senlis était petit, du moins pour un château royal mais, en revanche, l'auberge des Trois Pots, sa voisine, était grande et d'agréable habitation. Le roi, quand il était à Senlis, y logeait volontiers ses invités de marque et, tout naturellement, Démétrios y avait été installé, le séjour dans une abbaye ne lui étant pas agréable, ni permis à un orthodoxe. Il l'avait déclaré franchement à Louis XI qui bien qu'étant lui-même d'une extrême piété pouvait comprendre les raisons d'un homme de la valeur du médecin grec.

Esteban était parti en éclaireur tandis que Fiora s'entretenait avec le roi, pour annoncer l'arrivée de la jeune femme et celle-ci en entrant dans l'auberge trouva une agréable chambre toute préparée pour la recevoir. Elle en fut touchée mais c'est l'accueil de Démétrios qui l'émut le plus. Pour la première fois depuis qu'ils se connaissaient, il l'embrassa. En la voyant venir vers lui avec un visage pâle et bouleversé, il avait compris que c'était de ce geste-là dont elle avait besoin puisqu'elle était momentanément privée du refuge que représentait Léonarde. Mais, quand elle éclata en sanglots dans ses bras, il s'inquiéta :

— Que t'est-il arrivé ? Le roi t'aurait-il mal reçue ?

Son regard cherchait celui de Commynes, témoin de la scène et qui écarta les bras en haussant les épaules pour traduire son ignorance :

— Donna Fiora n'a pas dit un mot depuis que nous avons quitté la Victoire. Néanmoins, il semble bien que notre sire l'ait reçue avec faveur. Et moi, je ne souhaite que l'aider et si je peux quelque chose, je suis tout disposé à me conduire en ami véritable si l'on veut bien m'accepter...

Fiora s'écarta, prit le mouchoir que lui offrait Démétrios, essuya ses yeux et se moucha :

— Pardonnez-moi tous les deux, je viens de me conduire comme une enfant et j'en ai honte. Messire de Commynes... une amitié spontanément donnée est un cadeau du ciel et je l'accepte aussi simplement qu'elle m'a été offerte. Si le roi ne réclame pas votre présence ce soir, accepteriez-vous de souper avec nous ?

L'aimable visage du seigneur flamand s'illumina d'un large sourire... et Fiora en conclut que la cuisine de l'auberge devait lui être avantageusement connue.

— Très volontiers ! D'autant que cette longue route que nous avons courue ensemble m'a affamé et si vous m'acceptez tout poudreux ?...

— Venez vous rafraîchir dans ma chambre, proposa courtoisement Démétrios, et si vous souhaitez dormir ici...

— Excellente idée ! Je rejoindrai l'abbaye demain à l'aube. L'important est d'être là quand le roi sortira de la messe.

En dehors de la sympathie que lui inspirait Commynes, Fiora, tout en faisant disparaître la poussière de la route et en enfilant sa robe de lin brodée de feuilles vertes, s'avouait que son invitation à souper n'était pas entièrement dénuée d'arrière-pensée. Conseiller privé et très écouté de Louis XI, le sir d'Argenton devait savoir à quoi s'en tenir au sujet de Philippe et la jeune femme voulait apprendre à tout prix ce qui s'était passé. Elle s'en voulait d'éprouver tant d'angoisse pour le sort d'un homme qu'elle s'efforçait de chasser de son cœur, mais ce même cœur, sourd à toute raison, à toute sagesse et même à toute rancune ne voulait savoir qu'une chose : Philippe serait peut-être mort demain. Et cette idée lui était insupportable. Si Philippe ne respirait plus quelque part dans le monde, fût-ce au bout de la terre, Fiora savait bien qu'il manquerait quelque chose à sa propre vie. Amour ou haine, les deux extrêmes des sentiments humains mettaient dans une existence la pincée sel, de poivre et d'épices qui en font toute la saveur... Il fallait que messire de Selongey continuât d'exister !

Durant tout le début du repas, Fiora sut retenir les questions qui lui brûlaient les lèvres pour ne pas rompre le plaisir de son invité. Tout en dégustant une tourte aux poireaux et à la crème, des écrevisses de la Nonette et une carpe farcie provenant d'un étang voisin, Commynes et Démétrios parlaient de toutes sortes de choses en hommes qui se connaissent déjà et s'apprécient. En dépit de son jeune âge, le seigneur d'Argenton possédait une belle culture et, surtout, adorait parler politique. Il approuvait fort Louis XI de refuser le conflit ouvert avec le roi anglais. Ses troupes se contentaient d'accompagner les marches et contremarches d'un ennemi qui, visiblement, hésitait à engager le combat. Certes, l'armée anglaise était belle, bien armée et ses fameux archers n'avaient rien perdu de leur adresse mais, depuis le débarquement à Calais, l'envahisseur n'avait trouvé devant lui que terre brûlée et villes abandonnées. Les réfugiés d'Arras et de la région environnante, dont Louis XI avait ordonné la destruction pour affamer l'Anglais, avaient trouvé asile, vivres et argent à Amiens ou à Beauvais par exemple car, s'il voulait réduire l'ennemi à la portion congrue, le roi n'entendait pas que le menu peuple eût trop à souffrir.

— A présent, conclut Commynes en attaquant gaillardement un jambon cuit sous la cendre, Edouard et les siens en sont à peu près où le roi voulait les amener : ils ont dévoré toutes leurs provisions et, comme ils ne peuvent se nourrir sur le pays, leurs ventres commencent à sonner creux... ce qui, grâce à Dieu, n'est pas encore notre lot ! Tâtez de ce cochon, donna Fiora, il est sublime. Maître Auburtin s'est surpassé...

— Le duc de Bourgogne n'a-t-il pas ravitaillé son beau-frère quand il est venu le rejoindre ? demanda Démétrios.

— Il n'avait avec lui que cinquante cavaliers et les villes de Flandres lui avaient refusé leur aide...

— Est-ce à ce moment-là que le comte de Selongey a été fait prisonnier ? demanda Fiora d'une voix qu'elle espérait paisible.

Les yeux des deux hommes se tournèrent vers elle mais elle ne les vit pas. Chauffant entre ses deux mains son gobelet de vin, elle en humait l'arôme d'un air distrait sans paraître s'apercevoir du silence qui venait de tomber.

— C'est un peu plus tard, répondit calmement Commynes comme si la question de Fiora s'inscrivait tout naturellement dans le droit-fil de son récit. Sous Beauvais. Des espions du Téméraire avaient dû apprendre que notre sire, pour se délasser un peu l'esprit, voulait certain jour chasser la sarcelle près du Therain sans grande escorte. Messire de Selongey s'est placé en embuscade avec quelques hommes dans les broussailles d'une maison en ruine. Quand le roi est apparu, il s'est jeté sur lui, l'a désarçonné et il brandissait déjà une hache d'armes au-dessus de sa tête quand Robert Cunningham, que vous avez vu tout à l'heure et à qui cette partie de chasse n'inspirait pas confiance, a surgi soudain avec une douzaine d'Ecossais. Selongey ne cessait d'insulter notre sire. Il a été maîtrisé ainsi que son écuyer Mathieu de Prame, tandis que ses hommes étaient tués sur place. Les prisonniers ont été conduits d'abord dans la prison de l'évêque de Beauvais puis au château de Compiègne où ils sont gardés au secret en attendant un jugement qui ne saurait tarder...

— Mais, est-ce qu'en temps de guerre il n'est plus coutume de mettre les seigneurs prisonniers à rançon ?

— Sans doute, néanmoins ce n'était pas une action de guerre mais bien un assassinat froidement prémédité. Le roi n'était pas armé. J'ajoute qu'une telle témérité ne m'étonne pas de ce fou de Selongey. Il ignore tout de la diplomatie et ne connaît qu'un seul argument : tuer ! ajouta Commynes avec une nuance de dédain qui fit rougir Fiora. En outre, il voue à son maître une dévotion aveugle, sourde, impénétrable à tout raisonnement. Même Dieu passe après son prince dont il ne distingue aucun des défauts, dont il ne comprend pas et ne comprendra jamais qu'il court délibérément à un abîme où s'engloutira inéluctablement ce grand duché dont il prétend faire un royaume...

Toute gaieté avait soudain déserté le visage de Commynes. L'œil assombri, la bouche amère il ne regardait aucun de ses compagnons et Fiora eut l'impression soudaine qu'il ne s'adressait pas à eux mais à lui-même. Aussi fut-ce très doucement qu'elle reprit :

— Comment êtes-vous si bien au fait des affaires de Bourgogne, messire ? Vous parlez du duc Charles comme si vous le connaissiez personnellement...

La main de Démétrios venait de s'appuyer sur celle de Fiora pour la mettre en garde contre quelque chose mais il était déjà trop tard. Philippe de Commynes tourna vers elle un regard qu'elle ne parvint pas à déchiffrer. Il lui sembla tout de même qu'il contenait de la douleur et, cependant, ce fut avec un sourire qu'on lui répondit :

— Je suis flamand, donna Fiora. Mon père Colart de Commynes fut gouverneur de Cassel, bailli de Gand, souverain bailli de Flandre et chevalier de la Toison d'or. Le duc Philippe était mon parrain et j'ai été élevé à sa cour. A dix-sept ans, en 1464, j'ai été attaché à la personne du comte de Charolais qui, en devenant duc de Bourgogne, a fait de moi son conseiller et son chambellan. Mais je savais déjà qu'aucune entente ne serait longtemps possible entre moi et un maître incapable d'entendre un conseil de sagesse ou de modération. Si vous aviez comme moi assisté à la destruction de Dinant, au massacre méthodique de tous ses habitants, hommes, femmes, enfants, vieillards et jusqu'aux nouveau-nés, et cela parce que ces malheureux avaient osé élever la voix contre leur suzerain, vous sauriez ce que je veux dire... J'avais envie de vomir mais lui considérait tout cela d'un œil froidement satisfait. J'ai revu à Liège ce genre de tuerie où nul ne trouvait grâce, même les nonnes cloîtrées, même les êtres les plus pitoyables...

— Ainsi, dit Fiora sans songer à cacher sa surprise, vous étiez bourguignon ?...

Le sourire de Commynes se fit sarcastique :

— Et je suis à présent français. Un transfuge, n'est-ce pas ? Le Téméraire dirait un traître et pourtant je ne crois pas mériter cette épithète. On ne trahit que ce que l'on admire, que l'on estime ou que l'on aime, et je n'ai jamais éprouvé pour Charles aucun de ces trois sentiments. Tout ce qu'il souhaite inspirer, d'ailleurs, c'est la crainte...

— Quand avez-vous rencontré le roi Louis ?

— A la bataille de Montlhéry d'abord, où je l'ai vu combattre vaillamment et sans jamais cesser de ménager autant que faire se pouvait la vie et le sang de ses soldats. Je l'ai admiré. Puis je l'ai revu à cette malheureuse entrevue de Péronne, ce piège où il s'était fourvoyé pour une fois et où, pendant des heures, la mort est restée suspendue sur sa tête sans qu'il en parût effrayé. Il a dépensé des trésors de diplomatie et j'ai compris alors quel génie l'habitait. Je l'ai estimé à sa valeur je crois et j'ai alors tout fait pour retenir la colère aveugle du Téméraire. Le roi m'en a témoigné de la reconnaissance....

— On dit, fit Démétrios, que le Téméraire l'a obligé à l'accompagner à Liège et à assister à la punition de ses habitants... qui étaient pourtant ses amis de la veille. Il serait resté fort serein, en la circonstance, à ce que l'on dit...

— C'est un étonnant comédien et j'avoue qu'elle me fascine, cette « universelle aragne » qui tisse patiemment, soigneusement la toile où les insectes étourdis se feront prendre. Après Péronne j'ai accompli pour le Téméraire diverses missions en Angleterre, en Bretagne, en Castille, sans jamais recevoir autre chose que des critiques amères ou des rebuffades. En même temps, je voyais se développer une politique impitoyable et démentielle. De quoi le Téméraire n'a-t-il pas rêvé ? L'Empire ! L'hégémonie de l'Europe ! Obtenir de l'empereur Frédéric III qu'il le reconnaisse pour son héritier en lieu et place de son propre fils ! A présent, le royaume pour lequel il lui faut la Lorraine qui unirait les pays de par-deçà aux pays de par-delà... mais j'étais déjà parti. Une mission inutile où j'ai failli laisser ma vie pour rien m'a décidé : le roi Louis m'appelait. Dans la nuit du 8 au 9 août 1472, il vient d'y avoir trois ans, je l'ai rejoint en Anjou, aux Ponts-de-Cé. Et je ne regrette rien...

— Qu'adviendrait-il de vous si d'aventure le Téméraire s'emparait de vous ? fit Démétrios.

— Ma fin serait sans doute exemplaire. D'ailleurs, en attaquant le roi, Philippe de Selongey escomptait faire coup double et me ramener chargé de chaînes car il veut ma mort plus encore, je crois, que son maître. Malheureusement pour lui, je n'apprécie guère la chasse... et c'est lui qui est captif à présent.

— Vous le connaissez bien ? murmura Fiora.

— Assez bien en effet. Il n'a que deux ans de plus que moi et nous avons été longtemps compagnons d'armes. Cependant nous n'avons jamais été de vrais amis : nous sommes par trop différents.

— Néanmoins, il vous est peut-être arrivé de rencontrer sa femme ?

La surprise que manifesta Commynes était trop absolue pour n'être pas sincère.

— Sa femme? Je n'ai jamais entendu dire qu'il fût marié! A ma connaissance, il a refusé nombre de partis, parfois brillants, mais il n'aurait eu que bien peu de temps à consacrer à cette malheureuse...

— Pourquoi dites-vous malheureuse?

— Ce n'est pas un destin bien plaisant que de vivre isolée dans un château bourguignon ou d'augmenter le cercle de dames éloignées de leurs époux qui entourent, à Gand, à Bruges, à Bruxelles ou à Lille la duchesse Marguerite et sa belle-fille Marie. L'époque n'est guère propice à la félicité des couples! Ainsi de moi: depuis deux ans et demi que j'ai convolé, je n'ai guère rencontré dame Hélène, ma belle épouse. Quand elle n'est pas auprès de la reine Charlotte qui vit à Amboise avec ses enfants, elle réside sur cette terre d'Argenton qui m'est venue d'elle et où elle se plaît.

— Et... vous ne lui manquez pas? lança Fiora avec un brin d'insolence.

— Si c'est le cas, elle est trop sage et trop bien élevée pour jamais l'exprimer.

— Alors, changeons la proposition s'il vous plaît: elle ne vous manque pas?

Commynes, toute sa bonne humeur retrouvée, éclata de rire:

— Je vois qu'il faut vous faire plaisir, donna Fiora! Je pourrais vous dire que notre sire ne m'en laisse ni le temps ni le loisir et ce serait vérité. Pourtant, il m'arrive, certains soirs quand la campagne sent bon et que le ciel est plein d'étoiles, de regretter son absence car elle est douce, jolie et fraîche... aussi blonde que vous êtes brune... mais de caractère beaucoup plus paisible, si vous me pardonnez cette petite méchanceté.

Il commençait à se faire tard. Commynes, qui venait de liquider un saladier de fraises et de mûres en le faisant passer avec trois doigts d'une bonne eau-de-vie de prune, prit congé de ses nouveaux amis et rejoignit la chambre qu'on lui avait préparée. Fiora écouta décroître le bruit de ses pas dans la longue galerie, dominant la cour centrale, qui desservait les divers appartements puis, s'étant assurée que le sire d'Argenton était bien rentré chez lui, elle revint vers Démétrios qui, accoudé à la fenêtre, écoutait les cloches de la cathédrale proche sonner le couvre-feu, ayant auparavant soufflé les chandelles qui éclairaient la table. Mais la nuit était assez claire pour que l'on pût se priver d'éclairage. Fiora s'installa auprès du Grec et demanda :

— En vérité, je ne sais que penser de cet homme. Il me déroute. Il semble la franchise, la loyauté, l'honnêteté mêmes et il doit être facile de lui accorder son amitié, pourtant...

— Tu ne vas pas, à présent, lui reprocher d'avoir abandonné le Téméraire pour le roi Louis ?

— Ne le devrions-nous pas ? Dans toutes les langues du monde, c'est un traître ?

— Pas dans la mienne, car la faute n'incombe pas au sire de Commynes mais bien à ce prince démesuré, fou d'orgueil et inaccessible à tout sentiment humain qui n'a pas su retenir un tel serviteur. Car je te le dis, c'est un grand serviteur que ce Commynes et il est allé naturellement vers une intelligence en laquelle il reconnaissait la sienne. Il a l'étoffe d'un homme d'État et Louis XI ne s'y est pas trompé... Il sait que l'on a les dévouements que l'on mérite. Le Téméraire ne le sait pas et ne le saura jamais...

— Il a su s'attacher pourtant... messire de Selongey, murmura Fiora avec amertume...

— Parce qu'ils se ressemblent : ce sont des hommes de guerre, de ces féodaux que ceux de Florence redoutent et méprisent un peu parce qu'ils achètent leurs services. Ton Philippe est le reflet que le Téméraire peut voir s'il lui arrive de se regarder au miroir.

— Ce n'est pas mon Philippe !

— Et cependant ton cœur est ravagé d'angoisse depuis que tu le sais voué à l'échafaud. Ne dis pas non. Je lis en toi comme dans un livre, tu le sais bien.

— Tu lis aussi dans l'avenir. Va-t-il mourir ?

— Je n'en sais rien. Pour te répondre, il faudrait que je sois auprès de lui...

— Mais tu es près de moi ! Que vois-tu ?

— Une longue route, le fracas des batailles... du sang et des larmes. M'écouteras-tu, Fiora, si je t'ordonne de retourner à Paris, auprès de Léonarde et des Nardi ? Les combats qui se préparent sont trop rudes pour une femme. Je t'aime assez pour souhaiter te les épargner.

— Je ne veux pas être épargnée, fit-elle avec une soudaine violence. Je hais le Téméraire plus encore aujourd'hui que je ne le haïssais hier. Et si Philippe venait à mourir à cause de lui...

Un bruit de course dans la rue lui coupa la parole. Elle reconnut la silhouette trapue d'Esteban qui rentrait à l'auberge après une soirée passée sans doute dans quelque cabaret avec les soldats qui protégeaient la ville. Depuis qu'il avait quitté Paris, le Castillan aspirait l'odeur violente de la guerre par tous les pores de sa peau et il ne perdait jamais une occasion de s'approcher des troupes pour partager, ne fût-ce qu'un instant, une vie pour laquelle il avait de tout temps été créé. Démétrios n'ignorait rien de cette attirance. Il fallait qu'Esteban fût vraiment attaché à lui pour résister à son envie de s'engager. Mais résisterait-il encore longtemps dans ce pays où l'on rencontrait plus d'hommes d'armes que de civils ?

Du haut de la fenêtre, il l'appela et lui ordonna de monter le rejoindre.

— De toute façon, je serais venu, dit Esteban en entrant dans la chambre, car j'avais quelque chose à dire à donna Fiora.

— A moi ?

— A tous les deux serait plus juste. Le moine espagnol !

— Eh bien ?

— Il est ici. Peu avant la fermeture des portes je l'ai vu entrer, monté sur une mule. Il s'est allé loger chez l'archiprêtre de la cathédrale.

— Quel moine espagnol ? demanda Démétrios qui tombait des nues. Tout de même pas... ?

— Si, fit le Castillan avec un rictus féroce. C'est bien ça. Donna Fiora l'a vu à la messe de l'Assomption à Notre-Dame de Paris et moi je l'ai suivi ensuite et j'ai fait parler l'un des moines chez qui il habitait. Il paraîtrait qu'il vient ici pour voir le roi.

Démétrios demeura silencieux quelques instants, le temps sans doute de se faire à l'idée de voir Ignacio Ortega resurgir dans sa vie :

— Eh bien, soupira-t-il enfin, il ne nous manquait plus que ça ! Esteban, mon garçon, je suis désolé mais il va falloir que tu surveilles cet olibrius de près...

— Ça va, fit le garçon avec désinvolture. On sera dès la première messe à la cathédrale ! Une de plus une de moins...

CHAPITRE VII

LOUIS, PAR LA GRÂCE DE DIEU ROI DE FRANCE...

Trois jours plus tard, le roi tenait sa cour au château de Senlis. Cour étrange, dont les dames étaient absentes à l'exception d'une seule et qui ressemblait plus à un conseil de guerre qu'à l'habituelle réunion d'un souverain qui souhaite prêter l'oreille aux doléances de son peuple. Il y avait là plus d'armures que de pourpoints et de justaucorps. A peu près seul de son espèce, Louis XI portait une longue robe vert sombre ouverte devant pour laisser passer ses jambes maigres vêtues de chausses noires et ses pieds chaussés de poulaines de cuir qu'il tenait croisés. Sur le chapeau dont la pointe offrait un parallèle amusant avec son long nez, les médailles brillaient, astiquées. Ainsi vêtu, il offrait un contraste frappant avec les cottes de soie multicolores, les chaînes d'or dont se parait son entourage, et les tenues superbes de la Garde Écossaise. Quelques-uns de ses amis se tenaient auprès de lui : le vieux seigneur du Bouchage et le seigneur du Lude qu'il avait surnommé « Jean des Habilités », Tanneguy du Chastel, mais aucun de ceux-là n'était vraiment appelé en ses conseils. Seul, Commynes, le plus jeune pourtant, pouvait, à Senlis, se targuer de ce titre auprès d'un souverain dont on disait que « son cheval portait tout son Conseil ». Il était debout auprès de lui, prêt à répondre au moindre signe... Un grand lévrier blanc, « Cher Ami », le favori, était couché aux pieds de son maître qui siégeait sous un dais fleurdelisé.

Seule exception féminine dans cette assemblée d'hommes, et parce qu'elle y avait été conviée impérieusement, Fiora, vêtue de noir, ses cheveux sévèrement tressés couverts d'une coiffe basse en velours dont les pans n'en laissaient pas dépasser une mèche, était debout auprès de Démétrios dont la haute silhouette la masquait en partie. Rarement, elle s'était sentie aussi fébrile car depuis trois jours elle tournait en rond dans sa chambre d'auberge sans parvenir à entreprendre quoi que ce soit de valable, hantée par la pensée qu'à chaque instant Philippe pouvait être conduit au supplice, et se raccrochant au faible espoir que lui avaient laissé les dernières paroles du roi : « Nous reparlerons de tout cela à loisir... »

Elle avait espéré d'abord que Démétrios serait mandé auprès du souverain et qu'elle pourrait l'accompagner, mais il n'en avait rien été.

— Je croyais qu'il ne pouvait pas se passer de toi ? fit-elle presque agressive.

— Il ne peut surtout pas se passer de l'onguent que je lui ai concocté avec des feuilles de sureau et de ronce broyées dans la graisse fine et que l'on applique sur ses hémorroïdes après lavage avec une décoction froide de millepertuis. Il s'en trouve à merveille...

— Tellement bien qu'il n'aurait plus même besoin de toi ! N'importe quel médicastre peut se servir de ta recette...

— A condition de la connaître et je ne donne jamais mes compositions. Sauf à toi, bien sûr. Sois tranquille, le roi aura encore besoin de moi...

L'avant-veille, n'y tenant plus, Fiora avait réclamé son cheval. Elle savait que Compiègne n'était pas loin et elle voulait s'y rendre dans l'espoir d'apprendre quelque chose, si peu que ce soit, sur Philippe, mais elle s'était aperçue, alors, que s'il était aisé d'entrer dans Senlis, il l'était beaucoup moins d'en sortir sans un ordre du roi ou du gouverneur de la ville. La voyant au bord des larmes, Démétrios s'était efforcé de la réconforter.

- Prends patience! Je suis persuadé que messire de Selongey n'est pas en danger immédiat. En te faisant venir, notre sire, comme dit le jeune Commynes, avait bien une idée derrière la tête puisqu'il n'ignore rien des liens matrimoniaux qui t'attachent à son prisonnier. Il faut lui laisser le temps de l'exprimer...

- Parlons-en de Commynes! Lui aussi a complètement disparu! On ne l'a pas revu.

On le revit au matin de ce troisième jour. C'est lui qui vint signifier aux deux étrangers de se rendre au château pour le plaid royal. Quant à Esteban, il était demeuré fermement suspendu aux basques de fray Ignacio grâce à qui il n'avait pas raté un seul office. L'unique promenade un peu divertissante avait été quand le moine, voulant se rendre à l'abbaye de la Victoire, s'était fait refouler par les gardes de la ville. En dépit de la protection de l'archiprêtre, lui aussi devait attendre que le roi soit disposé à le recevoir. Mais sa présence irritait Fiora qui, par crainte de le rencontrer, ne mit pas le pied hors de l'auberge des Trois Pots.

Louis XI semblait d'excellente humeur ce matin-là. De sa place, Fiora pouvait le voir rire et bavarder amicalement avec le sire du Lude. Il accueillit avec faveur quelques suppliques de bourgeois venus faire appel à sa justice et distribua de larges aumônes à la prieure d'un couvent de l'extérieur qui avait subi des déprédations du fait des mouvements de troupes. Cela fait, le roi se leva :

- Messeigneurs, dit-il en frottant l'une contre l'autre ses longues mains sèches, nous avons pour vous des nouvelles qui réjouiront le cœur de tous nos bons sujets comme elles ont réjoui le nôtre. La menace que faisait peser sur notre royaume l'ambition folle de notre cousin de Bourgogne qui a convaincu l'Anglais de passer la mer pour s'emparer de notre pays, cette menace vient de s'éloigner. Il y a eu grave dispute suivie de brouille entre le roi Edouard et Charles le Hardi qui lui est venu reprocher de ne point faire marcher ses troupes contre nous et d'accueillir avec faveur l'idée d'un accord. Notre beau cousin de Bourgogne qui était revenu à Péronne est parti, hier, rejoindre son armée en Luxembourg sans esprit de retour. Demain nous irons rendre grâce au Seigneur Dieu et à Madame la benoîte Sainte Vierge, notre protectrice, et les prier afin qu'ils veuillent bien épargner à notre bon peuple douleur et affliction car c'est laide chose que la guerre...

Les acclamations emplirent la salle faisant voltiger la rangée de bannières pendues en haut des murs. Fiora et Démétrios, surtout pour ne pas se faire remarquer, joignirent leurs voix aux autres d'autant plus volontiers pour la jeune femme qu'elle voyait là une excellente occasion d'essayer d'obtenir la grâce de Philippe, indignement abandonné par ce maître qu'il aimait tant et qui, apparemment, n'avait rien tenté pour l'arracher de sa prison.

Elle était sur le point de se diriger vers le trône quand, à la porte de la salle, un huissier royal frappa le sol par trois fois de son bâton et lança d'une voix forte :

— Plaise au roi recevoir Mgr l'archiprêtre de la cathédrale et Sa Révérence le prieur de l'abbaye Saint-Vincent qui souhaitent présenter à lui un saint moine venu de Rome !

Sur un signe de Louis XI, les portes s'ouvrirent pour laisser passer les trois religieux.

A la vue du moine espagnol, Fiora eut un frisson de répulsion et d'horreur comme si une vipère venait de se dresser sur son chemin. Il était toujours le même. Plein de dédain et d'arrogance, il s'avançait entre les deux dignitaires, les mains enfouies au fond de ses manches, ne regardant personne sinon ce roi qui s'était levé pour accueillir des hommes d'Église. Le dôme dénudé de son crâne luisait dans la lumière pauvre de ce jour chargé de nuages et, en entendant gronder le tonnerre dans le lointain, Fiora se demanda si Dieu lui-même n'avait pas choisi de mettre le roi de France en garde contre l'être malfaisant qui marchait à sa rencontre...

Louis, par la grâce de Dieu roi de France... 187

A mesure qu'il s'avançait, « Cher Ami » se redressait. Quittant sa pose élégante d'animal héraldique, le chien se leva et gronda. Le roi posa vivement sa main sur son collier orfévré :

— Paix, mon fils, paix ! Recouche-toi !

Mais Fiora remarqua que les yeux de Louis XI avaient curieusement rétréci. De mauvaise grâce, en montrant les dents, « Cher Ami » obéit. Le moine ne lui avait pas fait l'honneur d'un regard et même répondit à peine au salut plein de révérence que lui adressait le roi.

— Cet homme doit être fou, chuchota Démétrios. Quelle curieuse façon de se présenter devant un souverain ! Ma parole, il se prend pour le pape !

— Je ne suis pas même certaine qu'il ne se croie pas un peu au-dessus. Mais chut !...

Louis XI, en effet, adressait une bienvenue aimable au voyageur venu de la ville sanctifiée par le tombeau de l'Apôtre et ajoutait :

— C'est toujours une grande joie, pour un cœur chrétien, d'accueillir un envoyé de notre Très-Saint-Père.

— Ce n'est pas pour te réjouir que le pape Sixte m'envoie vers toi, roi de France, car son cœur est lourd et plein de colère.

— De colère contre nous ? Cela est impossible. Nous ne nous souvenons pas d'avoir en quelque point que ce soit offensé le vicaire du Christ...

— Ta mémoire est courte, roi, et surtout complaisante. Tu oublies bien facilement que, depuis sept ans, tu détiens en dure prison un prince de la sainte Église. Le pape m'envoie t'ordonner de libérer sur l'heure le cardinal Balue !

Le visage de Louis XI se ferma et un éclair jaillit de sous sa paupière :

— Jean Balue est un traître qui méritait la mort car il n'a pas craint de comploter contre nous avec les gens de Bourgogne. Contre nous qui, d'un fils de meunier, avons fait un prélat couvert de richesse et d'honneurs, contre nous qui avons demandé et obtenu pour lui le chapeau de cardinal. Qu'il se tienne satisfait d'être encore en vie !

— C'est croupir au fond d'une cage, comme une bête fauve, que tu appelles être en vie ? Tu n'avais aucun droit de porter la main sur un homme de Dieu qui relève uniquement du pape.

— Nous avons tous les droits et le pape le sait bien qui a accepté voici trois ans le Concordat de Tours ! Nous serions tout disposé à faire un geste susceptible d'alléger le cœur de Sa Sainteté à condition qu'il ne s'agisse pas des affaires du royaume. Et il s'agit précisément d'une affaire du royaume...

— Tu refuses d'élargir le cardinal ?

— Positivement !

— Consens-tu toutefois à lire la lettre que t'adresse Sixte IV ?

— Une lettre ? Que n'avez-vous commencé par là, révérend frère...

Fray Ignacio tira de sa manche un mince rouleau de parchemin attaché d'un ruban blanc et scellé d'un large sceau doré que Louis XI reçut avec révérence et dont il baisa même le sceau avant de se tourner vers son chancelier pour qu'il décachette le message. A cet instant, Fiora bouscula Démétrios et s'élança sur le moine qui, déséquilibré, tomba à terre, laissant échapper le long couteau qui, dans sa main, venait de remplacer le parchemin. Les yeux vifs de la jeune femme rivés à fray Ignacio avaient entrevu l'arme, l'espace d'un éclair, et sa réaction avait été immédiate ; foncer droit devant elle avec une seule idée : écarter du roi la menace de mort qu'elle venait d'entrevoir. Le lévrier avait réagi avec la même impétuosité et, les pattes sur la poitrine du moine, il tenait sa gorge sous la menace de ses crocs. Fiora cependant se relevait, ramassait le poignard et, genou en terre, l'offrait à Louis XI :

— Sire, cet homme voulait tuer le roi !

Sans rien dire, celui-ci saisit l'arme et l'examina, prenant tout son temps et apparemment peu pressé de rappeler son chien qui grondait toujours, ce qui, d'ailleurs, paraissait inquiéter assez peu fray Ignacio. Si son visage n'était plus qu'un masque de fureur impuissante c'est uniquement parce qu'il venait de reconnaître Fiora :

— La Florentine ! cracha-t-il. La sorcière damnée ! Elle est ici et elle tente de m'imputer ses intentions criminelles !... C'est elle, c'est elle qui a apporté ce poignard, c'est elle qui...

— Qui s'apprêtait à nous tuer ? fit paisiblement Louis XI. Je suis avant tout ami de la logique et de la vraisemblance. Si l'idée de donna Fiora était de nous navrer, elle en avait tout le loisir l'autre jour à l'abbaye de la Victoire. Nous avons longuement parlé ensemble tête à tête. Ce que nous aimerions savoir plutôt, c'est en quelles circonstances elle a pu rencontrer cet étrange serviteur de Dieu.

Ayant déjà mis genou en terre, Fiora levait vers le roi ses grands yeux gris dont aucun nuage ne troublait la limpidité :

— S'il plaît au roi de m'entendre, je lui dirai tout.

— Et nous l'entendrons avec plaisir. Tout enfant déjà nous aimions fort les histoires de brigands. Messire de Commynes, veillez donc à conduire donna Fiora dans notre oratoire où nous la rejoindrons sous peu... A présent, « Cher Ami », retourne te coucher. Tu nous as bien servi et tu auras ta récompense. Capitaine Kennedy !

L'officier qui commandait la Garde Écossaise vint se placer auprès du moine qui, toujours à terre, n'osait se relever par peur des crocs du lévrier qui, bien qu'ayant obéi, grondait toujours :

— Aux ordres du roi ! Qu'ordonne-t-il ?

— A Dieu ne plaise que nous trempions nos mains dans le sang de cet assassin. Ainsi tu voulais mourir pour Balue, pauvre fou ?

— Je ne le connais même pas ! C'est pour ma reine, Isabelle de Castille que je suis prêt à périr. Tes soldats foulent et meurtrissent les terres qui sont siennes...

— Pas depuis longtemps et par mariage. Sans compter que la libre Catalogne ne lui a jamais appartenu. C'est à l'Aragon que nous avons eu affaire. Il serait bon que chez les frères du grand saint Dominique on apprenne un peu l'histoire et la géographie ? Hé ? Mais je ne te crois pas. La vérité c'est que le pape Sixte t'envoie. Il est l'allié du Téméraire et rien ne le réjouirait tant que notre mort. Qu'obtiendrait-il si tu avais réussi ?

— Qu'est-ce que j'en sais ? Tu es l'Antéchrist, le suppôt de Satan ! Tôt ou tard, tu recevras la punition de tes crimes, tôt ou tard tu sauras ce que pèse la malédiction. Pour avoir osé porter la main sur moi, tu seras excommunié, tu seras...

— Et pourquoi mon royaume ne serait-il pas mis en interdit ? ironisa Louis XI. Dieu que ce moine est fatigant ! Kennedy, mon ami, ôtez-le de là avant que la colère ne nous gagne...

— Et que faut-il en faire ?

— Faites-le conduire en notre château de Loches, sous bonne escorte. Il s'y trouve, si nous ne faisons pas erreur, une cage vide dans la salle où soupire ce cher Jean Balue. Mettez-les ensemble. Ils feront ainsi connaissance puisque apparemment ce fol est venu implorer la grâce d'un homme qu'il n'avait jamais vu. Ils devraient s'entendre.

Écumant de rage et de fureur, crachant le venin et l'anathème, fray Ignacio fut entraîné par quatre solides Écossais qui le portaient plus qu'ils ne l'encadraient. Les pieds du moine battaient l'air de façon grotesque... « Cher Ami » apaisé s'était recouché aux pieds du roi. Commynes prit Fiora par le bras :

— Vous venez, dit-il. Je crois qu'il n'y a plus rien à voir.

Elle le suivit sans se faire prier. Les hurlements de son ennemi résonnaient dans son cœur comme des chants d'allégresse... Ce moine qui semblait attaché à ses traces comme une malédiction, vivant rappel de la fureur aveugle qui l'avait précipitée en enfer, voilà qu'elle en était délivrée ! Elle ne savait pas où était ce château de

Loches mais, où qu'il soit, il mettait au moins entre elle et son ennemi l'épaisseur de ses murailles, de ses portes solides, de ses cachots profonds et de ses chaînes dans les cages...

— Il faut que cet homme soit fou, commenta Commynes. Venir attaquer notre sire au cœur de son royaume, dans l'un de ses châteaux, au milieu de ses gardes, de ses serviteurs et de ses amis ? Comment espérait-il en réchapper s'il avait réussi ?

— Le mieux du monde, j'imagine. Il se croit à la fois l'épée et la foudre de Dieu. En chaque prince temporel il voit un tyran. Il comptait sur la joie reconnaissante des esclaves libérés...

— Eh bien, si c'est là tout ce que le pape trouve à nous envoyer comme ambassadeur ! Je le croyais habile ?

— Il l'est peut-être plus que vous ne le pensez ? Réfléchissez : si l'attentat avait réussi, Sixte IV était débarrassé du plus puissant allié de Florence et donc d'un ennemi dangereux. Et comme fray Ignacio a échoué, il est débarrassé de toute façon d'un homme encombrant et dont il ne savait peut-être plus que faire lui-même. Ces fanatiques ont du bon — si j'ose dire — quand on sait s'en servir.

Commynes considéra Fiora avec une sincère stupeur puis éclata de rire :

— Moi qui me prenais pour un fin politique, je reçois là bonne leçon... Ah ! maître Olivier, veuillez nous laisser pénétrer chez le roi. Cette jeune dame doit l'attendre dans son oratoire.

La dernière phrase s'adressait à un homme qui sortait de l'appartement royal, tenant sous le bras un petit coffre. Vêtu de noir, le cheveu brun coupé court, le visage étroit d'une statue de bois, il avait des lèvres minces et des yeux qui possédaient l'immobilité et l'indéfinissable couleur d'un marais. Il s'inclina un rien trop bas et Fiora qui n'aimait pas sa figure le jugea obséquieux. La voix d'ailleurs était un peu trop douce :

— Monseigneur le prince de Talmont n'a pas besoin

qu'un modeste barbier le laisse pénétrer chez son maître. Il n'a qu'à paraître en personne!

Fiora crut déceler une trace de fiel dans ces dernières paroles. L'homme cependant ouvrait la porte avec une nouvelle courbette.

— Allons donc, maître Olivier! protesta Commynes avec un léger haussement d'épaules. Lorsque vous en décidez autrement, nul ne saurait entrer ici.

— Qui est-ce? demanda Fiora quand la porte se fut refermée sur eux et qu'ils se retrouvèrent dans une sorte d'antichambre meublée d'un seul coffre mais ornée de belles tapisseries.

— Le barbier de notre sire. Il se nomme Olivier le Daim et il est flamand comme moi mais il y a près de vingt ans qu'il est au service du roi et celui-ci apprécie beaucoup ses talents d'organisateur d'une maison. Il a en charge la préparation des voyages et déplacements et, grâce à lui, le roi retrouve toujours, où qu'il aille, ses affaires à la même place. Il est aussi de sens subtil et ne quitte jamais son maître. Il formerait même avec le secrétaire piémontais Alberto Magalotti une sorte... de... conseil étroit dont notre sire ne dédaignerait point d'écouter les avis.

— Il est si important avec si peu d'apparence?

— L'apparence n'a aucune influence sur le roi Louis et je ne suis pas certain que le Daim ait beaucoup de pouvoir, pourtant il convient de s'en méfier. Certains l'ont surnommé Olivier le diable. Mais vous voici à destination.

Après avoir traversé une chambre d'une grande sobriété dont les plus beaux ornements étaient certainement les chiens qui dormaient sur les tapis, Commynes fit entrer Fiora dans le petit oratoire dont la richesse frappa la jeune femme : tentures précieuses et panneaux peints — tous amovibles car, suivant la coutume du temps, la chapelle du roi comme ses meubles le suivaient dans ses différentes résidences — entouraient un autel drapé de brocart sur lequel s'élevait une croix de pierre auprès d'une statuette d'or représentant Notre-Dame de Cléry à laquelle

Louis XI vouait une dévotion toute particulière et d'une autre, en argent, à l'effigie de saint Michel au nom duquel le roi avait, le 1ᵉʳ août 1469, fondé à Amboise un ordre de chevalerie. Le collier à coquilles de cet ordre reposait sur la précieuse nappe d'autel, Louis XI se contentant d'ordinaire de porter une médaille au bout d'une simple chaîne. D'autres effigies de saints garnissaient de petites consoles au mur, certaines anciennes et une presque neuve représentant sainte Angadresme, la patronne de la ville de Beauvais qui avait opposé victorieuse défense aux troupes du Téméraire en 1472. La statuette avait été offerte au souverain par l'héroïne locale, Jeanne Laisné, dite « Jeanne Hachette », qui avait mené femmes et enfants au combat des remparts... Les couleurs chaudes d'un vitrail faisaient vivre tous ces objets.

— Que c'est beau! soupira Fiora. Voilà enfin une pièce digne du roi de France!

— Justement parce que c'est la seule où notre sire ne le soit plus. Il n'est ici que l'humble serviteur de Dieu.

— Par saint Louis, mon aïeul vénéré, il vous arrive de dire de grandes choses, Commynes! fit le roi qui venait d'entrer. A présent, me laissez avec donna Fiora mais attendez dans ma chambre...

Il s'agenouilla pour une courte prière et la jeune femme crut bon de l'imiter, ce qui fait qu'en se relevant il la trouva à genoux et lui tendit la main pour l'aider à se relever. Quand elle fut debout, il garda un instant ses doigts dans les siens, plongeant son regard songeur dans celui de la jeune femme.

— Alors? Ce moine espagnol? D'où le connaissiez-vous?

— De Florence où il tentait de saper le pouvoir de Monseigneur Lorenzo sur l'ordre du pape Sixte qui souhaite donner notre cité à son neveu, Girolamo Riario...

— Nous connaissons assez bien les idées de Sa Sainteté et c'est de vous qu'il est question.

— C'est une longue histoire, sire...

Les yeux du roi s'élevèrent vers la croix de pierre de l'autel :

— Dieu n'est jamais pressé. Nous non plus lorsqu'il s'agit du bien de l'État. Parlez !

Sans plus insister, Fiora entama la pénible histoire de ses relations avec Fray Ignacio. Elle le fit aussi objectivement que possible, sans essayer de foncer des couleurs déjà bien assez sombres. Elle savait qu'avec un homme de la trempe et surtout de l'intelligence de Louis XI, un récit clair, exempt de toute passion, serait mieux perçu qu'un lamento dramatique.

— Ainsi le seigneur Médicis a fait chasser ce moine de Florence, fit-il lorsque Fiora se tut. Bien sûr, c'est toujours délicate entreprise que frapper un membre de la sainte Église mais il nous paraît un peu désinvolte de n'avoir pas mis ce fanatique hors d'état de nuire. Quand le pape néglige ce qu'il doit aux princes chrétiens, il est du devoir de ceux-ci de mettre leurs terres, leurs gens et leur personne à l'abri. Fray Ignacio Ortega va pouvoir réfléchir longuement sur les dangers qu'il y a à mélanger les genres : ou l'on est un homme de Dieu, ou l'on est un espion et un assassin.

— Il est peut-être aisé de passer de l'un à l'autre dès l'instant où l'on se mêle de politique et je crois savoir que beaucoup de prêtres s'en occupent ?

— Et le pape plus encore que tous les autres ! Je crains qu'il ne soit un souverain temporel beaucoup plus qu'un père spirituel. En outre, il ne nous aime pas. C'est notre beau cousin, le duc Charles, qui a ses préférences. Il l'a clairement prouvé en lançant son légat, l'évêque de Forli Alessandro Nanni, entre lui et l'Empereur lors de l'affaire de Neuss. Grâce à l'habileté de celui-ci, il n'y a eu ni vainqueur ni vaincu. On s'est réconciliés, du bout des lèvres sans doute, mais le Téméraire a pu retirer ses troupes qu'en ce qui nous concerne nous trouvions fort bien là où elles étaient. Il se trouvait libre alors de s'occuper de nous...

— Mais il n'en a rien fait ?

— Il est difficile de faire la guerre quand on manque d'argent et de troupes fraîches. Ce moine devait être un bon moyen d'en finir une fois pour toutes avec le roi de France...

— Le roi est-il certain... qu'il ne pourra pas s'échapper ?

Louis XI plissa des yeux, laissant filtrer une lueur de gaieté et sourit :

— Si nous en avons le loisir dans les temps à venir, nous vous présenterons notre château de Loches. Viendrait-il des ailes à ce moine, qu'il ne pourrait s'en envoler. Mais assez parlé de châtiment ! Vous nous avez sauvé la vie et nous souhaitons vous en témoigner une gratitude à la mesure du service rendu. Que voulez-vous ?

Derechef Fiora plia le genou puis, inclinant la tête :

— Je sais que je vais demander beaucoup au roi mais tout ce que je désire c'est la vie... et la liberté du comte de Selongey.

Le silence qui suivit fut si pesant que la jeune femme frissonna et, sans oser relever les yeux, ajouta d'une voix faible mais cependant audible :

— Je ne désire rien d'autre, sire...

Toujours sans rien dire, Louis XI prit à deux doigts le menton de Fiora et considéra longuement les grands yeux gris aux cils desquels perlait une larme.

— Pauvre enfant ! soupira-t-il doucement. Amour vous tient en plus cruelle prison que ne sont les geôles de Loches ! Non, n'ajoutez rien !... Nous étions persuadé, en venant dans cette chapelle, que vous demanderiez la grâce de cet homme. Nous vous devons trop pour vous la refuser... bien que cela contrarie les espoirs que nous avions misés sur vous. Relevez-vous !

Il se détournait, allait prendre la statuette de sainte Angadresme qu'il scruta comme s'il pensait y trouver un défaut.

— Sire, commença Fiora, la reconnaissance que je...

— Non ! Ne remerciez pas ! Peut-être... ne méritons-nous

pas autant de gratitude que vous l'imaginez... En vous faisant venir ici, nous avions pensé, surtout vous ayant vue, que vous seriez pour nous... un bon otage, tout à fait de nature à déterminer le sire de Selongey à nous servir. Vous nous avez laissé entendre que notre prisonnier ne tenait pas à vous à ce point-là ! Dès lors, nous avions conçu un autre plan : obtenir vos services contre le Téméraire en vous faisant espérer sa grâce. Ce maudit moine et son poignard sont venus se mettre tout à la traverse... Enfin ! soupira-t-il, demain vous serez conduite à Compiègne auprès de...

— Que le roi me pardonne de l'interrompre, sire, mais je crois que nous ne nous comprenons pas. L'idée de la mort de celui que je croyais mon époux m'était insupportable. Il vivra et j'en remercie la clémence du roi mais je ne veux rien d'autre. N'ai-je pas dit l'autre jour à Votre Majesté que j'étais disposée à la servir si, ce faisant, je pouvais assouvir la haine que j'éprouve pour le duc de Bourgogne ? Rien n'est changé.

Louis XI baisa dévotement la précieuse figurine avant de la replacer sur son support. Sans se retourner vers Fiora il demanda :

— Vous ne souhaitez pas lui porter vous-même la nouvelle inespérée de sa libération ? Ce serait, il me semble, belle et noble vengeance ?

— Non sire. Je ne veux même pas le revoir pour ne point risquer de retomber sous le charme où il m'a tenue captive. En frappant le maître qu'il chérit plus que tout au monde, je serai mieux vengée...

— Et dans ce but, vous feriez... n'importe quoi ? Jusqu'à... vous donner à un autre homme ?

— Si mon mariage ne fut qu'un leurre, je n'ai pas à redouter l'adultère. Que le roi ordonne ! J'obéirai.

— Soit. Allez rejoindre messire Lascaris. Ce soir, vous souperez tous deux à notre table, en petit comité, ce dont personne ne s'étonnera après ce que vous avez accompli ce jour pour le royaume. Vous saurez plus tard, ce que vous aurez à faire...

S'agenouillant à nouveau devant l'autel scintillant, Louis XI s'abîma dans une profonde oraison. Fiora salua à la fois Dieu et le roi puis se retira à reculons...

L'orage qui avait menacé en grondant tout le jour, tournant autour de la ville et des grandes forêts qui l'environnaient, creva quand vint le soir, déversant sur toutes choses de véritables cataractes. Chaque rue se transforma en ruisseau et les gouttières en autant de petites cascades. Le tonnerre fulminait de majestueuses imprécations et les éclairs succédaient aux éclairs... Il n'y avait plus âme qui vive dans les rues. Seuls, les soldats de garde aux remparts recevaient la douche stoïquement. Après l'étouffante chaleur qui rendait les armures si pesantes, l'énorme averse devait être délicieusement rafraîchissante.

Posté derrière la fenêtre de sa chambre, le roi Louis considérait l'orage avec satisfaction : il songeait à son « bon frère », le roi Edouard IV d'Angleterre qui, le ventre creux et les pieds dans l'eau, devait attendre avec quelque impatience à présent la conclusion de l'accord secret que lord Howard et John Cheyney étaient venus six jours plus tôt établir avec lui. Ces deux-là, dont il était convenu qu'ils resteraient comme otages jusqu'à ce que l'armée anglaise eût repassé la mer, étaient les seuls qui ne devaient pas souffrir beaucoup de la faim : avant de les renvoyer à leur maître, on les avait nourris et abreuvés royalement, circonstance qui devait donner quelque chaleur à leurs propos...

— Les Anglais doivent nous attendre comme le messie ! déclara le roi en se frottant les mains. Tant d'eau et pas une goutte de bière ou de vin pour se remonter le moral...

— Espérons tout de même que la pluie cessera de tomber d'ici demain. Si c'est toujours demain que nous partons pour Amiens ? dit Commynes.

— Bien sûr que nous partons demain. L'entrevue avec Edouard est prévue pour le 29 de ce mois à Picquigny et nous avons d'ici là beaucoup de choses à mettre au point.

Demain aussi, j'ordonnerai à Tristan Lhermite, notre Grand Prévôt, de remettre en liberté le sire de Selongey et de le faire accompagner, sous bonne escorte jusqu'à Vervins. Là on le relâchera en lui faisant savoir que le Téméraire est à Namur. Il le rejoindra ainsi sans peine...

— Vous libérez cet homme qui a voulu vous tuer ? Sire, est-ce bien raisonnable ?

— Donna Fiora m'a sauvé la vie et c'est sa liberté qu'elle a demandée en récompense.

— Pourquoi ? C'est insensé !

— Elle est sa femme. C'est pourquoi j'avais voulu la voir... Allons Commynes, ne fais pas cette tête ! En libérant ce tranche-montagne je réalise, je crois, la meilleure affaire de ma vie. Donna Fiora croit son époux bigame — et il l'est peut-être après tout ! Elle ne sait pas au juste si elle l'aime ou si elle le hait. Une chose est certaine : elle ne veut plus le voir. Mais ce qui est beaucoup plus manifeste, c'est l'exécration qu'elle voue à Bourgogne dont elle a juré la mort. Je vais lui en fournir les moyens.

— Comment cela ?

— Je vais l'envoyer à Campobasso qui est l'un des principaux chefs de guerre du Téméraire mais qui n'a pas l'air de savoir exactement de quel côté sa tartine est beurrée...

— Je vois : elle représente le petit morceau de beurre chargé d'expliquer à ce condottiere que les vaches françaises produisent de meilleur lait et plus abondant que les vaches bourguignonnes ?

Louis XI se mit à rire et assena une bonne claque dans le dos de son jeune conseiller.

— Il y a plaisir à causer avec vous, messire Philippe... encore que votre métaphore champêtre ne convienne guère à pareille beauté. On dit Campobasso fort porté sur les dames et celle-ci, merveille, vient d'Italie, comme lui.

— Ne va-t-elle pas courir de bien grands périls ? Pour rejoindre le Napolitain, il va lui falloir traverser des régions infestées de soldats ? Elle est jeune... et fragile pour être ainsi lancée dans une fournaise, ajouta Commynes gravement.

Si gravement même que le roi fronça les sourcils.

— Pâques-Dieu, mon compère, tu es en train de tomber amoureux ? Souviens-toi que ton cœur appartient tout entier à dame Hélène, ta gracieuse épouse. La belle Florentine n'est pas pour toi.

— Vous préférez en faire don à ce reître ?

— Eh oui ! Rarement j'ai eu en main si belle arme et si bien trempée. Rassure-toi, elle sera protégée... A présent, allons remercier Dieu de toutes les bontés dont il nous comble et puis mettons-nous au lit. Demain, avant de partir, je verrai donna Fiora pour lui donner mes instructions.

— Si elle réussit, que ferez-vous pour elle ?

— Au lendemain de la mort du Téméraire, elle pourra demander ce qu'elle voudra. En outre, je lui destine certain petit château entouré d'une belle terre qui n'est point éloigné de notre manoir de Plessis-lez-Tours...

— Doux Jésus, sire ! fit Commynes scandalisé. Vous ne songeriez pas à en faire...

— Notre maîtresse ?... Hé, hé !... Ce n'est pas l'envie qui nous en manquerait mais nous avons juré de ne plus toucher autre femme que Madame la Reine et c'est un serment que nous entendons respecter. Néanmoins, le voisinage d'une fille d'Ève à la fois belle et intelligente est un plaisir qu'un honnête roi peut s'accorder. D'autant que le pays de Loire est bien le cadre idéal pour tant de grâce et de charme.

— J'en demeure d'accord, sire, mais... Selongey, bigame ou pas, dans tout cela ?

— Il faut espérer que, si le Téméraire trépasse, son plus fidèle chevalier n'aura pas le mauvais goût de lui survivre. Et nous pourrions alors envisager de marier sa veuve à quelque fidèle serviteur...

— Qui, bien sûr, ne serait pas moi ! grogna Commynes.

— Me prendriez-vous pour le Grand Turc, mon ami ? Je vous ai déjà marié... et fort bien marié. Ne pleurez pas !

Poussant une collection de soupirs qui en disaient long sur ce qu'il pensait des projets de son maître touchant la belle Fiora, le sire d'Argenton s'en alla coucher non sans avoir prié son valet d'aller lui chercher en cuisine quelques tranches de pâté ou de venaison escortées d'un flacon de vin. Les peines de cœur lui donnaient toujours faim...

Le soleil ne reparut pas le lendemain. Il demeura caché derrière d'épais nuages sombres, tellement tristes qu'ils ne pouvaient s'empêcher de verser, de temps en temps, quelques pleurs en forme de crachin qui détrempaient peut-être plus sûrement que les trombes d'eau de la veille... Cela n'arrangeait pas les chemins dont certains se transformaient en fondrières, mais le roi Louis n'en ordonna pas moins le départ en direction d'Amiens où Tanneguy du Châtel, qui y commandait d'importants effectifs, l'avait précédé.

Debout sur le rempart à la porte nord de la ville, Fiora, enveloppée d'une mante noire à capuchon qui la préservait de la pluie, regardait défiler le train du roi, s'émerveillant de la puissance qu'avait su réunir ce petit homme aux yeux vifs qui menait son royaume avec la sûreté de main d'un bon cocher, sans paraître se soucier des fondrières que creusaient sous les roues de son char les grands féodaux encore acharnés à se tailler la plus grosse part d'un gâteau en forme d'étoile qui s'appelait la France. Il est vrai qu'il disposait pour cela d'une puissance nouvelle et encore inconnue : une armée permanente, née des Compagnies d'Ordonnance créées par son père et qu'il avait su mener à un point de perfection rare. Cette armée se composait de quatre mille lances – la lance étant une unité tactique formée d'un homme d'armes, de son page, de son coutillier, de deux archers et d'un valet d'épée – s'ajoutaient la Garde Écossaise et la Garde Française. Outre cela, vingt mille francs – archers et artilleurs, plus six mille gens d'armes fournis par les seigneurs français. Sans oublier les canons, la redoutable artillerie dont les frères Bureau avaient doté la France sous Charles VII et que Louis XI avait améliorée encore. Tout cela formait, entre Dieppe et Reims, un long rideau de fer et de feu capable de résister victorieusement à l'armée anglaise.

Fiora, bien sûr, ne vit passer que les deux gardes royales précédant et suivant Louis XI qui chevauchait à la tête d'un groupe chatoyant de pennons, de cottes d'armes et de caparaçons joyeusement coloriés. Lui-même était à demi armé, portant avec la cotte de mailles courte une demi-cuirasse, des cuissards, des grèves et des solerets d'acier bleu. Pas de heaume empanaché cependant, mais un chapeau de feutre noir au bord retroussé et orné d'une médaille de saint Michel mais que cerclait la couronne d'or. Ainsi, il était plus simplement équipé que n'importe lequel de ses gardes mais il eût pu se dispenser de l'insigne royal car son maintien fier et son élégance de cavalier [1] ne laissaient planer aucun doute sur sa qualité : il était bien le roi. Quant à ses bagages, ils auraient pu être ceux d'un roi mage. Outre les chariots qui transportaient son lit démontable, sa chaise de commodités, ses tapisseries, sa chapelle et ses chiens, d'autres en interminable file portaient les lourds coffres pleins d'or qui avaient remplacé les barils parisiens ; d'autres encore chargés de victuailles de toutes sortes et de nombreux tonneaux, emplis de vin cette fois, étaient destinés à apaiser la faim de l'armée anglaise comme l'or la soif d'Edouard et de quelques-uns de ses barons. Des ribaudes suivaient, à pied ou en charrettes, afin de soutenir le moral des troupes comme cela se pratiquait dans toutes les armées du monde. Ainsi s'en allait le roi de France bouter l'Anglais hors de son royaume sans crainte d'y laisser seulement la vie du moindre de ses hommes. Néanmoins, l'oriflamme de saint Denis l'accompagnait comme il se devait en marchant vers un ennemi.

Le cœur un peu serré, Fiora vit passer Démétrios qui

---

1. Il était bien plus royal à cheval qu'à pied.

chevauchait auprès de Philippe de Commynes. Louis XI était trop satisfait des soins prodigués par le médecin grec pour lui permettre d'accompagner son amie :

— Il se peut que je vous autorise à la rejoindre dans quelque temps, lorsque je serai guéri. Jusque-là me suivrez !

Ni les prières de Démétrios ni celles de Fiora n'avaient pu fléchir cette volonté. Non sans raison, le roi estimait que Lorenzo de Médicis lui avait dépêché un médecin pour s'occuper de lui et pas pour courir les chemins avec une jolie femme.

— N'ayez crainte, ajouta-t-il en manière de consolation, vous serez présent pour l'hallali. Je sais que vous y tenez !

Force avait été de s'incliner mais Fiora, cependant, n'irait pas sans protection au-devant de son destin : Démétrios avait ordonné à Esteban de la suivre sans rencontrer d'ailleurs la moindre protestation. Le belliqueux Castillan n'était guère tenté par les combats à coups de jambons, de pâtés, de futailles et d'écus d'or tels que les affectionnait le roi Louis. Fiora, elle, s'en allait vers ce foudre de guerre, ce prince de la tempête et de ses fureurs qu'était le duc de Bourgogne. La balance, en dépit du dévouement qu'il portait à son maître, penchait irrésistiblement du côté de la jeune femme.

Jugeant d'ailleurs qu'Esteban constituait une escorte un peu mince, Louis XI avait commis à la garde de son ambassadrice occulte l'un des meilleurs sergents de sa Garde Écossaise, Douglas Mortimer, surnommé Mortimer-la-Bourrasque, qui possédait peut-être le plus affreux caractère de tout le régiment... peut-être parce qu'il n'avait pas eu l'honneur de voir le jour dans les Highlands vénérés mais bien à Plaimpied, au sud de Bourges, des amours passionnées puis légitimes d'un certain Francis Mortimer. Celui-ci avait fait ses premières armes comme jeune écuyer à la bataille de Baugé, où les cinq mille Écossais venus au secours du dauphin Charles – plus tard Charles VII – s'étaient couverts de gloire sous la bannière de John Stuart, comte de Buchan. Leur chef s'était retrouvé un jour connétable de France et comte d'Aubigny, non loin de Bourges, où il s'était établi. Le jeune Francis avait continué, le pli étant pris, à en découdre au service de la France, sous Buchan puis sous le Breton Richemont avec une parenthèse exaltante au service de Jehanne la Pucelle, l'envoyée de Dieu qui montrait courage d'homme mais dont le regard bleu avait tant de lumière... Tout cela ne lui avait guère laissé de temps à dépenser au service de l'amour et il s'était écoulé près de vingt ans avant que le guerrier se retrouvât captif d'un autre regard bleu et des blonds cheveux de Marguerite Lalliée, la jeune veuve d'un hobereau des environs d'Aubigny. Douglas était issu de ce coup de foudre mais, s'il avait toujours porté à sa mère tendresse et vénération, il ne pouvait s'empêcher de lui reprocher secrètement d'avoir fait de lui un des membres les plus représentatifs de cette race hybride, les Écossais-Berrichons, qui avaient proliféré autour d'Aubigny et de Bourges.

Aussi, fermement déterminé à ne pas perpétuer les Mortimer avant d'avoir eu la chance de retourner dans les Hautes Terres, le sergent la Bourrasque s'était-il consacré exclusivement à son métier de soldat en refusant avec obstination de s'apercevoir que villes et campagnes, sans compter la cour, offraient à son choix nombre de jolies jeunes filles et même de moins jeunes tout aussi charmantes. Pour l'hygiène, les ribaudes lui convenaient parfaitement. Quand l'envie lui en venait, il en prenait une sans y attacher plus d'importance que s'il s'agissait d'un gobelet de vin. Néanmoins, il la choisissait avec autant de soin que sa boisson.

Parvenu ainsi à l'âge de quarante ans, Douglas Mortimer élevait à près de six pieds sa tignasse roussâtre en accord parfait avec la longue moustache qui barrait son visage tanné, les épais sourcils qui abritaient ses yeux noisette — ceux de sa mère la Berrichonne! — et un nez d'une pureté si parfaitement romaine que l'on s'était longtemps demandé, en famille, où il était allé le chercher. Brave comme tous les chevaliers de la Table Ronde, fort comme plusieurs Turcs, la Bourrasque savait dresser un cheval et montait comme un Mongol, tirait à l'arc mieux que Robin des bois, faisait sauter la tête d'un homme, casque compris, d'un seul coup de hache, maniait la lance, l'épée, la masse et le fléau d'armes avec une adresse qui confinait à la perfection et s'offrait par-dessus le marché le luxe d'être intelligent. Louis XI, pour lequel il avait déjà rempli quelques missions, l'avait choisi à cause de ces talents variés, bien sûr, mais aussi pour une autre raison : Mortimer qui avait déjà beaucoup voyagé au service de son maître connaissait la France, la Bourgogne, la Lorraine et tous autres pays limitrophes comme sa propre poche.

Un peu perplexe en face de cette force de la nature qui posait sur elle un regard d'une parfaite indifférence, Fiora demanda timidement si son guide n'était pas trop contrarié de quitter son régiment et son splendide équipement pour veiller sur une simple femme.

— Pas cette fois, répondit calmement la Bourrasque. Les Anglais, je les aime mieux au bout de ma lance qu'au bout d'une cuillère à pot ! Les Bourguignons sont plus amusants.

Esteban, lui, était franchement furieux :

— Je suis capable de vous défendre en toutes circonstances et contre n'importe quel ennemi, donna Fiora, et je n'ai pas besoin de cette montagne de muscles ! Sa présence est une offense à mon courage et à mon dévouement !

Démétrios entreprit de le calmer :

— Le roi ne te connaît pas. En outre, donna Fiora peut être exposée à de graves périls contre lesquels vous ne serez pas trop de deux. Enfin, tu pourrais penser à moi !

— Je sais, maître ! Crois-tu qu'il ne me soit pas pénible de te quitter ? Même pour peu de temps ?

— Ce n'est pas cela que je veux dire. Qu'un autre prenne ma place auprès de celle que je considère un peu comme ma fille est contrariant pour les projets que nous avons formés ensemble.

— Tu n'as rien à craindre, intervint Fiora qui rejoignait à cet instant les deux hommes dans la cour du château où le départ se préparait après un ultime entretien avec le roi. Où est ton don de double vue, Démétrios ? Le rideau de l'avenir ne se lève-t-il plus pour toi ?

— Je peux lire dans l'avenir des autres mais pas dans le mien.

— Eh bien, lis dans le mien ! Ne vois-tu rien de ce qui m'attend ? Souviens-toi du bal au palais Médicis !

— Tu n'étais pour moi qu'une inconnue alors. L'affection trouble la vue du mage. Tu m'es devenue chère, petite Fiora...

Émue, la jeune femme prit les mains du Grec et se haussa sur la pointe des pieds pour poser un baiser sur sa joue. C'était la première fois qu'il faisait allusion à un lien affectif entre eux et elle en était touchée :

— Tu me rejoindras bientôt, j'en suis certaine. Le roi me l'a promis !

Sans répondre, Démétrios avait posé ses deux mains sur la tête de Fiora en un geste qui était une bénédiction.

— De toute façon je te rejoindrai. Avec ou sans la permission du roi...

Puis, se détournant, il était parti à grands pas rejoindre son cheval et Philippe de Commynes qui, déjà en selle, lui faisait signe de se hâter. Fiora et Esteban se rendirent alors, en silence, jusqu'au chemin de ronde des remparts d'où, à présent, ils regardaient s'égrener l'interminable cortège. Celui-ci s'estompa peu à peu, ses brillantes couleurs brouillées dans la brume que formait la petite pluie fine et persistante...

— Allons nous préparer maintenant ! soupira Fiora. Notre Écossais doit déjà nous attendre à l'auberge en trépignant...

En fait, Mortimer ne trépignait pas le moins du monde. Installé dans la grande salle, il vidait philosophiquement quelques pintes de bière tiède dans la meilleure tradition britannique. Posées devant lui, sur un banc, ses sacoches voisinaient avec une longue et large pièce de laine rousse grossièrement tissée dans laquelle un fil rouge et un fil vert dessinaient des carreaux et qui servait à la fois de manteau, d'écharpe et de couverture à l'Écossais. Vêtu de daim gris, il avait remplacé le grand béret à plumes de héron qui était d'uniforme par un autre, plus petit et en même tissu que son manteau, garni de plumes de faisan. Une dague et une longue épée pendaient de chaque côté de sa ceinture.

Ainsi équipé, Douglas Mortimer était superbe et majestueux à souhait ainsi qu'en témoignaient les yeux ronds de la jeune servante qui le contemplait, un doigt dans la bouche, sans qu'il y prêtât d'ailleurs la moindre attention. Mais, voyant entrer Fiora, il se leva, vida son pot, jeta une pièce sur la table, reprit son bagage et se dirigea vers la jeune femme :

— Prêt! fit-il sobrement. L'étape de ce soir est à Villers-en-Retz [1] !

— L'étape de ce soir est à Paris, dit Fiora doucement mais fermement. J'ai à y faire!

— Pas question! grogna l'Écossais. Le roi a ordonné : je vous conduis en Lorraine.

— Tout à fait d'accord mais il n'a pas précisé par quel chemin. Nous passerons par Paris!

— C'est du temps perdu. Quand le roi ordonne, on exécute. Le roi a dit en Lorraine, on va en Lorraine!

La voix du sergent la Bourrasque commençait à prendre quelque ampleur. Fiora comprit qu'il était temps pour elle d'user de cette vertu de patience que Démétrios proclamait souveraine en toutes choses :

— Écoutez, messire Mortimer : j'ai laissé à Paris, avec une jambe cassée, une femme qui m'a servi de mère, que j'aime infiniment, qui doit être en peine de moi et qui a le droit de savoir où je m'en vais. Je ne veux pas partir sans l'embrasser. Est-ce que vous pouvez comprendre cela?

---

1. De nos jours Villers-Cotterêts.

— Je ne comprends rien que les ordres du roi. Si vous vouliez faire le détour de Paris, il fallait le lui dire.

— Mais enfin qu'est-ce que cela peut vous faire de passer par un chemin ou par un autre ? s'écria Fiora qui commençait à perdre sa précieuse patience.

— A moi, rien, mais à mon cheval cela fait quinze lieues de plus et parfaitement inutiles. Sans compter le temps que nous allons perdre là-bas ! Ah, vous êtes bien une femme, hurla Mortimer dont la moustache commençait à se hérisser de fureur. Vous saurez que lorsque l'on a l'honneur...

Ils se dressaient l'un en face de l'autre comme des coqs de combat. Esteban se glissa entre les deux et prit Fiora aux épaules, tournant délibérément le dos à l'Écossais :

— Écoutez-moi, donna Fiora ! Vous savez combien je vous suis attaché et croyez bien que je n'ai aucune envie de donner raison à cet Écossais entêté mais il vaut mieux ne pas retourner rue des Lombards.

— Vous voulez que je parte pour une aventure dont je ne reviendrai peut-être pas sans embrasser ma chère Léonarde ? Oh, Esteban, je vous croyais un homme de cœur !

— Et je prétends l'être mais c'est à dame Léonarde que je pense. Sa jambe ne peut être encore guérie. Il y faudrait un miracle. Donc il ne peut être question de l'emmener. Si vous allez la rejoindre, elle vous posera des questions, s'inquiétera. Ce qui n'est pas le cas pour le moment. Elle vous croit auprès du roi et de mon maître. Ne pensez-vous pas qu'il est préférable de ne pas troubler la paix de son cœur ? D'autre part, j'ignore de quelle mission vous avez été investie et je ne veux pas le savoir, mais elle le désirera. Que lui direz-vous ?

Fiora se détourna lentement et les mains d'Esteban retombèrent. Il y eut un silence que Mortimer eut le bon goût de ne pas troubler, devinant peut-être que son adversaire était vaincue. Ce qui était le cas. Fiora savait bien qu'Esteban avait raison. Elle n'avait jamais rien su cacher à Léonarde quand celle-ci voulait savoir quelque chose.

Comment lui dire que le roi l'envoyait en Lorraine pour y séduire « par tous les moyens » l'un des capitaines du Téméraire et l'amener à la trahison pure et simple ? Léonarde pousserait les hauts cris, se mettrait en travers et peut-être que toutes deux en viendraient à une dispute, peut-être à une brouille que la jeune femme ne pourrait supporter... Et, pour le moment, elle avait besoin de tout son courage. Relevant les yeux, elle vit qu'Esteban l'observait. Douglas Mortimer, se désintéressant de la question, était allé vers la porte ouverte qu'il obstruait de sa puissante carrure et regardait tomber la pluie.

— Vous avez raison, mon ami. Mieux vaut laisser dame Léonarde vivre doucement sa convalescence dans le jardin de dame Agnelle. D'ailleurs, cela convient mieux à son âge que les rudesses des grands chemins et, ainsi, elle priera pour nous en toute quiétude... Messire Mortimer ! appela-t-elle.

L'Écossais se retourna :

— Madame ?

— Nous partirons quand vous voudrez... pour nous rendre là où vous l'avez décidé.

On fit étape, ce soir-là, à Villers-en-Retz.

Troisième partie

LES MERCENAIRES

CHAPITRE VIII

UN CONDOTTIERE

La pluie ne cessait pas. Le temps, détraqué, faisait de la fin de ce mois d'août une sorte d'automne précoce et apocalyptique où les grondements du tonnerre alternaient avec des pluies diluviennes et des sautes de vent violentes. Il fallait s'estimer heureux quand on ne recevait sur le dos que ce fin crachin qui enveloppait le paysage d'un brouillard d'eau. Cela trempait tout autant qu'un gros orage mais c'était, à tout prendre, plus facile à supporter. Fiora, enveloppée de sa grande mante noire à capuchon en dépit de la chaleur encore lourde, et Esteban sous son manteau de cheval faisaient le gros dos, mais la Bourrasque, comme s'il se sentait dans son élément, allait son chemin, drapé dans sa couverture sans perdre un pouce de sa taille. Bien droit sur sa selle, la plume en bataille, il menait son cheval par les chemins transformés en bourbiers et en fondrières avec autant de dignité que s'il eût escorté le roi. Sa large carrure coupait le vent devant Fiora lui bouchant un paysage qui, à vrai dire, n'avait rien de réconfortant. La Champagne que l'on traversait de part en part avait terriblement souffert des dernières guerres et en dépit de la poigne du roi Louis qui faisait régner au moins la sécurité, l'effort de redressement demeurait faible. Même à Reims, la ville royale, la ville du sacre, la misère montrait son visage blême. Des villages entiers avaient été brûlés que l'on s'efforçait de reconstruire mais la pluie incessante ne permettait guère de distinguer ce que l'on rebâtissait de ce qui était en ruine.

Après Reims ce fut pire. Crayeuse et désolée, la campagne montrait de grandes plaques blanchâtres entre les touffes de végétation. Il n'y avait pas d'auberges. Seuls, de maigres prieurés accueillaient le voyageur et, en dépit de leur bonne volonté, ne pouvaient lui offrir que des fruits, du miel et du fromage plus l'abri d'une grange qui ne contenait guère de paille. Néanmoins, Mortimer récompensait cette hospitalité royalement en homme qui a reçu des ordres et les exécute à la lettre plus qu'en généreux seigneur : chaque fois qu'il devait se séparer d'une pièce d'or, ses sourcils se fronçaient et sa moustache se tortillait sur une grimace.

— Je parierais qu'il est avare, chuchota Esteban un matin où l'on quittait l'un de ces pauvres relais. Le roi doit le savoir et a ordonné en conséquence. Sans cela cet olibrius aurait été capable de nous laisser mourir de faim et coucher à la belle étoile.

Les relations entre Fiora et son guide ne s'étaient guère améliorées. Une seconde algarade avait eu lieu à Senlis même, quand la jeune femme avait refusé fermement la litière que l'Écossais lui destinait et, ouvrant son manteau, avait montré son costume de garçon.

— C'est une dame que j'escorte, fulmina-t-il. Pas un galopin !

— Vous escortez Fiora Beltrami, lui déclara tranquillement la jeune femme, et cela m'étonnerait beaucoup que le roi ait pris la peine de vous dire comment je devais m'habiller et par quel moyen de locomotion je voyagerai. Je monte à cheval depuis ma plus tendre enfance et n'ai aucune envie de passer des heures secouée comme prunier en août dans cette espèce de boîte. Nous irons d'ailleurs plus vite !

Ce dernier argument avait emporté la décision mais, depuis, Douglas Mortimer n'adressait la parole à sa compagne que lorsque c'était tout à fait indispensable. Matin et soir, il la saluait sans piper mot.

Avec Esteban, les relations n'étaient pas plus chaleureuses. L'Écossais et le Castillan faisaient assaut de morgue et, eût-on dit, l'impossible pour être désagréables l'un envers l'autre. C'est ainsi qu'Esteban ayant découvert que Mortimer détestait l'entendre chanter, entreprit de charmer les longueurs de la route en régalant ses compagnons de toutes les ballades, romances et cantilènes qu'il avait pu emmagasiner depuis son enfance. Il avait d'ailleurs une voix agréable mais pour rien au monde Mortimer n'en aurait convenu. Il se contenta de dire à haute et intelligible voix qu'il pleuvrait sans doute moins si Esteban consentait à se taire.

Néanmoins, Fiora et son mentor furent bien obligés de reconnaître que la présence de la Bourrasque n'avait rien de superflu. Il allait son chemin avec sûreté, sans jamais se tromper et quand, au passage d'un petit bois, une demi-douzaine de brigands tomba sur les voyageurs avec l'intention évidente de les soulager de leurs biens, ils furent obligés de constater que le sergent la Bourrasque valait une escouade à lui tout seul. A la vue de l'ennemi, il entra dans une sorte de fureur sacrée et, poussant un hurlement à faire tomber des murailles s'il y en avait eu en vue, il fondit l'épée haute sur les nouveaux venus. En un clin d'œil il en coucha trois à terre pour l'éternité, ce que voyant, les trois autres s'enfuirent sans demander leur reste poursuivis par les tonitruantes malédictions d'un gosier digne d'avoir vu le jour à Glenlivet, berceau des Mortimer. Ces vociférations vouaient leurs descendances au pire destin après avoir émis des doutes insultants sur la qualité de leurs pères et mères. Esteban, aussi éberlué que les brigands, n'avait même pas eu le temps de tirer sa propre lame... Il ne put que joindre ses compliments – pas très sincères car il se sentait frustré – à ceux de Fiora tout autant abasourdie que lui-même :

– Si le roi en a seulement une douzaine comme vous, dit

celle-ci, il devrait pouvoir aplatir les armées de Bourgogne en une seule bataille...

— Nous sommes tous comme ça ! Je n'ai rien fait d'extraordinaire, répondit Mortimer redevenu instantanément aussi froid qu'il était bouillant la minute précédente.

Il ajouta, avec une désarmante simplicité :

— Nous, Écossais, sommes les meilleurs soldats du monde.

Puis rajustant son bonnet qui avait résisté victorieusement à une hache envoyée perfidement et à tout hasard, il reprit le chemin un instant interrompu suivi avec une sorte de respect par ses deux compagnons.

Lorsque l'on atteignit la Meuse qui, dans cette région, marquait la frontière entre le royaume de France et les états du duc de Bourgogne, Fiora pensa que l'heure était venue de se séparer de Mortimer, un des membres de la fameuse Garde Écossaise ayant bien peu de chance d'être accueilli aimablement sur les terres du Téméraire. Le pont et la petite ville de Dun était déjà en vue, et elle arrêta son cheval.

— Puisque c'est ici la Bourgogne, n'est-il pas temps de nous quitter, messire Douglas ?

Il s'arrêta lui aussi et tourna vers la jeune femme un regard glacé :

— Campobasso tient garnison à Thionville. Je vous conduis jusque-là. Le roi veut savoir comment vous serez reçue : ces mercenaires italiens sont des gens dont il convient de se méfier.

— Pourquoi seraient-ils moins honorables que d'autres ? demanda sèchement Fiora atteinte dans son amour-propre florentin.

— Justement parce que ce sont des mercenaires. Ils vont au plus offrant et, dans le combat, sont fort ménagers de leur sang, plus encore de leur vie. En tout cas, Campobasso n'a jamais passé pour un parangon de vertu. S'il en allait autrement, voulez-vous me dire ce que nous ferions ici ?

— S'il était si facile de le détourner de ses devoirs, voulez-vous me dire pourquoi l'on m'aurait envoyée ? riposta la jeune femme. Un sac d'or aurait suffi. Cela dit je suis... très heureuse de vous conserver comme guide.

— J'aimerais bien en être sûr, marmotta l'Écossais en rendant la main à sa monture.

Un moment plus tard, après de brèves palabres avec le capitaine commandant la petite place de Doulcon qui, face à Dun, surveillait le vieux pont bâti jadis par les légions romaines, et après avoir acquitté le droit de passage, Fiora et ses compagnons franchissaient ledit pont pour entrer dans la ville. Celle-ci marquait la frontière de l'ancien duché de Luxembourg devenu terre bourguignonne depuis qu'en 1441 la duchesse Élisabeth de Görlitz l'avait cédé au père du Téméraire. Pas pour son bien. La campagne se révélait plus misérable peut-être que la Champagne, ravagée qu'elle était tour à tour par les Français trop proches et par l'occupant bourguignon.

Contrairement à ce que pensaient les trois voyageurs, ils n'eurent aucune peine à se faire admettre. A la dernière étape, Fiora avait troqué son costume de garçon pour une robe et une coiffure de femme. Sa beauté, son élégance et l'air martial de ses deux compagnons impressionnèrent visiblement l'officier qui commandait la garde du pont. S'il montra quelque surprise en se trouvant en face d'une noble dame d'au-delà des Alpes et s'il émit quelques doutes sur l'agrément qu'elle pouvait trouver à parcourir un pays à ce point abandonné du ciel, il s'inclina lorsque la jeune femme dit calmement :

— Le comte de Campobasso que vous connaissez peut-être est mon cousin et je désire le rejoindre au plus tôt...

— Il aura sans doute grande joie d'une aussi belle visite mais, jusqu'à Thionville où il se trouve, le chemin n'est guère sûr pour une femme. Je serai heureux de vous faire escorter car, s'il vous arrivait malheur, il ne me le pardonnerait sans doute pas.

— Un laissez-passer sera amplement suffisant, capitaine. Mon écuyer et mon secrétaire sont de taille à me défendre en cas de mauvaise rencontre...

— Je ne mets nullement en doute leur valeur mais un laissez-passer ne suffira pas si vous tombez sur un parti de soldats en train de fourrager car la plupart ne savent pas lire. Croyez-moi, le tabard de Bourgogne sur les épaules de deux solides gaillards vous sera d'une plus grande aide que tous les papiers du monde.

Et c'est ainsi que le lendemain, après avoir accepté pour la nuit l'hospitalité de l'officier et enchanté sa mémoire pour de longues semaines, Fiora, qui s'en allait travailler à la perte du duc de Bourgogne, quitta Dun sous la garde de ses couleurs. Dans deux jours, si rien ne se mettait à la traverse, elle rejoindrait celui dont elle avait mission de faire un traître...

Le surlendemain, vers la fin du jour, deux hommes jouaient aux échecs dans la salle haute du château de Thionville. Bien que le jour ne fût pas encore éteint, un haut chandelier de fer forgé portant une douzaine de chandelles éclairait le jeu d'ébène et d'ivoire. Dans la grandiose cheminée, un feu flambait pour tenter de combattre l'humidité. Construit au siècle précédent pour les ducs de Luxembourg, le château avec ses murs énormes était une solide forteresse capable de supporter n'importe quel assaut. En effet Thionville et sa région formaient un coin enfoncé dans le duché de Lorraine avec lequel les Luxembourg n'étaient pas toujours d'accord. Il fallait que la cité et ses défenses fussent à la hauteur de leur mission et elles l'étaient, mais le confort intérieur avait ce quelque chose de spartiate qui est l'apanage des bâtiments militaires.

La salle où jouaient les deux hommes n'échappait pas à cette règle. En dehors de la petite table où reposait le jeu et des deux chaises à bras garnies de daim sur lesquelles ils étaient assis, l'ameublement se composait strictement d'un grand coffre de bois noirci par le temps et de deux trophées d'armes anciennes. Une tapisserie qui aurait gagné à être trois ou quatre fois plus grande et quelques bannières aux couleurs passées accrochées très haut sous la voûte faisaient ce qu'elles pouvaient pour réchauffer une salle construite pour les grandes assemblées et où les deux hommes semblaient un peu perdus. Les fenêtres, hautes et étroites, s'ouvraient au fond de profondes embrasures comportant chacune deux bancs de pierre et il fallait vraiment un soleil éclatant pour qu'elles donnassent un éclairage convenable. Par temps gris, elles ne dispensaient qu'un jour pauvre auquel il convenait de suppléer. D'où le feu et les bougies.

Les deux hommes, pour différents qu'ils fussent, étaient également remarquables. L'un était grand, bien bâti avec cette sorte de grâce animale des grands fauves. Sous la tunique de daim noir qui le vêtait on devinait une musculature longue, déliée, une souplesse d'homme entraîné à tous les exercices du corps. Ses épais cheveux noirs s'argentaient aux tempes et adoucissaient un peu un visage aux traits durs, au teint basané, sillonné de cicatrices qui en déparaient l'harmonie classique, à l'œil noir, vif et perçant : c'était Campobasso. L'autre, nettement plus petit mais bâti en force, avait la peau couleur de terre cuite et les cheveux diversement colorés d'un qui a passé sa vie sous le soleil. L'œil vif lui aussi mais d'un vert foncé qui devenait presque jaune autour de la pupille, il ne quittait pratiquement jamais la cotte aux mailles brillantes qui apparaissait sous un tabard rouge à ses armes : c'était son collègue et ami, Galeotto.

Cola di Monforte, comte de Campobasso, appartenait à une antique famille des environs de Naples qui s'était attachée à la fortune de la maison d'Anjou. D'étranges bruits couraient sur lui et les siens. On disait que son père était mort lépreux et qu'il avait tué sa femme infidèle dont il avait eu cependant deux fils. Quand, en 1442, le « bon roi René » qui régnait sur Naples et sur la Lorraine avait été chassé, par Alphonse d'Aragon, de son royaume méditerranéen sur lequel veillait le Vésuve, Campobasso, alors âgé de dix-huit ans et attaché à la suite de Jean de Calabre, le fils aîné de René, ami de surcroît de son fils Nicolas, avait quitté sans regret une terre pauvre et qui ne rapportait guère pour les doux horizons de la Provence et de l'Anjou. Du château de Tarascon à celui d'Angers, Campobasso avait suivi la fortune de Nicolas de Calabre devenu duc de Lorraine à la mort de son père Jean. Cela lui avait valu de devenir maître et seigneur du château de Pierrefort, à Martaincourt, une vigoureuse forteresse dominant de ses hautes murailles la pittoresque vallée de l'Esch où il tenait garnison comme un prince. En effet, condottiere dans l'âme, attaché à la guerre autant qu'à l'argent, Campobasso n'était pas parti seul de ses terres campaniennes mais avec quelques-uns de ses vassaux qui lui composaient l'agréable début d'une petite armée avec laquelle il convenait de compter car, bien équipée et bien entraînée par un homme pour qui les armes n'avaient plus de secrets, elle composa rapidement une « condotta » de valeur.

Peut-être Campobasso serait-il demeuré fidèle à la maison d'Anjou si, à la fin de juillet 1473, le jeune duc Nicolas n'était mort subitement. Si vite même que l'on parla d'empoisonnement mais il fallait un successeur. La noblesse lorraine porta la couronne ducale à la fille aînée du vieux roi René, Yolande, veuve du comte Ferry de Vaudémont, mais celle-ci ne souhaitait pas régner : elle vivait de ses souvenirs dans son château de Joinville. Cependant elle avait un fils de vingt-deux ans auquel, tout naturellement, elle transmit ses droits héréditaires. Celui-ci devint le duc René II.

Mais ce maître-là ne convenait pas à Campobasso. Il le jugeait trop frêle, trop aimable, trop « damoiseau ». En revanche, quand en septembre et à Luxembourg, alors qu'il faisait encore partie de la garde de René II, il rencontra le duc de Bourgogne, il pensa que c'était là le chef qui correspondait à ses vœux. Il connaissait d'ailleurs le Téméraire pour l'avoir rencontré, huit ans plus tôt, lorsqu'il prenait la tête de cette fameuse Ligue du Bien Public montée contre le roi de France et dont faisaient partie Jean de Calabre, alors duc de Lorraine, et son fils Nicolas. Il s'en fallait de deux ans que Charles ne s'installât sur le trône de son père mais son arrogance et sa splendeur séduisirent Campobasso. Devenu le Grand-Duc d'Occident, il l'éblouit.

Résultat : toujours en cette année 1473 mais en décembre, le Téméraire mettait pied à terre dans la cour du château de Pierrefort où le condottiere l'accueillait. Le Bourguignon n'eut aucune peine à détourner son hôte du service de « l'Enfant », car celui-ci n'attendait que cela. Royalement payé et couvert de présents par le plus fastueux des princes, Campobasso accepta le poste de commandement des troupes lombardes qu'il se chargeait d'aller recruter à Milan.

En dépit des apparences, c'était à peine une trahison. Charles de Bourgogne se disait le meilleur ami du jeune René qu'il avait obligé à accepter sa protection « contre les menées du roi de France ». Protection qui coûtait au jeune souverain quatre de ses meilleures villes où s'installèrent des garnisons « protectrices », essentiellement bourguignonnes et entièrement tyranniques.

« L'Enfant » cependant ne s'y trompa pas et, trois mois plus tard, il faisait incendier le donjon de Pierrefort en l'absence de son propriétaire – il n'eut pas le temps de détruire le reste – privant ainsi le château du Napolitain de sa meilleure défense.

Pour consoler Campobasso le Téméraire lui promit que, la Lorraine soumise, il pourrait choisir telle ville qui lui conviendrait. Son intention était en effet d'écraser le petit duc pour s'assurer ses terres qui étaient le meilleur lien pour unir les Pays-Bas à la Bourgogne proprement dite.

Promesse encore à tenir, en cette fin d'année 1475, car, depuis, le Téméraire n'avait cessé de guerroyer et Campobasso de le servir avec un talent et une fidélité qui semblaient à toute épreuve.

Jacopo Galeotto était moins compliqué. Condottiere au service du duc de Milan, il rejoignit sans se faire prier l'armée bourguignonne au siège de Neuss lorsque Campobasso vint le lui demander. Les deux hommes étaient liés d'amitié et se complétaient car, si l'un et l'autre étaient des guerriers endurcis et des cavaliers émérites, Galeotto possédait un talent supplémentaire et bien utile : c'était un ingénieur traînant après lui une troupe de charpentiers habiles à construire tours de siège, béliers et autres machines de guerre – et ces engins firent merveille au siège de Neuss mais sans parvenir à vaincre la résistance acharnée des habitants et de la garnison. Galeotto, bien sûr, en conçut quelque rancœur cependant que Campobasso commençait à se poser des questions. Il avait vu la superbe armée bourguignonne bloquée durant des mois devant un caillou têtu et s'y user sans résultat intéressant. Or, gagner à Neuss, c'était mettre l'empereur à genoux et c'était ouvrir l'Allemagne à ses appétits. Au lieu de cela, il avait fallu se replier sous la bénédiction d'un évêque italien ce qui n'était qu'une mince consolation pour qui espérait un gros butin.

Campobasso y pensait encore. Il y avait à présent deux grandes heures qu'il jouait aux échecs avec son ami sans s'intéresser vraiment au jeu. Son esprit était ailleurs. Soudain, il se leva. Si brusquement que l'échiquier se renversa. Les pièces noires et blanches roulèrent sur le dallage qu'aucun tapis ne réchauffait.

– C'est malin! grogna Galeotto. Le prochain coup, tu étais échec et mat mais tu ne comprendras jamais que s'obstiner à défendre sa reine est une erreur.

– Excuse-moi. Je joue mal, c'est vrai, mais je ne suis pas à ce que je fais.

– Où es-tu alors ?

Sans répondre, le condottiere alla jusqu'à l'une des fenêtres qui dominaient la Moselle et en considéra un instant le flot vif qui reflétait un ciel désespérément gris. Au-delà du pont gardé par ses mercenaires, il pouvait distinguer quelques faibles lumières jaunes qui s'allumaient dans le vieux quartier juif presque désert d'ailleurs car, si les ducs de Luxembourg avaient montré aux enfants d'Israël une certaine tolérance, il n'en allait pas de même avec le duc de Bourgogne. Les plus jeunes d'entre eux étaient partis pour rejoindre les colonies juives de Francfort ou de Cologne. Seuls, quelques vieux restaient pour le service de l'antique synagogue et ils étaient les seuls, dans une ville où Campobasso faisait peser une férule impitoyable, à se féliciter de sa présence. Habitué depuis toujours aux ghettos des cités italiennes, le commandant de la place n'avait pas jugé utile d'exterminer quelques vieillards qui avaient d'ailleurs eu la bonne idée de lui acheter leur tranquillité.

Galeotto rejoignit son ami près de la fenêtre et considéra un instant la grisaille extérieure :

— Que trouves-tu de si passionnant à regarder tomber la pluie sur la rivière ?

— Ce n'est pas la pluie que je regarde : ce sont nos hommes. Ils sont tous nés au-delà des Alpes et ils sont tous aussi malheureux que moi.

— Malheureux ? En voilà un mot dans ta bouche ! Qu'est-ce qui te gêne ?

— Tout ! Et d'abord cette ville où tout est noir ! Noir comme cette terre où il ne pousse rien...

— Mais qui nous donne du fer avec lequel on forge des armes. Ce n'est pas un mince avantage.

— Tu crois ? Moi je donnerais tout le fer du monde pour revoir la baie de Naples et mes collines sous le soleil...

— Nous sommes condottieri, fit Galeotto en haussant les épaules avec philosophie. Un jour ici, un jour là et si la paye est bonne...

— Tu la trouves bonne, toi ? Nous n'avons rien touché depuis Neuss où nous espérions si beau butin. Ensuite, nous sommes venus ici pour nous refaire mais le pays n'est pas celui de Cocagne. N'importe, nous espérions la France que nous devions conquérir de compte à demi avec les Anglais et tu as entendu ce qu'a dit ce moine que nous avons pris ce matin : le roi Édouard, gavé d'argent et de vins français, a repassé la mer et nous, nous restons là comme des imbéciles dans ce nid à chauves-souris suspendu au-dessus de la Lorraine... dans laquelle nous n'avons pas le droit d'entrer !

— Il y a pourtant des Bourguignons en Lorraine. Nous tenons quatre villes...

— Nous ? As-tu oublié que nous ne sommes que des mercenaires ? Le duc Charles réserve les bonnes places à ceux de son proche entourage, à des seigneurs nés sur son terroir, pas à des coureurs d'aventures comme nous...

— Nous n'en avons pas moins un poste de confiance. Et la place n'est pas si mauvaise... ou bien es-tu en train de me dire que tu préférerais servir le roi Louis ? Alors là je t'arrête ! Louis XI n'a que faire de nous. Il possède peut-être la meilleure armée du monde, une armée permanente entretenue toute l'année sur le pied de guerre et il ne s'en sert même pas. Celui-là, c'est avec sa cervelle qu'il se bat !

— Il a pourtant des mercenaires. Sa fameuse Garde Écossaise...

— La plupart de ses hommes sont nés en France. Ils sont devenus plus français que les vrais...

— Mais ils sont couverts de privilèges, d'honneurs et d'or...

— Sans doute mais ils sont fidèles, ce que nous ne sommes ni l'un ni l'autre. Après tout fais-toi écossais si le cœur t'en dit !

— Ne sois pas stupide. Nous avons l'un et l'autre des hommes qui attendent de nous profit et gloire. Si nous...

L'entrée d'un page trempé dont les longs cheveux noirs dégouttaient d'eau sous un bonnet à la plume réduite de moitié lui coupa la parole. C'était un garçon d'une douzaine d'années, beau comme un ange mais dont le regard insolent avouait une assurance nettement au-dessus de son âge et de sa condition. Ce regard ignora Galeotto pour se poser, câlin et vaguement complice sur Campobasso qui sourit :

— Que veux-tu, Virginio ?

— J'apporte des nouvelles, Monseigneur...

— Des nouvelles du duc ? s'écria le condottiere avec une hâte qui lui mit le feu aux joues.

Le page haussa les épaules :

— Rien d'aussi important, Monseigneur. Trois voyageurs viennent d'arriver à la porte de France : deux hommes et une femme. La femme dit qu'elle est votre cousine ?

— Ma cousine ? Du diable si j'ai encore une cousine ! Comment est-elle ? Jeune ?

— Je crois...

— Belle ?

Le page haussa de nouveau les épaules avec un dédain qui amusa Galeotto.

— A ta place, fit-il, je demanderais à voir. Ce cher Virginio est mauvais juge en matière de femmes. Et puis une cousine qui t'arrive ainsi du bout du monde, cela mérite quelques égards.

— Si Monseigneur dit qu'il ne la connaît pas, ce ne peut être qu'une espionne. Je vais dire au corps de garde qu'on les jette en prison, elle et ses compagnons...

Avant que Campobasso ait trouvé le temps de répondre, Galeotto avait empoigné le page par le col de son tabard armorié et le soulevait de terre :

— Hé ! là, moucheron ! Pas si vite ! Depuis quand est-ce que tu donnes des ordres ici ? Pour que cette femme te déplaise tant, elle doit être intéressante...

— Repose-le ! fit Campobasso. Et toi, Virginio, va chercher ces gens et amène-les-moi. Ou plutôt amène la femme et laisse les hommes au corps de garde. A propos, où est Salvestro ?

D'une voix soudain enrouée, le page qui se massait la gorge en jetant à Galeotto des regards furieux répondit :

— Votre écuyer est chez le bourgmestre. Celui-ci a tué un cochon et il a oublié d'en envoyer la moitié au château.

— Dans ces cas-là il faut prendre le cochon tout entier. Je ferai des reproches à Salvestro. Va à présent !

— Tu lui laisses prendre un peu trop de place, dit Galeotto quand le garçon eut disparu. Il y a tout de même des femmes ici, sans compter les ribaudes de la troupe...

— Aucune de ces femelles n'est aussi belle que lui, fit le comte avec un sourire ambigu. Il a le corps d'un jeune dieu grec... et il aime l'amour.

— Un jour viendra où tu ne pourras plus t'en faire obéir. Tu devrais l'envoyer rejoindre ton fils à Pierrefort car si un jour le duc venait à s'apercevoir...

— Ai-je encore assez d'importance à ses yeux pour qu'il s'occupe de ce qui se passe dans mon lit ? fit Campobasso avec amertume. Je me demande parfois si lui-même n'en fait pas autant ? Jamais aucune femme ne franchit le seuil de sa chambre ou de sa tente...

— Il n'en a pas besoin. Le père a eu tellement de maîtresses qu'il en a dégoûté le fils. Et puis, on dit qu'il ne peut oublier sa première épouse, Isabelle de Bourbon. Même la seconde qui est cependant désirable n'a pu obtenir de lui qu'un intérêt poli. Il est vrai que l'on dit aussi qu'elle n'était pas vierge quand il l'a épousée... Par tous les saints du ciel !

Les yeux de Galeotto venaient de s'arrondir en même temps que la porte s'ouvrait pour livrer passage à Fiora. Elle se tenait debout au seuil, enveloppée de sa grande mante noire où brillaient les gouttelettes de pluie, le capuchon rejeté en arrière libérant sa tête fine que ses nattes brillantes où s'attachait un voile vert couronnaient superbement. Hautaine, elle posait ses grands yeux gris sur ces deux hommes qui la contemplaient, muets d'admiration.

— Voilà votre cousine, Monseigneur, lança Virginio. Sa voix mauvaise rompit le charme.

— Qu'elle soit la bienvenue ! murmura Campobasso comme du fond d'un rêve. Va-t'en, Virginio !... Toi aussi, Galeotto !

— Que je... commença l'autre, sidéré.

— Je veux être seul un moment... avec ma belle cousine, coupa le comte qui ne quittait pas Fiora des yeux. Sois sans crainte, tu pourras la revoir au souper... mais ce premier instant m'appartient.

Il demeura debout en face de la jeune femme jusqu'à ce que les deux autres eussent quitté la pièce dans un silence que troublait à peine le bruit du feu dans la cheminée. Fiora n'avait pas encore prononcé une seule parole et lui ne disait plus rien. Simplement il la regardait... comme si le temps venait de s'arrêter, comme si toute sa vie était suspendue à ce regard. Et ce fut Fiora qui rompit le silence.

— Ne m'offrirez-vous pas, dit-elle doucement, de m'asseoir auprès du feu ? Je suis trempée...

— Et moi je suis impardonnable...

Il s'empressait à présent, conduisait sa visiteuse près de la cheminée, tisonnait les bûches qui s'écoulèrent en une multitude de braises étincelantes, ajoutait du bois avec des mains qui tremblaient un peu, avançait l'un des sièges recouverts de daim, enfin aidait Fiora à se débarrasser de sa mante mouillée. Ne sachant qu'en faire, il la mit sur son bras et frappa dans ses mains. Virginio, qui ne devait pas être loin, apparut instantanément :

— Encore toi ? Est-ce qu'il n'y a plus de valets dans ce château ?... Porte ce vêtement dans ma chambre où tu le mettras à sécher devant le feu. Et puis va aux cuisines : fais-nous porter du vin et veille à ce que l'on serve promptement le souper !

Le page arracha le manteau plus qu'il ne le prit et partit en courant, des larmes de rage au fond des yeux. Campobasso revint vers Fiora et s'assit devant elle sur la marche de l'âtre.

— Ainsi nous sommes cousins ? C'est à n'y pas croire ! fit-il avec un sourire plus émerveillé que sceptique. Êtes-vous napolitaine ?

— Non, florentine. Je me nomme Fiora Beltrami. Mon père était l'un des puissants citoyens de Florence...

— Était ?

— Je l'ai perdu voici quelques mois. Quant à notre cousinage il est, je crois, assez lointain et remonterait à une aïeule venue de Naples. Les Florentins prenant rarement femme hors de Toscane, le fait était assez exceptionnel pour qu'on en ait gardé le souvenir.

— Remercions donc cette aïeule ! Personnellement je sais peu de chose sur les femmes de ma famille, hormis que certaines furent assez turbulentes. Mais que faites-vous si loin de votre ville ? Ce n'est tout de même pas pour me rejoindre que vous avez fait ce long voyage ?

— Non. Je vous l'ai dit : mon père est mort... et les Médicis m'ont chassée pour s'emparer de sa fortune. J'ai cherché refuge en France où il avait... de grandes amitiés...

— Si grandes que cela ?

— Je crois qu'il ne saurait en exister de plus hautes. C'est dans cet entour que j'ai entendu prononcer votre nom pour la première fois et la fantaisie m'est venue, à moi qui n'ai plus de famille, de vous voir de plus près... L'été me semblait une bonne saison pour voyager. Hélas, le ciel n'était pas du tout de cet avis !

Elle se leva pour s'approcher du feu et les yeux de l'homme qui la regardait se mirent à briller d'un éclat sombre. La robe de fin drap, souple comme un gant, qui la revêtait épousait les formes d'une gorge exquise, ronde et ferme, la finesse d'une taille dont on avait envie de prendre la mesure. C'était plus une fantaisie de couturière parisienne qu'une robe vraiment à la mode mais Agnelle avait pressé Fiora d'acheter cette robe qui semblait peinte sur son corps, du moins jusqu'aux hanches, avant de s'évaser pour finir en une courte traîne que l'on pouvait attacher au poignet.

— Néanmoins, vous êtes arrivée jusqu'ici. Puis-je demander si vous regrettez ce pénible voyage ?

Elle le regarda entre ses cils rapprochés et se mit à rire, un rire aussi doux que le roucoulement d'une colombe :

— Vous voulez savoir si je suis déçue ? Eh bien non... Vous êtes... très beau, messire mon cousin, mais je pense que vous ne l'ignorez pas et que plus d'une belle dame vous en a persuadé. Telle est du moins votre réputation.

— J'ignorais que cette réputation fût allée jusqu'en France ?

— Il faut bien qu'il en soit ainsi puisque je suis là. J'ai voulu vérifier... Mais n'en soyez pas surpris : à Florence les femmes sont accoutumées à dire librement ce qu'elles pensent, et ce qu'elles désirent. Il se trouve que je suis libre de faire ce qu'il me plaît...

Se moquait-elle de lui ? Campobasso l'envisagea un instant mais il était déjà au-delà de tout raisonnement clair et ne savait plus qu'une chose : cette fille qui lui tombait du ciel ou qui lui venait de l'enfer, il fallait qu'elle soit à lui. Jamais il n'avait vu de femme aussi belle, aussi séduisante. Elle lui faisait bouillir le sang et il n'aimait pas attendre... Se levant d'un brusque coup de reins, il posa ses mains sur les hanches de Fiora pour la rapprocher de lui :

— Sais-tu, fit-il en italien, qu'il peut être dangereux de me plaire... un peu trop ?

— Pourquoi dangereux ? Je n'ai peur de rien, répondit-elle dans la même langue. Moins encore depuis que je t'ai vu. A cet instant j'ai espéré que tu me trouverais belle...

— Belle ?...

Il voulut se pencher sur sa bouche, grisé par l'étrange odeur de fleur, d'herbe et de laine mouillée qui émanait de ce corps souple qu'il sentait vivre entre ses doigts, mais déjà elle lui échappait en tournoyant sur elle-même comme pour une figure de danse.

— Ne me regardez pas comme si vous étiez un loup affamé et moi une pauvre agnelle, cousin ! fit-elle en souriant. Songez que je viens de faire un long voyage et que c'est plutôt à moi d'être affamée ! Nourrissez-moi, cousin ! Nous aurons tout le temps de... causer après, non ?

Avec l'impression de s'échapper d'un rêve, Campobasso se secoua comme s'il sortait de l'eau et se tourna vers Fiora, craignant qu'elle n'ait été qu'un mirage, mais elle était toujours là. Les bras haut levés, ce qui faisait saillir ses seins, elle détachait les épingles qui retenaient son voile et sa chevelure :

— Mes cheveux sont tout mouillés et me coulent dans le cou ! dit-elle en riant.

Instantanément, la masse noire et luisante glissa sur ses épaules et le long de son corps. L'homme qui la dévorait des yeux pensa que, dans cette robe verte, avec ses longs cheveux humides, elle ressemblait à une sirène et il la désira plus encore. Mais il résista à l'envie qui lui venait de se jeter sur elle, de déchirer sa robe et de la prendre tout de suite, sur les dalles de pierre. En bon Napolitain, il savait apprécier la savoureuse souffrance de l'attente, à condition qu'elle ne dure pas trop longtemps et, sur ce point, il était rassuré. Son orgueil de mâle lui soufflait que cette affolante sorcière aux yeux couleur de nuages n'était apparue que pour s'offrir à lui... Et puis ne venait-elle pas de France ? Cette France où elle avouait avoir de si hautes amitiés ?

Il levait les mains pour appeler de nouveau quand la porte s'ouvrit, livrant passage à des valets chargés de tréteaux, d'un plateau de bois et de nappes pour dresser la table. Virginio les suivait et ses yeux sombres s'arrêtèrent d'abord, pleins de haine, sur Fiora qui, devant le feu, faisait sécher ses cheveux, puis sur son maître avec une interrogation muette qui fit sourire celui-ci. Campobasso jouissait cruellement de la jalousie qu'il sentait bouillonner dans l'âme de son page.

— Où va-t-elle coucher ? demanda Virginio en désignant la jeune femme d'un mouvement de tête dédaigneux.

— Donna Fiora, répondit le condottiere en appuyant sur l'appellation, couchera dans ma chambre, bien entendu. C'est la seule convenable avec celle du seigneur Galeotto. Tu veilleras à ce que les draps soient changés...

— Et vous alors ? Où coucherez-vous ?

— *Chi lo sa ?...* Peut-être dans ma chambre ? Pourquoi pas ?

— Et moi ? fit le garçon avec insolence.

— Toi ?... Où tu voudras. Tiens... avec Salvestro quand il reviendra de chez son bourgmestre...

Le garçon devint très pâle et ses yeux noirs lancèrent des éclairs :

— Je la tuerai, tu entends, fit-il entre ses dents serrées. Je la tuerai si tu y touches...

D'un doigt négligent, Campobasso caressa la joue duvetée du page et son sourire s'accentua, découvrant des dents fortes et blanches, de vraies dents de carnassier :

— Alors j'aurai le regret de te faire pendre, mon petit Virginio, fit-il doucement. C'est d'ailleurs ce qui t'arriverait si elle était victime du moindre accident... Avoue que ce serait dommage car nous pourrions avoir encore de belles heures tous les deux. Songes-y !

— Mais enfin qu'est-ce qu'elle est, cette femme, pour prendre tout d'un coup la meilleure place ici ?

— Comment ? Tu ne le sais pas encore ? Mais... c'est ma cousine et j'ai toujours eu l'esprit de famille. Comme tous ceux qui n'en ont pas beaucoup.

La voix de Fiora résonnait, chaude et musicale à travers la vaste salle :

— A propos, mon beau cousin, me direz-vous ce que vous comptez faire de mes gens ? Vous n'allez pas, j'imagine, les laisser toute la nuit dans votre corps de garde ? Le voyage aura été aussi peu agréable pour eux que pour moi.

— Pardonnez-moi ! Je les avais oubliés. Va les chercher, Virginio !... que je voie à quoi ils ressemblent, ajouta-t-il *sotto voce*.

Un moment plus tard, le Castillan et l'Écossais faisaient leur entrée dans la salle qui, avec sa table disposée pour le repas et les suppléments de chandelles et de torches que l'on y avait allumés, avait perdu son aspect glacial. Des odeurs de viandes cuites les accompagnaient :

— Voici Esteban, présenta Fiora. Il est tout à la fois mon écuyer, mon secrétaire, mon mentor et mon garde du corps. Et voici Denis Mercier qui a bien voulu me servir de guide depuis Paris.

Le condottiere considéra les deux hommes avec intérêt. Esteban avec sa tête carrée, son nez cassé, ses cheveux drus et son corps trapu était l'image même du soldat de fortune tel qu'il aimait à en recruter. Et n'avait guère l'aspect d'un secrétaire. Quant à l'autre avec ses épaules de corsaire et son air arrogant, il sentait le militaire plus encore que son compagnon...

— Pour connaître si bien les chemins, tu es de par ici ? demanda-t-il à Mortimer qui, sans se soucier de formules de politesse excessives, répondit paisiblement :

— Non. Je suis du Berry mais j'ai beaucoup voyagé.

— Tant que ça ? Un bon guide peut être très précieux. Je pourrais sûrement t'employer... à moins que tu ne préfères rentrer chez toi. A qui es-tu ?

— A personne. Mais j'ai ma maison et mes habitudes et dès l'instant où ma mission est remplie...

« Le diable m'emporte, pensa Campobasso, si ce géant n'appartient pas à la fameuse Garde Écossaise du roi Louis ? En ce cas, la belle cousine pourrait être... une messagère ? » Et comme des valets entraient portant bassins, aiguières et serviettes, immédiatement suivis de Galeotto qui avait fait quelque toilette, il déclara :

— Passons nous laver les mains, ma belle cousine et puis à table !

— Tu pourrais me présenter ! grogna Galeotto dont la figure, rasée de frais, montrait quelques estafilades.

— C'est trop juste. Donna Fiora, voici le seigneur Jacopo Galeotto, de Milan, qui commande avec moi le corps des Lombards de Mgr le duc de Bourgogne. Donna Fiora Beltrami, de Florence.

— Ah Florence ! soupira le capitaine avec âme, je l'ai visitée, jadis quand le duc Galeazzo-Maria Sforza et la duchesse Bona sont allés visiter les seigneurs de Médicis ! Quelle fête nous avons eue ! Quelles belles joutes ! Quels vins ! Quelles femmes... C'était en...

— En 1471, il y a quatre ans, dit Fiora avec un sourire en voyant s'éclaircir sous cette précision qui affirmait sa qualité de Florentine le visage un instant soucieux de Campobasso. Votre duchesse Bona était bien belle! Mon père a eu l'honneur de danser avec elle...

Et l'on prit place à table en évoquant la splendeur du Magnifique pour le plus grand plaisir de Fiora, heureuse de pouvoir parler de sa ville bien-aimée, de cette Florence qui lui avait fait tant de mal et dont, pourtant, l'image et le souvenir ne quitteraient jamais son cœur...

Deux heures plus tard, debout dans l'embrasure de la fenêtre étroite de la chambre où on l'avait conduite, Fiora attendait Campobasso. Elle savait qu'il viendrait car il n'y avait pas à se tromper sur le regard appuyé qu'il avait eu, tout à l'heure, en lui baisant la main pour un « bonsoir » hypocrite. Elle y était résignée car Commynes, sur l'ordre du roi, lui avait tracé, du condottiere napolitain, un portrait à l'acide d'une extraordinaire fidélité. Elle savait sa propre situation ambiguë et aussi qu'elle avait affaire à un homme emporté et sans patience. Si elle se refusait après l'avoir si bien ensorcelé, elle risquait de le subir de force. Mieux valait lui laisser croire encore qu'elle était séduite : elle n'en aurait que plus de puissance...

Mais elle n'avait pas voulu se coucher et c'est debout qu'elle l'attendait. Le lit à courtines rouges, datant du siècle précédent et au moins assez vaste pour quatre personnes, que l'on avait ouvert, demeurerait vide aussi longtemps qu'elle le désirerait. Son orgueil, en effet, refusait de recommencer les prémices de la scène affreuse vécue chez Pippa, dans le bordel du quartier Santo Spirito : la fille offerte plus qu'à demi nue, telle une venaison sur un plat...

Autour de ses épaules qui frissonnaient malgré elle, comme si l'on eût été en plein hiver, elle serrait une écharpe. Elle n'avait pas peur pourtant. Campobasso allait être le troisième homme à posséder son corps, après Philippe et l'affreux Pietro. L'un lui avait apporté l'éblouissement de l'amour comblé, l'autre l'horreur d'un viol sadique dont elle gardait le souvenir épouvanté. Entre ces deux extrêmes, Campobasso n'avait guère de chance de laisser une trace quelconque. Elle l'attendait avec l'indifférence qui devait être celle d'une courtisane car elle acceptait de jouer ce rôle. Son corps était le piège tendu en vue de la perte d'un prince. Il fallait engluer le condottiere assez fortement pour le détacher entièrement du Téméraire. Néanmoins, c'était une chance – et Fiora l'admettait volontiers – que l'homme ne soit pas dépourvu de séduction.

A Florence... un siècle plut tôt, Démétrios lui avait promis de l'armer pour les combats à venir et il avait tenu parole. Un soir, sur le bateau qui les avait conduits en Provence, il avait dessiné pour elle un corps masculin en lui indiquant les zones érogènes. Il l'avait fait avec la froideur et le détachement d'un professeur d'anatomie en face d'une élève et celle-ci avait reçu son enseignement dans le même esprit...

– Dans certains pays d'Afrique et d'Orient, les filles sont éduquées dès le jeune âge en vue des plaisirs de l'homme, lui dit-il alors, et ce n'est pas une mauvaise chose car le pouvoir de la femme s'en trouve renforcé. Même une créature aussi belle que toi peut avoir besoin d'être initiée. Tu n'en seras que plus redoutable.

En outre, le Grec avait composé pour elle un parfum dont il lui avait recommandé de se servir avec modération et uniquement dans certaines circonstances.

– Les femmes de harem en usent pour exciter les sens de leur seigneur et maître mais, avait ajouté Démétrios avec une satisfaction d'inventeur, je lui ai apporté quelques perfectionnements.

Ce soir, pour la première fois, Fiora en avait mis. Très peu, juste, du bout du doigt, une goutte derrière l'oreille et une entre les seins. C'était peu mais elle avait tout de même l'impression d'embaumer comme une cassolette allumée. Elle en tirait plus d'assurance, sans doute, mais aussi la bizarre impression d'avoir changé de personnalité, d'être en train de se dédoubler en quelque sorte. Son âme s'éloignait un peu d'un corps dont elle allait pouvoir contrôler froidement les réactions et le comportement...

Au-dehors s'éteignaient les bruits de cette ville inconnue. Les feux qui mettaient un reflet rougeâtre au plafond de la chambre étaient ceux des postes de garde échelonnés sur les remparts et au long de la Moselle. Les cris que se renvoyaient les sentinelles étaient en dialecte lombard, si proche du toscan que la jeune femme ne pouvait s'empêcher d'en éprouver du plaisir... La cité luxembourgeoise, muette et noire au fond de la nuit, disparaissait complètement. Les troupes qui l'occupaient lui imposaient ainsi leur propre couleur...

La porte, en s'ouvrant, grinça légèrement. En dépit de son courage, Fiora sentit un frisson glacé courir le long de son dos. L'instant difficile était venu, l'instant où il fallait, plus que jamais, demeurer maîtresse d'elle-même...

De l'ombre se détacha une ombre plus dense que le reflet lointain de la veilleuse effleura à peine :

— Vous n'êtes pas encore au lit ? fit Campobasso. Ne saviez-vous pas que... j'allais venir ?

— Si fait... mais je ne me couche jamais pour attendre une visite. Ce serait me placer en état d'infériorité...

— Il y a visite et visite et je n'ai pas conscience que ma présence dans cette chambre en soit une... J'espérais...

Elle lui fit face brusquement, les yeux chargés d'éclairs.

— Quoi ? Me trouver dans ce lit, nue et les jambes écartées, n'attendant que votre bon plaisir ?

— Par San Gennaro ! Quelle violence soudaine ! Ne pouvons-nous reprendre notre conversation de tout à l'heure là où nous l'avions laissée ? Souvenez-vous ! J'allais vous prendre dans mes bras...

Elle s'attendait à une réaction brutale et il n'en était rien. Sa voix n'était au contraire que douceur et prière. Il était si près d'elle que Fiora pouvait entendre sa respiration courte et retint un sourire de triomphe : se pouvait-il qu'elle l'eût enchaîné si vite, alors même qu'il n'avait rien reçu d'elle sinon le droit de baiser sa main ? Le fauve était-il déjà rendu à sa merci ? Elle eut la tentation de l'éprouver en le renvoyant avec hauteur mais une phrase de son cher Platon délaissé depuis des mois lui revint en mémoire : « Donne et tu recevras... »

— Eh bien qu'attendez-vous ? fit-elle avec un sourire provocant. Ou bien... préférez-vous me déshabiller d'abord ?

Elle sentit frémir les mains qu'il posait déjà sur sa taille. Puis elles remontèrent, caressèrent sa gorge au passage, saisirent le décolleté de la robe et tirèrent... L'étoffe se déchira jusqu'à la taille mais, déjà, Campobasso serrait Fiora contre lui, enfouissait son visage dans la masse des cheveux noirs dénoués, couvrant son cou de baisers dévorants puis s'emparait de ses lèvres avant de l'emporter jusqu'au lit où il acheva de réduire sa robe à l'état de haillons avant de se jeter sur son corps dénudé... comme une bête assoiffée sur un ruisseau frais.

Emportée dans un ouragan de caresses et de baisers, Fiora, la première explosion de brutalité passée, découvrit que ce fauve pouvait être un amant passionné, et sachant jouer d'un corps féminin avec brio. Elle attendait un soudard, elle eut un amoureux. Elle avait cru pouvoir garder la tête froide mais, trahie par ses sens, elle dut laisser à plusieurs reprises le plaisir la rouler dans sa vague brûlante. Et la nuit allait vers sa fin quand le sommeil, à son tour, la vainquit et lui fit oublier que si elle avait, elle aussi, remporté une victoire, celle-ci ressemblait beaucoup à une victoire à la Pyrrhus.

L'oreille collée derrière la porte de la chambre, le page Virginio, ses dents plantées dans son poing et défaillant presque de rage impuissante, avait compté toutes les plaintes, tous les soupirs, tous les râles que le jeu ardent de l'amour avait arrachés à ce couple invisible...

Quand les tambours de la diane sonnèrent le réveil des soldats, Campobasso, trop entraîné aux combats de Vénus pour qu'une nuit d'amour l'ensevelît dans le sommeil au point de l'empêcher d'entendre, glissa du lit en prenant soin de ne pas éveiller Fiora, passa sa chemise et ses chausses puis gagna la grande salle où l'attendait déjà Salvestro, son écuyer.

— Va me chercher les deux hommes qui accompagnaient hier donna Fiora! ordonna-t-il tout en dévorant un quignon de pain resté sur la table. Puis tu amèneras une vingtaine de soldats dans l'escalier.

Esteban et Mortimer furent là presque aussitôt. L'inquiétude avait tenu le Castillan éveillé toute la nuit; quant à l'Écossais, il était habitué lui aussi à s'éveiller avec le jour.

— Vous allez pouvoir rentrer chez vous, leur dit Campobasso. Donna Fiora n'a plus besoin de vos services.

— Pardonnez-moi, monseigneur, fit Esteban dont le visage venait de se fermer, mais je suis à son service depuis longtemps et, si elle n'a plus besoin de moi, c'est à elle de me le signifier! Jamais je ne la quitterai de mon plein gré... ou sur un ordre étranger!

— J'ai reçu, moi aussi, l'ordre de veiller sur elle, dit tranquillement Mortimer, et j'ai pour habitude d'aller toujours jusqu'au bout de mon devoir.

— Un grand mot pour un guide. Tu étais chargé de la conduire jusqu'à moi? Eh bien voilà qui est fait! Tu peux partir.

— Vous m'avez mal compris : je dois la conduire partout où elle souhaitera se rendre. Elle aura encore besoin de moi.

— Inutile de jouer au plus fin avec moi, je sais qui tu es : l'un des gardes écossais du roi de France. Alors écoute ceci : tu vas retourner vers ton maître et tu le remercieras grandement pour le beau cadeau qu'il m'a envoyé. Tu ajouteras que j'espère, un jour, pouvoir lui en marquer ma gratitude... lorsque donna Fiora sera devenue la comtesse de Campobasso. Va à présent! Quant à toi, ajouta-t-il à l'adresse d'Esteban, tu as entendu : je vais épouser ta maîtresse et je peux t'assurer que je saurai la défendre de tous périls. Je te conseille de suivre ton compagnon.

– Et si je refuse ? grogna le Castillan qui sentait monter sa colère.

– C'est tout simple : avant une heure tu seras pendu.

– Je n'ai pas envie, moi non plus de repartir, articula Mortimer. Où alors, allez chercher donna Fiora. D'elle j'accepterai un ordre...

Il avait tourné les yeux vers Esteban et celui-ci lut sans peine que la Bourrasque était sur le point de se déchaîner. Entre eux deux, le condottiere désarmé ne pèserait pas lourd... Mais Campobasso soupirait d'un air excédé :

– Dieu que vous êtes fatigants !

Il frappa dans ses mains et, aussitôt, une vingtaine d'hommes armés pénétrèrent dans la salle :

– Vous n'aurez pas le dernier mot avec moi. Partez tranquillement et séparons-nous bons amis. Mes hommes vous donneront quelques vivres pour la route... et vous pourrez vous partager ceci.

Il détacha la bourse attachée à sa ceinture et la lança vers les deux hommes mais aucune main ne se tendit pour la saisir et son contenu se déversa sur les dalles. A nouveau l'Écossais consulta son compagnon du regard puis, haussant les épaules, déclara :

– Partons ! Je ferai vos commissions à mon supérieur... toutes vos commissions !

– Parfait ! On va donc vous accompagner hors des portes de la ville.

Mortimer et Esteban partirent sans se retourner, suivis par les soldats. Salvestro fermait la marche. Quand ils eurent disparu, Campobasso se mit en devoir de récupérer les pièces d'or qui avaient roulé à terre, les remit dans la bourse qu'il fit sauter dans sa main avec satisfaction tout en se dirigeant vers la chambre.

Fiora dormait toujours dans la masse brillante de ses cheveux en désordre qui sertissaient son corps charmant.

Le comte la contempla un instant puis, ôtant ses vêtements, il se glissa auprès d'elle et, appuyé sur un coude, il se mit doucement à la caresser. Elle gémit, sans ouvrir les yeux, s'étira pour mieux s'offrir à la main qui glissait sur elle, dispensatrice d'un plaisir dont elle sentait déjà la chaleur monter au creux de ses reins. Quand elle commença à se tordre avec une plainte heureuse, il entra en elle pour la rejoindre dans le spasme suprême...

CHAPITRE IX

L'ARRESTATION

Durant trois jours et trois nuits, Campobasso et Fiora demeurèrent enfermés dans le double isolement de leur chambre et des rideaux du lit. Seul Salvestro franchissait, deux fois le jour, la porte de celle-ci pour apporter des repas mais sans jamais rien voir de ce qui se passait derrière ceux-là. Galeotto avait été chargé d'assurer le commandement et de veiller à l'ordre dans Thionville. Il s'en acquittait avec hargne, serrant les poings quand il lui arrivait de tourner les yeux vers certaine fenêtre close où il imaginait bien qu'on ne faisait point pénitence.

Ces heures ardentes, Fiora les vécut entièrement dans les bras de son amant. Il la gardait contre lui pour dormir, pour la faire manger et boire et quand, au bout de vingt-quatre heures, elle réclama un bain, la porta lui-même dans le bassin que le vieil écuyer avait rempli d'eau fraîche, la lava, la sécha sans cesser de lui prodiguer caresses et baisers. Quand il ne lui faisait pas l'amour, il la regardait avec émerveillement, touchait ses paupières, ses lèvres, son cou, ses seins, ses pieds et ses mains, et lui murmurait des mots d'amour qu'elle ne comprenait pas toujours.

Jamais la jeune femme n'avait imaginé qu'elle allait allumer pareille passion. Cet homme n'était jamais comblé, jamais rassasié et la possession, au lieu d'apaiser ses sens, semblait les exaspérer et décupler son désir au point, parfois, d'effrayer Fiora. Il dormait peu et ne la laissait lui échapper dans le sommeil que durant de courts laps de temps : une heure ou deux après quoi elle le retrouvait plus affamé d'elle que jamais :

— Tu es à moi pour toujours, lui dit-il un soir en la serrant à l'étouffer. Je ferai de toi ma femme...

Prise de court par cette déclaration inattendue, elle choisit le parti de rire.

— Tu veux m'épouser ?... et je ne sais même pas ton prénom...

— Cola... ici, on dit Nicolas comme le jeune duc que j'ai perdu et que j'aimais servir. Mais je ne veux de toi d'autres mots que d'amour.

— Je ne crois pas avoir dit que je t'aimais ? Seulement que tu me plaisais...

— Qu'importe si ta bouche ne le dit pas ! Ton corps, lui, le crie sans cesse, ton corps qui m'appelle, ton corps que je fais chanter, vibrer, crier même. Cela vaut toutes les fadaises des poètes. Et d'ailleurs tu m'aimes déjà sans même t'en rendre compte...

— Peut-être, mais tant que je ne m'en rendrai pas compte, je ne t'épouserai pas...

Nouant ses poings dans ses cheveux il lui tira cruellement la tête en arrière :

— Tu en aimes un autre ? Dis-moi ! Est-ce que tu aimes un autre homme ? Allons, réponds !

Emporté par une fureur subite, il planta ses dents à la naissance de son cou. Les yeux soudain pleins de larmes, Fiora poussa un cri de douleur...

— Pourquoi serais-je ici... si c'était le cas ?

Il la lâcha, vit que des larmes coulaient et que sa peau portait une marque rouge...

— Pardon ! pardon mon amour !... Je deviens fou... Tu brûles mon sang et tu me donnes des joies que je n'ai jamais connues avec aucune femme. Et toi, dis-moi... un autre homme t'a-t-il jamais donné autant de plaisir ? Dis-moi ! Je veux savoir...

— Non, murmura Fiora en pensant qu'elle ne mentait qu'à peine car sa nuit de noces avait été brève auprès de ce déchaînement de passion, de cette orgie d'amour qu'elle vivait et qui l'épuisait mais qui, curieusement, lui rendait toute sa présence d'esprit.

Elle avait pleinement conscience de la dualité existant entre sa tête et un corps dont elle ne pouvait contrôler les réactions. Et sa tête lui disait qu'elle n'aurait plus jamais besoin d'utiliser le parfum de Démétrios dont la senteur avait disparu depuis des heures et que Campobasso était bel et bien son prisonnier. Entre elle et un duc dont d'ailleurs le service lui plaisait moins qu'il ne l'avait cru, le condottiere n'hésiterait pas... mais tandis qu'il léchait la petite blessure de son épaule, Fiora pensa, repue d'amour, qu'elle aimerait voir s'achever cette claustration à deux que rien ne semblait susceptible de faire cesser.

Pourtant, au matin du quatrième jour, le vantail de la porte retentit des coups que lui portait un gantelet de fer. En même temps, la voix rude de Galeotto braillait :

— Sors d'ici... Cola ! Il faut que je te parle et c'est urgent !

Campobasso s'arracha du lit nu, traversa la chambre et courut ouvrir. Il reçut en plein visage le regard furieux de son ami.

— Que se passe-t-il ?
— Le page a disparu !
— C'est cela ta nouvelle ? Qu'il aille au diable et que...
— Non. Ce n'est pas seulement cela : le duc Charles est à son château de Soleuvre, à douze lieues d'ici. Que crois-tu qu'il va se passer si ce damné Virginio est allé lui raconter que tu délaisses ton commandement parce que tu ne peux plus t'arrêter de baiser une espionne du roi de France ?

La main de Campobasso fila comme un serpent jusqu'à la gorge de son compagnon qu'elle serra furieusement :

— Je t'interdis de parler ainsi, tu m'entends ? Elle sera ma femme !

— Alors, si tu veux qu'elle vive assez longtemps pour ça, tu ferais bien de la renvoyer d'où elle vient ! rugit Galeotto en s'arrachant à la poigne de son ami.

— Jamais je ne la renverrai !

— Alors mets-la à l'abri mais fais quelque chose. Le gamin a dû partir dans la journée d'hier...

Le comte réfléchit un instant puis grogna :

— Tu as peut-être raison. Envoie-moi Salvestro et donne l'ordre qu'on cherche une litière et que l'on prépare une escorte : dix hommes !

— A quoi penses-tu ?

— Je vais la faire conduire à Pierrefort !

— En plein pays lorrain donc en pays ennemi ? Tu es fou ?

— Justement. Le Téméraire n'ira pas la chercher là si ce sale petit bougre est allé me dénoncer. Pierrefort m'appartient toujours comme nous appartiennent toujours les villes que ce jeune imbécile de René II nous a laissé occuper.

L'heure qui suivit fut difficile pour Fiora. Non que les projets de son amant lui déplussent particulièrement — car elle était prête à n'importe quoi pour dormir une grande nuit tranquille — mais les choses se gâtèrent quand il lui avoua qu'il avait renvoyé ses compagnons de route. Il dut faire face à une fureur tout italienne qui le stupéfia quelques instants.

— De quel droit t'es-tu permis de renvoyer mes serviteurs ? criait-elle. Parce que tu as couché avec moi, tu t'imagines que tu peux tout faire, tout détruire de ce qui est ma vie ? Esteban m'est attaché depuis longtemps et tu l'as renvoyé comme un valet indélicat ! Je ne te pardonnerai jamais et je refuse de rester ici plus longtemps !

— Calme-toi, je t'en supplie. Tu vas partir, je viens de te le dire...

— Sans doute, mais pas comme tu l'entends ! Si tu crois que je vais me laisser enfermer dans ton château, tu te trompes lourdement. Fais-moi seller un cheval et adieu !

— Tu es folle ! Où iras-tu...

— A présent que je n'ai plus de guide ? Je vais te surprendre : j'irai rejoindre le duc de Bourgogne !

— Il te fera pendre !

— Crois-tu ? M'as-tu fait pendre, toi, quand je suis arrivée, parfaite inconnue et même un peu suspecte ? Non. Tu m'as mise dans ton lit et j'ai accepté car je te croyais un homme. Mais tu es là à trembler comme un gamin parce que, peut-être, ton page est allé te dénoncer. Le Téméraire me paraît d'une autre envergure... et ce pourrait être amusant d'essayer de le séduire.

Envahi d'une rage soudaine, il la prit à la gorge :

— Sale petite putain ! Tu en as assez de moi, n'est-ce pas ? Un lit princier serait plus intéressant que le mien ?... Mais je ne te laisserai pas faire. Je t'ai dit que je voulais te garder et je te garderai !

— Tu... garderas mon cadavre... alors ! souffla-t-elle à demi étranglée.

Comprenant qu'il était en train de la tuer, Campobasso la lâcha mais ce fut pour l'expédier à terre d'une bourrade :

— Tu feras ce que j'ai dit ! Lève-toi et habille-toi... si tu ne veux pas que je te fasse habiller par mes hommes...

Elle se releva en effet mais ce fut pour lui éclater de rire au nez :

— Voilà qui serait amusant ! Bonne idée ! Appelle donc tes hommes ! Quelques archers en guise de chambrières, cela peut être drôle...

L'absurde défi le calma net mais réveilla son ardeur. D'un geste brutal il la saisit dans ses bras, la poussa contre l'une des colonnes du lit et la prit debout avec tant de violence qu'elle cria de douleur.

— Ne me pousse pas à bout, Fiora ! Jamais je n'accepterai de te perdre, tu entends ? Je veux pouvoir te posséder encore et encore chaque fois que j'en aurai envie et pour cela il faut que je te cache, que je t'éloigne du danger. Si le duc ordonnait ta mort, je serais capable de le tuer... Je t'aime, comprends-tu ? Je t'aime, je t'aime, je t'aime !...

— Que vas-tu faire ? demanda-t-elle un moment plus tard tandis qu'avec des gestes redevenus caressants il l'aidait à s'habiller.

— Dès que tu auras quitté Thionville, je partirai pour Soleuvre et je verrai le duc sans attendre qu'il m'appelle. Je lui dirai à quel point je tiens à toi et aussi que je veux faire de toi ma femme. Il n'osera plus, dès lors, s'en prendre à toi. Il a trop besoin des troupes que je commande. Alors, je t'enverrai chercher et nous nous marierons...

— Pourquoi ne pas le quitter au lieu de braver sa colère ? Pars avec moi !

Il hésita, visiblement tenté car la pensée de voir s'éloigner de lui, même pour peu de temps, cette femme adorable le déchirait mais il fallait bien, enfin, que la raison reprît ses droits...

— Je ne peux pas, avoua-t-il. J'ai à payer mes hommes et le duc me doit de l'or...

— Un autre t'en donnerait peut-être davantage ?...

— Je sais... et il se peut que j'y vienne un jour. Mais pour l'instant, j'entends recevoir mon dû. Le Téméraire a envoyé en Lombardie le Grand Bâtard Antoine, son demi-frère et son meilleur capitaine, pour ramener des mercenaires. J'entends que les miens soient payés avant ces nouveaux venus...

Fiora n'insista pas. Une idée lui venait : elle allait se laisser conduire où il l'avait décidé. De là elle trouverait sûrement un moyen de s'enfuir et, s'il tenait à elle autant qu'il le disait, Campobasso abandonnerait tout pour la rejoindre...

Une heure plus tard, étendue sur les coussins d'une litière un peu antique mais solide et dont les rideaux de cuir fermaient hermétiquement, Fiora quittait Thionville dont elle n'avait pratiquement rien vu et traversait le camp planté au bord de la Moselle pour tous les soldats qui n'avaient pas trouvé place dans la ville. Salvestro, indifférent à son ordinaire, chevauchait auprès d'elle cependant qu'une escorte de dix hommes partagée en deux groupes précédait et suivait l'attelage. Par précaution, les hommes d'armes portaient, au lieu du tabard vert à croix de Saint-André blanche qui était de Bourgogne, la cotte d'armes à la double croix de Lorraine... On prit la direction du sud à vive allure. Il fallait couvrir dans la journée la petite vingtaine de lieues qui séparaient la ville luxembourgeoise du château lorrain de Campobasso. Quitte à arriver au cœur de la nuit, le condottiere préférant de beaucoup que cette arrivée se fît dans l'obscurité.

Bâti au siècle précédent par Pierre de Bar, le château de Pierrefort, baptisé selon son géniteur, dressait ses murailles sur un éperon dominant un vallon encaissé qui formait une voie naturelle entre le Barrois et la Moselle. C'était un pentagone d'environ vingt mille mètres carrés défendu par quatre tours représentant chacune un échantillon de l'architecture militaire de l'époque : une tour carrée, une tour ronde, une tour à bec et enfin une grosse tour octogone : le donjon. C'était cette tour que la colère du duc René II avait à demi détruite mais le château n'avait que peu souffert de l'incendie [1]. Donnant, au nord et à l'est, sur un ravin abrupt, il était bordé, au sud et à l'ouest, par de larges et profonds fossés qu'enjambait un pont dormant sur lequel venait s'abattre le grand pont-levis. Une première ligne de défense, faite de palissades et d'échauguettes de bois qui avaient brûlé en partie, précédait les fossés. C'était à la fois un ouvrage d'art et une puissante forteresse où Campobasso gardait une garnison d'une vingtaine d'hommes sous le commandement d'un de ses fils...

Mais Fiora ne vit rien de ces abords, pas plus d'ailleurs que de la route suivie car, sans souci des cahots de la litière sur le chemin raboteux, elle dormit comme une souche tout au long du voyage et n'ouvrit les yeux qu'au

---

[1]. Pierrefort est encore debout en partie, mais il renferme une exploitation agricole qui ne l'améliore pas.

bruit apocalyptique du pont-levis qui s'abaissait et de la herse que l'on relevait. La troupe passa sous l'arc brisé de la porte, pénétra dans une cour immense qu'éclairaient mal quelques pots à feu et s'arrêta enfin devant l'entrée d'un beau logis dont les fenêtres étaient élégamment sculptées et portaient sous le gable les armes des anciens seigneurs de Bar.

Un jeune homme qui ressemblait à Campobasso, vêtu de cuir sous une cotte de mailles brillantes, se tenait debout sur le seuil.

– Salut à toi, Salvestro, vieux brigand! cria-t-il joyeusement. Tu as bien failli recevoir quelques carreaux d'arbalète avec tes cottes lorraines. En voilà une idée?

– La Bourgogne n'est pas en odeur de sainteté. C'était plus prudent...

– Et quel bon vent t'amène?

– Un vent qui va te remporter, messire Angelo. Ton père te réclame et m'envoie tenir Pierrefort à ta place.

– Dis-tu vrai? Je vais enfin quitter ce nid de hiboux et revoir la guerre? Vive Dieu! Voilà des jours que j'attends ça!

Les deux hommes s'embrassèrent, se bourrèrent de quelques coups de poing en riant puis Angelo demanda:

– Qu'est-ce qu'il y a dans cette litière?

– Le précieux trésor de ton père. Celle qui sera bientôt la dame de ces lieux: ta future belle-mère, quoi!

Ouvrant les rideaux de la litière, il offrit la main à Fiora pour l'aider à descendre. Mal réveillée, la jeune femme clignait des yeux dans la lumière des torches que tenaient deux valets.

– Sommes-nous arrivés? demanda-t-elle.

– Oui, madonna. Voici messire Angelo qui est l'aîné des fils de Mgr Cola.

Mais, déjà, le jeune homme s'inclinait, avec une grâce inattendue chez un homme vêtu d'acier et s'emparait de la main de la jeune femme.

– Il n'y a qu'un instant, je croyais être heureux de

m'éloigner d'ici, belle dame. Mais voilà que l'envie m'en passe puisque vous allez rester alors que je m'en vais!

— Merci de votre accueil, messire! Je n'espérais pas rencontrer un galant homme dans cette forteresse...

— Moi non plus, fit Salvestro goguenard. Tu as fait des progrès dans l'art de parler aux dames, gamin. Quant à la guerre, n'y compte pas trop! Le duc Charles qui est à Soleuvre a dépêché, paraît-il, messire Hugonet, son chancelier, à Vervins pour y discuter de la paix avec les envoyés du roi de France.

Toute gaieté s'effaça du visage du jeune homme :

— La paix? Le Téméraire veut la paix avec son plus mortel ennemi? C'est à n'y pas croire! Le Français lui a repris la Picardie et ses troupes ont attaqué le nord de la Franche-Comté depuis la fin de la trêve, en mai.

— Il a d'autres chats à fouetter et préfère sans doute tenir Louis XI à distance même au moyen d'une paix boiteuse. On dit qu'à l'appel du duc René de Lorraine, les Suisses et les Alsaciens sont entrés aussi dans la Franche-Comté qu'ils ravagent. Après tout, tu pourrais bien l'avoir quand même, ta guerre! acheva-t-il avec un sourire narquois.

— Tout cela est fort intéressant, messieurs, dit Fiora avec un sourire qui corrigea son rappel à l'ordre, mais j'aimerais assez entrer dans cette maison... et souper si possible?

— Pardonnez-nous, fit Angelo, vous avez mille fois raison. Mais vous arrivez bien car j'ai chassé tout le jour et j'allais me mettre à table.

— Vous pouvez chasser alors que cette forteresse bourguignonne en pays lorrain doit être en péril continuel?

— Nous ne sommes pas vraiment en Lorraine mais à la frontière du duché et de la France. Comme cette frontière n'est pas très bien délimitée, je vis à peu près tranquille mais vous le serez plus encore si nous sommes en paix avec Louis XI... Et le duché ne bouge pas. René II a rejoint le roi. Mais entrons!

En pénétrant dans le logis, Fiora découvrit que l'on pouvait être homme de guerre et homme de goût. Des tapis et de grandes tentures brodées habillaient la salle où ne manquaient ni les meubles, ni les coussins, ni les beaux objets. Elle en fit compliment à son jeune hôte ajoutant que Thionville, cependant ancien château ducal, n'offrait rien de comparable.

– Mon père ne fait qu'y passer. Il s'en accommode simplement. Ici, c'est chez lui, comme d'ailleurs à Ainvelle-aux-Jars, non loin de Neufchâteau où il ne va guère, se contentant d'y maintenir mon frère et un bailli chargé de récupérer les impôts mais où le château mériterait qu'on fît quelques aménagements. Vous vous en chargerez sans doute puisque vous allez devenir son épouse ? Ce dont je me réjouis sincèrement...

Fiora fit honneur au souper de poissons et de venaison qu'on lui servit et se déclara ensuite satisfaite de la chambre que l'on venait de préparer pour elle, une pièce agréable avec ses rideaux à grands ramages et la tapisserie mille fleurs qui enjolivait le panneau faisant face aux fenêtres... Celles-ci, malheureusement, donnaient sur la seule cour comme les autres fenêtres du logis.

La jeune femme s'y enferma à clé, craignant que ce jeune homme, qui la contemplait avec un plaisir évident, ne voulut vérifier par lui-même les charmes dont son père se voulait captif. Mais personne ne vint frapper et elle s'en trouva grandement soulagée.

Livrée à elle-même pour la première fois depuis des jours – et surtout des nuits! –, Fiora employa une grande partie de celle-ci à réfléchir. Ayant dormi toute la journée, elle n'avait plus sommeil et se retrouvait l'esprit clair pour faire face à une situation tout à fait inattendue. En arrivant à Thionville, elle espérait plaire à Campobasso, sans doute, mais de façon paisible, se l'attacher peu à peu et l'amener doucement là où Louis XI voulait le voir venir : abandonner la cause du Téméraire et rentrer en France avec elle, en emmenant, bien sûr, ceux de ses soldats qui lui étaient attachés. Le tout avec l'appât d'une honnête quantité d'or...

Cela aurait pu, aurait dû marcher si deux facteurs nouveaux ne s'étaient présentés : d'abord la présence de Galeotto, de ses hommes d'armes et d'une partie de l'armée bourguignonne dans la cité luxembourgeoise : ils auraient empêché Campobasso de partir par tous les moyens. Ensuite la passion insensée qu'elle avait allumée dans le cœur et dans les sens du condottiere. Violente, exclusive, voire dangereuse, elle avait joué dans le sens contraire de ce qu'espérait Fiora : au lieu de la suivre, Campobasso n'avait plus pensé qu'à une chose : garder pour lui seul celle qu'il aimait, la cacher le temps qu'il le faudrait puis l'épouser au grand jour : tout cela sans quitter pour autant le clan bourguignon. D'ailleurs, si la paix avec la France était faite, sa trahison ne serait que de peu de prix et le priverait des grands avantages offerts sans doute par un prince lancé à la conquête d'un royaume. Et maintenant, Fiora se retrouvait au cœur d'un pays inconnu, enfermée dans un château fort sans aucune possibilité d'assistance pour en réchapper. Privée de l'astuce d'Esteban et de la force prodigieuse de Mortimer ainsi que de leur courage à tous les deux, elle était presque désarmée car elle se voyait mal tentant sur le vieux Salvestro une entreprise de séduction dans l'espoir de se faire ouvrir la porte.

Où se trouvaient-ils, à cette heure, le Castillan et l'Écossais ? Campobasso les avait fait reconduire, d'après ce qu'il en avait dit, à une lieue de Thionville. On ne leur avait restitué leurs armes qu'à ce moment-là et ceux qui les accompagnaient avaient pu les voir s'éloigner en direction de la France. Y étaient-ils déjà arrivés et les choses s'étaient-elles passées comme on le lui avait raconté ? Leur avait-on « vraiment » rendu leurs armes ou bien les avait-on égorgés sans plus de façon ? Fiora connaissait assez son amant, à présent, pour savoir que tout était à redouter de son génie tortueux...

S'il n'en était rien – et elle l'espérait de tout son cœur – Douglas Mortimer devait être en train de revenir à bride abattue vers son roi pour lui rendre compte de sa mission. Mais Esteban ? Était-il parti avec lui dans l'espoir de ramener un quelconque secours ? Fiora en doutait un peu. Le Castillan lui était attaché. En outre, pour rien au monde, il n'eût transgressé un ordre de Démétrios et celui qu'il en avait reçu était formel : veiller sur Fiora en tout temps et en toutes occasions. Peut-être n'était-il pas si loin qu'on le pensait ?... En tout cas, une chose était certaine : il fallait parvenir à sortir d'ici, coûte que coûte. Peut-être alors, apprenant qu'elle lui avait échappé, Campobasso se lancerait-il à sa recherche, privant ainsi le Téméraire d'un de ses meilleurs capitaines ? De toute façon, elle ne voulait plus être le jouet de cet homme et revivre ces jours et ces nuits qu'elle ne pouvait même plus évoquer sans honte : elle s'était conduite comme une courtisane sans doute, s'y étant d'ailleurs préparée mais le pire est qu'elle y avait pris plaisir. Elle avait découvert qu'elle pouvait aimer les jeux de l'amour sans en éprouver le sentiment, tout comme un garçon, et qu'un parfait inconnu, s'il était habile, saurait faire vibrer ses sens et lui faire oublier un instant qu'elle était autre chose qu'une chair avide de jouissances.

Et ce fut en pensant à sa prochaine évasion qu'elle finit par s'endormir, si profondément même qu'elle n'entendit pas, au petit matin, le jeune Angelo partir avec l'escorte qui l'avait amenée.

Quand il eut quitté le château, Salvestro fit baisser la herse et relever le pont-levis. Puis, jetant un rapide coup d'œil à la fenêtre derrière laquelle dormait cette femme qui avait envoûté son maître, il esquissa un sourire, haussa les épaules et s'en alla inspecter les quartiers et les armes des hommes chargés de garder la forteresse. Fiora ne le savait pas encore mais elle était prisonnière d'un vieux soldat qui ne l'aimait pas et qui ferait tout pour qu'elle comprenne bien le rôle qu'on lui attribuait : celui d'un bel objet entièrement voué au repos du guerrier et à ses plaisirs. Rien de plus!

Elle s'aperçut très vite du sort qui lui était fait. Dès le matin, constatant que, pour une fois il ne pleuvait pas et que le ciel était presque clair, elle demanda un cheval pour faire un tour dans les environs. On lui répondit alors que c'était impossible, les promenades à cheval ou à pied n'étant pas compatibles avec la défense d'une place forte frontalière. Et on lui désigna l'escalier qui, près de la porte d'entrée, montait d'un seul jet jusqu'au chemin de ronde. Mais quand elle commença à en gravir les degrés, elle entendit sonner derrière elle les pas ferrés des deux soldats chargés de l'accompagner. Et c'est escortée de leur présence vigilante qu'elle parcourut le chemin de ronde du château à pas lents, regardant à peine le paysage alentour qui cependant n'était pas sans charme, envahie qu'elle était par une sensation désagréable.

Ce fut pis encore quand, redescendant, elle s'aperçut que deux maçons étaient occupés à sceller des barreaux à la fenêtre de sa chambre sous la surveillance attentive de Salvestro. Emportée par une brusque colère, elle courut à lui :

— Qui vous a permis de faire cela ? Ignorez-vous que votre maître souhaite que je devienne son épouse ?

— Soyez sans crainte : personne ne vous manquera de respect dans ce château mais, voyez-vous, je ne suis pas certain que vous ayez, vous, très envie de devenir sa femme et, comme il tient à vous, je veux être assuré que vous serez prête à le recevoir quand il le souhaitera.

— Quelle sottise ! Ne suis-je pas venue à lui de bon gré ?

— Sans doute... mais dans quel but ? Parce que vous rêviez de lui depuis longtemps ? Je ne crois pas cela : vous êtes toute jeune et lui sera bientôt vieux.

— Ne savez-vous pas que je suis sa cousine ?

— C'est possible... mais ce n'est pas certain. Quant à moi, j'ai reçu mission de vous garder et je vous garderai, au besoin contre vous-même. Et croyez bien qu'il m'en coûte! Sans vous je serais à ses côtés pour la guerre qui se prépare.

— Quelle guerre? On est en train de signer la paix...

— Et moi je vous dis que le duc va repartir en guerre.

— A la mauvaise saison? Comme c'est vraisemblable!

— C'est sans importance pour d'authentiques soldats. Voulez-vous rentrer à présent?

— Je me plaindrai du sort que l'on m'a fait ici!

— Mais le maître, lui, ne se plaindra pas : ce qu'il veut, c'est vous avoir dans son lit, et moi je veillerai à ce que vous n'en sortiez pas, justement, de ce lit!

Furieuse, Fiora rentra au logis en se donnant le plaisir dérisoire de faire claquer la porte derrière elle.

Et les jours, et les nuits se mirent à couler, tristes, gris, tous pareils et étouffants d'ennui. Le temps avait repris ses couleurs désolantes et l'été s'était achevé dans les grandes pluies et les vents démesurés de l'équinoxe. Pierrefort, environné de nuages et de tourbillons, ressemblait à un vaisseau dans la tempête et Fiora aimait alors à monter sur les remparts pour le plaisir violent de se laisser fouetter par les bourrasques. Elle rêvait d'être emportée par l'une d'elles et de pouvoir, comme un oiseau, voler par-dessus les créneaux pour se plonger dans la campagne détrempée comme elle eût plongé dans la mer... Mais il fallait toujours redescendre... et au logis elle étouffait.

Elle passait de longues heures assise dans la salle, au coin de l'immense cheminée où le bois brûlait tout le jour, sans rien faire, le regard perdu dans le jeu capricieux des flammes. Elle n'avait aucun moyen de s'occuper car on ne trouvait pas un livre dans ce château ni rien qui permît de broder ou d'occuper ses mains à quelque ouvrage. La nuit, Salvestro l'enfermait à clé dans sa chambre et couchait en travers de la porte pour plus de sûreté encore : Fiora pouvait l'entendre ronfler comme une toupie d'Allemagne. Entre-temps n'ayant rien à se dire, ils n'échangeaient que peu de mots. La seule péripétie notable était représentée par les nouvelles que, deux fois la semaine,

Salvestro envoyait chercher à Toul ou à l'abbaye de Domèvre quand on allait aux provisions.

Ainsi que l'avait prédit le vieil écuyer, le Téméraire avait levé son étendard violet et noir et rouvert les portes de la guerre. Après avoir envoyé, le 15 septembre, au jeune duc René un manifeste qui n'était rien d'autre que la plus belliqueuse des déclarations, il avait pris le commandement de son armée et commençait à envahir la Lorraine. Il était précédé par un premier corps de troupes aux ordres du maréchal de Luxembourg et de Campobasso qui avaient mis le siège devant Conflans-en-Jarnisy. René II était parti pour la France afin d'essayer d'obtenir l'aide de Louis XI sans y croire tout à fait puisque le roi venait de signer la paix de Soleuvre avec la Bourgogne. L'écho des combats faisait frémir le vieux Salvestro comme un cheval de bataille qui entend la trompette et le rendait plus désagréable encore s'il était possible.

Une nuit, Fiora fut réveillée par le vacarme de la herse et du pont. Il y eut le galop d'un cheval, des cris. Elle sauta à bas de son lit et enfilait sa chemise pour aller voir ce qui se passait mais n'eut qu'à peine le temps de se poser des questions. Déjà Campobasso, le casque sous le bras, son armure dégouttante et le regard étincelant était entré. Un instant ils se regardèrent en silence puis, laissant tomber son heaume et arrachant ses gantelets, il marcha vers elle...

— Il fallait que je vienne! dit-il. Conflans se passera de moi pendant une vingtaine d'heures...

— Tu veux dire... que tu as abandonné ton poste pour venir jusqu'ici?

— Oui... au risque de me déshonorer mais je n'en pouvais plus... J'ai besoin de toi... plus encore que de l'air que je respire. Viens m'aider à ôter cette ferraille! J'ai deux heures environ.

Au lieu d'obtempérer, elle s'empara d'une grande écharpe pour en couvrir son trop mince vêtement, croisa les bras sur sa poitrine et s'adossa à la fenêtre :

— Non ! C'est un peu trop facile de tomber ici comme la foudre en déclarant que tu as besoin de moi ! Eh bien, vois-tu, moi, je n'ai nullement besoin de toi, aucune envie de toi et, si tu me veux, il faudra me faire violence !

Décontenancé par sa réaction, il ne sut que balbutier penaud :

— Mais... Fiora... nous nous aimons ! As-tu déjà oublié Thionville, notre chambre... et comme nous nous sommes aimés ?

— Je n'oublie rien. Toi, en revanche, tu sembles avoir perdu de vue ce que l'on doit à une femme de ma qualité. Que suis-je ici ? Une fille soumise à ton bon plaisir ? Regarde ces barreaux à ma fenêtre ! Sais-tu que je n'ai le droit de prendre l'air que sur le chemin de ronde et flanquée de deux gardes ? Sais-tu que ton écuyer couche en travers de ma porte ?...

— N'en sois pas fâchée, je t'en supplie ! C'est moi qui ai donné ces ordres à Salvestro. Il le fallait... pour ta sûreté !

— Qu'est-ce que ma sûreté peut bien venir faire ici ?

— Il faut comprendre ! Outre que cette place n'est pas absolument sûre, je ne pouvais te laisser seule au milieu d'une garnison sans prendre quelques précautions. Je sais trop qu'aucun homme n'est à l'abri de ta beauté. Ceux d'ici sont faits comme les autres et, après boire, une fenêtre est vite escaladée... Salvestro !

Le vieux soldat apparut aussitôt. Il devait être collé contre la porte, comme d'habitude...

— Aide-moi à enlever tout ça ! lui ordonna Campobasso.

— Peine superflue, ricana Fiora car tu repartiras comme tu es venu. Je n'accepterais jamais d'être traitée comme une ribaude !

— Je te traite comme ma femme, un point c'est tout.

— Vraiment ? On dit que tu l'as tuée ! Vas-tu recommencer ?

— Vous êtes bien indulgent, Monseigneur, de discuter avec cette créature, grogna Salvestro qui achevait d'ôter les pièces d'armure. Je vais vous la maintenir et vous en userez à votre plaisir...

Mais Campobasso, d'une bourrade, l'envoya balader sur le mur :

– Va me chercher du vin ! Ensuite, ferme cette porte à clé et reviens me quérir dans deux heures. Que l'on me tienne un cheval frais !

Pendant ce temps, l'esprit de Fiora travaillait. Deux heures, ce n'était pas beaucoup. Et, même, ce n'était pas suffisant... Que se passerait-il si elle réussissait à l'empêcher de repartir ? Il serait déshonoré, certes, mais de cela elle ne se souciait d'aucune façon... Et le jeu en valait, comme on dit, la chandelle...

Lorsque Salvestro eut rapporté le vin et que le bruit de la clé tournant dans la serrure se fut fait entendre, elle se mit à rire. Il restait là, à quelques pas d'elle, le front soucieux, remâchant visiblement l'accusation qu'elle lui avait jetée à la tête :

– Cesse de rire ! Qui t'a dit...

– Que tu as tué ta femme ? Mais mon cher, cela fait partie de ta légende. Au surplus, cela ne me préoccupe en rien !

– Qu'est-ce qui te préoccupe alors ?

– Toi, peut-être ! Je n'aime pas être traitée comme une esclave captive mais j'aimerais assez tenir pour assuré d'être réellement ta maîtresse... dans tous les sens du terme.

– Alors, mets-moi à l'épreuve ! Commande ! J'obéirai... Mais, je t'en supplie, ne te refuse pas !

– Soit ! je consens à t'éprouver. Je t'ordonne de rester où tu es et de n'en bouger sous aucun prétexte avant que je ne te le dise.

– Que veux-tu faire ?

– Juger de ton obéissance. Tu ne bougeras pas, sinon...

Lentement, très lentement, sans le quitter des yeux, elle ôta l'écharpe de ses épaules, dénoua le ruban de sa chemise et la laissa glisser à terre, puis s'étira voluptueusement en soulevant la masse lustrée de ses cheveux. Campobasso était devenu violet :

– Fiora! implora-t-il.
– Non, tu ne bouges pas!

Sans se hâter, gracieuse et nue, elle alla jusqu'au coffre sur lequel Salvestro avait posé le vin, s'en versa un gobelet et le but à petites gorgées sans cesser de sourire à l'homme qu'elle torturait ainsi. Il tomba à genoux et cria son nom :
– Fiora! Le temps passe! Cesse ce jeu cruel!
– C'est vrai : tu as soif! Attends!... Je vais te faire boire.

Cette fois elle se détourna pour remplir la coupe d'étain mais, en même temps, prit sur le coffre son aumônière dans laquelle elle gardait son parfum ainsi qu'une petite fiole, cadeau de Démétrios, bien entendu, et qui contenait un somnifère dont elle versa deux gouttes. Ses grands cheveux formaient un abri suffisant pour que Campobasso ne vît pas ce qu'elle faisait. Enfin, élevant la coupe entre ses deux mains, elle s'approcha de lui et lui tendit le vin.
– Bois! fit-elle doucement. Pendant ce temps, je vais te déshabiller. Ensuite... nous irons au lit!

Il avala le breuvage d'un trait puis, jetant la coupe, enleva la jeune femme dans ses bras et alla s'effondrer avec elle sur le lit qui protesta. Mais l'effet du somnifère n'était pas assez rapide pour que Fiora évitât l'assaut furieux que son amant lui infligea.

Quand il fut endormi, elle se glissa hors du lit, s'en fut rincer le gobelet avec un peu de vin qu'elle jeta par la fenêtre, en reversa dans le récipient qu'elle posa au chevet et vida le restant du pot au-dehors. La pluie faisait rage et diluerait les traces. Puis elle revint se coucher, but un peu de vin, renversa la coupe sur les draps, et fit semblant de dormir.

Naturellement, quand Salvestro entra pour rappeler son maître au devoir, il fut impossible de le réveiller :
– Il a bu comme une éponge, soupira Fiora. Il est ivre mort!
– Il est surtout ivre de fatigue. Et vous y êtes pour quelque chose... N'importe! Il faut qu'il reparte sinon il est perdu. Aidez-moi à l'habiller!

Détournant les yeux pour ne pas voir Fiora se lever, il commençait déjà à passer les chausses au corps inerte qui émettait des grognements de protestation entre deux ronflements. A eux deux, ils réussirent à l'habiller puis Salvestro alla chercher le sergent qui commandait la petite garnison pour qu'il l'aide à enfermer Campobasso dans son armure. Cachant sa déception, Fiora les regardait faire. Elle découvrait que la pire ruse féminine était impuissante contre le dévouement aveugle d'un vieux serviteur.

Habillé et armé, le condottiere fut hissé et attaché sur un cheval que Salvestro, qui s'était équipé en un clin d'œil, prit par la bride :

— Je vais le reconduire jusqu'à ce qu'il se réveille. S'il faut aller jusqu'à Conflans, j'irai jusqu'à Conflans, dit-il au sergent.

Et, se penchant sur sa selle, il lui glissa quelques mots à l'oreille et quitta le château.

Avec un haussement d'épaules résigné, Fiora retourna se coucher dans son lit taché de vin...

Salvestro revint dans la journée. Campobasso avait repris conscience à l'aube et regagnait son camp à francs étriers, sans rien comprendre à ce qui lui était arrivé.

Cependant son escapade allait avoir, pour son orgueil, de rudes conséquences. Durant cette nuit, du secours était arrivé à Gratien d'Aguerre, le vaillant gouverneur de Conflans, en la personne de Gérard d'Avilliers, gouverneur de la ville frontière de Briey [1] qui venait à son aide avec une partie de ses troupes. Campobasso réussit néanmoins à regagner son camp mais ce fut pour voir arriver sur ses arrières le duc René II en personne, revenu de France avec quatre cents lances (environ deux mille cinq cents hommes) placées sous le commandement de Georges de La Tremoille, qui lança sur lui cette force nouvelle

---

1. Le dessin des frontières du Luxembourg, de la Lorraine et de la France est alors extrêmement tortueux, avec des poches et des redans qui en rendent l'appréhension assez difficile.

augmentée d'un corps de chevaliers et d'arbalétriers lorrains. Comprenant qu'il allait y laisser la vie, le condottiere se hâta de lever le siège... et essuya l'une des plus terribles colères du duc de Bourgogne. Traité de lâche et d'incapable, Campobasso, la rage au cœur, ne put que courber le dos sous l'orage en jurant qu'il se rattraperait.

Quand la nouvelle en parvint à Pierrefort, Salvestro jeta feu et flammes et Fiora fut un instant en danger :

— Il me tuera peut-être ensuite mais s'il recommence pareille folie pour vous, je jure que je vous étranglerai de mes mains ! brailla-t-il en lui mettant sous le nez deux puissantes tenailles velues capables de briser le cou d'un ours mais qu'elle considéra froidement :

— Vous me rendriez peut-être service, fit-elle. Croyez-vous que je puisse aimer ce genre de vie ?

Et, haussant les épaules, elle tourna les talons et se dirigea vers la chapelle attenante au logis. Les bâtisseurs du château avaient dû être des gens fort pieux car, outre cette chapelle, un oratoire avait été édifié entre les cuisines et le corps de garde à l'usage des serviteurs et des soldats.

Ce n'était pas la première fois que Fiora entrait dans le petit sanctuaire mal éclairé, lourdement voûté d'ogives dont personne ne prenait soin. Un autel nu, une croix de pierre et, sur les murs, des fresques en partie désagrégées par l'humidité, un vieux banc mangé des vers... c'était tout ce que l'on y voyait. Pourtant la jeune femme aimait à y venir à cause de la qualité de silence qu'elle y trouvait. Et elle restait assise de longues heures sur le vieux banc sans prier – elle en avait perdu l'habitude et n'essayait même pas de la retrouver – les mains nouées sur ses genoux, cherchant à démêler un fil clair dans l'écheveau embrouillé de sa vie naufragée.

Ce brin lumineux auquel, avec obstination, elle s'était accrochée durant tant de jours, c'était l'amour de Philippe mais cela même n'avait plus de sens puisqu'il était marié, ou remarié. Elle n'avait plus le droit de penser à lui et, malgré tout, il était toujours au fond de son cœur, comme la pointe de flèche qu'aucun chirurgien ne saurait arracher sans causer la mort du patient. Et Dieu sait si elle en souffrait parfois! L'espérance qu'elle avait emportée avec elle en quittant Florence s'était éteinte sans parvenir à guérir l'invisible blessure qu'empoisonnait à présent le souvenir de Campobasso et des joies charnelles qu'elle en avait reçues. Que ferait-elle quand le Téméraire aurait reçu son châtiment? Le couvent? A aucun prix! Le souvenir de Santa Lucia renforçait la répulsion qu'elle avait toujours eue pour la vie monastique. Rejoindre Démétrios et continuer avec lui son errance à la recherche du savoir? Cela ne la tentait guère et d'ailleurs Démétrios n'avait pas besoin d'elle. Alors... mourir serait peut-être la meilleure solution, mais à condition que cette mort vînt la prendre sous le ciel de Florence afin que ses cendres pussent reposer dans la terre même qui recouvrait le corps du seul homme qui l'eût aimée vraiment et sans rien demander en échange : Francesco Beltrami... son père. Quant à Campobasso, jamais plus il ne la toucherait, dût-elle se tuer si c'était la seule façon de l'éviter.

Cette décision, elle la changea en serment quand on apprit ce qui s'était passé à Briey tandis que le duc Charles, à la tête du gros de son armée, descendait vers le sud pour contourner Nancy et s'attaquer à Épinal. Campobasso chargé de réduire la ville frontière s'y était attaqué avec la rage et la fureur nées de son humiliation. Briey n'avait pour garnison que quatre-vingts Allemands et ses habitants, plus la troupe que lui avait laissée René II avant de repartir quêter d'autres soldats car, ayant conscience de la faiblesse de son armée, il l'avait répartie dans ses villes principales avant de s'éloigner. L'artillerie non plus n'était pas fameuse : trois ou quatre pièces. Le condottiere avec ses six mille hommes l'emporta sans beaucoup de peine mais il se souvenait de l'aide que Gérard d'Avilliers, le gouverneur, avait apportée à Conflans. Une fois entré dans la ville qui s'était défendue courageusement et que ses soudards mettaient au pillage, il fit pendre à des arbres tous les soldats de la garnison sous les yeux de leurs chefs et surtout de Gérard d'Avilliers dont un bras avait été emporté par un boulet de canon. L'horreur submergeait la Lorraine en ce mois d'octobre tandis que le Téméraire, qui avait tourné la capitale par Custines et la Neuveville, ravageait le sud du duché qu'il voulait s'assurer avant d'attaquer Nancy. Toute la Lorraine en criait vers le ciel tandis que son peuple essayait de fuir la férocité des vainqueurs.

Du haut des remparts de Pierrefort, Fiora pouvait voir des files de paysans misérables, n'ayant plus ni toit ni foyer, traînant avec eux des enfants et des vieillards, des blessés aussi et se cherchant au moins un abri contre cette pluie qui ne cessait pas et qui grossissait rivières et ruisseaux. Certains venaient vers le château, suppliant qu'on voulût bien leur ouvrir et les secourir mais Salvestro était impitoyable et les chassait à coups de pierres et de flèches, sans se soucier de la fureur écœurée de Fiora.

— Quelle sorte de mère t'a porté, vieux misérable! lui jeta-t-elle à la face devant ses archers. Même les loups ne tuent que s'ils ont faim. Toi et ton ignoble maître, vous tuez par plaisir parce que vous vous croyez à l'abri du châtiment...

— Mon ignoble maître ? Tu ne le trouves pas si affreux quand il te baise, sale petite putain florentine. Je sais quelle chanson tu chantes quand il te couvre. Et il y reviendra encore!

— Jamais, tu entends? Jamais plus il ne me touchera. Sur le salut de mon âme!

— Ton âme ? ricana le vieux. Il ne lui reste plus grand-chose à perdre! Celle d'une coureuse de routes, d'une espionne prête à faire n'importe quoi. Ôte-toi de là avant que je ne perde patience.

Alors, à toute volée, elle le gifla puis lui cracha au visage avant de s'enfuir en courant, poursuivie par la voix rauque de fureur de Salvestro :

— Il va venir! Il va venir bientôt, celui qui est ton maître et le mien, et je saurai quoi lui dire!

Haussant les épaules, elle courut s'enfermer dans sa chambre mais elle passa d'abord par la cuisine où elle rafla un couteau, bien décidée à s'en servir contre quiconque l'attaquerait et, s'il n'y avait plus d'espoir, contre elle-même.

Mais Campobasso ne revint pas... Ce qui vint, par un matin chargé de brume des premiers jours de novembre, ce fut, sous la bannière de Bourgogne, une troupe de cavaliers escortant un officier déjà âgé, à la mine hautaine, devant lequel il fallut bien ouvrir les portes quand il eut crié :

— De par Monseigneur Charles, prince et duc de Bourgogne, comte de Charolais, moi, Olivier de La Marche, chevalier de l'honorable ordre de la Toison d'or et capitaine des gardes de mondit seigneur le duc, vous somme d'ouvrir à notre requête l'accès de ce château !

Rassemblant en hâte un piquet d'honneur et passant son meilleur tabard, Salvestro fit abaisser le pont et lever la herse. Aussitôt les cavaliers s'engouffrèrent et s'avancèrent jusqu'au milieu de la cour.

— J'ai à parler, dit le chef, à celui qui commande cette place.

— C'est moi, monseigneur. Salvestro da Canale, écuyer de Mgr le comte de Campobasso et tout à votre service.

— Je l'entends bien ainsi. Vous devez me remettre une femme, une certaine Fiora Beltrami. Elle est bien ici ?

— Certes... mais j'ai reçu ordre de veiller sur elle et de la garder par-devers moi tant que mon maître ne me donnera pas ordre de la libérer.

Le capitaine se pencha et, sans effort apparent, saisit Salvestro par le col de sa tunique et le souleva de terre :

— Moi, c'est au duc de Bourgogne que j'obéis et il m'a commandé de quérir cette femme et de la lui amener ! As-tu entendu ?

— Il a très bien entendu, coupa la voix froide de Fiora qui s'avança de quelques pas hors du logis. Je suis Fiora Beltrami. Que me voulez-vous ?

Sans songer à cacher sa surprise en face de cette mince jeune femme à l'allure fière et toute de noir vêtue qui posait sur lui le calme regard des plus grands yeux qu'il ait jamais vus, Olivier de La Marche baissa involontairement le ton pour déclarer :

— J'ai ordre de vous arrêter et de vous conduire par-devers mon maître.

— M'arrêter ? Ai-je donc commis quelque crime ?

— Je l'ignore. Êtes-vous prête à me suivre de bon gré ?

— Et même avec plaisir ! fit-elle avec un étroit sourire dont elle adressa la fin à Salvestro qui luttait visiblement contre une colère. Puis-je emporter ce qui m'appartient ? C'est peu de chose, d'ailleurs.

— Sans doute. Un de mes hommes va vous assister. Pendant ce temps j'entends qu'on amène ici un cheval tout sellé.

Un moment plus tard, Fiora revenait, enveloppée de sa mante noire et suivie d'un soldat qui portait son léger bagage. Un cheval attendait. Elle se dirigea vers lui mais le capitaine qui avait mis pied à terre s'interposa. Il tenait à la main une cordelette :

— Je dois vous attacher. Si vous promettez de ne pas tenter de vous échapper, je lierai vos mains devant vous...

— Ah !... C'est à ce point ?

— Oui.

— Bien... De toute façon, soupira-t-elle, je vous ai dit que j'étais heureuse de quitter cette prison.

— Même si une autre vous attend ?

— Quelle qu'elle soit, je suis certaine de m'y plaire davantage.

Ses poignets une fois liés, on l'aida à enfourcher son cheval et l'officier disposa même son manteau autour d'elle, rabattant le capuchon sur sa tête pour la garantir de la pluie. Puis, remontant en selle, il prit la bride du cheval de la jeune femme qu'il passa au-dessus de son gantelet.

— Avez-vous le droit de me dire où vous me conduisez ?

demanda Fiora tandis que, côte à côte avec La Marche, elle franchissait la porterie de Pierrefort.

— Il n'y a là aucun secret. Je vous conduis devant Nancy au camp de Monseigneur le duc. Nous y serons ce soir.

— Alors, tout est bien ainsi.

Sous l'abri de la capuche, elle se permit un sourire. Tout valait mieux que demeurer la captive de Campobasso, même si cela signifiait l'échec de sa mission. Elle allait enfin approcher ce prince fabuleux dont ses amis ne disaient jamais assez de bien et ses ennemis jamais assez de mal, ce Charles le Hardi ou le Téméraire auquel Philippe de Selongey était enchaîné par son serment de chevalier de la Toison d'or et sa foi féodale... cet homme enfin que Démétrios et elle-même avaient juré de tuer. Et voilà qu'elle était à présent sa prisonnière et que c'était lui qui, peut-être, la ferait mourir. Mais, au fond, c'était sans importance... à condition, toutefois, que le destin ne la remît pas en présence de Philippe... Il ne fallait pas que la blessure secrète se remît à saigner si elle voulait affronter la mort d'un front serein.

CHAPITRE X

DEVANT NANCY...

Des hauteurs du village de Laxou, Fiora vit s'étendre à ses pieds deux villes. L'une, faite de tentes aux couleurs vives surmontées de flammes aux teintes assorties, disposées autour d'une bâtisse à demi écroulée entre de minces tours pointues ; l'autre, couronnée de fumées, dressait ses remparts et ses tours, défendus par des fossés et des ouvrages de terre. Rangés en ligne devant l'une et sur les murailles de l'autre, des canons tiraient dont le vacarme s'accompagnait de cris. Des hommes s'agitaient de part et d'autre. En dépit du temps gris, on voyait briller les armes et les cuirasses. Des hommes tombaient sur les parapets des tranchées creusées devant la ville de toile et sur les boulevards[1] de la ville de pierre dans laquelle on pouvait voir flamber, avec de hautes flammes rouges et des nuages de fumée noire, ce qui devait être une maison...

Nancy n'était pas une très grande ville. Cinq à six mille habitants vivaient dans ce quadrilatère long d'environ six cents mètres sur quatre cents, mais c'était tout de même la capitale du duché de Lorraine et une noble ville pour la défense de laquelle ses princes avaient édifié de hauts murs dont de grands hourds de bois protégeaient les cré-

1. Ces boulevards se présentaient comme de grosses masses de terre reposant sur des estacades de pieux de chênes disposés en quinconces. Ils étaient destinés à renforcer les postes de guet.

neaux. Peu de tours cependant : en dehors de celles, jumelles, qui défendaient la porte de la Craffe – celle du nord – et la porte Saint-Nicolas – celle du sud – et les deux poternes, celle que l'on appelait Sarate et la poterne Saint-Jean, quatre tours seulement : celle du Vannier au nord-est, celle de Sar au nord-est ; celle du Terreau, plein ouest, et enfin la grande tour, véritable donjon qui commandait, au sud-est, la route vers la commanderie Saint-Jean. Plus, bien sûr, celles qui défendaient le palais ducal sur le long côté est regardant vers la Meurthe.

Cinquante ans plus tôt, le duc Charles II, conscient des progrès de l'artillerie et du fait que les vieilles murailles droites et les fossés ne formaient plus pour sa ville une défense suffisante, avait ordonné, pour éloigner l'ennemi de la base des remparts et protéger les portes tout en permettant des sorties, la construction de ces « bellewarts » – ou boulevards. On avait renforcé les loges de guet et, un peu plus tard, le duc Jean II avait érigé les tours jumelles à poivrières d'ardoise qui défendaient la porte de la Craffe [1]. Et telle qu'elle était, la capitale lorraine résistait fièrement aux assauts de l'armée bourguignonne... Une armée qui, cependant, grâce à des contingents luxembourgeois, comtois, savoyards et anglais, était redevenue puissante et redoutable et qui, de Metz [2] par le nord ou de Franche-Comté par le sud, pouvait recevoir aide et ravitaillement, ce qui n'était pas le cas de la cité investie : dès le début du siège, Campobasso avait capturé les troupeaux qui paissaient hors des murs. Combien de temps, dans ces conditions et par cet automne froid et pluvieux, Nancy résisterait-elle ?

Apparemment insoucieux de la canonnade, Olivier de La Marche dirigea sa prisonnière vers l'immense camp et traversa les divers quartiers où travaillaient nombre de corps de métiers : armuriers, charrons, bourreliers, charpentiers, couteliers, boulangers, bouchers et même un apo-

---

1. La seule qui existe encore.
2. L'évêque de Metz était l'allié au Téméraire.

thicaire. Une armée, c'était alors un gros bourg où ne manquaient ni les tavernes ni les ribaudes dont le campement se trouvait un peu à l'écart sur les bords de l'étang Saint-Jean. Le duc Charles en avait réduit le nombre à trente par compagnie mais cela faisait encore pas mal de monde.

Avec la tombée du jour – et le jour baissait vite par ce novembre maussade – les bouches à feu cessèrent de tirer. Les assaillants regagnèrent leur camp en rapportant leurs blessés, ceux tout au moins qui n'étaient pas au-delà de tout secours humain. Dans la cité assiégée, les cloches de Saint-Epvre et de Saint-Georges sonnèrent l'Angélus et, d'un côté comme de l'autre, les têtes se découvrirent tandis que l'on s'immobilisait pour une courte prière. L'escorte de Fiora fit de même... Enfin, passé les anciennes fortifications de la vieille commanderie des chevaliers de Saint-Jean de Jérusalem, qui se trouvaient à environ douze cents mètres des remparts, on découvrit, gardé militairement, un groupe de tentes fastueuses rangées autour de la plus grande, un immense tref pourpre dont la pointe centrale était surmontée d'une bulle d'or couronnée. Une grande bannière violet, noir et argent était plantée tout auprès et un peuple d'écuyers, de valets et de pages habillés aux armes de Bourgogne s'agitait autour. Les autres tentes portaient les armes du duc de Clèves, du prince de Tarente, de divers ambassadeurs et de nombreux chevaliers de la Toison d'or mais celle qui était la plus proche du logis ducal était un peu plus grande que les autres, d'une riche teinte violette surmontée d'une croix d'or et abritait le légat du pape, Alessandro Nanni, évêque de Forli.

Toutes ces habitations provisoires, dont certaines auraient pu rivaliser avec de vraies maisons pour la solidité et l'élégance, étaient, à cette heure, pleines d'activité cependant que dans les bâtiments encore debout de la commanderie, les cuisiniers poussaient leurs feux sous les rôtis et les ragoûts dont les parfums épicés emplissaient l'air. Cela donnait lieu à un joyeux brouhaha grâce auquel on pouvait oublier un peu que l'on était en guerre...

L'apparition du capitaine des gardes menant en bride une belle jeune femme vêtue de noir aux poignets entravés suscita plus que de l'intérêt mais, apparemment sourd et insensible aux appels et aux questions de ses compagnons d'armes, Olivier de La Marche poursuivit son chemin sans même tourner la tête. Fiora, elle non plus, ne regardait rien ni personne. Très droite sur son cheval, elle avait l'attitude hautaine d'une reine captive et ne vit pas, à quelques pas d'elle, deux chevaliers dont l'un aidait l'autre à se débarrasser d'un heaume cabossé. Une immense stupeur figea un instant le visage du premier qui, du coup, arracha le casque un peu trop vite :

– Doucement, s'il te plaît ! protesta Philippe de Selongey. Tu as failli m'arracher le nez !

– Regarde !... et dis-moi si, par hasard, je n'aurais pas des visions ?

De son bras tendu, Mathieu de Prame désignait les deux cavaliers qui se dirigeaient vers la tente du duc. Sous son hâle Philippe rougit brusquement.

– Ce n'est pas possible ! Cela ne peut pas être elle ? murmura-t-il. Si elle était encore vivante, que ferait-elle ici ? Et prisonnière ?

– Je ne sais pas. Mais crois-tu que pareille ressemblance soit possible ? J'aurais cru cette beauté unique...

– Il faut savoir !

Philippe s'élança, mais déjà La Marche et sa captive avaient mis pied à terre devant la demeure ducale où veillaient des gardes et étaient entrés. Les lances se croisèrent silencieusement devant Selongey quand il voulut pénétrer à son tour.

– Je veux entrer ! protesta-t-il. Il faut je voie Monseigneur le duc sur l'heure !

– Impossible ! Messire Olivier vient de donner ordre de ne laisser passer quiconque après lui.

— Mais enfin, cette femme qui vient de pénétrer avec lui les mains liées, qui est-elle ?

— Je l'ignore...

Avec fureur, Selongey arracha son gantelet et le jeta à terre. Prame, qui l'avait rejoint, s'efforça de l'apaiser :

— Calme-toi ! La colère ne te servirait à rien. Il suffit d'attendre qu'elle sorte... Le duc ne va pas la garder éternellement chez lui...

— Tu as raison... Attendons !

Et tous deux allèrent s'asseoir sur le tronc d'un des nombreux arbres qui avaient été abattus...

Pendant ce temps Fiora, après avoir attendu quelques instants seule dans une sorte d'antichambre tendue de velours pourpre, accédait, toujours guidée par le capitaine des gardes, à une pièce somptueuse, tendue d'une toile entièrement brodée d'or qui brillait comme une mitre d'évêque. Au milieu, éclairé par un candélabre où brûlaient une profusion de cierges, et par des lampes de cristal, une sorte de trône se dressait sous un baldaquin de pourpre frappé des armes de Bourgogne. Sur ce trône, un homme était assis que Fiora reconnut aussitôt pour l'avoir entendu décrire par sa nourrice : « Il a le visage large et coloré au menton puissant, aux yeux sombres et dominateurs. Ses cheveux sont noirs et drus... » Cet homme, c'était le Téméraire.

Il portait une longue robe de velours rouge ceinturée d'or, réchauffée d'un collet d'hermine sur lequel s'étalait le collier de la Toison d'or. A son bonnet de même velours brillait un joyau étrange et fascinant : une aigrette de diamants retenue par un petit carquois fait de perles et de rubis, et la prisonnière pensa qu'il ressemblait à l'un de ces princes de légendes dont son père lui contait les belles histoires quand elle était enfant. Très certainement l'empereur n'était pas plus imposant que lui. Cependant, elle n'en eut pas peur et même elle eut un peu envie de rire en pensant que, depuis des mois, elle rêvait d'abattre cet homme défendu par une armée de gardes et une autre de serviteurs, plus encore que par sa propre légende. Elle, simple fille sans aucune puissance, et son ami Démétrios, un médecin grec vieillissant, ils avaient juré de tuer le Grand Duc d'Occident sans même savoir s'ils pourraient un jour l'approcher... Et voilà qu'elle était devant lui, mais captive, liée de cordes et que, sans doute, elle ne vivrait pas assez pour voir se lever la prochaine aurore, car ce visage sombre, ces yeux chargés d'éclairs qui la considéraient en silence n'augureraient rien de bon. Mais elle n'avait toujours pas peur.

— Ainsi, dit-il enfin d'une voix grave et sonore qui aurait pu être celle d'un chanteur, ainsi tu es la fille pour laquelle un de mes meilleurs capitaines oublie ses devoirs et abandonne son poste devant une ville assiégée ? D'où sors-tu donc pour ne pas savoir que l'on s'incline devant un prince ?

— Une femme ne s'incline pas, monseigneur, et je ne saurais saluer comme il convient avec les mains liées. Je cherche d'ailleurs, depuis que l'on m'est venu chercher, la raison de ceci, ajouta-t-elle en élevant ses poignets entravés. Je n'ai, que je sache, tué ni volé personne ?

— Tu es une espionne au service de mon beau cousin, le roi Louis de France. C'est pire à mes yeux.

— Vraiment ? N'ai-je pas entendu dire qu'une trêve de neuf années avait été signée à Soleuvre entre le roi et Votre Seigneurie ? Je pensais qu'il était possible de voyager à son aise dès l'instant où les armes se sont tues ?

— Ici elles parlent encore. Ainsi, tu as eu fantaisie de visiter les frontières et singulièrement une ville où, comme par hasard, était concentrée une grande partie de notre armée ?

— J'ai eu le désir de rencontrer le seul cousin qui me reste, oui monseigneur.

— Cousin ! Campobasso est ton cousin ?

— Je ne vois pas en quoi, dit Fiora avec un demi-sourire, ce lien de parenté peut offenser le puissant duc de Bourgogne. Et puisque nous parlons d'offense, j'aimerais,

Monseigneur, que vous cessiez de me tutoyer. Je suis de bonne naissance et le roi Louis que j'ai rencontré, en effet, m'a toujours parlé avec déférence. Je n'ai pas entendu dire que Sa Majesté soit de moins bonne maison que Votre Seigneurie.

Devant l'audace de cette femme dont les grands yeux gris le considéraient avec une ironique insolence, la colère de Charles éclata. Le visage soudain aussi rouge que sa robe, il se dressa debout et ordonna :

— La Marche! Obligez cette femme à s'agenouiller devant nous et faites-lui comprendre que sa vie ne tient qu'à un fil. Elle a tout intérêt à cesser d'exciter ainsi notre colère!

Sans un mot, le capitaine des gardes vint derrière Fiora et pesa sur ses épaules jusqu'à ce que ses genoux plient. Ils tombèrent assez rudement sur le tapis mais la jeune femme ne baissa pas la tête pour autant.

— Il eût été plus simple, dit-elle, de me délier les mains. Vous auriez pu constater alors, monseigneur, que je sais saluer un prince comme il convient de le faire. Un geste obtenu par force n'a jamais été signe de respect... Cela dit, faites-moi exécuter si cela peut vous satisfaire.

Ce tranquille courage éteignit la fureur de Charles. C'était, en effet, de toutes les vertus, celle qu'il appréciait le plus :

— Vous ne craignez pas la mort?

— Pourquoi la craindrais-je? La vie ne m'a rien apporté qui mérite d'être regretté.

Le Téméraire s'approcha et se pencha un peu pour scruter les profondeurs de ce regard qui ne fuyait pas le sien. Soudain, il tira de sa ceinture une dague dont la poignée d'or était enrichie de pierreries et en appuya la pointe sur le cou de la jeune femme :

— Je vous accorde le temps de dire une prière!

— C'est inutile, murmura Fiora. Dieu n'a rien à me pardonner car je ne crois pas l'avoir jamais offensé gravement. Lui, en revanche, s'est plu à me faire souffrir. S'il consent à entendre de moi une prière, qu'il me réunisse à mon père assassiné!

Elle ferma les yeux, attendant que l'arme s'enfonce mais déjà elle s'éloignait. D'un geste vif, le duc trancha les cordes qui liaient les mains de la jeune femme:

— Je crois, pardieu, que vous dites vrai, fit-il d'une voix sombre. Vous n'avez pas peur... Sors, La Marche! Et vous, relevez-vous!

Mais Fiora n'eut pas le temps d'exécuter cet ordre: Campobasso venait de faire irruption dans la pièce. Il vit Fiora à genoux et le duc, un poignard à la main:

— Monseigneur! cria-t-il. Pour l'amour de Dieu ne touchez pas à cette jeune femme! Je l'aime et je veux l'épouser!

Il se précipitait vers Fiora, la relevait et, passant un bras autour de ses épaules, il reprit:

— Ne la rendez pas responsable des fautes que j'ai pu commettre, mon prince! Sans bien s'en rendre compte, elle a allumé en moi un feu dévorant qui ne me laisse ni trêve ni repos. Je ne peux plus vivre sans elle et...

— Dehors! hurla le duc. Qui t'a donné l'audace d'entrer ici sans y être appelé? Où sont mes gardes?... La Marche!

— Non, n'appelez pas, Monseigneur! pria Campobasso avec un regard douloureux à Fiora qui l'avait repoussé. Je ne cherche en rien à offenser Votre Seigneurie mais on m'a dit que vous aviez fait conduire ici donna Fiora et à la pensée qu'elle était livrée sans défense à votre colère...

— Sans défense? Je trouve, moi, qu'elle s'en tire fort bien? Qui t'a prévenu?

— Mon écuyer, Salvestro da Canale, que j'avais chargé de la garder en mon château de Pierrefort. Il a suivi l'escorte qui l'amenait ici. Ne me la prenez pas, Monseigneur, je vous en conjure, car elle ne mérite pas l'irritation où je vous vois. Comprenez! Nous sommes l'un à l'autre, nous nous aimons et il ne manque, à notre bonheur, que la permission de notre prince et la bénédiction...

— Et pourquoi pas ma permission à moi? claironna une

voix furieuse dont le son fit manquer un battement au cœur de Fiora. Mal contenu par Olivier de La Marche et un page qui faisaient de courageux efforts pour le maîtriser, Philippe de Selongey venait de faire irruption à son tour dans la tente ducale. Le visage du duc devint couleur de brique :

— Selongey maintenant ? gronda-t-il. Ah ça, mais on entre ici comme dans un moulin ! Que venez-vous faire ici ? Sortez !

Au lieu d'obéir, Philippe mit un genou en terre mais sans baisser la tête et sans perdre un pouce de sa fierté :

— Je demande excuse, monseigneur, pour ce manquement à l'étiquette ! Votre Seigneurie me connaît : elle sait combien je lui suis fidèle et attaché mais il fallait que je vienne et je n'ai pas pu m'en empêcher quand j'ai vu ce reître forcer votre porte...

— Personne apparemment n'aurait pu vous en empêcher ! J'attends à présent que vous me disiez ce que vous venez faire ici. Avez-vous cru — et ce serait une bonne excuse — que Campobasso en voulait à notre vie ?

— Non, monseigneur. Je viens réclamer ce qui m'appartient. Cette jeune dame est ma femme !

Un boulet tombant au milieu de la tente princière n'eût pas causé surprise aussi grande. Le duc considéra un instant chacun des trois personnages de cette étrange scène avec un regard qui ne présageait rien de bon puis retourna, plus sombre que jamais, siéger sur son trône. Campobasso réagit le premier. Tirant son épée, il voulut se jeter sur Philippe qui se relevait sur un geste du duc :

— Par tous les diables de l'enfer, tu mens, misérable ! Mais tu ne me la prendras pas...

— Assez ! cria le duc et déjà Olivier de La Marche avait bondi sur le condottiere et lui arrachait son épée cependant que son maître reprenait : On n'assassine pas, chez moi ! Pour avoir osé dégainer devant moi, vous devriez être puni, comte de Campobasso ! Retirez-vous !

— Mais, monseigneur...

— Ne m'obligez pas à répéter si vous voulez éviter la honte d'être jeté dehors !... Et maintenant Selongey à nous deux ! Faites très attention à ce que vous allez dire car il n'a jamais été permis à quiconque de se moquer de moi et moins encore à ceux qui sont dans ma faveur.

— Dieu me garde de jamais vous déplaire, mon prince. Depuis l'enfance je suis votre féal et je mourrai avant d'avoir usé à votre encontre d'une ironie qui serait sacrilège à mes yeux.

— Je te crois, Philippe ! En ce cas, réponds sans crainte : tu prétends que cette femme est tienne ?

— Je l'ai épousée à Florence où vous m'aviez envoyé auprès des Médicis, en février dernier. Son père, Francesco Beltrami, était alors l'un des deux ou trois hommes les plus riches et les plus puissants de la ville. Nous nous sommes mariés...

— Afin de pouvoir offrir au trésor de guerre de Votre Seigneurie les cent mille florins d'or qui constituaient ma dot et que les Fugger d'Augsbourg vous ont versés ! coupa Fiora enfin parvenue à maîtriser l'émotion ressentie quand Philippe était apparu devant elle, tellement semblable au souvenir qu'elle en gardait et pourtant différent.

Cela tenait peut-être à cette armure qu'il portait avec aisance et qu'elle ne lui avait jamais vue, à ces cheveux plus courts, à ces traits creusés par la fatigue, à cette petite cicatrice qui entaillait sa joue mais son cœur avait bondi vers lui et la blessure secrète saignait à nouveau en dépit de la joie fugitive éprouvée lorsqu'il avait revendiqué son titre d'époux. Une joie qui s'était vite effacée. Reniée et abandonnée jadis, trompée à présent puisqu'une autre femme portait son nom, Fiora appela sa rancune au secours de ce cœur trop faible.

— Certes, admit Selongey, et je n'ai pas caché à votre père l'usage auquel je destinais cette somme importante mais je vous ai épousée pour une autre raison, Fiora. Souvenez-vous !

— N'allez pas prétendre aujourd'hui que vous m'aimiez

alors que vous ne vouliez de moi qu'une seule nuit ? Vous m'avez abandonnée sans esprit de retour au lendemain de nos noces pour revenir à la seule femme que vous aimiez réellement et que vous avez dû épouser dès que vous m'avez crue morte. En admettant que vous ne l'eussiez point épousée avant ?...

— Une autre femme ? Moi j'ai épousé quelqu'un d'autre ? Moi, Philippe de Selongey, chevalier de la Toison d'or, je serais bigame ?

— Je ne vois pas d'autre terme à employer. Ou alors expliquez-moi qui est cette Béatrice qui règne en votre château de Selongey. On m'a appris là-bas qu'elle en était la dame...

— Béatrice ? s'écria Philippe. Elle est encore là ?

— Et pourquoi donc n'y serait-elle pas si elle est chez elle ?

Selongey se mit à rire de bon cœur, une petite flamme de gaieté soudain allumée dans ses yeux noisette.

— Je la croyais rentrée depuis longtemps chez ses parents. Sachez qu'elle est ma belle-sœur et rien de plus.

— Quand dites-vous la vérité et quand mentez-vous ? Une belle-sœur, cela suppose au moins un frère et vous avez dit à mon père que vous n'aviez aucune famille.

— Et c'était vrai. Mon frère aîné, Amaury, a été tué à la bataille de Montlhéry, il y a dix ans. Sa veuve espérait, je ne vous le cache pas, que je l'épouserais, ainsi que cela se fait assez couramment dans nos familles. Mais je n'ai jamais pu me résoudre à prendre pour femme qui je aimais pas. Vous, Fiora... je vous aimais.

— Vous m'aimiez... et cependant vous êtes parti sans me laisser l'espoir de vous revoir un jour.

— Je suis revenu pourtant et ce fut pour apprendre quelle catastrophe s'était abattue sur vous. On vous disait morte. Je n'avais aucune raison d'en douter.

— Philippe !... Mon Dieu... je vous ai tant haï !

A la fois bouleversée et envahie d'une joie presque trop forte après tout ce qu'elle avait enduré, Fiora, oubliant la présence du prince, tendait déjà les mains vers son amour retrouvé et Philippe allait peut-être s'élancer vers elle quand la voix froide du Téméraire, qui les observait en silence, les cloua sur place.

— C'est une belle histoire sans doute mais puisque, Madame, vous avez l'honneur d'être la comtesse de Selongey, voulez-vous m'expliquer comment il se fait que vous soyez aussi la maîtresse du comte de Campobasso et une maîtresse assez ardemment aimée pour qu'il souhaite l'épouser lui-même ?

Comme s'ils s'éveillaient d'un songe, ils se tournèrent vers lui du même mouvement automatique. La joyeuse lumière du bonheur vacilla et s'éteignit dans l'âme de Fiora comme elle venait de s'éteindre dans les yeux de Philippe ; la jeune femme comprit que ce prince, qui les dominait de sa splendeur quasi barbare, allait tout faire pour lui arracher l'homme qu'elle aimait et elle se prépara à combattre.

— N'ayant plus personne au monde, pourquoi n'aurais-je pas recherché le seul parent qui me restât, même si ce n'était qu'un lointain cousin ? fit-elle calmement.

— Et votre hâte était si grande que vous n'avez pas hésité à venir le trouver à Thionville, au milieu de nos armées ? Comment saviez-vous où il était ?

— Il suffisait de savoir où se situaient ces armées. Les faits et gestes d'un aussi grand prince que Votre Seigneurie sont vite connus. En allant vers l'endroit où résidait le duc de Bourgogne, on pouvait espérer rencontrer l'un de ses principaux capitaines. Il n'était que d'interroger en chemin...

— Et l'idée de rejoindre celui que vous aviez épousé ne vous effleurait pas ?

— J'ai déjà dit que je ne croyais plus à la réalité de notre mariage. D'ailleurs... je pensais qu'il n'était plus de ce monde. Il avait assuré à mon père que, pour effacer la mésalliance dont il marquait son nom en le donnant à la fille... d'un marchand, il espérait trouver au combat une mort honorable...

Le duc se tourna vers Philippe qui, le regard au loin, avait écouté sans rien dire, aussi froid que son armure.

— Est-ce vrai ?

— Que je voulais mourir ? Oui, monseigneur mais j'avais présumé de mes forces et surtout je n'avais pas prévu que j'aimerais autant. Au lendemain de notre mariage, je savais déjà que je n'accepterais pas de ne plus la revoir et qu'il faudrait qu'un jour ou l'autre je revienne...

Il parlait comme du fond d'un rêve, de cette étrange voix blanche et détachée de ceux que Démétrios soumettait à son pouvoir hypnotique. Fiora voulut aller vers lui mais un geste impérieux du Téméraire l'en empêcha.

— Vous m'aimiez donc vraiment, Philippe ? Pourquoi n'avoir rien dit ? Pourquoi être parti sans un mot, sans...

— Assez ! s'écria le duc. Je ne vous ai pas autorisée à parler au comte de Selongey. Dites-moi plutôt d'où vous veniez quand vous avez atteint Thionville ?

— De France, bien entendu. Après la mort de mon père j'ai rejoint à Paris messer Agnolo Nardi, son frère de lait qui tient rue des Lombards le comptoir et la banque Beltrami...

— Des marchands ! Des boutiquiers ! fit le duc avec un écrasant dédain. Voilà ce que vous avez épousé, Philippe de Selongey, vous dont les ancêtres étaient aux croisades ! La fille est belle, j'en conviens, mais il en est d'autres...

— Ces autres vous apportent-elles en mariage cent mille florins d'or ? gronda Fiora souffletée par ce mépris. Chez nous, la noblesse tient à honneur de contribuer à la richesse de l'État en menant de grandes affaires et plus d'une Florentine a épousé un prince.

— Baissez le ton, s'il vous plaît ! Vous n'êtes pas ici devant l'un de ces Médicis nés à l'ombre d'un comptoir ! En outre, vous oubliez un peu facilement que vous avez été dénoncée comme étant une espionne de Louis XI chargée par lui de séduire Campobasso... et que vous avez scrupuleusement accompli votre mission. Nierez-vous qu'au soir même de votre arrivée chez votre « cousin » vous l'avez accueilli dans votre lit ? Nierez-vous que durant trois jours et trois nuits les portes de votre chambre ne se sont point ouvertes ? Nierez-vous qu'il vous a fait conduire à son château de Pierrefort où, pour coucher encore avec vous, il a abandonné son poste devant Conflans ? Tout à l'heure encore, n'était-il pas à cette même place, prêt à se traîner à genoux pour que je vous rende à lui et lui accorde de vous épouser ? « Nous nous aimons, disait-il. Nous sommes l'un à l'autre »... Que vous faut-il de plus ? Dois-je l'appeler pour qu'il nous conte ici, par le menu, ce que furent ces jours et ces nuits de Thionville ?

Brusquement, Selongey perdit son immobilité de statue et plia un genou :

— Avec votre permission, monseigneur, je me retirerai.

Et sans attendre son congé, il tourna les talons et quitta la tente. Sa figure était celle d'un homme que l'on vient de frapper à mort. Fiora, envahie par le désespoir, le regarda sortir mais ses yeux étaient secs. Pour rien au monde, elle ne laisserait voir sa souffrance à cet homme féroce qui attendait sans doute des cris, des pleurs et des supplications mais pas ce silence atterré qui changeait la jeune femme en statue. Quand Philippe eut disparu, elle se tourna vers le duc, très droite dans sa longue robe noire et leva vers sa splendeur pourpre ses yeux aussi gris que le ciel d'hiver :

— Il semblerait, monseigneur, qu'il fasse meilleur servir un prince né derrière un comptoir que le Grand Duc d'Occident. Votre Altesse déteste sans doute messire de Selongey ?

— Lui ? Il a notre estime et notre amitié.

— C'est l'évidence même. Que serait-ce si vous le haïssiez ?

— Ne vous flattez pas trop. Il préférera souffrir que

vivre aussi publiquement bafoué. L'adultère, chez nous, est puni de mort.

— Sauf quand il est princier, si j'en crois la légende du père de Votre Seigneurie. Eh bien, faites-moi exécuter : cela arrangera tout.

— Et serait d'un bon exemple car je hais l'adultère et vous me faites horreur, si belle que vous soyez! Nous verrons la suite à donner à ceci. Pour l'instant, vous allez rester dans ce camp sous bonne garde. Ceux qui veilleront sur vous m'en répondront sur leur tête car je ne vous permettrai pas d'échapper au sort que vous méritez. Mais pour l'heure, nous avons une ville à prendre... Soyez cependant certaine que nous ne vous oublierons pas!

Remise à nouveau au seigneur de La Marche, elle allait sortir quand le Téméraire l'arrêta :

— Un instant! Avant que de vous rendre en France, aviez-vous déjà quitté Florence?

— Non, monseigneur. Jamais...

— Bizarre!... Il me semble pourtant vous avoir déjà vue... il y a fort longtemps...

— On dit qu'en ce bas monde nous avons tous un sosie, Votre Seigneurie aura rencontré une femme qui me ressemble... Dans une rue peut-être?... Ou dans quelque marché? Ou derrière un comptoir?...

Haussant les épaules, il lui fit signe de sortir. Alors sans incliner la tête si peu que ce soit, elle lui offrit la plus gracieuse et la plus parfaite des révérences puis quitta le pavillon ducal environnée de gardes. La nuit était venue mais les entours du grand tref étaient éclairés par de nombreuses torches et de larges feux près desquels se chauffaient les hommes étaient allumés un peu partout.

Quand Fiora apparut au-dehors, Campobasso, qui attendait sur ce même tronc d'arbre où s'étaient assis tout à l'heure Philippe et Mathieu, s'élança vers elle mais La Marche l'écarta :

— Éloignez-vous! Les ordres de Monseigneur le duc sont formels : aucun entretien n'est permis...

— Où la conduisez-vous ?

— Ici près, mais ceux qui seront chargés de veiller sur elle en répondront sur leur vie... Il vous est interdit de l'approcher.

Le condottiere recula comme si on l'avait frappé : Fiora était passée devant lui sans même lui accorder un regard. Alors il voulut s'élancer vers l'intérieur du pavillon mais, prévoyant son geste, les gardes avaient déjà croisé leurs lances... Fou de rage, il les insulta sans réussir à troubler leur impassibilité, ce que voyant il s'élança sur les traces de l'escorte afin d'apprendre au moins où l'on conduisait celle qu'il aimait.

Il n'alla pas loin. Derrière le grand tref pourpre, des tentes beaucoup moins spacieuses étaient attribuées à certains des officiers de la maison ducale. Ce fut dans l'une de celles-ci, laissée libre par la mort récente de son propriétaire, que La Marche fit entrer sa prisonnière, éclairant d'une torche prise au-dehors un intérieur assez confortable où se voyaient un lit de camp garni de coussins et de couvertures, deux coffres dont l'un contenait des ustensiles de toilette, un grand chandelier de fer, un brasero éteint et un tapis posé sur le plancher qui isolait la tente de l'herbe rase sur laquelle on l'avait plantée. Une provision de bois attendait contre l'une des parois...

L'un des soldats alluma le feu tandis qu'à l'aide de sa torche le capitaine des gardes enflammait les chandelles :

— Je vais vous faire porter à souper, dit La Marche à Fiora qui s'était assise, frissonnante, sur le lit. J'enverrai aussi votre bagage et, demain, une femme viendra s'occuper de vous.

— Grand merci. Mais pourquoi tant de soins ? Ne suis-je pas prisonnière ?

— Nous n'avons guère de cachots à notre disposition. En outre, les ordres de monseigneur sont que vous ne manquiez de rien. Je dois y veiller personnellement...

— C'est trop de bonté... mais consentiriez-vous à y mettre un comble en me disant où loge messire de Selongey ? Est-ce loin d'ici ?...

— Je n'ai pas le droit de vous l'apprendre, madame. Vous êtes ici au secret en quelque sorte avec défense d'en sortir ou de communiquer avec qui que ce soit en dehors de moi ou de qui aura la permission d'entrer...

Fiora hocha la tête, signifiant qu'elle avait compris puis se leva et alla offrir ses mains froides à la chaleur du brasero qui emplissait son étroit logis d'une bonne odeur de bois brûlé. La tête vide comme cela doit être lorsque l'on a subi un naufrage, elle n'essayait même pas de penser, uniquement occupée de sentir son corps transi et douloureux se réchauffer lentement. Dans ses os et dans sa chair, elle ressentait une immense fatigue qui allait jusqu'à une sorte de souffrance; tout cela bien au-delà de la lassitude procurée par une chevauchée de cinq ou six lieues, mais le passage avait été cruel d'une joie éblouissante à un profond chagrin et Fiora ne désirait plus qu'une seule chose : dormir! plonger pour des heures dans ce sommeil des bêtes harassées qui ressemble à la mort! Tôt ou tard, il faut bien émerger mais il arrive alors que le courage et les forces soient restaurés. Sinon, il ne reste plus qu'à chercher un sommeil plus profond encore et, surtout, irrémédiable...

Elle allait se jeter sur son lit quand, dans l'encadrement de toile, un jeune garçon, vêtu avec élégance d'un justaucorps de velours violet brodé d'argent sur des chausses gris clair et des bottes courtes de daim violet, apparut un plateau entre les mains :

— La noble dame m'accorde-t-elle permission d'entrer ? demanda-t-il en s'inclinant avec aisance.

Il avait parlé italien et Fiora, presque machinalement, lui sourit. C'était le premier mâle qui la traitait avec respect.

— Bien sûr ! fit-elle. Est-ce que nous serions compatriotes ?

— Pas tout à fait. Je suis romain : Battista Colonna, des princes de Paliano, page de mon cousin, le comte de Celano, mais récemment passé au service de Mgr le duc de Bourgogne. A présent, si vous y consentez, madame, nous parlerons français pour ne pas inquiéter les sentinelles, ajouta-t-il dans cette langue tout en posant son plateau sur un coffre.

— Le service du comte de Celano ne vous convenait plus ?

— Ce n'est pas cela mais je chante assez bien et Mgr Charles, qui entretient un chœur de jeunes chanteurs, aime que je joigne ma voix aux leurs. Je suis, pour ainsi dire, prêté.

— Et l'on vous a chargé de m'apporter à souper, vous qui êtes de très noble famille si je vous ai compris ? Qui vous a donné l'ordre ?

— Messire Olivier de La Marche. Nous n'avons guère au camp que des valets d'armes et faute de femme sachant servir une noble dame florentine, messire Olivier a pensé qu'il vous serait plus... quel terme a-t-il employé ?... Ah oui : réconfortant d'être servie par un garçon né dans la péninsule.

— Voilà une attention que je n'aurais jamais imaginée il y a seulement cinq minutes. J'espère seulement que le duc Charles n'en sera point contrarié ?

— Messire Olivier ne fait jamais rien sans l'autorisation de monseigneur. A présent, donna Fiora, je vous souhaite bon appétit et un bon repos !

— Vous connaissez mon nom ?

— Messire Olivier n'oublie jamais rien, fit le jeune Colonna avec un salut qui était presque une pirouette et un joyeux sourire.

Un peu revigorée par la visite inattendue de ce gamin — il pouvait avoir une douzaine d'années — chaleureux et charmant, Fiora remercia mentalement l'impassible capitaine de la garde ducale en se promettant bien de le faire de vive voix quand l'occasion lui en serait donnée. Puis elle découvrit qu'elle avait faim et dévora littéralement le pâté d'anguilles, les rissoles et les fruits séchés que le page avait apportés avec une petite cruche de vin de Bourgogne. Après quoi, se jetant tout habillée sur le lit en s'enveloppant d'une couverture, elle laissa sa fatigue l'emporter vers un paradis paisible où les anges chantaient la gloire de la bienheureuse Vierge Marie... Dans sa chambre somptueuse, le Téméraire, le menton dans la main, écoutait la maîtrise de sa chapelle composée de vingt-quatre jeunes garçons sous la direction du maître Adam Busnois, interpréter un motet à Notre-Dame... Les voix célestes emplissaient la nuit froide annonciatrice d'un hiver précoce et dans l'immense camp étendu bien au-delà de l'étang Saint-Jean jusqu'au pied des coteaux de Malzéville, chacun retenait son souffle pour puiser dans tant de beauté un peu de réconfort pour les combats à venir.

Durant plusieurs jours, Fiora demeura enfermée sous sa tente sans voir personne d'autre que le jeune Battista Colonna qui lui apportait ses repas et la fille visiblement terrifiée et apparemment muette qui venait vaquer à un semblant de ménage, lui portant du bois et de l'eau, nettoyant l'âtre et les bassins sans que Fiora réussît à lui tirer seulement une parole.

Heureusement, Battista était un peu plus bavard. Fiora, à demi assourdie par la canonnade qui faisait rage tout le jour, apprit de lui que Nancy se défendait bien. Le bâtard de Calabre qui en était le gouverneur était un habile homme de guerre. Non content d'avoir, à l'approche de l'armée bourguignonne, fait ajouter aux bastions, demi-lunes, redoutes et contrescarpes déjà existant des terrasses, des cavaliers[1] et des parapets en tout genre, son artillerie, aux mains d'un maître canonnier nommé Desmoulins qui était peut-être le meilleur artificier de son siècle, rendait coup pour coup à l'assaillant. Les deux canons que Desmoulins avait fait monter sur la Grande Tour regardant la commanderie avaient déjà obligé deux fois le Téméraire à changer la place de ses tentes et mis en pièces le « Courtois », la longue couleu-

1. Ouvrage de fortification dominant des retranchements à l'arrière.

vrine avec laquelle les Bourguignons attaquaient ladite tour et celle de la porte Saint-Nicolas. Le jeune Romain ne cachait pas qu'un certain découragement commençait à poindre chez les assaillants. Allait-on recommencer l'interminable siège de Neuss ? Dans la ville, par ailleurs, l'espoir renaissait en dépit des réserves de vivres qui commençaient à diminuer. La pluie d'ailleurs venait à l'aide des gens de Nancy, transformant le camp ennemi en cloaque...

Malheureusement pour eux, les Bourguignons reçurent du renfort : le Grand Bâtard Antoine de Bourgogne, demi-frère du Téméraire et son meilleur général, arriva du sud, amenant avec lui les troupes lombardes fraîches qu'il était allé chercher à Milan. Avec son aide, Charles put achever l'encerclement de la cité, trop serré pour que le moindre ravitaillement pût être apporté...

— Est-ce à dire, demanda Fiora, que le siège va bientôt s'achever ou sommes-nous ici pour des mois ?

— J'espère pour vous que la résistance des Lorrains ne sera pas éternelle. Cette tente est assez agréable mais à condition d'en sortir plus que vous ne le faites.

En effet, Fiora avait le droit, la nuit venue et sous la surveillance étroite des soldats qui veillaient à sa porte, de sortir quelques minutes pour respirer un peu d'air frais. Le reste du temps, elle pouvait ouvrir les rideaux masquant la porte mais pas davantage. En général, elle ne profitait guère de la permission pour éviter les paquets de pluie que le vent charriait. Néanmoins, la remarque du page l'inquiéta :

— Voulez-vous dire que je ne sortirai pas d'ici avant que Nancy ne se soit rendue ?

Battista hésita un instant puis, baissant la voix, répondit en italien :

— C'est tout à fait exact. Je ne devrais pas vous le dire mais après tout vous avez, selon moi, le droit de savoir ce qui vous concerne : Campobasso a attaqué messire de

Selongey et les deux hommes ont commencé à se battre quand Monseigneur le duc est intervenu. Il leur a commandé de remettre l'issue de leur querelle jusqu'à ce que l'armée soit entrée dans Nancy, ajoutant qu'il ne voulait pas risquer d'avoir l'un, ou peut-être deux de ses meilleurs capitaines, hors d'état de servir. Et même en faisant peser sur eux sa colère, il a eu du mal à en venir à bout. Il a fallu qu'il menace... de vous faire exécuter immédiatement. Cela les a calmés net. Chacun est reparti vers son commandement...

– Sauriez-vous me dire quand cela est arrivé ?

– Le lendemain matin de votre venue et je ne sais, en vérité, lequel des deux était le plus acharné. Si on les avait laissés faire, ils s'entre-tuaient. Aussi, pour éviter que cela ne se reproduise, monseigneur en a envoyé un à l'est et l'autre à l'ouest...

– Merci de m'avoir renseignée, dit Fiora. Vous agissez envers moi en ami véritable et j'en suis extrêmement touchée. Puis-je encore vous demander quelque chose ?

– Si c'est en mon pouvoir... et ne contrarie pas trop mes ordres.

– J'espère que non. Je voudrais que vous acceptiez de me prévenir au cas où... il arriverait quelque chose au comte de Selongey.

Le jeune Colonna lui sourit et son étroit visage, brun comme une châtaigne, s'illumina puis, s'inclinant bien bas devant Fiora, il lui fit un beau salut :

– Ce fut toujours dans mon intention... Madame la comtesse ! C'est trop naturel...

La gentillesse de cet enfant était bien le seul rayon de soleil qui mît un peu de chaleur dans les jours uniformément gris et tristes de la jeune femme. Les heures s'écoulaient lentes, interminables, toutes semblables. Un couvent avec sa rigidité eût été préférable à cette prison de toile d'où l'on ne voyait rien mais où l'on entendait tout. Le crépitement de la pluie alternait avec le bruit du canon, les cris de joie ou de douleur et le vacarme des assauts sans cesse repoussés. L'écho des prières aussi arrivait jusqu'à la captive car la tente du légat papal était proche et il y avait eu l'énorme explosion de joie suscitée par l'arrivée triomphale du Grand Bâtard de Bourgogne. Enfin, et c'était au moins agréable, Fiora entendit plusieurs fois chanter la maîtrise que dominait parfois la voix sonore de Battista. Mais Fiora avait tout de même l'impression déprimante d'être l'une de ces recluses comme elle en avait vu deux à Paris, qui vivent toute leur existence entre quatre murs de pierres que l'on maçonne autour d'elles et qui n'ont plus, sur la vie, que la vue très limitée d'une étroite fenêtre par laquelle leur arrivent les dons de la charité, et l'ouïe de ce qui se passe autour de ce tombeau à peine ouvert que l'on boucherait tout à fait à leur mort. Sans le jeune Colonna elle se fût crue oubliée mais elle ne savait plus très bien si elle souhaitait tellement la fin du siège qui ouvrirait sa prison – sans doute pour une autre et peut-être pour l'échafaud – et qui serait le signal du combat à mort auquel se livreraient les deux hommes qui déchiraient sa vie...

Un soir où le tintamarre avait été particulièrement fort et où elle avait même entendu rugir, non loin d'elle, la voix du Téméraire, elle attendit Battista avec plus d'impatience encore que de coutume pour savoir ce qui se passait et, quand elle entendit des pas, elle jeta le livre d'heures qu'elle avait trouvé dans l'un des coffres et qui était la seule lecture à sa disposition, donc sa seule distraction même si les prières qui s'y trouvaient n'éveillaient guère d'écho sensible dans son cœur.

Elle le vit apparaître dans l'ombre de la porte et constata qu'il avait tiré son bonnet jusque sur son nez.

– Fait-il donc si mauvais ? lui dit-elle gaiement. Je n'entends pourtant pas la pluie...

Sans répondre, il posa le plateau couvert d'une serviette à terre et, presque d'un même mouvement, arracha son bonnet et tira une dague de sa ceinture en s'avançant dans le cercle de lumière dispensée par le candélabre :

— Vous n'êtes pas Battista ? s'exclama Fiora. Qui êtes-vous ?

En même temps qu'elle posait la question, elle le reconnut. C'était le page de Campobasso, ce Virginio dont elle n'avait pu oublier le regard haineux et qui, à présent, dardait sur elle des yeux flambant d'une joie féroce :

— Qui je suis ? Je suis ta mort, ribaude ! grinça-t-il, en continuant à avancer lentement, un pas après l'autre, dégustant cet instant qu'il avait dû appeler de toutes ses forces durant des jours.

Une seule chose le troublait un peu : la femme ne manifestait aucun signe de crainte.

— Remettez cette dague au fourreau et allez-vous-en ! s'écria Fiora. Je n'ai qu'à appeler...

— Tu peux toujours appeler. J'ai endormi tes gardes avec du vin drogué. Tu n'as plus devant ta porte que deux paquets inertes et tu ne m'échapperas pas.

— Pourquoi voulez-vous me tuer ? Que vous ai-je fait ?

— Je veux te tuer pour être sûr que Campobasso ne retournera plus jamais dans ton lit. Avant toi, je régnais sur lui. Il aimait mes baisers et mes caresses et puis, tu es venue... A présent, quand nous faisons l'amour, son esprit est absent et ça je ne peux pas le supporter.

Virginio se détendit soudain comme un ressort et fondit sur Fiora, la dague haute. De toutes ses forces, celle-ci hurla :

— A l'aide ! A moi !... Au secours !...

Elle tendait toutes ses forces pour écarter la lame meurtrière mais le page était grand pour son âge et bien entraîné alors que la claustration avait ôté à Fiora une partie de ses moyens. Il allait avoir le dessus et, dans une seconde, l'arme s'enfoncerait dans sa gorge. Elle ferma les yeux appelant encore à l'aide.

— J'arrive ! cria une voix qui lui parut celle même d'un ange.

Virginio fut arraché d'elle, désarmé, jeté à terre et bientôt il se tordit sous le genou vigoureux qui coinçait sa poitrine.

— Un peu jeune, l'ami, pour faire un assassin ! dit Esteban mais, apparemment, la valeur n'attend pas le nombre des années. Et maintenant qu'est-ce qu'on va faire de toi ?

— S'il vous plaît, messire, tenez-le-moi et prêtez-moi votre dague que je lui règle son compte, fit Battista qui apparaissait en chemise, couvert de boue et se frottant la tête où se gonflait une énorme bosse. Cette brute m'a assommé, dépouillé de mes vêtements et de mon plateau et, si j'ai bien compris, il a mis aussi les gardes hors d'état de servir ?

— Vous êtes dans le vrai. Mais si vous voulez m'en croire, vous feriez mieux d'aller chercher du secours... Je peux très bien tenir encore quelque temps. Je ne fatigue pas.

— Vous devez avoir raison. On ne peut pas étouffer l'affaire surtout quand on s'en prend aux soldats de monseigneur... et à son otage préféré. Le duc nous a tous rendus responsables de donna Fiora sur nos têtes...

Et Battista, s'enveloppant dans la couverture que lui tendait Fiora, repartit en courant et en appelant « A la garde ! ». Cependant, la jeune femme qui n'avait pas encore bien retrouvé ses esprits vint s'accroupir auprès d'Esteban qui maintenait toujours Virginio à terre en lui pointant une dague sur la gorge et considéra non sans stupeur la cotte verte à croix de Saint-André blanche serrée par un ceinturon sur une chemise de mailles, la longue épée qui pendait à son côté et le chapel de fer qui avait roulé à terre quand il s'était jeté sur le page.

— Esteban ! soupira-t-elle. Mais c'est un miracle ! Vous voilà bourguignon à présent ?

— C'est tout récent, donna Fiora ! fit-il avec un sourire aussi paisible que s'ils s'étaient quittés la veille. Mais je n'en ferai pas moins un bon soldat, ajouta-t-il avec un clin d'œil qui conseillait la prudence. Vous allez bien depuis notre dernière rencontre ? C'était... en Avignon, je crois ? Quant à moi, en faisant une ronde, j'ai vu ce gredin qui assommait un page, lui volait ses habits et son plateau, revêtait l'un et prenait l'autre et je l'ai suivi pour voir ce qu'il comptait faire. J'ai vu... mais c'est une vraie chance de vous rencontrer ! Si j'avais pu supposer que vous étiez là, en plein milieu de ce camp !...

Fiora avait compris à quoi rimait ce bavardage à bâtons rompus : même mis hors d'état de nuire, Virginio restait dangereux car il avait malheureusement une langue de vipère et savait s'en servir.

Ils causèrent ainsi sur un ton superficiel et parfaitement irréaliste jusqu'à ce que revînt Battista toujours aussi sale. Mais cette fois, La Marche en personne l'accompagnait avec quelques-uns de ses gardes. Le garçon fut remis debout sans douceur tandis que le Castillan faisait toute une affaire d'épousseter ses genouillères. Le capitaine des gardes était visiblement furieux :

— De soldats endormis, un page attaqué ! Qu'est-ce que cela signifie ? Et d'abord qui es-tu ?

— Virginio Fulgosi, sire capitaine. Je suis attaché à la personne de Mgr le comte de Campobasso, fit le jeune prisonnier qui visiblement reprenait son aplomb. C'est sur son ordre que je suis venu ici... Cette... cette femme avait fait tenir à mon maître un billet le suppliant de la faire évader...

— Curieuse façon de faire évader quelqu'un en l'attaquant avec ça ! s'écria Fiora indignée en brandissant la dague tachée de sang et la blessure qu'elle avait reçue à la main en se défendant. Ce misérable a tenté de me tuer et sans ce brave homme, ajouta-t-elle en désignant Esteban qui avait recoiffé son chapel et qui prenait un air modeste, je serais morte à l'heure qu'il est. Interrogez-le : il vous dira comment cela s'est passé... Ensuite vous pourrez toujours demander à Campobasso quels ordres il a donnés à ce garçon...

— Elle ment ! hurla Virginio qui se tordait comme une couleuvre sous la poigne des hommes qui le maintenaient. Cet homme et elle se connaissent. C'est un de ses anciens amants !

La gifle que lui asséna le Castillan avait de quoi assommer un bœuf mais sa voix n'était que vertueuse indignation quand il proclama :

— Bien sûr que je connais donna Fiora depuis longtemps ! Elle était haute comme trois pommes, quand je l'ai vue pour la première fois, à Florence chez son noble père. Et je connais aussi donna Léonarda, sa pieuse gouvernante, et Mgr le prince Lascaris, son grand-oncle... et je voudrais bien savoir ce qu'elle fait ici au milieu de tous ces hommes d'armes et à la merci du premier coquin venu !

— C'est bien, l'ami ! Nous verrons ce que Monseigneur le duc pensera de tout cela. Tu vas venir avec moi pour lui raconter ce qui s'est passé. Ensuite je ferai appeler messire Campobasso... Donna Fiora, je vous demande excuses pour tout ceci. Je vais vous envoyer maître Matteo de Clerici, le médecin de monseigneur, pour panser votre blessure.

— N'en faites rien, messire Olivier. Ce n'est pas profond et je saurai soigner moi-même cette écorchure. Mais je vous remercie de votre courtoisie et je vous recommande ce brave garçon, qui ne peut être qu'une excellente recrue pour l'armée de Monseigneur le duc : c'est un cœur vaillant et un bras solide.

Elle n'avait plus qu'un désir : être seule puisqu'il était impossible de parler avec Esteban mais, de le savoir près d'elle, veillant sur elle, était d'un grand réconfort. Ce qui ne l'empêchait pas de griller de curiosité. Par quel incroyable cheminement le Castillan en était-il venu à s'engager dans l'armée bourguignonne ? Il avait dit cette péripétie récente : mais qu'avait-il fait durant ces deux mois ?... Incapable de trouver une réponse, elle mangea un peu de viande froide, une ou deux cuillerées de confiture et alla s'étendre sur son lit, y étalant son manteau pour suppléer la couverture qu'elle avait donnée à Battista. Pour la première fois depuis bien des nuits, son sommeil fut paisible, confiant, tant il faut peu de chose à un être jeune pour se sentir en sécurité. Pour qu'Esteban ait pu arriver à point nommé et sauver Fiora d'une mort certaine, c'est qu'une providence veillait sur elle. Mais ce secours venu de l'au-delà, elle ne l'attribuait pas à Dieu. Non parce qu'elle n'y croyait plus – elle n'avait jamais cessé de croire – mais parce que le Tout-Puissant semblait ne s'occuper des humains que pour les submerger de souffrances et d'épreuves. Non, si quelqu'un, là-bas, veillait sur elle, ce ne pouvait être que l'âme douloureuse de l'homme qui lui avait consacré sa vie, de ce Francesco Beltrami qu'elle ne cesserait jamais d'appeler son père.

Quand il revint, le lendemain, Battista apportait un plein panier de mauvaises nouvelles : d'abord, Philippe de Selongey avait été blessé – légèrement il est vrai – au cours d'une sortie tentée par les assiégés pour faire entrer un convoi de vivres par la porte de la Craffe. Ensuite, le page Virginio que Campobasso, fou de rage, avait ordonné d'exécuter, avait été sauvé par l'intervention du Téméraire en personne. Selon le duc, il n'était pas du tout certain qu'il n'ait pas dit la vérité et qu'il n'y eût pas tentative d'évasion. Le garçon avait été remis au prévôt de l'armée en attendant que l'affaire fût tirée au clair. Enfin, la pluie diluvienne avait provoqué un glissement de terrain qui avait enseveli toute une compagnie. L'armée, exaspérée par ce temps abominable, était à deux doigts de la rébellion et, selon le page, l'évêque de Metz, Georges de Bade, qui aurait voulu voir son frère le margrave devenir au moins gouverneur de Lorraine, ne cessait de parcourir le camp pour exhorter les hommes à la patience affirmant que le camp abondait en vivres, ces vivres qui manquaient cruellement à la ville bloquée...

– Mais, enfin, dit Fiora, leur fameux duc René, où est-il ? Ne va-t-il pas venir au secours de sa capitale affamée ?

– Je crois qu'il voudrait bien mais ne peut pas. Il est en France pour essayer d'obtenir du secours et des troupes du roi Louis mais celui-ci, si j'ai bien compris, ne tient pas du tout à rompre encore une fois les accords signés à Soleuvre...

— La place d'un chef est à la tête de ses troupes, surtout quand le combat est désespéré. Quant à vos Bourguignons je ne vois pas de quoi ils se plaignent : ils n'ont qu'à attendre tranquillement que la ville meure de faim. Est-ce si difficile ?

— Peut-être pas, mais c'est le second hiver qu'ils voient venir à se geler devant des portes qui refusent de s'ouvrir. Ils n'ont pas digéré Neuss et Nancy ne leur inspire aucune confiance. Il faut comprendre !

La dernière mauvaise nouvelle surgit en la personne du capitaine des gardes : le duc Charles ordonnait qu'on lui amenât sa prisonnière. Sans un mot, Fiora prit son manteau, jeta le capuchon sur sa tête et suivit l'officier à travers les rafales de pluie dans lesquelles le camp commençait à se dissoudre...

Elle trouva le duc dans une pièce plus petite que celle où il l'avait reçue la première fois. C'était, tendu de précieuses tapisseries d'Arras parfilées d'or, une sorte de cabinet d'armes. Le duc s'y tenait assis en compagnie d'un petit homme tout rond dont la figure avenante couronnée de courts cheveux gris frisottants était surmontée d'une mitre violette brodée d'or. Des flots de cendal couleur d'améthyste emballaient un corps qui donnait l'impression d'être ovoïde. Une grande croix d'or et de rubis pendait à son cou au bout d'un ruban assorti à la robe d'où dépassaient de petits pieds chaussés de pantoufles de velours et de petites mains blanches et dodues que l'anneau pastoral avait l'air d'écraser.

Comprenant que ce devait être là le légat papal, Fiora plia le genou devant lui, se donnant ainsi le plaisir de faire attendre un instant au Téméraire le salut qu'elle lui devait. Quand elle lui eut rendu cet hommage de politesse, elle attendit calmement ce qui allait suivre.

— Voici, dit le duc d'un ton bref, la femme dont j'ai parlé à Votre Eminence et dont on ne sait trop ni qui elle est ni d'où elle vient. Elle se nomme Fiora Beltrami, secrètement épousée paraît-il par le comte de Selongey, notre fidèle serviteur, mais il semblerait qu'elle soit aussi une espionne de Louis de France qui, dans un but obscur, est devenue la maîtresse du comte de Campobasso. Elle l'a rendue à moitié fou et il a provoqué en duel, comme vous le savez, messire Philippe...

– J'ai cru comprendre, coupa l'évêque avec un demi-sourire, qu'ils s'étaient provoqués mutuellement. On dit qu'ils se sont empoignés comme charretiers dans une taverne et qu'il a fallu cinq hommes pour les séparer...

– Certes, certes!... Il n'en demeure pas moins qu'il y a là, pour la paix de cette armée, un danger que j'ai voulu éloigner en ordonnant aux deux adversaires de remettre le combat après la chute de Nancy. Ils y ont consenti mais, en dépit de la parole donnée, un page de Campobasso s'est introduit la nuit dernière chez cette femme. Il y a eu bataille et, à présent, on parle... trop. Les esprits sont en émoi...

– J'en demeure d'accord, mais, mon fils, ce grand émoi me semble venir davantage de ce siège interminable et du temps détestable que nous envoie le Seigneur Dieu pour notre pénitence à tous.

Fiora regarda Alessandro Nanni avec étonnement. Ses précédentes relations avec le moine Ignacio Ortega lui avaient donné une idée toute différente de ce que pouvait être un envoyé de Sixte IV. Celui-là semblait à la fois aimable et plein d'humour. Le froncement de sourcils du Téméraire la convainquit de ce que cette impression était la bonne.

– Quoi qu'il en soit, reprit le duc, il faut que cette situation scandaleuse cesse. Le mariage de Selongey et de cette femme a été célébré à Florence dans le secret. En outre, il n'est pas valable à nos yeux. Selongey a violé le droit féodal qui lui interdisait de contracter union sans l'assentiment de son suzerain, c'est-à-dire nous!

– C'est une faute sans doute mais je crains, mon fils, qu'aux yeux de Dieu il en aille autrement. Qui vous a mariés, mon enfant?

— Le prieur du couvent San Francesco à Fiesole, Eminence.

— Vous étiez consentante ou contrainte ?

— Consentante... et si heureuse !

— Et messire de Selongey ? Était-il heureux lui aussi ?

— Il le disait... mais peut-être vaudrait-il mieux le lui demander. Il avait juré de m'aimer et de n'aimer que moi. Il se peut qu'il ait menti...

— Vous en aviez juré autant ? Et cependant, si ce que l'on rapporte est vrai...

— Je me suis donnée au comte de Campobasso, c'est exact. Je croyais mon mariage nul... et je pensais avoir été bafouée.

— L'aimez-vous donc, lui aussi ?

— Non... murmura Fiora qui sentit ses joues s'enflammer, mais... j'ai été... trahie par la nature et j'avoue y avoir pris plaisir.

— Je vois... et je vous sais gré de votre franchise. A présent, monseigneur, je souhaiterais apprendre de vous comment vous entendez faire cesser ce que vous appelez... « une situation scandaleuse » puisque, à l'exception des intéressés, de Votre Seigneurie et de moi-même, personne jusqu'à présent n'en sait rien ?

— Elle l'est à mes yeux, et devrait l'être aussi à ceux de Votre Eminence, fit le duc avec hauteur. Certes, Selongey et Campobasso n'ont pas donné la véritable raison de leur querelle et le duel découle naturellement de la rixe qui les a opposés. C'est à l'issue de la rencontre qu'il nous faudra prendre une décision : si Selongey l'emporte il n'en demeure pas moins l'époux d'une femme adultère et celle-ci devra être exécutée...

— N'est-ce pas une solution un peu... excessive ? Donna Fiora me semble avoir quelques excuses et, avant de la livrer à l'épée du bourreau...

— Je ne souhaite pas en venir là car, même en la faisant mourir au fond d'une prison, il en resterait toujours une trace. Voilà pourquoi je fais appel à Votre Eminence. En tant que légat de Sa Sainteté Sixte IV, vous avez tous pouvoirs pour prononcer l'annulation du mariage. Ainsi, et quelle que soit l'issue du combat, cette créature pourra aller se faire pendre ailleurs et, s'il plaît à Campobasso de la ramasser, personne n'y verra d'inconvénients.

Dans un bruissement soyeux, Mgr Nanni se leva brusquement et, bien que debout il fût vraiment petit, il revêtit une impressionnante majesté qui dut frapper Charles de Bourgogne car il se leva à son tour :

— Vous faites, il me semble, très bon marché de la vie d'une femme et des sacrements du Seigneur, fit sévèrement le légat. Nul n'a le droit de séparer, fût-ce par le glaive, ceux qui se sont unis devant Dieu de bonne foi. Si votre Selongey a été assez bête pour s'estimer amoindri par un mariage avec la fille d'un riche Florentin, il est l'unique responsable de ce qui lui arrive. Un autre a pris ce qu'il dédaignait et c'est tant pis pour lui. Qu'il s'en explique avec cet autre et qu'ils s'entre-tuent est leur affaire. Mais je refuse que cette pauvre enfant, déjà bien éprouvée, devienne leur victime expiatoire. Attendons l'issue du duel. Si, à ce moment, l'un des deux époux demande l'annulation, j'étudierai la question. Pas avant !

— Je peux vous prédire que Philippe désirera cette annulation. Il ne peut souhaiter demeurer uni à une telle femme !

— Surtout si vous l'y contraignez. Songez seulement qu'il va se battre pour elle...

— Pas pour elle ! Pour son honneur bafoué !

— L'honneur paraît infiniment plus précieux quand il a d'aussi beaux yeux !

— Eminence ! protesta le duc indigné, votre indulgence envers cette créature est, en vérité, excessive, déroutante. Est-ce parce qu'elle est italienne, comme vous ?

— Je pourrais m'estimer offensé si je ne savais à quels excès peut vous porter la colère, monseigneur. En tout cas, je serais fort surpris que cet étrange mari vous laisse conduire sa femme à l'échafaud.

— Alors, ce sera l'annulation. Je saurai bien l'en

convaincre car il est digne d'une princesse et cette fille de marchands...

— Pourrait alors avoir le regret de vous réclamer, coupa Fiora, les cent mille florins d'or de sa dot ! Vous voyez, monseigneur, vous n'avez d'autre solution que de la faire exécuter...

Elle salua l'évêque puis, jetant au Téméraire que la colère empourprait un regard de mépris glacial, elle tourna les talons et sortit de la tente...

Peut-être aurait-elle eu à pâtir de la colère qu'elle avait allumée chez le duc si un événement inattendu ne s'était produit presque simultanément : dans la ville assiégée, les trompettes et les tambours se mirent à battre la chamade, ce qui était signe certain que Nancy souhaitait se rendre et le duc Charles en éprouva une grande joie.

On apprit, plus tard, qu'une lettre du duc René était parvenue à entrer dans la cité : « Puisque pour mon malheur, écrivait le jeune prince, je me trouve réduit à ne pouvoir rien faire pour votre bien et à ne pouvoir rien tenter pour ma gloire, je vous exhorte par l'intérêt même de la patrie pour laquelle vous vous êtes sacrifiés, de ne point prodiguer davantage votre sang par de plus longs efforts qui vous conduiraient à des pertes plus grandes et à une capitulation moins favorable... »

Ce message que tous écoutèrent en pleurant n'entama pas la résolution du gouverneur : le bâtard de Calabre voulait se battre encore, car les fortifications n'étaient pas endommagées ni le peuple effrayé. On pouvait tenir encore deux mois et, dans deux mois, le Téméraire se découragerait... mais les échevins et tout le conseil de la ville furent d'avis qu'il fallait obéir au duc dont on savait qu'il était à présent retiré chez sa mère, Yolande de Vaudémont, au château de Joinville. On ne viendrait jamais à bout de cette grande armée. Mieux valait essayer d'obtenir une capitulation honorable.

Le gouverneur brisa son épée et en jeta les morceaux devant les robes rouges des magistrats. C'était le 29 novembre 1475...

Quatrième partie

LA COURSE À L'ABÎME

CHAPITRE XI

LE DUEL

Le lendemain 30 novembre, jour de la Saint-André qui était le protecteur de la Bourgogne, le duc Charles fit son entrée dans Nancy à huit heures du matin par la porte de la Craffe. Le temps gris mais sans pluie, apportait au moins cet apaisement au peuple muet et en grand deuil qui regardait, contenu par une double haie d'infanterie étirée sur toute la longueur de la ville et jusqu'à la porte Saint-Nicolas par laquelle, la veille, était sortie la garnison avec les honneurs de la guerre.

Le Téméraire avait tenu à assister en personne à ce départ. Il avait pour ainsi dire passé en revue les deux mille Allemands qui repartaient vers l'Alsace, les six cents Gascons vers la France et les quelque deux mille Lorrains dont les uns rentraient chez eux et les autres allaient renforcer la garnison de Bitche. Le bâtard de Calabre vint le dernier, escorté uniquement du banneret qui portait son étendard. Armé de toutes pièces, à cheval mais tête nue, altier et superbe, il vint au petit trot de son destrier jusqu'au Téméraire et lui jeta :

— S'il n'avait tenu qu'à moi, tu te serais cassé les dents sur cette ville, Charles de Bourgogne. J'en jure Dieu! Mais les bourgeois tiennent à la vie plus qu'à l'honneur. Que vas-tu en faire ? Les passer tous au fil de l'épée ?

— Non pas. Je me suis engagé à maintenir Nancy dans la possession de ses privilèges et de la régir selon ses anciennes coutumes. J'en ferai la capitale de mon royaume. Pourquoi, toi qui es vaillant et de sang royal n'en redeviendrais-tu pas le gouverneur ? J'aime les hommes de valeur.

— Moi aussi et c'est pourquoi je pars. Il ne sera jamais dit, tant que je vivrai, qu'un prince lorrain, même bâtard, se sera incliné devant toi...

— D'autres le feront peut-être ? Tu sais que ton grand-père, le vieux roi René, songe à me léguer la Provence par testament afin que soit reformé l'antique royaume burgonde ?

— Libre à lui. Nous n'avons que faire de la Provence. Seule la Lorraine nous intéresse et tu n'en as pas fini avec nous !

Enlevant son cheval, le bâtard de Calabre partit au galop sur la route de France. Une tache de boue projetée par les sabots du destrier vint maculer le manteau de velours rouge que le Téméraire portait sur son armure... Celui-ci fronça le sourcil mais l'ombre qui passait sur son visage se dissipa rapidement :

— Nancy est à nous, mes fidèles ! lança-t-il à pleine voix. Songeons à présent à y faire notre joyeuse entrée ! Et que l'on sache que quiconque molestera l'un des habitants ou l'attaquera dans ses biens sera puni de mort !

A sa surprise, ce même soir décidément fertile en événements, Fiora apprenait que le légat du pape avait obtenu qu'elle fût placée sous sa protection immédiate et qu'elle suivît tous ses déplacements jusqu'à ce que l'issue du combat entre Selongey et Campobasso permît de statuer sur son sort. Le jeune Colonna demeurait momentanément attaché à son service et elle comptait bien obtenir de l'aimable prélat qu'on lui rendît Esteban.

Aussi, dès le lever du jour, Battista la conduisit rejoindre la petite troupe de prêtres et de moines qui composaient l'escorte de Mgr Nanni. Annoncée pour le commun des mortels comme une dame pèlerine désireuse de se recueillir devant les reliques de saint Epvre, elle prit place dans la litière de voyage du prélat cependant que celui-ci enfourchait une mule pour faire, dans la ville, une entrée plus proche du cœur des habitants. Par une de ces délicatesses inattendues et dont il avait le secret, le Téméraire avait décidé que Dieu, en la personne du légat, entrerait le premier dans la cité conquise avec l'espoir que ce geste apaiserait quelques rancœurs et disposerait favorablement pour lui les cœurs de ces ennemis d'hier dont, en toute bonne foi, il souhaitait faire les loyaux sujets de demain.

Aucune manifestation de joie, cependant, n'accueillit ce prélat qui précédait le vainqueur mais, devant lui, la foule, d'un mouvement unanime, s'agenouilla sous sa main bénissante :

— Reprenez espoir, mes enfants, répétait-il avec une pitié qui ressemblait à de la tendresse, le duc Charles ne vous veut aucun mal et vous n'aurez point à souffrir de son fait...

Derrière les rideaux de la litière frappée aux armes papales, Fiora regardait ces gens vêtus de noir, ces visages creusés par les privations, ces maisons dont certaines montraient des toits crevés par les boulets de canon et d'autres de plus graves blessures. L'odeur de la mort et des incendies semblait attachée aux murailles et elle eut honte d'entrer ainsi, cachée sans doute, mais présente, dans ce cortège qui préludait à celui du vainqueur. Heureusement, la litière pénétra directement dans le palais ducal qui se composait alors de quatre bâtiments ordonnés autour d'une cour centrale [1] et s'arrêta dans ladite cour tandis que le légat allait prendre place dans la collégiale Saint-Georges, voisine immédiate du palais, pour y accueillir le nouveau maître. Battista Colonna apparut aussitôt devant Fiora :

— Les fourriers de monseigneur Charles ont travaillé toute la nuit pour préparer des logements. Il y en a un

---

1. Il n'en reste rien. Le duc René II l'a fait reconstruire en partie et il a été complété par ses successeurs.

pour vous. Voulez-vous qu'on vous le montre tout de suite ou préférez-vous regarder la « joyeuse entrée » ?

— Ce que j'en ai aperçu jusqu'ici n'augure pas une franche liesse mais je préfère néanmoins assister à l'arrivée du duc...

Elle eut juste le temps de gagner, dans une grande salle déserte, une fenêtre du premier étage : les six trompettes d'argent qui ouvraient la marche sonnaient sous la porte de la Craffe. Derrière elles venaient une centaine d'hommes d'armes précédant une compagnie de chevaliers empanachés sous les flammes brillantes de leurs pennons diversement colorés. Le Téméraire apparut à quelques pas derrière eux et sa splendeur coupa le souffle des assistants : montant son cheval favori, le Moro, caparaçonné de pourpre et d'or, il portait un ample manteau entièrement brodé d'or qui s'étalait sur la croupe du cheval, le grand collier de la Toison d'or et, sur la tête, la plus fabuleuse coiffure qui se puisse admirer : une haute barrette de velours couverte de perles, entourée d'une guirlande de rubis et de diamants et surmontée d'un fermail composé de trois gros rubis, célèbres d'ailleurs, et que l'on appelait les Trois Frères, de quatre perles énormes et d'un diamant pyramidal qui captait le moindre reflet lumineux. Sous ce chapeau de parade, plus précieux sans doute que la couronne impériale, le Grand Duc d'Occident rayonnait d'orgueil et jouissait visiblement de la stupeur émerveillée de la foule [1] attendant des acclamations qui ne venaient pas : rien qu'un chuchotement qui courait sur la foule comme une risée de vent sur de l'eau calme... Dans le miroir de sa mémoire, Fiora revit la silhouette grise du roi de France et pensa qu'en vérité la comparaison n'était pas à l'avantage de celui-ci ; mais il n'était pas certain qu'une intelligence égale, un esprit aussi acéré fussent cachés sous cette éblouissante apparence de prince de légende...

---

[1]. Cette fantastique coiffure, prise par les Suisses à Grandson fut vendue par eux aux Fugger d'Augsbourg.

Derrière le duc, sur des chevaux de parade magnifiquement caparaçonnés venaient le duc Engelbert de Nassau, le Grand Bâtard Antoine, le comte de Chimay Philippe de Croy, le duc Jean de Clèves, le prince de Tarente, le comte de Marle, fils du Connétable de Saint-Pol qui ignorait encore que son père, livré par le traité de Soleuvre au roi de France — qu'il avait abondamment trahi d'ailleurs —, était enfermé à la Bastille et subissait un jugement qui le mènerait à l'échafaud, Jean de Rubempré, seigneur de Bièvres, et beaucoup d'autres parmi lesquels, avec un serrement de cœur, Fiora reconnut Philippe...

Il n'avait pas sacrifié au souci d'élégance des autres seigneurs. Sous le tabard à ses armes — aigles d'argent sur champ d'azur — qui habillaient aussi son destrier, il portait le harnois de guerre. Seule, la visière relevée du casque ceint d'une couronne comtale permettait de reconnaître son profil arrogant. Retenant d'une main ferme son cheval qui encensait, il allait son chemin d'un air absent, ne regardant rien ni personne mais, dans le cadre d'acier bleu, son visage était très pâle et Fiora se souvint qu'il avait été blessé l'avant-veille... Son regard s'attacha à cette fière silhouette qui s'éloignait et elle ne vit pas, un peu après, Campobasso, rutilant et doré sur tranche, qui chevauchait en compagnie du marquis de Hochberg, du comte de Rothelin et de Jacopo Galeotto.

Mais lui l'aperçut et, pour qu'elle le regardât, s'agita tellement sur sa selle que son cheval fit un écart et bouscula ceux de ses voisins, d'où il résulta quelque désordre et Fiora, machinalement, tourna les yeux de ce côté. Alors quand elle reconnut Campobasso, elle se recula vivement et quitta la fenêtre. La seule vue de cet homme qui avait possédé son corps lui répugnait à présent parce qu'elle y prenait la mesure de sa propre honte. Elle aurait donné n'importe quoi pour qu'il n'y eût pas de Thionville dans son existence.

— J'en ai assez, dit-elle à Battista qui était rentré avec elle, et j'aimerais gagner mon appartement.

— Êtes-vous si pressée ? Vous savez que des gardes vont être placés à votre porte comme il y en avait devant la tente ?

— Je n'ai guère d'illusions sur mon sort, Battista. Le duc me déteste et ne souhaite qu'une chose : me voir disparaître de son horizon, que ce soit par la mort ou par l'annulation...

— C'est possible... mais vous, que souhaitez-vous ? Vous n'êtes pas beaucoup plus âgée que moi et c'est bien prématuré pour désirer mourir...

— Je ne le désire pas mais je suis lasse de lutter contre un destin qui ne cesse de m'accabler. J'avais un père et je ne l'ai plus ; j'avais un époux et je l'ai perdu, par sa faute autant que par la mienne, et je m'aperçois qu'à vouloir me venger j'ai tout perdu. Alors, ce qui peut arriver est de peu d'importance. Je crois, voyez-vous, Battista, que je suis surtout très, très fatiguée... Je voudrais dormir et ne plus jamais me réveiller...

— Ce n'est pas raisonnable. Deux hommes vont se battre pour vous, pour votre amour...

— Non : pour leur amour-propre. Ce n'est pas du tout la même chose...

Cependant, arrivé devant la collégiale Saint-Georges [1], le duc Charles mit pied à terre et confia, selon la coutume du pays, son cheval à un chanoine, après quoi le prévôt du chapitre, Jean d'Haraucourt, le conduisit dans l'église pour y entendre la messe et y prêter le serment qu'au jour de leur couronnement prêtaient toujours les ducs de Lorraine. Il aurait pu s'en dispenser mais il tenait, pour rassurer les populations, à ne négliger aucune des coutumes locales pensant qu'on lui en saurait gré.

Agenouillé devant l'autel scintillant, il savourait pleinement son heure de gloire car, pour la première fois, les pays de par-deçà et les pays de par-delà se trouvaient unis grâce à ce chaînon manquant que constituait la Lorraine.

---

1. Elle n'existe plus.

Bientôt l'Empereur, dont il espérait fiancer le fils à sa fille, poserait sur sa tête une royale couronne et la Bourgogne, enfin détachée du vieux tronc capétien comme de toute obédience impériale, voguerait librement vers le destin prodigieux auquel lui donnaient droit sa puissance et sa richesse... Bientôt... mais pas encore tout de suite. Restait à faire payer aux cantons suisses, ce ramassis de bouviers et de manants, l'audace dont ils avaient fait preuve, en lui ôtant le comté de Ferrette, en attaquant sa Comté Franche et en s'aventurant sur les terres de la duchesse Yolande de Savoie, sa fidèle alliée. Et cela ne tarderait pas. Ensuite, après un temps de repos qui permettrait au nouveau roi de lever la plus grande armée du monde, on irait jeter à bas du trône aux fleurs de lis le trop subtil Louis XI, et la France aurait enfin un souverain digne de sa grandeur passée...

Ainsi rêvait le Téméraire dans cette église où, hier encore, s'élevaient les prières pour que Dieu éloigne, du vieux pays lorrain, l'envahisseur et son armée, mais Charles ne doutait pas une seconde d'amener promptement ses nouveaux sujets à remercier le ciel de leur avoir donné pour maître un prince si fastueux, si magnanime et si vaillant. Cela les changerait de « l'Enfant », ce pauvre petit René II qui, au lieu de mourir au combat, avait préféré courir se réfugier dans les jupes de sa mère pour y pleurer son impuissance...

Tandis que s'ordonnaient un grand banquet et une fête publique pour tenter de faire oublier passagèrement aux Nancéens leurs morts et leurs maisons détruites, Fiora, dans la chambre qu'on lui avait donnée et qui se situait dans une des tours regardant vers la Meurthe, recevait la visite de Mgr Nanni. Elle le remercia de la protection qu'il lui accordait et grâce à laquelle, bien certainement, on lui avait donné ce logis au lieu d'une prison.

— Je n'y suis pas pour grand-chose, mon enfant. Même si cela lui déplaît souverainement, le duc ne peut faire que vous ne soyez la très légitime comtesse de Selongey. Il vous doit des égards.

— Il n'en caresse pas moins l'idée de me faire exécuter, ce qui aurait le double avantage de libérer Philippe et d'effacer cette histoire de dot que, de toute évidence, il n'apprécie guère.

— Soyez sûre qu'alors vous auriez droit à tous les honneurs dus à votre rang, fit le prélat avec un sourire, mais nous n'en sommes pas là. Je dirai même que votre plus grande chance d'échapper au bourreau réside dans cette dette que le duc a envers vous. Cent mille florins sont une somme énorme... et il est tout à fait incapable de la restituer. Son sens chevaleresque s'oppose à ce qui serait une manière peu élégante de se débarrasser d'un créancier. C'est ce que je suis venu vous dire pour vous rassurer un peu... et aussi que le duel entre le comte de Selongey et Campobasso aura lieu demain soir, à minuit, dans le pourpris du château, sans autres témoins que le duc lui-même, vous, moi, deux assistants qui seront Galeotto pour le Napolitain, et messire Mathieu de Prame pour votre époux. Le Grand Bâtard Antoine tiendra le rôle de juge d'armes. Le combat sera... à outrance.

— Ce qui veut dire ?

— Que seule la mort de l'un ou l'autre adversaire pourra y mettre fin.

Un filet glacé coula le long du dos de Fiora qui frissonna comme si le vent d'hiver était entré dans sa chambre pour l'envelopper de froidure :

— C'est épouvantable, articula-t-elle. Ce n'est pas possible ! Le duc ne peut pas accepter une chose pareille ?... Je ne veux pas y croire. C'est monstrueux !

— Il le faudra bien pourtant. Vous ignorez tout des lois féodales de ces pays. J'admets d'ailleurs que les coutumes de nos gens d'au-delà des Alpes ne sont pas meilleures sinon pires : chez nous on loue des spadassins pour se débarrasser d'un ennemi...

— Qu'elles soient meilleures ou pires, je ne veux pas le savoir.

Et tournant le dos au légat elle marcha rapidement vers

la porte de la chambre, l'ouvrit et repoussa violemment les hallebardes qui se croisaient devant elle :

— Je veux voir le duc! fit-elle avec hauteur. Et si vous tentez de m'en empêcher, je crierai si fort que l'on viendra. Je dirai alors que vous avez essayé de me tuer!

— Mon enfant, plaida Alessandro Nanni alarmé, vous n'y pensez pas?

— Je ne pense qu'à cela! Conduisez-moi sinon je saurai bien trouver seule mon chemin.

Le petit évêque trottinait à ses côtés en essayant de la retenir mais c'était impossible : Fiora avait décidé que, ce soir, elle verrait le Téméraire et ainsi, l'une courant et l'autre presque à bout de souffle ou peu s'en fallait, ils parvinrent jusqu'à l'antichambre où veillaient une demi-douzaine de gardes. Olivier de La Marche s'y promenait en compagnie du valet de chambre du duc, Charles de Visen. L'entrée tumultueuse de la jeune femme les arrêta :

— Annoncez-moi à monseigneur! ordonna-t-elle aussi sèchement que si elle se fût adressée à un serviteur. Je veux le voir!

— C'est impossible, fit La Marche. Monseigneur est en conférence avec l'ambassadeur de Milan et vous n'avez rien à faire ici! Gardes, ramenez cette femme chez elle!

— Ne me touchez pas! cria Fiora. Il est urgent que je le voie : il y va de la vie d'un homme!

— Et moi je vous dis...

— Qu'est-ce que c'est? Quel est ce bruit?

La porte venait de s'ouvrir sous la main du Téméraire. Il embrassa la scène d'un coup d'œil, vit Fiora qui se débattait aux mains des soldats et le légat qui faisait de dérisoires efforts pour la raisonner :

— Encore vous! fit-il. Vous forcez ma porte à présent? Je croyais, éminence, que vous répondiez de cette folle?

— Je ne peux répondre des élans du cœur, fit Nanni avec un soupir. Et donna Fiora est très, très émue...

— Eh bien, voyons cette émotion! Entrez, tous les deux!

Sans un regard pour la vaste pièce dont les domestiques

de Charles avaient fait une splendeur d'or et de pourpre ordonnée autour d'une admirable tapisserie où des milliers de fleurs cernaient les armes de Bourgogne, ni pour l'élégant personnage qui se tenait debout auprès d'un dressoir orné de deux statues d'or, Fiora dès le seuil offrit au duc une profonde révérence :

— Monseigneur, pria-t-elle, je viens d'apprendre que le duel doit avoir lieu demain. Je supplie Votre Seigneurie de l'empêcher...

— Une rencontre où l'honneur de deux chevaliers est engagé ? Il faut être une fille de marchands pour songer à cela...

— Il faut être surtout une femme soucieuse de justice... et une femme qui aime. Messire de Selongey est blessé : le combat ne sera pas égal.

— Vous savez cela aussi ? Pour quelqu'un que j'ai mis au secret, vous n'ignorez apparemment rien de ce qui se passe dans mon armée ? fit le duc avec l'ombre d'un sourire qui emplit d'espérance le cœur de la jeune femme. Rassurez-vous, la blessure de Selongey est bénigne.

— Mais c'est un combat à outrance !

— Et alors ?

Les jambes de Fiora se dérobèrent sous elle ; elle tomba à genoux et cacha son visage dans ses mains :

— Par pitié, monseigneur !... Faites de moi ce que vous voulez, jetez-moi en prison, livrez-moi au bourreau mais empêchez cette horreur ! Je ne veux pas le voir mourir !

Il y eut un silence que troublait seulement le bruit de la respiration de la jeune femme. Mgr Nanni se penchait déjà vers elle pour la réconforter mais le duc l'arrêta d'un geste puis, lentement, il vint à Fiora :

— Vous l'aimez à ce point ?... Alors pourquoi Campobasso ?

— Par vengeance... et pour le détacher de vous... de vous pour le service duquel Philippe est toujours prêt à tout sacrifier. Il n'a voulu de moi qu'une fortune pour vos armes... et une seule nuit.

Il se pencha, prit les deux mains qu'elle gardait obstinément devant son visage et l'obligea doucement à se relever :

— Vous me détestez, n'est-ce pas ?

Elle n'hésita qu'à peine et répondit, ses yeux gris dans les yeux noirs du prince :

— Oui... Sans vous, je serais heureuse !

— Sans moi, vous ne le connaîtriez même pas. Que serait-il allé faire à Florence ? Rentrez chez vous, à présent, et priez Dieu ! Je sais que vous semblez décidée à vous passer de son secours mais Mgr Nanni réussira peut-être à vous convaincre de vous tourner vers Lui. Il arrive qu'il exauce les prières... Quant au duel, je n'ai même pas la possibilité de le retarder : aucun des adversaires n'y consentirait...

Guidée par le légat qui avait pris son bras, elle se dirigeait vers la porte mais, avant de la franchir, elle se retourna :

— Ne pourrais-je au moins... lui parler ?

— S'il y consent, je ne m'y opposerai pas. Dois-je aussi accorder permission à Campobasso qui ne cesse de réclamer un instant d'entretien avec vous ?

— S'il vous plaît, monseigneur... à aucun prix ! Je voudrais... ne plus le voir jamais. Mais je vous remercie de permettre que je rencontre Philippe...

Ils étaient face à face à présent, dans ce qui avait été l'oratoire des duchesses de Lorraine, un petit sanctuaire de pierre grise que le faste bourguignon avait déjà rhabillé d'azur, d'argent, d'une très belle statue de la Vierge et de quelques reliquaires devant lesquels, à l'entrée de Fiora, Philippe priait, à genoux.

Au léger grincement de la porte, il s'était levé et, une main posée sur la table de communion, il regardait la jeune femme venir à lui mais elle s'arrêta à quelques pas.

— Je ne souhaitais pas vous rencontrer, dit Selongey d'une voix basse où Fiora crut percevoir une lassitude.

Mais le duc a insisté sans d'ailleurs m'en donner la raison.

— C'est moi qui l'en ai prié. Je voulais vous voir avant que... oh, Philippe, vous êtes blessé!

La tempe droite, en effet, portait une écorchure tout juste refermée autour de laquelle la peau avait bleui mais Philippe haussa les épaules :

— Si c'est de cette estafilade que vous souhaitiez me parler...

— Un peu oui... mais surtout de ce duel qui m'épouvante. Est-il indispensable que vous vous battiez...

— Avec votre amant ? J'espère bien le tuer! J'ai quinze ans de moins que lui et ce n'est pas cette égratignure qui m'en empêchera. Vous avez peur, dites-vous ? Alors vous auriez dû comprendre qu'en venant prier pour lui vous ne feriez qu'accroître mon envie de l'abattre.

— Prier pour lui ? C'est une pensée qui ne m'effleurait même pas. C'est pour vous que je tremble...

— Vous êtes bien bonne mais vous devriez plutôt vous inquiéter pour ce batteur d'estrade, car je ne le ménagerai pas et il trouvera cela très déplaisant. Inhabituel surtout : un condottiere, chacun le sait, est fort ménager d'une vie qu'il entend conserver pour pouvoir jouir à l'aise, sur ses vieux jours, des fruits de ses services mercenaires...

— J'ai supplié le duc d'empêcher ce combat.

— Il vous a ri au nez, j'imagine ? Croyez-vous que je puisse endurer qu'un homme vienne à la cour de mon prince réclamer ma femme comme son bien ?

— Votre femme? dit Fiora avec amertume. Dans votre esprit je ne l'aurai été que durant quelques heures mais jamais, au grand jamais vous n'avez imaginé de vivre avec moi, de faire de moi la compagne de tous vos instants. Croyez-vous que j'ignore les termes de ce contrat insensé que vous avez arraché à la faiblesse de mon père et par quel moyen, indigne d'un chevalier, vous avez emporté la victoire ? Dans tous les pays du monde cela s'appelle du chantage!

— Je vous voulais à tout prix et j'aurais employé tous les moyens, même les pires...

— N'est-ce pas ce que vous avez fait ?

Il détourna la tête pour ne plus rencontrer ce regard étincelant de colère où il ne pouvait lire que sa condamnation.

— Je l'avoue à ma honte mais vous m'avez rendu fou...

— Moi ou ma fortune ?

— Je croyais vous avoir prouvé que je vous aimais ?

— Vous me l'avez prouvé ? Était-ce preuve suffisante que cette nuit où vous avez fait de moi une femme, après quoi vous vous êtes enfui comme un voleur sans vous demander, même un seul instant, si vous ne me laissiez pas irrémédiablement blessée ? Vous emportiez une lettre de change et une mèche de cheveux, m'a-t-on dit. C'était cela votre victoire...

— Je suis revenu à Florence.

— Vous l'avez déjà dit et cela non plus ne prouve rien. Vous avez écouté, en regardant brûler mon palais, les premiers ragots venus et vous êtes reparti, avec de grands soupirs sans doute mais, ces soupirs, je ne suis pas certaine qu'ils n'étaient pas de soulagement. Vous vous retrouviez veuf avec, devant vous, un nouvel avenir.

— Ce n'est pas vrai. Je suis revenu parce que je vous aimais, parce que je voulais vous revoir...

— C'est sans doute ce que vous avez essayé de vous faire croire à vous-même ? Si vous m'aviez aimée... comme moi je vous aimais, vous auriez détruit Florence, pierre par pierre, vous auriez creusé la terre avec vos ongles jusqu'à ce que vous eussiez retrouvé au moins mon cadavre mais vous êtes reparti tranquillement. L'histoire était finie, il n'y avait plus le moindre Beltrami au monde pour vous rappeler que, pour l'amour de votre maître, vous étiez allé jusqu'à souiller les aigles d'argent de vos armes en épousant l'enfant de l'inceste et de l'adultère, la fille de Marie de Brévailles. Vous n'aviez plus besoin de mourir comme vous l'aviez annoncé emphatiquement à mon père... et d'ailleurs, je suis bien obligée de constater que vous n'êtes pas mort !

— Et vous me le reprochez ? Vous me haïssez à ce point ?

— Décidément, vous n'avez rien compris...

L'une des broderies dorées que l'on avait tendues sur les murs de l'oratoire venait de se soulever sous la main du Téméraire qui s'avança vers Fiora, trop surprise par cette soudaine apparition pour songer au moindre salut. Philippe, lui, était devenu très rouge et voulut s'approcher de son maître mais celui-ci l'écarta d'un geste.

— Va-t'en Philippe ! Et songe à te confesser avant d'affronter Campobasso ! Je te verrai plus tard...

— Monseigneur ! Il faut que je vous dise... que je vous explique...

— Il n'y a rien à expliquer. J'ai tout compris. Laisse-moi avec elle !

Avec un dernier regard à Fiora, Philippe baissa la tête et quitta la chapelle dont les dalles résonnaient sous ses solerets d'acier sans que le duc eût seulement tourné les yeux vers lui. Charles fixait la jeune femme avec l'expression de qui vient de trouver la solution d'un problème difficile. Il vint jusqu'à elle et, avec des gestes d'une grande douceur, ôta les longues épingles qui maintenaient sa coiffure. Quand les lourds cheveux retombèrent le long du cou mince, il recula de quelques pas :

— Jean de Brévailles ! Je savais bien que ce visage appartenait à mon passé mais je ne le croyais pas si lointain ! Cela fait combien d'années ?

— Que vous avez refusé leur vie à une mère désespérée ? Dix-huit dans quelques jours. Je suis née très peu de temps avant leur mort. Ce qui m'étonne, c'est que vous en ayez conservé le souvenir ?

— Cela est, pourtant. Je l'aimais bien avant que la pure image de ce garçon fier et beau ne s'abîme dans la honte et le déshonneur...

— Pourquoi, monseigneur, n'ajoutez-vous pas, dans le sang, celui que vos bourreaux ont fait couler sur ce vieil échafaud que j'ai vu à Dijon ? Encore n'était-ce pas assez : il fallait aussi la boue, l'ordure, l'ignoble tombe où par votre ordre on les a jetés et où j'ai failli mourir...

— L'ordre venait de mon père, pas de moi.

— Mais vous n'avez rien fait pour y changer quoi que ce soit ! Si un homme, un de ces marchands que Votre Seigneurie dédaigne si hautement ne s'était trouvé là pour exercer cette pitié qui aurait dû être le fait du prince, je me serais dissoute au fond du même cloaque. Cet homme m'a recueillie, nourrie, éduquée, aimée... Il a voulu faire de moi sa fille et, ce dernier printemps, il en est mort après avoir été obligé de me marier à messire de Selongey qui avait percé son secret...

Le visage brun du prince devint couleur de brique et son regard s'enflamma :

— Ne me dites pas que Philipe, la loyauté, la droiture, l'honneur mêmes, que Philippe, chevalier de la Toison d'or a osé employer pareil moyen ?...

— Pour vous rapporter l'argent que lui avait refusé Lorenzo de Médicis, il eût été capable de pis encore. Il vous est attaché corps et âme, même si cela me déchire le cœur de le reconnaître. Et vous savez à présent pourquoi il n'a voulu de moi qu'une nuit, pourquoi je devais couler ma vie entière à Florence sans jamais paraître en Bourgogne, afin que nul ici n'apprenne qu'il avait été jusqu'à souiller son nom en épousant la fille des Brévailles, et vous moins encore que quiconque... vous, son véritable dieu !

— Taisez-vous ! Par saint Georges, je vous ordonne de vous taire !

Les mains sur les oreilles, le duc alla s'effondrer sur l'une des deux chaires armoriées qui se faisaient vis-à-vis dans le chœur. Il resta là un moment, respirant difficilement comme un homme qui étouffe et ouvrant d'un geste brusque le col de sa longue robe fourrée de martre. Il ferma les yeux puis, quand le souffle devint plus régulier, il darda son regard noir sur Fiora :

— Vous avez admis tout à l'heure que vous me détestiez. Le mot était faible n'est-ce pas ? Vous me haïssez ?... et c'est pour me nuire que vous avez séduit Campobasso ?

— Au point où nous en sommes, monseigneur, il serait absurde de mentir : je n'ai qu'une seule tête à vous offrir. Et puis, à la vérité, je ne me sens plus tellement envie de vivre.

— Vous voulez mourir ?

— Cela arrangerait si bien les choses...

— C'est à moi d'en juger... Sortez à présent et laissez-moi prier ! J'ai, sur mon honneur, grand besoin de prier...

Après une génuflexion qui s'adressait au duc aussi bien qu'à Dieu, Fiora quitta l'oratoire dont elle referma très lentement la porte derrière elle. Assez lentement pour voir que le Téméraire s'était laissé tomber à genoux sur la marche de l'autel et avait enfoui sa tête dans ses mains. Au mouvement des épaules, on pouvait même supposer qu'il pleurait...

Il était près de minuit, le lendemain soir, quand Battista Colonna vint chercher Fiora dans sa chambre. Silencieusement, éclairés par la lanterne que le page balançait dans sa main, la jeune femme et son guide parcoururent des salles, des galeries, descendirent des escaliers en colimaçon qui semblaient interminables et finalement débouchèrent dans le pourpris du palais dont les quelques arbres, dépouillés par l'hiver, montraient à nu leurs branches tordues, soulignées d'un léger liseré blanc. Il était tombé de la neige dans la journée et elle avait couvert l'enclos d'une mince couche floconneuse.

Autour de ce qui était, au printemps, un doux tapis d'herbe émaillé de fleurs où les dames aimaient à venir s'asseoir pour deviser, entendre des vers ou danser des rondes, se tenaient quelques hommes enveloppés de longs manteaux noirs, comme Fiora elle-même, qui les faisaient semblables à des fantômes. Deux d'entre eux étaient assis sur des escabeaux que l'on avait apportés là : c'étaient le duc Charles et le légat. Un troisième siège, auprès de ce dernier, attendait Fiora qui y prit place après avoir salué silencieusement le prélat, le prince et un homme d'une cinquantaine d'années et de haute mine qui se tenait debout auprès du Téméraire et dont elle savait qu'il était son demi-frère, ce Grand Bâtard Antoine qui, par ses exploits avait élevé sa naissance illégitime à la hauteur d'une légende. Personne ne disait mot...

Dans la flaque de lumière dispensée par les torches que portaient trois valets noirs – et peut-être muets – apparurent les deux adversaires. Leurs armures cannelées, forgées toutes deux par les célèbres Missaglia de Milan les appariaient et, à première vue, on ne put les reconnaître que grâce à ceux qui les accompagnaient : Mathieu de Prame pour Selongey et Galeotto pour Campobasso. Ils étaient sensiblement de même taille. Chacun d'eux était armé d'une épée et d'une dague...

D'un même mouvement, ils vinrent mettre genou en terre devant le duc et le légat. Le premier ne bougea pas mais quand le second leva la main pour un geste de bénédiction, Philippe ôta le grand bacinet qui emprisonnait sa tête et le jeta à terre affirmant ainsi son intention de combattre sans sa protection...

— Souhaitez-vous tellement vous faire tuer ? demanda le Téméraire d'une voix sourde où perçait une angoisse. Reprenez ce casque !...

— Avec votre permission, monseigneur, je n'en ferai rien. Nous ne sommes pas ici pour bosseler de l'acier. L'un de nous n'en sortira pas vivant. Ce sera plus facile ainsi...

— Comme il vous plaira mais vous vous infligez là un grave désavantage... à moins que votre adversaire ne montre pareil dédain de la vie ?...

Tous les regards se tournèrent vers Campobasso qui paraissait changé en statue. Son hésitation était palpable mais il tourna les yeux vers Fiora et lut dans son regard tant d'implacable mépris qu'il se décida et libéra également sa tête :

— Après tout, pourquoi pas ? fit-il avec un haussement d'épaules...

Tous deux se relevèrent ensuite et vinrent se mettre aux ordres du Grand Bâtard qui leur assigna une place à chacun puis se recula et se tourna vers le duc. Celui-ci fit un signe d'assentiment :

— Allez, messeigneurs, et que Dieu juge de vos causes laquelle est la meilleure.

Comme dans une figure de danse bien réglée, les deux lourdes épées se levèrent en même temps et Fiora enfonça ses ongles dans sa main, le cœur étreint d'une angoisse mortelle. Hors de leurs carapaces de fer les deux têtes nues paraissaient étrangement fragiles. Qu'une épée s'abattît sur l'une d'elles et c'était la mort assurée, les deux hommes se battant avec une violence qui donnait la juste mesure de la haine qu'ils se portaient. Le jardin clos résonnait du choc des armes d'où naissaient parfois des étincelles. Leur habileté était sensiblement égale et le duel risquait de durer longtemps. Selongey était peut-être plus rapide et plus souple, mais Campobasso possédait une plus longue expérience car ce n'était pas la première fois qu'il affrontait un homme en combat singulier et il était impossible de prédire lequel, finalement, aurait le dessus...

Fiora aurait voulu fermer les yeux, ne rien voir, mais cela lui était impossible : il lui fallait regarder... Parfois son regard glissait, plein d'appréhension, vers le visage immobile du Téméraire dans lequel, seuls, les yeux semblaient vivre. Ils étincelaient, ces yeux, en suivant les phases de la lutte qui, pour son âme guerrière, devait être un spectacle de choix et une amère rancœur s'empara de Fiora. Comment avait-elle pu être assez stupide pour aller lui demander d'interdire un duel dont il avait dû se promettre beaucoup de plaisir et qu'il appréciait à présent, en connaisseur averti ? L'émotion de cette femme affolée avait dû l'amuser comme l'amusait sans doute l'anxiété qu'il devinait... De toute façon, et quelle que soit l'issue du combat, Fiora avait perdu tout espoir en l'avenir. Sa vie était définitivement saccagée car elle n'accepterait jamais d'être le prix d'une victoire du condottiere sur l'homme qu'elle aimait et, si Philippe l'emportait, il la rejetterait loin de lui à tout jamais.

— Qu'il vive, mon Dieu ! implora-t-elle, retrouvant soudain à cet instant de péril extrême le recours désespéré à la prière, qu'il vive et je le libérerai de moi. Je demanderai l'annulation de ce mariage insensé !...

Elle avait froid jusqu'à l'âme. La neige qui couvrait le pourpris et qui, sous les pas des duellistes, n'était plus que boue, lui glaçait les pieds et la faisait trembler. C'était comme si tout ce froid s'insinuait dans ses veines pour remonter sournoisement jusqu'au cœur...

Le souffle des deux hommes s'écourtait et devenait bruyant. Le combat durait, durait et, à tant frapper, la lourde épée devait à présent peser dix fois son poids dans les muscles fatigués. Les coups semblaient moins violents et aucune blessure n'apparaissait sur l'un ni sur l'autre. Fiora reprenait espoir. Le duc allait-il enfin arrêter cette lutte par trop égale ? Soudain, en voulant éviter une charge de son adversaire, Philippe recula, glissa, tomba lourdement sur le dos. Déjà Campobasso allait se précipiter sur lui, l'épée haute pour frapper à la tête, quand la jeune femme, avec un cri d'épouvante, se jeta entre les deux hommes, bousculant Campobasso dont l'épée s'abattit sur son épaule tandis que le bras vêtu de fer la frappait à la tête. Elle sentit une douleur fulgurante mais s'évanouit aussitôt, emportant dans les profondeurs apaisantes de l'inconscient l'écho des clameurs qui s'élevaient autour d'elle ; puis elle ne sut plus rien de ce monde impitoyable des hommes, contre la cruauté duquel elle venait de se briser volontairement...

En reprenant conscience, elle retrouva la douleur. Son épaule, que des mains cependant douces maniaient lentement, la faisait affreusement souffrir comme si l'on était en train de la lui arracher. Sa tête aussi lui faisait mal et les sons y résonnaient tels qu'une cloche vide... Elle ouvrit péniblement les yeux et vit qu'on l'avait ramenée dans sa chambre du palais et qu'un homme en qui elle reconnut Matteo de Clerici, le médecin ducal, était penché sur elle et lui donnait des soins :

— Aucun os ne semble brisé, commentait-il en italien. L'épaisseur du manteau et de la robe ont un peu amorti le coup, porté d'ailleurs avec une arme dont le tranchant s'émoussait, mais c'est un vrai miracle que l'épaule n'ait pas été arrachée... Ah! je crois qu'elle revient à elle!

— Vous êtes certain que sa vie n'est pas en danger? fit la voix du duc Charles et Fiora, en dépit des brumes qui lui obscurcissaient le cerveau, découvrit qu'il employait l'italien avec aisance.

— A moins de complications, certainement pas. J'ai enduit la blessure d'un baume qui devrait apaiser la douleur et aider à cicatriser les chairs. Quant au coup reçu à la tête, c'est chose bénigne : une bosse qui est déjà d'un joli bleu...

— Philippe, souffla Fiora... Est-ce que... Philippe est vivant?

La puissante silhouette noire du Téméraire émergea de l'ombre et apparut dans la clarté des chandelles allumées au chevet du lit :

— Sain et sauf... de même que son adversaire d'ailleurs. Mais quelle folie que ce geste! Croyez-vous sincèrement que j'aurais laissé Campobasso égorger Selongey?

L'expression du visage de Fiora indiqua clairement le doute, et elle murmura :

— Le combat n'était-il pas à outrance?

— J'ai toujours le droit d'arrêter un duel quand bon me semble. Je savais que l'un comme l'autre aurait beaucoup de mal à venir à bout de son ennemi et j'espérais que la fatigue finirait par avoir le dessus. J'avoue que, cependant, j'eusse préféré que l'on gardât les casques...

— Ne... pouviez-vous... ordonner qu'on... les remît?

— Cela, non. Chacun a le droit de se battre de la façon qui lui convient...

— Monseigneur! reprocha le médecin, ma patiente a perdu beaucoup de sang et elle a besoin de repos. Je vais lui faire absorber une potion qui la fera dormir et nous verrons, au jour, comment se comporte la plaie...

— Un moment encore... s'il vous plaît, dit Fiora. Je voudrais vous demander... monseigneur... de parler pour moi à Sa Grandeur le légat. Je... je demande l'annulation... de mon mariage...

— Vous voulez?...

— Oui... et le plus tôt sera le mieux. Dites à messire de Selongey... qu'il est délié de tout engagement.. envers moi. Ainsi que... vous-même. Mon père... savait que cet or vous était destiné... Je ne reviendrai plus sur un don... qu'il a fait librement!

Épuisée par l'effort qu'elle venait de s'imposer, elle ferma les yeux, ne vit pas le duc se pencher sur elle, mais elle sentit la chaleur de sa main quand il y emprisonna la sienne:

— Ne hâtez rien, je vous en supplie! Vous n'êtes pas vous-même en ce moment...

— Parce que j'ai perdu... toute agressivité? fit la jeune femme avec un pâle sourire.

— Peut-être. Nous reparlerons de tout cela quand vous serez rétablie. Je dois vous dire que Selongey est là, dehors. Voulez-vous lui permettre d'entrer?

— Non... non! Ni lui... ni l'autre! Par pitié!

— Vous avez droit à beaucoup mieux que de la pitié, mais il en sera comme vous le désirez. Reposez-vous!

— Il en est plus que temps, en effet, dit aigrement le médecin. D'autre part, il conviendrait de trouver une femme pour veiller donna Fiora. En dehors des filles de cuisine, ce palais est plein d'hommes et je ne compte pas les deux mille filles de joie qui poursuivent notre armée. Les soins d'une femme de bien seraient...

— Souhaitables? Je partage votre avis et m'en occuperai dès le matin. En attendant, ne lui mesurez pas vos soins...

Après son départ, Matteo de Clerici fit absorber à la blessée une tisane qu'il venait de préparer sur le feu de la cheminée et dans laquelle il versa quelques gouttes d'un flacon qu'il avait apporté avec lui.

La drogue devait être efficace car, à peine la dernière gorgée avalée, Fiora s'endormit profondément...

Derrière la porte de la chambre, le duc avait retrouvé Philippe qui arpentait nerveusement le dallage : il était visible qu'il avait pleuré :

— Comment va-t-elle ? interrogea-t-il. Puis-je la voir ?

— Elle n'est pas en danger immédiat mais tu ne saurais entrer, Philippe.

— Pourquoi ?

— Parce qu'elle ne le veut pas.

— C'est l'autre qu'elle attend ? s'écria le jeune homme avec fureur. Il n'est pas loin : Olivier de La Marche le retient au bas de cet escalier...

— Elle ne veut voir ni l'un ni l'autre... et elle désire expressément que je sollicite du légat l'annulation de votre mariage. Elle te fait savoir que tu es délié, envers elle, de tout engagement. Ce sont là ses propres paroles et je crois qu'elle a raison.

— Monseigneur ! protesta Selongey. N'aurai-je pas, moi aussi, la possibilité de parler ? Cela me concerne, il me semble ?

— Baisse le ton, s'il te plaît ! C'est au duc de Bourgogne que tu t'adresses. Au duc de Bourgogne qui est en droit de te demander compte de ta conduite : d'abord tu t'es marié sans ma permission, ensuite, tu as usé de chantage pour obtenir la main d'une malheureuse née dans la honte et que le plus misérable de mes sujets eût été libre de refuser pour épouse. Tu mériterais que je t'oblige à rendre ta Toison d'or. A présent, je t'interdis de chercher à la revoir et plus encore à l'approcher. Contente-toi de savoir qu'elle t'a sauvé la vie et va-t'en ! Oublie-la !

— Si vous croyez que c'est facile ! s'exclama Selongey avec amertume. Voilà des mois que j'essaie car je la croyais morte. Et puis je l'ai revue et j'ai senti...

— Vos sentiments ne m'intéressent en rien. Moi, votre prince, je vous ordonne, sous peine de déshonneur public, de vous détourner à jamais d'une femme adultère, née de l'inceste et de surcroît espionne de notre beau cousin de France.

— Qu'allez-vous faire d'elle ? Vous n'allez pas au moins lui faire de mal ? Elle est si jeune et elle a tant souffert !

— Cela dépendra de votre obéissance. Tout à l'heure, je verrai le légat mais vous, préparez-vous à partir pour la Savoie où la duchesse Yolande, envahie par les gens des Cantons, appelle au secours. Vous lui annoncerez notre venue prochaine et resterez auprès d'elle jusqu'à ce que je vous rappelle. Il faut qu'avant midi vous ayez quitté Nancy avec cinquante lances !

— Monseigneur, par grâce ! Elle est innocente et vous ne l'ignorez pas.

— Beaucoup moins que vous ne le croyez. De toute façon, ce mariage doit être dissous. Ne m'obligez pas par votre obstination à la faire disparaître elle-même ! Sachez que je la tiendrai dorénavant sous mon regard pour m'assurer de votre obéissance.

— Vous a-t-elle jamais fait défaut ? Laissez-moi au moins lui dire adieu ? Je lui dois la vie !

— Non... vous ne pourriez plus partir et je vous ai donné un ordre.

La mort dans l'âme, Philippe salua et se retira avec un dernier regard sur ce panneau de bois derrière lequel reposait la seule femme qu'il eût jamais aimée. Il se dirigea vers l'escalier mais, sur le point de descendre, se ravisa :

— Un mot encore, monseigneur. Je désire que l'on vende tous mes biens. Fiora n'a plus rien et je ne le supporte pas. Faites au moins cela pour moi !

— Vraiment ? Comment vivrez-vous puisque c'est vous alors qui n'aurez plus rien ?

— Votre victoire définitivement assise, mon prince, j'irais offrir mon épée au doge de Venise. Une fortune, cela peut se reconstituer au hasard d'une guerre... à moins que tout ne s'y achève.

Saluant derechef mais avec une raideur qui traduisait bien sa colère contenue, Selongey disparut enfin dans les profondeurs de l'escalier, suivi des yeux par le Téméraire qui se prit à sourire :

– C'est ce que nous verrons... fit-il.

La maison de l'échevin Georges Marqueiz, dans la rue Ville-Vieille et près de l'église Saint-Epvre, était l'une des plus belles de Nancy et n'avait pas souffert des bombardements. C'est là qu'au matin on transporta Fiora encore à demi inconsciente afin qu'elle y reçût des soins féminins impossibles à assurer dans un palais transformé en caserne. Dame Nicole, l'aimable épouse du magistrat, avait accepté très volontiers de donner au nouveau maître ce gage de bonne volonté. C'était une grande femme dont les cheveux blonds blanchissaient harmonieusement, sans beauté réelle, mais elle avait des yeux bruns pleins de chaleur et un charmant sourire. La blessée n'eut aucune peine à gagner son cœur et fut elle-même conquise sur-le-champ.

Cependant, le nouveau duc déployait toutes ses grâces – et quand il le voulait, il en avait beaucoup – pour séduire ses nouveaux sujets. On ne vit que fêtes et réjouissances. Charles se répandait en libéralités, en magnificences et en caresses. Il convoqua, dans son nouveau palais, les états de Lorraine où il prononça un discours mémorable :

– ... On s'apercevra bientôt que je cherchais par mes armes bien plus votre félicité que la mienne, dit-il à ces gens qu'il avait affamés et dont il avait réduit quelques-uns à coucher dans des décombres, la Providence qui vous a soumis à mes lois vous réservait sans doute le bonheur de vivre sous mon gouvernement ; vous allez en effet désormais retrouver votre nation opulente, heureuse, tranquille et cette ville, maintenant le centre de mes états, sera le lieu de ma résidence. Je vais l'embellir d'un superbe palais, l'augmenter d'un grand nombre d'édifices, pousser ses remparts jusqu'à Tombelaine et lui donner le même lustre sous mon règne que Rome en reçut autrefois sous l'empire d'Auguste...

Il terminait en demandant une assurance d'inviolable attachement à sa personne et l'assemblée, enthousiasmée, n'attendit même pas qu'il en ait terminé pour lui jurer fidélité.

— C'est quelque chose que devenir la capitale d'un grand royaume, dit Nicole Marqueiz à sa pensionnaire. Quand on sait à quelle richesse ont atteint Bruges, Lille et Dijon, cela donne à rêver...

— N'aimez-vous pas votre jeune duc?

— Il est charmant mais c'est un enfant, comme dit monseigneur Charles. Il n'est pas de taille à se mesurer à un tel prince. Il faut vivre avec son temps, que voulez-vous!

Une partie de la noblesse lorraine se rallia d'ailleurs au nouveau seigneur. Cela choquait quelque peu Fiora qui se rétablissait doucement et qui commençait à se demander ce qu'il en adviendrait d'elle-même. Battista Colonna venait chaque jour prendre de ses nouvelles et causer avec elle. Il lui avait appris le départ de Philippe pour la Savoie et aussi la scène violente qui, à cause d'elle, avait opposé Campobasso au duc Charles. Le condottiere, ayant su que Fiora demandait l'annulation de son mariage, conçut de grands espoirs et exigea qu'on lui accordât le titre de fiancé, réclamant du même coup l'autorisation d'aller visiter chaque jour celle qu'il considérait comme la future comtesse de Campobasso.

— Monseigneur, raconta Battista, lui a déclaré qu'il n'était nullement question que vous puissiez l'épouser, qu'en ce qui le concernait il s'y opposait formellement et que, d'ailleurs, il entendait vous garder par-devers lui comme otage...

— Comme otage? Mais de quoi? et pourquoi?

— Je ne saurais vous en dire plus, madonna. C'est le

terme que Monseigneur Charles a employé. Toujours est-il que Campobasso est parti en claquant les portes et en jurant que, de sa vie, il ne servirait un prince qui ne reconnaissait pas à leur valeur les services rendus.

– Parti ? Mais pour où ?

– Vous n'allez pas me croire : pour Saint-Jacques-de-Compostelle où il veut faire pèlerinage !

Fiora éclata de rire, Campobasso sous la bure et le chapeau du pèlerin lui semblait une image du plus haut comique.

– Et il s'y rend avec toute sa troupe de mercenaires ? Cela va faire un beau cortège !

– Je crois qu'il va laisser sa *condotta* à son château de Pierrefort, ce qui le dispensera de la payer. On dit que, depuis pas mal de temps déjà, il réserve pour lui-même l'argent qu'il perçoit du duc. Il a annoncé aussi qu'il comptait rendre visite au duc de Bretagne qui serait un peu son parent...

– N'importe quoi ! soupira Fiora mais en son for intérieur, elle était plutôt satisfaite.

D'une part d'être débarrassée d'un homme qu'elle jugeait à présent plus qu'encombrant et ensuite d'avoir, somme toute, parfaitement accompli sa mission. En effet, connaissant le condottiere comme elle le connaissait, le grand saint Jacques et le duc de Bretagne devaient se résumer en un seul personnage : le roi de France, auprès duquel, très certainement, Campobasso allait déverser ses griefs. Et c'était bien à cela qu'elle avait souhaité l'amener. Ce qui lui permit de se réjouir pleinement d'en avoir terminé avec une aventure qu'elle jugeait peu glorieuse...

En revanche, cette excellente nouvelle s'accompagnait d'une autre... qui l'était moins. Peu de temps après l'entrée à Nancy, elle avait demandé au légat qu'on lui retrouve Esteban afin qu'il puisse reprendre son service auprès d'elle. Or, le jeune Colonna lui apprit que le Castillan était introuvable. Il semblait qu'au lendemain du soir où il avait sauvé Fiora du poignard de Virginio, Esteban se fût volatilisé. Ni le chef de la compagnie où il s'était engagé ni les autres soldats ne savaient ce qu'il était devenu... Et Fiora, à l'inquiétude qu'elle en éprouva, comprit qu'à son humble place, le Castillan avait gagné une petite partie de son cœur, comme Démétrios et comme tous ceux qui s'étaient comportés envers elle en amis véritables.

Cette disparition faisait qu'elle se sentait plus déracinée que jamais et elle ne comprenait pas pourquoi le duc tenait tant à la garder auprès de lui. Ne l'avait-il dit que pour se débarrasser de Campobasso ou bien cette histoire d'otage était-elle sérieuse ? Du fond de ce lit étranger, dans cette maison étrangère au cœur d'une ville et d'un pays étrangers, la jeune femme ne souhaitait plus que de retourner à Paris pour y rejoindre sa chère Léonarde dont l'absence lui était de plus en plus pénible. Noël approchait et elle appréhendait à présent cette douce fête où se réunissent ceux qui s'aiment. Pour elle ce serait le Noël de la solitude, le premier qu'elle allait vivre sans son père et sans Léonarde. Même Philippe, cette ombre d'époux, était au loin, perdu à jamais pour elle... A dix-huit ans, le cœur n'a pas encore oublié les tendres joies de l'enfance ni la douceur du foyer paternel et Fiora, durant la nuit entière, pleura, elle dont l'orgueil détestait les larmes, sur les cendres, encore chaudes, de son palais incendié et de son bonheur détruit.

– Moi aussi je suis séparé des miens, lui confia au matin Battista en remarquant ses yeux rougis, et si vous ne souhaitez pas vous mêler à vos hôtes pour la fête, je pourrais m'en venir et vous chanter de jolies chansons de chez nous...

Ce qui eut pour conséquence immédiate de la faire pleurer de plus belle à sa grande confusion. En vérité, elle devenait d'une affligeante sensibilité ! Elle embrassa l'enfant sur les deux joues pour le remercier de son amitié.

Or, à la veille de la Nativité, trois cavaliers qui ne ressemblaient en rien aux rois mages, surgirent des chemins enneigés et franchirent la porte de la Craffe : un homme, une femme et un jeune garçon. C'étaient, dans l'ordre : Douglas Mortimer superbe sous son harnois de la Garde Écossaise mais de fort méchante humeur de se présenter en pareille compagnie, Léonarde, juchée sur une mule et emmitouflée de lainages et de fourrures, aussi sereine que son compagnon était grognon, enfin le jeune Florent, l'apprenti banquier gagné par le démon de l'aventure, qui s'était pendu aux basques de la vieille demoiselle en refusant farouchement de s'en séparer avec, bien sûr, au fond de son cœur innocent, l'espoir de revoir la belle dame de ses pensées...

Tout ce monde se retrouva bientôt devant Olivier de La Marche un peu déconcerté par cette arrivée pittoresque :

— Je dois remettre à Monseigneur le duc une lettre du roi de France et en attendre réponse, dit Mortimer du ton rogue qui lui était habituel.

— Vous serez conduit à lui dans un instant... mais quelles sont ces personnes ? Vous voyagez en famille ?

Avant que l'Écossais qui avait viré au rouge brique ait libéré les mots que la colère coinçait dans sa gorge, Léonarde s'était chargée de la réponse.

— Moi, de la famille de cet ours mal léché ? Sachez, sire capitaine, qu'il a seulement été chargé par Sa Majesté le roi de nous protéger, moi et ce jeune homme, au long du voyage depuis Paris. Sachez aussi que je désire voir votre maître. Je suis la gouvernante de donna Fiora Beltrami qu'il retient prisonnière et je suis venue la chercher car il ne convient pas qu'une jeune dame de sa qualité se trouve seule en compagnie de soudards !

— Je vois, dit La Marche. Et celui-là ? ajouta-t-il en désignant Florent.

— Mon jeune valet, ou mon page comme il vous plaira. Je suis dame Léonarde Mercet, déclara-t-elle du ton altier qu'elle eût employé pour dire : je suis la reine d'Espagne.

— Vous m'en direz tant ! fit le capitaine, mi-figue, mi-raisin. Votre nom, messire ?

— Douglas Mortimer, des Mortimer de Glen Livet, officier de la Garde Écossaise du roi Très-Chrétien, Louis, onzième du nom, lança celui-ci en homme qui sait ce qu'il représente...

La Marche d'ailleurs s'inclina :

— Veuillez me suivre !

Quelques instants plus tard, l'Écossais et la vieille fille pliaient le genou devant le Téméraire qui, superbe à son habitude, donnait ses audiences du mardi dans la salle des états de Lorraine. Si Léonarde fut impressionnée par le faste qui l'entourait, elle n'en montra rien et ce fut un regard fort paisible qu'elle posa sur l'homme dont on disait qu'il faisait trembler la moitié de l'Europe.

Avec tout le cérémonial requis par le protocole, Mortimer, familier des usages de cour, remit au duc de Bourgogne une lettre aux termes de laquelle Louis XI, après l'avoir félicité de sa victoire sur Nancy et l'assurant de sa fraternelle affection, demandait que soit remise à son envoyé « très noble et très gracieuse dame Fiora Beltrami dont nous tenions le défunt père en très particulière estime et amitié et dont nous avons appris avec inquiétude qu'elle s'était aventurée jusqu'en Lorraine pour y retrouver un sien cousin. Cette jeune dame étant chère à notre cœur paternel, nous déplorerions qu'il lui fût advenu dommage ou peine et nous considérerions comme une particulière marque d'amitié qu'elle soit confiée à notre messager et à la dame qui l'accompagne afin d'être ramenée au-delà de la ville frontière de Neufchâteau où le seigneur comte de Roussillon pourra s'en charger et la faire conduire en sûreté jusqu'à nous... ». Suivaient les effusions rituelles mais le Téméraire n'en parcourut pas moins la royale épître avec un air manifestement renfrogné. Neufchâteau, qui d'ailleurs s'était rendu à lui, ne se trouvait qu'à quinze lieues de Nancy et le comte de Roussillon, l'un des meilleurs capitaines du roi, n'avait pas coutume de ne commander qu'une poignée d'hommes.

Charles laissa la lettre s'enrouler sur elle-même avant

de la tendre à son secrétaire puis considéra un instant les deux personnages qui attendaient son bon plaisir :

— Nous sommes heureux d'apprendre, dit-il enfin, que les frontières de France sont si bien gardées et, en vérité, nous n'en avons jamais douté. Quant à donna Fiora, nous concevons parfaitement qu'elle soit chère au cœur de notre cousin le roi Louis. Malheureusement, nous ne la détenons pas par-devers nous...

Il prit un temps sans paraître s'apercevoir de la pâleur soudaine de Léonarde et de l'angoisse qui montait dans ses yeux, ni d'ailleurs des sourcils froncés de Mortimer.

— Et puis, reprit-il, nous ne la connaissons pas en tant que telle. Nous n'avons ici que la comtesse de Selongey, épouse de l'un de nos meilleurs capitaines et nous sommes étonné que le roi ignore ce détail. Mais il est bien certain que nous ne saurions remettre au roi de France une grande dame de Bourgogne. Nous en écrirons dans ce sens à notre cher et aimé cousin. En attendant, sire Mortimer, vous êtes notre hôte jusqu'après les fêtes de Noël qu'il ne conviendrait pas de vous faire passer dans la froidure des grands chemins. Quant à vous, madame, vous allez être conduite sur l'heure auprès de votre élève tenue de garder la chambre à la suite d'un... léger accident.

Quand, un moment plus tard, Nicole Marqueiz introduisit Léonarde auprès d'elle, Fiora, incrédule, ferma les yeux en les serrant très fort comme il arrive lorsque l'on se trouve en présence d'une lumière trop violente, mais déjà celle-ci s'était élancée vers elle et l'avait prise dans ses bras :

— Mon agneau ! Enfin je vous retrouve !

Les quatre mois de séparation qu'elles venaient de subir leur paraissaient à présent quatre siècles et pendant un long moment ce fut un festival de questions à bâtons rompus et d'embrassades. Chacune avait tellement à raconter que l'on ne savait plus par quel bout commencer...

— Nous n'y arriverons jamais, dit Fiora, si nous ne

En outre Démétrios a tiré l'horoscope de ce prince et ce qu'il y a lu l'a si fort attaché à lui qu'il ne veut plus le quitter. Le roi y a consenti. Quant à Esteban, il est allé rejoindre son maître et nous avons fait route ensemble jusqu'à Saint-Dizier...

— Ainsi Démétrios m'abandonne? dit Fiora avec un peu de tristesse. Je croyais que nous avions conclu un pacte? Mais apparemment mon sort l'intéresse moins que celui de « l'Enfant »...

— L'enfant?

— C'est ainsi que le duc Charles appelle celui qu'il vient de déposséder de ses terres et de sa couronne.

— Il est assuré que lui n'a rien d'un enfant. C'est un homme impressionnant. Mais ne croyez-vous pas qu'il serait temps de m'apprendre ce que vous avez fait de tout ce temps passé sans votre vieille Léonarde?

Le récit de Fiora fut plus long. Elle le fit honnêtement, sans concessions pour elle-même ou pour sa pudeur et il advint que, parfois, Léonarde rougît à l'écouter mais quand ce fut fini, celle-ci se contenta de se moucher vigoureusement, ce qui chez elle était signe de grande émotion et s'en vint embrasser sa Fiora sur le front.

— J'aimerais bien vous voir oublier tout cela au plus vite, mon agneau, mais ce me paraît difficile avec ce duc Charles qui tient essentiellement à vous garder par-devers lui.

— Il a dit à Campobasso que j'étais un otage.

— J'ai bien entendu. Mais alors pourquoi donc répond-il hautement à cet insupportable Mortimer que la place de la dame de Selongey est auprès de lui? D'autant que, si je vous ai bien comprise, vous venez de renoncer à cet honneur en demandant l'annulation de votre mariage?

— C'est étrange, en effet, mais ne me demandez pas de vous expliquer le Téméraire. Personne n'est en mesure de le faire, je crois... et peut-être non plus lui-même!

La nuit venue, les deux femmes, laissant les Marqueiz aller entendre à Saint-Epvre la messe de minuit, suivirent

Le duel

mettons un peu d'ordre dans nos propos. Commen[t] vous pu savoir que j'étais ici ?

— La réponse tient en un seul nom : Esteban.

Léonarde expliqua comment, chassés par Campo[basso] le Castillan et l'Écossais avaient résolu de se séparer pour retourner rendre compte au roi de l'issue de sa [mis]sion, l'autre pour rester aux alentours de Thionville [ou] même dans la ville afin de surveiller ce qui se passai[t au] château. Quand Fiora était partie pour Pierrefort, il a[vait] suivi, de loin, l'escorte de la jeune femme et grâce à [un] peu d'argent il avait trouvé asile chez l'un des paysans [qui] ravitaillaient le château en bois ou en fourrage. L'entr[ée] en scène d'Olivier de La Marche ne lui avait pas échap[pé] et, comme à l'aller, il avait suivi Fiora jusqu'au cam[p] bourguignon où il s'était engagé dans une compagnie franche afin de pouvoir circuler dans le camp.

L'arrivée de la jeune femme avait suscité au moins la curiosité et Esteban situa très vite l'endroit où elle était enfermée. Cela lui permit de la sauver du poignard de Virginio mais, après la prise de Nancy et comprenant qu'il ne pouvait rien faire avec ses seules forces, il s'enfuit en pleine nuit, brûlant les étapes, et rentra à Paris d'où Agnolo Nardi l'avait emmené chez le roi au château de Plessis-lez-Tours... avec Léonarde qui avait fermement insisté pour les accompagner.

— Étant désormais en paix avec la Bourgogne, poursuivit Léonarde, notre sire a pensé que rien ne s'opposait à ce qu'il vous réclame. Je crois que le roi a beaucoup d'estime pour vous et nous étions tous fort affligés de votre sort.

— Vous n'aviez pas tout à fait tort de l'être. Mais vous ne me parlez point de Démétrios ? Est-il toujours auprès du roi Louis ?

— Non. Il est au château de Joinville, pas bien loin d'ici avec le duc René II de Lorraine. Le roi l'a « prêté » au jeune duc pour qu'il prodigue ses soins à la vieille princesse de Vaudémont, sa grand-mère, qui est fort malade.

Battista Colonna venu, au nom du duc Charles, les convier à l'office de la collégiale Saint-Georges.

C'était la première fois, depuis Notre-Dame de Paris, que Fiora assistait à une messe. Mais sa paix avec Dieu était faite puisqu'il avait permis que Philippe ne succombât pas sous l'épée de Campobasso et, dans cette église illuminée qui, avec ses grandes brassées de houx et de gui, ressemblait à quelque forêt enchantée, elle se laissa bercer par les voix angéliques des jeunes chanteurs de Bourgogne... Scintillant de ses plus beaux joyaux, le Téméraire étalait dans le chœur la fabuleuse splendeur d'un manteau tissé d'or et semé de pierreries. Autour de lui ses officiers, bien qu'ayant revêtu leurs plus riches atours, passaient inaperçus...

— Est-il permis à un homme né de la femme de se glorifier lui-même à ce point ? murmura Léonarde.

— Je crois, répondit Fiora, qu'il considère tout cela comme très naturel. N'est-il pas le Grand Duc d'Occident et, si j'en crois les rumeurs, il pourrait être bientôt roi. Mais les fêtes de ce soir ne constituent pour lui qu'une étape. Battista m'a dit que, d'ici peu, il va reprendre les armes pour libérer les terres de la duchesse de Savoie et tirer vengeance des Suisses qui se sont emparés de son comté de Ferrette[1] et ont mis à mal la Comté Franche...

— Que va-t-il faire de nous en ce cas ? Pense-t-il vous traîner à sa suite comme ces reines de l'Antiquité que l'on attachait au char du vainqueur ?

— On ne se sépare pas d'un otage et il prétend que j'en suis un. Je pense d'ailleurs que ce ne sera pas plus pénible pour nous que pour ces ambassadeurs étrangers que vous voyez auprès de lui et qui doivent le suivre partout...

Des « chut ! » énergiques rappelèrent aux deux femmes qu'une église n'est pas un endroit pour causer. Elles se le tinrent pour dit et joignirent leurs voix à celles des fidèles qui entonnaient un chant de Noël.

La fête passée, il leur fallut faire face à un problème

---

1. Le Landgraviat de Haute-Alsace.

quand, au moment de partir, Mortimer vint leur faire ses adieux et réclamer Florent qu'il devait emmener : le duc n'autorisait aucun Français à demeurer dans son entourage. Le garçon pleura, pria, supplia, mais rien n'y fit, jusqu'à ce que l'Écossais lui déclarât de sa voix tranquille :

— On vous fait beaucoup d'honneur en vous traitant en homme. Après tout, je peux peut-être obtenir du duc qu'il laisse le gamin pleurnicheur que vous êtes dans les jupes des dames ?

Ce fut magique. Florent devint très pâle puis alla faire son baluchon. Quand il revint en silence saluer Fiora et Léonarde, il leur lança un regard si désespéré que la vieille fille, une fois le garçon parti, s'exclama :

— Ce Mortimer est assommant mais, au moins, il n'est pas amoureux de vous, contrairement à tant d'autres – et vous n'imaginez pas comme je trouve cela reposant...

CHAPITRE XII

LES TROMPES DE LA MORT

Les tourbillons de neige balayaient le col de Jougne où la trace du chemin ne se voyait presque plus. Depuis que l'on avait quitté Pontarlier et le fort château de Joux où le sire d'Arbon, qui le tenait pour le duc, avait reçu son maître en mettant sa cave et son garde-manger au pillage, le vent s'était levé jusqu'à devenir tempête tandis que l'armée montait péniblement vers la ligne de faîte entre le Rhône et le Rhin.

L'armée ? En fait c'était un monde qui s'étirait interminablement sur la route jurassienne. Cela évoquait l'Exode car, outre les vingt mille hommes de troupe sous divers capitaines, il y avait des centaines de chariots transportant les tentes et les pavillons d'apparat, les tapisseries, les coffres de joyaux, les vêtements somptueux, les manuscrits, l'argenterie, l'argent monnayé, le fabuleux trésor qui composait la chapelle ducale avec les statues d'or des douze apôtres, les châsses et les objets de culte, tous précieux, sans compter les prêtres et les chantres, enfin tout l'attirail de la Chancellerie avec ses gratte-papier et son chancelier Hugonet, les meubles et encore bien d'autres choses... Tout cela destiné à démontrer, non seulement aux Suisses mais à l'Europe entière, que la puissance, la force et l'organisation bourguignonnes étaient sans rivales au monde. D'ailleurs, dans l'esprit du duc Charles, cette guerre qu'il entamait devait être rapide et sans appel :

une simple expédition punitive destinée à asseoir sa puissance plus solidement que jamais.

En haut du col, les pieds dans la neige, le Téméraire regardait défiler ce train immense qui faisait chanter son orgueil. Il n'était plus le duc de Bourgogne, il était Hannibal franchissant les Alpes en plein hiver et peu lui importait qu'il s'agît du Jura! Son seul regret était sans doute qu'il n'y ait pas le moindre éléphant...

Il était là depuis des heures, insensible aux bourrasques de neige et au vent coupant, contemplant avec avidité cette affirmation de sa souveraineté que traduisaient les bannières, pennons et oriflammes. Ceux qui passaient devant lui s'efforçaient de les tenir droits et de redresser l'échine en dépit de la tourmente. Et apparemment, il n'était pas question qu'il quittât la place...

A son côté, son frère Antoine et, un peu en arrière, emmitouflés jusqu'aux yeux, ceux dont il faisait sa société habituelle depuis que l'on était sortis de Nancy : l'ambassadeur milanais Jean-Pierre Panigarola, et enveloppé d'un grand manteau doublé de martre, les cheveux entièrement cachés par un vaste chaperon de velours rubis, un mince jeune homme qui n'était autre que Fiora. On avait dû laisser à Salins Olivier de La Marche, atteint de dysenterie.

La veille du jour où l'on allait quitter Nancy, c'est-à-dire le 10 janvier, le Téméraire avait appelé auprès de lui la jeune femme, tout à fait remise de sa blessure. Il l'avait reçue seul à seule dans son cabinet d'armes où il examinait un nouveau type d'arbalète qu'un armurier allemand lui avait fait porter.

— Donna Fiora, dit-il sans se retourner, vous avez appris, je pense, que nous partons demain pour châtier les Suisses pillards et envahisseurs? J'ai décidé que vous voyageriez en compagnie de messire Panigarola, ambassadeur de Mgr le duc de Milan, qui est l'un des hommes les plus sages et les plus aimables qu'il m'ait été donné de connaître et, comme il n'est jamais bien loin de moi, c'est dire que nous cheminerons assez souvent de compagnie.

— Monseigneur, coupa Fiora, pardonnez-moi de vous interrompre, mais pourquoi tenez-vous tant à m'emmener... et sous quel nom ? Suis-je un otage et, dans ce cas, pourquoi ? Vous avez dit à Douglas Mortimer que j'étais la comtesse de Selongey et cependant Votre Seigneurie sait très bien que j'ai demandé l'annulation. Une annulation qu'elle souhaite d'ailleurs autant que moi.

Tenant toujours son arbalète, le duc se retourna et considéra la jeune femme d'un œil amusé :

— Vous avez pourtant été bien élevée, donna Fiora ! Ne vous a-t-on pas appris que l'on ne questionnait jamais un souverain ? Voilà, il me semble, une belle série de questions ?... Mais, pour une fois, je vais répondre... à condition que vous m'accordiez une faveur...

— Une faveur ? De moi au puissant duc de Bourgogne ?

— Mais oui. Je vous dirai tout à l'heure ce que je souhaite. Pour l'instant, voyons ce que vous m'avez demandé... Êtes-vous un otage ? En un certain sens oui. Vous savoir sous ma main... et peut-être en danger, vous assure à vous une certaine tranquillité et à moi l'obéissance de deux hommes...

— Deux ? Campobasso est parti à ce que l'on m'a dit.

— Il reviendra. L'important est que Selongey et lui ne passent pas leur temps à s'entre-tuer et à vous chercher aux quatre horizons. Parlons à présent de cette annulation ! Le légat s'est rendu auprès de l'empereur Frédéric pour m'assurer de sa neutralité durant la guerre que j'entreprends. Il réglera cette question à son retour. Donc, jusqu'à ce moment, vous avez droit au titre de comtesse de Selongey.

— Ce n'est pas du tout mon sentiment et je ne veux pas le porter.

— Comme il vous plaira. C'est donc sous votre nom florentin que vous serez présentée demain à l'ambassadeur. Votre gouvernante voyagera dans son chariot le plus confortable. Quant à vous... et c'est là que j'en viens à cette faveur dont nous parlions, vous me suivrez à cheval... si toutefois vous savez monter.

— Vous avez bien voulu admettre, monseigneur, que j'ai été bien élevée.

— C'est parfait mais ce sera mieux encore si vous acceptez de revêtir le costume que l'on a dû, à cette heure, déposer chez vous. Un costume... de garçon.

Fiora se mit à rire :

— Si c'est cela que vous désirez, monseigneur, c'est bien peu de chose. Je possède déjà un costume masculin grâce auquel j'ai voyagé plus commodément depuis Florence.

— Si vous y êtes accoutumée, ce n'en est que mieux mais je souhaite vraiment vous voir porter celui que j'ai envoyé. C'est... la raison profonde du désir que j'ai de vous garder auprès de moi durant cette campagne...

En rentrant chez les Marqueiz, Fiora trouva, en effet, étalées sur son lit, des chausses collantes de soie noire, de fines chemises brodées et une tunique de velours d'un beau rouge profond sur la manche de laquelle étaient brodées les grandes armes de Bourgogne chargées d'un lambel d'argent à trois pendants qui la laissèrent perplexe. Un chaperon de même velours, frappé d'une médaille d'or représentant saint Georges, une lourde chaîne d'or, un superbe manteau de cheval de fin drap noir doublé de martre et des bottes de daim noir fourrées accompagnaient ces vêtements, mais la jeune femme ne leur accorda qu'une attention distraite. Elle contemplait toujours le pourpoint quand Léonarde entra, les bras chargés de vêtements qu'elle allait mettre dans un coffre et Fiora pensa qu'elle pourrait peut-être l'éclairer :

— Vous êtes bourguignonne, dit-elle. Alors vous devez savoir quel est cet écu ? Monseigneur Charles m'a fait porter ces vêtements tout à l'heure. Je dois les revêtir et chevaucher près de lui.

Léonarde prit la tunique mais ne répondit pas tout de

suite. D'un doigt songeur, elle suivait le dessin compliqué de la broderie et, quand elle laissa retomber le vêtement, Fiora eut l'impression qu'elle avait pâli :

— Eh bien ? fit-elle avec impatience.

— Plus personne n'arbore ces armes. Elles étaient celles de Monseigneur Charles quand il n'était que comte de Charolais. Le lambel d'argent est la marque du fils aîné... Je suppose qu'étant son écuyer, Jean de Brévailles a dû en porter de semblables...

— Ah !

C'était donc cela ! Le lendemain, à la halte de Neufchâteau où le Téméraire devait prendre le commandement de l'armée, Fiora s'approcha du prince tandis qu'il faisait vérifier les fers de son cheval :

— Je vous ai obéi, monseigneur, dit-elle, mais j'avoue ne pas comprendre le pourquoi de ce costume. Est-ce... pour accentuer une ressemblance ?

— Oui, répondit le duc en italien. Il m'est doux, pour cette guerre, d'avoir à mes côtés l'image d'un compagnon d'autrefois... d'un compagnon que j'aimais.

— Que vous aimiez ? protesta Fiora indignée. Vous osez dire cela quand vous n'avez rien fait pour le sauver ?

— Je ne pouvais rien faire. Le crime était sans pardon possible car il offensait Dieu autant que l'humanité. Mieux valait, cent fois, que cette tête tombât sur l'échafaud plutôt que l'enfouir dans quelque cul-de-basse-fosse. Jean était mon ami. Nous avons lu Plutarque ensemble, navigué ensemble au large de Gorcum, jouté ensemble, bu et ri ensemble. Il pouvait espérer de mon amitié un grand état, une belle alliance et cependant... cependant, continua-t-il avec une brusque flambée de colère, il est parti sans même un mot, il a rejeté tout cela, renié tout cela pour le corps d'une femme qui était sa sœur. Alors que je le croyais pur, il était comme tous les autres, comme mon père que le premier jupon venu mettait en folie... pire que tous les autres !

— Non, dit Fiora doucement. Il était seulement victime

d'un amour impossible, défendu... mais c'était tout de même de l'amour.

Il la regarda avec, dans les yeux, une sorte d'égarement.

— Vous croyez ?

— J'en suis certaine. Et vous aussi monseigneur... sinon, pourquoi serais-je auprès de vous et sous ces vêtements ?

— C'est vrai. Il m'a... beaucoup manqué. Vous me donnez l'illusion de sa présence, d'autant plus précieuse que vous avez l'âge qu'il avait alors... Eh bien, ajouta-t-il en français, est-ce enfin fini ?

Le maréchal-ferrant avait achevé son ouvrage. Le duc s'enleva en selle et rejoignit, au trot, le Grand Bâtard qui l'appelait. Fiora le regarda s'éloigner sans parvenir à comprendre d'où venait le bizarre sentiment, assez proche de la pitié, qu'elle éprouvait soudainement...

Depuis, il s'était montré plein de gentillesse à son égard, surtout pendant les quinze jours que l'on avait passés à Besançon pour adjoindre à l'armée quelques compagnies comtoises. Il était même étonnant de constater que, du jour où il avait su la vérité sur la naissance de Fiora, le duc avait complètement changé d'attitude envers elle. De hargneux et méprisant, il s'était fait presque amical alors que le contraire eût été plus normal. Parfois, le soir, il l'invitait à venir écouter ses chanteurs et même, ayant découvert qu'elle savait jouer du luth et possédait une jolie voix, il la faisait chanter en duo avec Battista Colonna et il lui arrivait de chanter avec eux. Les seuls bénéficiaires de ces concerts intimes étaient Antoine de Bourgogne et l'ambassadeur milanais.

Fiora noua vite amitié avec Jean-Pierre Panigarola. C'était un homme d'une quarantaine d'années, avec ce visage étroit et méditatif que l'on voit à certaines statues de saints – mais il n'en avait que l'apparence. Fin, cultivé, sachant manier l'humour, il était un observateur attentif de la nature humaine et un excellent diplomate. Presque chaque jour, il écrivait de longues lettres au duc de Milan,

Galeazzo-Maria Sforza, son maître, et Fiora découvrit rapidement qu'il connaissait le Téméraire mieux que ses propres frères. De même qu'il semblait se retrouver fort aisément dans la politique sinueuse de Louis XI, auprès duquel il avait rempli avec succès des fonctions d'ambassadeur avant que la mort de Francesco Sforza, père du duc actuel, grand chef d'État et ami du roi de France, ne vînt renverser les alliances et tourner Milan vers la Bourgogne.

Le faux garçon, nourri de Platon, de Sophocle et d'Hésiode, l'enchantait d'autant plus qu'il savait parfaitement que c'était une femme ravissante et qu'il appréciait les filles d'Ève en amateur éclairé de la beauté sous toutes ses formes.

— Vous devriez être florentin, lui dit un soir Fiora en riant. Je crois que vous en avez les qualités et peut-être les défauts...

— Je me trouve fort bien d'être milanais, encore que notre ville ne se puisse comparer à la cité du Lys Rouge. Néanmoins, j'avoue que je vous envie le seigneur Lorenzo! Quelle intelligence! quelle profondeur de vues! Je ne vois guère que le roi de France pour lui être comparé...

— N'admirez-vous donc pas Monseigneur Charles?

Panigarola hocha la tête et se mit à contempler d'un air songeur la coupe de précieux verre de Venise emplie de vin à travers laquelle les flammes d'un chandelier faisaient scintiller des rubis :

— Il me fascine et il m'effraie. Il est le dernier représentant d'une époque révolue, d'une race en voie de disparition. Le dernier féodal, le dernier chevalier peut-être, l'élève de Jacques de Lalaing toujours captif des exploits de ce paladin errant qui usa sa vie à courir l'Europe pour y rompre des lances en joutes et tournois et se mesurer aux meilleures épées connues. La vie de chaque jour avec ses contraintes, ses petitesses aussi lui échappe complètement. Il a été trop riche et trop puissant trop tôt... Il ne s'est jamais soucié de ses peuples destinés seulement, selon lui, à produire richesse et puissance guerrière et il est triste de penser que de l'énorme fortune léguée par son père, le duc Philippe, il ne reste rien à l'exception des joyaux et des objets précieux...

— Rien ? Je sais qu'il lui arrive de faire appel à des banques étrangères, mais je ne pensais pas... ?

— Qu'il en était là ? Malheureusement si. Il vit dans un rêve de gloire et d'hégémonie quasi européenne car il se veut le plus grand capitaine de son temps. Malheureusement pour lui, il est affronté à un roi qui est peut-être l'homme le plus intelligent et le moins pourvu de scrupules qui soit. Le superbe bourdon doré pourrait bien se prendre dans la toile que tisse patiemment « l'universelle aragne »...

— Mais le roi Louis n'a-t-il pas signé la trêve de Soleuvre ?

— Bien sûr que si, mais vous ne vous imaginez pas qu'il se tient tranquille pour autant ? Certes, ses troupes ne bougent pas des frontières et il a refusé d'aider le duc de Lorraine pour ne pas renier sa signature de façon trop évidente, mais il fait la guerre autrement.

— Comment cela ?

— La fille de Francesco Beltrami... que j'ai eu le plaisir de connaître, devrait me comprendre aisément car la guerre du roi Louis est une guerre économique. Il a certes une puissante armée, mais c'est son or qu'il fait marcher et soyez certaine que les Suisses que nous allons attaquer étourdiment en ont reçu une bonne part. En outre, Louis anémie le commerce flamand et les foires bourguignonnes par une concurrence systématique. Ses navires détournent les bateaux génois et vénitiens des ports bourguignons d'Anvers et de l'Écluse qui approvisionnent Bruges, ce qui enrage les Flamands. Il interdit les expéditions de blé. Sa main est partout... Il a réussi à réconcilier Sigismond d'Autriche et les Cantons, cependant ennemis farouches jusque-là. Il a renvoyé, toujours avec de l'or, les Anglais hors de France...

— Il n'y avait pas que de l'or. Il y avait du vin et des victuailles...
— Je sais. Les Parisiens en ont même fait une chanson.

> *J'ai vu roi d'Angleterre*
> *Amener son gros ost*
> *Pour la française terre*
> *Conquérir bref et tôt*
> *Le roi voyant l'affaire*
> *Si bon vin leur donna*
> *Que l'autre sans rien faire*
> *Content s'en retourna*

— Inutile d'ajouter que Monseigneur Charles a trouvé proprement scandaleuses et la chanson et la manière de se débarrasser d'un ennemi, ajouta Panigarola en riant...

Grâce à lui, ce soir-là, Fiora ne s'abandonna pas trop aux regrets et au désenchantement qui ne pouvaient que l'assaillir : il y avait un an tout juste qu'elle avait mis sa main dans celle de Philippe et s'était unie à lui en croyant fermement que c'était pour toujours. Mais la fin de la nuit fut plus pénible car en dépit de la fatigue d'une journée de cheval par un temps affreux, elle ne réussit pas à trouver un seul instant de sommeil...

Le 11 février 1476, le Téméraire remporta, sans coup férir d'ailleurs, sa première victoire. L'interminable cortège de ses troupes franchit le col de Jougne et vint s'installer dans Orbe qui était à trois lieues et demie du col et à pareille distance de Grandson, but premier de l'expédition. En même temps, les lances italiennes de Pierre de Lignana, qui constituaient l'avant-garde et s'étaient dirigées vers le lac Léman, récupérèrent Romont sur les confédérés. Mais le plus important c'était Grandson, une ville et un fort château situés à l'extrémité sud du lac de Neuchâtel.

En fait et en l'occurrence, le Téméraire ne voulait que reprendre ce qui, un an auparavant, était de son obédience. En 1475, les gens des cantons de Berne, Bâle et Lucerne, décidés à conquérir le pays de Vaud appartenant à la Savoie, ont fait sauter ce verrou bourguignon dont le seigneur, Hughes de Chalon-Orange, s'ennuyait alors devant Neuss avec le reste de l'armée du duc Charles. Grandson, solidement défendue par le bailli Pierre de Jougne mais envahie par les paysans refluant des campagnes, n'a pas résisté longtemps à la famine et à l'artillerie lourde des Suisses. A l'automne, le pays de Vaud tout entier tombait dans leurs mains alors sans tendresse. Seule Genève échappait à la dévastation en payant une rançon de 26 000 florins d'or qui coûta leurs bijoux aux dames de la ville et leurs cloches aux églises...

Le 19, on arrive enfin devant Grandson par un temps vraiment affreux : il pleut, il neige et il fait froid :

— On ne peut pas dire que la France et la Bourgogne vous aient réservé leurs plus beaux sourires, fit Léonarde que Fiora avait rejointe dans son chariot tandis que tentes et pavillons se montaient. A part la canicule, vous n'avez guère connu que la pluie, le vent et les pires intempéries... Vit-on jamais automne et hiver semblables ?

— Vous avez peut-être un peu oublié votre jeunesse, répondit Fiora. A Florence le temps est si doux !... Il est vrai que lorsque l'on a perdu quelque chose ou quelqu'un on ne se souvient plus que de ses qualités.

Le Téméraire avait choisi d'établir son camp près de Giez. Ses pavillons de pourpre et d'or couronnèrent superbement une colline [1] tandis que cinq cents autres tentes d'une grande richesse et des centaines de bannières multicolores étalaient sur les environs le plus fabuleux des tapis. Le reste du camp, celui en « rase campagne », couvrait la plaine en demi-cercle, entre la ville et la montagne, et s'étendait jusqu'à l'Arnon, une

---

1. Si superbement que le souvenir en est resté et que la colline s'appelle encore aujourd'hui « le Duc de Bourgogne »...

étroite rivière débouchant dans le lac près d'une lieue plus loin.

— Grandson ne devrait nous donner aucun mal, confia le duc Charles à Panigarola et à Fiora tandis qu'ensemble ils regardaient la nuit tomber sur le lac dont les lointains se perdaient dans une brume glacée et la ville tassée derrière les cinq tours de son château. Depuis trois semaines déjà, les bourgeois se sont emparés du chef de la garnison bernoise, Brandolphe de Stein, et nous l'ont livré... Il est captif en Bourgogne.

— Comment se fait-il alors que les portes ne soient pas grandes ouvertes et qu'aucune délégation ne soit encore venue à vous, monseigneur ? fit l'ambassadeur. Je crois, moi, qu'ils vont se défendre durement. Ce sont de bons soldats que les Suisses...

— Ces bouviers, ces paysans ? lança le duc méprisant. Nous n'aurons aucune peine à les balayer. Qu'ils prennent garde à ma colère car je pourrais porter la guerre dans les cantons de la Haute Ligue [1].

— Ce que je ne saurais conseiller à Votre Seigneurie car, dans certains d'entre eux, la rudesse des montagnes double la valeur des hommes...

— C'est ce que nous verrons !

Le siège de Grandson dura neuf jours, neuf jours pendant lesquels bombardes, couleuvrines et fauconneaux dirigèrent, même la nuit, un feu meurtrier sur la petite cité. A l'intérieur du château, des incendies se produisirent, allumés par des brandons enflammés et par l'explosion de la soute à poudre qui détruisit en partie le beau logis seigneurial... La fin était d'ailleurs prévisible, cinq cents hommes ne pouvant lutter contre quinze mille. Bientôt, bloquée de toutes parts et démoralisée d'ailleurs par l'absence de son chef, la garnison se rendit. Alors commença l'horreur...

---

1. Berne, Fribourg, Bâle, Zurich, Lucerne, Uri, Schwyz, Soleure et Unterwalden composaient la Haute Ligue cependant que dix villes alsaciennes formaient la Basse Ligue, ennemie elle aussi du Téméraire après les exactions de son bailli, Pierre de Hagenbach.

Debout derrière le duc au milieu des seigneurs qui composaient son état-major, Fiora, Panigarola et Battista Colonna, pétrifiés, assistaient au carnage. Du haut de la tour Pierre, les Bourguignons précipitaient les soixante-dix défenseurs du chemin de ronde au milieu des rires et des quolibets en criant très fort qu'il était temps pour eux d'apprendre à voler sans ailes... Cependant, au pied des murailles, les quatre cents autres soldats de la garnison étaient pendus par grappes de trois ou quatre aux arbres d'un bois situé aux abords du château ou bien noyés dans le lac avec une pierre au cou...

L'ambassadeur milanais ne put retenir une protestation indignée :

— Est-ce façon, monseigneur, de traiter des soldats ? Ils se sont battus parce que c'était leur devoir. Pardonnez-moi mais ceci est indigne d'un grand chef de guerre.

— Allons ! Ces gens ne méritent pas d'autre traitement. Souvenez-vous que leurs pareils ont dévasté plusieurs cités du pays de Vaud... Il en arrivera autant d'ailleurs à tous les Suisses qui me tomberont sous la main.

— Encore une fois, monseigneur, ce sont des soldats ! et ils se sont rendus...

— Je vous trouve bien sensible, Panigarola ? Cela servira de leçon à ce ramassis de marchands, de toucheurs de bœufs et de chasseurs...

— Certains de ces chasseurs traquent l'aigle et l'ours.

— Et je dis, moi, que c'est une infamie ! cria Fiora qui ne pouvait plus contenir son indignation. Tuer des hommes désarmés est une lâcheté à laquelle je refuse d'assister plus longtemps !

Tournant les talons et bousculant ses voisins, elle prit sa course en direction du camp, gagna sa tente où Léonarde lisait ses heures et y pénétra en trombe :

— Venez, Léonarde ! Nous partons. Je vais chercher des chevaux. Emballez vite le peu que nous possédons et préparez-vous !

— Que se passe-t-il ?

— Le duc Charles est en train de faire assassiner les malheureux qui se sont rendus ce matin. Il arrivera ce qu'il arrivera mais je ne resterai pas auprès de ce bourreau une minute de plus !

— Enfin ! soupira la vieille demoiselle en se précipitant sur un sac de cuir qu'elle se mit en devoir de remplir. Voilà des jours que j'espérais cela !

— Vous êtes contente de partir ? Par le temps qu'il fait et alors que je ne sais même pas où nous allons ?

— Il tomberait des hallebardes et des grêlons gros comme le poing que je me précipiterais dehors quand même. Quant à savoir où nous allons, je vous le dirai tout à l'heure. Allez chercher les chevaux !

Un moment plus tard, les deux femmes galopaient sur la route de Montagny dans l'intention de refaire le chemin parcouru à l'aller et de repasser le col de Jougne puisque c'était le seul itinéraire qu'elles connussent. La route défoncée par le passage de l'armée et de l'artillerie serait au moins facile à suivre...

Soudain, à un détour du chemin, elles virent se dresser devant elles ce qui leur parut être un mur de fer : une cinquantaine de chevaliers armés de toutes pièces, en tête desquels Fiora, dont le cœur manqua un battement, reconnut les aigles d'argent sur champ d'azur. D'ailleurs, la visière relevée du casque ne laissait aucun doute sur l'identité de son propriétaire. Fiora hésita un instant mais constata vite que toute échappatoire était impossible et elle décida de faire front...

En dépit de son déguisement, Philippe la reconnut aussitôt.

— Vous ?... Et dans cet équipage ? Mais où prétendez-vous aller ? Et avant que Fiora ait pu répondre, il ajoutait : je suis heureux de vous revoir, dame Léonarde, mais je vous croyais plus de sens.

Il avança son cheval jusqu'à toucher celui de Fiora et ne put s'empêcher de sourire :

— Quel charmant garçon vous êtes ! Mais, pour l'amour du ciel, dites-moi ce que vous faites là ?

— C'est assez évident il me semble ? Je pars, je m'enfuis, je me sauve ! L'otage a pris la clé des champs ! lança-t-elle avec colère. Pour tout l'or du monde, je ne resterai pas un instant de plus, quoi qu'il puisse arriver, auprès de ce monstre qu'est votre duc !

— Le duc un monstre ? Mais que vous a-t-il fait ?

— A moi ? rien... encore qu'il y ait peut-être matière à discussion, mais là n'est pas la question. Je viens de voir comment il traite les soldats de Grandson dont la seule faute est d'avoir osé lui résister. Ils se sont rendus à merci et on les massacre, par dizaines. On les jette du haut des remparts, on les pend ou les noie afin qu'il n'en reste plus un seul pour appeler sur votre maître la vengeance du ciel. Ce qui n'empêche qu'elle l'atteindra un jour !

Le silence qui suivit traduisit la gêne de Philippe qui avait pâli :

— Quand la colère le prend, il peut être effrayant, je le sais et...

— En colère, lui ? Pas le moins du monde. Il sourit et même il rit tant il trouve plaisant le spectacle...

— Il semble d'ailleurs coutumier du fait, dit paisiblement Léonarde. J'ai entendu parler de ses exploits à Dinant et à Liège où il n'a même pas accordé la vie sauve aux chats !

— Laissez, chère Léonarde ! Vous ne convaincrez pas messire de Selongey. Le Téméraire est son dieu... mais moi qui préfère en servir un plus clément, je vous prie de nous livrer passage afin que nous puissions continuer notre voyage.

— Etes-vous si pressées ? temporisa Philippe. J'avoue que j'espérais vous voir en rejoignant le camp...

— Nous n'avons plus grand-chose à nous dire, Philippe. J'ai demandé que notre mariage soit annulé. Ainsi vous serez libre et le cher duc sera content. Je crois qu'il vous tient en réserve quelque grande dame...

— Que voulez-vous que j'en fasse ? cria Selongey que le ton de persiflage de la jeune femme agaçait. Quant à cette annulation, je n'en veux pas. Je n'ai aimé et n'aimerai jamais que vous, Fiora, et quoi que vous ayez pu faire...

— Ce que « j'ai » pu faire ? Apparemment ce serait vous qui auriez quelque chose à me reprocher ?

— Il me semble, oui ! Avez-vous déjà oublié... Thionville ?

— Inutile de crier et de réjouir vos compagnons avec nos querelles. J'en vois plus d'un sourire. Il est vrai que les distractions anodines sont plutôt rares dans ce pays. Mais, dans quelques instants vous pourrez leur offrir beaucoup mieux : des arbres supportent des grappes humaines. Le duc vous expliquera que c'est le summum du comique. A présent, je veux passer !

— Je ne vous laisserai pas partir ! dit Philippe en s'emparant de la bride du cheval de Fiora.

A cet instant d'ailleurs, un nouveau cavalier, lancé au galop, débouchait du tournant de la route et dut faire preuve d'une réelle science équestre pour arrêter sa monture avant la collision.

— Donna Fiora ! s'écria Battista Colonna. Dieu soit loué ! je vous retrouve !

— Vous me cherchiez ?

— Monseigneur vous cherche. Il ordonne que vous rentriez au camp immédiatement. J'ai ordre de vous ramener à tout prix.

— Voilà qui est fait, Battista. A présent, vous pouvez retourner dire à votre maître que je refuse de revenir. Il a exigé que je le suive dans cette guerre mais je ne m'en sens vraiment plus le courage. J'en ai vu plus que je n'en peux supporter. Dites-le-lui !...

— Ah !

Le jeune garçon devint très rouge et détourna la tête.

— C'est là votre dernier mot ? murmura-t-il.

— Absolument... Pardonnez-moi, Battista ! Je sais que je vous confie là une mauvaise commission mais...

— Je crois qu'elle est même plus mauvaise encore que vous ne l'imaginez, intervint Philippe. Que se passera-t-il si donna Fiora ne revient pas avec nous, Colonna? Je jurerais que vous en répondez... peut-être même sur votre tête?

— Ce n'est pas possible! protesta Fiora. Il ne peut pas rendre cet enfant responsable de ma conduite?

— C'est très possible au contraire. Quand le duc Charles entre en fureur, il ne raisonne plus, ne se contrôle plus... et vous l'avez peut-être offensé gravement? Que lui avez-vous dit?

— Je ne sais plus exactement mais je crois que j'ai parlé d'infamie... de lâcheté... Battista, je vous en prie, dites-moi la vérité! Messire de Selongey a-t-il raison?

Pour toute réponse le jeune Colonna baissa la tête...

— C'est indigne! fit Fiora avec dégoût. Comment peut-on abuser à ce point de son pouvoir! Et vous, Philippe, comment pouvez-vous servir un tel maître?

— Je connais ses défauts mais aussi ses qualités. En outre, il a reçu mon allégeance lorsqu'il m'a armé chevalier et derechef lorsqu'il m'a conféré la Toison d'or...

— Moi aussi j'ai reçu votre serment, dit Fiora doucement.

— L'un ne me délie pas de l'autre. Je reviens vers lui pour me battre à ses côtés contre les Suisses dont l'armée se rassemble. D'autre part, j'ai un message de la duchesse de Savoie qui a quitté Turin pour sa ville de Genève. Il faut que je le voie... mais vous, si cela vous est trop pénible, partez! Rentrez en Bourgogne! Allez m'attendre à Selongey! Je vais ramener Battista et croyez-moi, il ne lui arrivera rien! C'est moi qui en réponds!

Un instant ils se regardèrent au fond des yeux et, dans le cœur de Fiora, quelque chose s'épanouit, s'illumina. Se pouvait-il que les temps douloureux eussent pris fin et que le bonheur pût renaître? Le regard de Philippe était brûlant d'amour comme il l'était durant la nuit de Fiesole et, pour ce regard-là, Fiora savait qu'elle était déjà prête à endurer bien des souffrances... Elle lui sourit avec une tendresse infinie...

— A moins qu'il ne vous supprime tous les deux ? C'est un risque que je ne veux pas courir... Rentrons, Battista ! Et vous, Philippe, poursuivez votre chemin mais... s'il vous plaît... prenez bien soin de vous!

Elle posa sa main sur le gantelet de fer et une joyeuse étincelle s'alluma dans les yeux noisette du jeune homme :

— Allez donc parler d'amour à la dame de vos pensées sous cette ferraille! murmura-t-il. Ne pensez plus à cette stupide annulation, ma douce! Vous êtes mon épouse bien-aimée... et il faudra bien que le Téméraire s'y fasse!

Un quart d'heure plus tard, Fiora et Léonarde avaient regagné le camp des Bourguignons. Battista Colonna les déposa chez elles et s'en allait rendre compte de sa mission lorsque, sur le point de quitter la jeune femme, il mit genou en terre devant elle :

— Je n'oublierai jamais ce que vous venez de faire pour moi, madonna. Vous pourrez me demander ma vie si un jour vous en avez besoin...

— Voilà un jour qui ne viendra jamais, Battista, mais je vous remercie tout de même!

Quand elle l'eut vu s'éloigner, elle se tourna vers Léonarde qui, avec la grande philosophie qui était sienne, sortait les vêtements des sacs pour les replacer dans les coffres :

— Qu'entendiez-vous tout à l'heure quand vous m'avez dit que nous parlerions plus tard de l'endroit où nous pourrions aller ?

Léonarde ne répondit pas tout de suite comme si elle hésitait puis, tirant d'un étui de velours un rouleau de parchemin, elle le garda entre ses mains :

— Je pensais ne vous donner ceci que lorsque nous aurions recouvré notre liberté mais, dans le fond, je peux aussi bien vous le remettre maintenant : le roi Louis vous a fait don d'un petit castel en pays de Loire, non loin de sa demeure de Plessis-lez-Tours pour vous remercier des peines endurées à son service. Il y a ici le titre de propriété... et un message du roi...

Elle lui tendit le rouleau que Fiora repoussa :

— Je ne crois pas que je l'habiterai jamais. Ma vie, après tout, pourrait bien se fixer en Bourgogne. Oh, Léonarde, vous n'imaginez pas comme je suis heureuse ! Je n'aurais jamais imaginé que c'était encore possible. Il me semble que je reviens à la vie après une longue, longue maladie... Nous renverrons ceci au roi avec un beau remerciement.

— Sans doute, sans doute... mais ne nous hâtons pas ! Quelque chose me dit que vous n'en avez pas encore fini avec Monseigneur Charles. C'est un homme avec lequel il faut compter...

Et Léonarde rangea soigneusement l'étui de velours rouge.

A la grande surprise de Fiora, le Téméraire, lorsqu'il la revit le lendemain, ne fit aucune allusion à ce qui s'était passé mais il dit au jeune Colonna, assez haut pour être entendu de la jeune femme.

— Ce que j'ai exprimé hier vaut pour demain. Je t'ai confié une personne que je tiens à garder, Battista ! Veille à ce qu'elle ne s'écarte plus...

Le sourire de la jeune femme réconforta l'enfant. Pour rien au monde, à présent, Fiora ne s'éloignerait du camp bourguignon puisque Philippe l'avait réintégré...

Ô la joie de le voir venir avec le Grand Bâtard pour prendre les ordres dans le pavillon ducal, de rencontrer son regard et son sourire ! Un instant, ils furent seuls tous les deux et la foule chamarrée qui se pressait autour du Téméraire disparut. Mais ce fut très court et il fallut bien revenir sur terre. Philippe allait repartir avec Antoine et l'avant-garde de l'armée que le duc chargeait, afin de préparer son avance prochaine vers Neuchâtel, de s'emparer du château de Vaumarcus, clé du passage le long du lac.

En effet, la longue plaine accidentée qui s'étendait entre les monts du Jura et l'immense nappe d'eau était large d'une demi-lieue à la hauteur de Grandson mais allait en se rétrécissant pour se trouver enfin coupée par un éperon boisé qui, de la montagne, descendait jusqu'au rivage. Deux routes seulement permettaient de franchir cet obstacle : l'une, la « Via Detra » qui suivait au flanc de la montagne le tracé d'une ancienne voie romaine et l'autre qui longeait le lac dont les lointains se perdaient vers le nord. Vaumarcus commandait cette seconde voie...

Le duc expliqua :

— Notre belle cousine Madame la duchesse de Savoie nous a donné avis des bruits qui courent le pays de Vaud. Quelques milliers d'hommes des Cantons menés par ceux de Berne se rassembleraient à Neuchâtel pour marcher ensuite contre nous. Ils ne sont guère à craindre pour les guerriers que nous sommes mais nous allons tout de même les gagner de vitesse...

— Pourquoi ne pas les attendre ici ? fit le Grand Bâtard. Le camp est bien protégé, tant par le cours de l'Arnon et par les fossés et autres ouvrages que nous avons établis que par nos canons. En outre, ces montagnards ont peu de cavalerie. La nôtre, en plaine, pourrait s'éployer largement...

— Peut-être mais je crois que notre meilleure alliée est la rapidité. Allez vous assurer de Vaumarcus pour nous y appuyer au besoin. Ensuite je mettrai l'armée en marche. L'effet de surprise jouera pleinement et nous tomberons sur Neuchâtel avant même que ces gens aient formé de véritables corps de troupe.

— Donc vous levez le camp ?

— Non. Rien ne presse. Je vous l'ai dit, la vitesse est notre arme la meilleure et nous ne pouvons nous encombrer des chariots de bagages, des registres de la Chancellerie et de toutes ces femmes que nous traînons après nous. Croyez-moi, nous allons faire là une promenade militaire et nous serons devant Neuchâtel sans avoir peut-être besoin de tirer l'épée.

— Emmenez-vous les ambassadeurs[1] ?

---

1. Inquiet, le duc de Milan avait envoyé en effet trois ambassadeurs extraordinaires, un Palavicini, un Visconti et un Grimaldi pour être encore mieux informé. Le Téméraire refusa de les garder et les renvoya à Orbe.

— Pour ce qui me concerne, dit Panigarola, je suivrai monseigneur à moins qu'il ne me le défende. Ne suis-je pas les yeux et les oreilles de mon noble maître ? Sa voix aussi parfois...

— Vous êtes plus qu'un ambassadeur car nous avons de l'amitié pour vous, fit le duc aimablement. Vous serez à nos côtés...

— Puis-je espérer que vous y serez seul ? fit audacieusement Philippe les yeux sur Fiora. Certains pages me semblent un peu fragiles pour le poids de l'armure...

Le Milanais surprit ce regard et sourit :

— Monseigneur le duc laisse au camp ses trésors. Avec sa permission, j'en ferai autant de celui qu'il m'a confié.

Le lendemain 1ᵉʳ mars, le château de Vaumarcus tombait sans coup férir aux mains des Bourguignons qui y placèrent garnison et, à l'aube du samedi 2 mars, l'armée s'ébranla pour ce que le duc avait appelé « une promenade militaire »...

Le souvenir de ce matin frileux devait rester longtemps gravé dans la mémoire de Fiora. Debout au seuil de sa tente, serrant autour d'elle le grand manteau fourré que le duc Charles lui avait donné, elle le regarda s'éloigner dans la plaine, statue de fer couronnée d'un lion d'or, sur le puissant destrier le Moro, son cheval favori que le caparaçon d'acier changeait en bête apocalyptique et sous la flamme ondoyante de son étendard haut tenu par un chevalier banneret. Autour de lui, des chevaliers de la Toison d'or que distinguaient seulement leurs écus : un monde fantastique de griffons, de léopards, d'alérions, de taureaux, de chimères et de sirènes... Une fleur de lis d'or dont les pointes étaient des pierres précieuses dansait sur la tête du cheval ducal, symbole dérisoire et jamais abandonné de ce sang royal français que cependant le Téméraire abhorrait...

Le jour qui se lève est gris, le ciel blême... Sur la gauche, le mont Aubert et le Chasseron sont encore enneigés et le lac a des reflets de mercure... Tout là-bas, l'avant-garde, revenue de Vaumarcus, serpente à travers les vignes sur la « via Detra » cependant que le gros de l'armée contourne Grandson pour suivre le chemin de la rive et finir par disparaître. Mais cette armée semble bizarre à celle qui l'observe : le duc n'a pas pris soin de la ranger en bataille ; elle progresse sans discipline et même avec une sorte de laisser-aller. Il est vrai qu'en principe on ne va pas se battre mais parcourir une certaine distance pour aller surprendre les Suisses chez eux... C'est tout juste si l'on n'espère pas les trouver à table.

Ce que le Téméraire n'imagine pas un seul instant, c'est qu'à Neuchâtel s'est rassemblée une armée qui réunit des soldats d'élite, les meilleurs d'un pays qui en comporte presque autant que d'habitants mâles. Il y a là ceux de Bâle, venus avec un contingent de Strasbourg, ceux de Fribourg, de Soleure, de Bienne, de Baden et de Thurgovie. L'avoyer Hassfürter a mené de Lucerne mille neuf cents hommes. Heinrich Göldli et Hans Waldmann ont conduit les gens de Zurich tandis que Schachnachthal et Hallwyll sont à la tête des sept mille hommes de Berne. Schwyz a envoyé le tiers de sa population sous le commandement de Rudolph Reding, soit mille deux cents hommes et les petits cantons montagnards d'Uri et d'Unterwalden chacun cinq cents. En tout quinze à vingt mille hommes qui, eux aussi et à la même heure que les Bourguignons, se sont mis en marche vers Grandson pour venger leurs frères massacrés... Charles va trouver en face de lui la plus redoutable infanterie d'Europe mais il ne le sait pas encore et il devise agréablement au long du chemin avec son autre demi-frère Baudoin, avec le prince d'Orange, avec Jean de Lalaing et Olivier de La Baume...

Vers midi, Fiora et Battista qui jouaient aux échecs s'arrêtèrent et se tournèrent d'un même mouvement vers le nord. Dans le lointain, un bruit étrange se faisait entendre : une sorte de long mugissement que la distance atténuait mais qui, sur place, devait être effrayant. Cela s'arrêtait puis reprenait et la jeune femme sentit un frisson glacé courir le long de son dos :

— Qu'est-ce que c'est ? demanda-t-elle.

— Ma foi, je n'en sais rien, dit Léonarde qui cousait assise auprès de la table et qui, à tout hasard, fit un signe de croix.

— J'ai entendu dire, fit le page d'une voix changée, que les montagnards suisses ont de grandes trompes dans lesquelles ils soufflent et que l'on peut entendre à plusieurs lieues... Si c'est bien cela, c'est que...

— Que le duc, qui ne s'y attend pas, a rencontré les Suisses, acheva Fiora... Mon Dieu ! Ce bruit terrible vous glace le sang.

Ensemble, la jeune femme et l'enfant sortirent. Le meuglement s'était tu et c'était à présent le silence. Dans Grandson où, sur la rive, les cadavres des suppliciés n'avaient pas été dépendus, on n'apercevait aucun mouvement. Sur les chemins de ronde, les gardes étaient immobiles écoutant eux aussi... Puis, il s'éleva une grande rumeur...

— C'est trop loin pour voir quelque chose, dit Battista, mais on se bat là-bas !...

Plus personne, dès lors, ne parla. Le cœur serré, Fiora pensait à Philippe. Sa vaillance était connue. Il devait être au plus chaud de la bataille, toujours prêt à donner sa vie pour son duc... Alors, elle alla s'agenouiller auprès de Léonarde qui priait et partagea de tout son cœur son oraison...

Ce fut vers le milieu de l'après-midi que la catastrophe se produisit. On vit soudain l'armée bourguignonne, semblable à une énorme vague étalée sur la plaine, refluer en désordre, hommes, chevaux et voitures mêlés dans une effroyable confusion tandis que rugissaient de nouveau — et tellement plus proches ! — les terribles trompes d'Uri et de Lucerne que, cependant, un énorme « Sauve qui peut ! » réussissait à couvrir.

— En fuite ! articula Battista effondré. L'armée est en fuite !...

Ce qui suivit fut, pour Fiora, comme un mauvais rêve. Panigarola surgit couvert de poussière avec des taches de sang :

— Vite ! Aux chevaux ! Il faut rejoindre le duc !...

Quelques instants plus tard, Fiora se retrouva, galopant en direction d'Orbe avec Léonarde, Battista et l'ambassadeur qu'avaient rejoints son secrétaire, ses serviteurs et ses chevaux. Ils n'étaient pas seuls d'ailleurs : tous ceux qui avaient la garde du camp fuyaient, à pied, à cheval ou en voiture, sans trop savoir où ils allaient mais terrifiés par les rugissements qui se rapprochaient...

— Que s'est-il passé ? demanda Fiora.

— Une chose invraisemblable : alors que certaines de nos troupes effectuaient un repli, celui-ci a été pris pour une fuite par les troupes qui montaient en ligne. D'autant que des bandes de Suisses sortant de la forêt s'apprêtaient à attaquer par le flanc. Tout de suite ça a été la panique... une déroute sans précédent, impensable et absurde. Les deux tiers de l'armée ont fui sans avoir combattu...

— Vous avez donc rencontré les Suisses ?

— Oui. Et, je l'avoue, c'était assez effrayant. J'ai vu surgir tout à coup une phalange énorme : quelque huit mille hommes marchant au coude à coude, dardant devant eux des piques deux fois plus longues que nos lances, un gigantesque hérisson sur lequel flottaient trente bannières vertes et un grand étendard blanc. Ces gens combattent bras nus, vêtus de demi-cuirasses sur des jaques de cuir, la tête couverte de chapeaux de fer. Ils ont le visage rasé et des anneaux d'or aux oreilles. Ils ont l'air sortis d'un conte fantastique... et ils ont semé la terreur...

Se retournant sur sa selle, Fiora aperçut l'immense camp abandonné avec ses tentes magnifiques, son énorme matériel et ses canons. Un rayon de soleil rouge, apparu soudain entre deux nuages gris, fit étinceler la sphère d'or sur les grands pavillons pourpres du Téméraire :

— Est-ce que... le duc Charles abandonne vraiment tout ceci ?

Panigarola haussa les épaules :

— Cela aussi est insensé, n'est-ce pas ? Mais nous avons eu assez de mal à l'empêcher de se jeter seul au milieu des ennemis. On l'a entraîné de force... Quant à ce camp, les Suisses vont ramasser à coup sûr le plus fabuleux butin de l'Histoire [1]...

« Je crois, ajouta-t-il en retenant son cheval que nous pouvons ralentir. Personne ne nous poursuit... Les Suisses ont peu de cavalerie. En outre, le pillage va les occuper un long moment.

— Où est Monseigneur le duc ? demanda Battista.

— Devant nous. C'est à Nozeroy, en France-Comté que nous le rejoindrons. Mais nous prendrons quelque repos à l'hospice de Jougne. Je crois, fit-il avec un demi-sourire, que donna Léonarde appréciera.

— J'apprécie déjà beaucoup, messire ambassadeur, que vous m'épargniez les joies du galop bien que ce soit toujours intéressant de faire une nouvelle expérience...

Une poignée d'hommes resserrés autour d'un prince

---

[1]. Fabuleux, en effet. Outre la totalité du camp avec ses pavillons, ses vivres, ses chevaux, ses armes, ses canons et tout un matériel suffisant pour équiper une armée, les Suisses s'emparèrent des statues d'or, des reliquaires et autres objets précieux de la Chapelle ducale, du chapelet de Philippe le Bon fait de pierres précieuses, de la vaisselle d'argent, du Grand Sceau de l'État et de celui du Grand Bâtard Antoine, de centaines de vêtements brodés d'or, de tapisseries admirables, du siège doré du duc et de son fabuleux chapeau de parade, enfin de ses joyaux uniques au monde : le Grand Diamant de Bourgogne qui ne sera jamais retrouvé, celui qui deviendra le « Sancy », un grand diamant jonquille que l'on appellera « le Florentin », la « Rose d'York », la « Plumette » faite de perles, de rubis et de diamants, les « Trois frères » déjà cités, des perles énormes : la « Pérégrine » et la « Non Pareille », l'ordre de la Jarretière du duc orné de diamants et de perles, son collier de Grand maître de la Toison d'or, fabuleux joyaux pesant plusieurs kilos, d'autres joyaux encore composant un trésor digne des *Mille et Une Nuits*, les plus riches habits du Téméraire, ses coffres d'or et d'argent monnayés et cent autres choses. En résumé une pluie de richesses qui s'abattit sur la Suisse et dont on peut affirmer qu'elle constitua un bon début pour la fortune des Cantons. Encore faut-il ajouter que les Fugger purent acheter à des prix plus que raisonnables, à des gens qui n'en connaissaient pas la valeur, des joyaux qui se chiffreraient aujourd'hui en millions de dollars. Disons enfin que les musées helvétiques possèdent nombre d'objets provenant de Grandson. D'autres pièces se retrouvent dans le trésor de Vienne et certains joyaux ont fait partie des bijoux de la Couronne de France, de ceux d'Angleterre, d'Autriche et de Toscane. Le « Sancy » racheté par le président Giscard d'Estaing a fait retour à la France.

éperdu de chagrin et d'impuissante fureur, c'est tout ce qui, dans la nuit, atteignit la petite ville de Nozeroy, dressée sur sa colline balayée par les vents comme une main tendue vers le ciel. L'armée, la grande armée réunie par le duc Charles n'était plus qu'un souvenir. Non qu'elle comptât beaucoup de morts mais, à la suite des troupes italiennes qui avaient pris peur, toutes les autres s'étaient égaillées, éparpillées, dispersées dans toutes les directions. En quittant lui-même le champ de bataille, le duc avait donné des ordres pour qu'on tentât d'endiguer un peu cette panique mais c'était à peu près impossible. Les soldats, sourds et aveugles, avaient fui comme une horde de cerfs devant un incendie de forêt.

Au matin blême, les braves Comtois de la petite cité virent passer devant eux, toujours magnifique sous ses armes splendides, un homme pâle qui semblait vidé de toute vie et dont le regard fixé loin devant lui ne regardait personne. Il allait son chemin dans la neige qui étouffait le bruit des pas du cheval, marchant vers le château qui allait l'accueillir et chacun s'inclinait devant lui. Mais des chuchotements couraient dans le vent du matin car, parmi ceux des chevaliers qui escortaient le duc, ne se trouvait pas le seigneur de Nozeroy, Hughes de Chalon-Orange. Pour qu'il ne fût pas là afin d'ouvrir sa demeure au maître qu'il aimait, il fallait qu'il lui fût advenu quelque malheur et la tristesse pesa sur Nozeroy autant et plus que les sombres nuages du ciel [1]. On saluait mais, presque en se cachant, on se signait comme devant un convoi funèbre. Et le château se referma sur ce prince qui venait de regarder en face et pour la première fois le visage de la défaite... Il semblait frappé à mort.

Pourtant, quand Panigarola et ses compagnons le rejoignirent, un peu plus tard, ils trouvèrent un homme bouillonnant d'activité. Il envoyait sur toutes les routes pour qu'on lui ramène autant de fuyards que possible, il expédiait des messagers en Lorraine et en Luxembourg pour

---

1. Les Suisses devaient renvoyer plus tard son corps au duc Charles.

qu'on lui acheminât de l'artillerie, en Bourgogne et à Besançon pour avoir des vivres et de l'argent. Et surtout il parlait, il parlait, lui si volontiers silencieux. Il expliquait : cette bataille de Grandson n'était qu'un accident dû à la lâcheté de ses soldats italiens d'abord mais aussi picards, anglais et wallons. Dès qu'il aurait reconstitué de nouvelles troupes, avec d'authentiques braves cette fois, il retournerait combattre les Suisses :

— Dans huit jours au plus, déclara-t-il à Panigarola sidéré, nous reformerons le camp à Salins, à deux lieues d'ici. Olivier de La Marche à qui j'en ai écrit et qui doit être guéri prendra toutes les dispositions nécessaires...

Puis, se tournant vers Fiora qui le regardait avec de grands yeux incrédules :

— Pour votre première guerre vous n'avez pas eu de chance mais je vous promets que vous verrez mieux bientôt... très bientôt.

— Monseigneur, murmura-t-elle, pardonnez-moi d'oser vous questionner mais... sait-on des nouvelles de... du comte de Selongey ?

La flamme de gaieté factice se voila dans les yeux sombres du duc Charles.

— Non... et pas davantage de mon frère Antoine avec lequel il combattait. J'espère sincèrement qu'aucun mal ne leur est advenu car j'ai vu disparaître dans la mêlée le prince d'Orange qui avait aussi en charge une partie de l'avant-garde... Peut-être aurons-nous bientôt des nouvelles.

On en eut vers la fin du jour quand le Grand Bâtard Antoine fit son entrée dans la ville, amenant avec lui un fort escadron. A son côté, chevauchait Mathieu de Prame, livide et les yeux encore bouffis de larmes, qui vint s'abattre plutôt que s'agenouiller devant le duc. Ce qu'il avait à dire tenait en peu de mots : il avait vu Philippe de Selongey tomber, submergé par ce qui ressemblait à une lame de fond mais, emporté lui-même par l'irrésistible reflux suscité par la panique, il lui avait été impossible de lui porter secours et pas davantage de rechercher son corps.

De derrière lui, Charles entendit un faible cri, à peine une plainte. Se retournant, son regard rencontra celui de Fiora dilaté par la douleur. Elle ne pleurait pas, ne vacillait pas comme il arrive lorsque l'on va s'évanouir ; elle semblait changée en statue et seul le léger tremblement de ses lèvres disait qu'elle vivait encore. Alors, passant un bras paternel autour des épaules tétanisées :

– Viens, mon enfant, dit-il avec beaucoup de douceur, viens ! Allons pleurer ensemble...

Et il sortit avec elle...

CHAPITRE XIII

DANS UNE TENTE ABANDONNÉE...

Une étrange amitié se noua, dès lors, entre ce souverain rongé par tous les démons de l'orgueil et de la honte, auquel sa lourde défaite venait d'enseigner le doute, et cette jeune femme qui avait perdu son unique raison d'espérer. Nul ne put jamais savoir ce qui se dit durant les longues heures qu'ils passèrent ensemble dans la petite chapelle du château sous la garde du seul Battista Colonna, raide d'orgueil en dépit de la fatigue qui le ravageait...

Au matin, Fiora, les yeux secs et résolus, tendit à Léonarde une paire de ciseaux et lui ordonna de lui couper les cheveux à la hauteur du cou, à la mode italienne :

— Le duc Charles, déclara-t-elle pour mettre fin aux protestations de sa vieille amie, a juré de ne plus raser sa barbe tant qu'il n'aura pas vengé son honneur et tiré des Suisses une éclatante revanche. Moi, je ne quitterai plus le costume de garçon parce que j'ai résolu de suivre monseigneur partout où il ira jusqu'à ce que...

— Jusqu'à ce que la mort vous prenne comme elle a pris messire Philippe ? fit Léonarde navrée. Oh, mon agneau, n'existe-t-il pas d'autre chemin pour vous que celui-là ? Vous êtes si jeune !

— Quelle voie voudriez-vous que je suive ? Celle du couvent comme font beaucoup de celles dont le cœur ne peut guérir ? Je n'en ai jamais eu le goût et l'ai moins encore à présent s'il se peut.

— Qui vous dit que votre cœur ne guérira jamais ? Souvenez-vous : quand vous avez connu le comte de Selongey, vous étiez amoureuse de Giuliano de Médicis et très jalouse de monna Simonetta ?

— J'aimais tout ce qui brillait et Giuliano brillait de tant de feux ! Mais ils se sont éteints quand Philippe est apparu et j'ai compris alors que je n'aimais pas Giuliano...

— Combien j'aurais souhaité que vous ne l'apprissiez jamais ! soupira Léonarde ! Mais pour en revenir au duc, n'aviez-vous pas juré d'en tirer vengeance ?

— Je ne l'ai pas oublié mais... comment vous dire ? Il me semble qu'il est en train de se détruire lui-même et j'éprouve la même impression que lorsque j'ai vu Pierre de Brévailles cloué à sa chaise, devenu un mort vivant. Il ne demandait qu'à mourir. Lui laisser la vie était une punition plus cruelle. Démétrios qui peut voir l'avenir penserait peut-être la même chose que moi...

— C'est possible mais ce n'est pas certain. Démétrios est plus dur que vous ne le croyez. Cela dit, n'allez pas croire que je cherche à vous lancer de nouveau à la poursuite d'une vengeance que j'ai toujours redoutée. Si vous avez compris qu'il vaut mieux laisser faire Dieu...

— Dieu ? Il vient de me prendre l'homme que j'aime à l'instant même où nous nous retrouvions enfin. Je crois, décidément, qu'il n'a pas beaucoup d'amitié pour moi. Non, ne dites rien et surtout laissez-moi faire ce que j'ai décidé ! Et pour commencer, voulez-vous couper mes cheveux ou préférez-vous que je le fasse moi-même ?

— Sûrement pas ! Au moins ils ne seront pas massacrés.

Avec décision, Léonarde s'empara des ciseaux et d'un peigne puis, la mine farouche, commença à tailler dans l'épaisse chevelure en pensant, pour empêcher sa main de trembler, que des cheveux, après tout, cela repousse...

Quand Fiora rejoignit le duc le lendemain, vêtue de la tunique de velours noir qu'il lui avait envoyée, il la regarda mettre genou à terre devant lui comme l'eût fait un garçon et lui sourit :

— Quel dommage de ne pouvoir vous armer chevalier ! Mais je peux au moins faire ceci...

Il alla prendre dans un coffre ouvert une dague richement damasquinée dont la poignée était ornée d'améthyste et, faisant se relever Fiora, accrocha lui-même l'arme à sa ceinture :

— Deux de mes serviteurs, voyant le désastre, ont réussi à sauver un chariot dans lequel ils ont entassé tout ce qui leur tombait sous la main. Ceci en faisait partie. Quand nous irons au combat, je vous donnerai d'autres armes...

— Je ne veux pas d'autres armes, monseigneur. Je n'en saurais que faire. Je veux seulement vous suivre comme fait l'ambassadeur de Milan qui est toujours auprès de vous.

— Il estime que c'est encore la meilleure place pour pouvoir décrire les événements à son maître [1]. En outre j'aime causer avec lui. Mais, ajouta-t-il d'une voix où perçait une émotion, votre présence me sera douce, je l'avoue. Même si en cela je fais preuve d'un insupportable égoïsme... Je crois que je vais avoir bien besoin d'amitié...

Les jours qui suivirent furent en effet des jours sombres. Les conséquences de la défaite commençaient à se manifester par une sorte de refroidissement dans les relations diplomatiques. En dépit des lettres de Panigarola, le duc de Milan auquel on demandait de nouveaux mercenaires répondit par de vagues excuses et n'envoya rien. Le vieux René, qui devait léguer au Téméraire son comté de Provence et sa couronne de roi de Sicile et de Jérusalem, fit volte-face et, poussé par les agents de Louis XI, commença à s'intéresser à son petit-fils, ce jeune duc René à qui l'on avait pris la Lorraine.

Cependant le duc Charles subissait le contrecoup moral de ce qu'il appelait sa honte, et après une courte période d'agitation fébrile, il tomba dans une crise de noire mélan-

---

1. Le rôle d'un ambassadeur était alors assez exactement celui d'un correspondant de guerre pour un grand journal.

colie. Il s'enferma chez lui, ne tolérant personne à ses côtés. Il restait étendu, refusant la nourriture mais buvant beaucoup de vin, lui qui n'en buvait que très peu. Il ne se lavait plus et, dans son visage creusé où la barbe naissante mettait son ombre noire, les yeux sombres brûlaient d'un feu désespéré...

– Il est assez sujet à ces crises de dépression, confia le Milanais à la jeune femme. C'est son sang portugais qui les lui apporte. Là-bas on appelle cela la « saudade » mais j'avoue que celle-ci est plus grave que les autres. Il faudrait faire quelque chose mais quoi ?

– Il aime tant la musique ! Pourquoi ne pas lui amener les chanteurs de sa chapelle ?

– Pardonnez-moi cette image hardie, ma chère Fiora, mais le diable seul sait où ils sont, ceux-là !

– Croyez-vous qu'il soit possible de trouver un luth ou une guitare dans cette cité des vents ?

Le château du défunt Hughes de Chalon était mieux pourvu que Fiora ne le pensait et le soir même, tenant un luth d'une main et Battista Colonna de l'autre, elle s'installa sur le coin d'un coffre dans la petite pièce qui servait d'antichambre et, après un court conciliabule avec son jeune compagnon, entama le prélude d'une chanson française déjà ancienne mais que l'on chantait un peu partout en Europe. Gardant un œil inquiet sur la porte close, Battista se mit à chanter :

> *Le roi Loys est sur le pont*
> *Tenant sa fille en son giron*
> *Elle lui demande un cavalier*
> *Qui n'a pas vaillant six deniers...*

Mais cette première strophe n'était pas achevée que la porte volait plus qu'elle ne s'ouvrait sous la main furieuse du Téméraire qui apparut, titubant, la bouche mauvaise et l'œil injecté de sang :

– Qui ose ici chanter un roi Louis quel qu'il soit ?

— C'est moi, monseigneur, qui ai demandé à Battista de faire entendre cette mélodie, dit Fiora tranquillement.

— Vous vous croyez tout permis apparemment ? Je vous ai montré trop d'indulgente faiblesse et...

— C'est à vous-même que vous montrez trop de faiblesse, monseigneur. J'ai voulu vous rappeler que, tandis que vous vous laissez aller à une mélancolie hors de saison, le roi de France, lui, est toujours à l'ouvrage.

La main levée pour frapper retomba sans force le long du corps et peu à peu la fureur quitta le regard trouble que la jeune femme osait fixer. Le duc se détourna enfin pour regagner sa chambre.

— Que l'on aille chercher mes valets et que l'on m'apporte un bain ! ordonna-t-il. Quant à vous deux, continuez à chanter mais trouvez autre chose !

Le concert improvisé dura jusqu'à ce que Charles de Visen, le valet de chambre du duc, vint dire aux jeunes musiciens que son maître venait de s'endormir et qu'ils pouvaient rentrer chez eux. Il était minuit passé.

— Vous avez fait là du bon ouvrage, leur dit Panigarola qui était venu s'installer auprès d'eux pour les entendre. Je gage que la crise est passée et que demain monseigneur aura retrouvé toute son activité.

Au matin, en effet, après avoir expédié quelques dépêches dont l'une ordonnait de prendre les cloches des églises de Bourgogne pour les porter aux fondeurs de canons, le duc décida que l'on quitterait sur l'heure Nozeroy pour gagner Lausanne où il voulait réunir la nouvelle armée avec laquelle il comptait aller assiéger Berne, cheville ouvrière de son désastre, Berne où le magistrat le plus influent de la ville, Nicolas de Diesbach, menait le parti français avec son compère Jost de Silinen, tous deux amis personnels de Louis XI.

— Tant que je n'aurai pas détruit Berne, les armes de Bourgogne ne retrouveront pas leur éclat, déclara le Téméraire, et il se lança dans la préparation minutieuse de cette nouvelle campagne où il espérait restaurer sa gloire ternie.

Le Grand Bâtard Antoine et le prince de Tarente, qui avaient réussi à regrouper une partie des fuyards, choisirent d'installer le camp sur un large plateau dominant le lac Léman entre Romanet et Le Mont. On y monta la grande maison de bois qui avait abrité le duc Charles devant Neuss et qui, moins somptueuse sans doute que les pavillons perdus, en offrait tout autant de confort. Autour de ce bâtiment campèrent les nouvelles troupes que l'on avait commandées. Il en vint trois mille d'Angleterre, six mille de Bologne, six mille de Liège et du Luxembourg, enfin six mille « Savoisiens » que la duchesse Yolande amena elle-même, de Genève, à son allié le duc de Bourgogne.

La vue de cette belle femme blonde, qui avait à peu près l'âge du Téméraire, étonna Fiora. Elle ne ressemblait en rien à son frère Louis XI et montrait une féminité épanouie et rayonnante qui n'était pas sans charme. En la voyant s'avancer, souriante et les deux mains tendues vers son allié préféré, Fiora comprit soudain pourquoi cette princesse française joignait ses armes à celles du pire ennemi de son frère.

– Elle l'aime, n'est-ce pas? dit-elle à Panigarola.

– Cela n'a jamais fait pour moi aucun doute mais je la trouve bien imprudente. Le roi Louis est à Lyon et rassemble une armée de ses fidèles Dauphinois à Grenoble. Quant à mon maître, le duc de Milan, je sais qu'il a envoyé des messagers à Louis pour lui proposer un accord... et tenter de s'approprier la Savoie.

– Est-ce que vous ne devriez pas prévenir le duc Charles?

– Je n'ai reçu aucune commission officielle. En outre, s'il était question de prendre la Savoie, je serais fort étonné que le roi nous la laisse. Il n'empêche et je le répète que je trouve la belle duchesse bien peu sage...

Néanmoins, elle apportait avec elle le printemps qui éclata soudain avec l'irrésistible ardeur de la nature, le long des chemins défoncés par les charrois de guerre, sur ces terres où plus d'un village avait été rasé. L'herbe repoussait, verte et tendre sur les blessures de la terre et au milieu des ruines. Le lac, gigantesque miroir du ciel d'un bleu léger, avait des moirures d'argent et sur ses bords les amandiers et les pommiers refleurissaient. L'air était léger avec, au plein du jour, les douceurs caressantes d'un soleil peut-être décidé à faire oublier le désastreux automne et le rude hiver. A Lausanne que les malheurs avaient épargnée, la vie bouillonnait dans les rues aussi bien que dans les jardins où tout s'épanouissait. Les ambassadeurs étrangers s'y pressaient avec leur suite car il était impossible de les héberger au camp. Panigarola et ses confrères vénitiens, napolitains, gênois et autres gens d'Italie avaient élu domicile à l'auberge du Lion d'or, la plus belle de la ville. Les autres hôtelleries et les couvents étaient pleins et les marchands affluaient attirés par tant de nobles personnages.

Le point culminant fut l'arrivée commune du légat Alessandro Nanni et du protonotaire apostolique Hessler, envoyés tous deux par l'empereur pour conclure le mariage du prince Maximilien avec la jeune Marie de Bourgogne, héritière des Grands Ducs d'Occident. La messe de Pâques, célébrée dans la cathédrale de Lausanne le 14 avril, en revêtit un éclat exceptionnel.

Fiora y assista, en vêtements féminins cette fois, ses cheveux coupés cachés par un hennin de toile d'argent voilé de noir comme il convenait à son grand deuil. La veille et en présence du légat, le duc Charles l'avait, pour faire taire peut-être les inévitables bruits que sa présence auprès de lui faisait courir, reconnue solennellement pour « très noble et très haute dame comtesse de Selongey, veuve de messire Philippe de Selongey, chevalier de la Toison d'or, mort vaillamment, accablé sous le nombre sur le champ désastreux de Grandson pour l'honneur de nos armes. Puis il avait ajouté : « Désormais seule au monde, Mme de Selongey a fait vœu de nous suivre au combat afin d'y prendre part, au nom de son défunt époux, à l'éclatante vengeance qu'avec l'aide de Dieu nous allons tirer d'un ennemi indigne du sang qu'il a versé. »

Durant tout l'office pascal, Fiora eut conscience, comme elle l'avait eue la veille, de nombreux regards fixés sur elle avec plus de curiosité sans doute que de sympathie mais elle s'en souciait peu. Qu'est-ce qui pouvait avoir la moindre importance à présent que Philippe avait quitté ce monde, que ses yeux à lui ne la regarderaient plus, que ses mains ne la toucheraient plus ? Qu'on la jugeât bien ou mal ne signifiait rien. Hormis le jeune Battista et Panigarola, il n'y avait aucun de ces gens qui lui tînt par quelque lien que ce soit. Hormis le duc aussi bien sûr, mais elle n'arrivait pas à analyser le sentiment qui l'attachait à lui. C'était une sorte de fascination où entrait de la pitié et cette attirance qu'exercent ceux, très rares, dont le destin exceptionnel semble prometteur de grandes catastrophes. Il était seul à poursuivre un rêve chimérique et démesuré au milieu d'une Europe positive où la plus grande puissance, désertant les vieilles lois chevaleresques, appartenait aux plus habiles et aux plus riches... Une voix secrète soufflait à la jeune femme que l'ange de la mort suivait les pas du Téméraire et que, sans en avoir conscience, c'était l'ombre de ses ailes noires qu'il essayait de fuir, que c'était contre elle qu'il se débattait.

Depuis Nozeroy, sa santé demeurait chancelante. Il souffrait d'une fièvre constante et de maux d'estomac, passait des nuits au milieu de ses hommes sans quitter l'armure et avalait au matin les tisanes que lui préparaient Matteo de Clerici et un autre médecin envoyé par la duchesse de Savoie, inquiète de cet état, mais ce n'étaient pas ces maux, nés surtout d'un système nerveux détraqué qui menaçaient la vie du prince. Le mal résidait dans son âme qui ne parvenait plus à croire en son étoile...

Au sortir de la cathédrale, Fiora, suivie de Léonarde aussi raide et hautaine qu'une duègne espagnole, regagnait l'auberge du Lion d'or où Panigarola lui avait trouvé une chambre. Le duc ne voulait pas qu'elle séjournât alors au camp où régnait trop souvent l'indiscipline et où les rixes étaient nombreuses. Soudain elle eut l'impression que quelqu'un s'était attaché à ses pas. Elle pressa l'allure et entendit que l'on courait derrière elle. Alors, s'arrêtant brusquement, elle se retourna. Un homme d'armes était en face d'elle en qui, avec stupeur, elle reconnut Christophe de Brévailles. Il avait les yeux pleins de larmes.

— Pourquoi, fit-il avec un mélange de colère et de douleur, pourquoi m'avez-vous caché votre mariage ? Quand nous nous sommes rencontrés, vous m'avez menti ! Dans quel but ?

— Cela avait-il de l'importance ? Souvenez-vous : vous veniez de fuir votre monastère et vous vouliez être soldat. Qu'aviez-vous à faire de ma vie passée ?

— Rien, bien sûr... mais c'est en vous voyant, je crois, que j'ai tant désiré une autre vie. Acquérir la gloire, la fortune et ensuite vous rechercher afin de...

— N'en dites pas plus ! Vous saviez très bien que rien ne serait jamais possible entre nous. Vous êtes mon oncle, que cela vous plaise ou non, et moi, à présent que tout est accompli, je ne veux plus même me souvenir qu'il existe encore au monde des Brévailles.

— Tout est accompli ? Que voulez-vous dire ?

— Que Regnault du Hamel est mort, mort de peur en me voyant une nuit paraître à son chevet. Quant à votre père...

En quelques mots, Fiora raconta le retour de Marguerite au château de ses ancêtres et ce que toutes deux y avaient trouvé :

— Votre mère est en paix, ajouta-t-elle et même je crois qu'elle a retrouvé quelque chose qui ressemble au bonheur...

— Mais vous, coupa Léonarde qui observait le jeune homme avec attention, vous qui espériez tant de la vie militaire, êtes-vous plus heureux que dans votre couvent ?

— Oui, parce que j'ai trop souffert à Cîteaux mais

j'avoue volontiers que je n'aime pas beaucoup plus ce que je fais. Quand je vous ai quittés, je me suis enrôlé, en me donnant pour fils d'un artisan de Dôle, dans les troupes du comte de Chimay. Et j'ai assez vite compris mon erreur : j'enviais la vie brillante des chevaliers mais moi, n'ayant plus droit à mon propre nom, je n'avais rien à espérer que vieillir sous le harnois, au milieu des soldats avec le droit d'appeler une ribaude pour apaiser mes besoins d'amour. Et puis la guerre me fait horreur... J'ai vu trop d'atrocités...

— Alors, allez-vous-en ! fit Fiora d'une voix pressante. Rentrez chez vous ! Votre mère sera heureuse de vous revoir et vous n'avez plus rien à redouter de votre père...

Christophe secoua ses épaules comme pour en chasser la lourde tristesse qui l'accablait :

— Vous oubliez mes vœux rompus ! Je suis un moine en rupture de monastère. Que je reparaisse en Bourgogne et l'on me ramènera au couvent où je serai condamné à l'*in pace* jusqu'à ce que la mort me prenne. Je préfère encore qu'elle me trouve sur le champ de bataille, à la face du ciel plutôt qu'au fond d'une oubliette...

— Je peux peut-être vous aider encore. Le légat du pape est ici et je le connais. Si j'obtiens que vous soyez délié de vos vœux, rentrerez-vous à Brévailles ?

Christophe détourna la tête pour que son interlocutrice ne puisse lire dans son regard :

— Peut-être... mais pas maintenant ! Le duc va attaquer les Suisses et l'on dit que vous serez auprès de lui. Je veux y être aussi.

— Christophe ! soupira Fiora, il faut que vous cessiez à tout jamais de penser à moi. Cela ne me cause aucune joie et me gêne. Puisque vous avez appris mon mariage, vous savez aussi que je suis veuve...

— Vous pourrez dire ce que vous voulez. On ne commande pas à son cœur...

— Je le sais mieux que vous car j'aime d'un amour unique celui que la mort m'a enlevé et tant que j'aurai la vie, je ne cesserai pas de l'aimer. La seule chose que je souhaite, c'est le rejoindre... A présent disons-nous adieu...

— Un moment, fit Léonarde. N'oubliez pas votre promesse de parler au légat !

— C'est vrai. Sous quel nom êtes-vous engagé chez le comte de Chimay ?

— Christophe Laîné. Un grand nom comme vous voyez, fit amèrement le jeune homme.

— Tous les grands noms sont sortis d'un autre, nettement plus petit, dit Fiora avec sévérité. Même ceux des rois. Vous auriez peut-être pu faire quelque chose de celui-là mais, puisque vous regrettez le vôtre, je vais tenter de vous le rendre afin que vous puissiez rentrer chez vous en toute tranquillité...

— Vous me méprisez, n'est-ce pas ? murmura Christophe devenu tout rouge. Mme de Selongey n'a que dédain pour moi ?

— Non mais j'avoue que vous me décevez ! Il serait temps que vous deveniez un homme...

— Alors gardez votre aide et ne vous occupez plus de moi ! cria-t-il, soudain furieux et, avant que l'on ait pu le retenir, il avait fait volte-face et s'enfuyait en courant. Fiora eut un mouvement pour le suivre mais Léonarde la retint...

— Eh bien ? fit-elle, allez-vous vous mettre à courir par les rues avec une robe à traîne et un hennin haut comme une flèche de cathédrale ? Laissez ce garçon faire comme il désire même s'il ne sait pas très bien ce qu'il veut... en dehors du fait qu'il est amoureux de vous et souhaiterait ne vous quitter ni de jour ni de nuit.

— Ce dont je ne veux pas. Le mieux est, je crois, que je parle à Mgr Nanni...

— N'en faites rien pour l'instant ! Si le jeune Brévailles décide finalement de rentrer chez lui, il saura bien venir vous le dire.

Cette rencontre troubla tout de même Fiora. L'idée que

sa bonne action de l'été précédent semblait tourner mal lui était insupportable et elle regretta plus que jamais l'absence de Démétrios qui savait toujours dans quelle direction il fallait se diriger, mais Démétrios semblait l'avoir abandonnée pour s'attacher à ce jeune duc de Lorraine qui accumulait les catastrophes. Fiora n'était pas très sûre de ne pas lui en vouloir.

Dans les jours suivants, le duc Charles tomba sérieusement malade et Christophe sortit de la pensée de Fiora. Atteint d'une gastrite aiguë et d'hydropisie, les jambes enflées, défiguré par la douleur, le prince fut ramené d'urgence à Lausanne où la duchesse de Savoie lui fit préparer un appartement au château. Durant trois jours et trois nuits, on craignit sérieusement pour sa vie et ses médecins ne quittaient plus son chevet. La ville fit silence, suspendue à ce souffle haletant dont on ne savait pas s'il allait s'éteindre tout à coup.

— Si encore on avait quelque bonne nouvelle à lui porter, soupira Panigarola, cela le ranimerait un peu mais toutes celles qui arrivent sont détestables. En Lorraine, les troupes du duc René, sous les ordres du bâtard de Vaudémont, ont repris Épinal ainsi que Vezelise, Thenod et le Pont-Saint-Vincent. Personne, bien sûr, n'ose le lui dire. Ce serait peut-être empoisonner ses dernières heures.

— C'est à ce point ?

— Autant qu'on puisse le savoir. La duchesse Yolande monte la garde et ferait la sourde oreille s'il réclamait l'un de nous deux, ou tous les deux. Mais on le dit inconscient. Seul, le Grand Bâtard peut l'approcher et, hier soir, je l'ai vu sortir avec des larmes dans les yeux...

— Quel dommage ! A Florence, j'avais un ami, un grand médecin de Byzance capable de miracles...

— A Florence ? Il a dû perdre de son talent alors, car votre ville natale est en deuil, ma chère Fiora.

— En deuil ? Ce n'est pas... Monseigneur Lorenzo ?

— Non. C'est une jeune femme merveilleusement belle à ce que l'on dit et peut-être la connaissiez-vous ? On l'avait surnommée là-bas l'Étoile de Gênes...

— Simonetta ! souffla Fiora atterrée. Simonetta est morte ?

— Il y a peu de jours, dans la villa des Médicis à Piombino où on l'avait conduite dans l'espoir que l'air de la mer la guérirait, mais tout a été inutile. On l'a portée en terre le surlendemain à l'église d'Ognissanti au milieu d'un peuple en larmes...

Ainsi la prédiction de Démétrios venait de se confirmer ! Elle crut entendre la voix profonde du Grec au soir du bal tandis que tous deux regardaient Simonetta et Giuliano se sourire et se parler à voix basse : « Elle n'a plus que quinze mois à vivre. Alors Florence sera dans l'affliction mais vous ne le verrez pas... » Sincèrement désolée, Fiora pensa que Giuliano de Médicis devait être bien malheureux.... Et aussi que le monde fragile et charmant de sa jeunesse continuait de s'abîmer, peut-être de se détruire. Florence avait vécu ses plus belles fêtes, ses plus douces heures parce que c'était le sourire de Simonetta qui les inspirait.

> *Qui veut être heureux se hâte*
> *Car nul n'est sûr du lendemain*

disait la chanson prophétique de Lorenzo. Fiora pensa que, par deux fois, le bonheur était passé auprès d'elle sans qu'elle pût le saisir. Il ne repasserait pas une troisième fois...

Contrairement à ce que l'on craignait, le Téméraire se rétablit, rasa sa barbe et revint à ses affaires. Le 6 mai, encore convalescent, il signait en privé, dans sa chambre, avec le protonotaire Hessler et en présence de Mgr Nanni, l'accord de mariage entre sa fille et le fils de l'empereur. Le mariage devrait avoir lieu en novembre à Cologne ou à Aix-la-Chapelle.

C'était la seule bonne nouvelle.

Les mauvaises par ailleurs affluaient. Les Suisses poursuivaient leurs combats contre la Savoie. Les gens du

Valais tenaient la haute vallée du Rhône et, dans le Val d'Aoste, les troupes vénitiennes et lombardes recrutées pour le Téméraire ne pouvaient franchir le col du Grand-Saint-Bernard. Envoyé contre les Valaisans, le beau-frère de Yolande, le vaillant comte de Romont, avait dû battre en retraite et les Suisses avaient envahi l'est et le sud du lac Léman. De Lausanne on pouvait voir les incendies qu'ils avaient allumés... Enfin il fallut bien avouer au duc ce qui s'était passé en Lorraine.

Charles était trop faible encore pour piquer l'une de ses colères dévastatrices mais il pressa ses préparatifs. Trois jours après l'accord de mariage, il montait à cheval vêtu d'une tunique de soie brodée d'or et doublée de martre – le poids de l'armure était encore trop lourd pour ses épaules amaigries et pendant quatre longues heures alla passer la revue de ses troupes dont il avait modifié l'armement. Ainsi ses hommes avaient reçu des piques aussi longues que celles des Suisses et il avait réduit sa cavalerie. L'effectif était d'environ vingt mille combattants dont un tiers de mercenaires peu sûrs et un quart de Savoisiens fermement décidés, eux, à se battre jusqu'au dernier. Il fut décidé que le 27 mai on se mettrait en route pour Berne. L'armée, elle, allait prendre position à Morrens, à environ une lieue au nord de Lausanne. La veille du départ, Fiora, qui rejoignait le duc avec Panigarola, fit ses adieux à Léonarde qui devait rester à l'auberge du Lion d'or en compagnie de Battista. Car, bien sûr, il ne pouvait être question d'emmener la vieille demoiselle dans cette expédition militaire.

Ce furent des adieux muets. Sachant toute prière inutile devant la farouche détermination de la jeune femme, Léonarde embrassa Fiora sans rien dire mais elle la serra très fort contre elle et des larmes coulaient lentement sur son visage.

– N'ayez pas trop peur, donna Léonarda, rassura Panigarola qui vint la saluer après la sortie de Fiora. Je veillerai sur elle. Il est bien rare que l'on tue un ambassadeur...

— Mais on dit... que les Suisses ont juré de ne pas faire de prisonniers!

C'était exact. Dans tous les cantons, on avait levé un homme sur deux, ce qui représentait une puissante armée et tous avaient fait serment de tuer sur-le-champ leurs captifs.

— Sans doute. Et monseigneur en a dit autant mais je ne serai pas prisonnier non plus et donna Fiora demeurera auprès de moi. La bannière de Milan est connue. Sa vipère sera pour nous deux une bonne protection...

— Je sais que vous êtes bon et que vous l'aimez bien, messire ambassadeur,... mais elle veut mourir... et elle est l'enfant de mon cœur.

Il prit les deux mains de la vieille demoiselle et les serra :

— Je saurai bien l'en empêcher. Et puis... elle ne sait pas ce que c'est que se trouver au cœur d'une bataille. Si courageuse soit-elle, l'instinct de conservation sera le plus fort...

— Je ne la comprends plus. Faut-il qu'elle aime encore Philippe de Selongey pour en arriver là!...

— Il n'arrive jamais que ce que Dieu a voulu. Priez pour elle... mais ne vous tourmentez pas outre mesure!

Lui, cependant, n'était pas sans inquiétude. Cette campagne était une folie plus grave encore que celle de Grandson. Vaincre les Suisses ne rapporterait rien à Charles, ou si peu, alors qu'une défaite serait irrémédiable. Il eût été si simple de s'asseoir autour d'une table et de discuter... mais comment faire entendre raison à un homme obsédé par les blessures de son orgueil ? « Mourir plutôt que d'accepter la honte!... » Il ne cessait de répéter cela et tout ce que Panigarola put obtenir de lui c'était que l'armée avancerait avec une sage lenteur. En revanche, il fut impossible de l'empêcher, au lieu de se diriger droit sur Berne, d'aller mettre le siège devant la petite ville forte de Morat, au bord du lac du même nom.

— Comment ne comprend-il pas, confia le Milanais à

Fiora, qu'il va user ses forces contre cette taupinière au lieu de marcher droit sur l'ennemi ? A Grandson il n'a pas su attendre enfermé dans son camp retranché, cette fois il va s'arrêter, ce qui donnera aux Suisses tout le temps de le prendre à revers...

Mais le duc était au-delà de tout raisonnement logique. Il voulait abattre tout ce qui se trouvait sur son chemin et qui portait le nom de Suisse. Le 11 juin, il faisait investir Morat et installer son camp au bord du petit lac qu'une mince arête montagneuse séparait de celui de Neuchâtel...

Au matin du samedi 22 juin, Panigarola et Fiora, au trot paisible de leurs chevaux, effectuaient une promenade sur les arrières du camp. Il ne faisait pas beau et même il pleuvait mais ni l'un ni l'autre ne se supportait plus dans les tentes où il régnait une accablante chaleur. Il y avait eu une petite escarmouche dans la nuit du 20 au 21 mais rien de sérieux et tout était tranquille. La campagne, verte et boisée, était belle et fraîche et, en tournant le dos au camp, il était possible d'oublier un instant que l'on y était en guerre. Fiora avait même retiré le chapeau de fer que le duc l'obligeait à porter. Elle en aurait fait volontiers autant de la chemise de mailles dont il l'avait nantie quand elle lui avait refusé de s'introduire dans une armure, en disant qu'elle serait incapable de bouger sous une telle carapace. Mais Panigarola ne le lui aurait pas permis.

Les deux cavaliers avaient traversé le camp en répondant gaiement aux saluts et aux sourires qu'ils récoltaient. La jeune femme était populaire dans l'armée. Non parce qu'elle était la seule de son sexe – le Téméraire, en effet, avait fait chasser les ribaudes avant le départ de Lausanne – mais parce que l'on admirait son courage, sa gentillesse et ce vœu qu'elle avait fait de porter au combat les armes de son époux défunt pour que les aigles d'argent de Selongey puissent encore flotter au vent d'une bataille.

Fiora et son compagnon en dépit de la mise en garde des sentinelles avaient franchi la ligne de défense et atteignaient une petite éminence quand, soudain, la pluie s'arrêta et le ciel parut s'éclairer. Secouant sa tête mouillée, la jeune femme lui offrit un sourire et allait dire quelque chose quand l'ambassadeur s'écria :

– Regardez! Par Dieu... nous allons être balayés!

Des forêts avoisinantes, les Suisses jaillissaient par centaines, par milliers, arquebusiers devant, piquiers derrière. Ils couraient vers le camp ennemi qui ne les attendait pas. D'un même mouvement les deux amis firent volter leurs chevaux et foncèrent vers les palissades en hurlant à pleins poumons :

– Alerte!... Nous sommes attaqués, alerte! Le camp se referma derrière eux et avant même qu'ils eussent atteint la tente ducale, les canons et les arquebuses commençaient à tonner, étouffant l'appel lugubre des trompes montagnardes qui se faisaient entendre.

Le Téméraire était avec son médecin quand Fiora et Panigarola firent irruption chez lui.

– Vite! Mes armes, ordonna-t-il. Et tandis qu'un écuyer allait chercher son cheval, l'ambassadeur et Matteo de Clerici le bouclèrent dans son armure. Puis tous sortirent de la tente, sautèrent en selle et coururent sus à l'ennemi derrière le grand étendard que brandissait Jacques van der Maes. La bataille déjà faisait rage, les palissades étaient enfoncées, les lignes bourguignonnes rompues. Et tout de suite, Fiora épouvantée se trouva au centre d'une mêlée furieuse dans laquelle, tout à coup, elle vit s'abattre l'oriflamme de Bourgogne et celui qui la portait. Elle fit reculer son cheval pour échapper à ce piège, sans même songer à décrocher la hache d'armes qui pendait à sa selle. L'animal affolé s'enfuit vers le lac où les troupes lombardes se jetaient par paquets. Les mercenaires savaient déterminer infailliblement quand une bataille était perdue et s'efforçaient de préserver leur vie. Le lion d'or du cimier ducal était invisible et Panigarola lui-même avait disparu emporté sans doute par le flot...

Atteint d'un carreau d'arbalète, le cheval de Fiora

s'abattit. Elle s'en dégageait péniblement quand elle vit un gros Suisse qui fonçait sur elle avec une longue pique. La mort était là, devant elle, et elle en eut horreur. Pour ne pas la voir, elle ferma les yeux et, soudain, elle se sentit bousculée, jetée à terre. Un corps tomba sur le sien, qu'elle repoussa avec un cri. C'est alors qu'elle vit le Suisse courir vers une autre victime en brandissant sa pique tachée de sang... et qu'elle reconnut celui qui en avait été percé à sa place :

– Christophe !... Oh ! mon Dieu, c'est Christophe !...

La poitrine du jeune homme était couverte de sang et un filet sombre commençait à couler au coin de ses lèvres mais il ouvrit les yeux et réussit à sourire.

– Vous voyez bien... qu'il fallait me laisser faire... ce que je voulais, fit-il péniblement. Sauvez-vous, Fiora ! L'armée... est en fuite mais... la tente du duc est proche... Allez vous y cacher... et si l'on vous trouve... dites que vous êtes une femme... Il faut gagner du temps.

– Ne parlez plus ! Je vais vous tirer jusque-là, chercher de quoi vous soigner. On dirait que les Suisses s'éloignent...

– Ils... poursuivent le duc et moi... je n'ai plus... besoin... de rien. Je... je... vous... aime...

Ce fut le dernier mot. La tête de Christophe roula sur son épaule. Fiora, désolée, ferma doucement les yeux gris, semblables aux siens, que la mort n'avait pas clos, puis posa un baiser léger sur la bouche entrouverte.

Voulant regarder où en étaient les choses elle vit trouble et s'aperçut ainsi qu'elle pleurait. Elle essuya ses yeux du revers de sa main, avisa une épée abandonnée sur l'herbe et s'en saisit. La grande tente rouge – le duc en avait fait refaire une autre presque aussi belle que celle perdue à Grandson – n'était pas loin en effet et le chemin presque dégagé. Se relevant, elle allait courir vers cet abri quand un homme se dressa devant elle, brandissant une masse d'arme. Elle esquiva le coup en se baissant puis, presque d'instinct, son bras armé se détendit avec une force décuplée par la peur et la rage. L'épée s'enfonça dans le ventre du soldat qui s'écroula avec un râle de douleur. Alors, abandonnant l'arme, Fiora courut jusqu'au pavillon ducal, s'y engouffra et alla s'abattre secouée de sanglots sur le lit aux draps froissés que personne ne referait.

Combien de temps dura cette espèce de crise qui l'avait secouée des pieds à la tête quand elle avait compris qu'elle venait de tuer un homme ? Une heure ou quelques minutes ? Elle était incapable de l'évaluer et cela aurait pu durer longtemps encore si une main posée sur son épaule et qui la secouait sans ménagement n'était venue l'arracher de sa prostration :

– Assez pleuré ! fit une voix rude. Levez-vous et dites qui vous êtes...

Au son de cette voix, elle sursauta et, en un instant, elle fut debout, face à Démétrios qui la considérait avec stupeur.

– Ce n'est pas possible ? exhala-t-elle, hésitant à reconnaître le Grec dans ce guerrier casqué et couvert d'une tunique de cuir renforcée de plaques de métal. Ça ne peut pas être... toi ?

– Pourquoi pas ? fit-il durement. Serait-ce plus étonnant que de te retrouver dans cette tente ? Ainsi les bruits que l'on colporte sont vrais ? Comment croire une chose pareille ?

– S'il te plaît... De quoi parles-tu ? s'écria-t-elle, la joie de ces retrouvailles coupée net par la sévérité du ton et plus encore par celle du regard. Quelle est cette chose que l'on ne peut pas croire ?

– Que tu sois la maîtresse du Téméraire ! Mais il faut bien se rendre à l'évidence puisque je te trouve en train de te lamenter sur son lit...

– Moi ? La maîtresse du duc Charles ? Qui dit cela ?

– Tout le monde. On parle beaucoup dans cette région de l'Europe d'une jeune femme déguisée en garçon qui suit le Bourguignon partout, dont il ne peut se passer, qui a accès auprès de lui de jour comme de nuit et qui...

— En voilà assez ! Me connais-tu donc si mal pour croire une telle vilenie ? Ceux qui colportent ces ragots démontrent en tout cas ceci : c'est qu'ils ne connaissent absolument pas le duc. Jamais, à l'exception de sa duchesse, il ne touche une femme. Jamais il n'a eu de maîtresse. Les débauches de son père lui en ont inspiré l'horreur.

— En ce cas, que fais-tu auprès de lui ?

— Tu ne trouves pas que tu poses beaucoup de questions ? A mon tour à présent de te demander ce que tu fais là ? Aux dernières nouvelles que m'a données Léonarde tu t'étais pris d'une immense amitié pour René de Lorraine au point de ne plus le quitter d'une semelle ? Et te voici chez les Suisses ?

— Pour une excellente raison : le duc René est ici. Il a chargé les Bourguignons en fuite à la tête d'un corps de cavalerie alsacienne et, comme d'habitude, j'étais avec lui. Il sera là dans un instant.

— Qu'est-ce que tu veux que ça me fasse ? Oh, je sais ! il paraît que c'est un garçon de bel avenir ? Tu aurais pressenti en lui un grand capitaine ? Le moins que l'on puisse dire est qu'il n'en donne guère l'impression. Dès qu'il essuie une défaite, il se sauve à toutes jambes sous prétexte d'aller chercher du renfort... et on ne le revoit plus. Pendant ce temps les Lorrains ont supporté tout le poids de la guerre... Le duc Charles qui l'appelle « l'Enfant » sait ce qu'il dit — et, si je comprends bien, tu es devenu sa nourrice ?

Démétrios se mit à rire, d'un rire qui avait quelque chose de féroce.

— C'est facile d'accuser quand on ne sait comment se défendre ? As-tu oublié le serment du sang ?

— Non, je ne l'ai pas oublié et j'ai rempli, moi, la mission dont m'avait chargée le roi Louis. J'ai détaché Campobasso du parti bourguignon et Dieu sait ce qu'il m'en a coûté ! Dieu et Esteban d'ailleurs, car je suppose qu'il t'a rejoint ?

— Oui. Il m'a dit en effet ce que tu avais dû supporter...

— Sans lui, je serais morte, mais les dangers que j'ai courus ne t'ont pas beaucoup empêché de dormir. J'ai failli être exécutée par le duc et j'ai manqué mourir sous l'épée de Campobasso... enfin j'ai perdu... Philippe... que je venais de retrouver et c'était pour essayer de le rejoindre et aussi pour que ses couleurs paraissent encore auprès de l'étendard de Bourgogne que je suis ici.

Les larmes qui enrouaient sa voix augmentaient sa colère car elle s'en voulait de trahir ainsi sa faiblesse devant cet homme. Elle l'avait cru son ami mais il avait suffi que ce misérable petit duc lorrain passât entre eux pour le changer en ennemi impitoyable.

— Bravo! Je vois que tu es devenue une bonne Bourguignonne, l'amie même de ce prince dont tu avais juré la mort?

— Je ne suis pas son amie mais il s'est montré bon pour moi. Il a essayé d'apaiser ma douleur et, même, il m'a avoué pourquoi il n'avait pas sauvé Jean de Brévailles que cependant il aimait...

— Et tu l'as cru, bien sûr. C'est si facile quand on a envie de croire!

— Et si facile de nier l'évidence quand on tient à rester aveugle! Seulement j'attends encore de voir ce que tu as fait, toi, pour tenir le serment?

— Plus que tu ne crois peut-être. Je sais que René II a été désigné par le destin pour vaincre le Téméraire et c'est ce qu'il vient d'effectuer aujourd'hui... Ton duc est en fuite et je te ferai remarquer qu'il t'a abandonnée.

— Si le tien a vaincu, ce n'est certes pas tout seul. Je dirai même que tout le mérite en revient aux Suisses. Mais, Démétrios, si tu tiens tant à la mort de Charles de Bourgogne, pourquoi donc ne cherches-tu pas à l'approcher? Un médecin étranger, ce serait d'autant plus facile qu'il est malade. Vas-y et tue-le?... Non? Cela ne te dit rien? Évidemment, tu n'en sortirais pas vivant et quelque chose me dit que tu tiens à la vie désormais.

— Pas plus qu'avant mais j'ai encore à faire. Par ailleurs, toi, il te serait facile d'en délivrer la terre qu'il écrase de son orgueil et de sa folie. Avec ceci, par exemple...

Du sac de peau qui pendait à sa ceinture, Démétrios tira une petite fiole qu'il fit miroiter à la lumière d'un chandelier :

— Trois gouttes et le Téméraire n'aura plus le loisir de faire massacrer ses peuples, à commencer par ses soldats! Tu entends ces cris? Les Suisses tiennent leur parole et égorgent tout ce qui leur tombe sous la main. Il en aurait fait autant s'il avait vaincu. C'est un monstre assoiffé de sang...

Il aurait pu parler longtemps ainsi mais Fiora ne l'écoutait pas. Elle regardait avec dégoût briller la petite fiole au bout des doigts du Grec.

— Non. Jamais tu ne feras de moi une empoisonneuse! Je te l'ai déclaré à Florence, le poison est une arme ignoble.

— Soit! soupira Démétrios en posant le minuscule flacon sur une table. Tu peux employer tel moyen qui te plaira mais sache ceci : c'est seulement quand le Téméraire aura cessé de vivre que je te rendrai ton mari.

— Mon mari ?... Philippe? Philippe serait encore vivant?

— Oui. J'étais à Grandson moi aussi — sans le duc René pour une fois. J'ai trouvé Selongey sur le champ de bataille. Je l'ai relevé, soigné... et caché en un lieu où tu ne saurais le retrouver sans mon aide.

— Philippe vivant !... Mon Dieu! Il vous arrive donc parfois d'entendre une prière et de l'exaucer ?...

— Laisse donc Dieu où il est! Le temps presse. Il faut que le Téméraire disparaisse, tu entends ?... Tu peux penser de moi ce que tu veux, mais tu es la seule qui puisse l'approcher. Alors agis! Il faut qu'il meure...

Brusquement, Fiora recouvra tout son sang-froid. Fièrement redressée, elle toisa celui qu'elle avait cru si longtemps son ami :

– Quel homme es-tu donc, Démétrios Lascaris, pour oser employer pareil moyen ? Ta haine aveugle ne te permet plus de juger sainement et j'ai l'horreur à présent de ce sang que tu as mêlé au mien...

– T'est-il donc si cher, ce Selongey dont tu sais pourtant bien qu'il t'a oubliée. Souviens-toi de la jeune femme...

– La veuve de son frère aîné mort voici des années. Encore que je ne discerne pas en quoi cela te regarde. Va ton chemin et laisse-moi suivre le mien.

A cet instant, deux hommes pénétrèrent ensemble dans la tente. L'un était Panigarola, couvert de boue et de sang, l'autre un jeune homme blond et mince, aux yeux bleus, portant sur son armure une tunique de drap d'or marquée d'une double croix blanche dont les manches étaient à ses couleurs, blanc et rouge. Voyant Démétrios mettre genou en terre devant lui, Fiora comprit que c'était le duc René...

– Elle est ici ! s'écria le Milanais en courant prendre Fiora par la main. Monseigneur, voici la jeune femme dont je vous ai parlé et, grâce à Dieu, elle est toujours vivante !

– Vous m'en voyez ravi, messire Panigarola. En vérité il eût été dommage qu'il arrivât malheur à une aussi jolie dame... et je comprends que vous ayez pris tant de risques pour la retrouver...

– Le risque n'était pas si grand, monseigneur, dès l'instant où j'ai reconnu votre bannière. Je savais que vous feriez respecter la mienne.

– Où irions-nous si nous nous mettions à présent à exterminer les diplomates ? Allez en sûreté maintenant. Mon banneret et quatre cavaliers vont vous reconduire hors d'ici... Je vous salue, madame, et j'espère sincèrement qu'il me sera donné de vous revoir... dans des circonstances moins tragiques...

Sans répondre, Fiora plia le genou devant René et sortit sans un regard pour Démétrios...

Mais ce qu'il lui fallut traverser ensuite lui mit le cœur au bord des lèvres. Partout on égorgeait, on assommait, on tirait des flèches sur les malheureux qui essayaient de fuir par le lac. C'était une effroyable vision, un enfer abominable et elle finit par fermer les yeux très fort en appuyant ses deux mains sur ses oreilles pour ne plus entendre les cris et les râles d'agonie, laissant Panigarola qui avait saisi la bride de son cheval le conduire en même temps que le sien. C'est seulement quand elle entendit faiblir ces affreuses plaintes qu'elle comprit que l'on s'éloignait du champ de mort.

– Vous pouvez ouvrir les yeux, dit calmement le Milanais, nous sommes seuls...

Elle obéit et s'efforça de lui sourire mais cet effort méritoire ne donna pas grand résultat.

– Comment vous remercier ? Vous êtes revenu pour moi dans cet enfer ?

– J'étais le seul à pouvoir le faire. Le duc a pu fuir entouré de quelques lances. Jamais je ne l'ai vu aussi éperdu, presque hagard... Je crois qu'il se serait laissé tuer sur place si plusieurs chevaliers ne l'avaient entraîné... Mais pensons à vous ! Si vous vous sentez mieux, Fiora, nous allons regagner Lausanne aussi vite que possible. D'après les bruits qui me sont parvenus, les Suisses, après cette victoire acquise, vont fondre sur la ville pour la mettre à sac... Il faut aller chercher donna Léonarda et le jeune Battista.

Fiora lui lança un coup d'œil épouvanté et lança son cheval au galop. Il ne manquerait plus qu'on lui tuât sa chère Léonarde !...

CHAPITRE XIV

L'ÉTANG GELÉ...

Trois jours plus tard, après un voyage mouvementé qui les avait contraints à remonter vers Orbe pour éviter les bandes incontrôlées et féroces qui se dirigeaient sur Lausanne, Panigarola, Fiora, Léonarde et Battista arrivaient dans la cité montagnarde de Saint-Claude, pittoresquement accrochée à des pentes rocheuses au-dessus du confluent de la Bienne et du Tacon. La ville, composée surtout d'artistes « ymagiers » et de tailleurs de pierre regroupés en une solide corporation, se serrait autour de ses torrents et de la grande abbaye bénédictine dont, au XIIe siècle, saint Claude, faiseur de miracles, avait été l'abbé. Ce furent les portes de ce monastère qui s'ouvrirent devant l'ambassadeur de Milan et ses compagnons.

Ils y trouvèrent le Grand Bâtard Antoine qui venait juste de descendre de cheval et qui, sans plus de façons, sauta au cou de Panigarola pour l'embrasser :

— Sire ambassadeur, vous direz à votre maître que je lui ai grande reconnaissance. Sans ce superbe coursier qu'il m'a donné, je laissais la vie à Morat. Sa rapidité m'a sauvé...

— Votre valeur aussi, monseigneur. Êtes-vous seul ici ? Je croyais que le duc avait décidé d'y venir ?

— C'était son idée en effet mais il en a changé. Apprenant que la duchesse de Savoie s'était réfugiée avec ses enfants dans son château de Gex, il s'y est rendu avec le sire de Givry et messire Olivier de La Marche pour convaincre Mme Yolande de le suivre en Bourgogne.

— En Bourgogne ? Pour quoi faire ?

— Je crois qu'il tient à s'assurer de sa fidélité.

— Ah !... Et... comment est-il ?

— Tout furieux. Il ne décolère pas. Il jure qu'avant peu il aura réuni une armée de cent cinquante mille hommes pour fondre sur les Cantons et les ravager de fond en comble... Je crains, ajouta Antoine de Bourgogne avec tristesse que sa raison ne soit atteinte...

— Non, monseigneur... mais il rêve ! Il n'a jamais cessé de rêver. D'empire d'abord, puis de l'antique royaume lotharingien. Et c'est ce rêve qu'il poursuit à travers la haine que lui inspirent les Suisses. Fasse Dieu que le réveil final ne soit pas trop cruel ! Sait-on combien d'hommes ont été perdus ?

— Vous voulez dire massacrés ? Plusieurs milliers parmi lesquels Jean de Luxembourg, Somerset et la majeure partie des archers anglais. Galeotto qui a résisté aussi longtemps qu'il a pu devant la tente ducale a réussi à percer avec deux compagnies et à fuir. Ajoutez à cela que, cette fois encore, les Suisses ont fait main basse sur tout notre camp et sur notre artillerie neuve, comme à Grandson. C'est un désastre, pire encore que le premier...

— Puis-je demander quels sont vos ordres à présent, monseigneur ? Attendrez-vous le duc ici ?

— Non. Je pars demain pour Salins afin d'y rallier les survivants de Morat. S'il y en a !... Il m'y rejoindra. Voulez-vous faire route avec moi ?

— Avec plaisir si mes compagnes ne sont pas trop épuisées.

Pendant ce temps, dans la maison des hôtes où elles avaient été conduites dès l'entrée de l'abbaye, Léonarde, à l'aide de chandelle fondue, soignait son séant pas encore habitué à ces galopades éperdues à califourchon mais sans pour autant cesser de bougonner et de vouer Démétrios à tous les feux de l'enfer. Elle n'avait pas décoléré depuis que Fiora lui avait raconté son entrevue avec le Grec.

— Il faut que ce vieux fou ait perdu l'esprit ! Je ne vous ai jamais caché ce que je pense de la vengeance et, en dépit de cela, je vous ai laissée faire. Grâce à Dieu, il ne vous a pas été accordé de salir vos mains...

— Mes mains sont sales, Léonarde. J'ai tué un homme.

— C'était lui ou vous et cela fait la différence. Mais aller froidement empoisonner, ou poignarder ou étrangler un être vivant, j'étais bien certaine que vous ne le feriez jamais.

— J'aurais poignardé du Hamel sans hésiter et, pour ce qui est du duc, j'aurais pu le tuer devant Nancy quand, superbe et arrogant, il m'accablait de son mépris et disposait de moi comme d'un meuble. Je ne l'ai pas fait parce que, en retrouvant Philippe, je n'ai pas eu... le courage de me condamner à mort en assassinant le Téméraire. Mon amour était plus fort que ma haine, et puis, ensuite, j'ai compris bien des choses au point même de pardonner au duc de n'avoir pas gracié mes parents. A présent l'idée de tuer cet homme malade, affaibli, frappé dans tout ce qui faisait son orgueil et sa gloire, cette idée me fait horreur. Et pourtant...

— Pourtant quoi ? Vous n'allez pas faire cela ?

Fiora dégrafa sa tunique, l'ôta et la jeta sur l'une des deux couchettes monacales qui meublaient la chambre, puis alla prendre, dans le coffre de cuir qui suivait Léonarde partout et en quelques circonstances que ce soient, un miroir à main pour s'y regarder :

— Mes cheveux repoussent. Il va falloir...

— Les recouper ? Ne comptez pas sur moi pour cela, et d'ailleurs je vous le défends. Votre époux est vivant. Que dirait-il en vous retrouvant tondue ? Il est temps de redevenir une femme, Fiora !

— Pour quoi faire ? Je ne reverrai Philippe que si...

Elle avait pris, à sa ceinture, la dague précieuse dont le

Téméraire lui avait fait présent et, l'air absent, en caressait doucement la lame brillante. Léonarde pâlit :

— Je vous quitte sur l'heure, Fiora, si vous ne me jurez d'abandonner cette idée insensée. Tuez le duc et vous serez pendue sur-le-champ : je ne veux pas voir ça ! Quant à Démétrios...

— Je sais déjà ce que vous en pensez ! dit Fiora avec un demi-sourire. Vous n'avez parlé que de lui depuis que nous avons quitté Lausanne...

— Peut-être, mais j'ai encore à dire ceci : vous n'avez pas à lui obéir. L'ignominie de son marché de lâche vous délie de tout lien envers lui.

— Mais Philippe ?

— Il ne lui arrivera rien de mal tant que son geôlier espérera voir son chantage réussir. Ce qu'il faut, c'est essayer de savoir où se trouve le duc de Lorraine : Démétrios ne sera pas loin et je saurai qu'en faire.

— Vous avez sans doute raison mais comment savoir où est René II ? D'après Panigarola, il ne cesse de se déplacer...

— Alors il faut rester auprès du duc Charles... et de ce cher ambassadeur qui sait toujours tout. Ils ont tous deux leurs espions et c'est là que nous aurons les meilleurs renseignements.

— Pourquoi ne pas rejoindre le roi à Lyon et lui demander de rappeler Démétrios ? C'est son médecin et...

— Et rien ne dit qu'il obtempérera. En outre, souvenez-vous que le jeune Colonna répond sur sa tête de votre présence ?

— Après tant de catastrophes, croyez-vous que le duc Charles pense encore à cela ?

— Mieux vaut ne rien hasarder avec un homme tel que lui. Et malheureusement il tient à vous... assez pour avoir ordonné à un fils de prince de veiller sur la vieille bourgeoise que je suis. S'il revoyait Battista sans vous...

Panigarola confirma les vues de la vieille demoiselle. D'après le Grand Bâtard, Charles s'était inquiété de

« Madame de Selongey » en des termes qui ne laissaient aucun doute sur le prix qu'il y attachait. Fiora pensa qu'il n'y avait rien à ajouter à cela et qu'elle avait tout intérêt à suivre les conseils de Léonarde.

Victime de ses propres avis, celle-ci en fut réduite à faire fondre double quantité de chandelle : le lendemain, on repartait pour Salins en compagnie du Grand Bâtard. En dépit des menaces de Démétrios, Fiora se sentait plus heureuse qu'elle ne l'avait été depuis longtemps. Le plus important n'était-il pas que Philippe fût vivant, qu'il respirât quelque part sous le même ciel qu'elle ? La nuit sombre de son avenir s'éclairait d'une chaude lueur d'espérance. Enfin, elle avait une immense confiance dans la sagesse de Léonarde... Avec son aide, elle commençait à croire qu'il lui serait possible de vaincre Démétrios, peut-être en utilisant ses armes favorites : la patience et la ruse.

Quand, le 2 juillet, le Téméraire à la tête de quelques cavaliers fit son entrée dans Salins, Fiora eut peine à le reconnaître. Comme il avait changé en quelques jours ! Ce visage bouffi, ces yeux las marqués de poches, cette bouche amère, ce regard vitrifié... Était-ce bien le même homme ? Sans l'armure dorée et le casque au lion d'or couronné, elle eût douté d'être en face du duc de Bourgogne. Pourtant il souriait et saluait de la main les gens de sa ville qui l'acclamaient éblouis par cette image somptueuse à laquelle le soleil arrachait des éclairs.

En voyant s'approcher Fiora et Panigarola qui venaient le saluer, il eut pour eux un vrai sourire, chaud et communicatif et les embrassa tour à tour. Il semblait extraordinairement heureux de les revoir et les garda auprès de lui jusqu'au soir. Durant le souper qu'ils prirent ensemble et avec le Grand Bâtard, il fut d'une gaieté charmante qui confondit ses invités. Ses projets étaient immenses et il rejetait, avec dédain, la responsabilité de la défaite de Morat sur le manque de courage de ses troupes qui n'avaient su, une fois de plus, que tourner casaque et prendre la fuite.

— Monseigneur, intercéda Panigarola, montrez-leur quelque pitié. Beaucoup sont morts...

— ... Qui ne le seraient pas s'ils s'étaient bien battus et ceux de ma maison ont été les plus mauvais. Rien d'étonnant : beaucoup étaient des Français mais je vais battre le rappel de ma noblesse fieffée de toute la Bourgogne. Je sais déjà pouvoir compter...

Il alignait des chiffres, formait des escadrons, confiait des commandements à des chefs dont on ne savait pas au juste s'ils étaient déjà morts ou encore vivants...

— J'ai eu l'impression de souper avec des fantômes, confia Fiora au Milanais. Cette grande armée dont il parle existe-t-elle ailleurs que dans son imagination ? J'ai peur qu'il ne soit encore malade.

— Moi aussi. En tout cas, une chose m'étonne ? Où est passé le capitaine de sa garde qui en principe ne le quitte pas ? Il paraît qu'il aurait été envoyé en mission ? Et comme il était avec lui à Gex, je me demande ce que cela peut être ?

Il allait l'apprendre trois jours après quand les échos du château retentirent des clameurs furieuses du Téméraire : Olivier de La Marche venait d'arriver avec un détachement de ses gardes et le duc braillait à tous les échos qu'il allait lui faire « ôter la tête »... En voyant accourir Panigarola visiblement bouleversé, Fiora qui se promenait avec Léonarde au bord de la Furieuse, le torrent qui longeait toute la ville de Salins, comprit qu'il se passait quelque chose de grave.

— Je commence vraiment à croire qu'il est dément, s'écria l'ambassadeur. Il vient de commettre la pire des folies : alors qu'en quittant le château de Gex, il a embrassé la duchesse de Savoie en lui jurant une amitié éternelle, il a, en même temps, commandé à Olivier de La Marche de s'assurer de sa personne ainsi que de celles de ses enfants alors qu'elle se rendait à Genève auprès de son beau-frère l'évêque.

— Il a fait arrêter la duchesse Yolande ? Mais pourquoi faire[1] ?

— Elle avait refusé de le suivre en Bourgogne et il espérait ainsi tenir fermement la Savoie. Malheureusement, un serviteur a caché le prince héritier Philibert et son jeune frère dans un champ de blé. Ils sont à Genève à présent et j'imagine d'ici le bruit qu'y fait l'évêque. Je gage qu'on va parler du baiser de Judas et que le roi Louis, qui lui n'est pas fou, va sauter sur l'occasion de s'ériger en protecteur de sa sœur et de ses neveux. C'est un coup à faire de la Savoie l'ennemie mortelle de notre duc... Comme s'il n'en avait pas assez !

— Où est la duchesse ?

— Pas très loin d'ici : au château de Rochefort près de Dôle. Quant à La Marche, qui a manqué la moitié de sa mission, je le vois mal parti...

Il garda cependant sa tête. Le duc Charles avait trop de soucis pour s'attarder longtemps sur cet épisode : les Suisses continuaient leurs exploits. Après avoir mis Lausanne à sac, ils s'apprêtaient à prendre le chemin de Genève quand le roi de France intervint. Morat l'avait ravi mais il ne tenait pas du tout à ce que les Suisses continuassent à piétiner l'héritage de son neveu : en foi de quoi il envoya son outil préféré : un sac d'or plus une petite armée à Chambéry pour leur rappeler que, même s'il ne faisait pas souvent la guerre, il n'en possédait pas moins tous les moyens de la déchaîner. Peu de temps après, la Savoie et les Cantons signaient un traité de paix.

— Quel grand homme ! s'écria Panigarola enthousiasmé. En voilà au moins un qui ne considère pas la guerre comme le dernier des beaux-arts !

Ce n'était évidemment pas l'avis du Téméraire qui avait réuni à Salins les états de Haute-Bourgogne pour leur expliquer la nécessité de lui venir en aide dans sa guerre contre les Suisses, cette guerre à laquelle il ne vou-

1. Transportée au château de Rouvres, la duchesse devait être délivrée quelques semaines plus tard par Charles d'Amboise envoyé par Louis XI.

lait pas renoncer. Il fit alors à ses sujets un superbe discours, appuyé sur Tite-Live et sur les grands exemples de combats perdus et de guerres gagnées. Il n'avait entrepris tout cela que pour les protéger, eux, leurs femmes, leurs enfants et leurs biens contre le danger mortel des Suisses et des Français. Il fit tant et si bien que son auditoire presque en larmes s'engagea à financer la protection des frontières mais à deux conditions : que le duc cessât de s'exposer en personne et qu'il conclût la paix dès que l'occasion s'en présenterait. Charles jura tout ce que l'on voulut et se remit au travail avec enthousiasme :

— Donna Fiora, déclara-t-il à la jeune femme un soir où, comme cela lui arrivait de plus en plus souvent, elle venait de chanter en compagnie de Battista, quand j'aurai vaincu tous ces croquants et leur aurai repris mes biens, je ferai de vous une princesse. Vous pourrez choisir dans mes états celui qui vous plaira le mieux. Et je vous rendrai votre dot.

— Je n'en demande pas tant, monseigneur. Vivre en paix dans le souvenir de mon époux — elle avait jugé plus prudent, en effet, de ne lui rien révéler de ce qu'elle avait appris — est tout ce que je désire. Je n'aime pas la guerre et qui gouverne un état doit toujours s'y préparer.

— Celle-ci sera la dernière. Ensuite, je ferai de vous le plus bel ornement de ma cour...

Fiora ne répondit rien, trouvant à cette phrase une résonance étrange. D'ailleurs l'attitude de Charles envers elle se modifiait encore. Il lui demanda de reprendre les vêtements féminins qui, même s'ils étaient de grand deuil, « mettaient si bien sa beauté en valeur ». Non seulement elle n'avait plus à essuyer ses colères mais il était envers elle d'une galanterie extrême, lui offrait des présents, l'interrogeait sur son enfance, ses études, sur la vie qu'elle menait dans cette Florence dont il rêvait souvent et dont il ne désespérait pas d'y entrer un jour en maître, car, parfois, il songeait même à conquérir l'Italie...

— Je crois, Dieu me pardonne, qu'il est tombé amoureux de vous, déclara Panigarola en regardant Fiora déployer une pièce d'un magnifique satin gris pâle broché d'or qu'un chevaucheur venait de rapporter de Dijon.

— Est-ce que vous n'avez pas un peu trop d'imagination ?

— Sûrement pas. Je ne saurais d'ailleurs le lui reprocher mais je ne suis pas certain que ce soit pour votre plus grand bonheur. Dans l'état d'exaltation où je le vois, une grande passion chez un homme dont on a toujours vanté la chasteté pourrait se révéler dangereuse.

— Que faudrait-il faire alors ?

— Fuir ! Le plus vite et le plus loin possible. Je vous y aiderai... tant que je serai là tout au moins.

— Est-ce que vous songeriez à partir ?

— Je crains fort d'être rappelé un jour prochain. Les conséquences de Morat sont désastreuses et la politique de mon pays est en train de changer. Milan se rapproche de la France et si mon prince rompt ses relations avec la Bourgogne..

Fiora garda le silence un instant. L'idée de voir cet ami discret s'éloigner lui faisait peine. Rejetant le tissu brillant elle marcha lentement jusqu'à la fenêtre qu'un somptueux coucher de soleil incendiait :

— Si vous partez, il vous faudra emmener Battista car je ne resterai pas non plus. De toute façon, je ne suivrai pas le duc dans une autre guerre. J'ai vu Grandson et Morat : cela me suffit.

Néanmoins, dans les jours qui suivirent, le duc se montra plus calme. Il décida de quitter Salins pour le château de La Rivière, grande bâtisse féodale hérissée de tours et pourvue d'un imposant appareil militaire, située à trois ou quatre lieues de Pontarlier, sur un haut plateau jurassien assez triste mais suffisamment vaste pour que l'on y rassemblât une armée. Sa maison et ses familiers l'y suivirent. Fiora y trouva un appartement plus riche qu'elle n'en avait eu depuis longtemps mais c'en était fini des jours paisibles de Salins où, dans la calme fraîcheur des montagnes, les rescapés de Morat avaient pu prendre un peu de repos et retrouver leur souffle.

Les premières nouvelles qui arrivèrent à La Rivière jetèrent le Téméraire hors de lui. Alors que les états de Bourgogne avaient accepté de l'aider, ceux de Flandres, réunis à Gand, avaient non seulement refusé de lui apporter quelque aide que ce fût mais encore prétendaient rogner sur les sommes précédemment allouées à l'armée sous prétexte qu'il n'y avait plus d'armée.

— Plus d'armée! vociféra le duc. Ces misérables Flamands verront bientôt si je n'ai plus d'armée! Je marcherai contre leurs insolentes cités dès que j'aurai châtié les bouviers des Cantons. Quant à cet âne de chancelier Hugonet qui s'est laissé tenir pareil langage il en répondra sur sa propre fortune. Je vais faire saisir ses biens...

Plus grave encore : le duc René II dont la grand-mère, la vieille princesse de Vaudémont, venait de mourir en lui léguant une fortune avait enrôlé des mercenaires suisses et alsaciens, obtenu de la ville de Strasbourg qu'elle lui prêtât son artillerie et venait de libérer Lunéville. On prétendait qu'il allait se diriger sur Nancy pour en chasser les Bourguignons.

Cette nouvelle fit battre plus vite le cœur de Fiora. Elle savait où était Démétrios. Il fallait maintenant voir aux moyens de le rejoindre au plus tôt.

— Cela ne va pas être facile, dit Léonarde, soucieuse. Sortir à la fois de ce château plus fermé qu'un coffre de marchand et de ce camp qui se forme autour et qui grandit chaque jour pose un problème difficile à résoudre car, avec ce grand amour que vous porte le duc – et même si vous ne vous en êtes pas encore rendu compte – vous êtes aussi surveillée que si vous étiez sa fiancée...

— Il faudra tout de même bien trouver un moyen. Je ne vais pas me laisser emmener encore par-delà les monts quand c'est à Nancy que je dois aller?

Cette dernière crainte fut vite effacée. Une fois sa colère passée, le duc Charles changea ses plans du tout au tout :

plus question de courir sus aux Cantons avec lesquels d'ailleurs semblaient s'amorcer timidement quelques bruits de pourparlers. Désormais c'était vers le nord qu'il allait falloir marcher pour chasser définitivement de Lorraine les hommes de René II, car la Lorraine était le lien des deux Bourgognes, le maillon indispensable et trop chèrement acquis pour le laisser se rompre...

— Voilà qui simplifie les choses, commenta Léonarde. Nous ne savions pas comment nous rendre à Nancy et voici que l'on se propose de nous y conduire. L'armée se rassemble tous les jours. Bientôt nous partirons...

Le vaste plateau en effet se peuplait presque à vue d'œil. La Bourgogne tenait ses promesses et envoyait des troupes et des armes. On vit venir des Picards, des Wallons et des Luxembourgeois, quelques Anglais aussi obtenus non sans peine du roi Édouard par la duchesse Marguerite. Galeotto rejoignit l'un des premiers avec ses lances et ses charpentiers. Les soldats s'installaient dans les villages et les hameaux dont les habitants retenaient leur souffle en dépit des ordres sévères du Téméraire touchant le vol, le viol ou le pillage. D'autres campaient directement sous la tente et leurs feux de cuisine, la nuit venue, s'échevelaient sous le vent venu des montagnes. Le château s'emplissait de seigneurs et de capitaines qui y menaient grand bruit. Ce n'étaient que colloques, conciliabules, beuveries aussi il faut bien le dire, et Fiora ne quittait plus son appartement où Panigarola venait souvent se réfugier quand il était las des récits d'exploits guerriers. Elle ne voyait presque plus le duc et ne s'en plaignait pas. Le temps n'était plus aux chansons : le bruit des armes avait pris leur place et emplissait tout. Les oiseaux eux-mêmes et les animaux des bois fuyaient vers la montagne... Et puis, un matin, Panigarola vint faire ses adieux à Fiora.

En le voyant paraître botté et son manteau de cheval sur le bras, la jeune femme comprit ce qu'il en était avant même qu'il n'ait ouvert la bouche :

— Ne me dites pas que vous partez ?

— C'est bien cela pourtant. Le duc vient de me donner mon congé avec plus de bonne grâce d'ailleurs que je n'aurais osé l'espérer dans de telles circonstances...

— Milan et la Bourgogne ne sont plus alliées ?

— Non. Il est déjà inespéré que nous ne soyons pas en guerre. Monseigneur a bien voulu me dire qu'il me regretterait...

— Il n'est pas le seul. Je suis... navrée de vous perdre, mon ami. Nous reverrons-nous jamais ?

— Pourquoi pas ? Milan n'est pas si loin et je tiens à ce que vous sachiez que ma maison sera toujours prête à vous accueillir.

— Sauf si vous n'y êtes pas. Qui dit que l'on ne vous enverra pas demain chez le Grand Khan ?

— Il y a peu de chance : sa langue m'est inconnue. Mais... je suis venu aussi vous communiquer la nouvelle que je viens d'apprendre de Galeotto : Campobasso revient !

— Ici ?

— Peut-être pas. Mais il a écrit au duc pour lui proposer de reprendre du service avec sa condotta. Cela représente près de deux mille hommes et sa proposition a été accueillie avec transport.

Fiora rejoignit Léonarde qui cousait près de la fenêtre.

— Vous avez entendu ? Il faut que nous nous préparions à partir sur l'heure. Attendez-nous un moment, mon ami, nous ferons route ensemble !...

Elle se précipitait déjà vers un coffre qu'elle ouvrit.

— Je vous en prie, n'en faites rien. J'avais prévu votre réaction et j'ai demandé la permission de vous emmener. Monseigneur refuse formellement de vous laisser partir.

Laissant retomber le couvercle, Fiora hésita un instant puis marcha vers la porte :

— Il ne me le refusera pas à moi. Je ne veux plus rester ici, au milieu de tous ces hommes d'armes, dont les regards souvent me déplaisent, à attendre que Campobasso ne s'empare à nouveau de moi.

— N'y allez pas, Fiora ! Ce sera inutile. Tout ce que vous y gagnerez sera peut-être de vous retrouver tout à fait prisonnière.

— Mais enfin, il y a peu, vous me proposiez de m'aider à fuir ?

— En effet !... mais je ne savais pas tout. Et même je ne savais rien. Plus jamais le duc Charles ne vous autorisera à vous éloigner de lui. Et si vous prenez la fuite, vous savez quelle sera la conséquence ?

— C'est insensé ! s'écria Léonarde. Ce n'est plus de l'amour, c'est de la rage.

— Ni l'un ni l'autre, donna Léonarde... C'est de la superstition. Quand nous avons séjourné à Besançon, l'hiver passé, un rabbin versé dans la kabbale a dit à monseigneur que la mort ne l'atteindrait pas tant que vous seriez auprès de lui, Fiora. Voilà pourquoi il vous a reconnue si hautement pour la dame de Selongey car cela fait de vous une Bourguignonne ; pourquoi il veut vous garder à sa cour quand la guerre aura pris fin ; pourquoi enfin Battista doit mourir si vous prenez la fuite. Vous êtes devenue comme son ange gardien.

D'abord médusée, Fiora éclata brusquement de rire :

— Moi, son ange gardien ? Moi qui en quittant Florence ne rêvait que de le tuer ?... Il y a là de quoi me faire revenir à mes premières idées.

— N'essayez pas car vous n'y parviendrez pas quoi que vous fassiez. La lame du poignard cassera, le poison sera sans effet...

— Mais enfin vous croyez à ces folies, vous, si logique et si bon philosophe ? Qui vous a dit cela ? Le duc ?

— Non. Le Grand Bâtard que je priais d'intercéder pour vous et qui, depuis longtemps, a demandé que l'on vous rende votre liberté.

— Il faudrait alors que Battista rentre chez lui. Après tout il est romain, cet enfant, et il n'appartient pas vraiment à la maison de Bourgogne. Son maître n'était-il pas le comte de Celano ?

– Qui a disparu à Grandson et dont on ne sait ce qu'il est devenu. Mais je vous en prie calmez-vous! Rien n'est encore perdu. En vous quittant, je dois m'arrêter à Saint-Claude pour y attendre Mgr Nanni. Le légat espère toujours arriver à conclure la paix entre la Bourgogne et les Cantons. Le pape et l'empereur y sont attachés et il a désiré me rencontrer. Nous verrons ensemble ce que nous pouvons faire. Le jeune Colonna pourrait être rappelé à Rome... par un deuil familial, par exemple?

– Vous pensez obtenir du légat qu'il profère un aussi gros mensonge?

En dépit de la gravité du moment, Panigarola se mit à rire.

– Ma chère enfant, apprenez qu'en politique comme en diplomatie, le mensonge et la vérité sont des notions tout à fait abstraites. Il n'y a que le résultat qui compte... et Mgr Nanni est l'un des meilleurs diplomates que je connaisse. Ainsi donc prenez patience!... et permettez à un vieil ami de vous embrasser car vous lui êtes devenue chère. Portez-vous bien, donna Léonarda!

– Je n'y manquerai pas, messire, fit celle-ci avec une petite révérence et j'en souhaite tout autant à Votre Excellence!

Le soir venu, le duc Charles, à la surprise de Fiora, se fit annoncer chez elle. Et elle constata du premier regard qu'il était triste.

– Je viens vous demander à souper, donna Fiora, dit-il en prenant sa main pour la relever de sa révérence. Et, à moins que cela ne vous contrarie, on servira ici.

– Monseigneur ne sait-il pas qu'il est chez lui?

– Ne soyez pas si cérémonieuse. Vous devez être aussi affligée que moi. N'avons-nous pas perdu un ami?

– Je ne crois pas. Vous avez perdu l'ambassadeur, non l'ami qui vous reste certainement attaché.

– Puissiez-vous dire vrai mais je mesure à ces défections combien la gloire de la Bourgogne est ternie. Il est urgent qu'une grande victoire lui restitue tout son éclat. Heureusement vous me restez.

En dépit de ce qu'avait dit Panigarola, Fiora ne put s'empêcher de tenter sa chance :

— Tenez-vous vraiment à m'emmener encore en guerre, monseigneur ? J'en suis... affreusement lasse ! La guerre me fait horreur...

— Vous voulez me quitter, vous aussi ? Qu'est devenu mon jeune écuyer si vaillant ? Qu'est devenue la dame de Selongey qui tenait tant à maintenir auprès des miennes les couleurs de son époux ?

— Elle a vu verser trop de sang. Ne lui accorderez-vous pas de se retirer à Selongey ?

— Pour y vivre dans la solitude d'un château campagnard ? Non, donna Fiora, je ne crois pas que cela vous tente. Il y a autre chose n'est-ce pas ? Cette amitié qui m'était si douce n'était qu'un leurre ? Comme les autres vous voulez me fuir parce que vous me croyez fini, détruit...

Il s'énervait. Sa voix montait déjà. Devinant alors qu'il lui fallait prendre le dessus, Fiora s'écria :

— Vous avez raison : il y a autre chose. Campobasso va vous revenir et moi je ne veux plus jamais revoir cet homme ! C'est pour cela que je vous demande mon congé...

— Ce n'est donc que cela ? Alors rassurez-vous. Je promets que vous ne le verrez pas. Il est vrai qu'il a demandé à reprendre du service sous ma bannière. C'est un bon capitaine et j'ai malheureusement besoin de ses soldats mais il ne viendra pas ici. Je lui ai ordonné d'aller prendre position entre Thionville et Metz où il attendra le prince de Croÿ et le duc Engelbert de Nassau qui vont venir des Pays-Bas avec cinq mille hommes de pied. Dans peu de jours il faut que nous ayons quitté La Rivière. L'Enfant a mis le siège devant Nancy et je veux le prendre à revers. Vous serez auprès de moi comme naguère mais Olivier de La Marche aura ordre de veiller sur vous et de vous tenir à l'écart lorsque Campobasso viendra me voir. Mais je ne veux pas que vous me quittiez. Il *faut,* vous entendez, il faut que vous demeuriez à mes côtés. Ne me demandez pas pourquoi!

Et, oubliant qu'il s'était invité à souper, le Téméraire s'enfuit. La porte retomba derrière lui et le bruit s'en prolongea un instant dans le silence qui s'était établi dans la chambre.

— Eh bien! soupira Léonarde. Nous souperons seules!

— J'aime autant cela mais avouez tout de même que c'est effrayant! Jamais je ne pourrai lui échapper...

— N'y pensez pas! Vous ne devez plus avoir en tête qu'une seule idée: nous allons partir pour Nancy. N'est-ce pas là le principal? Ce serait bien le diable si dans le tohu-bohu d'une guerre nous n'arrivions pas à fausser compagnie à monseigneur. Et si le jeune Colonna n'est pas encore parti, eh bien, nous l'enlèverons.

— Léonarde, dit Fiora avec conviction, vous m'étonnerez toujours. Enlever Battista?

— Pourquoi pas? Ce pourrait être très amusant...

Le 25 septembre au matin, l'armée si péniblement reconstituée quittait La Rivière... D'aucuns auraient dit une apparence d'armée tant le contraste était poignant avec la superbe machine de guerre que deux semblants de bataille avaient réduite en miettes. Vieux soldats recuits au feu des mitrailles et jeunes recrues, la Bourgogne, la Picardie, le Luxembourg et le Hainaut avaient apporté tout ce qu'ils pouvaient fournir pour les adjoindre aux lances fidèles de Galeotto, le seul mercenaire dont la loyauté n'eût jamais fait défaut. Mais c'étaient les troupes de la dernière chance. Qu'une nouvelle défaite les disperse ou les anéantisse et il n'y aurait plus rien, plus même de Bourgogne dont les clochers vides n'avaient plus de bronze à fournir. Dix mille hommes, pas plus, c'est tout ce que le Téméraire traîne après lui et sur lesquels il compte pour chasser une fois de plus l'Enfant de sa terre natale.

Sous le chaperon noir qu'elle a repris pour cacher ses

cheveux déjà longs, Fiora chevauche à la queue du cheval du Téméraire et en compagnie de Battista. Elle est si sombre que le page n'ose même plus chanter. Panigarola lui manque. Sa culture et sa philosophie en faisaient un compagnon inégalable grâce à qui le plus long chemin se parcourait sans peine. Les nouvelles qu'elle en avait reçues n'étaient pas des meilleures : en arrivant à Saint-Claude, le légat papal avait dû se coucher sous les assauts d'une bronchite jointe à une attaque de goutte. Il n'était pas près de rejoindre le duc Charles...

Celui-ci bouillait d'impatience. Savoir René II devant Nancy le rendait malade et aussi l'obligatoire lenteur d'une armée dont tous les membres n'étaient pas montés, tant s'en faut ! Quatre à cinq lieues par jour, sous le poids des armes, c'était tout ce que l'on pouvait demander à l'infanterie alors que le Téméraire rêvait de voler comme l'aigle pour fondre enfin sur son ennemi.

Par Levier, Ornans, Besançon et Vesoul, on atteignit les confins de la Lorraine où l'on s'enfonça vers l'ouest afin d'éviter les villes déjà reconquises par René. Le Téméraire ne voulait pas gaspiller ses forces. Il voulait d'abord Nancy et, pour cela, il fallait qu'il rejoigne les troupes de Campobasso, de Chimay et de Nassau auxquelles il avait donné l'ordre de venir à sa rencontre à Toul... Le 7 octobre, il faisait son entrée dans Neufchâteau... à l'instant même où René II entrait dans sa capitale retrouvée et en chassait le gouverneur bourguignon, Jean de Rubempré seigneur de Bièvres. Fou de rage, le duc Charles faillit tuer le messager qui lui en apportait la nouvelle...

Néanmoins, son armée grossissait. Quand il eut fait, à Toul, sa jonction avec Campobasso – qui d'ailleurs se fit attendre – et récupéré les troupes – environ quinze cents hommes – évacuées de Nancy par Jean de Rubempré, il se vit à la tête d'un effectif de dix-huit mille soldats. C'était plus que n'en pouvait aligner le jeune duc de Lorraine et tous les espoirs demeuraient permis. D'autant que le 17, les Bourguignons battaient une partie de ses gens à Pont-à-Mousson. La route de Nancy était ouverte...

Charles crut tout de bon que son étoile enfuie brillait à nouveau au-dessus de sa tête quand il apprit que René venait, une fois de plus, de quitter Nancy pour se procurer un surcroît de troupes. Celui-ci laissait la ville aux plus coriaces de ses fidèles : Gérard d'Avilliers, les frères d'Aguerre, Petit-Jean de Vaudémont, renforcés de deux capitaines gascons : Pied-de-Fer et Fortune. Deux mille hommes avec eux :

– Nous tiendrons au moins deux mois, lui dirent-ils, mais faites vite ! Sinon, ensuite, ce sera la faim qui nous décimera...

Jean de Rubempré, en effet, et la garnison en grande partie anglaise de la ville avaient résisté près de deux mois au duc René. Depuis que celui-ci y était entré, elle n'avait guère eu le temps de refaire des approvisionnements qui faisaient déjà cruellement défaut puisque l'on en était venu à manger les chevaux, et pas davantage de réparer ses murailles écornées. Aussi, quand, le 22 octobre, le Téméraire investit la ville et fit reconstruire auprès de la Commanderie Saint-Jean sa maison de bois, était-il sûr que la victoire était à portée de sa main.

– Nous fêterons Noël au palais comme l'an passé, dit-il joyeusement à Fiora, et je donnerai une si belle fête que vous dédaignerez le souvenir de celles des Médicis...

Elle le remercia d'un sourire machinal mais le cœur n'y était pas. A nouveau, il était avec elle amical, chaleureux, allant jusqu'à les installer, Léonarde et elle, dans une chambre de son logis de campagne. De même, il avait tenu sa parole et elle n'avait pas revu Campobasso. Elle lui était reconnaissante mais pas moins désorientée. Ce René II qui fuyait tel un mirage dès que l'on croyait s'approcher de lui en venait à l'exaspérer. Où était-il à présent ? A Strasbourg, à Berne, à Fribourg, Dieu sait où parmi les Cantons ? Démétrios était-il toujours avec lui ?

Et Philippe ? Où était Philippe ? Était-il guéri de ses blessures et, en ce cas, le retenait-on dans quelque prison ? Les points d'interrogation se succédaient dans l'esprit découragé de la jeune femme et elle ne voyait pas où il fallait en chercher les réponses.

— Si le duc de Lorraine est parti chercher du secours, il finira bien par revenir, prédisait Léonarde toujours pratique. Cessez de vous tourmenter ; vous ne changerez rien à cette histoire insensée que le duc Charles nous oblige à écrire avec lui...

— Savez-vous à quoi je pense ? Je me demande si Démétrios n'est pas dans Nancy. Une cité assiégée a besoin d'un bon médecin tandis qu'un jeune prince en parfaite santé peut s'en passer...

— Cela n'a rien d'impossible. Mais je ne vois pas comment vous pourriez entrer dans cette ville pour vous en assurer ?

Soir après soir, de la fenêtre de sa chambre, Fiora regardait le jour tomber sur Nancy avec le désir toujours plus ardent d'y pénétrer. Elle en venait à penser que ces murs meurtris par le tir des bouches à feu et cependant toujours debout retenaient aussi l'homme qu'elle aimait. Mais comment arriver jusque-là sans essuyer le feu des défenseurs ou se faire tuer par les assaillants ? Et elle s'effrayait quand, en fin de journée, le rouge soleil d'automne habillait les remparts de flamme et de sang...

La ville se défendait farouchement. Des attaques incessantes harcelaient le camp bourguignon qui, chaque fois, y laissait des hommes. Le bâtard de Vaudémont que la légende commençait à auréoler avait même réussi, dans la nuit de la Toussaint, à s'approcher du quartier général des assaillants et le logis du Téméraire n'avait échappé à l'incendie que de justesse. Vaudémont s'était fondu dans la nuit avec ses hommes sans en laisser un seul sur le terrain mais des cadavres marquaient son passage.

Et puis l'hiver, avec un mois d'avance, arriva comme une tempête et mit tout le monde d'accord en ensevelissant sous ses nappes de neige et ses écharpes de brume assiégeants et assiégés. En une nuit, tout fut blanc ; les ruisseaux et l'étang Saint-Jean se figèrent et la Meurthe elle-même se mit à charrier des glaçons. La faim et ses souffrances s'installèrent dans Nancy, le froid, la maladie et la peur dans le camp des Bourguignons. Chaque jour qui se levait révélait des désertions.

Inquiet, Antoine de Bourgogne tenta de faire entendre raison à son frère :

— Pourquoi vous obstiner à cette campagne d'hiver ? Nous perdons des soldats tous les jours. Levons le camp et allons nous abriter en Luxembourg. Au printemps nous reviendrons...

— Ce serait donner à René le temps de refaire une armée, à Nancy celui de se ravitailler. Non, mon frère. J'ai décidé de passer Noël dans cette damnée ville dont je voulais faire la capitale d'un empire. Ils ne tiendront plus longtemps. Ils ont mangé les chevaux. A présent ils mangent les chiens, les chats et même les rats...

Ce n'était que trop vrai. Nancy endurait vaillamment son martyre, brûlait ses meubles pour avoir un peu moins froid et tentait des sorties désespérées dans l'espoir de récupérer un peu de nourriture... Les Bourguignons en manquaient moins car ils contrôlaient, au nord de la ville, la route de Metz et du Luxembourg par où leur venait le ravitaillement. Le trésor de guerre, en effet, se trouvait à Luxembourg. Campobasso, Chimay et Nassau surveillaient cette route avec défense formelle d'en bouger. C'était le duc qui, chaque matin, s'en allait visiter les capitaines et les différents ouvrages avancés.

Fiora appréciait ces dispositions : elles tenaient Campobasso éloigné du camp de la Commanderie et lui permettaient de sortir sans craindre de mauvaises rencontres. Car dans la maison de bois, l'atmosphère, enfumée par les braseros, lui paraissait difficile à supporter. « Nous sortirons de là fumés comme des jambons », grognait Léonarde, et chaque jour, en compagnie de Battista, elle s'obligeait à une courte promenade autour de l'étang Saint-Jean ou vers le bois de Saurupt. C'est ainsi qu'un jour où, profitant d'un rarissime rayon de soleil, elle s'était avancée jusqu'à la lisière du bois, elle vit un bûcheron occupé à débiter un arbre dont il entassait les morceaux dans une sorte de traîneau. Elle eut l'envie soudaine de lui parler et s'approcha :

— Vous êtes de par ici, brave homme ? Il n'y a pourtant plus beaucoup de maisons aux alentours.

— J'habite assez loin mais, par ce fichu temps, faut bien trouver d' quoi s' chauffer, pas vrai ?

L'homme s'était redressé et se frottait les reins et, du haut de sa grande taille, considérait la jeune femme avec, dans ses yeux bleus, une lueur amusée. En dépit d'une barbe et d'une moustache envahissantes, Fiora stupéfaite reconnut Douglas Mortimer... Jetant un rapide regard autour d'elle pour voir où était Battista elle le vit bander l'arc qu'il emportait toujours avec lui par précaution pour tirer un vol de corbeaux. Il ne pouvait pas l'entendre :

— Qu'est-ce que vous faites là ? chuchota-t-elle.

— Vous voyez, je m'occupe. Ce n'est pas facile de vous rencontrer dites donc ? Le roi s'inquiète de vous et se demande si vous n'êtes pas devenue bourguignonne ? On lui a parlé d'une jeune femme qui ne quitte plus le Téméraire. Vous êtes sa maîtresse ?

— Ne dites pas de sottises : le duc n'a pas de maîtresse. Mais il tient à moi parce qu'il voit en moi une sorte de talisman.

La figure barbue se fendit d'un large sourire :

— Si vous étiez à Grandson et à Morat vous êtes en effet un sacré talisman.

— On lui a prédit que la mort ne l'atteindrait pas tant que je serai avec lui...

— Je vois. Mais vous avez des jambes et quelque chose qui ressemble à une intelligence. Pourquoi, depuis le temps, ne vous êtes-vous pas encore échappée ?

— Regardez cet enfant qui tire des corbeaux ! Si je m'enfuis, il sera exécuté.

— Ah !... C'est en effet un problème qu'il faut essayer de résoudre. Mais c'est aussi une chance que vous soyez venue jusqu'ici. Voilà plusieurs jours que je vais au camp proposer du bois, ou des lièvres comme hier. Je voulais qu'on s'habitue à me voir. Je continuerai d'ailleurs mais j'avais à vous dire ceci : le roi veut que je vous sorte de là car le danger augmente et il redoute pour vous...

— Remerciez-le mais, pour l'instant, je n'ai rien à craindre. Ce que je voudrais savoir, c'est où se trouve le duc René ? Le savez-vous ?

— Il est encore assez loin, je crois, mais il sera ici avant la fin de l'année. C'est ça, le danger.

— Je ne le redoute pas. Pourriez-vous me dire si Démétrios Lascaris est encore avec lui ?

— Le médecin grec ? Il ne le quitte pas. Dites, vous ne croyez pas que nous avons assez causé ?

— Encore une question : pourquoi Campobasso est-il revenu ?

— Pour l'argent... et pour vous. Prenez garde ! c'est un truand qui a réussi à dégoûter jusqu'au roi qui l'a renvoyé. Il désertera certainement quand l'heure sera venue. Le Roi vous est reconnaissant de ce que vous avez fait mais il craint que vous n'en soyez victime. Campobasso vous veut, à tout prix, alors, à présent que nous nous sommes vus, ne bougez plus de votre logis. Je vais essayer de veiller sur vous mais, de toute façon, ce ne sera plus long.

Depuis un moment déjà, Mortimer avait repris sa cognée. Battista qui avait tué deux corbeaux revenait avec son gibier. Fiora le félicita de son adresse.

— Vous comptez les manger ? On dit que c'est très dur.

— Pas si on les fait bouillir assez longtemps, mais je comptais les offrir à ce pauvre homme. Le gibier est rare en ce moment.

Le faux bûcheron accepta le présent avec une gratitude touchante et un accent de terroir qui amusa tellement Fiora qu'elle préféra s'éloigner rapidement avec le page que les bénédictions de l'homme poursuivaient... Cette présence faisait plaisir à la jeune femme et l'inquiétait en même temps. Si Mortimer était pris, il serait pendu comme espion ainsi que cela venait d'arriver à un maître d'hôtel du duc René, un gentilhomme provençal nommé Suffren de Baschi [1] qui avait été découvert alors qu'il tentait de faire entrer dans la ville de la poudre et de la viande. Une curieuse histoire d'ailleurs! Le duc Charles dans un premier mouvement de colère avait ordonné qu'on le branche. Le Grand Bâtard, le sire de Chimay et Campobasso avaient prié qu'on lui laissât la vie mais, tandis que les deux premiers poursuivaient le prince de leurs objurgations, Campobasso le fit pendre séance tenante. Il est vrai que le malheureux avait crié à ses avocats « Dites au duc de m'accorder un instant d'entretien en tête à tête. Il donnerait un duché s'il savait ce que je peux lui révéler... » Après ce que Mortimer lui avait appris, Fiora tira une conclusion simple : Suffren savait que le condottiere allait trahir et c'était cela qu'il voulait révéler au duc.

Dans les jours qui suivirent, Fiora ne quitta pas sa chambre et tint compagnie à Léonarde qui avait pris un rhume en allant aider Matteo de Clerici à soigner les malades. Il y eut d'ailleurs grande assemblée en l'honneur du protonotaire Hessler venu apporter une lettre et des joyaux de la part du prince Maximilien pour sa fiancée Marie de Bourgogne. Le duc et ses capitaines s'efforcèrent de lui faire aussi bonne chère que possible étant donné les moyens restreints dont on disposait. Fiora, elle, se garda bien de paraître car elle avait aperçu Campobasso parmi les autres. Et puis, elle avait espéré que Mgr Nanni accompagnerait, comme d'habitude, l'abbé de Xanten, mais Hessler était seul et plus aucune nouvelle n'était venue de Panigarola. Elle pensa que le légat, étant déjà âgé, il était peut-être mort?

Et puis Noël vint, le plus tragique que l'on vit jamais pour les belligérants. Nancy crevait de faim et en était à

1. Un ancêtre du bailli de Suffren.

arracher les charpentes des maisons démolies pour obtenir un peu de chaleur autre que celle des incendies allumés par l'artillerie bourguignonne et que l'eau gelée empêchait d'éteindre mais dans le camp la situation n'était guère meilleure. Chaque jour passé coûtait des hommes. Le froid impitoyable les paralysait, leur gelait les pieds et les tuait par centaines. Les désertions atteignaient un taux alarmant et, dans cette nuit de la Nativité qu'il s'était promis de fêter dans le palais des ducs de Lorraine, le duc Charles, après avoir entendu la messe, erra jusqu'à l'aube au milieu de ses soldats en compagnie de son médecin et du Grand Bâtard, s'efforçant de les réconforter, distribuant du vin, de l'eau-de-vie, des médicaments et tançant les capitaines qui, selon lui, ne savaient pas prendre soin de leurs hommes pour au moins les maintenir en vie :

— Il faut vraiment vous être fidèle, monseigneur, lui lança Galeotto. Partout en Europe on célèbre la venue de l'Enfant Jésus et nous nous sommes là à crever de misère et de maladies devant cette putain de ville qui préférera se laisser détruire jusqu'à la dernière pierre plutôt que se rendre. Ne vaut-il pas mieux partir avant que la mort ne nous prenne tous ?

— Il est un autre Enfant devant lequel nous ne fuirons jamais et je sais qu'il approche. Plutôt la mort !...

Après la messe du jour où personne ne chanta, le duc fit appeler Fiora.

— J'ai regrets et chagrin de vous avoir obligée à me suivre, madame de Selongey, dit-il — c'était la première fois qu'il l'appelait ainsi — et je vous en demande pardon du fond du cœur... Je sais... que je n'ai plus grand-chose à attendre de la Fortune et peut-être ai-je lassé la patience de Dieu. Pourtant, je ne trouve pas le courage de me séparer de vous...

— A cause de la prédiction du rabbin ? questionna Fiora doucement.

— Ah, vous savez cela ? Mais vous vous trompez. Mourir au combat est désormais tout ce que je souhaite. La

Bourgogne dont je rêvais... demeurera un rêve. Quand le Lorrain viendra, il ne me restera peut-être que cinq mille hommes. Non, si je vous demande de m'accompagner encore c'est pour garder devant mes yeux, le plus longtemps possible, une image de pure beauté. Vous comprenez ?

— Ne perdez pas courage, monseigneur ! Cela ne vous ressemble pas. Vous êtes le grand duc d'Occident, vous êtes...

— Ce prince que vous haïssiez ? Vous souvenez-vous ?

— Il y a longtemps que j'ai changé d'avis. Mon époux vous aimait tant !...

— Merci, mais cessons de nous attrister. C'est Noël aujourd'hui et je voulais vous faire un présent... digne de vous.

Détachant de son cou une mince chaîne d'or, il la passa à celui de Fiora. Elle soutenait un diamant pyramidal d'une rare teinte bleutée.

— Gardez ceci en mémoire de moi car il est bien certain, ajouta-t-il avec un sourire, que vous ne reverrez jamais votre dot.

— Monseigneur ! Je ne puis accepter...

— Oh mais si, vous pouvez parce que je le veux. A présent retirez-vous et envoyez-moi Olivier de La Marche...

Profondément émue, Fiora regagna sa chambre lentement, la main posée sur la pierre encore chaude. Elle avait compris que le rêveur venait enfin de s'éveiller et qu'il considérait avec une froide lucidité les dangers qui le menaçaient. Il était le sanglier acculé par la meute, il le savait et il ne ferait rien pour échapper à son destin, rien d'autre que de se défendre jusqu'au bout. Mais il ne se laisserait jamais prendre vivant...

Comme il arrive dans les grands drames, une note burlesque apparut dans les derniers jours de l'année sous l'aspect du roi Alphonse V du Portugal, cousin du duc. Il venait proposer ses bons offices pour reconcilier son beau cousin avec le roi de France dans le but d'obtenir de ce dernier une aide financière dans sa lutte contre la reine de Castille. Le duc Charles le regarda comme s'il tombait de la lune :

— Aidez-moi d'abord à prendre Nancy ? fit-il en haussant les épaules. L'autre ouvrit de grands yeux puis, comprenant qu'il n'avait rien à attendre, s'éclipsa sans demander son reste.

Dans la nuit de la Saint-Sylvestre, Campobasso déserta, emmenant avec lui ses deux fils et trois cents cavaliers. Il allait rejoindre le duc de Lorraine qui n'était plus qu'à deux journées de marche pour lui demander, comme prix de sa trahison, la ville de Commercy. Il s'attendait à une réception chaleureuse, il ne trouva que des visages glacés. Les chefs suisses qui entouraient René II lui déclarèrent brutalement qu'ils n'entendaient pas combattre aux côtés d'un traître. On l'envoya garder le pont de Bouxières qui commandait le passage vers la Meurthe à une petite lieue au-dessus de Nancy :

— Vous m'accueillerez peut-être plus chaleureusement si je vous apporte la tête du Téméraire ? leur lança-t-il, furieux.

— Ce serait grand dommage que si noble tête tombât dans des mains aussi sales! riposta Oswald de Thierstein.

Le 4 janvier 1477, l'armée lorraine s'installa à Saint-Nicolas-de-Port, un faubourg de Nancy, après en avoir massacré la garnison bourguignonne. La bataille était pour le lendemain.

Au matin de ce dimanche, Fiora regardait tomber la neige. Il faisait moins froid mais toute la campagne était blanche et le vent soulevait des tourbillons immaculés. Ni elle ni Léonarde n'avaient dormi de la nuit. C'était sans doute la délivrance qui leur arrivait mais elles n'en étaient pas moins angoissées comme à l'approche d'une catastrophe... L'une après l'autre, les compagnies quittaient le camp pour aller prendre position et s'enfonçaient dans la tourmente comme une armée de fantômes...

Après la messe qu'elles entendirent auprès de lui, le duc Charles leur fit ses adieux puis se livra à ses écuyers pour revêtir la lourde armure.

Soudain, comme l'un d'eux lui passait son heaume, le lion d'or du cimier tomba. Impassible, le Téméraire regarda, sur la prairie rouge et bleu du tapis, ce symbole de la grandeur de la Bourgogne, puis plongea son regard dans celui du Grand Bâtard :

— *Hoc est signum Dei !*[1] dit-il seulement tandis que son valet de chambre se hâtait de fixer à nouveau l'ornement. Puis il coiffa le casque et se disposait à sortir quand Battista apparut et vint mettre un genou en terre devant le prince :

— Faites-moi donner des armes, monseigneur ! Je veux être auprès de vous pour cette bataille...

— Ne t'ai-je pas confié une mission ? Celle de veiller sur une dame.

— Donna Fiora n'a plus besoin de moi et je veux combattre à vos côtés. Je suis un Colonna ! Mon nom me donne droit au danger.

— Il en sera comme tu le désires, mon enfant, fit le duc tandis qu'un pâle sourire passait sur son visage immobile. Qu'on lui donne des armes ! Adieu... adieu à tous !

Il sortit. Le Moro, son beau destrier noir, l'attendait, superbement caparaçonné au milieu d'un groupe de gentilshommes. Il l'enfourcha, fit aux deux femmes un salut de la main et se mit en marche avec ses compagnons. Fiora vit le lion d'or et le grand étendard violet et noir s'effacer puis disparaître dans la tourmente de neige.

— Vous devriez rentrer, dit Léonarde. Il fait encore froid.

— Rien qu'un moment encore...

Elle ne voulait pas que sa vieille amie vît les larmes qui coulaient de ses yeux et fit quelques pas. L'attaque, alors, fut soudaine : trois cavaliers apparurent ; l'un d'eux s'empara d'elle et la jeta en travers de sa selle sans se sou-

---

1. C'est un signe de Dieu !

cier de ses cris puis il tourna bride et s'enfuit aussi vite que le permettait la neige déjà épaisse.

— J'ai assez attendu, cria-t-il. A présent tu es à moi et pour toujours !

Mais elle n'avait pas eu besoin de l'entendre. Elle avait déjà reconnu Campobasso et, sans cesser de crier, se mit à se débattre pour essayer de glisser à terre, ce qui ralentit la course de son ravisseur.

— Assommez-la, mon père ! conseilla l'un des cavaliers. Une bosse n'a jamais tué une femme et nous devons faire vite.

— Tuez-moi donc ! hurla Fiora. Cela m'évitera de le faire moi-même car jamais plus je ne t'appartiendrai. Tu me fais horreur...

Elle se meurtrissait à l'acier de l'armure mais n'en continuait pas moins sa défense désespérée. Le condottiere allait peut-être suivre le conseil d'Angelo quand trois autres cavaliers surgirent de l'impalpable rideau blanc et barrèrent le chemin.

— A nous deux, Campobasso ! Je sais déjà que tu es un traître. Je vais voir à présent si tu es vraiment un lâche ! déclara Philippe de Selongey. C'est ma femme que tu enlèves et tu vas le payer de ta vie...

— Viens la prendre si tu la veux ! fit le ravisseur en s'efforçant de redresser Fiora contre lui pour s'en faire un rempart. Mais la voix de Philippe avait galvanisé la jeune femme. Toutes griffes dehors, elle s'attaqua furieusemet au visage que la visière relevée du casque découvrait. Campobasso poussa un hurlement et desserra son étreinte. Elle en profita pour lui échapper et glissa dans la neige...

— Belle défense ! apprécia la voix traînante de Douglas Mortimer, mais écartez-vous car nous n'en avons pas fini avec ces gens.

Le troisième cavalier, qui était Esteban, avait d'ailleurs sauté à terre pour relever la jeune femme et l'installer contre un moignon d'arbre.

— Ça va ? fit-il.

— Oui... mais d'où sortez-vous ?

— On vous le dira plus tard. Pour l'instant on a besoin de moi...

Il remonta à cheval et rejoignit les deux autres. Le combat était déjà engagé entre Selongey et son ennemi et les armures résonnaient sous le choc de la hache que maniait Philippe et du fléau d'armes qu'avait empoigné son adversaire. Mortimer luttait contre Angelo et le troisième cavalier qui était Giovanni, l'autre fils. Esteban courut vers celui-ci.

Accrochée à son arbre, l'estomac noué d'angoisse mais ne sentant ni le froid ni l'humidité qui envahissaient ses vêtements Fiora suivait le furieux combat qui se livrait sous ses yeux. Elle s'efforçait de garder confiance : le miracle qui venait de se produire ne pouvait pas être vain. Il fallait que la victoire restât à la juste cause...

Soudain, dominant les injures qu'échangeaient les combattants, il y eut un cri d'agonie sitôt suivi d'un hurlement de douleur :

— Giovanni ! hurla Campobasso.

Déjà le corps sans vie roulait dans la neige qui devint rouge. Esteban, armé plus légèrement que ses compagnons, avait sauté en croupe de son adversaire et, soulevant son casque, lui avait tranché la gorge. En même temps, l'instant où l'attention du condottiere avait été détournée suffit à Philippe pour asséner un coup de hache qui enfonça le casque et blessa le Napolitain à la tête... mais il resta en selle. Ce que voyant, Angelo se déroba devant la masse d'arme de Mortimer, saisit la bride du cheval de son père et l'entraîna :

— Au large, mon père ! Nous ne gagnerons pas !

Les deux cavaliers disparurent en direction du nord...

Philippe avait déjà arraché son heaume et courait vers sa femme qu'il prit dans ses bras.

— Mon amour ! Tu n'as rien ?... Il ne t'a pas blessée ?

— Non... Oh, Philippe, est-ce bien toi ? J'ai tant désespéré de te revoir jamais... Je croyais...

Mais il lui fermait la bouche d'un baiser passionné, la serrant contre sa poitrine vêtue de fer avec une force qui lui arracha un gémissement.

— Vous allez l'écraser, remarqua tranquillement Mortimer, et à mon avis ce serait dommage. Laissez-la vivre un peu.

Philippe lâcha Fiora et se mit à rire :

— Tu as raison, compagnon, mais un trop grand bonheur peut rendre fou. Je vous la confie : prenez-en bien soin...

— Philippe ! cria Fiora voyant qu'il remettait le pied à l'étrier, tu ne vas pas me quitter ?

Elle se leva, courut à lui mais il était déjà en selle et son sourire s'effaça :

— Il le faut, Fiora ! On se bat là-bas et mon prince n'a guère de chances d'emporter la journée. Je dois le rejoindre ! Merci à vous, amis, et merci à monseigneur René qui, en vrai chevalier, m'a permis de rejoindre les miens une fois ma femme à l'abri...

— Philippe ! hurla Fiora à s'en faire éclater le cœur, reste ! Tu vas te faire tuer !

— J'espère bien que non, parce que je t'aime !

Il piqua des deux et Fiora voulut s'élancer sur sa trace mais Mortimer la saisit à bras-le-corps et la retint :

— Restez tranquille ! fit-il rudement. Il ne vous pardonnerait pas de ne pas le comprendre : il y va de son honneur !

Au même instant, le mugissement lugubre des grandes trompes montagnardes se fit entendre. Il était un peu plus de midi et la bataille était engagée...

Elle ne dura guère en dépit de la défense désespérée de la petite armée bourguignonne. Tel un bélier gigantesque, la phalange suisse hérissée de piques avait jailli de la forêt de Saurupt pour enfoncer par le travers les troupes ennemies qui devaient faire face en même temps à l'assaut frontal des Lorrains. Deux ou trois fois encore, tandis que l'armée se débandait, que Galeotto blessé se retirait vers la

Meurthe avec ce qu'il restait de ses hommes, on aperçut dans la mêlée le Téméraire qui se battait furieusement avant de disparaître...

Au pas lent de son cheval, Démétrios longeait le ruisseau Saint-Jean, se dirigeant vers l'étang du même nom. Les cadavres couvraient le sol où la neige, sous les piétinements, était devenue boue sanglante. Déjà les pillards, habituels vautours des champs de mort, étaient à l'ouvrage cependant que sonnaient éperdument toutes les cloches de la ville délivrée.

En arrivant près de l'étang, le Grec crut entendre une plainte, un faible appel. Il mit pied à terre et prit son sac de médecine. L'étang était gelé mais la glace avait cédé par endroits sous le poids des corps sans vie. Avec précaution, il s'avança parmi les roseaux, tâtant le sol de la pointe du pied avant de le poser. La plainte se fit plus proche et, soudain, il le vit. Couché au milieu des plantes givrées, les pieds trempant dans l'eau, son armure dorée souillée de sang. Le Téméraire était là, devant lui, une longue pique enfoncée dans sa poitrine, une autre transperçant l'une de ses cuisses. Le casque au lion d'or reposait contre son épaule mais Démétrios n'avait pas besoin de cet emblème pour reconnaître l'homme qu'il haïssait depuis si longtemps.

Le blessé sentit sa présence et ouvrit les yeux :

— Sauve... Bourgogne ! souffla-t-il et Démétrios se pencha. Son ennemi était là, pantelant, à sa merci. Il n'avait qu'un geste à faire pour assouvir enfin sa vengeance et déjà sa main cherchait à sa ceinture la poignée de la dague mais il entendit :

— Au nom du Dieu vivant... aidez-moi !

Alors, le Grec se souvint qu'il était médecin et qu'en aucun cas un médecin n'a le droit de tuer. Ses mains qui allaient frapper n'étaient pas faites pour cela mais pour panser les plaies, pour soigner et pour guérir... et le goût amer de la vengeance quitta sa bouche. Empoignant l'arme qui clouait le corps au sol, il la tira lentement avant de la jeter au loin, puis il déboucla l'armure et l'ôta avec d'infinies précautions :

— Ne bougez pas, dit-il. Je suis médecin... Je vais vous soigner puis j'irai chercher de l'aide...

Il se détourna et se releva pour chercher son sac qu'il avait déposé derrière lui. Le coup arriva à cet instant. Lancée d'une main sûre, une hache vint s'enfoncer dans le crâne de Charles qu'elle ouvrit. Le duc expira aussitôt et Démétrios, stupéfait, regarda fuir l'assassin. Il n'y avait plus rien à faire. Cette fois, le Téméraire était bien mort... et la Bourgogne avec lui sans doute.

Le Grec resta là un moment, à le contempler, cherchant en face de cette dépouille tragique à retrouver sa vieille hargne. Les armes de Lorraine qu'il portait sur sa manche le préservaient des hommes à la recherche d'un butin quelconque et l'on s'écartait de sa silhouette noire penchée sur ce nid de roseaux où commençait à se dissoudre ce qui avait été le plus fastueux des princes d'Europe...

— Vous n'avez pas pu le tuer, vous non plus ? fit une voix froide et, levant les yeux, Démétrios vit Léonarde qui le regardait les bras croisés, serrant autour d'elle une grande pièce d'étoffe grise...

— Non, fit-il avec une humilité nouvelle — non, je n'ai pas pu. Je suis médecin avant tout...

— Et vous vouliez qu'elle le tue, elle, cette innocente dont, mieux que personne, vous saviez ce qu'elle avait souffert ? C'est facile, n'est-ce pas, de dire : « Tue !... Poignarde ! Empoisonne ! » lorsque l'on est soi-même à l'abri et en sécurité ? Elle risquait la torture, l'échafaud, mais cela vous était égal. Et vous avez osé exercer sur elle le plus odieux des chantages...

— Ne m'accablez pas, dame Léonarde ! La pensée qu'elle ait pu devenir son amie me bouleversait. Elle avait juré de m'aider à le détruire... !

— Et vous fondiez vos espoirs sur une enfant, vous avez osé aller jusqu'à faire de l'homme qu'elle aime l'objet d'un marché ignoble ? Et vous vous imaginiez que je vous laisserais faire ? Je ne vous aimais pas, Démétrios ; à présent je vous hais...

— Je ne peux pas vous en vouloir. Esteban, lui aussi, s'est tourné contre moi ; il a aidé Philippe de Selongey à s'échapper et il a obtenu pour lui la protection de Guillaume de Diesbach et du duc René. A présent tout est fini. Demandez pardon pour moi à Fiora et dites-lui qu'en dépit de ce qu'elle a pu penser je l'aimais bien.

— Où allez-vous ?

— Je ne sais pas. Vers qui pourrait avoir encore besoin de moi. Peut-être le roi Louis...

— C'est de peu d'importance. Ce qui compte, c'est que ce soit très loin. Elle vous pardonnerait peut-être. Moi, je ne peux pas...

— Bien sûr...

Comme si c'eût été un effort immense, il se hissa sur son cheval. En un instant, ses épaules s'étaient voûtées et il eut dix ans de plus. Une fois en selle, il se retourna vers la femme qui le regardait dressée au bord de l'étang gelé, semblable à quelque impitoyable statue de la justice...

— Adieu, dame Léonarde !

— Adieu ser Démétrios ! Je ne peux rien vous souhaiter de mieux que la paix du cœur mais il faut pour cela changer de route...

Le soir même, à la lumière des torches, le duc René, au pas paisible de la Dame, sa jument blanche, faisait son entrée dans Nancy pour aller rendre grâce à la collégiale Saint-Georges. La ville était plus qu'à moitié ruinée et le palais ducal sans toit : on l'avait brûlé. Devant le couvent des Dames pêcheresses, on avait fait une pyramide avec les ossements des chevaux, des chiens et des chats que l'on avait mangés durant le siège mais, grâce aux provisions du camp bourguignon, la faim s'éloignait. Elle ne serait bientôt plus qu'un mauvais souvenir...

Les prisonniers étaient nombreux : le Grand Bâtard et son autre demi-frère Baudoin, le comte de Chimay, Olivier de La Marche, Jean de Chalon-Orbe, le seigneur de Blamont, le margrave de Roeteln et son beau-frère Philippe de Fontenoy, Philippe de Selongey et la fleur de la cavalerie bourguignonne. Ils seraient mis à rançon mais, par la grâce du duc René, Fiora, le soir même, retrouvait à la fois son époux et la chambre qu'elle avait occupée un an plus tôt dans la maison de Georges et Nicole Marqueiz...

Le duc René, cependant, n'était pas satisfait : on n'avait pas retrouvé le duc de Bourgogne et la seule idée qu'il pouvait être encore en vie mettait en péril sa victoire. Si le Téméraire avait pu fuir en Luxembourg ou ailleurs la couronne de Lorraine ne serait jamais solide sur sa tête.

Or, le lendemain, tandis que le peuple de Nancy tout entier pillait le camp bourguignon, un enfant vint aux genoux de René : c'était Battista Colonna :

— Je crois savoir où est le duc, monseigneur, car je l'ai vu tomber... Je peux guider les recherches.

On le suivit jusqu'à l'étang Saint-Jean où, parmi des dizaines de cadavres entièrement dépouillés, gisait un corps nu à moitié pris par les glaces et à peine reconnaissable. Le crâne était fendu jusqu'à la mâchoire, le corps troué de cent blessures et à demi écrasé par les chevaux, une joue dévorée par un loup ou par un chien. Auprès de lui gisait Jean de Rubempré qui avait été gouverneur de Lorraine. Les deux corps furent recueillis pieusement dans des draps blancs et rapportés dans Nancy, l'un chez un bourgeois nommé Hughes, et le duc chez Georges Marqueiz. On l'y lava, on le vêtit d'une longue robe de soie brodée, on couvrit sa tête blessée d'un bonnet de velours rouge puis on l'étendit sur un lit de parade couvert et drapé de velours noir, mains jointes, quatre torches brûlant aux angles du lit. Un autel avait été dressé dans la chambre et tous furent admis à venir saluer celui qui avait été le dernier Grand Duc d'Occident.

Le duc René vint à son tour, portant, selon l'usage des anciens preux, une barbe de fils d'or qui descendait jusqu'à sa ceinture, ultime marque de respect envers un adversaire vaincu. Il considéra un instant la dépouille mortelle, prit sa main droite et avec un soupir :

— A la mienne volonté, beau cousin, que votre malheur et le mien ne vous eût réduit en cet état...

Puis il s'inclina profondément et sortit pour aller rendre la vie à sa Lorraine martyrisée. Le lendemain, le Téméraire était inhumé dans la Collégiale Saint-Georges tendue de drap noir et en présence de tous les habitants de la ville portant à la main un cierge allumé [1]. Tout était bien fini...

Dans leur chambre que le feu réchauffait mal, Philippe et Fiora venaient de s'aimer. Étendus, épaule contre épaule et main dans la main, ils goûtaient le bienheureux anéantissement des corps que la grande vague du plaisir vient de rejeter sur la grève blanche des draps froissés, mais ils ne dormaient pas. Ils n'en avaient envie ni l'un ni l'autre car il leur semblait que jamais ils ne réussiraient à rattraper tout ce temps perdu. Ils avaient l'impression que, par leurs mains jointes, le même sang coulait de l'un à l'autre.

Se redressant sur un coude, Philippe caressa du bout du doigt le beau visage aux yeux clos, posa un baiser sur les pointes roses des seins et passa une main tendre sur la peau bien tendue du ventre plat :

— J'espère que tu me donneras bientôt un fils, murmura-t-il contre la conque fragile de l'oreille. Il est temps, ne crois-tu pas, que nous songions à fonder une famille ?

Elle s'étira et bâilla puis, tournant la tête, colla ses lèvres à celles de son époux.

— Es-tu si pressé ? fit-elle en reprenant son souffle. Ne pouvons-nous songer simplement à nous aimer ? J'ai bien le temps d'avoir mal au cœur !... N'avons-nous pas toute la vie devant nous ?

— Sans doute, mais quand je t'aurai ramenée à Selon-

---

1. Il est à présent à Bruges.

gey, j'aimerais savoir que, dans ce joli corps, une petite flamme s'est allumée. Quel homme amoureux ne souhaite se fondre avec la femme aimée pour donner le jour à un enfant. Et jamais femme ne fut aimée autant que je t'aime... Mon amour, ma douce, ma belle, quand je serai loin de toi il me serait si doux...

Les derniers mots se fondirent dans un baiser ardent que Philippe prolongea le long du cou de Fiora en même temps que sa main écartait doucement ses jambes. Mais une sorte de signal d'alarme venait de s'allumer dans l'esprit de la jeune femme et, glissant hors du bras qui l'enserrait, elle s'éloigna un peu et demeura assise sur le pied du lit, les jambes repliées, considérant le grand corps étendu que de nouvelles cicatrices avaient marqué.

— Quand tu seras loin de moi ? Qu'est-ce que cela veut dire ? As-tu déjà l'intention de me quitter alors que nous venons seulement de nous retrouver ?

— Il le faudra bien, mon cœur, soupira-t-il. Le duc est mort mais la Bourgogne existe encore. Elle porte un nom : la princesse Marie que la ville de Gand tient captive avec la duchesse Marguerite. C'est le devoir de ceux qui ont été les compagnons de son père d'aller lui offrir leurs bras et leurs épées...

— La princesse Marie ? Mais elle n'a besoin de personne ! N'est-elle pas fiancée au fils de l'empereur Frédéric ? Je pense qu'il est tout de même assez grand pour veiller aux intérêts de sa future femme ?

— Après ce qui vient de se passer, je ne suis pas certain que Frédéric considère toujours cette alliance comme profitable. La Bourgogne est exsangue... et les filles du roi de France sont fort riches. Ne te fâche pas, Fiora et reviens dans mes bras ! J'ai un devoir à remplir et ma femme doit le comprendre.

Il tentait de l'attirer à lui, mais elle frappa sur les mains tendues vers elle et sauta du lit...

— Non, Philippe. Ne compte pas sur ma compréhension. Durant tout ce temps où nous avons été éloignés l'un de l'autre, j'ai trop souffert pour accepter une nouvelle séparation... Tu es décidément l'homme des amours brèves! Quand tu m'as épousée tu ne voulais de moi qu'une nuit d'amour et maintenant, après seulement trois nuits, tu ne songes déjà qu'à repartir ? Mais je n'ai rien à faire de ta princesse! Elle a encore des palais, des gardes, un énorme héritage et un fiancé impérial par-dessus le marché. Et il faudrait que, moi, j'accepte d'aller m'enterrer dans un château perdu en compagnie d'une belle-sœur qui me détestera sans doute, pendant que tu iras caracoler en Flandres et jouer les preux chevaliers venus au secours de la veuve et de l'orpheline ? Eh bien n'y compte pas!...

— Fiora, s'écria Philippe, tu ne comprends pas. Mon amour pour toi qui est ardent et profond n'est pas en jeu. Tu sais bien que toi seule comptes pour moi...

— Après la princesse Marie!

— Non, bien avant, mais nous devons à la mémoire de son père de tout faire pour la sauver des dangers qui la menacent. Je ne vais pas partir demain. Mais dans quelques jours nous irons à Selongey où je t'installerai en souveraine maîtresse. Et il se peut que je ne sois pas longtemps absent. Je reviendrai...

— Pour la naissance de ton premier enfant ? Eh bien non, je ne suis pas d'accord. Emmène-moi!...

— C'est impossible. Tu n'en as pas encore assez de la guerre ?

— Plus qu'assez car je n'ignore pas qu'elle fait beaucoup plus de veuves encore qu'elle ne fabrique de héros. Alors tu restes avec moi... ou je m'en vais!

Il se leva d'un bond, courut à elle et voulut la prendre dans ses bras.

— Folle que tu es, fit-il tendrement, où irais-tu ?

— Chez moi. Agnolo Nardi, qui gère les intérêts français de la banque Beltrami, songeait à m'acheter un domaine. Bien mieux, le roi Louis m'a fait présent d'un château près de Plessis-lez-Tours. C'est là que je vais aller, Philippe... et c'est là que tu viendras me chercher quand tu auras décidé d'être pour moi un époux, un amant... enfin, autre chose qu'un courant d'air...

— Fiora ! Tes conditions sont inacceptables. Je suis bourguignon et n'ai rien à faire en France. Jamais je n'irai !...

— Même pour me reprendre ?

— Même pour te reprendre...

— Alors, adieu... car c'est la seule preuve d'amour que j'attends de toi.

Il avait pâli jusqu'aux lèvres mais ses yeux dorés flambaient de colère :

— Tu n'as pas le droit de faire cela. Tu es ma femme et tu dois m'obéir...

Elle le considéra un instant, luttant contre l'envie de mettre un terme à cette dispute, de se réfugier dans ses bras et de renouer avec lui le tendre duo interrompu, mais il avait malencontreusement prononcé le mot qu'il ne fallait pas dire : obéir !

— Mon père lui-même qui avait tous les droits n'a jamais réclamé de moi l'obéissance. Si être ta femme ne signifie que cela pour toi, mieux vaut nous séparer. Un mariage peut s'annuler, je ne le sais que trop, et dussé-je aller jusqu'à Rome, je ferai briser le nôtre... à moins que tu ne viennes à moi !

Arrachant du lit une couverture, Fiora y blottit sa nudité et se jeta hors de la chambre tiède en réprimant farouchement les sanglots qui montaient dans sa gorge.

Saint-Mandé, 12 août 1988.

Achevé d'imprimer sur les presses de

à Saint-Amand-Montrond (Cher)
en novembre 2004

POCKET - 12, avenue d'Italie - 75627 Paris Cedex 13
Tél. : 01-44-16-05-00

— N° d'imp. : 45135. —
Dépôt légal : octobre 1991.
Suite du premier tirage : novembre 2004.

Imprimé en France